Third Edition

Advertising Management

David A. Aaker   John G. Myers

University of California at Berkeley

Prentice-Hall, Inc., Englewood Cliffs, New Jersey 07632

Library of Congress Cataloging-in-Publication Data

Aaker, David A.
    Advertising management.

    Includes bibliographies and index.
    1. Advertising—Management. I. Myers, John G.
(date). II. Title.
HF5823.A13 1986   659.1   86-20520
ISBN 0-13-016023-7

Editorial/production supervision
and interior design: **Cheryl Smith**
Cover design: **Wanda Lubelska**
Manufacturing buyer: **Ed O'Dougherty**

Printed in the United States of America

10 9 8 7 6 5 4 3 2 1

ISBN 0-13-016023-7 01

Prentice-Hall International (UK) Limited, *London*
Prentice-Hall of Australia Pty. Limited, *Sydney*
Prentice-Hall Canada Inc., *Toronto*
Prentice-Hall Hispanoamericana, S.A., *Mexico*
Prentice-Hall of India Private Limited, *New Delhi*
Prentice-Hall of Japan, Inc., *Tokyo*
Prentice-Hall of Southeast Asia Pte. Ltd., *Singapore*
Editora Prentice-Hall do Brasil, Ltda., *Rio de Janeiro*

Contents

iii

Preface

Advertising is a fascinating and important subject. The health of many businesses depends on the generation of effective advertising. Yet the key to developing effective advertising and, indeed, determining exactly how advertising works is illusive to academic researchers and practitioners alike. Advertising also catches the imagination of people outside the industry. Everyone seems to have opinions on advertisements and finds it easy to attach labels to them, such as fun, humorous, warm, entertaining, persuasive, boring, contrived, or irritating.

This third edition of *Advertising Management* has been extensively updated and revised. However, the basic thrust of the book remains. The overriding objective is again to provide an approach to the management of advertising that is sophisticated, thoughtful, and state of the art while being practical and relevant to planning, decision making, and control. The focus is on decision making, specifically those decisions involved with setting advertising budgets and objectives, creating advertising campaigns, developing media strategies, and measuring advertising results. The book again draws on and attempts to integrate three related disciplines: behavioral science, marketing and advertising research, and management science.

Advertising is basically communication and persuasion and as such has long leaned on the insights of psychology and the study of consumer behavior. Thus, it is natural to look to theories, concepts, and research findings from psychology to help understand and manage the process. The fact is that developments in recent years have provided new ways of modeling advertising that show great promise.

Marketing and advertising research techniques and methodologies underlie the approach of this book. In all phases of the advertising process from objective setting through campaign creation and media selection to copy and campaign evaluation, research provides the thrust. Even governmental concerns about deception in advertising are turning to research. The array of research techniques is both comprehensive and powerful. It is imperative that a practitioner be familiar with these techniques and understand their roles and limitations.

The quantitative models of management science are a part of modern advertising management as well. They provide structure, definition, and measurement to what otherwise might be rich but abstract behavioral theories or intuitive and practical approaches to complex decision areas.

CHANGES IN THE THIRD EDITION

In most chapters, new concepts, models, techniques, and research findings have been added together with fresh examples of problems and approaches from the "real world." In particular, the copy-testing chapter, Chapter 14, now presents a spectrum of copy-test methods. The application of split-cable testing to budget and copy decisions is presented and illustrated. There is now a separate chapter on creative styles (Chapter 12), in which the creative philosophy and the approach of four classic advertisers of the past and five currently successful practitioners are detailed.

Two chapters new to the third edition were stimulated by advances in behavioral theories. One, Chapter 9, discusses seven models of information processing and attitude change, including peripheral processing, cognitive response, category-based evaluation, and the mere exposure models. Another, Chapter 10, focuses on the feeling response to advertising, an exciting area of study that shows promise of shedding light on an important area of advertising. Included are topics such as the attitude toward the ad, the association of feelings with the brand, and the possibility of the advertising transforming the use experience.

In this edition, each chapter begins with a quotation or excerpt from a famous person or work intended to capture a major theme in the chapter, or otherwise generate additional interest in the material.

THE ORGANIZATION AND CONTENT

The book is again divided into six parts, with each part except the final one containing an integrative case. Part I describes the field of advertising, introduces advertising planning and decision making, positions advertising within the organization, and presents materials on segmentation and the advertising budget. Part II focuses on setting advertising objectives. Advances from the fields of positioning, attitude research, and measurement are drawn on as they relate to objective setting.

Part III steps back and looks at communication, persuasion, and market processes, drawing heavily on models and theories from psychology. The intent is to provide a foundation from which creative options can be developed and tested. Part IV is involved with generating copy alternatives, producing advertisements, and copy testing. Part V turns to media selection decisions. Part VI is devoted to the legal issues of deceptive advertising that face an advertising decision maker and the social and economic issues that have always surrounded advertising and served to make it controversial.

THE TARGET AUDIENCE

This book is intended for users and potential users of advertising as well as for those who are preparing for a career in advertising. The book has been used successfully in both undergraduate and graduate courses in advertising, advertising management, communication management, and promotional management. It has also been used as the basis for training in at least two of the top ten advertising agencies in the world. The book does not presume any previous course.

ACKNOWLEDGMENTS

We would like to thank several people who helped immeasurably to improve this third edition, including John Deighton, Julie Edell, Manoj Hastak, Trudy Kehret-Ward, Dean Krugman, Thomas O'Guinn, Camille Schuster, Douglas Stayman, and Debra Stephens. They join those who helped us on prior editions, including Boris Becker, David Furse, Ewald Grether, Stephen Greyser, Harold Kassarjian, James Krum, Richard Lutz, Andrew Mitchell, William Mindak, Francesco Nicosia, Michael Ray, Allan Shocker, William Wilkie, and Terrance Witkowski. We also acknowledge the superb translation effort by Ikujiro Nonaka and Hisashi Ikegami, who translated the book into Japanese, and Roberto Alvarez del Blanco, who translated it into Spanish.

To all these people and others whose efforts and contributions now escape our memory, we offer our thanks. Our faculty colleagues and students at Berkeley have been a constant source of inspiration and encouragement throughout the development of the book and its revisions. Finally, we thank our wives and families for their support and understanding. To them the book is dedicated.

David A. Aaker

John G. Myers

1

The Field of Advertising Management

The trade of advertising is now so near to perfection that it is not easy to propose any improvements. (Samual Johnson, 1760)

The competent advertising man must understand psychology. The more he knows about it the better. He must learn that certain effects lead to certain reactions, and use that knowledge to increase results and avoid mistakes. Human nature is the same today as in the time of Caesar. So the principles of psychology are fixed and enduring. We learn, for instance, that curiosity is one of the strongest of human incentives. (Claude Hopkins, *Scientific Advertising,* 1926)

The field of advertising management is made up of a system of interacting organizations and institutions, all of which play a role in the advertising process. At the core of this system are advertisers, the organizations that provide the financial resources that support advertising. Advertisers are private or public-sector organizations that use mass media to accomplish an organizational objective. It is the decision to invest resources in purchasing time or space in such mass media as television, radio, newspapers, or magazines that basically distinguishes advertisers from nonadvertisers. Advertisers make use of mass media. Nonadvertisers do not.

Advertising management is heavily focused on the analysis, planning, control, and decision-making activities of this core institution—the advertiser. The advertiser provides the overall managerial direction and financial support for the development of advertising and the purchase of media time and space, even though many other institutions are involved in the process. A focal point is the development of an advertising program or plan for the advertiser. In cases where several different kinds of products or services are offered by the advertising organization, a separate program may be developed for each. The resulting advertisement is usually aired or placed several times, and the resulting schedule of exposures is referred to as an *advertising campaign*. The development and management of an advertising campaign associated with an advertiser's brand, product, or service is thus a major point of departure for advertising management.

In developing and managing an advertising campaign, the advertiser basically deals with numerous institutions, as Figure 1-1 illustrates. The advertising agency, the media, and the research suppliers are three supporting or *facilitating* institutions external to the advertiser's own organization. The agency and the research suppliers assist the advertiser in analyzing opportunities, creating and testing advertising ideas, and buying media time and space; the media, of course, supply the means by which to advertise. Others are, in effect, *control* institutions that interact with and affect the advertiser's decision-making activities in numerous ways. Government and competition are the two most important external control institutions. Most advertisers are affected by a wide range of government regulations concerning their products, services, and advertising. Direct or indirect competitors are usually present

Figure 1-1.   Major institutions involved in the field of advertising management

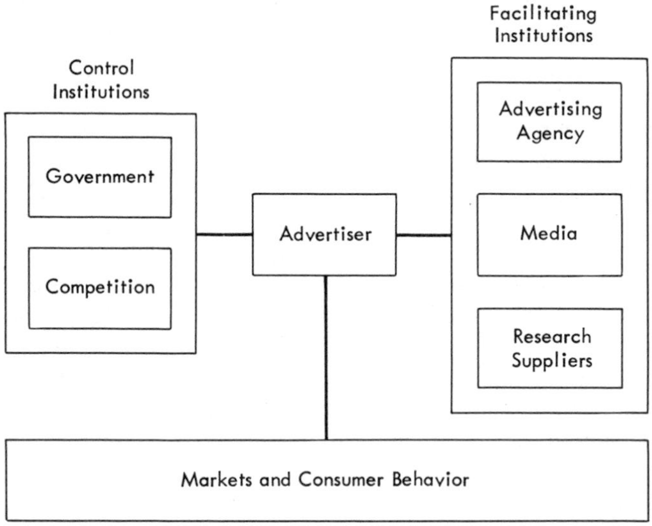

and serve as a major external control. What competitors do and how they react is thus an important part of advertising management.

The markets or consumers the advertiser is attempting to reach through advertising can be thought of as yet another kind of external institution that both facilitates and controls advertising. The concepts of *markets* and *consumers* will be used interchangeably to refer to any classification of individuals, organizations, or groups the advertiser is attempting to reach or "get a message to." Examples could be housewives, electronic engineers, automobile dealers, voters, hospital patients, government officials, or other industrial, retail, government, or nonprofit organizations. Without an existing or potential target for advertising messages, the rationale for advertising would not exist. The consumer is a controlling force, mainly through a whole range of behavioral possibilities, such as viewing or not viewing, buying or not buying, voting or not voting, and so on. It is the consumer, in this broad sense, to whom advertising campaigns are directed, media are used, advertising agencies create copy, and upon whom advertising research is done. The identification and understanding of markets and consumer behavior is thus also a vital part of advertising management.

In this chapter, background information is presented on advertisers and on the three major facilitating institutions: advertising agencies, the media, and research suppliers. A discussion of several perspectives on the subject of advertising, including the one adopted in this book, follows. The balance of the book, from the perspectives of Figure 1-1, deals, in one way or another, with advertising planning and decision making in the context of markets, competition, and governmental constraints.

THE ADVERTISER

The advertiser is the core institution of the field of advertising management, and expenditures of advertisers provide the basis for estimates of the size of the advertising industry. Expenditures by all advertisers in all media (newspapers, magazines, business papers, television, radio, direct mail, outdoor billboards, and so on) were estimated to be over $88 billion in 1984,[1] having more than tripled in the 9-year period after 1975, when they were about $28 billion. Although inflation accounted for much of this growth, it is still impressive. One estimate is that by the year 2000 advertising expenditures in the United States will reach $320 billion and will exceed $780 billion worldwide.[2]

The *Standard Directory of Advertisers*[3] listed 17,000 companies engaged in advertising in 1978. Most are small, private, or nonprofit organizations utilizing broadcast or print media on a local basis in the immediate region or metropolitan area in which they are located. Even this large figure excludes public service advertisements (PSAs),[4] nonpaid advertisements by nonprofit organizations, and classified advertisements in local newspapers purchased by private citizens. Advertisers utilizing local media, although large in number, do not account for the majority of advertising expenditures. In 1984, for example, local advertising that largely reflects media use by small advertisers accounted for about 44 percent of all advertising expenditures, whereas national advertising, reflecting large-scale users, accounted for the remaining 56 percent.[5]

Small- and large-scale advertisers can be distinguished according to the degree to which they use the facilitating institutions shown in Figure 1-1. Private citizens and many local small-scale advertisers, for example, buy media time or space directly and do not use an advertising agency or the services of a research supplier. The typical large national advertisers will have one or more advertising agencies under contract and will buy numerous types of research services, as well as conduct research on their own. In general, they make full use of the system shown in Figure 1-1, whereas small-scale advertisers, for budgetary reasons, use only parts of the system. Although many of the case examples, models, and research techniques and results presented in this book focus on the full system, and are thus most directly applicable to large-scale advertisers, the underlying principles involved are equally applicable to any advertiser, large or small, profit or nonprofit, and so on.

Advertisers differ according to the markets they serve, the goods and services they produce, and the media they use. In the private sector, advertisers can be distinguished according to whether they are predominantly *consumer, industrial,* or *retail* advertisers. Consumer advertisers are those mainly involved in the manufacture of durable or nondurable goods and services for consumer markets. Industrial advertisers predominantly manufacture and market products for industrial markets, and retailers often advertise locally to attract store patronage. Many large firms, such as General Motors, International Harvester, and Sears, Roebuck, service more than one market, which makes attempts to classify advertisers on this basis less meaningful. The media-use distinctions, however, are comparatively clear-cut. Retail advertisers, particularly at the local level, use newspaper advertising extensively. Consumer goods and services advertisers make heavy use of television, radio, and consumer magazines. Industrial advertisers generally make heavy use of trade magazines, business papers, direct mail, and trade shows. Industrial advertising is basically different, because its audience is made up of professionals who are often more willing and able to accept and process detailed information than is an audience made up of members of households.

About 55 percent of all national advertiser expenditures is accounted for by 99 private corporations and the federal government.[6] The top 100 advertisers in 1983 came from 15 industries. Table 1-1 shows the industries in rank order based on volume of dollars spent on advertising. The number of companies in each industry who were among the top 100 advertisers is also shown.

The top 10 national advertisers are shown in Table 1-2 for the years 1979 and 1984. In 1984, they accounted for over $6.4 billion of advertising investment, or more than 28 percent of all expenditures of the leading 100 national advertisers. As can be seen, eight of the companies retained their leadership position. Compared with 1979, General Foods and Warner-Lambert moved out of the top 10, and were

Table 1-1.   **Industries Represented by Top 100 Advertisers, 1983 (millions of dollars)**

RANK	INDUSTRY	ADVERTISING EXPENDITURES	NUMBER OF COMPANIES
1	Food	$ 3,914.8	18
2	Automotive	2,001.4	10
3	Pharmaceuticals	1,574.1	8
4	Tobacco	1,533.3	6
5	Soaps and cleaners	1,522.9	5
6	Retail chains	1,425.0	3
7	Communications and entertainment	1,020.0	7
8	Toiletries and cosmetics	948.3	7
9	Electronics and office equipment	866.8	8
10	Telephone equipment	667.5	3
11	Soft drinks	638.6	2
12	Chemicals and gasoline	627.9	4
13	Wine, beer, and liquor	617.8	5
14	Airlines	392.6	5
15	Gum and candy	252.6	3
	Miscellaneous	874.0	6
	Total	$18,877.6	100

Source: Adapted from *Advertising Age,* September 14, 1984, p. 8.

replaced by Beatrice Cos. and McDonald's. Some comments on several of the top 10 advertisers follow.

Procter & Gamble, the nation's largest private advertiser, invested nearly a billion dollars in advertising in 1984, and is estimated to pass the $1 billion mark by 1985. Like many manufacturers of consumer-packaged goods, the company relies heavily on television advertising. In 1983, however, some significant shifts

Table 1-2.   **Top Ten National Advertisers in 1979 and 1984 (millions of dollars)**

1979			1984		
Rank	Company	Expenditures	Rank	Company	Expenditures
1	Procter & Gamble	614.9	1	Procter & Gamble	872.0
2	General Foods	393.0	2	General Motors	763.8
3	Sears, Roebuck	379.3	3	Sears, Roebuck	746.9
4	General Motors	323.4	4	Beatrice Cos.	680.0
5	Philip Morris	291.2	5	R.J. Reynolds	678.1
6	K Mart Corp.	287.1	6	Philip Morris	570.4
7	R.J. Reynolds	258.1	7	AT&T	563.2
8	Warner-Lambert	220.2	8	Ford Motor Co.	559.4
9	AT&T	219.8	9	K Mart Corp.	554.4
10	Ford Motor Co.	215.0	10	McDonald's Corp.	480.0
		3,202.0			6,468.2

Source: Advertising Age, September 11, 1981, p. 1 and September 26, 1985, p. 1.

into cable and syndicated TV programming took place. Although about 77 percent ($596 million) of total spending went into television, network TV spending was reduced 14 percent in that year. The company spent almost 16 percent ($123.2 million) in "unmeasured media," which includes cable, direct mail, collateral materials, co-op advertising, trade show promotions, point-of-purchase, and transit advertising. Television is, nevertheless, a preferred medium for advertising because products are bought on a repetitive, short-purchase-cycle basis, and television provides the best means of achieving an impact and maintaining consumer loyalty. In 1983, P & G had 69 established consumer product lines, plus hundreds of products sold to institutions.

In 1983, Procter & Gamble had two exceptionally large new-product introductions, Always feminine hygiene, and Citrus Hill Select orange juice. Each was supported by a $100 million budget, which broke all previous records for the heaviest spending on new-product introductions. Among the more heavily advertised established brands were Tide ($25.5 million), Pampers ($23.6 million), Crest Gel ($37.0 million), Secret and Sure deodorant ($31.7 million), Folgers coffee (about $20 million), and a pharmaceutical product acquired in an acquisition, Encaprin (about $25 million).

In contrast, General Motors, the second largest advertiser, spends much of its advertising dollars on print media. Its products are relatively expensive and are regarded by most consumers as major purchases. General Motors spent only about 38 percent of its budget on television in 1983 and used magazine, newspaper, radio, and outdoor advertising much more extensively than did Procter & Gamble. A manufacturer of durable goods will typically be more inclined toward print media than will a manufacturer of packaged goods, because a durable product is more complex and requires longer and more detailed copy. In 1983, General Motors had a record sales and profit year and reorganized into "small car" and "large car" groups. Chevrolet, Pontiac, and GM Canada divisions came under "small car," and Buick, Oldsmobile, and Cadillac under "large car." Advertising expenditures were allocated as follows: Chevrolet, $178 million; Buick, $48.6 million; Oldsmobile, $45.5 million; Pontiac, $55 million; and Cadillac, $22.5 million. An example of a classic 1915 Cadillac advertisement designed to communicate an image of quality is shown in Figure 1-2.

Sears, Roebuck, the third largest advertiser in 1984, represents advertising by a giant retail chain. As shown in Table 1-2, a second large retail chain, K-Mart, is also among the top 10 advertisers. In 1983, the largest part of Sears, Roebuck's national advertising expenditures, $508.1 million (about 69 percent), went into catalogs, direct mail, and other "unmeasured" media. Catalogs have been an important promotional vehicle ever since the company was founded. The balance of Sears, Roebuck's national advertising effort in that year went for television, magazine, radio, and outdoor advertising. Their national effort really began in 1967. They started a $5 million magazine campaign for a number of hardware and software items. Since then advertising budgets for such familiar names as Craftsman tools, Allstate insurance, and tire, battery, and appliance products has grown con-

Figure 1-2.   **A classic 1915 advertisement communicating quality**

THE PENALTY of LEADERSHIP

IN EVERY FIELD OF HUMAN ENDEAVOR · HE THAT IS FIRST MUST PERPETUALLY LIVE IN THE WHITE LIGHT OF PUBLICITY ॐ WHETHER THE LEADERSHIP BE VESTED IN A MAN OR IN A MANUFACTURED PRODUCT · EMULA TION AND ENVY ARE EVER AT WORK ॐ IN ART · IN LITERATURE · IN MUSIC · IN INDUSTRY · THE REWARD AND THE PUNISHMENT ARE ALWAYS THE SAME ॐ THE REWARD IS WIDESPREAD RECOGNITION · THE PUNISHMENT FIERCE DENIAL AND DETRACTION ॐ WHEN A MAN'S WORK BECOMES A STANDARD FOR THE WHOLE WORLD IT ALSO BECOMES A TARGET FOR THE SHAFTS OF THE ENVIOUS FEW ॐ IF HIS WORK IS MERELY MEDIOCRE HE WILL BE LEFT SEVERELY ALONE ॐ IF HE ACHIEVE A MASTERPIECE · IT WILL SET A MILLION TONGUES A-WAG GING ॐ JEALOUSY DOES NOT PROTRUDE ITS FORKED TONGUE AT THE ARTIST WHO PRODUCES A COMMON PLACE PAINTING ॐ WHATSOEVER YOU WRITE · OR PAINT · OR PLAY · OR SING · OR BUILD · NO ONE WILL STRIVE TO SURPASS OR TO SLANDER YOU · UNLESS YOUR WORK BE STAMPED WITH THE SEAL OF GENIUS ॐ LONG LONG AFTER A GREAT WORK OR A GOOD WORK HAS BEEN DONE · THOSE WHO ARE DISAPPOINTED OR ENVI OUS CONTINUE TO CRY OUT THAT IT CANNOT BE DONE ॐ SPITEFUL LITTLE VOICES IN THE DOMAIN OF ART WERE RAISED AGAINST OUR OWN WHISTLER AS A MOUNTEBANK · LONG AFTER THE BIG WORLD HAD ACCLAIM ED HIM ITS GREATEST ARTISTIC GENIUS ॐ MULTITUDES FLOCKED TO BAYREUTH TO WORSHIP AT THE MUSICAL SHRINE OF WAGNER · WHILE THE LITTLE GROUP OF THOSE WHOM HE HAD DETHRONED AND DISPLACED ARGUED ANGRILY THAT HE WAS NO MUSICIAN AT ALL ॐ THE LITTLE WORLD CONTINUED TO PROTEST THAT FULTON COULD NEVER BUILD A STEAMBOAT · WHILE THE BIG WORLD FLOCKED TO THE RIVER BANKS TO SEE HIS BOAT STEAM BY ॐ THE LEADER IS ASSAILED BECAUSE HE IS A LEADER · AND THE EFFORT TO EQUAL HIM IS MERELY ADDED PROOF OF THAT LEADERSHIP ॐ FAILING TO EQUAL OR TO EXCEL · THE FOLLOWER SEEKS TO DEPRECIATE AND TO DESTROY · BUT ONLY CONFIRMS ONCE MORE THE SUPERIORITY OF THAT WHICH HE STRIVES TO SUP PLANT ॐ THERE IS NOTHING NEW IN THIS ॐ IT IS AS OLD AS THE WORLD AND AS OLD AS THE HUMAN PASSIONS ENVY · FEAR · GREED · AMBITION AND THE DESIRE TO SURPASS ॐ AND IT ALL AVAILS NOTHING ॐ IF THE LEADER TRULY LEADS HE REMAINS - THE LEADER ॐ MASTER POET · MASTER PAINTER · MASTER WORKMAN · EACH IN HIS TURN IS ASSAILED · AND EACH HOLDS HIS LAURELS THROUGH THE AGES ॐ THAT WHICH IS GOOD OR GREAT MAKES ITSELF KNOWN · NO MATTER HOW LOUD THE CLAMOR OF DENIAL ॐ THAT WHICH DESERVES TO LIVE · LIVES

siderably. A major new effort is the Sears Financial Network, including Allstate Insurance, Coldwell Banker Real Estate, and Dean Witter Financial Services Corporation. Millions of additional dollars spent primarily on local newspaper advertising are not included in the $746.9 million shown in Table 1-2.

Whereas national advertising for retailers such as department stores or food chains is the exception, local advertising is vital. Much local retail advertising features item and price listings, but some retailers take a broader view and emphasize store image. John Wanamaker, a retail executive in the early 1900s, was among the first to focus on store image, using such headlines as ''The quality is remembered long after the price is forgotten.''

Beatrice Companies, the fourth largest advertiser in 1984, is the result of the merger of three major corporations, Beatrice, Esmark, and Norton Simon. Esmark, with brands like Playtex and Danskin, first acquired Norton Simon, whose major subsidiaries, Hunt-Wesson and Swift, have familiar brands in catsup, tomato sauce, pudding, meats, peanut butter, and others. Beatrice, well known for Tropicana orange juice, La Choy, Samsonite luggage, and Culligen water treatment, acquired Esmark in August 1984 for about $2.8 billion. Avis Rent-A-Car is also a Beatrice company. A major effort begun in 1983 was launching a corporate identity campaign around the theme "You've known us all along," with advertising during both the Winter and Summer Olympics. The role of advertising is particularly interesting in this connection.

Nonprofit organizations, such as schools, colleges, churches, hospitals, and libraries, are increasingly making use of local advertising. They have many of the same problems as business firms. They must identify the groups they serve, determine their needs, develop products and services to satisfy those needs, and communicate with their constituencies. This communication can often be done most effectively by advertising. National advertising is also increasing among nonprofit organizations, particularly for fund-raising or behavior-change efforts by the major medical associations and such groups as Boy Scouts, Girl Scouts, and the United Fund. The federal government was the twenty-sixth largest advertiser in 1984, spending $287.8 million. The largest governmental advertising effort, $166.3 million, was for military recruiting efforts for each branch of the military services. The postal service spent $42.0 million and Am Trak spent $26.3 million in 1984.

An interesting new form of advertising, called *advocacy advertising*, began about 1973. Business institutions take a public position on controversial issues of social importance, aggressively state and defend their own viewpoints, and criticize those of their opponents. For example, Mobil Oil ran an ad in the October 23, 1975, *Wall Street Journal* advocating the end of controls on oil.[7] Professional groups, like lawyers, also, for the first time, were legally allowed to advertise their services and thus became yet another type of advertiser.

There are thus dozens of different types of advertisers and an equally large number of forms of advertising, including national, local, consumer, industrial, service, comparative, cooperative, corrective, advocacy, counter, and public service advertising. Each is discussed in various sections of the book. Those interested in retail, industrial, or sales-promotion activity can, for example, find more on these topics in Chapter 7 in the sections on short-term behavioral objectives.

Role of the Brand Manager

It will be helpful to describe briefly the position of a brand manager because, for many large advertisers, both industrial and consumer, such a position is central to the development of advertising. The brand manager, either directly or through a staff advertising manager, makes the advertising-policy decisions and interacts with the agency. The brand manager position has often been compared to the president's position in a small company. He or she is responsible for all marketing aspects of the brand and, internally, draws upon the full range of line and staff resources of the corporation. This includes such departments as sales, new product planning, marketing research, and so on. In many cases, the advertising budget is the most significant expenditure associated with marketing the brand. Externally, the brand manager usually represents the interests of just one corporation brand and oversees the development of the advertising and marketing program for it. This role is particularly important in the study of advertising management, even though it is not the only one for which the materials in this book are relevant. Basically, the concepts, models, and decision aids presented are completely general, even though they are often presented from the viewpoint of a brand manager in a consumer packaged-goods organization. It should also be emphasized that they apply when the object of the advertisement is other than a packaged consumer product; it may be a service, a political candidate, or a government program; or the target of the communication may be other than a consumer, such as an organization, an industrial buyer, a voter, or a client of an organization.

Those whose career orientations are toward brand management or analogous positions in retail firms will find the materials in this book most useful. There are thousands of brands and, analogously, thousands of brand managers. A further impression as to what is being "managed" by each can be gained by looking at the budgets of some of the brands of the four major national advertisers reviewed earlier. The brand advertising manager of each of these products is, in effect, managing a fairly good sized "company" within a company, and the success or failure of the advertising, as well as all other attendant tools associated with marketing the brand, are based on the skill with which he or she manages it.

A product or a specific version of a product—a brand—is thus a major reference point for the study of advertising management. We use the term "product" or the term "object" in a general sense throughout the book to refer to the reference point for advertising. It can be something tangible like Green Giant peas, a service like Allstate insurance, or even an idea like "Keep America Beautiful." As noted, the organizational role most often used to identify the manager of day-to-day advertising operations in a great number of cases is that of brand manager.

FACILITATING INSTITUTIONS

All advertisers, by definition, use some form of media to accomplish organizational objectives. Where significant amounts of media expenditures are involved, the advertiser will also use the services of an advertising agency and one or more research suppliers. Together, these three types of institutions make up the primary facilitating institutions of advertising management. In this section, we present an overview of the role, nature, and scope of these three institutions. Much of the organizational dynamics of advertising management is best understood by observing the role of the facilitating institutions in relation to the advertiser, as shown in Figure 1-3.

First, note that the advertising agency is represented in a position "between" the advertiser and the media. A major role of the advertising agency is the purchase of media time and space. The agency, on the one hand, is interacting with the advertiser and, on the other, with one or more media organizations. A second point to note is the role of research. Although not shown explicitly in Figure 1-3, most large firms, at each of the levels of advertiser, agency, and media, will have their own internal research departments, and each will also be purchasing research data

Figure 1-3.   **Role of facilitating institutions**

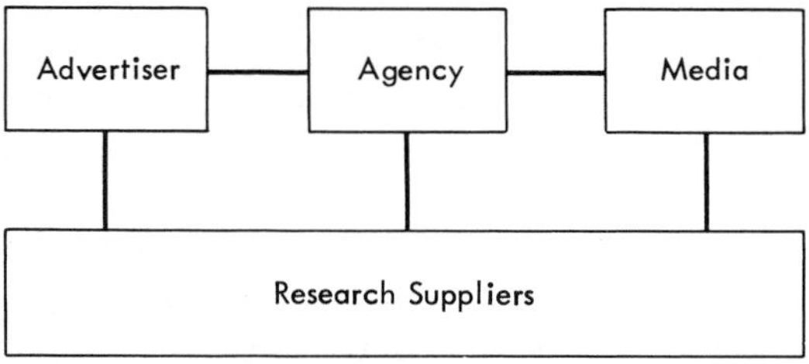

externally from some outside research supplier. The research input to the system is a vital aspect on which many of the formal models, theories, and decision aids presented in this book are based.

Another insight from Figure 1-3 is that a typical advertising campaign evolves from the activities of a project or planning group composed of representatives of the advertiser, the agency, and one or more research suppliers. Basically, many meetings of this group will take place over the course of campaign development. Oral presentations of creative ideas and media plans will be made by the agency representatives. Similarly, research suppliers will make oral presentations on the results of a consumer survey, a copy test, and so on. Much written and telephone communication also takes place during this process.

In the previous section, it was suggested that the brand manager was the major representative of the advertiser's interests. The analogous positions at each of the three facilitating-institution levels are the account executive for the agency, the media representative for media, and the project supervisor for research suppliers. Each level of the system is also represented by a professional trade association. For example, the Association of National Advertisers (ANA) represents advertiser interests; the American Association of Advertising Agencies (AAAA) serves the agency component; and associations like the National Association of Broadcasters (NAB), the American Newspaper Publishers Association (ANPA), the Magazine Publishers Association (MPA), the Direct Mail Marketing Association (DMMA), and the Outdoor Advertising Association of America (OAAA) serve the major media. The Advertising Research Foundation (ARF) is heavily concerned with the research aspects of the system.

The Advertising Agency

A unique aspect of advertising is the advertising agency, which, in most cases, makes the creative and media decisions. It also often supplies supportive market research and is even involved in the total marketing plan. In some advertiser-agency relationships, the agency acts quite autonomously in its area of expertise; in others, the advertiser remains involved in the creative and media decisions as the campaign progresses.

The first advertising agent, Volney B. Palmer, established an office in Philadelphia in 1841.[8] He was essentially an agent of the newspapers. For 25 percent of the cost, he sold space to advertisers in the various 1,400 newspapers throughout the country. He made no effort to help advertisers prepare copy, and the service he performed was really one of media selection. His knowledge of and access to the various newspapers were worth something to an advertiser.

Although the nature of an agency has changed considerably since Palmer's day, the method of compensation has persisted. The basic compensation for modern agencies is a fixed percentage of advertising billings, 15 percent, which they receive from the media in which the advertisements are placed. This percentage can be augmented to cover extra services the agency may perform, such as special market studies, but it has really been a remarkably durable and rigid system through the years. The system is criticized because it encourages the agency to recommend higher media budgets than may be appropriate. However, efforts to replace it with a cost-plus or performance-based system have been largely unsuccessful, and probably 70 to 80 percent of all agency billing is still done in this way.

By the turn of the century, agencies started to focus their attention on the creation of advertising for clients. Probably the first agency with a reputation for creative work was Lord and Thomas, which was blessed with two remarkable copywriters, John E. Kennedy and Claude Hopkins. Kennedy believed that advertising was salesmanship in print and always tried to provide a reason why people should buy the advertised goods. One of Kennedy's first tasks when he joined Lord and Thomas in 1898 was to recreate an advertisement for a new washer that had relied on the headline "Are you chained to the washtub?" appearing over a figure of a worn, disgruntled housewife shackled to a washtub.[9] Kennedy's advertisement showed a woman relaxing in a rocking chair while turning the crank of a washer. The copy emphasized the work of the ball bearings and the time and chapped hands the machine would save. The cost of the resulting inquiries decreased from $20 each to a few pennies.

Claude Hopkins, who joined Lord and Thomas in 1907, was regarded by many as the greatest creator of advertising who ever practiced the art. One year, soon after joining the firm, he made nearly $200,000 just writing copy.[10] He was particularly good at understanding the consumer and at integrating the advertising into the total marketing effort. His first account was Campbell's Pork & Beans.[11] He discovered, using his own research, that 94 percent of American housewives baked their own beans. Yet the advertisers of the day were focusing on the relative advantages of their own brands compared to competitors'. Hopkins' campaign argued against home baking, reminding housewives of the sixteen hours involved in preparing the beans and the probability of ending up with crisp beans on top and mushy beans below. His primary-demand appeal (getting people to buy the product—any brand) was enormously successful. In response to the competitive reaction, he boldly ran advertisements challenging consumers to "Try Our Rivals Too." He also secured distribution among restaurants and then advertised to the consumers the fact that restaurants had selected the Campbell brand. Hopkins knew the importance of developing an advertising program that was based on consumer desires. In his words, "Argue anything for your own advantage and people will resist to the limit. But seem unselfishly to consider your customers' desires and they will naturally flock to you.''[12]

Hopkins also took on the task of advertising the company's evaporated milk, a new product for Campbell.[13] In introducing the brand, Hopkins used a technique on which he often relied. He offered to buy housewives a ten-cent can as an indication of his confidence in the brand. In a single newspaper advertisement that ran in New York for one day only, he inserted a coupon that could be redeemed at a retail store for one can of milk. His idea proved to be brilliant. It provided incentives for people to try the product without tarnishing its image, as a fifty-cents-off coupon might have done. More important, it encouraged retailers to stock the brand to satisfy customer demands and to share in the profit represented by the offer. Entering a New York market dominated by another brand, the technique gained for Campbell 97 percent distribution practically overnight. More than 1,460,000 customers redeemed the coupon in the single New York advertisement. The $175,000 cost of the program was recovered in less than nine months, and Campbell captured the New York market.

The agencies grew in size and influence through the years as they demonstrated an ability to create effective advertising. Lord and Thomas grew from less than $1 million in billings in 1898 to more than $6 million in 1910, and to $14 million in 1924.[14] In 1984, Foote, Cone & Belding, the successor to Lord and Thomas, had worldwide billings of more than $1.802 billion.

Table 1-3 shows the top 10 advertising agencies in 1984.[15] As can be seen, Foote, Cone & Belding ranked in eighth place in that year based on world billings. Billings represent media costs, whereas income is the money retained by the agency, generally around 15 percent of billings. Young & Rubicam, the leader, had gross worldwide billings of over $3.202 billion, and tenth-ranked Doyle Dane Bernbach billed over $1.5 billion. Y & R employed 8,418 people in 1984. The largest agencies, like the large advertisers they serve, are best viewed as large multinational organizations with branch offices around the world, which derive a significant

Table 1-3.   **Top Ten U.S. Advertising Agencies, 1984 (millions of dollars)**

RANK[a]	AGENCY	WORLD BILLINGS	GROSS U.S. INCOME	GROSS INCOME OUTSIDE U.S.
1	Young & Rubicam	$3,202.1	$323.1	$157.0
2	Ogilvy & Mather Intl.	2,887.9	270.5	150.5
3	Ted Bates Worldwide	2,839.2	263.2	161.2
4	J. Walter Thompson Co.	2,706.7	218.2	187.6
5	Saatchi & Saatchi Compton	2,301.7	157.4	180.1
6	BBDO International	2,275.0	235.0	105.0
7	McCann-Erickson	2,169.4	118.5	206.7
8	Foote, Cone & Belding	1,802.3	196.9	71.6
9	Leo Burnett Co.	1,734.8	163.2	90.3
10	Doyle Dane Bernbach Intl.	1,510.6	154.1	64.2

[a] Based on world billings.

Source: Advertising Age, March 28, 1985, p. 1.

amount of their income from overseas operations. Some agencies are more international than others. As can be seen in Table 1-3, for example, Saatchi & Saatchi Comptom, based in London, and McCann-Erickson, a U.S.-based agency, derive more of their income from outside the United States. Others, like Foote, Cone & Belding, Leo Burnett, and Doyle Dane Bernbach, derive the bulk of their income from domestic operations. However, all are very large multimillion-dollar organizations employing thousands of people in the business of creating, researching, and placing advertising.

A survey of agency reputations was conducted for *Advertising Age* by SRI Research Center in the last quarter of 1984. A random sample of 300 advertising directors of companies with revenues over $25 million a year selling to the top 20 U.S. markets was interviewed. Six attributes of the agency were identified as most important: (1) creativity, (2) account executives, (3) media, (4) top management, (5) marketing, and (6) research. Table 1-4 shows the top three agencies on each attribute. J. Walter Thompson ranked first on five of the attributes, a reputation distinguished by its across-the-board strength. Ogilvy & Mather, Chiat/Day, and Doyle Dane Bernbach were perceived as strongest on creativity.

This survey also identified factors considered most important in assessing the strengths of an agency, and those on which agencies were perceived as weak. Figure

Table 1-4. **Agency Ranking on Six Attributes, 1984**

WHAT ARE THE MOST IMPORTANT AGENCY ATTRIBUTES?	WHICH AGENCIES ARE BEST AT THAT?
1. Creativity	1. Ogilvy & Mather 2. Chiat/Day 3. Doyle Dane Bernbach
2. Account executives	1. J. Walter Thompson 2. Ogilvy & Mather 3. Leo Burnett Co.
3. Media	1. J. Walter Thompson 2. Leo Burnett Co. 3. BBDO International Ogilvy & Mather
4. Top management	1. J. Walter Thompson 2. Ogilvy & Mather 3. Young & Rubicam
5. Marketing	1. J. Walter Thompson 2. Leo Burnett Co. 3. Ogilvy & Mather
6. Research	1. J. Walter Thompson 2. Ogilvy & Mather 3. BBDO International Leo Burnett

Source: Advertising Age, March 28, 1985, p. 6

1-4 shows the results. Creative talent and knowing the client's business were the two most important "necessary strengths" of an advertising agency. Quality of people was also very important. Not knowing client business, inadequate cost estimating, lack of creativity, poor account executives, and misrepresentation were most frequently mentioned as weak spots.

Agency Organization.   A modern agency employs three different types of people, in addition to those handling administration. The first is the creative services group, which includes copywriters, artists, and people concerned with advertising

Figure 1-4.   Advertising agency strengths and weaknesses

Necessary Agency Strengths

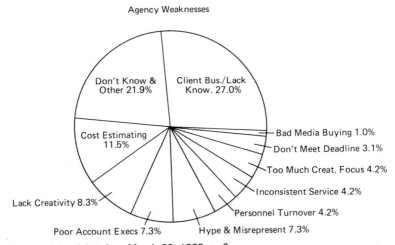

Agency Weaknesses

Source: Advertising Age, March 28, 1985, p. 6.

production. This group develops the advertising campaign, prepares the theme, and creates the actual advertisements. The second is the marketing services group, whose responsibility includes media and market research. This group contains the technical specialists—the psychologists who direct market research efforts and the operations researchers who develop the media buying models. The final group is the client services group, including account executives. An account executive is, in many respects, an agency's counterpart to a client's brand manager. An account executive is responsible for contact with the client. One of her or his important functions is to understand and perhaps contribute to the development of the client's advertising objective and to communicate it to the creative service and marketing service groups. As the advertising campaign is developed, the account executive obtains advice and decisions from the client as they are needed. In addition to these operating groups, there is usually a review board consisting of key agency people who review all campaigns generated within the agency.

The Full-Service Agency and Alternatives.   The dominant type of agency provides a full spectrum of services, including market research, new-product introduction plans, creative services, and media purchases, and is termed a *full-service agency*. An alternative to the full-service agency for large advertisers has recently appeared. Basically, it involves the replacement of the large agency with smaller specialized organizations, perhaps supplemented by a greater in-house client involvement in the process. It is stimulated by the development of organizations that specialize in media purchases and others that provide only creative services—the "creative boutiques." The rigidity of the 15 percent agency commission structure has also contributed to its development. Some companies feel that they do not use the full 15 percent worth of services.

Magnavox is a firm that has had experience with à la carte buying of advertising services. A Magnavox executive explained the reasoning behind the move, pointing out that the new wave of à la carte advertisers

> seems to be eliminating many costs related to agency middleman functions, such as account management and marketing and research processors. Along with the elimination of the full-service agency's overhead factors, this probably knocks off at least one-third of the 15% commission that the agency normally collects. The advertiser should be able to obtain the needed services for the remaining 10% and, if he does some of the media buying internally, for print, he can come in under 10%, as we have done. We also save the 15% agency commission on ad production, research, and other functions that an agency buys outside.[16]

The American Association of Advertising Agencies has set forth a position paper in which it presents the case for the full-service agency, arguing against "piecemealing." They identified 10 advantages of a full-service agency, including centralization of responsibility and accountability, simplified coordination and administration of a client's total advertising program, greater objectivity, sales-oriented creative work, synergistic experience, a stronger pool of talent, and a better working climate.

The Media

The amount of money spent on advertising in the various media from 1935 to 1984 is shown in Table 1-5. Through the years, the largest media category has been newspapers, which carried 27 percent of all advertising placed in 1984. The second largest medium in 1984 was television, which was nonexistent in 1945. Direct mail was the third largest medium, with expenditures of $13.8 billion. Thus, direct mail, a medium with low visibility in many respects, garnered more than twice as much advertising revenue as did radio. The strength of direct mail is its potential for pinpointing an audience and its capacity to present large quantities of advertising. Magazines represent another important medium. Business papers are primarily the trade magazines used by industrial advertisers and others who aim at nonconsumer audiences and, thus, for purposes of classification, could also be considered as magazines. Radio is yet another major media category.

Media developments have dramatically influenced the thrust of advertising through the years. Perhaps the most significant contribution to advertising was the development of the printing press by Gutenberg in 1438. Forty years later, in 1478, William Caxton printed the first English language advertisement, a handbill for a book of rules for the clergy at Easter.[17] The printing press, of course, made possible newspapers and magazines, the print media on which most advertising still relies.

The first important medium was newspapers. The earliest agencies, in the mid-nineteenth century, were essentially agents for newspapers. They provided a classic wholesaling function for the newspapers, each of which was too small by itself to sell space directly to the national advertisers. To a large extent, newspapers, particularly the smaller ones, still employ agents to sell their space to national advertisers, although these agents are now organizations distinct from agencies. However, the newspaper is really the domain of the local merchant. More than 80 percent of newspaper advertising is placed at the local level, and the most important newspaper advertisers are local retailers.

For all the attention television has received, it is nevertheless interesting that advertising for television in 1984 was exceeded by newspaper advertising. Furthermore, although the total share of newspaper advertising has declined since the advent of television, the decline has only amounted to a few percentage points. In 1984, about 27 percent of all advertising expenditures went into newspapers.

During the last decades of the 1800s, magazines began to assume increasing importance. In that period, Lord and Thomas concentrated on religious and agricultural periodicals, becoming the exclusive agent for many of them. After the Civil War, a young space salesman, J. Walter Thompson, decided to focus on the general magazine field, particularly the just-emerging area of women's magazines.[18] He provided advertisers with a list of several dozen from which they could choose. His choice of emphasis partly explains the phenomenal early success of the agency that still bears his name.

Until television arrived, magazines were the largest national advertising medium. With the advent of television, the magazine industry, and particularly the

Table 1-5.   **Estimated Advertising Expenditures in Major Media, 1935–1984 (millions of dollars)**

	1935	1945	1950	1955	1960	1965	1970	1975	1980	1984
Newspapers	761	919	2,070	3,077	3,681	4,426	5,704	8,442	15,615	23,744
National	148	203	518	712	778	784	891	1,221	2,335	3,007
Local	613	716	1,552	2,365	2,903	3,642	4,813	7,221	13,280	20,737
Magazines	130	344	478	691	909	1,161	1,292	1,465	3,225	4,932
Business papers	51	204	251	446	609	671	740	919	1,695	2,270
Television	—	—	171	1,035	1,627	2,515	3,596	5,263	11,330	19,874
National[a]	—	—	116	810	1,347	2,129	2,892	3,929	8,365	14,819
Local	—	—	55	225	280	386	704	1,334	2,965	5,055
Radio	113	424	605	545	693	917	1,308	1,980	3,690	5,813
National[a]	78	290	332	218	265	335	427	519	935	1,513
Local	35	134	273	327	428	582	881	1,461	2,755	4,300
Direct mail	282	290	803	1,299	1,830	2,324	2,766	4,124	7,655	13,800
Outdoor	31	72	142	192	203	180	234	335	610	872
Miscellaneous	342	555	1,122	1,793	2,342	2,985	3,848	5,571	10,795	16,775
Total national	890	1,740	3,260	5,380	7,305	9,340	11,350	15,340	30,435	49,590
Total local	830	1,100	2,440	3,770	4,655	5,910	8,200	12,820	24,315	38,490
Grand total	1,720	2,840	5,700	9,150	11,960	15,250	19,550	28,160	54,750	88,080

[a] Following is the breakdown for television, showing national and local expenditures on cable TV for 1984:

Network	8,562
Spot	5,453
Syndicated barter	400
Cable (national)	400
Local	5,055
Cable (local)	40
Total	19,874

Sources: "Twentieth Century Advertising and the Economy of Abundance," *Advertising Age,* April 30, 1980, Part 4, and *Advertising Age,* February 16, 1981, p. S-4, and May 6, 1985, p. 47.

mass-circulation magazines, began to feel the heavy pressure of competition. With the failure of such classic magazines as *The Saturday Evening Post, Look,* and finally *Life,* many began to question the long-term future of the magazine industry. Actually, magazines have considerable strength and vitality despite these visible setbacks. The year that the *Post* stopped publishing, twenty other magazines also merged or closed their doors, but more than 100 new ones appeared.[19] In 1950, magazine circulation was 140.2 per 100 population; twenty years later, it was 170.5 per 100 population and was still growing.[20]

The character of magazine publishing is changing, however. Despite the continued success of the *Reader's Digest,* whose circulation was more than 18 million in 1979, it is a fact that magazines are becoming more specialized.[21] They are aiming at special-interest groups and are often regional in scope. As a result, the audience is often more specialized also and is therefore desirable to an advertiser who is attempting to reach more specific audiences.

Magazines are innovating and attempting to capitalize on their physical contact with the audience to make their advertisements more effective.[22] Perfumed ink was used as early as 1957 for Baker's coconut in a *Better Homes & Garden* advertisement. Since then it has been used in advertisements for perfume, cologne, vodka, and soap. Recordings, such as Remington's "Music to Shave By," are included in advertisements. They are particularly effective in business advertisements that have a lengthy, detailed story to tell. Actual product samples have appeared in advertisements for Band-aids, candy, facial tissues, and computer software. Catalogs and other booklets have been included in magazine advertisements. These and other innovations reflect the willingness of magazines to build on their strengths.

Radio emerged in 1922 as an exciting, new, advertising medium. Its coverage of the 1922 World Series established it dramatically as a unique communication medium. The 1930s and 1940s were the golden years of radio. Without the competition of television, the network programs from the soap operas to the major evening shows starring such luminaries as Jack Benny, Eddie Cantor, Fred Allen, and Bing Crosby caught and held the attention of the American people. With the advent of television, however, radio went into the doldrums. But in the 1960s, radio started to make a comeback, finding a useful niche for itself by providing entertainment, news, and companionship, particularly for those in a car or otherwise occupied outside the home. It seemed to serve a purpose in a mobile and restless society. Radio's revitalization has been achieved by such programming innovations as talk shows, the all-news format, and hard-rock programs, and by such technological innovations as transistors, which make radios highly portable for people of all ages. Like magazines, radio has become more specialized as stations try to serve well-defined segments of the population. It has been particularly successful in developing a youth appeal. Like newspapers, it is a good medium for local advertisers, who provide radio with more than 60 percent of its advertising. One indication of the strength of radio is that the number of households with radios has increased from 44.8 million in 1952 to 76.5 million in 1979, and the number of autos with radios has increased from 23.5 million to 110.4 million in the same period.[23]

Television, delayed by World War II, began in the mid-1940s. In 1948, Milton Berle premiered his show, which was to dominate the ratings during the early years of commercial television. During the first decade of television, the advertiser usually sponsored and was identified with an entire program. This differs from the present practice of having several advertisers share a program. Advertisers were naturally attracted to this new medium because it provided an opportunity for presenting live demonstrations to large audiences. Television grew rapidly during the 1950s and 1960s. The number of homes with television sets in the top 50 markets increased from 6 million in 1950 to 30 million in 1960 and to 40 million in 1970.[24]

The advent of cable television, pay television, video recorders, and video discs promises to bring to television the same level of specialized audiences that magazines now deliver. The capability of offering programs to small special-interest audiences is rapidly emerging. These new technologies also provide for the entry of the "invited commercial." Viewers with the capability of bypassing commercials will only tend to watch commercials that are exceptionally entertaining, informative, or involving. Reaching this audience will require very different approaches to advertising creation and testing. Waiting in the wings are new developments in satellite transmission, with the ultimate prospect of reaching world audiences using visual approaches that are not tied to any particular language.

Like the top advertisers and top advertising agencies, there are top media companies. An important characteristic of the media industry is that most of the leading companies are diversified and are large conglomerates spanning all forms of media. Many of them also have significant revenues generated from nonmedia sources as well. For example, RCA, which owns NBC Broadcasting, derives only about 23 percent of its revenues from NBC. The industry is also very dynamic and is characterized by mergers, acquisitions, and divestitures of many kinds.

Table 1-6 shows the top 10 leading media companies in 1983 ranked on the basis of revenue generated from media operations. The three major broadcast networks, ABC, CBS, and NBC (owned by RCA), are among the leaders. American Broadcasting Company led the list for 1983 with over $2.8 billion in media revenue, representing 95.5 percent of all its revenues. Notice that CBS Inc., in second place, is a much larger company overall, and that only about 59 percent of its revenue comes from media. RCA, in turn, is about twice the size of CBS, with only about 23 percent of revenues generated by the NBC network.

To understand the media industry, it is important to appreciate that newspapers still dominate all other media in terms of revenue. Among the top 100 media companies in 1983, for example, newspapers accounted for $16.39 billion, about 39 percent. Knight-Ridder, Gannett, Times-Mirror, Advance Publications, Tribune, and Hearst are companies in the top 10 that are leading newspaper publishers. The New York Times, which placed eleventh in 1983, is another significant newspaper conglomerate. The leading newspaper company is Knight-Ridder, which, for ex-

Table 1-6. **Top Ten Media Companies, 1983**

RANK			1983 REVENUES (MILLIONS)		
1983	1982	COMPANY	Media	Total	% Media
1	1	American Broadcasting Co.	$2,815.2	$2,948.8	95.5
2	2	CBS Inc.	2,682.9	4,540.2	59.1
3	3	Time Inc.	2,248.5	2,717.0	82.3
4	4	RCA Corp.	2,090.0	8,980.0	23.3
5	7	Advance Publications	1,740.2	1,940.2	89.7
6	5	Gannett Co.	1,671.2	1,703.7	98.1
7	6	Times Mirror Co.	1,667.3	2,491.2	66.9
8	8	Knight-Ridder Newspapers	1,450.7	1,473.4	98.5
9	10	Tribune Co.	1,397.4	1,586.5	88.1
10	9	Hearst Corp.	1,116.0	N/A	N/A

Source: Advertising Age, June 28, 1984, p. 12.

ample, owns daily newspapers in 13 states. *San Jose Mercury News* in California is a good example of a Knight-Ridder publication. Knight-Ridder also owns television stations and cable networks.

The importance of magazines is reflected in the top group by Time Inc., publisher of *Time* magazine. Time Inc. also publishes *Discover, Fortune, Life, Money, People,* and *Sports Illustrated.* Time Inc. is, however, also the nation's leading cable company. Almost one-half of its total $2.2 billion of media revenue in 1983 came from its cable operations, such as Cinemax, producers of Home Box Office (HBO), and American Television and Communications, which in 1983 had 13 divisions nationwide. Not included in the leading 10 are some magazine companies that derive the bulk of their revenues solely from one or a few magazines, such as Reader's Digest Association ($190.5 million), National Geographic Society ($202 million), Playboy Enterprises ($150.2 million), Penthouse International ($153.0), and McCall Publishing ($121.6). Well-known book publishers are among the media conglomerates. McGraw-Hill, for example, received about 68 percent of total revenues from media, primarily from magazines ($381.2 million) such as *Business Week* and dozens of others in computing, chemical, electrical, medical, and other industries.

Various types of promotions can also be considered by the advertiser and represent yet another kind of media. The sales promotion industry has grown rapidly and was estimated to have reached the $40 billion level in 1980.[25] Like the major media, each form of promotional activity is represented by a professional trade association. Thus, the Promotion Marketing Association of America (PMAA) and the National Premium Sales Executive Association (NPSEA) focus on premiums, promotions, contests, couponing, sampling, price-offs, and cash refunds; the Point-of-Purchase Advertising Institute (POPAI) covers point-of-purchase and aisle display materials; the Specialty Advertising Association International (SAAI) is concerned with specialty advertising, such as imprinted business cards and gifts, and the Trade Show Bureau (TSB) with trade shows. Direct mail, represented by the Direct Mail Marketing Association (DMMA), is also often included in this category.

Research Suppliers

The final type of facilitating institution is made up of companies that supply research services to advertisers, advertising agencies, and the media. Currently, there are more than 500 firms in the United States[26] that supply all kinds of research information for advertising-planning purposes and for specific decisions, such as copy and media decisions.

The first advertising researchers developed methods for assessing the effectiveness of print advertising. Indeed, the progress of the field of advertising research closely parallels the development of each of the major media. The Audit Bureau of Circulations (ABC) was one of the earliest firms to develop the first audits of newspaper circulation in 1914. The notion of auditing circulation quickly spread to magazines, and Daniel Starch, a professor at Harvard University, developed the recognition method for measuring magazine readership in 1919. Later, in 1932, Starch founded the firm of Daniel Starch and Staff, which is still one of the largest supplier firms providing research on print advertising. It is now called Starch INRA Hooper.

Radio research, and broadcast ratings in general, first began in the 1920s, when Archibald Crossley started the Crossley Radio Ratings. The industry expanded greatly during the 1930s and 1940s, as politicians and advertisers realized the potential of radio for reaching national audiences. Frank Stanton, later to become president of CBS, began his career in radio research and, with Paul Lazarsfeld and others, initiated an office of radio research at Princeton University. Lazarsfeld later moved this office to Columbia University to form the Bureau of Applied Social Research.

Television research became one of the numerous specialties of the A. C. Nielsen Company, and it is particularly well known for its television program rating services. A. C. Nielsen, Sr., who founded the company in Chicago, began by developing auditing services of the movement of products through retail stores. This service is an important part of the current range of research services supplied by this company, and A. C. Nielsen has become by far the largest research supplier, with operations extending into many foreign countries. About 52 percent of Nielsen's 1984 research revenues of $491.0 million, for example, were generated from operations abroad.

From these early beginnings, research companies have sprung up to provide a wide variety of services to advertisers, ranging from consumer surveys and panels

Table 1-7.   **Top Ten Research Companies, 1984[a]**

RANK		COMPANY	RESEARCH REVENUES (MILLIONS)	PERCENT CHANGE VS. 1983	RESEARCH REVENUES FROM OUTSIDE U.S. (MILLIONS)
1984	1983				
1	1	A.C. Nielsen Co.	$ 491.0	5.9	$255.3 est
2	2	IMS International	151.4	10.1	83.9
3	3	SAMI	118.4	19.0	—
4	4	Arbitron Ratings Co.	105.8	12.3	—
5	5	Burke Marketing Services	66.0	9.8	1.7
6	8	M/A/R/C	37.6	39.8	—
7	7	Market Facts	35.9	26.7	—
8	12	Information Resources	35.8	69.7	—
9	9	NFO Research	29.5	10.1	—
10	10	NPD Group	29.2	17.7	—
		Total	$1,100.6	+22.1	$340.9

[a] For some companies, total revenues that include nonresearch activities are significantly higher than those shown in the table. Change from 1983 to 1984 includes revenue gains from acquisitions.

Source: Adapted from Jack J. Honomichl, ''The Nation's Top 40: Marketing/Advertising Research Companies,'' *Advertising Age,* May 23, 1985, p. 17.

to copy testing, audience measurement, and many others.[27] Table 1-7 shows the largest U.S. research companies in 1984, their research revenues, percent change from 1983, and the revenue generated outside the United States. These top 10 companies accounted for over $1.1 billion in the research revenue in that year, an overall increase of 22.1 percent from 1983. As can be seen, A. C. Nielsen is almost four times as large as the second-place IMS International and dominates the international operations as well. The first five companies shown have maintained their leading positions over the years and continue to be the largest research companies.

Most of the firms shown on the list provide data for advertising planning, implementation, and control purposes. Nielsen, IMS International, and SAMI (Selling Areas-Marketing Inc.) offer syndicated services to which advertisers subscribe on an ongoing basis. Auditing product movements in food and pharmaceuticals are good examples. Many maintain large consumer panels. NFO Research and the NPD Group are well known for their panel operations. Computer-assisted telephone interviewing (CATI) has grown considerably. Chilton Research Services is one of the nation's leaders in this service.

Some companies tend to specialize in either copy testing (ad testing is commonly called copy testing even though it is the whole advertisement that is usually tested, not just the copy) or audience measurement and provide information most useful for copy and media decision making. In broadcast, Burke Marketing Services, ASI Market Research, McCollum/Spielman, and the Gallup Organization are well known for their copy-testing services. Among the better known copy-testing services for print advertisements are those of Starch INRA Hooper. Concerning audience measurement, A. C. Nielsen and Arbitron are most prominent in broadcast. Simmons Market Research Bureau is one of the leaders in print audience measurement. Dozens of specialized services, such as Pulse and BAR (BAR monitors advertiser spending rates), are available for media planners. In print, ABC (Audit Bureau of Circulation) provides basic circulation and other data for magazines and newspapers, and BPA provides similar information for business, technical, and trade papers. SRDS (Standard Rate and Data Service), Simmons, and TGI (Target Group Index) provide very useful information on all media. Information Resources represents one of the newer forms of marketing research based on supermarket checkout scanners. Their service, called BehaviorScan, has grown rapidly. Management Decision Systems, acquired by Information Resources in 1985, focuses on computer decision-support system services.

Market research is a significant industry in the United States and is the source of much of the information used in advertising management. Throughout the book, we will show how research information enters at various stages of advertising management and discuss specific services in more detail. Here it is important to gain an initial impression of the diversity and range of such services and to appreciate the importance of their role in advertising management.[28]

PERSPECTIVES ON ADVERTISING

There is an extensive literature on advertising, made up of books, monographs, reports, journal articles, and speeches, most of which have been written since the turn of the century. David A. Revzan of the University of California lists more than 450 books on the subject of advertising written between 1900 and 1969.[29] There are at least six advertising handbooks, eight histories, and several biographical accounts of advertising people. In addition to handbooks and historical perspectives, advertising has been approached through a variety of paths and traditions. These different paths partly reflect the perspectives of such various disciplines as economics, psychology, social philosophy, and management. They also reflect the needs of the audiences to which they are addressed. Although many of the paths cross and some are ill defined, it is possible and useful to identify some of the main tracks that have been followed through the years.

Several books with an economic perspective, including Roland Vaile's *Economics of Advertising,* were published in the 1920s.[30] The depression of the 1930s increased public concern with the role advertising plays in our competitive economic system. Critics argued that advertising inhibits competition. In this environment, Harvard professor Neil Borden published a classic study of the economic effects of advertising.[31] The evaluation of advertising as an economic force in society has continued to receive attention over the years. A recent book in this tradition is Julian Simon's *Issues in the Economics of Advertising.*[32] The economic perspective tends to deal with aggregate statistics of firms and industries and is concerned with public-policy implications.

The writings of sociologists, religious leaders, philosophers, and politicians are also extensive, many reflecting critical views of advertising. Thus, in 1932, Arthur Kallet and F. J. Schlink published *100,000,000 Guinea Pigs,* followed by such works as A. S. J. Basker's *Advertising Reconsidered* in 1935, H. K. Kenner's *The Fight for Truth in Advertising* in 1936, Blake Clarke's *The Advertising Smoke Screen* in 1944, F. P. Bishop's *The Ethics of Advertising* in 1949, and later works like Vance Packard's *The Hidden Persuaders,* Francis X. Quin's *Ethics, Advertising and Responsibility,* and Sidney Margolius's *The Innocent Consumer vs. The Exploiters.*[33] Advertising is a controversial subject about which scholars, intellectuals, and businessmen tend to form strong and often contradictory opinions.[34]

Another approach to advertising, descriptive in nature, typifies the introductory texts covering the principles of advertising that have appeared from the early 1900s to the present time. They describe such institutions of advertising as advertising agencies and the various media, often from a historical perspective. The relative importance and the operation of these institutions is of central interest. Books of this type often also describe in some detail the physical process of creating advertising—the selection of type faces, the production process, and other practical particulars. The descriptive approach generally focuses on what advertising is in a macro sense and how it works at a detailed level.

Behavioral approaches to advertising can be traced to Walter Dill Scott's 1913 book, *The Psychology of Advertising.*[35] Since then, there has been a steady stream of books firmly tied to the behavioral disciplines, such as D. Lucas and C. E. Benson's *Psychology for Advertisers* in 1930 and, more recently, Edgar Crane's *Marketing Communications.*[36] This approach is largely concerned with the analysis of the communication process, using behavioral science theory and empirical findings. The interest in motivation research in the 1950s and consumer buyer behavior in the 1960s provided impetus to this area of thought. During the past decade, in particular, an enormous amount of progress has been made in using theories and models from psychology, social psychology, and sociology to help understand buyer behavior, the communication process, and the link between the two.

The research tradition in advertising parallels the development of the various media research services discussed earlier. It has also done much to motivate academic work on basic advertising research and studies of advertising effectiveness.

The managerial tradition is really more recent in origin. Perhaps the first book truly devoted to the subject of advertising management was a case book by Neil Borden and Martin Marshall, *Advertising Management: Text and Cases,* published in 1950 and revised in 1959.[37] This book, and the others that followed, approached the subject from the viewpoint of a manager faced with the tasks of preparing an advertising budget, deciding how to allocate funds to different media, and choosing among alternative copy strategies. These books were thus decision oriented and provided a contrast to the principles approach, in which the nature and role of advertising institutions and advertising techniques tended to be the point of emphasis.

Still another approach to advertising, even more recent in origin, is the model-building perspective originating from the fields of operations research and statistics. Although it had early predecessors, it really began in the late 1950s with the development of decision models concerned with allocating the media budget. Model building is so new that so far it is primarily represented in the literature in the form of monographs and journal articles.

The Approach of this Book

This book, like others, will touch on all these traditions, although its main thrust is really to blend the last four. The managerial perspective will largely motivate the book. The focus is on decision making, specifically those decisions that generate an advertising campaign. The book involves an attempt to analyze and structure systematically the various decision areas within advertising and to present material that shows promise of helping decision makers generate better alternatives and improve their decision-making process.

In doing this, the book will draw heavily on the models and theories that have originated from the behavioral disciplines and the more quantitative models that have emerged from operations research and statistics and the research techniques and approaches that underlie each. Our goal will be to extend and organize these models in such a way as to reveal their potential utility to decision makers. A deliberate effort will be made to integrate the two model-building traditions. It is the belief of the authors that integration will serve to maximize the strengths and minimize the limitations of the available models.

Many of the models introduced have considerable immediate or potential practical value. In general, however, models are introduced for their pedagogical value, as well as for their value as immediate practical aids to decision making. Therefore, in selecting models to be discussed, there is no demand that they be tested and completely operational; actually, relatively few are now well diffused through the business community. The fact is that well-conceived models do have significant pedagogical value. They provide a vocabulary and a structure that can make a complex decision area more understandable and accessible to a student. Thus, models are intended to enhance the learning process and upgrade discussions. They are not intended to provide a set of cookbook techniques that can be blindly followed in a particular situation.

The integration of research-based behavioral and quantitative models in a decision-making context is both exciting and challenging. The challenge is that a student must become familiar with management science modeling, philosophy, and techniques, be cognizant of consumer behavior and the workings of the market-place, and be aware of research tools and approaches. In writing this book, the authors have found that the insights to be gained from an integrative perspective far outweigh the frustrations involved. The hope is that seemingly detached and unrelated concepts, models, and decisions can eventually be seen as part of a whole that will help a manager become a more effective practitioner of modern-day advertising.

SUMMARY

There are four major advertising institutions with which the reader should be familiar: the advertiser, the advertising agency, the media, and the research suppliers. There is a wide variety of advertisers. Those who are classified as national advertisers spend the largest share of advertising dollars. The balance is spent by local advertisers. Advertisers can also be distinguished by the product type with which they are involved: consumer packaged goods, consumer durables, retail stores, or industrial products, for example.

In most cases, an advertising agency actually creates the advertisements and makes the media-allocation decisions. For this service, it receives from the various media 15 percent of the advertising billings it places. Claude Hopkins was an early copywriter who helped to generate a reputation for creating effective advertising for his agency. Modern agencies also try to achieve such reputations.

Media developments have dramatically influenced the thrust of advertising through the years. The printing press made possible newspapers and magazines, the major media before the advent of the broadcast media, television and radio. Radio in 1922 and television in 1948 provided a new dimension to advertising and sparked a period of growth. Despite the competition of the broadcast media, newspapers continue to be the largest medium, with more than $23.7 billion in advertising revenues in 1984. Television is second with over $19.8 billion, followed by direct-mail advertising. In the 1980s, the marriage of computers, mass communications, and satellite technologies will generate new types of teletext and videotex systems and create new opportunities and challenges for advertisers.

Modern advertising management is heavily involved with research, and a sizable industry of research supplier firms has grown up to serve the needs of advertisers, agencies, and the media. Today, over a billion dollars is spent annually on marketing and advertising research, and specialized services are associated with each of the major media.

Since the turn of the century, hundreds of books on advertising have been published, most of which can be categorized into different writing traditions. Some are historical and others descriptive in their orientation; still others represent the perspectives of economists, social philosophers, managers, behavioral scientists, and quantitative model builders. This book is motivated by the managerial perspective that focuses on the decisions that generate an advertising campaign. However, it also draws heavily on models originating in both the behavioral and quantitative disciplines. A major purpose of the book is to integrate these two model-building traditions to enhance their power and relevance to advertising decision makers. Thus, although it touches all the writing traditions, this book is really concerned with melding four perspectives: that of the manager, the behavioral scientist, the quantitative model builder, and the advertising researcher.

DISCUSSION QUESTIONS

1. Advertisers are defined as organizations that make use of mass media, whereas nonadvertisers do not. Are there any exceptions to this definition? In what other ways might advertisers and nonadvertisers be distinguished?

2. How will the role of advertising differ when the product involved is a consumer packaged product instead of a consumer durable? How will it differ for a retailer and an industrial advertiser? What part of the marketing program will advertising be assigned to in each case?

3. What similarities and differences would there be between the development of an advertising campaign for the Ford Foundation or the Forestry Service and Procter & Gamble or General Motors?

4. Consider the major institutions of advertising management given in Figure 1-1. Are there others that should be included? Write a brief statement explaining the primary roles of each institution.

5.   Do you believe that a company like Procter & Gamble should develop its own in-house agency, thereby keeping the 15 percent commission?

6.   Examine Table 1-5 for media trends. Why did outdoor media decline between 1955 and 1965? What is its likely future now? Why did total advertising expenditures increase so dramatically in 1950 and again in 1955 and 1984? Why did radio decline in 1955?

7.   Consumers will soon be able to purchase prerecorded videodiscs and engage in two-way communications via cable television systems. What are some of the implications of these developments for advertisers?

8.   Critics of advertising often wonder why certain advertisements are used. Outline the major research studies and research supplier services that would be involved in developing a major national campaign.

9.   Consider the different perspectives on advertising. For each, try to determine what would be regarded as the key issues. What types of experimental evidence would be of the greatest interest to each?

10.   Consider the problem of developing an advertising information system. What role would models have in the process?

11.   Concerning selecting an advertising agency, what agency attributes would you consider most important in picking an agency for a new Honda sports car?

NOTES

1. *Advertising Age,* May 6, 1985, p. 47.

2. Robert J. Coen, "Vast U.S. and Worldwide Ad Expenditures Expected," *Advertising Age,* November 13, 1980, p. 10.

3. *Standard Directory of Advertisers.* Skokie, Ill.: National Register Publishing Company, 1978. This directory, one of the so-called Red Books, is published annually by National Register, a subsidiary of Standard Rate and Data Service, and is a very useful reference to information on advertisers. A companion volume is *Standard Directory of Advertising Agencies.* Another useful reference to all aspects of the advertising industry is "Twentieth Century Advertising and the Economy of Abundance," *Advertising Age,* April 30, 1980.

4. The term PSA generally refers to advertisements sponsored by the Advertising Council, Washington, D.C., for federal government and other nonprofit organizations. There are, however, significant numbers of public-service announcements donated by media at the local level. None of this national or local advertising activity enters into estimates of the size of the advertising industry given here.

5. *Advertising Age,* May 6, 1985, p. 47.

6. *Advertising Age,* September 14, 1984, p. 8.

7. For a book on the subject, see S. P. Sethi, *Advocacy Advertising and Large Corporations.* Lexington, Mass.: D. C. Heath and Company, 1977.

8. Maurice J. Mandell, *Advertising* (Englewood Cliffs, N.J.: Prentice-Hall, 1968), p. 24.

9. Albert Lasker, *The Lasker Story* (Chicago: Chicago Advertising Publications, 1963), pp. 29–31.

10. Claude C. Hopkins, *My Life In Advertising* (Chicago: Chicago Advertising Publications, 1966), p. 172.

11. Ibid., pp. 101–105.

12. Ibid., p. 102.

13. Ibid., pp. 106–111.

14. Lasker, *The Lasker Story,* p. 38.

15. *Advertising Age,* March 28, 1985, p. 1.

16. "Advertising That Comes À La Carte," *Business Week,* May 1, 1971, p. 46.

17. Mandell, *Advertising,* p. 24.

18. *Advertising Age,* December 7, 1964, p. 32.

19. *Advertising Age,* October 20, 1969, p. 50.

20. *Advertising Age,* April 30, 1980, p. 270.

21. Ibid.

22. *Advertising Age,* October 20, 1969, p. 184.

23. *Advertising Age,* April 30, 1980, p. 268.

24. Ibid., p. 66.

25. Louis J. Haugh, "Sales Promotion Grows to $40 Billion Status," *Advertising Age,* April 30, 1980, p. 199ff.

26. For information on the marketing and advertising research supplier industry, see Bradford's *Directory of Marketing Research Agencies and Management Consultants in the U.S. and the World* (Fairfax, Va., biennial), and *International Directory of Marketing Research Houses and Services,* published by the New York Chapter of the American Marketing Association. Other useful information is contained in the *Roster of the American Marketing Association.* Recent marketing research texts also provide useful listings. See Donald R. Lehmann, *Market Research and Analysis* (Homewood, Ill.: Richard D. Irwin, 1979), pp. 138–148 and 161–171, and John G. Myers, William F. Massy, and Stephen A. Greyser, *Marketing Research and Knowledge Development* (Englewood Cliffs, N.J.: Prentice-Hall, 1980), pp. 101–166.

27. See *Advertising Age,* April 24, 1978.

28. See *Advertising Age,* March 17, 1984, p. M–17ff.

29. David A. Revzan, *Marketing Bibliography, Parts I and II* (Berkeley, Calif.: University of California Press, 1959). Supplement 1 published 1963; Supplement 2 published 1970.

30. Roland S. Vaile, *The Economics of Advertising* (New York: Ronald Press, 1927).

31. Neil H. Borden, *The Economic Effects of Advertising* (Homewood, Ill.: Richard D. Irwin, 1942).

32. Julian L. Simon, *Issues in the Economics of Advertising* (Urbana, Ill.: University of Illinois Press, 1970).

33. Arthur Kallet and F. J. Schlink, *100,000,000 Guinea Pigs* (New York: Vanguard Press, 1932); A. S. J. Basker, *Advertising Reconsidered* (London: P. S. King and Son, 1935); H. K. Kenner, *The Fight for Truth in Advertising* (New York: Roundtable Press, 1936); Blake Clarke, *The Advertising Smoke Screen* (New York: Harper & Row, 1944); F. P. Bishop, *The Ethics of Advertising* (London: Robert Hale, 1949); Vance Packard, *The Hidden Persuaders* (New York: David McKay, 1957); Francis X. Quin, *Ethics, Advertising and Responsibility* (Rome, N.Y.: Canterbury Press, 1963); and Sidney Margolius, *The Innocent Consumers vs. the Exploiters* (New York: Trident Press, 1967).

34. For a business perspective, see Francesco M. Nicosia, *Advertising, Management, and Society: A Business Point of View* (New York: McGraw-Hill, 1974).

35. Walter Dill Scott, *The Psychology of Advertising* (Boston: Small Maynard and Co., 1913).

36. D. Lucas and C. E. Benson, *Psychology for Advertisers* (New York: Harper & Bros., 1930); and Edgar Crane, *Marketing Communications,* 2nd ed. (New York: Wiley, 1972).

37. Neil H. Borden and Martin V. Marshall, *Advertising Management: Text and Cases,* rev. ed. (Homewood, Ill.: Richard D. Irwin, 1959).

2

Advertising Planning
and Decision Making

Plans are nothing, planning is everything. (Dwight D. Eisenhower)

Chapter 1 presented a broad view of the field of advertising management. The advertiser component is the core of the system, and many of the perspectives in this chapter and the balance of the book reflect the advertiser viewpoint. The person most responsible for advertising management is typically the brand manager, but the relevant titles will vary by organizational context, and we will henceforth use the more general term, advertising manager.

The major activities of advertising management are planning and decision making. In most instances, the advertising manager will be involved in the development, implementation, and overall management of an advertising plan. The development of an advertising plan essentially requires the generation and specification of alternatives. The alternatives can be various levels of expenditure, different kinds of objectives or strategy possibilities, and numerous kinds of options associated with copy creation and media choices. The essence of planning is thus to find out what the feasible alternatives are and reduce them to a set on which decisions can be made. Decision making involves choosing from among the alternatives. A complete advertising plan really reflects the end results of the planning and decision-making process and the decisions that have been arrived at in a particular product and market situation.

The planning and decision-making process begins with a thorough analysis of the situation facing the advertiser. This step is often called *situation analysis* to reflect the fact that the situation must be well understood before feasible alternatives are specified and decisions are made.

The first section of the chapter presents a framework for advertising planning and decision making. It is an elaboration of the advertising system model given in Chapter 1 and expands the advertiser component.

PLANNING FRAMEWORK

The major internal and external factors involved in advertising planning and decision making are shown in Figure 2-1. Internally, situation analysis, the marketing program, and the advertising plan are key considerations. As suggested in the

Figure 2-1.   **Factors involved in advertising planning and decision making**

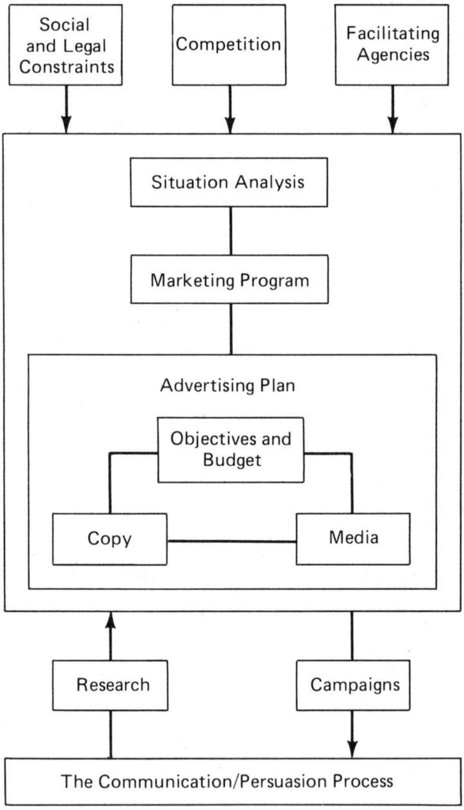

diagram, the three legs of advertising planning concern objective and budget, copy, and media considerations. Various external factors must also be considered. Most important is the communication/persuasion process shown at the bottom. The process of communication and persuasion in a particular product-market situation must be thoroughly understood if effective advertising is to be developed. As shown in the diagram, research is the means by which markets are analyzed, and campaigns are the means through which the organization communicates with markets. The other external factors involved in advertising planning and decision making are, as shown, social and legal constraints, competition, and the facilitating agencies.

The balance of this chapter addresses each of these factors. First, situation analysis is explained and discussed. Then a brief review of the marketing program and the major parts of the advertising plan is given. This is followed by sections on communication/persuasion processes, social and legal constraints, competition, facilitating agencies, and market segmentation strategy.

SITUATION ANALYSIS

The planning and decision-making process begins with a thorough analysis of the situation facing the advertiser. Situation analysis involves an analysis of all important factors operating in a particular situation. In many cases, this means that new research studies will be undertaken as well as relying on company history and experience.

AT&T, for example, developed a new strategy for its long-distance telephone services based on five years of research.[1] The research encompassed market segmentation studies, concept testing, and a large-scale field experiment. The field experiment focused on testing a new advertising campaign called "Cost of Visit." An existing "Reach Out" campaign, although successful, did not appear to get through to a large group of people who had reasons to call but were limiting their calls because of cost. Research based on annual surveys of 3,000 residential telephone users showed that most did not know the cost of a long-distance call or that it was possible to make less expensive calls in off-peak periods. Five copy alternatives were subsequently developed and tested, from which "Cost of Visit" was chosen. This campaign was credited with persuading customers to call during times that were both cheaper for them and more profitable for AT&T and, overall, was more effective than the "Reach Out" campaign. One estimate was that by switching $30 million in advertising from "Reach Out" to "Cost of Visit," an incremental gain in revenue of $22 million would result in the first year, and would top $100 million over five years.

This example highlights a "situation" in which advertising was undoubtedly a major factor, extensive research was done to study the situation, and large sums of money were involved in both research and advertising. A complete situation analysis will cover all marketing components and involve finding answers to dozens of questions about the nature and extent of demand, competition, environmental factors, product, costs, distribution, and the skills and financial resources of the firm. Table 2-1 provides a listing of topics and relevant questions that need to be answered for each topic.

Situation analysis invariably involves research of some kind. As noted in Table 2-1, for advertising planning and decision making, the principal thrust of research efforts will be on market analysis or, more broadly, the analysis of consumer motivation and behavior with respect to the product, service, idea, or object to be advertised. It is this kind of research that is most important in advertising, and many of the research approaches, techniques, models, and results presented throughout the book pertain to it. Many people in advertising are skeptical about the value of research, particularly with respect to the creative process of actually generating specific advertisements. Although research can slow up the process and, some would argue, can interfere with creativity and lead to mundane advertising, in most cases planning and decision making will be improved by research. Situation analysis can be based on conventional wisdom, managerial experience, or the creative team's inherent imaginative abilities, but current market and environmental conditions—what the situation is now—can only be adequately assessed by research. Such research flows from the company and its agency's research efforts, secondary data sources, and/or is purchased from research suppliers.

In many cases, a situation analysis is undertaken from the perspective of the total company or product line and will involve finding answers to dozens of questions including the history of the product, distribution, pricing, packaging, consumer analysis, competition, and many more. Several good planning guides are available on situation analysis.[2] Suffice it to say that situation analysis is generally the foundation for any well-developed marketing program, and the cornerstone for an advertising plan. The major parts of a typical marketing program are reviewed next.

MARKETING PROGRAM

Advertising planning and decision making take place in the context of an overall marketing program. The marketing program includes planning, implementation, and control functions for the total corporation or a particular decision-making unit or product line. The marketing plan will include a statement of marketing objectives and the spelling out of particular strategies and tactics to reach those objectives. The marketing objective should identify the segments to be served by the organization and how it is going to serve them. The needs and wants of consumers on which the firm will concentrate, such as the needs of working housewives for easily prepared meals, are identified and analyzed in preparing a marketing plan.

There are several marketing tools that can be used to help an organization achieve its marketing objectives. Its product or service can be developed or refined. A distribution network can help match an organization's output with its clientele. Pricing strategy is another marketing-decision variable. A sales force provides a

Table 2-1.   Topics and Questions Involved in Situation Analysis

A. Nature of demand

  1. How do buyers (consumer and industrial) *currently* go about buying existing products or services? Describe the main types of behavior patterns and attitudes.
     a. Number of stores shopped or industrial sources considered.
     b. Degree of overt information seeking.
     c. Degree of brand awareness and loyalty.
     d. Location of product category decision—home or point of sale.
     e. Location of brand decision—home or point of sale.
     f. Sources of product information and current awareness and knowledge levels.
     g. Who makes the purchase decision—male, female, adult, child, ·purchasing agent, buying committee, and so on?
     h. Who influences the decision maker?
     i. Individual or group decision (computers versus candy bar).
     j. Duration of the decision process (repeat, infrequent or new purchase situation).
     k. Buyer's interest, personal involvement or excitement regarding the purchase (hairpins versus trip to Caribbean).
     l. Risk or uncertainty of negative purchase outcome—high, medium, or low (specialized machinery versus hacksaw blades) (pencil versus hair coloring).
     m. Functional versus psychological considerations (electric drill versus new dress).
     n. Time of consumption (gum versus dining room furniture).
  2. Can the market be meaningfully segmented or broken into several homogeneous groups with respect to "what they want" and "how they buy"?
     Criteria:
     a. Age.
     b. Family life cycle.
     c. Geographic location.
     d. Heavy versus light users.
     e. Nature of the buying process.
     f. Product usage.

B. Extent of demand

  1. What is the size of the market (units and dollars) now, and what will the future hold?
  2. What are the current market shares, and what are the selective demand trends (units and dollars)?
  3. Is it best to analyze the market on an aggregate or on a segmented basis?

C. Nature of competition

  1. What is the present and future structure of competition?
     a. Number of competitors (5 versus 2,000).
     b. Market shares.
     c. Financial resources.
     d. Marketing resources and skills.
     e. Production resources and skills.

Table 2-1.   **Topics and Questions Involved in Situation Analysis** (*Continued*)

2. What are the current marketing programs of established competitors? Why are they successful or unsuccessful?
3. Is there an opportunity for another competitor? Why?
4. What are the anticipated retaliatory moves of competitors? Can they neutralize different marketing programs we might develop?

D. Environmental climate

1. What are the relevant social, political, economic, and technological trends?
2. How do you evaluate these trends? Do they represent opportunities or problems?

E. Stage of product life cycle

1. In what stage of the life cycle is the product category?
   a. What is the chronological age of the product category? (Younger more favorable than older?)
   b. What is the state of the consumers' knowledge of the product category? (More complete the knowledge—more unfavorable?)
2. What market characteristics support your stage of life cycle evaluation?

F. Cost structure of the industry

1. What is the amount and composition of the marginal or additional cost of supplying increased output?

G. Skills of the firm

1. Do we have the skills and experience to perform the functions necessary to be in this business?
   a. Marketing skills.
   b. Production skills.
   c. Management skills.
   d. Financial skills.
   e. R&D skills.
2. How do our skills compare to competitors?
   a. Production fit.
   b. Marketing fit.
   c. Etc.

H. Financial resources of the firm

1. Do we have the funds to support an effective marketing program?
2. Where are the funds coming from, and when will they be available?

Table 2-1.   **Topics and Questions Involved in Situation Analysis** (*Continued*)

I. Distribution structure

    1. What channels exist and can we gain access to the channels?
    2. Cost versus revenue from different channels?
    3. Feasibility of using multiple channels?
    4. Nature and degree of within and between channel competition?
    5. Trends of channel structure?
    6. Requirements of different channels for promotion and margin?
    7. Will it be profitable for particular channels to handle my product?

Source: Adapted from an unpublished note by Professor James R. Taylor of the University of Michigan. Used with permission.

communication device for personally dealing with an individual or a small group. Finally, there is the mass paid communication known as advertising.

Advertising is thus a part of the total marketing program. Such an observation may seem trivial, but there are many contexts in which this simple fact is forgotten. The result can be a marketing program in which the component parts work at cross-purposes instead of in a coordinated, synergistic manner. To show the importance of the need to coordinate advertising activities with other parts of the program, we will next discuss some features of the interaction of advertising with the other marketing variables.

Product

The product or more broadly the *object* of the advertising must be well understood. Is the product or thing to be advertised relatively new to the market or is the category an old and established one? What is the company's overall product policy in terms of the depth and breadth of its product line? Where does our brand fit in? Much analysis here concerns the product life cycle and how the advertising plan will be affected by the particular stage involved. It should be obvious, for example, that an advertising plan for a new brand, or a product at the early stages of the life cycle, will be very different from one developed for a mature or dying product. The plan must take this aspect of the overall marketing program into account.

Branding

The advertising plan must also take into account the company's branding policy. For example, a company might produce several variations of its product, all under a family or company name, such as those of the Campbell Soup Company or Del Monte Corporation, or produce those variations under different brand names, such as in the case of Procter & Gamble's detergent products—Duz, Tide, Biz, and so on. In the case of family branding, the advertising appropriation is made to the entire line with special attention periodically given to particular products in the line. For instance, Del Monte might feature canned corn or beans in some part of an overall campaign in support of the company's entire product line. In the individual branding case, each brand and the advertising budget, copy, and media decisions associated with it are treated largely independently. In fact, many corporations, such as the major soap and automobile companies, base their marketing organizations on the concept of *brand management* and actively encourage the brand managers to compete with one another for market share and consumer loyalty.

Pricing

When a firm develops a prestige product with a premium price, it is important that the advertising reinforce that idea of high quality and prestige. This can be done by associating the product with prestigious people, situations, or events. If the advertising objectives are written to encourage the use of advertising copy and advertising media incompatible with a prestige image, the whole marketing program may be jeopardized. Alternatively, when a firm offers a low-priced product, the job of advertising might be to stress the price differential by using hard-hitting copy.

Distribution

The role of advertising will also depend on the distribution channel selected. If door-to-door selling is employed, advertising may be used only to introduce the salesperson, or it may not be used at all. If wholesalers, retailers, or other middlemen are employed, different advertising strategies are available. The advertising and selling effort may be primarily directed to either the consumer or the trade. In the former case, the intent would then be to have consumer interest pull the merchandise through the distribution channel; in the latter case, distributor margins would get the emphasis, consumer advertising would be less, and the intent would be to push it through the channel. Generally, the nature and significance of advertising will differ according to whether the company is stressing a push or pull strategy and whether its distribution strategy is intensive (the use of many outlets to maximize customer convenience), exclusive (the use of a few outlets to maximize retailer interest), or selective (intermediate arrangements).

Personal Selling

Personal selling is another marketing tool that is primarily concerned with communication. Consequently, its relationship with advertising is particularly relevant. Personal selling is, of course, a far more effective communication method than advertising. The message and its presentation can be tailored to each prospect. Furthermore, interpersonal interactions can provide immediate feedback that permits the presentation to be adjusted. Advertising, on the other hand, is restricted to a communication message designed to appeal to large audiences, and it cannot be immediately altered if the message is not received as it was intended.

The advantage of advertising over personal selling is cost. Whereas a sales call may cost from $50 to $150, an advertisement exposure may cost only pennies. Consequently, the personal sales call can only be justified when the resulting impact will be large—when the product and a sale to one customer represent a significant amount of money or when a contact is being made with a retailer or wholesaler who may buy large amounts of a product. When a new product is to be introduced to hundreds of thousands of consumers, paid mass communication (advertising) is the most efficient method to use. Even when personal selling is appropriate, its effectiveness can often be enhanced if it is supported by advertising. A salesperson will be received more often and more sympathetically if the prospect has already learned about the firm and its product line from advertising.

Marketing-Mix Decisions

The marketing plan involves the allocation of the marketing budget to various components of the marketing mix. The effectiveness of the various elements of the marketing mix should be the factor that determines what share each receives of the total marketing budget. More specifically, the budget should be divided so that the marginal value of an extra budget increment will be the same in all components of the mix. Thus, a budget increment devoted to a reduced price should generate the same amount of extra sales as the same budget increment used for improving the product. If such a condition does not hold, dollars should be shifted to the area that will produce the higher incremental sales. The difficulty is, of course, to determine the sales response function for each of the various elements of the marketing mix.

The amount of the marketing budget allocated to advertising becomes the advertising budget. In evaluating the advertising budget, therefore, it is important to keep in mind that incremental amounts of money put into advertising must be more useful than the same amounts put into distribution or product refinement, or even reduced prices. Chapter 3 is devoted to a discussion of the budget and how the optimal budget level can be determined.

THE ADVERTISING PLAN

The major components of the advertising plan are shown in the Figure 2-1 framework. The advertising plan may be embedded within an overall marketing plan or, in some cases where advertising expenditures make up significant parts of the overall program, the advertising plan will dominate. In either event, advertising planning and decision making focus on three crucial areas: objectives and budget, copy, and media. Every advertising plan will, at a minimum, reflect planning, decisions, and commitments concerning each of these three major components. The broad purpose of advertising management is to develop, implement, and control an advertising plan. Planning as a process involves the generation and specification of alternatives. Decision making concerns the choice of the best alternative. Which strategy alternatives are feasible in a given situation? Which one should be adopted? What media mix will be most effective? These are some of the questions every advertising manager must address.

In an established-brand situation, analysis will involve a retrospective look at what has been done in the past and whether basic changes in the current plan are called for. In new-product situations, the manager may be essentially starting from scratch, and each aspect of the plan will require basic new thinking, significant amounts of new research information, and the development of entirely new advertising objectives and new copy and media strategies.

Alternatives with respect to objectives and the budget must first be carefully evaluated and specified. Then decisions with respect to what objectives and budget will be used must be made. Copy alternatives must be developed and analyzed. The decisions made at this stage take the form of the advertising campaign adopted in the particular situation. Finally, media alternatives need careful specification and analysis and decisions must be made on the media strategy to be adopted, made, and implemented. In each case, planning and decision making are involved.

Objectives and Budget

The pivotal aspect of any management plan is the development of operational objectives. An operational objective is one that provides useful criteria for decision making, generates standards to measure performance, and serves as a meaningful communication device. Objectives in advertising can be couched in many ways and still fulfill the functions of an operational objective. It is sometimes possible to develop objectives in terms of sales goals. Such goals are desirable because they appear to provide a readily accessible and absolute indication of advertising performance. However, because other marketing variables and competitors' actions can have an important impact on sales, it is often necessary to establish objectives in terms of intervening variables such as brand awareness, image, and attitude. The link between such intervening variables and advertising is more direct. Thus a significant increase in brand awareness can usually be identified with advertising. There are simply few other possible causes. To justify the use of intervening variables, a link must be established between them and subsequent sales. Much of Part II of this book will deal with the nature of that link.

An important part of the objective is the development of a precise, disciplined description of the target audience. It is often tempting to direct advertising at a broad audience; the implicit argument is that everyone is a potential customer. The risk is that a campaign directed at too wide an audience will have to have such a broad appeal that it will be of little interest to anyone and thus be ineffective. It is best to consider directing the advertising to more selected groups for which it is easier to develop relevant, stimulating copy. An advertiser need not be restricted to one objective and one campaign. It is quite possible to develop several campaigns, each directed at different segments of the market, or to develop one campaign based on multiple objectives.

The advertising budget decision is closely tied in with the objectives decision. Although there are many rules of thumb often used to decide on how much money to spend on advertising, the soundest rules involve beginning with a detailed specification of what a corporation is attempting to accomplish with advertising. It is only when the job to be done is well specified that the amount and nature of the effort—the amount of money to be invested in advertising—can be really determined.

In Chapter 3 we will examine some of the traditional approaches to the advertising budget decision and clarify how this decision is intimately related to objective setting and other decisions in advertising. The four following chapters, comprising Part II, will deal in depth with the broad topic of setting objectives and market positioning.

Copy

Copy planning and decision making are closely associated with the actual output—the advertisements themselves. A creative team must first develop a feasible set of copy alternatives and decide on a theme on which creative efforts will focus. As the creative process evolves, the theme is refined and made more and more specific until the actual advertisements on which the campaign will be based are created.

The theme involves such considerations as the tone of the campaign, its central message, and, perhaps, its spokesperson. A campaign can be light and humorous, it can be very serious, or it can rely heavily on creating a certain mood. A well-known spokesperson, such as Michael Landon representing Kodak, can be used to provide credibility and continuity.

The theme must eventually be translated into specific advertisements. Throughout the process, decisions have to be made concerning which different copy approaches, scripts, and final advertisements will be used. Copy tests, conducted in the laboratory or in the field, enable a creative team to check the evolving campaign continually against its objectives.

To develop effective copy and manage the process of copy creation and production, the advertising manager needs a basic understanding of communications, persuasion, and market processes. Advertising objectives must be translated into specific advertisements that will not only capture the attention of a target segment, but will also result in some significant attitudinal or behavioral impact.

Parts III and IV are devoted to these topics. Part III has four chapters that cover the perception process, information processing and attitude change, feeling response to advertising, and source, message, and social factors involved in communications and persuasion. Part IV focuses on creative styles of copy directors and agencies, a model of the copy creation and production process, and the important subject of copy testing.

Media

The media-allocation decision and media planning represent one of the few areas in advertising in which the use of mathematical models is well accepted. As a result, several models are available. The media-allocation decision will take several factors into consideration. One is the type of vehicle audience and how it matches the target audience of the campaign. Another is the ability of the vehicle to enhance the advertising impact, perhaps by creating a compatible mood or setting.

The type and nature of research information required to support media models differs somewhat from the perspectives of research in the case of copy decisions. A media planner is interested in questions concerning the reach and frequency of media alternatives, the effects of various vehicles, and matters involving learning and decay rates over the life of a campaign. Media research is thus a special topic that is treated, along with the development of various types of media models, in Part V. The decisions made in this area and in the other areas of objectives and copy constitute the final advertising plan. What should be clear is that advertising plans must all take these three major factors into consideration and will differ according to the decisions made in each area. The differences between advertising plans stem largely from differences in the external factors and the environmental situations that face advertisers. These external factors shape the advertising plan in many ways, and it is vital that they be analyzed in depth as the planning process proceeds.

THE COMMUNICATION/PERSUASION PROCESS

The most important factor to be considered in planning advertising is the communication/persuasion process. Figure 2-2 provides a simplified model of the communication/persuasion process. First, consumers are exposed to the advertisement. Exposure can result in information about the product or brand registering with the consumer. Advertisements can also generate feelings in an audience. Thus, both information and feelings are possible results of exposure to the advertisement. Each may in turn affect a person's attitude toward the brand or object of the advertising. Finally, attitude may affect his or her behavior.

Figure 2-2.   **An overview of the communication/persuation process**

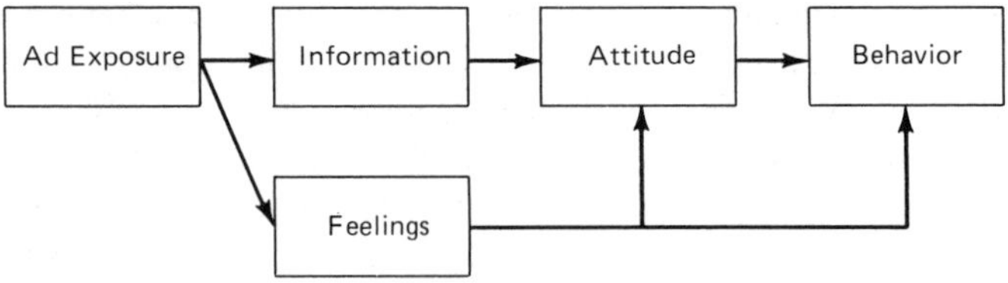

A major departure point is to understand how and why consumers acquire, process, and use advertising information. Although much has been researched and written about the effects of advertising and how it works, it is important to appreciate that this is a subject about which there are few definitive answers. There are many "theories" about the communication/persuasion process, many of them conflicting. For planning purposes, however, attention must be directed to this crucial factor and some depth of understanding attained for the particular product and market situation involved. It is also important at the planning stage to develop a good understanding of where advertising fits into the total pool of information and influence sources to which a consumer is exposed. Understanding information processing invariably leads to the need for understanding a wide range of other important psychological constructs, such as perception, learning, attitude formation and change, source effects, cognitive and affective response, and social factors such as personal influence. Four chapters in Part III are devoted to these topics.

Chapter 8 reviews theories of perception and perception processes. How are consumers likely to perceive advertising messages? How can attention be captured, and what interpretations are they likely to make of various components and parts of advertising? The perception process has long been recognized as the most significant barrier to effective communication. It is at this point that the sender does or does not get through to the receiver. Many forces and factors that affect perception are examined at length in Chapter 8.

Theories of information processing and attitude change are presented in Chapter 9. Much of the material draws on recent work of consumer behavior researchers in the area, particularly in extending our understanding of learning, memory, and memory functioning. How do consumers learn from advertising? Where does memory come in? What do we know about cognitive responses such as elaboration, counterarguing, source derogation, and so on? These topics are addressed in Chapter 9.

Chapter 10 focuses on theories and research to enhance understanding of the effects of feeling advertising, advertising that is explicitly designed to generate emotional responses in the audience, such as humor, fear, warmth, and so on. How does "transformational" advertising work? What do we know about using fear appeals? These are some of the things addressed in Chapter 10.

Chapter 11 begins with a review of theory and research on the effects of source components in advertising. Should a movie star, football players, or a typical consumer be used as a source? Then theories of message and message effects are reviewed. How can we build resistant attitudes, for example, or what kinds of advertising approaches can be used to communicate with a hostile audience? Another process examined in this chapter is personal influence and word-of-mouth advertising. In what advertising situations is personal influence likely to play a major role? It is often useful to conduct a *personal influence audit,* explained in this chapter as part of a general situation analysis.[3]

COMPETITION

Advertising planning and decision making are heavily affected by competition and the competitive situation facing the advertiser. Competition is such a pervasive factor that it will occur as a consideration in all phases of the advertising planning and decision-making process and the various topics treated in much of the balance of this book. A type of market-structure analysis that involves the development of perceptual maps of a market, for example, attempts to locate the relative perceptual positions of competitive brands. This topic is covered in detail in Chapter 5. Analogously, the concept of market share is useful in specifying advertising objectives explicitly takes the competitive factor into account. Situation analysis should usually include an analysis of what current share the brand now has (if it is an established brand), what share of a market is possible for a new brand, and from which competitors it will come? Analysis of the competitive factor is thus a crucial input to advertising planning and decision making.

Competition analysis can be extended in many ways. Basically, the planner will want to know the past, present, and likely future structure of competition. How many competitors are there? What market shares do they hold? What are their financial, marketing, and production resources? Will our position be (or is it) one of market leader, challenger, follower, or a comparatively small entry in the market?

Many companies have initiated their own tracking systems for monitoring competitive advertising. Byron G. Quann, group director of communications for the Information Systems Group of IBM, reports that the company became dissatisfied with publicly available information and developed their own tracking system. Print and television advertising are tracked for over 300 IBM competitors within 19 business groups used by the company. The research is done by two suppliers, the first providing a clipping service that scans 200 magazines and 130 newspapers, and the second providing tracking of radio and television commercials. In the latter case, tracking is done in the three major networks, cable, syndicated channels in major cities, and local stations in a number of selected cities.[4]

Opportunities for marketing and advertising can also be uncovered using competitive analysis. Is there a "hole" in the market not now being filled by a competitive offering? In other terms, is there a bundle of attributes that a consumer segment desires that some competitor has not yet targeted against? These types of questions need to be asked and answered in the initial stages of developing an advertising plan.

It will also be useful to study what competitors are currently doing in their advertising and marketing programs. As we will see, one of the ways to decide on the advertising budget, for example, is to spend at the rate of those competitors that are currently successful in the market situation. The analysis can be extended to a detailed look at what copy strategies are being used by competitors, what media mixes are currently used, and the changes that have taken place over time. Equally important is to know why certain competitors have failed to establish a place in the market. Why was their advertising program ineffective and/or what were the main reasons underlying product failure?

A final dimension of competitor analysis concerns the determination of retaliatory moves of competitors. How are they likely to react to our advertising plan? Can we anticipate major retaliatory moves designed to neutralize or suppress our efforts? Will competitors be likely to interfere with testing our advertising and try to confuse the results? An assessment of competition from these points of view is vital to the planning and decision-making process. A chapter is not devoted to competition in this book because it comes into play throughout most of the topics treated. On the one hand, it is important to look at competition as a precursor to the planning process, and on the other to appreciate that the development of plans and decision making with respect to objectives, budgets, copy, and media all must take into account the competitive factor.

FACILITATING AGENCIES

Another external factor identified in Figure 2-1 involves the agencies that facilitate the advertiser and provide the means to advertise. Recall that the nature and role of these types of agencies and institutions were reviewed in Chapter 1. From a situation-analysis viewpoint, the advertiser basically needs to know what kinds of facilitating agencies exist and the nature of the services they can provide. From a planning viewpoint, much local advertising, for example, is done without the services of an advertising agency or a research supplier. A national advertiser, on the other hand, may have under contract many different agencies and research suppliers, each serving one or more brands in a product line made up of several products.

Many advertising decisions involve choices among facilitating agency alternatives. What advertising agency should be chosen? What media should be used? What copy-test supplier will be best for our particular situation? Concerning the question of agency selection, for example, Cagley and Roberts[5] found that the "people factor" tends to dominate in agency selection. Characteristics such as the quality of personnel, reputation, integrity, mutual understanding, interpersonal compatibility, and synergism were very important. The study involved a mail questionnaire sent to 125 companies and ratings on 25 attributes ranging from "critically important" to "not important." Consideration of the facilitating agency factor is woven throughout many parts of the book. For example, the question of choosing a copy-test research supplier is treated at length in Chapter 14, and the question of what media and what media research services to use are the topics of Chapters 15 and 16.

SOCIAL AND LEGAL FACTORS

The final external factor in the planning framework concerns environmental, social and legal considerations. To a considerable extent, these exist as constraints on the development of an advertising plan and decision making.

In developing specific advertisements, there are certain legal constraints that must be considered. Deceptive advertising is forbidden by law. However, the determination of what is deceptive is often difficult, partly because different people can have different perceptions of the same advertisements. In guarding against deception, all types of perceptions must be considered. Furthermore, the letter and the spirit of the law on deceptive advertising is evolving rapidly. It is no small task to keep abreast of these developments. One solution is to create bland advertising that is vague and contains little specific information. However, such an approach can not only result in ineffective advertising, but it can lessen the social value of advertising by reducing the amount of useful information that it provides to the audience. Thus, an advertiser who attempts to provide specific, relevant information must be well aware of what constitutes deception in a legal and ethical sense and of other aspects of advertising regulation. Advertising regulation is the subject of Chapter 18.

Even more difficult considerations for a creative team are broad social and economic issues. Does advertising raise prices or inhibit competition? Also, issues such as the appropriateness of the use of sex or fear appeals are being examined. It has been suggested that women and minority groups are exploited in advertising by casting them in highly stereotyped roles. Another concern is that advertising, especially when it is more irritating than entertaining, is an intrusion into an already excessively polluted environment. A whole set of rules is emerging to cover advertising directed at children. These and other similar concerns, particularly those that affect copy and creative strategy, are developed more fully in Chapter 17.

SEGMENTATION STRATEGY

The term "market segmentation" was not coined until the latter part of the 1950s. Since then, however, it has had a major impact on marketing and advertising theory and practice. It is based on the rather trivial observation that all potential customers are not identical and that a firm should therefore either develop different marketing programs for different subgroups of the population or develop one program tailored to just a single subgroup. The fact that consumers differ and a single marketing program directed to all of them is not always the best strategy may seem rather obvious. Yet it is the essence of market segmentation that has the potential to improve dramatically the management of a wide variety of organizations.

Market segmentation strategy involves the development and pursuit of marketing programs directed at subgroups of the population that an organization or firm could potentially serve. A variety of marketing tools can be utilized to implement a segmentation strategy. Products and services can be developed and positioned for particular segments of the population. Distribution channels can be selected to reach certain groups. A pricing strategy can be designed to attract particular types of buyers. An advertising program can be created to appeal to certain types of consumers. Although the emphasis in this book is on the advertising plan, a segmentation strategy is not limited to any one element of the marketing program.

In some situations, the marketing program may involve subsegments. A strategic program may require a particular segmentation scheme. In implementing the accompanying advertising campaign, a more detailed breakdown of the market may be required. Suppose that an organization has decided to focus on the clothing needs of the style-conscious upper class and has selected retail outlets and product lines that will attract members of this group. In developing the advertising plan, it may be useful to divide this upper-class segment further on the basis of age, thus creating two subsegments—the young, upper-class woman and those who are older—each of which will tend to be exposed to different media and will be attracted by different appeals.

An example of the use of subsegments can also be drawn from the area of industrial marketing, which deals with the problems of marketing to organizations. Suppose that a new, small computer for use by small firms was to be developed and marketed. The market could be divided into banks, food stores, and other business categories. Assume that it was decided to develop one marketing program especially for small banks and a second program for individual food retailers. This would be a market-segmentation strategy. As the program directed at the banks evolved, it might be useful to develop subsegments; the decision makers in the bank might be divided into the officers and the data-processing personnel. Thus, two advertising campaigns would accompany the direct-sales programs. The one directed at the officers might explain the economic advantages of the new computer and would run in magazines that bank presidents tend to read. The other would be more specialized in content and would explain the technical aspects and potential advantages of the computer to the data-processing people. Such a campaign would appear in magazines favored by data-processing managers.

Concentration versus Differentiation Strategy

There are two different types of segmentation strategies. The first is the strategy of concentration in which the organization focuses on only one subgroup and develops a marketing program directed to it. The second is the strategy of differentiation in which two or more population subgroups are identified and marketing programs are developed for each. If segmentation is not employed and a single marketing program is developed and applied to all groups, the resulting marketing strategy is termed *undifferentiation* or *aggregation.*

If a strategy of concentration is pursued and a very large segment is the target, the approach is similar to one of undifferentiation in that an effort is made to reach a broad market. Such a strategy is enticing. Marketing decision makers often attempt to determine who the big users of the product are and then use that information to identify the target segment for a strategy of concentration. The problem is that competitors follow the same logic. They, too, have identified the segment with the "large" potential and are directing their efforts at it. As a result, the attractive segment might have several brands fighting for it, whereas there might be a smaller segment that no brand is attempting to serve. This phenomenon is very common and is called the *majority fallacy*.[6] The segment with the biggest potential is not always the most profitable. The fallacy is that competition is ignored in the analysis. It may be much more profitable to attempt to gain a small segment heretofore ignored, even if it represents only 5 percent of the market, than to fight 10 other brands for a share of a large segment that represents 70 percent of the market. It is obviously costly to do direct battle with large established competitors in a broadly based market segment.

A concentration strategy focusing on a smaller segment is particularly useful to a small firm that enters a market dominated by several larger ones. It may, in fact, be suicidal for the small company to compete with the larger ones for the large segment. However, if the small firm will concede the business represented by the large segment and discipline itself to direct its effort to a small segment with specialized needs, it may do very well. Furthermore, assuming that the smaller segment cannot really support two firms, the probability of losing the market to a competitor may then be rather small, since potential competitors will tend to avoid making an effort to secure a footing in this segment.

There are many examples of a concentration strategy. Midas Muffler does not attempt to satisfy the general service needs of car owners but concentrates instead on just servicing mufflers, a small part of total service needs. Successful computer companies, like Control Data, have not tried to attack IBM head-on: they have concentrated on research applications and other specialized markets. A boat manufacturer may specialize in one particular type of boat oriented to only a small segment of the entire boat market.

Under a strategy of differentiation, an organization does not restrict its efforts to a single segment but rather develops several marketing programs, each tailored to individual segments. These programs could differ with respect to the product lines. Perhaps the classic case of a differentiated marketing program involving product lines is the General Motors organization. Early in the company's life, General Motors decided to develop a prestige product line (Cadillacs), an economy line (Chevrolets), and several others to fill the gap between the two. The company thus covered the whole market but divided it into segments and developed a line for each segment. A differentiated segmentation strategy could, however, involve just the advertising campaign. The advertising could emphasize one brand attribute to one segment and a different brand advantage to another. Thus, a bicycle manufacturer might stress the recreational uses of its bicycle in the United States and its transportation value in Europe, where it is more frequently used for that purpose.

Segmentation is not always the optimal approach. It may be that a single product and appeal will be equally effective for everyone. Naturally, this type of strategy requires substantial resources. The Coca-Cola Company could be considered to be pursuing an undifferentiated marketing segmentation strategy. The product name, package, and advertising are designed to appeal to virtually everyone, as Figure 2-3 illustrates. It could be argued, however, that the Coca-Cola Company with its present variety of container types and sizes and its diet soft drinks has moved away from a pure strategy of undifferentiation. Such a move is partly a

Figure 2-3.   **An advertisement directed at a wide audience**

natural evolution. As a product class gains maturity, consumer needs often become more specialized and a segmentation strategy is a natural response of manufacturers to these needs.

The possibility of pursuing a strategy of differentiation by developing specialized marketing programs for various regions is well worth considering for many products. There are many examples of market strategies that were very successful in one part of the country but failed in another. In the 1950s, Rheingold beer, a dominant brand in New York, attempted to enter the southern California market. Management used the same marketing strategy it believed had been so successful in New York—a Miss Rheingold beauty personality, a dry-tasting product, and a distribution program that bypassed the wholesaler. Despite a splashy introduction, which resulted in almost complete exposure and significant trial rates, the brand folded after a three-year effort. The West Coast was not impressed with Miss Rheingold, the product, or the distribution strategy, and let the company know in a very direct way. Beer drinkers failed to buy in droves. The California market, as Rheingold and others have found, is significantly different from markets in New York, the Midwest, and the South.

Developing a Segmentation Strategy

The development of a segmentation strategy is sometimes aided by quantitative information obtained about the segments. Let's see how in the context of an example. Assume that a women's cosmetics manufacturer observed that a substantial and growing segment comprises women who believe that their role is or should be very different from the traditional role of wife and mother with interests subordinated to her family. The revised or "modern" role rather emphasizes independence and self-fulfillment.

The task is to develop an advertising strategy, indeed a total marketing program, aimed at the "modern" segment (and perhaps another aimed at the "traditional" segment). Knowing the identity of the target segment can suggest ways to make the advertising effort, as well as the total marketing program, more effective. Thus, advertising to the modern segment would not use the "housewife role" but would rather tend to use a model in a role setting reflecting an independent, fulfilling life-style not associated with the home. Some magazines and television programs will have thrusts and personalities that make them effective advertising vehicles for the modern segment. However, to develop the most effective marketing and advertising program possible, it would be useful to know more about the target segment. Thus, a study designed to describe the target segment in more depth is helpful.

Such a study was conducted by three researchers.[7] They mailed a questionnaire to 2,000 members of a mail panel, a group of people who have agreed to participate in mail surveys and are paid for their cooperation. One question served to identify the modern and traditional segments. It asked which of the following two ways of life was best:

1. A traditional marriage with the husband assuming the responsibility for providing for the family and the wife running the house and taking care of the children.

2. A marriage where husband and wife share responsibilities more: both work, both share homemaking and child responsibilities.

Forty-five percent of the respondents preferred a traditional arrangement and approximately 55 percent selected the modern or sharing alternative. The other questions profiled the modern woman in terms of demographics (like age, income, and education), life-style (as reflected by interests, opinions, and activities), media habits, and product usage. Selected questions are shown in Table 2-2.

The profile of the modern woman allows us to understand the segment more completely. The demographic profile indicates that the modern woman tends to be under 25, to have attended college, and to be employed. Such information could easily help in identifying advertising vehicles, as well as in making other decisions such as selecting retail outlets.

The life-style profile provides a relatively rich description of the modern woman. As expected, there are sharp differences between modern and traditional women concerning their "place" (questions 1 and 2). Questions 6 and 7 suggest that the modern woman tends to be more mobile and cosmopolitan. Question 9 indicates that even the modern woman views herself as "old-fashioned" in some respects, so that advertising appeals with an "old-fashioned" flavor may be acceptable. Questions 10 through 13 provide an indication of the activities in which the modern woman is engaged.

Media differences provide highly operational information helpful in media selection. Note the striking differences for heavy rock radio, *Glamour* magazine, and *Playboy* magazine.

Product usage information is often helpful. If the target segments are heavy users, their reactions to elements of the marketing program will be different than if they were light users. Heavier users, for example, will often be more knowledgeable and involved than light users, and, of course, they represent more sales potential. In this case the modern woman is a relatively heavy user of eye makeup and suntan lotion but not lipstick and hairspray. Usage of other products can suggest promotional tie-ins and provide additional life-style insights. The rather dramatic difference between the use of artificial sweeteners might suggest some attitude patterns that might be useful in product development. Perhaps a "natural" line of cosmetics should be considered.

To discuss the many possible bases for segmentation, it is useful to divide them into two categories, as shown in Table 2-3. Each provides a basis for understanding the structure of a market. The first, general consumer characteristics, contains variables that are not specific to any particular product or purchasing situation. In this category are demographics (age, family size, geographic location, and so on), culture, social class, and life-style. The second category has consumer characteristics that are specific to purchasing situations. Usage levels (heavy versus light users), brand loyalty, brand attitudes, and preferences are all defined in the context of a purchasing decision. A brief review of each type of variable is presented next.

Table 2-2.   **Profile of the Modern Woman**

CHARACTERISTIC	TRADITIONAL	MODERN
Demographic profile (% having characteristic)		
Age under 25	32	51
Age over 55	35	12
Education: some college	40	50
Employed	26	56
Income under $10,000	30	27
Income over $20,000	20	22
Dwelling unit: apartment	5	11
Life-style profile (% agreeing)		
1. A woman's place is in the home	68	30
2. The working world is no place for a woman	28	9
3. The father should be the boss in the house	81	59
4. I think the Women's Liberation movement is a good thing	41	61
5. There is too much emphasis on sex today	90	81
6. I would like to spend a year in London or Paris	25	39
7. We will probably move at least once in the next five years	32	41
8. I like sports cars	30	47
9. I have somewhat old-fashioned tastes and habits	91	81
10. I went to the movies at least once in the past year	68	79
11. I visited an art gallery or museum at least once last year	45	52
12. I went bowling at least once last year	30	39
13. I went to a pop concert at least once last year	7	18
14. I like to feel attractive to members of the opposite sex	79	89
15. I want to look different from others	66	72
Media differences (% exposed)		
Radio		
Heavy rock	8	20
Popular music	44	56
Television		
Waltons	42	32
Little House on the Prairie	33	24
Happy Days	16	20
Daytime game shows (in general)	12	8
Magazines		
Cosmopolitan	10	16
Glamour	7	13
Playboy	9	19
Redbook	27	34
Product usage (% using weekly or more often)		
Lipstick	87	80
Hairspray	62	56
Eye makeup	48	62
Suntan lotion (summer)	28	40
Artificial sweetener	33	8
Beer	9	12
Menthol-filter cigarettes	8	12
Gasoline	78	83

Source: Adapted from Fred D. Reynolds, Melvin R. Crask, and William D. Wells, "The Modern Feminine Life Style," *Journal of Marketing,* 41, July 1977, pp. 38–45.

Table 2-3. **Bases for Segmentation Strategies**

GENERAL CONSUMER CHARACTERISTICS	PRODUCT-RELATED CONSUMER CHARACTERISTICS
Age	Product usage
Income	Brand loyalty
Geographic location	Attitudes
Culture	Preferences
Life-style	

General Consumer Characteristics

Age. A very basic but useful demographic is age. The senior citizen market is large and growing and has a host of needs and wants not filled by existing products and services. Another important market is the young adult market profiled in Table 2-4. Note that the number of young adults is growing substantially faster than the population as a whole. Again it is useful to learn as much as possible about prospective target segments. Table 2-4 indicates that young adults are moving to the suburbs. It also provides information on their ownership of durables. The 18- to 24-year-old group has yet to buy some durables, but note that they do enjoy automobiles and room air conditioners.

Income. Another useful demographic is income. Table 2-5 profiles the high-income households. It shows that this segment has grown dramatically, although some of the growth, of course, reflects inflation. In 1974, fully 9.5 percent of households had incomes exceeding $25,000. The figure shows that geographically

Table 2-4. **Young Adults**

CHARACTERISTIC	18- TO 24-YEAR-OLDS	25- TO 34-YEAR-OLDS	ALL AGES
A growing segment (size in 000s)			
1970	24,455	25,146	204,335
1975	27,623	30,936	213,631
1980 (est.)	29,441	36,157	220,356
Where they live (% change 1970 to 1974)			
Total United States	15.7	18.3	4.1
Central cities	3.9	12.4	−1.9
Suburbs	28.3	23.5	8.4
Nonmetropolitan areas	15.1	18.0	5.4
What they own (% owning)			
One or more automobiles	88.4	89.7	82.8
Clothes dryer	50.5	62.1	51.6
Home food freezer	19.0	30.8	32.5
Kitchen range	57.5	70.5	73.5
Color TV	58.1	68.4	59.4
Room air conditioning	34.5	33.0	31.8

Source: Adapted from *Sales and Marketing Management*, April 11, 1977, p. A–12.

Table 2-5.   **High-Income Households: \$25,000+ Prospects**

A MUSHROOMING SEGMENT		\$25,000+ (000s)		ALL HOUSEHOLDS (000s)		
1959		336		55,990		
1964		601		60,080		
1969		1,986		66,612		
1974		6,563 (9.5%)		74,585		
Where they live	*Northeast*	*Midwest*	*South*	*West*		
1964	31.4	25.6	18.4	24.6		100%
1974	26.4	28.7	25.5	19.4		100%
What they own, as a percent of households who in 1975						
Owned two or more cars		22.0				
Took three or more vacation trips		27.6				
Bought a color table TV		25.4				
Stereo receiver amplifier		24.2				
Tape recorder		21.7				
Movie camera		21.7				
Hand-held calculator		26.2				

Source: Adapted from *Sales and Marketing Management,* April 11, 1977, p. A–14.

the growth areas for high-income households are the Midwest and especially the South. Although the high-income household represents 9.5 percent of all households, it is 27.6 percent of those households who took three or more vacation trips in 1975. Thus, for such costly products and services it should be considered an attractive segment.

Geographic Location.   Geographic location can often provide the basis for an effective segmentation strategy. A firm with modest resources can dominate, if it so chooses, a small geographic area. Its distribution within the limited area can be intense. Local media such as newspapers can be employed, and it is possible to buy space in regional editions of major national magazines and television spots near or within network television programs. The classic example of a concentration strategy is the local or regional organization that restricts itself geographically and attempts to tailor its marketing program to the needs of the people in that area. A local brewery or coffee manufacturer may compete with national brands, but only in a limited geographic area.

Culture.   Cultural factors are particularly important when multinational firms attempt to develop a segmentation strategy with the world as a market. Differences among cultures can affect product acceptance and advertising campaigns. The ''Pepsi Generation'' campaign, for example, was difficult to communicate to some cultures outside the United States.

Life-style.   A person's pattern of interests, opinions, and activities combine to represent his or her life-style. A knowledge of life-style can provide a very rich and meaningful picture of a person. It can indicate whether the person is interested in outdoor sports, shopping, culture, or reading. It can include information concerning attitudes and personality traits. Life-styles appeared in our cosmetics example as descriptors of a market segment. Life-style also can be used to define a segment. Revlon's "Charlie" cosmetic line is targeted at a life-style segment profiled as follows:

- Irreverent and unpretentious.
- Doesn't mind being a little outrageous or flamboyant.
- Breaks all the rules.
- Has her integrity based on her own standards.
- Can be tough, believes rules are secondary.
- A pacesetter, not a follower.
- Is very relaxed about sex.
- Is bored with typical fragrance advertising.
- Mixes Gucci and blue jeans; insists on individual taste, individual judgment.
- Has a sense of self and sense of commitment.

Figure 2-4 shows a Charlie advertisement.

Product-Related Consumer Characteristics

The second category of consumer characteristics is more closely associated with the purchasing process itself. Among the situation-specific segmentation variables are product usage, brand loyalty, store loyalty, attitudes, and preferences.

Usage.   A natural and powerful segmentation variable is product-class usage. Who are the heavy users of the product or service? Who are the light users? The most interesting of all are the nonusers. The challenge is to get them to try the product and, ultimately, become steady users. In fact, the marketing manager must address at least two problems: (1) to develop programs that attract members of the target group to try the product the first time; and (2) to develop products that this group will like well enough to buy regularly. Consequently, the nonusers should be of considerable interest to the marketing professional.

One segmentation scheme might involve heavy users, light users, and nonusers. Consider the market for a symphony. The nonusers group might be further divided into those who never attend a symphony under any conditions and those who are more positively disposed toward the symphony but have just never gotten around to going.

The heavy user is the crucial segment and the backbone of the operation. Although it may seem difficult to gain increased attendance from a group that already attends frequently, this segment should not be ignored. It might be possible, for example, to increase attendance by converting patrons (those who attend fre-

Figure 2-4.　**A campaign directed at a defined life-style**

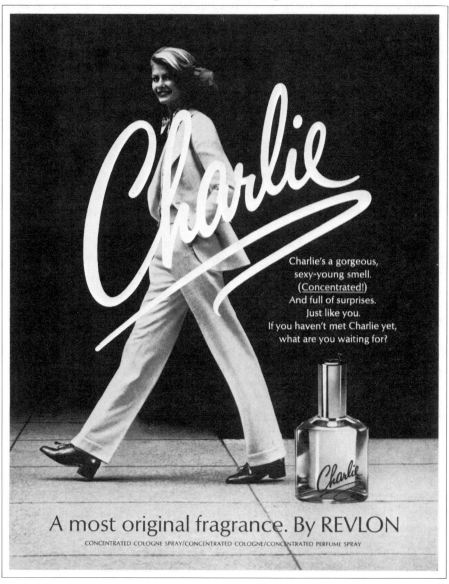

Courtesy of Revlon.

quently) to season ticket holders. Another alternative is to expand the season, thus providing more opportunities for attendance.

Those who attend less frequently need to be converted to more regular attendance. They might be attracted by special ticket plans that offer several performances but are something less than a season subscription. Future programs might be promoted to persons in this segment when they are actually in the theater, perhaps through program brochures and posters. The occasional attender could also be given an opportunity to make a commitment to attend another performance while still in the theater and the idea of another visit seems enticing.

The nonusers of the symphony who have a rigid, negative attitude are probably best forgotten. There is little chance that they could be persuaded to go, and even if they did, they would probably rarely attend. About the only way to approach this segment is to support music appreciation in the schools, so in future years, the size of this nonuser segment diminishes. Since this segment is probably large, discipline is required to ignore it.

The key segment is the nonuser who lacks strong negative opinions on symphonies. What type of marketing program will attract this segment? Perhaps the product can be modified. A series of special ''pops'' concerts with well-known and popular guest artists might be planned as a way to expose this group to symphonic music. A special price for one event, such as an outdoor concert, might appeal to this nonuser. Innovative advertising—perhaps in the sports or women's sections of the local newspapers—might succeed in reaching this segment.

This particular segmentation scheme is likely to be useful wherever the focus is on building up the market. Each person is classified according to usage, and a program is developed to increase the usage level.

The segments defined by usage usually require quite different marketing programs. So a program tailored to one of these segments can generate a substantially greater response than would a marketing program common to all segments. Of course, designing and implementing several marketing programs is costlier than developing one, but the resulting market response will often be significant enough to make it worthwhile.

Brand Loyalty. When a brand such as Tide is competing in a well-defined product class such as detergents, it is useful to consider brand loyalty as a basis for segmentation. The users of Tide can then be divided into those who are loyal buyers of the brand and those who are not. The nonloyal buyer tends to buy several brands, selecting, for example, the least expensive or the most convenient at the moment. Similarly, nonusers of Tide can be divided into those who are loyal to other brands and those who buy several other brands.

It is usually not easy to increase usage by turning nonloyal buyers into loyal buyers, since this tendency toward brand loyalty, with respect to a certain product class, has likely become ingrained over many years. The highest potential lies with the nonusers. The nonuser who is not loyal to another brand needs to be enticed to try the brand and thus to expand the *evoked set,* the group of brands he or she buys, to include the brand of interest. A special in-store display or a cents-off coupon might accomplish this task.

Buyers who are loyal to another brand will be very difficult and very costly to attract to a trial purchase. However, once attracted, there is an excellent chance of their becoming loyal buyers of the brand, since their tendency toward loyalty is not likely to change.

Obviously, however, a special display or a cents-off coupon is unlikely to attract the buyer who is loyal to another brand. He or she must be presented with a solid reason to change. If such a reason does exist, there is still the problem of communication, as the loyal buyer of one brand is not seeking information and, in fact, tends to avoid advertising for other brands. Thus, there is a trade-off. On the one hand, the loyal buyer of another brand is an appealing prospect because if converted she or he will generate sales dividends for several years. On the other hand, the loyal buyer is difficult and costly to attract.

Attitudes and Preferences.   Attitudes and preferences and many related psychological constructs such as motivations, perceptions, beliefs, product benefits, and so on, can also be used to segment markets. In the toothpaste market, for example, one segment tends to consider decay prevention most important, while others consider sensory-taste qualities, breath-freshening, or price, as most important. As a group, these variables are often called *intervening variables* to distinguish them from the more overt behavioral variables such as product usage or brand loyalty. A great deal of interest has been generated in looking at markets and market structure from this viewpoint, and much of the material in Chapters 4 to 6 pertains to viewing markets in this way.

Reaching Target Segments

There are two ways by which markets can be reached: controlled coverage and customer self-selection.[8]

In the controlled-coverage approach, the objective is to reach desired target segments and to avoid reaching those who are not in the target segments. Suppose that a segment is defined as "better golfers," and it is determined that they usually read *Golf Digest*. Suppose, further, that there are few readers of *Golf Digest* who are not in the target segment. Then an advertising campaign in *Golf Digest* would be an efficient way to communicate with the target segment. This concept applies to other marketing tools as well. A particular distribution outlet, such as the better sporting goods stores and golf course pro shops, may be selected to serve the target segment. Those who shop for golf equipment in department, hardware, or discount stores will deliberately not be exposed to the product. The use of a marketing program that reaches only target segments is often very efficient. The expense of reaching people who are not primary targets is avoided.

Customer self-selection is an alternative approach. Here the advertising program is directed to a mass audience of which the target segment may be only a small part. Those in the target segment are attracted to the marketing effort since it is tailored to them. Those not in the target group will probably avoid exposure, not because the program is unavailable to them, but because they either consciously or unconsciously choose to avoid it. For example, although ski equipment has a rather narrow appeal, a firm may run an advertisement about it in a mass circulation magazine. The target segment, all skiers, will be attracted to the advertisement if it is well done, but nonskiers will probably not be tempted to read it.

Again, the concept applies to other marketing tools. A product may be made available to the whole market through mass-merchandise outlets. However, if its features have been designed to appeal to a small segment, those in that segment will be the likely buyers, despite the fact that many others will have an opportunity to be exposed.

The use of controlled coverage usually is assumed to be the lowest cost alternative. However, there are two inefficiencies with controlled coverage. First, the approach encourages a manager to avoid mass-media promotional vehicles and mass-merchandising outlets. In terms of reaching large numbers, these advertising vehicles and store outlets are highly efficient. Even by increasing the cost to reflect those reached who are not among the audience of interest, it may still be the lower cost alternative. Second, the controlled-coverage approach forces a manager to make a real commitment about his or her segmentation strategy. If it is decided to rely exclusively on *Golf Digest* for the communication program, the manager excludes all those who do not read that particular magazine. Part of the segment he or she is really trying to reach may not read *Golf Digest*. By advertising in *Time* and permitting the audience of that magazine to generate the exact target group through self-selection, the manager will actually get a more optimal target segment that will, in fact, be larger than would be reached among the *Golf Digest* readers. This will tend to reduce the real cost of the larger-circulation vehicle.

SUMMARY

The predominant perspective of advertising management is that of the advertising or brand manager in the advertiser component of the overall system. The broad purpose of the manager is to develop, implement, and control an advertising plan. The major activities involved in these tasks are planning and decision making.

Planning involves the generation and specification of alternatives, and decision making concerns the choice process. Which alternative should be chosen? Which strategy is best in a particular situation? What copy theme should be used? What media mix will be most effective? And so on.

Advertising planning and decision making begins with a situation analysis. Situation analysis in advertising management requires consideration of a number of factors internal to, and external from, the advertising organization.

Internally, analysis should focus on the overall marketing program and how advertising will interact with the various components of the program. It is vital that the advertising plan be developed so as to mesh with and support the various components of the marketing mix. The advertising manager also needs to know the major areas of his or her planning and decision-making responsibilities. There are three areas of major importance: objectives-budget, copy, and media. Planning and decision making are required from each perspective, and the final advertising plan will reflect the various decisions made at each level.

Externally, the manager needs to engage in situation analysis with respect to the market conditions that are operating at the time and to assess the competitive, facilitating agency, and social and legal factors that will affect decision making and the development of the plan. Figure 2-1 organized these various factors as a planning and decision-making framework for which the situation with respect to each of them can be assessed.

The communication/persuasion process consists of exposure of consumers to the advertisement. Exposure can lead to retention of information in the ad and/or feelings aroused in the audience. Information and feelings can in turn affect the person's attitudes and behavior.

Competition is a pervasive factor in advertising planning and decision making. Situation analysis here requires careful assessment of the number of competitors, what market shares they currently hold, their financial and other strengths and weaknesses, and what advertising plans they are using.

Analysis of facilitating agencies requires, on the one hand, a basic knowledge of the alternatives that exist, and on the other, a knowledge of considerations that come into play in choosing among them.

The final factor to be accounted for in the situation analysis concerns the social and legal environment. Not only legal constraints must be considered, and the threats of governmental action if the advertising is found to be deceptive, but the situation with respect to broad social issues must be assessed. Advertising management must increasingly be concerned with these broader issues as well.

It is very important to determine whether the market can be broken down into actionable segments in the situation the manager faces. Market-segmentation strategy involves the development of marketing and advertising plans directed at one subgroup (concentration) or several subgroups (differentiation).

Analysis can be performed using a great many different variables and constructs as the basis for classifying people into segments. Several of them reflect general consumer characteristics, whereas others are product related or specific to the product being advertised.

DISCUSSION QUESTIONS

1. What are the basic differences between planning and decision making in advertising management? How does an advertising plan differ from an overall marketing plan? How do advertising decisions differ from other types of marketing decisions?

2. Outline the major components and considerations that you would include in your advertising plan if you were the brand manager of a brand

of gasoline, a major credit card, or a new electronic device for use in business computers. In what ways would the plans differ? In what ways would they be similar?

3. An important internal component in situation analysis is the overall marketing plan. Provide additional examples of how advertising interacts with the elements of the marketing plan.

4. Using the model in Figure 2-2, explain your reactions to a recent television advertisement.

5. Give an example of how a competitive situation would affect the development of an advertising plan for a museum, an airline company, and a telephone product.

6. Suppose in your assessment of the current advertising plan for your product you decided that the creative strategy was fundamentally weak. Which of the facilitating agencies would you look to as a possible source of the problem? Discuss some of the considerations in switching sources in this case.

7. Distinguish between controlled coverage and customer self-selection. Which approach would likely be most effective for the manufacturer of an expensive sports car?

8. What is the role of a supplemental segmentation variable? Focus on advertising campaigns with which you are familiar, and speculate about what may be the target segment and what supplemental segmentation variable might have been employed.

9. Some argue that usage is the most useful segmentation variable. Others believe that the benefit provided by the product or service is the most useful. Still others will refute both statements. What is your position? Why?

10. From what you now know about theories of learning and information processing, explain how advertising works.

11. Develop segmentation strategies for the following:
    a. Wristwatch company
    b. Manufacturer of electronic calculators
    c. College
    d. Police department
    e. Pleasure-boat company
    f. Large retail hardware store
    g. Church
    h. Hair spray

12. It has been said that an advertising manager lives in an environment of considerable uncertainty. Explain this statement. Do you agree? What are the chief avenues open to reduce uncertainty?

13.   It was stated in this chapter that it is often difficult to decide what is deception in advertising and what is not. Do you agree? What rules or principles should an advertiser use in deciding whether or not a message is likely to be considered "deceptive"?

NOTES

1. Alan P. Kuritsky, John D. C. Little, Alvin J. Silk, and Emily S. Bassman, "The Development, Testing, and Execution of New Marketing Strategy at AT&T Long Lines," *Interfaces,* 12, December 1982, pp. 22–37.

2. See "Outline for Developing an Advertising Plan," in Don E. Schultz and Dennis G. Martin, *Strategic Advertising Campaigns* (Chicago: Crain Books, 1979), pp. 13–16. For a parallel approach which is specific to advertising called "Advertising Opportunity Analysis," see Edward M. Tauber, "Point of View: How to Get Advertising Strategy from Research," *Journal of Advertising Research,* 20, October 1980, pp. 67–72.

3. A personal influence audit can be usefully done in conducting a situation analysis. See Chapter 11 for procedures involved in conducting a personal influence audit.

4. Byron G. Quann, "How IBM Assesses Its Business-to-Business Advertising," *Business Marketing,* January 1985, pp. 106–112.

5. James W. Cagley and C. Richard Roberts, "Criteria for Advertising Agency Selection: An Objective Appraisal," *Journal of Advertising Research,* 24, April–May 1984, pp. 27–31.

6. See Alfred A. Kuehn and Ralph L. Day, "Strategy of Product Quality," *Harvard Business Review,* 40, November–December 1962, pp. 100–110.

7. Fred D. Reynolds, Melvin R. Crask, and William D. Wells, "The Modern Feminine Life Style," *Journal of Marketing,* 41, July 1977, pp. 38–45.

8. These concepts are developed in the context of a normative mathematical model in Ronald E. Frank, William F. Massy, and Yoran Wind, *Market Segmentation* (Englewood Cliffs, N.J.: Prentice-Hall, 1972), especially in Chapter 8.

3

The Budget Decision

I know half the money I spend on advertising is wasted, but I can never find out which half. (John Wanamaker, founder of a department store)

The amount of money spent on advertising varies widely among companies even within the same industry. For example, while Noxell, with brand names like Cover Girl, Noxzema, and Lestoil, was spending over 20 percent of its 1985 sales on advertising, Avon was spending under 1 percent.[1] Among airlines, Delta spent 1.4 percent of its 1984 sales on advertising, while TWA spent 3.3 percent. Furthermore, firms often change their advertising expenditures radically from year to year.

What generates this wide variation in advertising expenditures among firms within the same industry and over time for the same firm? How do companies go about setting advertising budgets? How should they be setting or establishing their budgets? What set of models and techniques can be employed to improve their decision making? This chapter will be directed to these questions.

MARGINAL ANALYSIS

The theoretical underpinning of an advertising-budget decision is based on marginal analysis and is easily expressed. A firm would continue to add to the advertising budget as long as the incremental expenditures are exceeded by the marginal revenue they generate (see Figure 3-1). As pointed out in Chapter 2, such a marginal analysis could theoretically be applied to the other components of the marketing mix, such as personal selling, distribution, and pricing. A resulting optimal expenditure level could then be obtained for each component, which collectively would be the marketing mix. If the sum of these expenditures exceeded the available resources, the marketing budget for each would have to be scaled down. Each area would be constrained on the basis of the marginal revenue generated by the last dollar in its budget. If, for example, the last dollar put into personal selling generated $2 of profit, whereas the last dollar of advertising generated $3 of profit, it would probably be desirable to shift money from personal selling to advertising. Of course, personal selling and advertising cannot absorb investments in small increments, but the principle of marginal analysis is still valid.

Some Difficulties in Applying Marginal Analysis

There are, unfortunately, some difficulties in applying marginal analysis in practice. The assumption in the foregoing has been that it is appropriate to consider sales as a function of advertising expenditures, with advertising as the only input and immediate sales as the output. Such an assumption may be reasonable in some mail-order advertising. However, in other situations, it is more tenuous. Even when it does seem reasonable, the determination of the shape and parameters of the function is no easy task. This will be clear when estimation techniques are presented in the latter part of this chapter. Furthermore, even when a response curve does accurately represent a certain situation, there is no guarantee that it will continue to be valid in the future. The conditions of the market, including the competitive environment, change. As a result, the nature and shape of the response function also can change.

Figure 3-1.   **Graph of sales, profit, and advertising curves used in marginal analysis**

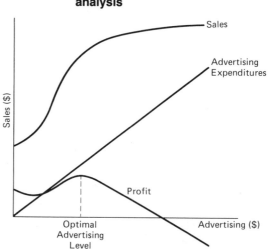

The assumption that sales are determined solely by advertising expenditures is obviously faulty in practically all situations. The nature of the advertising campaign, the copy used, and the media selected will usually influence the shape of the response curve. A strong creative effort will evoke a different response than a tasteless, misdirected campaign, even if the same expenditure levels are involved. Furthermore, it is difficult to sort out the effect of advertising from the effect of other forces that influence sales. Sales are, after all, a result of a company's total marketing and promotional effort as well as a number of environmental conditions, such as competitive actions and a host of economic, climatic, social, and cultural factors. If all factors including competitive activity remained constant except for advertising, it would be reasonable to consider advertising to be the only determinant of sales. The fact is, however, that such conditions do not hold in any real-world situation.

The dependent variable in the response function is sales—by implication, immediate sales. Although there are cases such as direct-mail advertising wherein the use of immediate sales is quite appropriate, in most instances there is a considerable lag between the time of the advertising and the time of the sales it might have helped stimulate. A consumer buying a car in June could have been affected by advertising for that car the previous fall. People may be affected by the reputation or image of a brand built up through advertising over a considerable period of time. Furthermore, advertising might attract buyers who become loyal customers for several years. Their immediate purchases may be only a small part of the value to the firm that enticed them to try the brand.

Extended Marginal Analysis

There are, in general, three ways in which firms can react to the difficulty of determining the response function in marginal analysis. They can, essentially, admit that the task is so formidable, at least given their expertise, that it is not worthwhile to pursue it and rely instead on other types of decision rules. Such rules may or may not reflect a marginal analysis. A second reaction is to attempt to determine a response function relating advertising expenditure to sales despite the difficulties. The argument is that, even if the result is imperfect, it might indeed provide some guidance; and the method at least has a theoretical basis. Furthermore, the exercise does not necessarily have to be expensive, so the risk is not excessive. The primary tools used, split-cable testing, field experimentation, and regression analysis, will be reviewed later in this chapter.

The third approach, which might be termed extended marginal analysis, is essentially to use marginal analysis but to describe the inputs and the outputs more completely. The inputs would thus be a complete description of the advertising program, the target audience, the creative approach, and the media used, plus any salient environmental conditions. The outputs would be what the audience learned, the impact on their attitudes, and the direct and indirect (through attitude change, for example) impact on buying decisions. Such an approach is, of course, ambitious and challenges our knowledge of how advertising operates and how the communication process functions. In part, the purpose of this book is to explore this type of direction. Accordingly, budget setting in such a framework will be reintroduced in Chapter 15.

In the following sections, the first two approaches will be more fully explored. Several practical methods of setting advertising budgets will be examined. Then various attempts to estimate the response function using experimentation and regression analysis will be presented.

BUDGETING DECISION RULES

There are several decision rules on which many firms draw in making budget decisions. Four such rules will be described. The rules are basically justified by arguing that budgets based on them are unlikely to be far from the actual optimal budget if a marginal analysis could be performed. In some cases, the rules are used in combination, the net budget being a compromise among several.

Percentage of Sales

One rule of thumb used in setting advertising budgets is the percentage of sales. Past sales or a forecast of future sales can be used as the base. A brand may have devoted 5 percent of its budget to advertising in the past. Thus, if the plan calls for doing $40 million worth of business next year, a $2 million advertising budget might be proposed. A similar decision could be based upon market share. For example, a brand could allocate $1 million for every share point it holds.

The percentage-of-sales guide is the most common approach to setting advertising budgets. A 1981 survey of 55 of the 100 leading consumer advertisers found that over 70% reported using some version of the percentage-of-sales method,[2] as did a similar survey of 92 British companies.[3]

If a firm or brand has been successful over several years using the percentage-of-sales approach, it might be assumed that the decision rule yielded budgets reasonably close to the optimal, so there is little incentive to change to another approach in setting budgets. The rule does tend to make explicit the marketing-mix decision, the allocation of the budget to the various elements of the marketing program. Furthermore, it provides comfort to a prudent financial executive who likes to know that her or his firm can afford the advertising. Finally, if competitors also use such a rule, it leads to a certain stability of advertising within the industry, which may be useful. If there is a ceiling on the size of the market, it is wise to avoid precipitating a war over advertising expenditures.

The major flaw in the method is that it does not rest on the premise that advertising can influence sales. In fact, sales or a sales estimate determine advertising expenditures. It can lead to excessive expenditures for large established brands and for over-the-hill brands that are basically servicing old loyal customers who will very likely continue to buy even if advertising support is withdrawn. It can, conversely, lead to inadequate budgets for promising healthy brands that could potentially become competitive with more advertising muscle.

The percentage-of-sales approach obviously needs to be modified in dynamic situations such as the following:

- When a brand is making a major repositioning move or reacting to one.
- When a brand becomes established and dominant.
- When a brand is just being introduced.

Making a Move.   When a brand decides to make a move, a substantial increase in advertising might be necessary, an increase that may not be justified by the percentage-of-sales logic. For example, when Phillip Morris purchased Miller's beer in 1972 and initiated a campaign to reposition it and increase its share, the advertising budget was dramatically increased. Similarly, when the effects of the Miller effort became evident, the other beer companies had to consider breaking out of their percentage-of-sales routine and react to the Miller move.

Established Brand.   When a brand becomes established and dominant, it can usually start reducing the percentage of sales allocated to advertising. As brand-name awareness becomes very high and the brand's image becomes very set, it is not usually necessary to advertise as heavily. Conversely, if a smaller brand is struggling to become known and is concerned about advertising at the minimal threshold level, it will often have to spend money at an artificially high percentage-of-sales level.

New Brand.   A new product, concept, or brand will have the special task of generating awareness and distribution from a zero level. As a result, it is usually necessary to make heavy investments in advertising during the first year or two of the brand's life. At Colgate-Palmolive, the guide is to base the advertising expenditures upon the total gross profit, which is the total sales less the product cost, as follows:[4]

- Advertising in first year equals twice the gross profit.
- Advertising in second year equals half the gross profit.
- Advertising in third and succeeding years equals 30 percent of the gross profit.

All You Can Afford

Firms with limited resources may decide to spend all that they can reasonably allocate to advertising after other unavoidable expenditures have been allocated. This rule usually ensures that they are not advertising too heavily, that advertising moneys are not being wasted. It thus does have some logic. Of course, if the value of more advertising could be demonstrated, extra money could usually be raised, so the limitation may be somewhat artificial.

Some larger firms also use this rule. They start with the sales forecast and budget all expenditures, including profit, except advertising. The advertising budget is what is left over. About all that can be said about such a rule, which is actually used in too many situations, is that it generates a financial plan that usually looks neat and attractive in an accounting sense. However, it rests on the assumption that sales are independent of the advertising expenditures. There is no realization that advertising may influence sales. The only reason advertising is included is that its absence would be difficult to justify.

Competitive Parity

Another common guide is to adjust the advertising budget so that it is comparable to those of competitors. The logic is that the collective minds of the firms in the industry will probably generate advertising budgets that are somewhat close to the optimal. Everyone could not be too far from the optimal. Furthermore, any departure from the industry norms could precipitate a spending war.

The problem here is that there is no guarantee that a group of firms is spending at an optimal level. Insofar as their spending habits are constant over time, and assuming that market conditions change over time, they are probably not spending at the optimal level. Even if they are, it is likely that the situations of individual firms are sufficiently unique so that the practices of their competitors should not be followed. In particular, a new small firm in the field might not receive the proportionate amount of impact for its advertising that a large established firm receives. The success of the larger firm may be due to many other factors in addition to advertising. Furthermore, the method does not consider such questions as differences in effectiveness of various campaigns or the efficiency of media placement.

Objective and Task

Objective and task, more an approach to budgeting than a simple decision rule, is used by two-thirds of the largest advertisers.[5] An advertising objective is first established in specific terms. For example, a firm may decide to attempt to increase the awareness of its brand in a certain population segment to 50 percent. The tasks that are required to accomplish this objective are then detailed. They might involve the development of a particular advertising campaign exposing the relevant audience an average of five times. The cost of obtaining these exposures then becomes the advertising budget. This approach is logical in that it assumes that there is a causal flow from advertising to sales. In effect, it represents an effort to introduce intervening variables such as awareness or attitude, which will presumably be indicators of future sales as well as immediate sales.

The major problem with this approach is that the link between the objective and immediate and future sales is often not spelled out. If the link were established, this approach would provide the basis for the extended marginal analysis mentioned earlier. In the next four chapters we will develop a framework for extending it in this direction so that it can indeed provide a logical, defensible basis for setting the advertising budget.

Budgeting Process in Large Firms

Figure 3-2 shows the organizational structure of a multibrand firm using a brand management system. Reporting to a marketing vice-president are brand managers who are responsible for the profitability of the brand and managers of marketing functional areas such as sales, advertising, and marketing research. Brand managers submit marketing plans, including an advertising budget, to the vice-president of marketing, who must make investment trade-off decisions between brands and the marketing function programs. At some higher level these proposals must also compete with those from groups such as manufacturing and engineering. The whole process involves bargaining, persuasion, and trade-off decisions.

Figure 3-2. **Simplified organization chart of a company employing the brand-management concept**

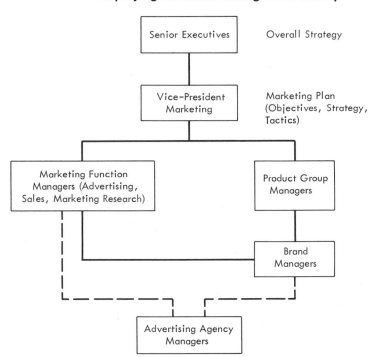

MARKET EXPERIMENTATION AND BUDGETING

A direct approach to estimating the sales response to advertising is to conduct field market experiments. Advertising expenditure levels are deliberately and systematically varied across areas. Sales changes are monitored through time, sometimes for several years, and related to advertising levels.

One of the best known sets of field experiments was conducted by Budweiser during the 1960s.[6] In one of their experiments seven advertising change treatments were used:

- −100 percent (no advertising)
- − 50 percent
- 0 percent (advertising was unchanged)
- + 50 percent
- +100 percent (the advertising expenditure was doubled)
- +150 percent
- +200 percent

Six marketing areas were assigned to each advertising treatment. The experiment ran for one year. Not only did "no advertising" result in the same sales level, but a −50 percent level actually resulted in a sales increase. One possible explanation was that there was a light-drinker segment for which reduced repetition was helpful. This experiment and others in the series resulted in substantial reductions in advertising expenditures, particularly on a per barrel basis, as Figure 3-3 illustrates.

Testing Advertising and Price

Sometimes it is useful to include marketing variables other than advertising in the experiment, particularly when the advertising response will depend on the levels of those other marketing variables. Eskin reports an experiment involving a new nutritional convenience food in which both advertising and price levels were tested.[7] A sample of 30 stores in each of four test cities was used. Two of the cities received a high advertising weight that was approximately twice that received by the other two cities. In addition, in each city the 30 test stores were split into three panels of ten stores, each matched as to store size and other factors. Each of these matched panels received one of three price treatments: a base price below 50 cents, a price 10 cents above the base, and a price 20 cents above it. The test ran for six months. Each month the unit sales per store was measured. The experimental design is summarized at the top of Figure 3-4.

The results are summarized at the bottom of Figure 3-4. Clearly, the higher advertising was very effective when the base price was used. In contrast, increased advertising had almost no effect at the highest price. Prior to the test, the belief was that the best candidates for a national program were the combinations of high price and high advertising and low price and low advertising. The logic was that a high

Figure 3-3.   **Advertising and sales, Budweiser beer; index 1954 = 100**

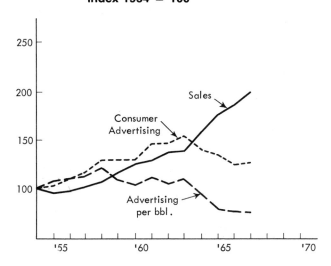

price was needed to provide margin to pay for the advertising. The test led to a very different conclusion, however—a low-price and high-advertising program.

In this case, the response to advertising depended upon the price level selected. If price had not been included in the experiment, a distorted impression might have emerged as to the advertising response. Inclusion of price, of course, also provided useful information about that marketing decision variable.

Problems with Market Experimentation

Experimental approaches are indeed useful and direct methods of obtaining information on sales-response curves. However, there are major problems associated with their use.

Experimentation is inherently expensive. There are several types of costs to consider. First, there are the obvious direct costs of setting up the experiment and collecting and analyzing the results. Second is the fact that management decisions are delayed by the research. The researcher is often in a dilemma. On the one hand, validity considerations demand a longer experiment. However, as the length increases, the timeliness of the results suffers. Furthermore, there is the very real likelihood that the situation will change (a major new product will emerge, for example) and the experimental results will not be applicable. Third, there is a security cost, particularly in new-product contexts. Competitors will have access to the nature and results of your experiments. Finally, an advertising test will invariably involve excess advertising in some areas and less than optimal in others. The costs of either situation can be very significant.

Figure 3-4.   **An advertising and price experiment**

Test Design

Advertising:	Low Weight						High Weight					
	Market 1			Market 2			Market 3			Market 4		
Price:	Base	+10c	+20c	Base	+10c	+20c	Base	+10c	+20c	Base	+10c	+20c
N =	(10)	(10)	(10)	(10)	(10)	(10)	(10)	(10)	(10)	(10)	(10)	(10)
Month												
1												
2												
3												
4												
5												
6												

Total no. of observations = 720
Measure = total sales/per store/by month

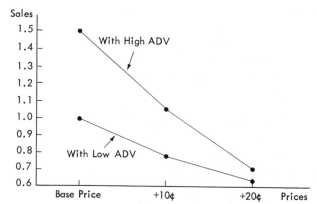

Source: Adapted from Gerald Eskin, "A Case for Test Market Experiments,"
Journal of Advertising Research, 15, April 1975, pp. 29, 31.

Market experiments are never "controlled" as well as would be desirable; there are a litany of things that can "go wrong." Retailers can run out of stock because of logistical problems or because they did not anticipate the impact of more advertising. Distributors or retailers in "low advertising treatment areas" can mount their own advertising or promotion campaign to replace the national advertising being withdrawn. They are more concerned with their marketing position than with any experiment. Competitors' marketing efforts, including new-product introductions, can confound the experiment. Further, competitors sometimes deliberately attempt to disrupt the test by radically changing some element of their competitive marketing strategy, such as their price or promotion effort.

Guidelines for Conducting Experiments

A list of guidelines for conducting experiments should include the following:

1. Use randomly selected control cities, areas, or stores so that the effects of advertising can be separated from all the other influences on sales. If possible, these control groups should be matched with the experimental groups on such dimensions as size or market share. For example, it would be useful to compare advertising levels across cities in which the advertised brand had comparable market-share positions.

2. Use before as well as after measures. If sales as a result of the experiment can be compared with "last year's sales" or "last month's sales," the results will be much more sensitive.

3. Use substantial differences in advertising expenditures. Do not try to compare a 10 or 20 percent change in advertising; rather, look at 50 or 100 percent changes.

4. Test reduced advertising as well as increased advertising. The payoff at Budweiser was from the reduced advertising tests.

5. Control or at least monitor other variables that might affect the interpretation. For example, price or other marketing variables might be included in the experiment. Or the experiment might be repeated for large stores and small stores. Outside, uncontrollable factors—most notably, competitive behavior—should be monitored.

6. Make sure that the test is run for an adequate time. A full year is often required when a mature brand is involved.

Split-Cable Testing

A relatively new and powerful technique for measuring advertising response is termed split-cable testing. Information Resources Inc.'s (IRI) BehaviorScan is one of the several split-cable testing operations (Burke and Nielsen being two others). BehaviorScan maintains a 3,000-member consumer panel in each of eight cities (such as Pittsfield, Massachusetts, and Marion, Indiana). All panelists carry ID cards that they present to supermarkets and drugstores when buying. Their purchases are all monitored by IRI, as is in-store activity such as special prices, features, and displays. The panelists have a device connected to their TV set that allows BehaviorScan to monitor what channel is tuned, and also to substitute one advertisement for another in what is called a "cut-in."

Panelists are divided into groups of panelists who are indistinguishable except that they are exposed to different advertising. They live in the same neighborhoods and shop at the same stores. The advertising budget test simply involves setting the advertising expenditure (or weight) levels, assigning each to a group of panelists, and monitoring the results.

The ability to control exposure levels and to monitor purchase activity provides the potential to conduct experiments that, unlike field experiments, are tightly controlled. Access to shelf space is guaranteed, so there is little concern about distribution problems. In-store activities that can confound results are at least monitored. The tests are hidden from competitors, which reduces the chance of disruption. The exact number of advertising exposures is known. In a field test, even if the expenditure level were known, the number of exposures could vary enormously. Purchases can be monitored accurately on a daily basis. First (trial) purchases, repeat purchases, coupon redemptions, and the time between purchases are all known.

Split-cable testing is certainly the state of the art and is undoubtedly the most effective way to measure the response function. However, it is not without limitations. First, it is relatively expensive. The test itself will cost at least $100,000 and probably many times more in addition to the in-house cost of the advertiser and the agency.

Second, it is often necessary to run a test for at least six months and perhaps several years. The carryover impact can easily involve six or more purchase cycles, which can extend the test for a year. Further, the need to measure the impact on brand goodwill and loyalty may take longer to determine. In one test of a health care brand with a national budget of $15 million, it took two years before the sales of the low-advertising group, receiving the equivalent of a $10 million budget, declined.[8] After one year it was actually above the other group. With a lengthy test, there is always the danger that conditions may change making the results obsolete and outmoded.

Third, the experiments can actually be overcontrolled.[9] Since distribution is controlled, there is no measure of the ability of the advertising to influence distribution. Thus, effective advertising could easily affect the retailer's initial opinion and decision to stock the brand and the enthusiasm with which it is pushed. The retailers could be exposed to the advertising themselves, or they could be influenced by consumer reaction to it. Yet the split-cable tests really provide little information about such an impact.

Fourth, there is a natural bias against conducting "down-weight" tests, whether split-cable or in the field.[10] Agencies basically get a commission on advertising and thus have a conflict of interest. Further, it is psychologically and logically inconsistent to be excited and positive about a new campaign and propose a budget reduction. Further, the product manager, who controls the advertising and is measured in part on short-run sales, views advertising as a way to protect short-term market position and react to competitor activities.

REGRESSION ANALYSIS AND BUDGETING

Another approach to estimating the advertising response curve is to look at the historical patterns of sales and advertising. When advertising changed in the past, what happened to sales? Or if the advertising level differed in different sales areas, how did sales differ? Such an approach is relatively inexpensive, as it uses data in hand.

A systematic way to analyze such patterns is through the use of regression analysis. A typical regression model could attempt to predict sales in one time period with the following types of explanatory (or independent) variables:

- Sales in the preceding period
- Advertising in the current period
- Advertising in the previous period
- Advertising two periods back
- Other marketing variables, such as distribution or price
- Measures of competitor advertising

Sales in the preceding period provide a measure of the existing market position that has probably been caused by the marketing program over a long period.

Advertising nearly always has an impact in future periods, representing future purchase cycles. The inclusion of previous advertising expenditures provides an attempt to measure this carryover effect of advertising. The advertising response would be the sum of the current impact and the carryover effect.

To isolate the impact of advertising it is necessary to include other marketing variables. Suppose, for example, that expenditures for promotion and advertising were potential causes of sales change. Unless promotion was included in the model, the apparent advertising effect might really represent a promotion effect. Similarly, unless some measure of competitor advertising is available, the apparent advertising impact may be distorted. An increase in advertising may have no impact on sales because competitor advertising increased dramatically. Without knowledge of competitor advertising, the advertising response might erroneously be thought to be low.

Problems with Regression Analysis

Regression analysis is sometimes useful, but on the whole it has been disappointing.[11] There are simply too many problems associated with its use. Perhaps the most difficult problem is to measure the carryover effect. The impact over one, two, or more periods simply gets swamped by all the other sources of sales variation. Further, in addition to the carryover effect, which could take months to dissipate, there is the long-run impact of advertising on the process of a brand's goodwill creation, persistence, and decay. There is often the fear that a sharp reduction in advertising may be felt only after years, when severe damage will have been done.

There are several other difficulties associated with regression analysis modeling in general and with the problem of measuring the carryover effect in particular. Among them are:

1.   There is often little variation in advertising except that due to seasonable factors. Without variation in advertising it is not possible to detect the impact of changes in advertising on sales. This problem is severe when a brand is overadvertising and it is so far out on the advertising response curve that there is no response to any change in advertising. In that case an extreme drop in advertising would be needed to detect any response, and such a variation is simply not in the data.

2.   The data may be faulty. For example, accounting sales data will represent shipments to retailers and not consumer purchases in response to advertising. Syndicated store movement data overcome this problem but are expensive and available only to consumer products firms. Accounting advertising data similarly represent billings by an agency and not exposures to ads. In fact, it is difficult to get any accurate measure of advertising exposures.

3.   Data describing other marketing variables are often not available or are expensive to obtain. Data describing competitor activities are rarely available. Annual data really are inadequate since the immediate and carryover effect of advertising usually occurs in months, not years.

4.   If a business uses the percentage-of-sales method of establishing a budget, a sales change could cause a change in advertising expenditures instead of the reverse (at least at the annual level).

SUMMARY

The theoretical underpinning of the advertising budget is based on marginal analysis and is easily expressed. A firm should continue to add to its advertising budget as long as the incremental expenditures are exceeded by the marginal revenue they generate. The determination of the functional relationship between advertising expenditures and sales, which is at the heart of marginal analysis, is most difficult for several reasons. First, the assumption that advertising expenditures affect immediate sales is often faulty. Second, the determination of the shape and parameters of the relationship is no easy task. Finally, the relationship changes through time.

Practical decision makers, in response to the problems of marginal analysis, have used several decision rules. The most widely used approach, which bases the advertising budget on some "percentage of sales," can lead to excessive expenditures for well-established brands and inadequate expenditures for new and promising brands. The objective and task approach, which will be extended and pursued in Part II, is based on the development of sound and defensible communication objectives. The final budget is also governed in some organizations by bargaining among individuals and groups within and outside the organization.

Marginal analysis requires determination of the sales response to advertising. One approach is to conduct field experiments by varying advertising levels in different test stores, cities, or areas. Field experiments encouraged Budweiser to reduce advertising in the 1960s. They tend to be costly both in money and time. Further, many factors can confound or mask the results, such as actions of retailers and competitors, the inability to deliver precise levels of advertising to test cities, and the impact of other marketing variables.

Another approach is split-cable testing, wherein advertising seen by matched panels of consumers is controlled and their purchases are monitored via store scanner systems. Split-cable testing scores high on validity and control but is fairly expensive, provides little information of the impact of the advertising on retailers, and can take from six months to two years, depending on the difficulty of measuring long-term effects.

A third approach, regression analysis, works with existing data and is thus inexpensive. However, it is rarely useful because of the lack of variability of the advertising data, the lack of data on confounding factors such as competitor actions and other marketing variables, the lack of data precisely measuring advertising and sales, and the difficulty of measuring the long-term impact of advertising.

APPENDIX

A Model of Adaptive Control

A model that uses experimental data as an explicit input to the budget decision was developed by John D. C. Little, a professor at MIT.[12] It recognizes that the relationship between advertising and sales changes over time with changing market conditions. As a result, the advertising budget decision should be updated accordingly.

The adaptive-control model starts by assuming a response curve and finding an optimal level of advertising expenditure, as in Figure 3-5. If the decision maker were confident about an estimate of the response function and if he or she believes it would not change over time, the problem would be solved. However, under more realistic conditions, it becomes desirable to obtain more information about the response curve. In particular, it is worthwhile to experiment by advertising at nonoptimal levels in a few test markets to gain such information. The new information from the experiments is added to the existing information on the sales response function to determine the current optimal advertising expenditure rate.

Assume that the advertising sales response function can be described by a specific mathematical function such as the following quadratic function:

$$S(A) = \alpha + \beta A - \gamma A^2 \tag{1}$$

where $S(A)$ = sales
A = advertising expenditures
α, β, γ = parameters

The first two terms in equation (1) represent the familiar straight-line, linear relationship. The third term adds a curvature. An example of equation (1) is the upside-down U shown in Figure 3-5.

If M is the gross margin of the product, then profit, P, will be

$$P = MS(A) - A \tag{2}$$

The value of advertising expenditures, A^*, that will maximize equation (2) can be found graphically or algebraically.[13]

Little has argued that the optimal advertising rate is relatively insensitive to γ as long as the parameter is set within reasonable bounds. Thus, Little assumes that γ is known and constant. He argues, however, that β is not likely to stay constant through time. Changes in competitive activity, product changes, changes in the quality of advertising, or shifts in economic conditions can result in changes in response β.

Figure 3-5 shows the nature of a sales experiment to derive estimates of β. It assumes at a particular time, t, the advertising rate $A(t)^*$ is considered to be optimal. All markets with the exception of a set receiving a lower rate, A_1, and a set receiving a higher rate, A_2, are subjected to this level of advertising.[14] The sales rate in the groups of markets at A_1 and A_2 provides information from which a revised estimate of the parameter β can be derived.[15]

Little compared the results of a computer-simulation version of the adaptive-control model with four other modeling alternatives. The model compared particularly well when contrasted with the results of assuming a constant advertising rate. These comparisons can be made by calculating how much the loss in profits would be in each case relative to having perfect information on the respective functions. In one case of assuming a constant rate, for example, losses amounted to 28.7 percent compared with only 1.5 percent for the adaptive-model formulation.

Figure 3-5.   **Sales experiment**

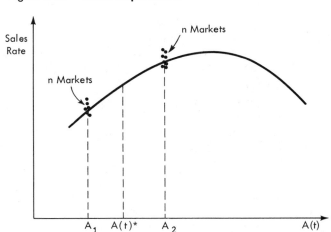

This model illustrates, among other things, the advantages of attempting to make objective measurements of relevant parameter values through experimental procedures and stresses the importance of repeated measurements. It is above all based on a recognition that an advertising manager faces a constantly changing environment and that he or she must adapt both plans and budget to those changing conditions. Many companies in effect are continuously experimenting and engaging in these types of marketing research studies, even though they may not be guided by formal decision rules. Although such research is bound to be costly, the effort is often worthwhile. The adaptive-control model provides an approach to answering the question of how much should be invested in such research, as well as how much to invest in advertising at any particular time.

DISCUSSION QUESTIONS

1. At the chapter outset, some large advertising expenditure differences were observed between firms in the same industry. Why would Noxell (Cover Girl, Noxzema) have twenty times the advertising-to-sales ratio as Avon? Why would TWA have over twice the advertising-to-sales ratio as Delta?

2. What exactly are the coordinates of the Figure 3-1 curve? How might they be measured?

3. In Figure 3-1, why is the sales curve S-shaped? Explain the gradually accelerating section on the lower half of the curve and the flattening out section on the upper half. Discuss the significance of this shape from the viewpoint of (a) a company, (b) an industry, and (c) the economy as a whole.

4. What is the percentage-of-sales budgeting approach? Why is it so widely used? Under what circumstances might it be inappropriate? Why?

5. What assumptions underlie the "all-you-can-afford" and "competitive-parity" approaches to setting advertising budgets?

6. Contact someone in a firm that does a signficant amount of advertising. What advertising budget-setting decision rule do they use? To what extent is the budget decision arrived at by the "bargaining process" referred to in connection with Figure 3-2?

7. Design a field experiment that would provide input data for the sales response to advertising function for a company selling men's razor blades. How much would the experiment likely cost? Identify other variables that might affect sales in your chosen test markets. What is the role, if any, of "laboratory experimentation" in this context?

8. Repeat Question 7 for a company selling technical instruments used in scientific laboratories and hospitals. How would the design differ? Should "industrial marketing" companies attempt to iden-

tify sales-response functions in connection with their advertising activities?

9.   Which kinds of firms are likely to invest in advertising and sales experiments? Why are experiments used infrequently? What are the problems and limitations of experiments? Why are experiments involving tests of reduced advertising expenditures so rare?

10. Suppose that you were a brand manager and had developed an experiment involving four Midwest test cities in which four levels of advertising expenditure were used over a six-month period. The resulting sales were compared with the sales during the same six months of the previous year. During your presentation to top management, you run into two challenges. First, the executive vice-president claims that the budget levels suggested by the model will not apply to your campaign in the East because response to advertising is different in that part of the country. Second, the advertising manager claims that the new campaign will have a much higher response than previous advertising and consequently the model output is of no relevance. How would you respond to these questions?

11. What are the two most important attributes of a split-cable test? In what sense might a split-cable test be overcontrolling? Under what circumstances would you worry about such a problem? What are the other disadvantages of split-cable testing?

12. What is the difference between a marginal analysis and a regression analysis?

13. Why might a regression model fit the data better if the log of advertising expenditures is used as the independent variable instead of the advertising expenditures?

14. Why would a regression analysis of a three-year sequence of monthly advertising expenditures and market share of a detergent be a less sensitive and valid way to determine advertising response than an experiment?

15. In the Koyck distributed lag regression model there is only one advertising term, current advertising. The coefficient of the previous period's sales becomes a measure of the carryover effect of advertising. The assumption is that sales are influenced by advertising and thus that past sales were "created" by previous advertising. Given that assumption, what would be the total impact of advertising if the advertising coefficient were 0.2 and the coefficient for the preceding year were 0.5? When might such an assumption be reasonable? [*Hint:* The series $1 + x + x^2 + x^3 + \cdots = 1/(1 - x)$.]

NOTES

1. *Advertising Age,* June 13, 1985 and September 26, 1985.

2. Charles H. Patti and Vincent Blasko, "Budgeting Practices of Big Advertisers," *Journal of Advertising Research,* 21, December 1981, pp. 23–29.

3. Colin Gilligan, "How British Advertisers Set Budgets," *Journal of Advertising Research,* 17, February 1977, pp. 47–49.

4. Barbara Brady, June Connolly, Les Quok, Karen Wachtel, and Peter Weiss, "Bright 'N Soft," unpublished paper, 1979.

5. Patti and Blasko, "Budgeting Practices."

6. Russell L. Ackoff and James R. Emshoff, "Advertising Research at Anheuser-Busch, Inc. (1963–68)," *Sloan Management Review,* Winter 1975, pp. 1–15.

7. Gerald J. Eskin, "A Case for Test Market Experiments," *Journal of Advertising Research,* 15, April 1975, pp. 27–33.

8. Reg Rhodes, "What AdTel Has Learned," presented to the American Marketing Association's New York Chapter, March 22, 1977.

9. Paul W. Farris and David J. Reibstein, "Overcontrol in Advertising Experiments," *Journal of Advertising Research,* 24, June–July 1984, pp. 37–44.

10. David A. Aaker and James M. Carman, "Are You Overadvertising?" *Journal of Advertising Research,* 22, August–September 1982, pp. 57–70.

11. Ibid.

12. John D. C. Little, "A Model of Adaptive Control of Promotional Spending," *Operations Research,* 14, November–December 1966, pp. 175–97.

13. Substituting equation (1) into equation (2) yields

$$P = M\alpha + M\beta A - M\gamma A^2 - A$$

Taking the derivative of P with respect to A and setting it equal to zero,

$$M\beta - 2M\gamma A - 1 = 0$$

Solving for A,

$$A^* = \frac{M\beta - 1}{2M\gamma}$$

14. The optimal gap between A_1 and A_2 and optimal number of test markets to use can be calculated. See Little, "Model of Adaptive Control," pp. 128–130.

15. Letting S_1 and S_2 be the observed mean sales rates in the groups of markets at A_1 and A_2, respectively, the experimental mean for (t) can be calculated as follows:

$$\hat{\beta}(t) = \frac{1}{A_1 - A_2} (\bar{S}_2 + \gamma A_2^2 - \bar{S}_1 - \gamma A_1^2)$$

The β to be used in determining the budget for the next time period, $t + 1$, is termed $\beta(t + 1)$. It is a weighted average of the β used in the current time period $\beta(t)$ and the estimate of β obtained from the experiment, $\hat{\beta}(t)$.

$$\beta(t + 1) = a\beta(t) + (1 - a)\hat{\beta}(t)$$

Thus, the decision rule defining the advertising rate in the next time period, $A(t + 1)^*$, is

$$A(t + 1)^* = \frac{M\beta(t + 1) - 1}{2M\gamma}$$

If the experiment were very accurate, a small value of a could be used and heavy reliance placed on the current experiment. If the accuracy of the experiment were low, a large value of a would be appropriate. In this case, the current rate would depend mostly on the rate used in the preceding time period, which in turn represents a summary of all past experience up to that time.

CASE FOR PART 1

Pacific Telephone & Telegraph Company*

For some years prior to 1972, PT&T had been concerned about the steadily rising rate of user calls for directory assistance (DA). Directory assistance service, for which the company did not charge, was expensive and cost the company in the neighborhood of $40 to $50 million per year. In one city alone, for example, daily volume of DA calls had increased in the peak month of September from 47,000 calls per day in 1969 to a projected 59,000 calls per day in 1972. Operators' attempts to use polite phrases in asking customers to reduce the incidence of DA dialing had not been successful. Other educational programs, internal control programs, and some limited advertising had been tried, but the volume of DA calls continued to rise.

The company decided in 1971 to develop a stronger and more direct advertising campaign and to test its effects in one market. Fresno, California, was chosen as the test city, and an eight-week advertising program was designed, made up of two television spots, radio spots, newspaper ads, and bill inserts. The principal themes of the ads were "Dial it yourself" and "The $40 million phone call." The campaign cost $14,000.

A summary of the essential procedure and phases of the study follows.

Phase I, Pre-Ad Campaign

An attitude survey of Fresno residents was run during May and June 1972 to determine attitudes and opinions about the company's cost of providing DA service and about possible charges for DA service. A total of 337 Fresno customers were interviewed by telephone.

Phase II, Ad Campaign

The campaign was run for two months, July and August 1972, and involved television and radio spots, newspaper ads, and a special bill insert. Advertising emphasized the cost of providing the service, the number of calls made for numbers in the directory, and points like, "If you're concerned about the cost of your telephone service, please look up numbers in the phone book whenever you can."

Phase III, Post-Ad Campaign

Phase III consisted of two additional studies: (1) an advertising awareness survey done in September to determine coverage of the advertising among heavy residence DA users, and (2) a post-ad campaign attitude survey, also done in September. The

* Courtesy of Pacific Telephone and Telegraph Company.

awareness survey involved 604 heavy-usage customers stratified by two-usage levels. One-half of the sample was randomly drawn from heavy users making 21 to 60 calls and one-half from very heavy users making 61 or more calls during May and June. The post-ad attitude survey was a telephone interview study of 333 residence customers, following the same procedures that had been used in the pre-ad phase. In all phases, detailed call tracking was established in four Fresno prefixes. Two of these prefixes had predominantly residential customers, and the other two had predominantly business customers. These data provided the primary information by which the company attempted to trace the effects of the advertising campaign on the actual behavior of customers with respect to DA rates.

Figure 1 shows monthly DA call volume in Fresno from January 1969 to November 1972. There is a marked regularity of seasonal patterning from year to year, and on this basis the company had forecast a projected volume without advertising. In September 1972, for example, the peak month of DA calls, the projection was about 59,000. Figure 1 shows that actual volume following the July–August campaign was only about 53,000, and the long-term growth pattern appeared to have been broken. The company calculated that the average volume decrease for the five months, July–November, was 9 percent.

Figure 2 shows that the trend in Fresno did not occur on a companywide basis during the period. The company overall was experiencing a growth rate during the period of about 7 percent over 1971, whereas Fresno, starting in August, showed a decrease to below 1971 volume. Some other highlights from the awareness and attitude study phases of the study were as follows:

Figure 1.   **Fresno directory assistance average business day volume**

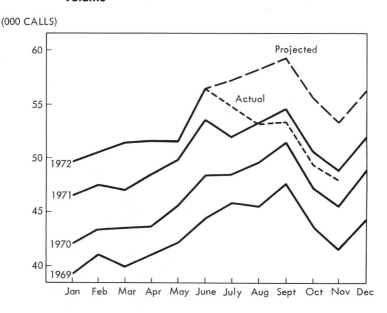

1. Among heavy users, ad recall was very high, about 75 percent. Four out of ten heavy users who had seen or heard advertising said that they used the directory more often than they did before seeing the ads; they acknowledged that exposure to the advertising was what motivated them to make fewer DA calls.

2. Some favorable shifts in attitudes and opinions about the cost of providing DA service and about possible DA charges were revealed in the attitude surveys. After the advertising, more people (26 percent versus 38 percent) said that DA service "costs a lot" for the company to provide. In the post-ad campaign survey, more people (48 percent versus 60 percent) said they would look up local numbers in the directory. This shift occurred almost entirely among respondents who said that they had seen or heard the test advertising. Finally, fewer respondents in the post-ad campaign survey felt that their reaction to the idea of a DA charge was "completely unreasonable" (43 percent versus 34 percent). These studies also provided valuable information on some of the demographic and life-style characteristics of heavy DA users compared with the general population; the heavy users tended to be younger, self-employed people in professional or managerial positions.

The results of the Fresno test were encouraging to company executives. It appeared that in Fresno the advertising campaign had had a significant and dramatic effect on call volume. An analysis was made of the cost savings resulting from the

Figure 2.   **Increase in average business day directory assistance volume, comparison of PT&T and Fresno (percentage change from 1971 to 1972)**

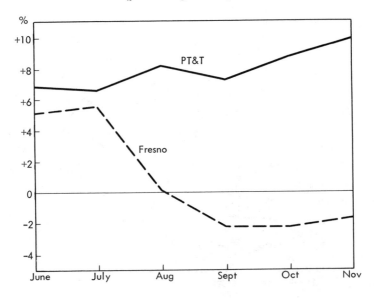

campaign in Fresno, and it was determined that, excluding overhead and equipment expenses, the company had saved $44,000 in wage and salary benefits over a five-month period as a result of the decreased volume. If the 9 percent call rate reduction could be maintained for one year, the savings would be $106,000. The production and media costs of the campaign were calculated to be $14,000.

Marketing Decisions

In the spring of 1972, the marketing planning group was attempting to determine what action should be taken for the coming year. A proposal vigorously put forward by one executive was that the company impose a minimal charge for DA assistance, which would be added to a customer's regular monthly bill, even though such a charge would be resisted by customers and the public utilities commission which would have to approve it. Another executive suggested that a system-wide campaign be developed along the lines of the Fresno campaign and be launched in the fall of 1972. It was estimated that throughout the system there were about 1 million DA calls daily and that the annual expense for operators and equipment handling these calls was about $55 million.

Although nobody knew precisely what a system-wide campaign would cost, the company's advertising agency had suggested that it would be about $500,000. The head of the marketing research group suggested a third alternative. He proposed that the company set aside additional funds for continued research on advertising effects on DA call volume and, in effect, repeat the Fresno experiment in other test markets before proceeding with a system-wide campaign or imposing a charge for the service. These executives were aware of the increasing amount of publicity being generated at the time by citizen groups against advertising by utility companies. Many of these groups were arguing that, because of the environmental and energy crisis, public utilities should be restricted from advertising. They claimed funds should be used to reduce customer telephone charges rather than be wasted on activities like advertising.

DISCUSSION QUESTIONS

1. Based on the figures given in the case, what is the economic value to the company of the advertising expenditures invested in the Fresno test market?

2. All other considerations aside, and assuming that a decision is made to launch a system-wide advertising campaign, how much money should the company invest in such a campaign?

3. In your own words, describe the Fresno test market experiment.

4. What problems do you see in the experimental design? How would you have changed it?

5. Discuss the assumption that the savings in Fresno could be projected to cover the full year.

6. What action should the marketing planning group have taken in the spring of 1972?

4

Setting Advertising Objectives

For an advertisement to be effective it must be noticed, read, comprehended, believed, and acted upon. (Daniel Starch, 1923)

For one who has no objective, nothing is relevant. (Confucius)

The pivotal aspect of any management effort is the development of meaning-ful objectives. Without good objectives, it is nearly impossible to guide and control decision making. Good performance may occasionally occur in the absence of objectives, but it can rarely be sustained. In the past, advertising has often been a free spirit within an organization, operating with little guidance or control. It has been able to resist the discipline of modern management because the actual creative decisions were usually made in another organization, the advertising agency. The challenge today is to bring effective management to the advertising process in such a way as to provide stimulation as well as direction to the creative effort. The key is the development of meaningful objectives. Part II is directed toward this end.

FUNCTION OF OBJECTIVES

Objectives serve several functions in modern management. One function is to operate as communication and coordination devices. They provide a vehicle by which the client, the agency account executive, and the creative team communicate.

They also serve to coordinate the efforts of such groups as copywriters, radio specialists, media buyers, and research specialists.

A second function of objectives is to provide a criterion for decision making. If two alternative campaigns are generated, one must be selected. Rather than relying on an executive's esthetic judgment (or on that of his or her spouse), he or she should be able to turn to the objective and select the criterion that will most readily achieve it. One test of the operationality of an objective is the degree to which it can act as a decision criterion.

A related function of an objective is to evaluate results. Thus, another test of objective operationality is whether it can be used to evaluate a campaign at its conclusion. This function implies that there needs to be a measure such as market share or brand awareness associated with the objective. At the end of the campaign, that measure is employed to evaluate the success of the campaign.

Sales as an Objective

Advertising objectives, like organizational objectives, should be operational. They should be effective criteria for decision making and should provide standards with which results can be compared. Furthermore, they should be effective communication tools, providing a line between strategic and tactical decisions.

A convenient and enticing advertising objective involves a construct like immediate sales or market share. The ultimate aim of advertising is often to help raise the level of some aggregate measure like immediate sales. The measure is usually readily available to "evaluate" the results of a campaign. Recall that much of the experimental research cited in the last chapter involved measures of immediate sales.

There are situations—mail-order advertising and some retail advertising, for example—when immediate sales are a good operational objective, and others in which they can play a role in guiding the advertising campaign. Chapter 7 will discuss in more detail such situations in which sales or market share make useful objectives. However, objectives that involve an increase in immediate sales are not operational in many cases for two reasons: (1) advertising is only one of many factors influencing sales, and (2) the contributory role of advertising often occurs primarily over the long run.

Advertising is only one of the many forces that influence sales, as Figure 4-1 illustrates. The other forces include price, distribution, packaging, product features, competitive actions, and changing buyer needs and tastes. It is extremely difficult to isolate the effect of advertising. Some argue that evaluating advertising only by its impact on sales is like attributing all the success (or failure) of a football team to the quarterback. The fact is that many other elements can affect the team's record—other plays, the competition, and the bounce of the ball. The implication is that the effect of the quarterback's performance should be measured by the things he alone can influence, such as how he throws the ball, how he calls the plays, and how he

Figure 4-1.   **Some of the factors influencing sales**

Advertising

Price

Distribution

Packaging   Sales

Product Features

Competition

Consumer Tastes

hands off. If, in a real-world situation, all factors remained constant except for advertising (for example, if competitive activity were static), then it would be feasible to rely exclusively on sales to measure advertising effectiveness. Since such a situation is, in reality, infeasible, we must start dealing with response variables that are associated more directly with the advertising stimulus.

The second reason involves the long-term effect of advertising on sales. If we believe that advertising generates a substantial lagged effect on sales, then the impact of an advertising campaign may not be known for certain until an unacceptable length of time has passed. For example, an important contribution of a one-year campaign might be its impact two or three years hence. As Figure 4-2 illustrates, advertising might attract buyers who will be loyal customers for several years, or it might start the development of positive attitudes that will culminate in a purchase much later. To determine this effect from sales data, it may be necessary to wait far beyond the end of the one-year campaign. Two problems are created. First, the difficulty of isolating the sales change caused by advertising becomes more severe as the time between the advertising expenditure and the sales response increases. Yet decisions must be made immediately and cannot wait for such data. Second, for more timely and accurate information, variables that respond more quickly to advertising input must be sought.

Thus, advertising objectives that emphasize sales are usually not very operational because they provide little practical guidance for decision makers. No one argues the desirability of a sales increase, but which campaign will (or did) generate such an increase? If an objective does not contribute useful criteria on which to base subsequent decisions, it cannot fulfill its basic functions.

Figure 4-2.   **Long-run impact of advertising**

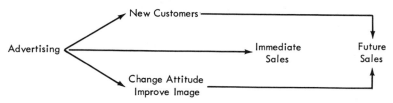

Toward Operational Objectives

If immediate sales do not form the basis of operational objectives in most situations, how does one proceed? The answer lies in part in three sets of questions. Addressing these questions in a careful, systematic way will often yield useful and effective objectives.

1. Who is the target segment?
2. What is the ultimate behavior within that segment that advertising is attempting to precipitate, reinforce, change, or influence?
3. What is the process that will lead to the desired behavior and what role can advertising play in the process? Is it necessary to create awareness, communicate information about the brand, create an image or attitude, or associate feelings or a type of user with a brand?

The first step is to identify the target audience. The specification of the target audience should be a part of the marketing objectives, e.g. the upscale buyers of stereo equipment. However, the segmentation description may need to be refined in the advertising context, i.e. those upscale buyers of stereo equipment who have not heard of Ajax Sound Products.

The second step involves the analysis of the ultimate desired behavior such as trial purchases of new customers, maintenance of loyalty of existing customers, creation of a more positive use experience, reduction of time between purchases, or the decision to visit a retailer. A part of the analysis should be an estimate of the long-term impact on the organization of such a behavior. What exactly is the value of the desired behavior? For example, the value of attracting a new customer to try a brand will depend upon the likelihood that the customer will like the brand and rebuy it.

The third step involves an analysis of the communication and decision process that will affect the desired behavior. Operationally, this usually involves using advertising-response measures that intervene between the incidence of the stimulus (advertising) and the ultimate behavioral response (certain purchase decisions) that is the focus of the advertising. Such response measures are called *intervening variables* and refer to a wide range of mental constructs such as awareness, brand knowledge, emotional feelings, and attitude. Thus, it might be that the key variable in inducing a new customer to try your brand is to inculcate high levels of brand awareness. The best way to maintain loyalty could be to strengthen an attitude. Even though the end goal is behavioral, the operational objective guiding decision making will often be specified in terms of one or more of such intervening variables. The determination of which intervening variables provide the best link to the desired behavior and which can be influenced economically by advertising is, of course, a challenge.

We start with the analysis of the desired behavior. After turning to the advertising response variables, we finally will discuss the segmentation specification.

BEHAVIORAL DYNAMICS

An understanding of market dynamics is necessary to an analysis of the ultimate behavior on which advertising should focus. An increase in sales or, more generally, an increase in product use (if the advertiser were a library or hospital, a sales measure would be inappropriate) can basically come from three sources: (1) from new customers attracted to the brand for the first time, (2) by increasing the loyalty of existing customers, and (3) by inducing existing customers to use more of the product class, either by increased usage or in new situations.

New Customers

Figure 4-3 shows a market divided into three segments. Segment E includes those who now buy our brand, brand A. Some members of segment E will buy only our brand, but many will probably also buy others, because they are either somewhat indifferent about a few brands or because they prefer other brands for some applications and our brand for others. They all buy our brand to some extent. Segment O contains those who buy other brands to the exclusion of ours. Some members of segment O will be loyal to another brand, and others will switch among other brands, but none is a buyer of our brand. Segment N members are not buyers of any brand in the product set. They get along without coffee, computers, lathes, or whatever product is involved.

The focus here is on increasing the size of segment E. One approach is to attract members of segment O to get them to try our brand. In Figure 4-4, Bulova is directing its campaign primarily to members of segment O. Such an effort may be difficult if the other brands are performing satisfactorily. However, it can be extremely worthwhile. If a "new trier" likes our brand, he or she could become a

Figure 4-3.   **Customer types**

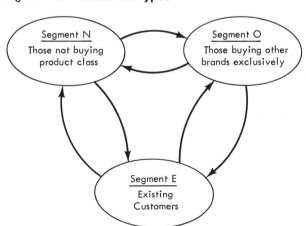

Figure 4-4.   **Attracting customers of competing brands**

HAVE YOU CAUGHT YOUR WATCH MAKING ADVANCES?

You become attached to your watch, you look after it, give it a home and what do you ask in return?

A little faithfulness.

But some watches are so ungrateful they'll pull a fast one. They'll lie and cheat until a man is forced to turn elsewhere.

Hopefully, to an Accutron® watch.

It has no balance wheel to get unbalanced and cause it to take liberties with its hands.

It has no mainspring to get unsprung and make it run out on you, altogether.

Instead, every Accutron watch has a tuning fork movement that's guaranteed to keep it faithful to within a minute a month.*

Month after month.

Even when nobody's looking.

ACCUTRON®BY BULOVA

Accutron Date/Day "BD". All stainless steel. Blue dial, silver and white markers. Date resets instantly. Protected against common watch hazards. $185. Other styles from $110.
*Timekeeping will be adjusted to this tolerance, if necessary, if returned to Accutron dealer from whom purchased within one year from date of purchase.

Courtesy of Bulova Watch Company.

customer, a member of segment E for many years. Determining the feasibility of this strategy will depend partly on how difficult this task will be.

Another approach is to attract people from segment N, those not now using the product class. An example of such an approach is the Pampers advertisement shown in Figure 4-5. The intent of that advertisement is to attract those using cloth diapers to a different type of diaper that they are not currently using. Such an approach might be particularly worthwhile to a large firm that already serves most of those buying the product class. The cost of obtaining a member from segment N will determine, in part, the advisability of this strategy. On the other hand, such a strategy will be less attractive to a smaller firm that runs the risk that the segment N member who is induced to try the product class may buy from a larger competitor. The smaller firm may therefore be content to let the larger firms attract people from segment N and confine itself to trying to obtain its new customers from segment O. The value of a segment O member will depend, of course, on how large a product-class buyer she or he ultimately becomes and on the share of these purchases eventually obtained by the advertiser.

A defensive strategy is also possible. Efforts could be made to reduce the flow from segment E to segment O. The goal would be to reduce the likelihood that a member of segment E would be tempted to try another brand and would, as a result, eventually stop using our brand. A large firm may also be concerned about customers moving from segment E to segment N. Existing users of the product could drop out of the market altogether. Some people, for example, stop shaving, grow beards, and stop buying any brand of shaving cream or razor blades.

Brand Loyalty

The members of segment E, the existing customers, will, in general, also be buying from competitors. Figure 4-6 shows the brand switching that could occur among existing customers. Some existing customers will be extremely loyal, buying from competitors only rarely if at all. For such customers, the goal would be to maintain their loyalty and reduce the likelihood that they would begin sharing their purchases with other brands and perhaps ultimately move to segment O. Advertising might attempt to remind them of the important features of the brand or to reinforce the use experience.

The Campbell's advertisement shown in Figure 4-7 may be in this category. It provides the opportunity for a user to express loyalty by obtaining a mug that in turn will help to reinforce the usage experience. Other customers may repeatedly switch among our brand and others. It may be possible to convince customers like these to become more loyal. If there are real brand advantages of which they may be unaware, such a task might be feasible. If, however, they are firmly convinced that several brands are equal, the effort may be difficult and costly. As before, the cost of generating the desired behavioral response must be balanced with its worth in terms of future purchase.

Figure 4-5.   **Attracting customers to the product class**

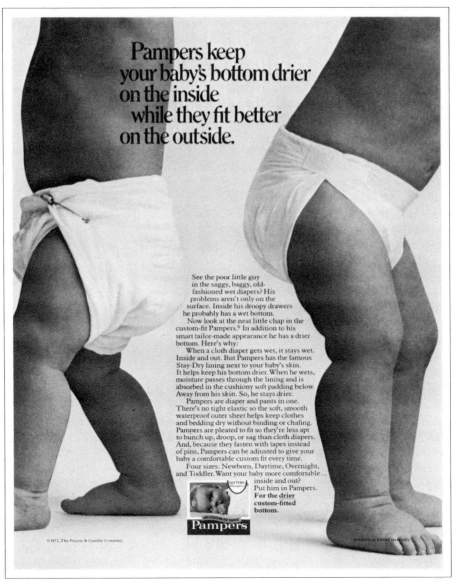

Increasing Usage

It is also possible to increase the usage of existing customers in the product class. In essence, the goal would be to reduce the time between purchases. Figure 4-8 shows a typical distribution of interpurchase times among existing customers. The effort would involve sliding the area under the curve to the left. Several approaches are available. Product use could be expanded by inducing people to use the product in a new application. For example, Scotch tape could be used for decorative as well as conventional purposes, or the combination of rum and iced tea might be suggested as a new drink, as in Figure 4-9. It may be possible to get existing customers to use the product in the familiar way but more frequently. Here the aim would usually be to do more than just induce an extra purchase; we would want to actually change long-term behavioral patterns so that the increased usage, at least for some customers, would continue over time. The value of advertising will then be represented by the increased usage. If the increased usage extends over a long time period, it will obviously be of greater value. As before, however, the value must be balanced against the cost involved.

Behavioral or Action Objectives

An analysis of market dynamics can lead to behavioral measures that by themselves can provide the basis for operational objectives. If the advertising's target is new customers, the goal may be to get new customers to try a brand for the first time. The results would be measured by the number of new customers attracted. Such an estimate could be obtained from a consumer panel or by a count of a cents-off coupon if that were a part of the advertising effort. The number of new triers, of course, is quite different from short-run sales. The quantity of sales in the short run represented by new customers is usually miniscule and will be swamped by the behavioral patterns of regular customers (Segment E).

The use of behavioral measures as objectives will be explored in detail in Chapter 7. They are often appropriate in retailing (store traffic measures), direct

Figure 4-6.   **Brand switching among existing customers**

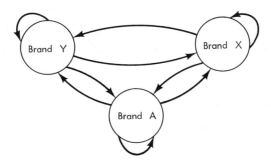

Figure 4-7.   **Maintaining brand loyalty**

Courtesy of Campbell Soup Company.

mail (responses or orders), and in lead generation for sales people especially in industrial marketing and sales promotion. Usually, however, it is useful to analyze also the communication and decision process relevant in a causal sense to the desired behavior and to identify intervening variables on which to base objectives. Of course, some situations could dictate the joint use of intervening and behavioral objectives.

ADVERTISING RESPONSE-VARIABLES INTERVENING BETWEEN ADVERTISING AND ACTION

Usually advertising is not well suited to directly precipitate action. Rather, it is better at conducting some communication, association, or persuasion task that will hopefully result in the desired action being precipitated. A communication results in the audience members learning something new or gaining an improved understanding or memory of some fact; i.e., Jello comes in a low-calorie form. Associations link a brand to concepts such as types of people, use situations, or feelings; i.e., driving a Dodge creates a carefree, exciting feeling. Persuasion involves creating or changing an attitude toward an object; i.e., I rather like that brand.

The identification and selection of the best advertising response variable upon which to base objectives is extremely difficult. There are countless numbers of advertising response variables to consider. Further, our understanding of both the given contexts and the communication and persuasion process is always incomplete. Nevertheless, there is still great pay-off to proceed in this direction.

To identify and use advertising response variables, the key questions to be addressed are:

1. What communication, association or persuasion task will be likely to precipitate the desired action?
2. How can this task best be conceptualized and measured?

In asking the first question, there are a set of intervening variables that are frequently useful. They include brand awareness, brand comprehension, brand image, brand attitude, and the association of feelings with a brand or use experience.

Figure 4-8. **Interpurchase time of existing customers**

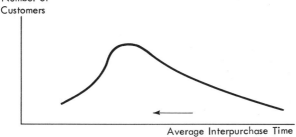

Figure 4-9.   **Suggesting a new use for the product**

Courtesy of Ogilvy & Mather Inc.

Brand Awareness

A basic communication task in which advertising excels is to create awareness. Awareness can be particularly needed when the goal is to stimulate a trial purchase perhaps of a new brand. The model is shown as Model A in Table 4-1. Advertising creates awareness in the new brand and the awareness will create the trial purchase after which the brand is on its own to gain acceptance. The awareness measure could be based upon a telephone survey where people are asked whether they have heard of the new brand and perhaps whether they know what type of product is involved (Yes, I've heard of Island Spice, it is a new tea). The percent answering correctly would be the awareness measure.

Awareness may also be an advertising response measure that could be instrumental at generating loyalty such as postulated in Model B in Table 4-1. Some low-involvement products like gum, soap, or beer are purchased without much thought or consideration. The choice is often based upon which brand is most familiar. One role of advertising is to get a brand to be more prominent in people's mind so that it is the choice in those no-thought choices. The goal could be to improve top-of-mind awareness—the percent of people who first mention the advertised brand when asked to list the brands of a product class they can recall.

Brand Comprehension

Another communication task for which advertising is well suited is to communicate facts about the brand, in particular about its attributes. Thus, it may be pivotal to communicate that the brand tastes fresher than competitors or that it rides better. Model C in Table 4-1 shows a new brand context in which trial purchase is not only dependent upon brand awareness but also learning about a key brand attribute. The brand perception on that attribute could be measured by asking respondents whether they agree or disagree that the brand has that attribute:

Agree Strongly $+3$ $+2$ $+1$ 0 -1 -2 -3 Disagree Strongly

In Model D in Table 4-1, the behavioral goal is to increase usage. The brand comprehension intervening variable is to communicate knowledge of a new application. Such a campaign was run by Arm & Hammer baking soda in 1972 who wanted to get people to use the product to deodorize refrigerators.[1] The percentage of households that reported having used the product in this application went from 1 percent to 57 percent in just 14 months. Later campaigns suggested its use as a sink, freezer, and cat-litter deodorizer.

In an industrial context, a goal might be to get organizations to purchase the advertised product. However, a realistic appraisal might indicate that a personal selling effort will play the key role in precipitating the decision. The role of advertising might then be to support the sales force by creating inquiries or by communicating information about the company as suggested by Models E and F in Table

Table 4-1. **Intervening and Behavorial Variables**

MODEL	*ADVERTISING VARIABLE*	*INTERVENING VARIABLES*	*BEHAVIORAL VARIABLES*
A	Advertising	→ Brand Awareness	→ Trial Purchase
B	Advertising	→ Brand Awareness	→ Loyalty
C	Advertising	→ Brand Awareness → Knowledge of Brand Attributes	→ Trial Purchase
D	Advertising	→ Knowledge of New Application	→ Increase Usage
E	Advertising		→ Sales Leads
F	Advertising	→ Knowledge About Company	→ Sales Via Personal Selling
G	Advertising	→ Associate Brand with User Type	→ Loyalty
H	Advertising	→ Brand Attitude	→ Loyalty
I	Advertising	→ Associate Feelings with Brand Use	→ Loyalty
J	Advertising	Brand Awareness → Knowledge of Brand Attributes → Brand Attitude	→ Trial Purchase
K	Advertising	→ Knowledge of Brand Attributes / → Brand Attitude	→ Trial Purchase

4-1. McGraw-Hill's advertisement, shown in Figure 4-10, dramatically illustrates the role that advertising can play in supporting the sales effort. It is useful to note that communication is not expected to play any significant direct role in precipitating purchase decisions. Thus, it would not be reasonable to measure its impact in terms of purchase decisions. Rather, it is linked causally with the reception that the salesperson receives, particularly on early visits.

Brand Image

Brand image includes the association of an attribute with a brand generated by brand comprehension, but it is broader. It also includes other types of associations as well. A brand, for example, can develop associations with a type of person or even another product. Thus, Charlie perfume, illustrated in Chapter 2 (Figure 2-4), is a perfume designed around a very specific type of female lifestyle. It is represented as Model G in Table 4-1. The Leading Edge Computer is associated with IBM by being positioned as a comparable computer at a lower price.

Chapter 5 will explore in more detail the nature of an image objective and a procedure for generating image objective alternatives and selecting among them. It will include a discussion of brand comprehension variables as a brand image is in part based upon people's perceptions of brands.

Brand Attitude

A brand attitude represents the like-dislike feeling toward a brand. Model H in Table 4-1 shows a case where loyalty is predicated upon increasing the attitude toward the object.

Attitude can be measured in a variety of ways as will be discussed in Chapter 6. One approach is to base it upon people's brand comprehension, perceptions of the brand with respect to specific attributes and characteristics. Another is to tap the like-dislike-dimensions as with this scale:

$$\text{Dislike} \quad -3 \quad -2 \quad -1 \quad 0 \quad +1 \quad +2 \quad +3 \quad \text{Like}$$

Still another, to base it upon behavioral intentions, is closer to a behavioral measure:

- I will definitely buy this brand
- I will probably buy this brand
- I might buy this brand
- I doubt that I will buy this brand
- I will not buy this brand

Chapter 6 will cover attitudes and their use in advertising objectives in detail. It will also include the role that brand comprehension has in creating and changing attitudes.

Figure 4-10. **Advertising's role in supporting the personal selling effort**

Courtesy of McGraw-Hill Publications Company.

Associating Feelings with Brands or Use Experiences

Sometimes the advertising objective can be to create feelings of warmth, energy, fun, anticipation, fear or concern, and associate those feelings with the brand and the use experience. Model I in Table 4-1 could represent a gum brand which is attempting to associate feelings of togetherness and happiness with its use.

There are well developed models, concepts, and measures that guide our use of image and attitude objectives. In contrast, the role of feelings is much less mature and far less is known about how they work or even if they do work. It is likely that feelings influence both image and attitude but it is not clear how the process takes place. Chapter 10 will present some emerging ideas about the feeling response to advertising. It suggests that in addition to measuring how audience members feel when being exposed to a commercial it might be useful to measure how they liked the commercial and their impressions of their use experience with the brand. The concept is that if feeling advertising (at least positive feeling advertising) is effective it will probably result in advertising that is liked and should impact upon the use experience.

More Complex Models and Multiple Objectives

In many contexts, there are two or more advertising responses that are needed for a desired behavior to occur. For example, Model J in Table 4-1 shows a trial purchase model that suggested that awareness can lead to trial purchase directly or through the creation of attribute knowledge and brand attitude. There are thus two routes to precipitating trial. Model K shows another multiple construct model, one in which there is no sequence implied. Two tasks are required but need not proceed the other.

When the advertising campaign can focus upon a single, well-defined objective, the communication task is made easier. When several objectives are introduced, there is always the danger that the campaign will become a compromise that will be ineffective with respect to all objectives.

However, it is often appropriate and necessary to deal with multiple objectives. Sometimes there is simply more than one objective that needs to be accomplished. These multiple objectives could require more than one advertising campaign, although such a need may not be determined until after the creative process has begun. At other times, a secondary objective might be necessary to justify the advertising. Thus, if the advertising was designed to attract store traffic during a weekend sale, a secondary objective might be to maintain top-of-mind awareness of the store. The secondary objective would not require a second campaign but would be an important part of the rationale for the advertising.

Multiple objectives could involve more than one target audience. For example, a computer company might need to gain awareness among one segment and to communicate the existence of a new product to another. Or there might be two communication tasks for the same target segment. For example, an industrial chemical company might need to generate sales leads for its salespeople and to establish an image of a solid company of substance.

The advertisement shown in Figure 4-11 has multiple objectives according to William D. Tyler, an *Advertising Age* columnist.[2] It was designed both to create brand-name registration and to position the brand along several dimensions. With respect to positioning, it stresses the English origin, emphasizes a dryness theme, and at the same time makes it seem fun to drink.

A distinction should be made between multiple objectives and multiple measures of the same objective. A reminder advertising campaign might be measured by short-term sales and by top-of-mind awareness using unaided recall techniques. Involved are two measures of the impact of the advertising upon immediate purchase of the product, rather than two objectives.

SPECIFYING THE TARGET SEGMENT

A basic question is the identity of the target segment. To whom is the advertising to be addressed? The target audience can be defined in many ways. Chapter 2 provided a more detailed discussion of segmentation and segmentation variables. Also, it introduced the concepts of general consumer characteristics like age, income, and life-style and product-specific consumer characteristics like usage, loyalty, and brand perceptions.

Of course, the marketing and firm objectives will usually have already considered the same question. Thus, the segmentation strategy may seem to be specified. The objective could be to provide a product line or service to small banks. However, just as an advertising goal is a subobjective, it may involve subsegments that are relevant to the communication task. For example, it might be appropriate to communicate cost savings for a computer model to bank presidents, software reliability to bank administrative personnel, and to ignore loan officers. Although the general marketing strategy would include all professionals in small banks, the advertising objectives could appropriately refine this group.

The behavioral measures discussed in this chapter such as usage and loyalty can define segments. A target thus could be the heavy user, the nonuser, the loyal user of our brand, or the group loyal to another brand. In Chapter 6, benefit segmentation will be explored where a target segment is defined by the benefits sought from a product. For example, a target segment might be those who are particularly concerned with the cost of operating a computer, whereas another segment might be interested primarily in the computer's speed.

The advertising response measures just presented can be particularly useful segmentation variables in the advertising context. Thus, the segments can be identified that are unaware of the brand, do not know or are not convinced that it has a key attribute, or have not yet developed a positive attitude. One or more of these segments can then be selected as the primary target. Such a segmentation choice can

Figure 4-11. **An advertisement with multiple objectives**

Courtesy of Rensfield Importers, Ltd.

make the advertising more effective since a campaign designed to create awareness will tend to be very different from one designed to communicate a product attribute.

DAGMAR

The approach to setting advertising objectives just outlined will be expanded upon in the next three chapters and in the balance of the book. Research findings, constructs, and measurement tools will be developed that will serve to make the approach effective and operational. In the balance of this chapter, the historical foundations for our approach to setting advertising objectives will be presented. It provides a rationale and basis for the introduction of advertising response measures in advertising objectives and for the concept of measuring over time such objectives.

There are several reasons for this diversion. First, the historical roots of the approach are not only interesting but provide a deeper understanding of thrust and scope. Second, they provide suggestions on implementation that are still useful and valid. Third, they provide a feel for the difficult issues that surround an effort to apply management science to an area in which subjectivity and creativity will always be important components of any strategy.

In 1961, Russell H. Colley wrote a book under the sponsorship of the Association of National Advertisers called *Defining Advertising Goals for Measured Advertising Results*.[3] The book introduced what has become known as the DAGMAR approach to advertising planning and included a precise method for selecting and quantifying goals and for using those goals to measure performance. The performance measurement feature had great appeal to managers of the 1960s, who were frustrated by the available methods for controlling advertising efforts and impatient with embryonic methods of developing sales-response models.

The DAGMAR approach can be summarized in its succinct statement defining an advertising goal. An advertising goal is a specific communication task, to be accomplished among a defined audience, in a given period of time. Note that a communication task is involved as opposed to a marketing task and that the goal is specific, involving an ambiguously defined task, among a defined audience, in a given time period.

A Communication Task

An advertising objective involves a communication task, something that advertising, by itself, can reasonably hope to accomplish. It is recognized that advertising is mass, paid communication that is intended to create awareness, impart information, develop attitudes, or induce action.

In DAGMAR, the communication task is based on a specific model of the communication process, as illustrated in Figure 4-12. The model suggests that there

Figure 4-12.   **A hierarchy-of-effects model
of the communication process**

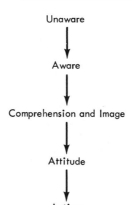

is a series of mental steps through which a brand or objects must climb to gain acceptance. An individual starts at some point by being unaware of a brand's presence in the market. The initial task of the brand is to gain awareness—to advance one step up the hierarchy.

The second step of brand comprehension involves the audience member learning something about the brand. What are its specific characteristics and appeals? In what way does it differ from its competitors? Whom is it supposed to benefit? The third step is the attitude (or conviction) step and intervenes between comprehension and final action. The action phase involves some overt move on the part of the buyer like trying a brand for the first time, visiting a showroom, or requesting information.

A communication model like the DAGMAR model with the implication that the audience member will sequentially pass through a set of steps is termed a "hierarchy-of-effects" model. A host of hierarchy models have been proposed. The AIDA model, developed in the 1920s, suggested that an effective personal sales presentation should attract attention, gain interest, create a desire, and precipitate action. The new adopter hierarchy model, conceived by rural sociologists, postulated five stages: awareness, interest, evaluation, trial, and adoption.

Another hierarchy model is particularly interesting because of its close ties with social psychological theory. Developed by Robert Lavidge and Gary Steiner,[4] it includes six stages: awareness, knowledge, liking, preference, conviction, and purchase. They divided this hierarchy into the three components corresponding to a social psychologist's concept of an attitude system. The first stage, consisting of the awareness and knowledge levels, is comparable to the cognitive or knowledge component of attitude. The affective component of an attitude, the like-dislike aspect, is represented in the Lavidge and Steiner hierarchy by the liking and preference levels. The remaining attitude component is the conative component, the action or motivation element, represented by the conviction and purchase levels, the final two levels in the hierarchy.

A Specific Task

We have mentioned that DAGMAR emphasizes the communication task of advertising as contrasted to the marketing objectives of the firm. The second important concept of DAGMAR is that the advertising goal be specific. It should be a written, measurable task involving a starting point, a defined audience, and a fixed time period.

Measurable.   DAGMAR needs to be made specific when actual goals are formulated. When brand comprehension is involved, for example, it is necessary to indicate exactly what appeal or image is to be communicated. Furthermore, the specification should include a description of the measurement procedure. If a high-protein cereal were trying to gain brand comprehension, managers could well decide to promote its protein content. However, merely mentioning its protein content is inadequate and open to different interpretations. Is the cereal to be perceived as one containing a full-day's supply as a protection against illness or as one that supplies more energy than other cereals? If a survey includes the request, "Rank the following cereals as to protein content," then brand comprehension could be quantified to mean the percentage who rated it first.

Benchmark.   President Lincoln has been quoted as saying, "If we could first know where we are and whither we are tending, we could better judge what to do and how to do it."[5] A basic aspect of establishing a goal and selecting a campaign to reach it is to know the starting conditions. Without a benchmark, it is most difficult to determine the optimal goal. The selection of an awareness-oriented goal might be a mistake if awareness is already high. Without a benchmark measure, such a circumstance could not be ascertained quantitatively. In addition, benchmarks can suggest how a certain goal can best be reached. For example, it would be useful to know whether the existing image needs to be changed, reinforced, diffused, or sharpened. A benchmark is also a prerequisite to the ultimate measurement of results, an essential part of any planning program and of DAGMAR in particular. Despite the obvious value of having benchmarks before goals are set, this is often not done. In fact, the key to DAGMAR is probably the generation of well-conceived benchmarks before advertising goals are determined. With such measures, the rest of the approach flows rather naturally.

The Target.   A key tenet of DAGMAR was that the target audience be well-defined. If the goal was to increase awareness, for example, it was essential to know the target audience precisely. Perhaps the goal was to increase awareness among the heavy user segment from 25% to 60% in a certain time period. The benchmark measure could not be developed without a specification of the target segment. Further, the campaign execution will normally depend on the identity of the target segment. The heavy user group will likely respond differently from a segment defined by a life-style profile.

Time Period. The objective should involve a particular time period, such as six months or one year. With a time period specified, a survey to generate a set of measures can be planned and anticipated. All parties involved will understand that the results will be available for evaluating the campaign, which could lead to a contraction, expansion, or change in the current effort. The length of the time period must fit into various constraints involving the planning cycle of both a company and an agency. However, the appropriate time necessary to generate the kind of cognitive response desired should also be considered.

Written. Finally, goals should be committed to paper. Under the discipline of writing clearly, basic shortcomings and misunderstandings become exposed, and it becomes easy to determine whether the goal contains the crucial aspects of the DAGMAR approach.

Suppose that the product of interest were an economy-priced bourbon. It has a bad quality image despite the fact that blind taste tests indicated that it does not have any real quality problems. An objective might be developed with respect to a scale ranging from -5 to $+5$ (inadequate taste to adequate taste). An admissible objective would be to increase the percentage of male bourbon drinkers in the United States who give a nonnegative rating on the scale from 5 to 25 percent in a 12-month period. Notice that this objective is measurable, has a starting point, a definite audience, and a fixed time period.

Implementation—The 6-M Approach

The DAGMAR book was not very specific in its advice to the person charged with its implementation. It did, however, provide guidelines that gave additional insight into its basic philosophy. One suggestion was that a systematic information-gathering process, termed the 6-M approach, be employed to analyze the market and product situation. The objective was to stimulate ideas or decision alternatives, thus guiding the manager toward more optimal decisions. The 6-M approach is structured around six categories of analysis: merchandise, markets, motives, messages, media, measurements.

Merchandise. Suggests an evaluation of the relative strengths and weaknesses of the product. What are the benefits offered by the product and how do they compare with those offered by the competition? Do any of these benefits stand out as significant contributors to the product's differential advantage?

Markets. Involves the present and potential users of the product and the intermediaries distributing it. One objective is to identify alternative segmentation strategies. As the preceding discussion suggested, many types of segmentation variables can be considered. Basic statistics covering the size and characteristics of the market usually provide a starting place. Consumption habits and buying influences are among the other variables that are usually introduced. A second consideration is intermediaries—the components of the distribution channel. The effect of advertising on distributors, wholesalers, and retailers is often overlooked. However, advertising has an important role to play for many products in influencing intermediaries. Basic questions should be asked. For example, what are the critical factors in sales growth? Are some associated with the trade? If so, what should advertising's role be?

Motives. Why do people buy? What rational and emotional reasons underlie purchase decisions? What motives are involved? What are the relevant consumption systems within which the product is imbedded? What are the goals of these consumption systems? The concept of the consumption system is often a useful device to gain understanding. When it is realized that orange juice is used not only at large and small breakfasts, but also with snacks, at cocktail parties, and so on, a feel is obtained for the heterogeneity of consumer motives. The goals of a breakfast are far different from those of a cocktail party, and the wants and needs of the consumer are also different.

Message. What alternative appeals could influence prospective consumers to purchase? What appeals have been used in the past by our product and by the competition? There is usually some value in being different, and it is essential to avoid being so similar to a previous competitor's advertisement that the appeal is transferred by the reader to the competitor's brand. For example, some automobile advertising benefits from similar competitor advertising.

Media. Refers to the media decisions and constraints that are involved. They can interact meaningfully with the segment selected and the appeal used.

Measurement. Refers to the measures that need to be obtained during this audit stage, not only to provide benchmarks to measure future progress, but also to provide real guidance in establishing objectives.

The DAGMAR Checklist

Another aid to those implementing the DAGMAR approach is a checklist of promotional tasks, partially reproduced as Table 4-2. The suggestion was to rate each of the promotional tasks in terms of its relative importance in the context of the product situation involved. Again, the intent was to stimulate ideas or decision alternatives, often the most difficult and crucial part of the decision process.

Following are two examples of the DAGMAR approach as presented in Colley's book. It is left to the reader to examine these examples critically to see if they satisfy the requirements of the approach as it has been presented here.

Table 4–2.   **Partial Checklist of Promotional Tasks**[a]

To what extent does the advertising aim at closing an immediate sale?
1. Perform the complete selling function (take the product through all the necessary steps toward a sale).
2. Close sales to prospects already partly sold through past advertising efforts (''ask for the order'' or ''clincher'' advertising).
3. Announce a special reason for ''buying now'' (price, premium, etc.).
4. *Remind* people to buy.
5. Tie in with some special buying event.
6. Stimulate impulse sales.

Does the avertising aim at near-term sales by moving the prospect, step by step, closer to a sale (so that when confronted with a buying situation the customer will ask for, reach for, or accept the advertised brand)?
7. Create awareness of existence of the product or brand.
8. Create *brand image* or favorable emotional disposition toward the brand.
9. Implant information or attitude regarding benefits and superior features of brand.
10. Combat or offset competitive claims.
11. Correct false impressions, misinformation, and other obstacles to sales.
12. Build familiarity and easy recognition of package or trademark.

Does the advertising aim at building a long-range consumer franchise?
13. Build confidence in company and brand, which is expected to pay off in years to come.
14. Build customer demand that places company in stronger position in relation to its distribution (not at the ''mercy of the marketplace'').
15. Place advertiser in position to select preferred distributors and dealers.
16. Secure universal distribution.
17. Establish a ''reputation platform'' for launching new brands or product lines.
18. Establish brand recognition and acceptance that will enable the company to open up new markets (geographic, price, age, sex).

How important are supplementary benefits of end-use advertising?
19. Aid salespeople in opening new accounts.
20. Aid salespeople in getting larger orders from wholesalers and retailers.
21. Aid salespeople in getting preferred display space.
22. Give salespeople an entree.
23. Build morale of company sales force.
24. Impress the trade.

---

[a] The complete list included 52 items.

Source: Russell H. Colley, *Defining Advertising Goals for Measured Advertising Results* (New York: Association of National Advertisers, 1961), pp. 61–68.

Overseas Airline Service[6]—A DAGMAR Case Study

The company is one of the smaller of several dozen airlines competing for American overseas airline passengers. It was recognized at the outset that it was impossible to compete with the giant airlines in advertising volume. The small budget would not permit the size of space, frequency, and media breadth used by the major airlines.

The copy and media strategy decided upon was, therefore, to concentrate on a particular segment of the audience, with a highly distinctive copy and art approach beamed at this particular audience.

Audience: experienced, sophisticated world travelers.

Message: the image of an airline that caters to a distinctive, discriminating, travel-wise audience.

Experience and judgment indicated that selling to the seasoned traveler was wise strategy. Not only does he or she make a more frequent customer, but his or her advice is sought and habits are emulated by the "first trippers."

Art and copy, in a highly distinctive style, were directed at attracting the attention and interest of the more experienced and sophisticated world travelers. In fact, a new name was coined and used extensively in the advertising to refer to such a person (TRAVOIR-FAIRE). Instead of featuring the more commonplace tourist attractions in the countries served, the advertising featured off-the-beaten-path scenes and unusual objects of art and interest. Whereas mass-appeal airlines were featuring hardware (make and speed of their jet service), advertising of the subject airline treated make and speed of ship in a subtle manner and emphasized distinctive items of decor, comfort, cuisine, and service.

In addition to the usual reports of opinion on advertising effectiveness that come through inquiries and comments made to ticket and travel agents, the company conducted an inexpensive attitude survey. Travel agents in selected cities furnished names and addresses of overseas travelers (two or more trips). Mail questionnaires were sent out periodically to a representative sample of several hundred such persons. Questions were directed toward determining the following information:

Awareness: What airlines can you name that offer all-jet service to _____ ?

Image: Which of these airlines would you rate as outstanding on the following? (A checklist of characteristics and features was included.)

Preference: On your next overseas trip, which of these airlines would you seriously consider? Why?

An unusually high return of questionnaires was received because of the offer of a free booklet of high interest to international travelers. Survey costs were small (several hundred dollars for each semiannual survey).

The results shown in the table indicate a steadily rising awareness, a growing image as portrayed in the advertising, and an increase in preference. This was ample indication that advertising had succeeded in conveying the intended message to the selected audience.

Survey Results (Percent)

	BEFORE ADVERTISING CAMPAIGN	END OF SIX MONTHS	END OF ONE YEAR
Awareness (have heard of company)	38	46	52
Image (luxury all-jet overseas service)	9	17	24
Preference (would seriously consider for next trip)	13	15	21

Electrical Appliances[7]—A DAGMAR Case Study

The following case example concerns electrical appliances but serves to illustrate other consumer durables such as automobiles or furniture.

The market is 26 million housewives who are logical prospects. A logical prospect is defined as an owner of an appliance three years old or more, plus new households formed by marriage and new home construction.

Marketing objective: Get sales action now, sell carloads of appliances this season, thus reducing substantial dealer and manufacturer inventories.

Advertising objective: Induce immediate action. The brand name and product advantages are already well known through consistent and effective advertising.

Advertising's task, at this particular stage, is to persuade housewives to visit dealers' showrooms and see a demonstration. A special ice cube tray is offered as an added inducement.

Specific advertising goal: To persuade 400,000 homemakers to visit 10,000 dealers in 4 weeks, an average of 40 prospects who will physically cross the threshold of each dealer's showroom.

Results were measured in several different dimensions. The media: sponsorship of special audience telecasts. The results: two telecasts drew a combined audience of 84 million people. Approximately 18 percent, or 15 million people, could play back the commercial messages. Nearly half a million took immediate action by walking into a dealer's showroom and purchasing the special offer. Advertising accomplished its assigned task by inducing consumers to visit the dealer's showroom. It is true that dealers sold a large volume of appliances during the special promotion. But advertising cannot claim all the credit since it was only one factor in the consummation of the sale. However, further research indicated that 44 percent of the people who bought a refrigerator gave advertising as the major factor in choice of brand.

Challenges to DAGMAR

DAGMAR had enormous visibility and influence. It really changed the way that advertising objectives were created and the way that advertising results were measured. It introduced the concept of communication objectives like awareness, comprehension, image, and attitude. The point was made that such goals are more appropriate for advertising than is some measure like sales which can have multiple causes. In introducing communication objectives, behavioral science constructs and models such as attitude models were drawn upon. DAGMAR also focused attention upon measurement encouraging people to create objectives so specific and operational that they can be measured. In doing so, it provided the potential to improve the communication between the creative teams and the advertising clients.

A measure of the significance of an idea is the degree of both theoretical and empirical controversy that it precipitates. By this measure DAGMAR has been most significant. There have been six different kinds of challenges to DAGMAR.

Sales Goal.   First, some purists believe that only a sales measure is relevant. As pointed out by Michael Halbert, one of the pioneering group at Du Pont engaged in the use of experimental-design approaches to measure advertising effect,[8]

> When a study using one of the goals just mentioned [e.g., increase awareness] is published and reported at a meeting, I sometimes get the unsocial urge to question the author with, "So what?" If he has shown that advertising does, in fact, increase brand name awareness or favorable attitude toward the company, on what grounds does this increase a justifiable use of the company's funds? The answer usually given is that more people will buy a product if they are aware of it or if they have a favorable attitude. But why leave this critical piece of inference out of the design of the original research?

For example, if awareness does not affect sales, why bother to measure it? If it does have a close relationship, why not measure sales directly? This is not the place to review the relevant arguments. Suffice it to say that there is a disagreement and that a more refined model of the communication process than is now available must eventually evolve.

Practicability.   A second objection focuses on the many implementation difficulties inherent in the DAGMAR approach. In particular, the 6-M approach and the checklist fall short of providing sufficient details to implement the approach. As Leo Bogart has observed, Colley provides broad outlines much like the dragonfly that, after showing a hippopotamus the relationship between wing movement and flying, was asked exactly how to do it and replied, "I'll give you the broad idea and you work out the details."[9] A level in the hierarchy to be attacked must be selected, and a campaign to influence those at that level must be developed. Neither of these tasks is easy.

Measurement Problems.   The third problem is measurement. What should we really measure when we speak of attitude, awareness, or brand comprehension? Substantial conceptual and measurement problems underlie all these constructs.

Noise in the System.   A fourth problem is noise that exists in the hierarchy model, just as it does in the other, more simple, response models involving immediate sales. We have argued that there are many causal factors other than advertising that determine sales. In a more complex model, it can be argued that there are many causal factors besides advertising that determine awareness. For example, variables such as competitive promotion or unplanned publicity can affect an awareness campaign.

Inhibiting the Great Idea.   The "great creative idea" is a dream or hope of many advertisers. DAGMAR is basically a rational, planned approach that, among other things, provides guidance to creative people. The problem is that if it does in fact have any influence on their work, it must also necessarily inhibit their efforts. When the creative approach of copywriters and art directors is inhibited, there is less likelihood that they will come up with a great idea and an increased probability of a pedestrian advertising campaign resulting. Of course, there might also be a lesser probability of a spectacularly ineffective advertising campaign.

Anthony Morgan, an agency research director, argues that the hierarchy model, which he terms the "HEAR-UNDERSTAND-DO" model, inhibits great advertising by emphasizing tests of recall, communication, and persuasion.[10] He gives two examples. First, a campaign with all music and warm human visuals which everyone loved failed to meet the "company standard" for the day-after-recall test (where on the day after ad exposure viewers are asked to recall specific copy points). A potentially great campaign was clearly being evaluated by the wrong criteria. A more appropriate model for this campaign might have been "SENSE-FEEL-RELATE." Chapter 10 will expand on this concept.

The second example is the Campbell Soup "Soup Is Good Food" campaign created to arrest a 10-year decline in per capita consumption of their Red & White line of soups. The campaign objectives were to communicate news, to change the perception of soup, and to increase consumption. The first commercials received the lowest persuasion scores (from a test measuring the impact of commercial exposure on attitudes and intentions) that any Campbell's commercial had ever scored. However, the campaign, which stimulated three years of sales increases, was designed not to have much initial impact but to withstand enormous repetitions and to work over time. The testing was simply inappropriate. The implication is that it can be dangerous to rely on testing based on the hierarchical model (or any other single conceptualization). Rather, conceptual and research flexibility needs to be employed.

Hierarchy Model of Communication Effect.   The sixth type of argument against the DAGMAR approach attacks the basic hierarchy model which postulates a set of sequential steps of awareness, comprehension, and attitude leading to action. The counter argument is that other models may hold in various contexts and that it is naive to apply the DAGMAR hierarchy models in all situations. For example, action can precede attitude formation and even comprehension with an impulse purchase of a low-involvement product. At this point there is general agreement that, indeed, the appropriate model will depend upon the situation and a key problem in many contexts is in fact to determine what that model is. However, the basic thrust of DAGMAR, the use of advertising response measures as the basis of objectives and the focus on measurement, does not depend upon the DAGMAR hierarchy model so the issue is not really that crucial as it may have once appeared.

We now turn to a practical implementation issue of the DAGMAR approach. To what level of the hierarchy should the advertising campaign be directed? Will it be more profitable to build up awareness than to move people from the awareness level to the comprehension level?

SELECTING THE RIGHT OBJECTIVE

Two attempts to apply DAGMAR are of particular interest for several reasons. First, they each are significant applications, supported by large investments of money and containing substantial empirical data. Second, their methodology has been reported. Finally, they both provide an approach to this crucial question: what hierarchy level should be emphasized or, more generally, which intervening variable should be the focus of the campaign?

The Leo Burnett Program: CAPP

CAPP, an acronym for continuous advertising planning program, was developed by the Leo Burnett advertising agency. As reported by John Maloney,[11] one of its architects, it is based on still another hierarchy-of-effect model consisting of unawareness, awareness, acceptance, preference, brand bought last, and brand satisfaction. Termed "the consumer demand profile," it is shown graphically in Figure 4-13. The acceptance level implies that the brand is acceptable to an individual; it meets his or her minimum requirements. Brand preference indicates the percentage of total product-class users who rate the brand, on a four-point scale, higher than any other brand. A unique element of the CAPP hierarchy is brand satisfaction, which is meant to reflect the performance of the brand after purchase and repeat buying.

A cross-sectional sample of 1,000 households, interviewed on a monthly basis, provided the data base. Information was obtained from each household on

Figure 4–13.   **Consumer demand profile**

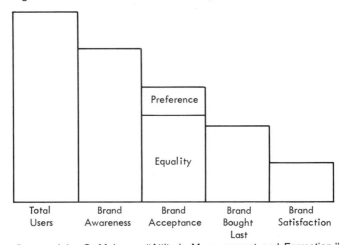

Source: John C. Maloney, "Attitude Measurement and Formation," paper presented at the Test Market Design and Measurement Workshop, American Marketing Association, Chicago, April 21, 1966.

their media habits and their location on the CAPP hierarchy with respect to the brands of interest. Monthly data provide a sensitive indicator of the response to the advertising campaign. Clearly, such time-series information has much greater and more timely interpretative power than measures restricted to immediately before and immediately after a campaign. If a substantial change is to be generated in a hierarchy measure, progress should be observed along the way and an appropriate campaign developed accordingly.

Which Hierarchy Level?   How can knowledge of the hierarchy profile and its trends be helpful in determining what level to attack? Maloney suggested an examination of the hierarchy patterns. The adjacent levels in the hierarchy were of particular interest. For example, if there were a small number of people who were aware of the brand (relative to the number of total users), then a worthwhile target could be to increase awareness. If a substantial number of people had accepted the brand, but only a few preferred it, perhaps it would be necessary to sharpen up the brand image in some respect. On the other hand, if there were a high degree of acceptance but a very low level of brand bought last, then it might become necessary to stimulate a trial purchase. If brand satisfaction is low compared to brand bought last, then perhaps there is a basic problem with the brand itself, and some very specific questions should be asked about its capacity to satisfy customer wants and needs. Essentially, the proposal is to consider the ratio of the size of adjacent levels, for example, the number of those who bought the brand last divided by the number who indicated brand satisfaction. A good level to consider is one for which this ratio involving the next lower level is high. This decision rule reflects the fact that it is usually worthwhile to concentrate on large segments and ignore smaller ones. It identifies that segment that contains large numbers of potential movers.

Naturally, it would be desirable to refine this decision rule by providing numerical guidelines. To do so, the profile histories associated with other brands in the product class would have to be considered to provide a frame of reference. The ultimate goal should be to expand the decision rule into a decision model that would make Maloney's suggestion explicit. Such a model will be developed, but in the context of a second example.

The General Motors Approach

Another major application of DAGMAR is the General Motors approach, as reported by Gail Smith.[12] The data base for this effort consists of six matched, cross-sectional surveys taken in September, October, December, January, March, and June. In the automobile industry, the impact of advertising effort is much more important in the fall than in the summer; therefore, the measurement schedule is adjusted accordingly. Seven types of information, shown in Table 4-3, were obtained in each survey. They included a hierarchy measure, product image, message registration, market behavior, product inventory, demographics, and media consumption.

Table 4-3.   **General Content of the Questionnaire Used to Establish Advertising Goals for General Motors Products**

  I. Preference levels by brand, by series of brand
        Awareness
        "Buying class"
        "Consideration class"
        First choice
 II. Product image
III. Message registration
        Specific product attributes
        Slogans
        Story line
 IV. Market behavior
        Shopping behavior, dealer visits
        Purchases
        Intentions
  V. Product inventory
        Content and condition
 VI. Demographics
VII. Media consumption
        Television: by hours per week, by selected programs
        Magazines: by hours per week, by selected magazines
        Radio: by hours per week, by time slot
        Newspapers: by hours per week, by type

Source: Gail Smith, "How GM Measures Ad Effectiveness," in Keith K. Cox, ed., *Readings in Market Research* (New York: Appleton-Century-Crofts, 1967), p. 172.

The hierarchy used by General Motors consisted of awareness, "buying class," "consideration class," and first choice. A brand is in a respondent's buying class if she or he considers it similar to or competitive with the brands she or he would actively consider when entering the market. Consideration class consists of those brands the respondent will favorably consider the next time he or she enters the market. Both of these measures are obtained through open-ended questions. The first choice is the one brand the respondent would select if a choice were made at the time the questionnaire was administered. Of course, this hierarchy was designed for a durable product and is quite suitable for other products of this nature.

The image section consists of 35 semantic differential questions measuring such dimensions as styling, prestige, and trade-in value. The message registration section measures the impact of the advertising. Did the slogans and the product attributes that were part of the advertising message get through to the audience? This information, in conjunction with the media consumption data, is, of course, interesting in itself. It provides the possibility of measuring the relative message impact of the various media. The market behavior section includes shopping behavior, purchases, and intentions. These kinds of constructs represent the ultimate payoff, and we shall attempt to use them to quantify the decision about which level to attack. The product inventory and demographic sections provide information that permits cross classification on the data, a basic approach to evaluating segmentation strategies. For example, the answers from young owners of foreign cars might be compared with responses from young owners of American cars.

Which Hierarchy Level?   The existence of such cross-sectional information provides a firm basis for the DAGMAR approach. However, to provide sensitive measures of the economic value of goal accomplishment, it is desirable to measure the same respondent at several points in time. Accordingly, General Motors questioned a subsample of the respondents in each survey 12 months later. One purpose is to obtain a measure of the accuracy of answers regarding planned shopping behavior, dealer visits, and so forth. Table 4-4 summarizes such information for a car, here called Watusi, which was developed by General Motors for the youth market.

The first column of Table 4-4 shows the sample proportion in each hierarchy level. The second indicates the probability that the respondent will visit a dealer. The third, the probability of a Watusi purchase, potentially provides the basis for an economic judgment about which level in the hierarchy would be the most profitable to attack. The table indicates that, if a respondent gave Watusi as a first choice, his or her probability of buying would be 0.56, whereas if the Watusi was only in the consideration class, the purchase probability would be 0.22. Thus, if someone who moves up to the "first choice" hierarchy level behaves like those already there, the latter's purchase probability would increase by

$$0.56 - 0.22 = 0.34$$

To determine the relative value of a campaign directed at those in the consideration class hierarchy level, it would also be necessary to weigh (1) the number of people in the consideration class hierarchy level, and (2) the cost and effectiveness of an advertising campaign designed to move them to the first choice hierarchy level.

Moving People up the Hierarchy.   How can advertising go about moving people from one hierarchy level to another? This problem will be addressed later in the book, in Chapter 6 in particular. However, it is useful to consider here the General Motors approach, which is based upon a 35-question semantic differential. Brand-image profiles for all people on each level are obtained and an average secured for

Table 4-4.   **Value of Preference Levels in Terms of Probability and Dealer Visitation and Purchase**

HIERARCHY LEVEL		PREFERENCE LEVEL PROPORTION	PROBABILITY WILL VISIT WATUSI DEALER	PROBABILITY WILL BUY WATUSI
5	Watusi first choice	0.05	0.840	0.560
4	Watusi in consideration class	0.07	0.620	0.220
3	Watusi in buying class	0.08	0.400	0.090
2	Aware of Watusi	0.14	0.240	0.050
1	Not aware of Watusi	0.66	0.015	0.004
	Total	1.00		

Source: Gail Smith, "How GM Measures Ad Effectiveness," in Keith K. Cox, ed., *Readings in Market Research* (New York: Appleton-Century-Crofts, 1967), p. 175.

each level. Table 4-5 shows such average profiles for those in the consideration class and the buying class. These average profiles are then compared and significant differences between them are noted. In Table 4-5, the largest difference is the image dimension labeled "trade-in value." Thus, it seems reasonable to work on this particular dimension to move the image of those in the buying class toward the image of those in the consideration class. The assumption is that, if an image can be so changed for an individual, he or she will change classes so that the new image will match the average image of "his or her class." Perhaps this is an extreme assumption. It places undue stress on the average. Obviously, there will be great variation about the mean. There will be some extreme values for each dimension, including trade-in value, that will overlap the adjacent classes. There are also likely to be other differences in members of adjacent classes that will not disappear even if one image dimension is altered. Nevertheless, this approach does have appeal. In the following three chapters it will be refined, extended, and related to formal models of attitude and market structure.

To implement these hypothetical conclusions properly, it is necessary to reach those in the level of interest, in this case, the buying class. The survey information reported in Table 4-3 includes a media-consumption section. Using these data, it may be possible to identify vehicles that will be effective in reaching those in the buying class. Furthermore, it may be possible to reach those in that class who have a low impression of the trade-in value of the Watusi automobile. Thus, to the extent

Table 4-5. **Ratings of Watusi, by Item, by Those Considering Watusi to Be in Their Buying Class**
(on scale of 1–100)

	BUT WILL NOT GIVE IT FAVORABLE CONSIDERATION	BUT WILL GIVE IT FAVORABLE CONSIDERATION	DIFFERENCE
Smooth riding	88	91	3
Styling	76	89	13
Overall comfort	81	87	6
Handling	83	86	3
Spacious interior	85	85	0
Luxurious interior	79	85	6
Quality of workmanship	80	83	3
Advanced engineering	77	83	6
Prestige	73	82	9
Value for the money	76	79	3
Trade-in value	59	77	18
Cost of upkeep and maintenance	63	67	4
Gas economy	58	58	0

Source: Gail Smith, "How GM Measures Ad Effectiveness," in Keith K. Cox, ed., *Readings in Market Research* (New York: Appleton-Century-Crofts, 1967), p. 176.

that vehicles can be so identified, the cost of changing the image of the average profile is minimized.

SUMMARY

Operational objectives provide criteria for decision making, standards against which to evaluate performance, and serve as a communication tool. Short-run sales usually do not provide the basis for operational objectives for two reasons: (1) advertising is usually only one of many factors influencing sales, and (2) the impact of advertising often occurs primarily over the long run.

The development of more operational objectives involves three considerations. First, the behavioral decisions or actions that advertising is attempting to influence need to be analyzed. The relevant behavior could be visiting a retailer, trying a new brand, increasing usage levels, maintaining existing brand loyalties, or donating money to a charity. Second, the communication and decision process that precedes and influences that behavior should be examined. This process will usually involve constructs like awareness, image, or attitude. Third, the specification of the target segment needs to be specified. Segment defining variables that are often useful include usage, benefits sought, awareness level, brand perceptions, and life-style.

This approach to setting objectives is a refinement and extension of an approach developed over a decade ago and known as DAGMAR. DAGMAR defines an advertising goal as a specific communication task to be accomplished among a defined audience in a given time period. Thus, a communication task is involved, as opposed to a marketing task, based on a hierarchy model of the communication process involving awareness, comprehension, attitude, and action. The goal is specific, with a definite measure, a starting point, a defined audience, and a fixed time period. To aid those implementing the approach, DAGMAR suggested that the decision maker analyze the situation in terms of merchandise, markets, motives, messages, media, and measurements.

By introducing behavioral science theory into advertising management, DAGMAR provides the framework for the development of more operational objectives. However, it has been challenged through the years on several fronts. Some critics believe that the only appropriate measure of advertising is sales. Another objection is that it is difficult to select a hierarchy level on which to base objectives and to know how to move people up the hierarchy. Others believe that the approach is limited by measurement problems and noise in the system. By providing guidance to operating people, DAGMAR is said to inhibit the development of "the great idea." Another criticism is that the hierarchy model of the communication process is not appropriate.

A crucial question in many advertising campaigns is to determine which intervening variable should be the focus of the campaign. One approach is to determine those hierarchy levels that have not yet been reached by large numbers of potential customers. An extension would not only consider the size of the segment, but the difficulty, and therefore cost, of moving them up the hierarchy, as well as the likelihood of their eventually making the desired decision (for example, to buy an automobile) once they have moved up.

DISCUSSION QUESTIONS

1. What are operational objectives? Consider various organizations. By research or by speculation, determine their objectives. Are they operational? Is profit maximization an operational business objective? Is sales maximization an operational advertising objective? Under what circumstances might it be?

2. Evaluate the judgment of a brand manager of Schlitz beer who decides that the goal of his advertising should be to remind people of the brand.

3. Why might advertising have an impact many years after it appears?

4. Distinguish between a communication objective and a marketing objective.

5. What is the difference between brand image, brand comprehension, and brand attitude?

6. How would you go about selecting which advertising response variable on which to base an advertising objective?

7. If awareness does not affect sales, why bother to measure it? If it does have a close relationship to sales, why not measure sales directly? Comment.

8. What is the "great idea" concept? Identify some campaigns that would qualify. Attempt to specify a set of DAGMAR objectives that might apply. Is DAGMAR inconsistent with the hope of obtaining a truly brilliant creative advertising campaign?

9. Under what circumstances is the hierarchy model most likely to hold? When will awareness precede and contribute to brand comprehension? When will brand comprehension precede and contribute to attitude? When will attitude change cause behavioral change? In particular, consider various product classes, various usage histories, and various decision processes.

10. Consider the CAPP data of Figure 4-13. Suppose that brand acceptance was 50 percent but brand preference was only 3 percent. What would be your diagnosis if you were a brand manager for a cereal? For an appliance? What if the brand awareness was 90 percent but brand acceptance was only 30 percent?

11. In the Watusi example, it was suggested that the "trade-in value" would be a good appeal to use. What were the assumptions that underlie

that conclusion? Given Table 4-5, under what conditions would it be worthwhile to focus on the "spacious interior"?

12. Two case studies were presented in the chapter, Overseas Airline Service and Electrical Appliances. Two more are presented with the appendix Regional Brand of Beer and Cranberries. For each of the four consider the following questions:
    a. Were the principles of DAGMAR followed to the letter?
    b. What objectives would you establish for the upcoming period?

APPENDIX: ADDITIONAL CASE STUDIES

Regional Brand of Beer

The subject brand of beer has been the largest selling brand in its headquarters market for generations. The company has gradually expanded distribution into contiguous markets and now distributes in over a dozen states. Company policy: avoid entering a new market until ready to go all out on advertising and distribution. The first year in a new market advertising expense, as a percentage of sales, will run three or four times the normal expenditure in an established market. It may take 2 or 3 years to reach the break-even point.

When first entering a new market, brand awareness is low. It is necessary to match or outspend the largest selling brand in order to capture a share of the consumer's attention and gradually woo him or her to try the brand. Management believes that anyone who is not prepared to enter competitive combat, quantitatively and qualitatively, is wasting money trying to open up new markets in this industry.

Advertising objective: deep and incessant exposure. The goal is to establish an 80 percent level of brand identity among moderate to heavy beer drinkers in the market area within 6 months and to maintain that level thereafter. Through a series of simple unaided and aided recall tests, consumers are asked to identify various brands of beer sold and advertised in the market area. Experience in past market introductions has shown that the brand has always succeeded in getting a firm foothold in a market where an 80 percent brand awareness level has been established. Once the brand name is established through "investment" advertising, expenditures as a percentage of the sales dollar return to a normal level.

Cranberries

A hypothetical trade association is made up of growers of cranberries, including many small producers who cannot afford to advertise individually. Consumption of cranberries is highly seasonal, traditionally during the Thanksgiving and Christmas seasons. A poor season, because of weather or other conditions, threatens to wipe out many producers who depend on this single crop for their livelihood. Land is unsuitable for crop diversification. Hence, the salvation of many growers lies in better marketing. Broad marketing objectives are (1) to increase consumption of cranberries, and (2) to diversify use of cranberries so that marketing activities are not crowded into one short season.

Marketing Strategy.   Develop new uses of product and create consumer demand through advertising, publicity, and promotion. The first step was to engage food technologists and home economists to develop delectable new recipes. Result: exciting new product, cranberry bread, was developed and tested.

Advertising Goals.   To spread the word among homemakers that cranberry bread is delicious, easy to bake, and a culinary accomplishment that will bring praise to the cook by all who taste it. Specifically, these one-year goals were set:

Awareness (have heard about cranberry bread)	*50 percent of market*
Favorable attitude (would like to bake it)	*25 percent of market*
Action (have baked it)	*10 percent of market*

Since advertising funds of cranberry growers were very limited, it was necessary to get participation and tie-in advertising of others who would benefit, such as flour millers and nut growers. With advertising as the pivotal force, retailers were willing to devote display space, food editors treated the new item editorially, and manufacturers of flour and other products were persuaded to include recipes on packages.

Proof of advertising performance was needed to convince all the cooperating groups of the success of the initial effort and of the advantages of continued support. The sales volume of cranberries was not, by itself, a suitable index of advertising effectiveness. The entire crop is always disposed of, if necessary, at distress prices. Furthermore, price received is not a reliable index since abundance of crops is governed by weather and other factors. Hence, measurement of the effectiveness of advertising alone was needed. Measurement was accomplished through a simple consumer panel survey to determine the percentage of homemakers who had heard about, wanted to try, or had actually baked the product. Results clearly indicated success of the first year's campaign and the desirability of continued promotional efforts, with emphasis on converting those who know about the product to repetitive users.

NOTES

1. Jack J. Honomichl, "The Ongoing Saga of 'Mother Baking Soda,' " *Advertising Age,* September 20, 1982, pp. M2–M3.

2. William D. Tyler, "Amazing, But It's True: Print Ads Are Getting More, Not Less, Gutzy," *Advertising Age,* March 5, 1973, p. 35.

3. Russell H. Colley, *Defining Advertising Goals for Measured Advertising Results* (New York: Association of National Advertisers, 1961).

4. Robert J. Lavidge and Gary A. Steiner, "A Model for Predictive Measurements of Advertising Effectiveness," *Journal of Marketing,* 25, October 1961, pp. 59–62.

5. Colley, *Defining Advertising Goals,* p. 31.

6. Ibid., p. 83.

7. Ibid., p. 73.

8. Michael Halbert, "What Do We Buy with an Advertising Dollar?," speech at the Ninth Annual Seminar in Marketing Management, Miami University, Oxford, Ohio, May 1961.

9. Leo Bogart, *Strategy in Advertising* (New York: Harcourt Brace Jovanovich, 1967).

10. Anthony I. Morgan, "Who's Killing the Great Advertising Campaigns of America?" *Journal of Advertising Research,* 24, December 1984–January 1985, pp. 33–37.

11. John C. Maloney, "Attitude Measurement and Formation," paper presented at the Test Market Design and Measurement Workshop, American Marketing Association, Chicago, April 21, 1966.

12. Gail Smith, "How GM Measures Ad Effectiveness," in Keith K. Cox, ed., *Readings in Market Research* (New York: Appleton-Century-Crofts, 1967).

5

Image and Competitive Position

I invented a slogan, "Be smart, get a fresh start with Ivory soap," because bathing, in its old ritualistic, anthropological sense, is getting rid of all your bad feelings, your sins, your immorality, and cleansing yourself, baptism, etc. (Ernst Dichter, describing his first motivation research study)

"They Laughed When I Sat Down at the Piano—But When I Started to Play. . ." (Author John Caples for International Correspondence School)

What does Sears mean to you? Or IBM? Or the First Community Bank? Or Kawasaki motorcycles? A brand name will have many associations. Some will be based on physical attributes. Others will reflect the fact that products are used to express life-styles, social positions, and professional roles. Still others will reflect associations involving product applications, types of people who might use the product, stores that carry the product, or salespeople who handle it. These associations will combine into an image or position.

Consumers tend to use images to reduce their mental work load and avoid having to reanalyze something each time they are exposed to it. A related idea is that of reputation. Just as an individual develops a reputation for consistency, trustworthiness, and so on, so too do brands, products, companies, and organizations. Basically, advertising can be used to mold and reinforce an image, and the decision as to what kind of an image should be developed is crucial to many advertising campaigns. This decision often means selecting those associations to build and emphasize and those associations which are to be removed or possibly deemphasized.

An image can be extremely rich or very simple. It can be very stable, based upon years of use experience and many associations, or it can be extremely unstable and dynamic. It can be very specific and well defined or it can be rather diffuse, meaning different things to different people. As might be expected, there is a long tradition of theoretical and empirical interest in the subject of images and imagery.[1] A popular definition of an image is the total impression of what a person or group of people think and know about an object. This overall impression is more than a set of facts, just as a picture of an outdoors scene creates a feeling and impression that is different from a description of each tree, stream, mountain, and cloud that make up the scene.

The terms "position" or "positioning" have recently been frequently used to mean "image," except that they imply a frame of reference for the image, the reference point usually being competition. It is important to understand that several levels of an organization can be thought of as "objects"—the company itself, its products, or its brands—that an image is associated with each, and that each can be positioned with respect to competitive alternatives. Thus, when the Bank of California positions itself as being smaller and friendlier than the Bank of America, it is focusing upon its image defined in the context of an attribute (friendliness) and a competitor (Bank of America). Such a context is usually implied when the term position is used instead of image.

Advertising objectives draw heavily upon four sets of constructs. One consists of behavioral constructs, such as trial purchases, store visits, or requests for information, and is the subject of Chapter 7. Such objectives are particularly relevant in retailing, mail order, industrial contexts, and sales promotion. Another includes attitude measurement and models, the subject of Chapter 6. Attitude models can help select the appropriate feature or attribute upon which to focus. For example, should the emphasis be upon our computer's performance characteristics or our service capability? Chapter 4 discussed a third construct, awareness. Often, especially in new product contexts, developing awareness is a primary job of advertising. In Chapter 14, the measurement of awareness using various recall methods will be discussed. In Chapter 8, the problems of gaining attention, so important in awareness advertising, will be considered. The fourth construct is image or positioning, the subject of this chapter.

In the first section several approaches to positioning will be presented. The discussion will then turn to several procedures that will lead to a possible positioning decision.

POSITIONING STRATEGIES

A positioning strategy can provide a focus in the development of an advertising campaign. The strategy can be conceived and implemented in a variety of ways that derive from the object attributes, competition, specific applications, the types of consumers involved, or the characteristics of the product class. Each represents a different approach to developing a positioning strategy, even though all of them have the ultimate objective of either developing or reinforcing an image in the mind of the audience. Seven approaches to positioning strategy will be presented: (1) using product characteristics or customer benefits, (2) the price-quality approach, (3) the use or applications approach, (4) the product-user approach, (5) the product-class approach, (6) the cultural symbol approach, and (7) the competitor approach.

Using Product Characteristics or Customer Benefits

Probably the most-used positioning strategy is to associate an object with a product characteristic or customer benefit. Imported automobiles illustrate the variety of product characteristics that can be employed and their power in image creation. Datsun and Toyota have emphasized economy and reliability and have become the leaders in the number of units sold. Volkswagen, the former leader and now in third position, emphasizes "value for the money." Volvo has stressed durability, showing commercials of "crash tests" and telling of the long average life of their cars. Fiat, in contrast, speaks of "European craftsmanship" and makes a distinct effort to position itself as a European car as opposed to a Japanese import. BMW attempts to put forth an image of performance in terms of handling and engineering efficiency. The tag line used by BMW is "the ultimate driving machine." BMW advertisements show the cars demonstrating their performance capabilities at a German race track.

Hughes Airwest positioned itself with respect to the product characteristic "courteous service" using radio commercials. In the radio spot an acapella choir replied yes to a series of 20 passengers' requests delivered in a rapid-fire manner. The commercial began by saying, "Hughes Airwest proudly presents the word passengers love to hear most, 'yes.' "

Sometimes a new product can be positioned with respect to a product characteristic that competitors have ignored. Brands of paper towels had emphasized absorbency until Viva was successfully introduced stressing durability. Viva demonstrations showed their product's durability and supported the claim that Viva "keeps on working."

Sometimes a product will attempt to position itself along two or more product characteristics simultaneously. In the toothpaste market, Crest became the leader decades ago by positioning itself as a cavity fighter, a position that was established by an endorsement by the American Dental Association. Since then, Crest has enjoyed a market share of up to 40 percent. However, several other successful entries have positioned themselves along two product characteristics. Aim, introduced as a good-tasting, cavity fighter, achieved a share of more than 10 percent. More recently, Aqua-fresh has been introduced by Beecham as a gel paste that offers both cavity-fighting and breath-freshening benefits. Aqua-fresh advertisements, such as in Figure 5-1, show people arguing whether to buy a breath-freshener or cavity-fighting dentifrice. Of course, the solution is Aqua-fresh.

It is always tempting to try to position along several product characteristics as it is frustrating to have some good product characteristics that are not communicated. However, advertising objectives that involve too many product characteristics can be most difficult to implement. The result can often be a fuzzy, confused image or, perhaps worse, advertising that is bypassed because it did not attract attention or interest.

Myers and Shocker[2] have made a distinction between physical characteristics, pseudo-physical characteristics, and benefits. Physical characteristics are the most objective and can be measured on some physical scale such as temperature, color intensity, sweetness, thickness, distance, dollars, acidity, saltiness, strength of fragrance, weight, and so on. Pseudo-physical characteristics, in contrast, reflect physical properties which are not easily measured. Examples are spiciness, smokey taste, tartness, type of fragrance (smells like a . . .), greasiness, creaminess, and shininess. Benefits refer to advantages that promote the well-being of the consumer or user. Ginger ale can be positioned as a product that "quenches thirst." Thirst-quenching is a benefit and provides the basis for this type of positioning strategy. Other examples are: does not harm the skin, satisfies hunger, easy to combine with other ingredients, stimulates, is convenient, and so on.

Positioning by Price-Quality

The price-quality product characteristic is so useful and pervasive that it is appropriate to consider it separately. In many product categories, there exist brands that deliberately attempt to offer more in terms of service, features, or performance. Manufacturers of such brands charge more, partly to cover higher costs and partly to help communicate the fact that they are of higher quality. Conversely, in the same product class there are usually other brands that appeal on the basis of price, although they might also try to be perceived as having comparable or at least adequate quality. In many product categories, the price-quality issue is so important that it needs to be considered in any positioning decision.

For example, in general merchandise stores, the department stores are at the top end. Neiman-Marcus, Bloomingdale's, and Saks Fifth Avenue are near the top followed by Macy's, Robinson's, Bullock's, Rich's, Filene's, Dayton's, Hudson's, and so on. Stores like Sears, Montgomery Ward, and J.C. Penney are positioned below the department stores but above the discount stores like K mart. Promotion by Sears directed at a more upbeat fashion image was thought to have hurt their "value" position and has probably caused some share declines over time.[3] Sears'

Figure 5-1. **Using two attributes**

"Are you kidding? Switch toothpastes? Lover boy here needs his fluoride paste."

"He can still get cavities. So he still needs a fluoride."

"Ah, Mom, I want a gel for fresh breath."

"We switched to Aqua-fresh. Now we fight cavities and freshen breath."

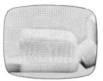

HERE'S HOW IT WORKS: Aqua-fresh gives you all the cavity-fighting fluoride of the leading paste...

And all the breath freshener of the leading gel...

Concentrated in one tooth-paste. That's double protection.

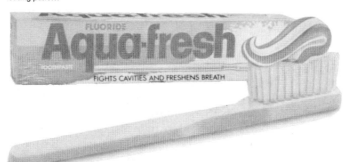

FLUORIDE

Aqua-fresh

FIGHTS CAVITIES AND FRESHENS BREATH

Double-protection Aqua-fresh® fights cavities and freshens breath.

Accepted
COUNCIL on DENTAL THERAPEUTICS
AMERICAN DENTAL ASSOCIATION

"Aqua-fresh has been shown to be an effective decay-preventive dentifrice that can be of significant value when used in a conscientiously applied program of oral hygiene and regular professional care." Council on Dental Therapeutics — American Dental Association.

© 1980, Beecham Inc.

recent five-year plan details a strategy of firmly returning to their positioning as a family, middle-class store offering top value. The plan also firmly noted that Sears is neither a discount nor a fashion store for the whimsical and affluent. Sears is just one advertiser that has faced the very tricky positioning task of retaining the image of low price while communicating a quality message. There is always the risk that the quality message will blunt the basic "low-price" position.

Positioning by Use or Application

Another way to communicate an image is to associate the product with a use or application. Campbell's Soup for many years positioned itself as a lunch-time product and used noontime radio extensively. The Bell Telephone Company more recently has associated long-distance calling with communicating with loved ones in its "Reach out and touch someone" campaign.

Products can, of course, have multiple positioning strategies, although increasing the number involves obvious difficulties and risks. Often a positioning-by-use strategy represents a second or third position for the brand, a position that deliberately attempts to expand the brand's market. Thus, Gatorade, a summer beverage for athletes who need to replace body fluids, has attempted to develop a positioning strategy for the winter months. The concept is to use Gatorade when flu attacks and the doctor says to drink plenty of fluids. Similarly, Quaker Oats has attempted to position their product as a natural whole-grain ingredient for recipes in addition to their breakfast food niche. Arm & Hammer baking soda has successfully positioned their product as an odor-destroying agent in refrigerators as the story board shown in Figure 5-2 illustrates.

Positioning by Product User

Another positioning approach is to associate a product with a user or a class of users. Thus, many cosmetic companies have used a model or personality to position their product. Brut fragrance, for example, has used Joe Namath. In Chapter 2, the use of a life-style profile by the Charlie line was noted. Makers of casual clothing like jeans have introduced "designer labels" such as Calvin Klein to develop a fashion image. The expectation is that the model or personality will influence the product's image by reflecting the characteristics and image of the model or personality communicated as a product user.

Johnson & Johnson repositioned its shampoo from one used for babies to one used by people who wash their hair frequently and therefore need a mild shampoo. This repositioning resulted in a market share that moved from 3 percent to 14 percent for Johnson & Johnson.

In 1970, Miller High Life was the "champagne of bottled beers" and had an image of a beer suitable for women to drink. In fact, it was purchased primarily by upper-class socioeconomic groups.[4] Philip Morris then purchased Miller and moved

Figure 5-2. Positioning by application

Product: ARM & HAMMER BAKING SODA   **DATE:** 5/30/80
Length: 30 SECONDS

Title: "THREE BOXES"
Commercial No.: ZCTB 4035

1. HARRY: (ON) Louise! Three boxes of Arm & Hammer Baking Soda?

2. LOUISE: (ON) Makes the house smell fresher, saves money.

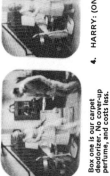

3. Box one is our carpet deodorizer. No cover-up perfume, and costs less.

4. HARRY: (ON) I like it.

5. LOUISE: (ON) Box two keeps the litter box fresher.

6. First baking soda — then litter.

7. HARRY: (ON) I like it.

8. LOUISE: (ON) Box three deodorizes our refrigerator...

9. (VO) better than the new gadgets and costs less.

10. (ON) Three boxes make the house fresher — and save money.

11. HARRY: (ON) I like it. I like it. BOTH: (ON) I like it.

12. ANNCR: (VO) Arm & Hammer Baking Soda.

130

the product out of the champagne bucket into the lunch bucket, repositioning it as a beer for the blue-collar working man who is the heavy beer drinker. The long-running campaign showed working men reaching the end of a hard day, designated as "Miller time," relaxing with a Miller beer. This campaign, which has run virtually unchanged since 1971, has been extremely successful. Miller went from a market share of 4 percent in 1971 to 15 percent in 1977.

Miller's Lite beer, introduced in 1975, used a similar positioning strategy. It was positioned as a beer for the heavy beer drinker who wants to drink a lot but dislikes that filled-up feeling. Thus, Miller's used convincing beer-drinking personalities such as Whitey Ford, Dick Butkus, and Mickey Spillane to communicate the fact that this beer was not as filling. In contrast, previous efforts by others to introduce low-calorie beers were dismal failures, partly because they emphasized the low-calorie aspect. One even claimed its beer had fewer calories than skim milk, and another featured a trim light beer personality.

Positioning by Product Class

Some products need to make critical positioning decisions that involve product-class associations. For example, Maxim freeze-dried coffee needed to position itself with respect to regular and instant coffee. Some margarines position themselves with respect to butter. Dried milk makers came out with instant breakfast positioned as a breakfast substitute and a virtually identical product positioned as a dietary meal substitute. The hand soap Caress by Lever Brothers positioned itself apart from the soap category toward a bath oil product.

The soft drink 7-Up was for a long time positioned as a soft drink that had a "fresh clean taste" that was "thirst-quenching." However, research uncovered the fact that most people did not regard 7-Up as a soft drink, but rather as a mixer beverage. The positioning strategy was then developed to position 7-Up as a soft drink, as a logical alternative to the "colas" but with a better taste. The successful Uncola campaign was the result.

Positioning by Cultural Symbols

Many advertisers use deeply entrenched cultural symbols to differentiate their brands from competitors. The essential task is to identify something that is very meaningful to people that other competitors are not using and associate the brand with that symbol. The Wells Fargo Bank, for example, uses a stagecoach pulled by a team of horses and very nostalgic background music to position itself as the bank that opened up the West. Advertising is filled with examples of this kind of positioning strategy. Marlboro cigarettes chose the American cowboy as the central focus to help differentiate their brand from competitors and developed the Marlboro Man. The Green Giant symbol was so successful that the packing company involved was renamed the Green Giant Company. Pillsbury's "doughboy" and dozens of other examples illustrate this type of positioning strategy.

Positioning by Competitor

In most positioning strategies, an explicit or implicit frame of reference is one or more competitors. In some cases the reference competitor(s) can be the dominant aspect of the positioning strategy. It is useful to consider positioning with respect to a competitor for two reasons. First, the competitor may have a firm, well-crystallized image developed over many years. The competitor's image can be used as a bridge to help communicate another image referenced to it. If someone wants to know where a particular address is, it is easier to say it is next to the Bank of America building than to describe the various streets to take to get there. Second, sometimes it is not important how good customers think you are; it is just important that they believe you are better than (or perhaps as good as) a given competitor.

Perhaps the most famous positioning strategy of this type was the Avis "We're number two, we try harder" campaign. The message was that the Hertz company was so big that they did not need to work hard. The strategy was to position Avis with Hertz as major car rental options, and therefore to position Avis away from National, which at the time was a close third to Avis.

Positioning with respect to a competitor can be an excellent way to create a position with respect to a product characteristic, especially price-quality. Thus, products that are difficult to evaluate, like liquor products, will often use an established competitor to help the positioning task. For example Sabroso, a coffee liqueur, positioned itself with the established brand, Kahlua, with respect to quality and also with respect to the type of liqueur. Its print advertisement showed the two bottles side by side and used the head, "Two great imported coffee liqueurs. One with a great price."

Positioning with respect to a competitor can be accomplished by comparative advertising, advertising in which a competitor is explicitly named and compared on one or more product characteristics. Pontiac has used this approach to position some of their cars as being comparable in gas mileage and price to leading import cars. Pontiac could attempt to position itself as having improved gas mileage without mentioning the competition, but it would be a very difficult task. As Figure 5-3 illustrates, by comparing Pontiac to a competitor that has a well-defined economy image, like a Volkswagen Rabbit, and using factual information such as EPA gas ratings, the communication task becomes easier.

DETERMINING THE POSITIONING STRATEGY

What should be our positioning strategy? The identification and selection of a positioning strategy can be difficult and complex. However, it becomes more manageable if it is supported by marketing research and decomposed into a six-step process.

Figure 5-3.   **A comparative advertisement**

PONTIAC TAKES ON THE IMPORTS

SUNBIRD vs. VW RABBIT

When it comes to good gas mileage at a good price, some people believe the Volkswagen Rabbit Custom is hard to beat.

But not all great little cars are designed overseas. One of the best comes from Pontiac.

SUNBIRD OFFERS BETTER MILEAGE.

Pontiac Sunbird rates ⟨24⟩ EPA EST. MPG, while the gas-powered Rabbit offers ⟨23⟩ EPA EST. MPG. Remember: Compare the "estimated mpg" to the "estimated mpg" of other cars. You may get different mileage depending on how fast you drive, weather conditions and trip length. Sunbird is equipped with GM-built engines produced by various divisions. See your dealer for details.

SUNBIRD HAS LOWER ANNUAL FUEL COSTS.

Based on the fuel economy sticker the government requires on every new car sold in America, Sunbird

"WHO'D EVER BELIEVE A RABBIT COULD BE BEATEN BY A PONTIAC?"

costs an estimated $24 less per year for gas than the Rabbit. The EPA bases annual fuel costs on each car's "estimated mpg" for 15,000 miles at 90¢ per gallon.

SUNBIRD HAS THE STANDARD FEATURES YOU WANT.

The spunky little Sunbird comes with Delco AM radio,* front bucket seats,

deluxe cushion steering wheel, tinted windows, whitewall tires, custom wheel covers, body side moldings, bumper strips and guards, Delco Freedom® battery and much more.

SUNBIRD IS PRICED $1202 LESS.

According to the government-required price sticker, Sunbird is priced at $4848 — while the Rabbit Custom is $6050. This base car comparison of manufacturer suggested retail prices includes optional automatic transmission. Sunbird price also includes dealer prep — the Rabbit does not. Taxes, license, destination charges and available equipment extra. Destination charges vary by location and affect comparison. *Level of standard equipment varies.*

Add it all up and see if you don't agree our Sunbird is the winner. Then hop on over to your Pontiac dealer's.

*Radio can be deleted for credit.

AND WINS BY $1226!

1. Identify the competitors.
2. Determine how the competitors are perceived and evaluated.
3. Determine the competitors' positions.
4. Analyze the customers.
5. Select the position.
6. Monitor the position.

In each of these steps one can employ marketing research techniques to provide needed information. Sometimes the marketing research approach provides a conceptualization that can be helpful even if the research is not conducted.

The first four steps or exercises provide a useful background. The final steps address the evaluation and measurement follow-up. Each step will be discussed in turn.

Identify the Competitors

A first step is to identify the competition. This step is not as simple as it might seem. Pepsi might define its competitors as follows:

1. Other cola drinks.
2. Nondiet soft drinks.
3. All soft drinks.
4. Nonalcoholic beverages.
5. All beverages except water.

A Triumph convertible might define its market in several ways:

1. Two-passenger, low-priced, imported, sports car convertibles.
2. Two-passenger, low-priced, imported sports cars.
3. Two-passenger, low- or medium-priced, imported sports cars.
4. Low- or medium-priced sports cars.
5. Low- or medium-priced imported cars.
6. Low- or medium-priced cars.

In most cases, there will be a primary group of competitors and one or more secondary competitors, and it will be useful to identify both categories. Thus, Coke will compete primarily with other colas, but other nondiet soft drinks and diet colas could be important as secondary competitors.

A knowledge of various ways to identify such groupings will be of conceptual as well as practical value. One approach is to determine from buyers of a product which other products they considered. For example, a sample of Triumph convertible buyers could be asked what other cars they considered and perhaps what other showrooms they actually visited. A Pepsi buyer might be asked to recall his or her last purchase of Pepsi and whether any other alternative went through his or her mind. Or the respondent could be asked what brand would have been purchased had

Pepsi been out of stock. The resulting analysis will identify the primary and secondary groups of competitive products. Instead of customers, retailers or buyers knowledgeable about customers could provide the information.

Another approach is the development of associations of products with use situations.[5] A respondent might be asked to keep a diary or to recall the use contexts for Pepsi. One might be with an afternoon snack. The respondent could then be asked to name all the beverages that would be appropriate to drink with an afternoon snack. For each beverage so identified, the respondent could be asked to identify appropriate use contexts so that the list of use contexts was more complete. This process would continue for perhaps 20 or 30 respondents until a large list of use contexts and beverages resulted. Another group of respondents would then be asked to make a judgment, perhaps on a seven-point scale, as to how appropriate each beverage would be for each use situation. Then groups of beverages could be clustered based upon their similarity of appropriate use situations. Thus, if Pepsi was regarded as appropriate with snacks, it would compete primarily with other beverages regarded as appropriate for snack occasions. If it was not regarded as appropriate for use with meals, it would be less competitive with beverages deemed more appropriate for meals. The same approach would work with an industrial product such as computers, which might be used in several rather distinct applications.

These two approaches suggest a conceptual basis for identifying competitors even when marketing research is not employed. The concept of alternatives from which customers choose and the concept of appropriateness to a use context can be used to understand the competitive environment. A management team or a group of experts, such as retailers or buyers who have an understanding of the customer, could employ one or both of these conceptual bases to identify competitive groupings.

Determine How the Competitors Are Perceived and Evaluated

To determine how competitor products are perceived, it is necessary to choose an appropriate set of product attributes for the comparison. The term ''attributes'' includes not only product characteristics and customer benefits, but also product associations such as product uses or product users. Thus for beer a relevant ''attribute'' could be the association of a brand with outdoor picnics as opposed to a nice restaurant. Another could be the association with athletes.

In any product category there are usually a host of attribute possibilities. Further, some can be difficult to specify. Consider the taste attribute of beer. Taste testers in a Consumer Union study considered the taste attribute but also the related attributes of smell, strength, and fullness. However, the strength of a beer is probably related to both its taste and its aroma characteristics, and perhaps also to its alcoholic content. Likewise, the notion of fullness is highly interrelated with the other attributes. Fullness can refer to the degree to which the drinker is left with a "full feeling" after consuming beer, to the visual color and texture of the product, and to a wide variety of other possible attributes.

The task is to identify potentially relevant attributes, to remove redundancies from the list, and then to select those that are most useful and relevant in describing brand images.

One approach to the generation of an attribute list is the *Kelly repertory grid*. The respondent is first given a deck of cards containing brand names from which all unfamiliar brands are culled. Three cards are then selected randomly from those remaining. The respondent is asked to identify the two brands that are most similar and to describe why those two brands are similar to each other and different from the third. The respondent is then asked to rate the remaining brands on the basis of the attributes thus identified. This procedure is repeated several times for each respondent. As a variant, respondents could be asked to select a preference between two brands and then asked why one brand was selected over the other.

Such a technique will often generate a rather long list of attributes, sometimes as many as several hundred and usually well over 40. The next step is to remove the redundancy from the list. In most cases there will be a set of words or phrases that will essentially mean the same thing. Such redundancies can be identified using logic and judgment.

Another approach is to remove redundancy through factor analysis.[6] Respondents are asked to rate each of the objects with respect to each attribute. For example, they might be asked to rate Budweiser on a seven-point scale as to the degree it is full bodied. Correlations between attributes are then calculated, and factor analysis essentially groups the attributes on the basis of those correlations.

After a list of nonredundant attributes is obtained, the next task is to select those that are the most meaningful and important to the customer's image of the competitive objects. The selected attributes should be those that are important and relevant to the customer in making distinctions between brands and in making purchasing decisions. One study found that the relevant attribute list for toothpaste was considered to include prevention of decay, taste, whitening capability, color and attractiveness of the product and its packaging, and price.[7] Chapter 6 on attitudes will discuss several approaches for selecting the most useful and meaningful attributes.

Determine the Competitors' Positions

Another useful exercise is to determine how competitors (including our own entry) are positioned. The primary focus of interest is how they are positioned with respect to the relevant attributes. What is the customer's image of the various competitors? We are also interested in how they are positioned with respect to each other. Which competitors are perceived as similar and which as different? Such judgments can be made subjectively. However, it is also possible to use research to help answer such questions empirically. Such research is termed *multidimensional scaling* because its goal is to scale objects on several dimensions (or attributes). Multidimensional scaling can be based upon either attribute data or nonattribute data. Approaches based on attribute data will be considered first.

Attribute-Based Multidimensional Scaling. The most direct way to determine images is simply to ask a sample of the target segment to scale the various objects on the attribute dimensions. One approach is to use a seven-point agree-or-disagree scale. For example, the respondent could be asked to express his or her agreement or disagreement with statements regarding the Chevette:

> With respect to its class I would consider the Chevette to be:
> Sporty
> Roomy
> Economical
> Good handling

Alternatively, perceptions of a brand's users or use contexts could be used to determine the brand image:

> I would expect the typical Chevette owner to be:
> Older
> Wealthy
> Independent
> Intelligent
> The Chevette is most appropriate for:
> Short neighborhood trips
> Commuting
> Cross-country trips

Another approach, the *semantic differential,* was used by Mindak to obtain the image of three beer brands.[8] The resulting profiles are shown in Figure 5-4. Notice that the image is not only obtained with respect to nine product attributes but also with respect to ten customer characteristics. Several observations emerge. Brand X is especially strong on the refreshing dimensions. Brand Z is weak across the board. The consumer profiles are really similar, which, in this case, was regarded as good news for the makers of brand X, who deliberately tried to appeal to a broad segment.

In generating such measures of image there are several potential problems and considerations of which one should be aware:

1. *Getting a relevant and meaningful attribute list.* The problems and approaches to generating a relevant attribute list have already been discussed. The most difficult job usually is to reduce a large attribute list by removing redundancies and emerging with interpretable, valid attributes or dimensions. If two or three exceptionally important attributes emerge,

Figure 5-4.   **Images and consumer profile for three brands**

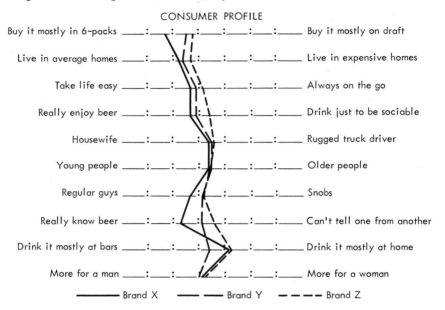

CONSUMER PROFILE

Buy it mostly in 6-packs	Buy it mostly on draft
Live in average homes	Live in expensive homes
Take life easy	Always on the go
Really enjoy beer	Drink just to be sociable
Housewife	Rugged truck driver
Young people	Older people
Regular guys	Snobs
Really know beer	Can't tell one from another
Drink it mostly at bars	Drink it mostly at home
More for a man	More for a woman

———— Brand X   — — Brand Y   – – – Brand Z

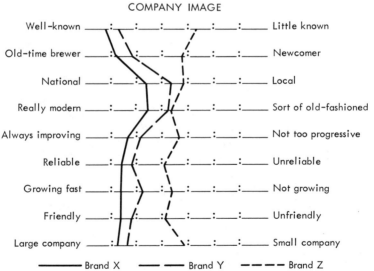

COMPANY IMAGE

Well-known	Little known
Old-time brewer	Newcomer
National	Local
Really modern	Sort of old-fashioned
Always improving	Not too progressive
Reliable	Unreliable
Growing fast	Not growing
Friendly	Unfriendly
Large company	Small company

———— Brand X   — — Brand Y   – – – Brand Z

Source: W. A. Mindak, "Fitting the Semantic Differential to the Marketing Problem," *Journal of Marketing,* 25, April 1961, pp. 31–32.

then it is possible and useful to plot the profiles in a two-dimensional portrayal. Such a plot is termed a perceptual map.

2. *The validity of the task.* Can a respondent actually position beers on an ''aged-a-long-time'' dimension? There could be several problems. One, a possible unfamiliarity with one or more of the brands, can be handled by asking the respondent to only evaluate familiar brands (although the degree to which a respondent is familiar with a brand might still be an issue). Another is the respondent's ability to understand operationally what ''aged'' means or how to evaluate a brand on this dimension. Any ambiguity in the scale or inability of a respondent to use the scale will affect the validity of the results.

3. *Differences among respondents.* The profile shown in Figure 5-4 represents the average score for the respondent group. However, the average hides the fact that subgroups within the population hold very different images with respect to one or more of the objects. Such diffused images can have important strategic implications. The task of sharpening a diffused image is much different from the task of changing a very tight, established one. A measure of dispersion, such as a standard error, or the raw frequency distribution, can allow the detection of respondent differences.

4. *Are the differences between objects significant and meaningful?* In comparing averages, whether the differences are statistically significant or discernible should be an issue. If the differences are not statistically significant, the sample size may be too small to make any managerial judgments. Of course, just the fact that the differences are statistically significant does not mean that they are large enough to be of managerial interest.

Non-Attribute-Based Multidimensional Scaling.   Attribute-based approaches have several conceptual disadvantages. A complete, valid, and relevant attribute list is not easy to generate. Furthermore, an object may be perceived or evaluated as a total whole that is not really decomposable in terms of attributes. These disadvantages lead us to the use of nonattribute data, that is, similarity data.

Similarity measures simply reflect the perceived similarity of two objects in the eyes of the respondents. For example, each respondent may be asked to rate the degree of similarity of each pair of objects. Thus, the respondent does not have an attribute list that implicitly suggests criteria to be included or excluded. The result, when averaged over all respondents, is a similarity rating for each object pair. A multidimensional scaling program then attempts to locate objects in a two- or three- (or more if necessary) dimensional space. Such a space is again termed a perceptual map. The program attempts to construct the perceptual map such that the two objects with the highest similarity are separated by the shortest distance, the object pair with the second highest similarity is separated by the second shortest distance, and so on. Of course, the programs will rarely be able to accomplish this goal, but many different perceptual maps are tried to get as close as possible.

A pilot study of car images used 50 owners of Granada and 50 nonowners.[9]

Between-object similarities were obtained for six cars and an "ideal car." The resulting perceptual map is shown in Figure 5-5. At the time of the study, Granada was attempting to position itself with Mercedes-Benz. Clearly, with respect to the sample used in this pilot study, that attempt was not very successful. Note that there was an effort to compare the perceptions of Granada owners with that of nonowners, as perceptions often differ considerably between such groups. In this case, however,

Figure 5-5.   **Similarity-based perceptual map**

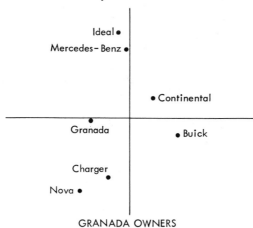

GRANADA OWNERS

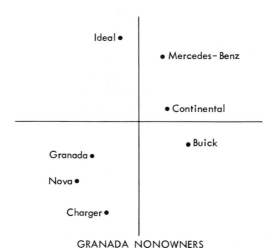

GRANADA NONOWNERS

Source: Robert E. Wilkes, "Product Positioning by Multidimensionnal Scaling," *Journal of Advertising Research,* 17, August 1977, p. 16.

they were very similar. Granada owners did have a tendency to position the Granada farther from a Nova than the nonowners.

The disadvantage of the similarity-based approach is that the interpretation of the dimensions does not have the attributes as a guide. Thus, in Figure 5-5 one horizontal axis might be determined ''prestige'' and the other horizontal axis ''size,'' but there are no attributes on which to base these judgments. Attribute data can be collected separately and correlated with the dimensions found in Figure 5-5, but it would be a distinctly separate analysis. The underlying perceptual map, of course, would still be based upon the similarity data.

Analyzing the Customers

The ultimate positioning decision specifies where in the perceptual map the brand should be positioned. Making that decision obviously requires knowing which areas in the map will be attractive to the customers. In most cases, customers will differ markedly as to the area in the perceptual map they prefer even if their perceptions of brands are similar. Thus, the task is usually to identify segments or clusters of customers based on their preferred locations in the perceptual maps. The decision will then involve selecting the segment or segments as well as the target position.

One approach to segmentation is to identify which attributes or customer benefits are most important and then identify groups of customers who value similar attributes or benefits. In Chapter 6, methods to identify important attributes or benefits will be discussed. Another approach uses the concept of an ''ideal object.'' An ideal object, illustrated in Figure 5-5, is an object the customer would prefer over all others, including objects that can be conceptualized but do not actually exist.[10] It is a combination of all the customer's preferred attribute levels. Customers who have similar ideal objects will form relevant segments.

It is often important to consider customers' preference for attributes in the context for the use context.[11] Preferences may be very sensitive to use context. In one study focus groups (structured discussions involving 8 to 10 people) and judgment were used to identify nine relevant use contexts for coffee:[12]

1.   To start the day
2.   Between meals
3.   Between meals with others
4.   With lunch
5.   With supper
6.   Dinner with guests
7.   In the evening
8.   To keep awake in the evening
9.   On weekends

In this study, there were differences across use occasion (Hill Brothers had a 7 percent share of breakfast use but only a 1.5 percent share of the remainder of the day). The major differences were found between A.M. coffee drinkers and P.M. coffee drinkers.

MAKING THE POSITIONING DECISION

The four steps or exercises should be conducted prior to making the actual positioning decision, as the results will nearly always contribute to the decision. The exercises can be done subjectively by the involved managers if necessary. Although marketing research will be more definitive, if research is not feasible or justifiable, the process should still be pursued. However, even with that background, it is still not possible to generate a cookbook solution to the positioning question. However, some guidelines or checkpoints can be offered.

1. *An economic analysis should guide the decision.* As was noted in Chapter 4, the success of any objective basically depends on two factors: the potential market size times the penetration probability. Unless both of these factors are favorable, success will be unlikely.

The market segment size should be worthwhile. If customers are to be attracted from other brands, those brands should have a large enough market share to justify the effort. If new buyers are to be attracted to the product class, a reasonable assessment should be made of the potential size of that growth area. If a new attribute is to be the basis for a campaign, a reasonable-sized segment should be interested. A survey of 1,250 consumers indicated that the initial thrust of 7-Up into the noncaffeine soft-drink market (which stimulated the introduction of noncaffeine colas) did tap a sizable segment. A total of 28 percent said that it makes a great deal of difference to them if their soft drink had caffeine.[13] In the same survey over 40 percent mentioned 7-Up when asked which noncaffeine soft drink first comes to mind—over four times greater than Pepsi Free.

The penetration probability indicates that there needs to be a competitive weakness to attack or a competitive advantage to exploit to generate a reasonable market penetration probability. An established brand will always find that the penetration probability will be higher among existing customers. The implication is that segments containing existing customers should be given high priority.

2. *Positioning usually implies a segmentation commitment.* Positioning usually means that an overt decision is being made to ignore parts of the market and to concentrate only on certain segments. Such an approach requires commitment and discipline, because it is not easy to turn your back on potential buyers. Yet the effect of generating a distinct, meaningful position is to focus on the target segments and not be constrained by the reaction of other segments.

There is always the possibility of deciding to engage in a strategy of undifferentiation—that of attempting to reach all segments. In that case, it might be reasonable to consider deliberately generating a "diffuse image," an image that will mean different things to different people. Such an approach is risky and difficult to implement and usually would only be used by a large brand with a very strong market position. The implementation could involve projecting a range of advantages while avoiding being identified with any one. Alternatively, there could be a conscious effort to avoid being explicit about any particular feature. Pictures of bottles of Coca-Cola superimposed with the words "It's the real thing," or Budweiser's claim that "Bud is the king of beers," or "Somebody still cares about quality" illustrate these strategies.

3. *If the advertising is working, stick with it.* An advertiser will often get tired of a positioning strategy and the advertising used to implement it and will consider making a change. However, the personality or image of a brand, like that of a person, evolves over many years, and the value of consistency through time cannot be overestimated. Some of the very successful, big-budget campaigns have run for 10, 20, or even 30 years. Larry Light, the executive vice-president of BBDO, a major New York advertising agency, said that the "biggest mistake marketers make is to change the personality of their advertising year after year. They end up with a schizophrenic personality at worst, or no personality at best."[14]

4. *Don't try to be something you are not.* It is tempting but naïve, and usually fatal, to decide on a positioning strategy that exploits a market need or opportunity but assumes that your product is something it is not. Before positioning a product, it is important to conduct blind taste tests, in-home or in-office use tests to make sure that the product can deliver what it promises and that it is compatible with a proposed image.

Consider Hamburger Helper, introduced in 1970 as an add-to-meat product that would generate a good-tasting, economical, skillet dinner. It did well during the early 1970s when meat prices were high, but in the mid-1970s, homemakers switched back to more exotic, expensive foods. Reacting to the resulting drop in sales, a decision was made to attempt to make Hamburger Helper more exotic by positioning it as a base for casseroles. However, the product—at least in the consumers' minds—could not deliver. The consumers continued to view it as an economical, reliable convenience food; furthermore, they felt that they did not need help in making casseroles. In a personality test, in which women were asked to view the product as though it were a person, the most prevalent characteristic ascribed to the product was "helpful."

5. *Consider symbols.* A symbol or set of symbols can have strong associations that should be considered when making positioning decisions. Symbols like the Marlboro Man or the Jolly Green Giant can help implement a campaign, of course, but there can be existing symbols already developed by the brand or organization that can be used. Their availability can affect the positioning decision. For example, Wells Fargo bank has used the Wells Fargo stagecoach with all its associations for many years. Figure 5-6 shows Wells Fargo associating the stagecoach with foreign settings thereby positioning the bank as a multinational. The Figure 5-6 advertisements are probably more interesting and effective than factual advertisements explaining a multinational capability.

Figure 5-6.   A symbolic theme carried out in four versions of a campaign

We're there, because you're there.

Wells Fargo Bank International, located at 40 Wall Street, is in the heart of the world's greatest concentration of multinational corporate headquarters.

Organized to assure personalized attention, this highly specialized, expert unit, dealing exclusively in international finance, is an integral part of the world-wide system of a $9

billion bank. Through this office, you're in direct contact with the financial resources of Wells Fargo Bank, the expertise in the Euro-dollar market of Wells Fargo Limited in London, and with branches, affiliates and representative offices around the world. For convenient service in New York, see Wells Fargo Bank International for your international banking needs

Wells Fargo Bank International

40 WALL STREET, NEW YORK, N.Y. 10005, TELEPHONE (212) 344-5400

If you're there, we're there.

Wells Fargo Bank

Where we are: Auckland, Bangkok, Buenos Aires, Bogota, Caracas, Dubai, Frankfurt, Hong Kong, Lima, London, Los Angeles, Luxembourg, Managua, Manila, Manizales, Mexico City, Miami, Nassau, New York, Ottawa, Panama City, Quito, San Francisco, San Salvador, Sao Paulo, Singapore, Sydney, Taipei, Tokyo. In London: Wells Fargo, Ltd. and Western American Bank, Europe Ltd.

WELLS FARGO BANK. SINCE 1852/ASSETS OVER $9 BILLION HEADQUARTERS: SAN FRANCISCO, CALIFORNIA 94104

144

Courtesy of Wells Fargo Bank.

Monitoring the Position

An image objective, like any advertising objective, should be operational, in that it should be measurable. To evaluate the advertising and to generate diagnostic information about future advertising strategies, it is necessary to monitor the position over time. A variety of techniques can be employed to make this measurement. Hamburger Helper used a ''personality test'' to learn more about the product. Such a test could also be employed to monitor any image changes. However, usually one of the more structured techniques of multidimensional scaling is applied.

John Morrill, a seasoned advertising executive, describes one effort to monitor images that is of interest because it is an industrial advertising setting.[15] He conducted telephone interviews with more than 1,000 buyers at dispersed locations. For each buyer, he determined what business publications were read regularly. On the basis of the readership information and a knowledge of advertisers' media schedules, the sample was divided into an exposed group and an unexposed group. Table 5-1 shows the results of one such study. Thus, 20 percent of the exposed group said that the advertiser provided the best technical assistance, whereas 14 percent of the unexposed group made the same judgment. However, only 4 percent of the respondents felt that the advertiser's competitors were best in the technical-assistance dimension.

BEYOND ATTRIBUTES

The emphasis has been on positioning strategies defined with respect to attributes. However, the task of creating an image often needs to move beyond attributes to include the ultimate consequences of product use and even the relationship of product use to people's life-styles, needs, and values. A positioning strategy that focuses only on attributes can be shallow and less effective than one that is based on a richer knowledge of the customer.

Life-Styles and Feelings

An understanding of relevant consumer life-styles and feelings related to a product helped Needham, Harper & Steers develop meaningful image objectives for Betty Crocker.[16] They conducted research involving more than 3,000 women, which focused not only upon the Betty Crocker image but also upon women's feelings about desserts in general. They found that 90 percent of the women were familiar with the Betty Crocker name. In general, Betty Crocker is viewed as a company that is:

> Honest and dependable
> Friendly and concerned about consumers
> A specialist in baked goods

Table 5-1. A Chemical Company: Opinions of Buyers about Three Competing Suppliers When Exposed and Unexposed to Their Advertising

| | PROPORTION OF BUYERS HOLDING THESE OPINIONS | | | | | |
| Opinions | About Company A, Which Ran 17 Pages of Advertising in One Year | | | About Companies B and C, Which Did Negligible Advertising in One Year | | |
	Exposed	Unexposed	Differential (%)	Exposed	Unexposed	Differential (%)
Preferred as supplier	0.37[a]	0.30	+ 23[b]	0.09	0.12	− 25[b]
Second and third choice as supplier	0.19	0.19	[b]	0.14	0.14	[b]
Willing to consider	0.56	0.50	+ 6	0.24	0.28	− 14[b]
Leads in quality	0.20	0.18	+ 11	0.03	0.03	[b]
Leads in price	0.05	0.07	− 29	0.03	0.03	[b]
Leads in delivery	0.18	0.15	+ 20	0.04	0.04	[b]
Best in your past experience	0.22	0.18	+ 22	0.05	0.05	[b]
Best technical assistance	0.20	0.14	+ 43	0.04	0.04	[b]
Salespeople lead in product knowledge	0.13	0.08	+ 63	0.05	0.05	[b]
Salespeople lead in service	0.11	0.09	+ 22	0.02	0.02	[b]
Most enthusiastic salespeople	0.12	0.06	+100	0.02	0.02	[b]
Share of market						
In customers	0.56	0.47	+ 19	0.20	0.23	− 13
In dollars	0.38	0.35	+ 9	0.13	0.19	− 32

[a] Read: 37% of the buyers exposed to A's advertising preferred A as supplier.
[b] No significant difference.

Source: John E. Morrill, "Industrial Advertising Pays Off," Harvard Business Review, March–April 1970, p. 13.

but

>Out of date
>Old and traditional
>A manufacturer of "old standby" products
>Not particularly contemporary or innovative

The conclusion was that the Betty Crocker image needed to be strengthened to become more modern and innovative and less old and stodgy.

To improve the Betty Crocker image, it was felt that an understanding was needed of the needs and life-style of today's women and how they relate to desserts. Thus, the research study was directed to basic questions about desserts. Why are they served? Who serves them? The answers are illuminating. Dessert users tend to be busy, active mothers who are devoted to their families. The primary reasons for serving dessert tend to be psychological and revolve around the family:

>Dessert is a way to show others you care.
>Dessert preparation is viewed as an important duty of a good wife and mother.
>Desserts are associated with and help to create happy family moments.

Two of the verbatim comments were:

>Our kids have the option of having it, you know, at dinner or later, and a lot of times they'll choose to have it at night, and it's kind of fun . . . you know, before bedtime, to all sit around and we share something together at the end of the day . . . and I think it's more than the food; it's—well, it's a social event.
>
>When you set it out, and you get your plates out and stuff like that, there's a lot of closeness and laughing.[17]

Clearly, ideas of family bonds, love, and good times are associated with desserts. As a result, the Betty Crocker image objective was to associate Betty Crocker uniquely with the positive aspects of today's families and their feelings about dessert. The promise was that Betty Crocker would help to make the desserts that contribute to happy family moments. The tone of the advertising was to be contemporary, appealing, and emotionally involving. Figure 5-7 shows one of the advertisements used.

THE MEANS-END CHAIN MODEL[18]

The means-end model focuses on the connection between product attributes, consumer consequences, and personal values:

Product Attributes ———— Consumer Consequences ———— Personal Values

Values represent the desired end states. They can have an external orientation ("feeling important" or "feeling accepted") or can relate to how one views oneself ("self-esteem," "happiness," "security," "neatness," "accomplishment"). Product attributes and consumer consequences represent the means that can be used to achieve the desired ends. Product attributes include measurable physical characteristics such as "miles per gallon" or "cooking speed" and subjective

Figure 5-7   **The "Bake Someone Happy" campaign**

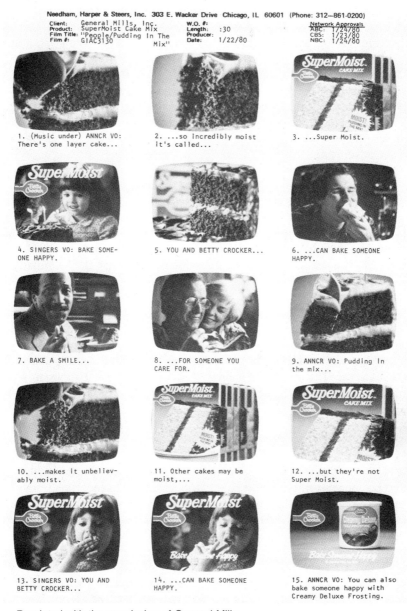

Needham, Harper & Steers, Inc.   303 E. Wacker Drive Chicago, IL 60601 (Phone: 312—861-0200)

Client: General Mills, Inc.
Product: SuperMoist Cake Mix
Film Title: "People/Pudding In The Mix"
Film #:   GIAC3130

W.O. #:
Length: :30
Producer:
Date: 1/22/80

Network Approvals
ABC: 1/24/80
CBS: 1/23/80
NBC: 1/24/80

1. (Music under) ANNCR VO: There's one layer cake...

2. ...so incredibly moist it's called...

3. ...Super Moist.

4. SINGERS VO: BAKE SOME-ONE HAPPY.

5. YOU AND BETTY CROCKER...

6. ...CAN BAKE SOMEONE HAPPY.

7. BAKE A SMILE...

8. ...FOR SOMEONE YOU CARE FOR.

9. ANNCR VO: Pudding in the mix...

10. ...makes it unbeliev-ably moist.

11. Other cakes may be moist,...

12. ...but they're not Super Moist.

13. SINGERS VO: YOU AND BETTY CROCKER...

14. ...CAN BAKE SOMEONE HAPPY.

15. ANNCR VO: You can also bake someone happy with Creamy Deluxe Frosting.

Reprinted with the permission of General Mills.

characteristics such as "tastes good," "strong flavor," or "stylish." Consumer consequences are any result occurring to the consumer. Consequences can be functional ("saves money" or "don't have to wash your hair every day") or can affect self-perceptions ("having more friends," "having fun," or "being more attractive").

The means-end chain model suggests that it is the associational network involving attributes, consequences, and values that really represent an image. Effective advertising should thus address all levels and not just be concerned with the product attributes. The major positive consumer consequences should be communicated verbally or visually, and the value level should provide the driving force behind the advertising.

One approach to eliciting a means-end chain can be illustrated using an airline example.[19] The process begins with a repertory grid exercise in which consumers are asked to state how two airlines out of a set of three are similar and how they differ. Consumers are then asked why an attribute such as "wide bodies" is preferred. One response might be "physical comfort." The consumer is then asked why "physical comfort" is desired. The answer could be to "get more done." Another "why" question yields a value, "feel better about self." Similarly, the "ground service" attribute leads to "save time," "reduce tension," "in control," and "feeling secure."

A campaign based on the ground service attribute would then address the consequences ("save time," "reduce tension," and "in control") and value ("feeling secure") dimensions. A mother needing personal service might be presented traveling with children. The theme is being "in control," being able to cope with the situation. The result is a feeling of security. The creative group will, of course, have knowledge of the total means-end structures as they develop the campaign.

THE BRAND PERSONALITY

Joseph Plummer, the research director of Young and Rubicam, indicates that there are three components to a brand image: attributes, consequences, and brand personality.[20] Think of a brand as if it were a person. Just as a person will have certain characteristics that define his or her personality, so can a brand. Thus, a brand could be characterized as modern or old-fashioned, or lively, or exotic.

Y & R developed a campaign for a Swedish insurance company which markets a low-involvement, avoidance product. A series of humorous commercials shows that most accidents could happen to anyone and actually are humorous and not really that tragic if looked at with the right perspective. The advertising created a personality of a firm that is approachable, warm, and most of all, human. Dr. Pepper made great sales progress during the 1970s by creating a personality of being original, fun, offbeat, and underdog.

Y & R conducts personality research on brands as if they were people. Consumers are asked to indicate which of a set of 50 "personality related" words and phrases they would use to describe each brand of interest. One test of this technique demonstrated that brands are perceived very differently. A total of 39 percent said that Holiday Inn was "cheerful," whereas only 6 percent said that Birds-Eye was "cheerful." Forty-two percent applied the "youthful" descriptor to Atari; only 3 percent applied it to Holiday Inn. Thirty-nine percent described Oil of Olay as "gentle," while no one applied it to Miller High Life. In profile, Holiday Inn was described as cheerful, friendly, ordinary, practical, modern, reliable, and honest.

In another study Y & R gave respondents a list of 29 animals and said: "If each of these brands was an animal, what one animal would it be?" They asked similar questions for 25 different activities, 17 fabrics, 35 occupations, 20 nationalities, and 21 magazines. Oil of Olay was associated with mink, France, secretary, silk, swimming, and *Vogue*. Kentucky Fried Chicken, in contrast, was associated with Puerto Rico, a zebra (recall the stripes on a Kentucky Fried Chicken bucket), a housewife dressed in denim, camping, and reading *TV Guide*.

SUMMARY

There are a variety of positioning strategies available to the advertiser. An object can be positioned as follows:

1. By attribute (Crest is a cavity fighter).
2. By price-quality (Sears is a "value" store).
3. By use or application (Gatorade is for flu attacks).
4. By product user (Miller is for the blue-collar, heavy beer drinker).
5. By product class (Carnation Instant Breakfast is a breakfast food).
6. By cultural symbol (Green Giant).
7. By competitor (Avis positions itself with Hertz).

Four exercises or steps should precede the selection of a positioning strategy. In the first, an effort should be made to identify the competitors. One approach is to consider what alternatives face the customer when a purchase decision is being made. Another is to consider associations of brands or purchase alternatives and use situations. In the second step, the attributes used to perceive and evaluate competitors are determined. One task is to reduce the attribute list to remove redundancy and to generate useful interpretable attributes. The third step involves the determination of the position of the various competitors. One approach is to scale the competitors on the various identified attributes. Another is to ask respondents to judge the similarity of pairs of objects. A perceptual map that locates the objects on two or three dimensions is a convenient way to portray the positioning. The fourth step involves customer analysis. What segmentation variables seem most relevant? What about benefit segmentation? What role does the product class play in the customer's life or business?

The positioning decision should involve an economic analysis of the potential target segments and the probability of affecting their behavior with advertising. Other suggestions include realizing that positioning involves a segmentation commitment, sticking to a strategy that is working, being sure that the product matches the positioning strategy, and consideration of available symbols that may contribute to image formation. Finally, consider the evaluation stage, where the position is monitored.

Positioning strategies are often defined with respect to attributes, but other constructs such as needs, life-styles, and values can play a useful role. Means-end models provide a rich picture of the associations between product attributes, consumer consequences, and values. The brand personality concept and its related research tools provide another way to conceptualize brand image.

DISCUSSION QUESTIONS

1. Consider six television and ten print advertisements. How are the products positioned?

2. Can you expand the list of seven positioning strategies mentioned in the text?

3. Obtain two examples of each of the positioning strategies discussed in the chapter.

4. Consider the following beer brands: Lowenbrau, Miller Lite, Coors, Coors Light, Schlitz, Schlitz Malt.
   a. In each case, write down what you think is the image the general public holds of that brand. Confine your answers to a few statements or phrases.
   b. Generate an attribute list for beer, using the Kelly repertory grid approach. Revise your answer to part (a).
   c. Identify the competitors of the listed brands of beer by asking consumers or potential consumers of that object what they would select if that object were not available.
   d. Determine the use situations relevant to beer, and for three use situations list other products that might be appropriate.

5. Consider all possible pairs of the following brands of soft drinks: 7-Up, Fresca, Diet 7-Up, Diet Pepsi, Coke, Orange Crush, your ideal brand.
   a. Rank order the brand pairs in terms of their similarity. Was the task a reasonable one? Are you comfortable with all your rankings?
   b. Pick several sets of three brands, identify the two most similar brands in the set, and explain why you regard them as the most similar. Using the Kelly repertory grid technique, generate a list of attributes relevant to this product class. Scale each of the

attributes in terms of how important they are to you in your choice of a soft drink.

   c. How would you say each of these brands is positioned?

6. What is a diffuse image? Give examples of brands that have a diffuse image.

7. What would be the characteristics of an ideal brand of toothpaste for you? How might the concept of an ideal brand be related to benefit segmentation? What brand did you buy last? Why? How would your ideal brand differ from this brand?

8. Budweiser is interested in entering the soft drink market. They have developed a new drink called Chelsea, which is a carbonated apple juice drink containing 0.5 percent alcohol. It is packaged in a glass bottle partially wrapped in foil, like some of the labels used on premium beers. What are the positioning alternatives open to Chelsea? How would you go about selecting the optimal one?

NOTES

1. See, for example, the 17 definitions of image given in J. G. Myers, *Consumer Image and Attitude* (Berkeley, Calif: Institute of Business and Economic Research, University of California, 1968), pp. 28–30.

2. James H. Myers and Allan D. Shocker, "Toward a Taxonomy of Product Attributes," Working Paper (Los Angeles: University of Southern California, June 1978), p. 3.

3. "Sears' New 5-year Plan: To Serve Middle America," *Advertising Age,* December 4, 1978.

4. "Miller's Fast Growth Upsets the Beer Industry," *Business Week,* November 8, 1976.

5. George S. Day, Allan D. Shocker, and Rajendra K. Srivastava, "Customer-Oriented Approaches to Identifying Product Markets," *Journal of Marketing,* 43, Fall 1979, pp. 8–19.

6. David A. Aaker and George S. Day, *Marketing Research* (New York: Wiley, 1980), Chap. 16.

7. Russell J. Haley, "Benefit Segmentation: A Decision Oriented Research Tool," *Journal of Marketing,* July 1968, pp. 30–35.

8. W. A. Mindak, "Fitting the Semantic Differential to the Marketing Problem," *Journal of Marketing,* 25, April 1961, pp. 28–33.

9. Robert E. Wilkes, "Product Positioning by Multidimensional Scaling," *Journal of Advertising Research,* 17, August 1977, pp. 15–18.

10. In Figure 5-5, an ideal point is shown as a point on the map. However, if an attribute-based multidimensional scaling was involved and a scale such as

Inexpensive to buy ⟷ Expensive to buy

were employed, the respondent would prefer to be as far to the right as possible. In that case the "ideal point" would actually appear in the perceptual map as an ideal direction or vector instead of as a point.

11. Rajendra K. Srivastava, Robert P. Leone, and Allan D. Shocker, "Market Structure Analysis: Hierarchical Clustering of Products Based on Substitution in Use," *Journal of Marketing,* 45, Summer 1981, pp. 38–48.

12. Glen L. Urban, Philip L. Johnson, and John R. Hauser, "Testing Competitive Market Structures," *Marketing Science,* 3, Spring 1984, pp. 83–112.

13. Joseph M. Winski, "No Caffeine—Choice: 7-Up," *Advertising Age,* May 30, 1983, p. 3.

14. "Style Is Substance for Ad Success: Light," *Advertising Age,* August 27, 1979, p. 3.

15. John E. Morrill, "Industrial Advertising Pays Off," *Harvard Business Review,* March–April 1970, pp. 8–14.

16. Keith Reinhard, "How We Make Advertising," presented to the Federal Trade Commission, May 11, 1979, pp. 22–25.

17. Ibid., p. 29.

18. Thomas J. Reynolds and Jonathan Gutman, "Advertising Is Image Management," *Journal of Advertising Research,* 25, February–March 1984, pp. 29–37; and Jonathan Gutman, "A Means-End Chain Model Based on Consumer Categorization Processes," *Journal of Marketing,* 46, Spring 1982, pp. 60–73. See also S. Young and B. Feigin, "Using the Benefit Chain for Improved Strategy Formulation," *Journal of Marketing,* 39, July, 1975, pp. 72–74.

19. Reynolds and Gutman, "Advertising Is Image Management," p. 32.

20. Joseph T. Plummer, "Brand Personality: A Strategic Concept for Multinational Advertising," presented to the AMA 1985 Winter Marketing Educators Conference, Phoenix, Ariz., February 1985.

6

Attitude and Market Structure

Said a tiger to a lion as they drank beside a pool, "Tell me, why do you roar like a fool?"

"That's not foolish," replied the lion with a twinkle in his eyes. "They call me king of all the beasts because I advertise."

A rabbit heard them talking and ran home like a streak. He thought he would try the lion's plan, but his roar was a squeak. A fox came to investigate—and had his lunch in the woods.

The moral: When you advertise, be sure you've got the goods! (Fable)

Chapter 5 presented various types of positioning strategy alternatives and a procedure for determining the positioning strategy. In this chapter, these ideas are extended and various approaches and techniques relating to attitude and market measurement presented. To know which strategy is best, we really need to know which attributes are the most important in a product-market situation. Also, we need to know whether a particular positioning strategy will really work. Are the attributes and images linked to overall attitudes? Do a consumer's beliefs about the attributes of a brand really influence the decision process? All these are questions about attitude and market structure.

The attitude construct is one of the most important ideas in advertising management. The basic argument is that consumers' purchases are governed by their attitudes toward product alternatives and that advertisers can do something to affect those attitudes. The construct really encompasses a system of interrelated subconstructs and the relations among them. In this chapter, measurement and structure issues will be the focus. Later chapters will examine questions of perceptual and attitude change processes.

The chapter begins with a brief overview of the attitude construct and various approaches to measuring attitude. This is followed by a section on how to identify the important attributes in a given product-market situation. Then some well-known models of attitude are presented, and some of the things to look out for in using the models are noted. The use of the attitude construct for segmentation and market planning and ideas on how attitude can be incorporated into a normative decision model round out the chapter.

ATTITUDE COMPONENTS AND MEASUREMENT

Attitude is a central concept to the entire field of social psychology, and theories and methods associated with its explanation and measurement have largely evolved from the work of social psychologists and psychometricians. Gordon W. Allport, for example, has stated that "Attitude is probably the most distinctive and indispensable concept in American social psychology. No other term appears more frequently in experimental and theoretical literature."[1] The most widely held view of the structure of an attitude is that it is made up of three closely interrelated components: cognitive (awareness, comprehension, knowledge), affective (evaluation, liking), and conative (action tendency). Measurement is usually focused on the middle component, assessing the degree of positive or negative feelings for an object. It is theoretically possible, however, to derive a measure of attitude from any one of the three components. For example, a person's intention to purchase a brand would be a measure of brand attitude.

Attitude can be measured directly by asking a respondent to indicate whether he or she likes or dislikes a brand or by attempting a direct assessment of the degree of like or dislike on a positive-negative scale. The indirect approaches rely on deriving a measure from other kinds of consumer response. For example, a consumer could be asked to judge a brand on the basis of several attributes or characteristics according to whether it was positive or negative on each, and the mean of her or his scores taken as the attitude measure. Such measures are called *derived measures* because they are based on a synthesis of factors and processes that underlie the attitude. They are in essence attitude models.

Much of the chapter involves derived attitude measures and attitude models in this sense. These models draw on the cognitive component of attitude.

Measures of Overall Attitude

The simplest way to measure overall attitude toward an object (brand, store, product class, or whatever) is to ask a respondent whether he or she likes or dislikes it. There are no explicit attribute criteria given on which the evaluation is made. Respondents are simply asked to answer "yes" or "no," and the responses are used to determine the brand attitude.

If interest centers on attempting to capture the degree of attitude, the question can be put in the form of a scale. For example, a respondent could be asked to express how much she or he liked a brand on a scale ranging from "very much" (1) to "very little" (7). Other terms could be used, such as "excellent-poor," or "good-bad." George S. Day,[2] a University of Toronto professor, for example, suggested the seven-point scale shown in Figure 6-1 as being particularly appropriate for durable products. He points out how segments of the scale might be used to identify whether the object is preferred, and whether or not it is likely to be considered if a purchase situation developed.

Another approach is to provide an explicit reference to a comparison stimulus or stimuli [for example, another brand(s) or company(s)]. Subjects can be asked to rank objects in the order of their preferences for them. An attitude for an object would then be the ranking it received. The attitude for a respondent group might be the percentage that ranked the object first or among the first three. By adding a scale such as "How much do you prefer brand A over brand B?" the relative distance between brands in terms of overall attitude might be determined. A variation of this technique to be given later in the chapter is called *paired comparisons*. Respondents make their judgments concerning the brand by considering pairs presented two at a time.

An important question is whether attitudes measured in these ways are related to brand choice and market behavior. Positive attitudes toward a brand will not always result in purchase behavior. A person can have a positive attitude for a brand and yet not be willing or able to buy it. Many teenagers have strong positive attitudes for a Porsche, but few are likely to be purchasers. Furthermore, situational events at the time of purchase and/or "impulsive" behavior can throw off short-run sales predictions made on the basis of attitude measures taken some time previous to the purchase occasion. However, if these types of cases are basically exceptions and are not dominant in the market or segment of interest, a strong relationship between attitude and purchase behavior should emerge.

Achenbaum[3] has demonstrated that attitude and usage levels are associated in several consumer product categories. Figure 6-2 shows the attitude-usage relationship for a brand of cigarettes, deodorant, gasoline, laxative, and a dental product. The data are based on impressive sample sizes usually involving over 1,000 respondents. For each of the four brands, the percentage using the brand is strongly related to the attitude toward it. For the dental product, the attitude profiles of current users are compared with those of former users. Current users tend to have

Figure 6-1.   **A relative rating scale for brand attitudes**

(1)	(2)	(3)	(4)	(5)	(6)	(7)
This brand is the best that is available.	I like this brand very much – but there's another just as good.	I like this brand – but others are better.	This brand is acceptable – but most other brands are better.	I neither like nor dislike this brand – it doesn't have any particular merits.	I don't like this brand very much – although it is not as bad as some.	I don't like this brand at all – it is one of the worst available.

Primary choice class

Secondary consideration class

Non-consideration class

Source: George S. Day, *Buyer Attitudes and Brand Choice Behavior* (New York: Columbia University Press, 1970), p. 160.

Figure 6-2. Attitude-usage relationships in several product categories

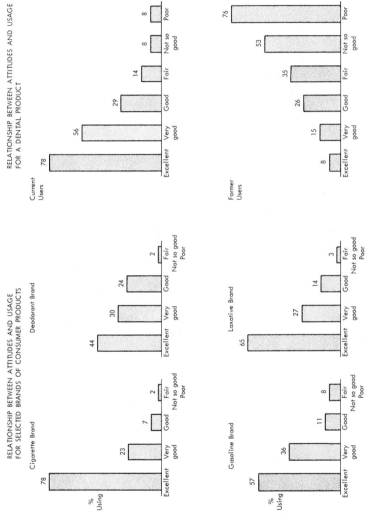

Source: Alvin A. Achenbaum, "Knowledge Is a Thing Called Measurement," in Lee Adler and Irving Crespi, eds., *Attitude Research at Sea* (Chicago: American Marketing Association, 1966), p. 113.

positive attitudes, whereas former users tend to have negative attitudes. Although not shown in Figure 6-2, Achenbaum reports the tendency for a third category of individuals—those who have never tried the brand—to have mainly neutral attitudes.[4]

OVERALL ATTITUDE AS AN OBJECTIVE

Why is the attitude construct so important in advertising? A simple answer is that millions of dollars of advertising and great financial risks ultimately depend on what happens to attitude. Brand attitude is the pillar on which the sales and profit fortunes of a giant corporation rest. Consider the stakes involved in the Coca-Cola Company's decision to change the taste of Coke in early 1985 in its battles with Pepsi.

Attitudes are used for objective setting, strategic decision making, and evaluating performance in advertising. A range of attitudes can be identified for a brand that has been on the market for a short period. Figure 6-3 suggests that seven attitude segments might be identified for the brand, ranging from segment 1, holding strong negative attitudes, through segment 4, holding neither positive nor negative attitudes, to segment 7, holding strong positive attitudes. The tails of the distribution represent attitude extremes. The majority fall in the middle segments, holding slight tendencies in either direction or no *predisposition* one way or another with respect to the brand. These segments represent alternative targets for an advertising campaign.

Segment 7 might represent a small group of relatively heavy users who have become satisfied with the brand and are strongly loyal to it. Attitude in this case could be a measure of brand loyalty. We would expect this group to express strong positive feelings to back up their behavior and purchasing patterns.

Segment 4, on the other hand, could hold no attitude for our brand for at least two reasons. First, it represents people who do not yet know that our brand exists. They have not learned of it from our advertising, from friends, or by any chance use

Figure 6-3.   **Attitude segments for a hypothetical brand**

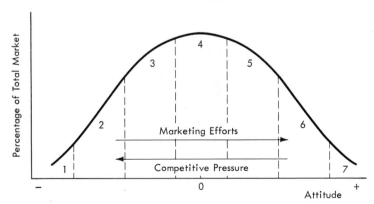

experience. Such people have not yet entered the *awareness* stage. Second, some people in this segment could be aware of the brand but be so uninvolved in purchasing with respect to the product class that no meaningful direction of predisposition exists. They could purchase it on one occasion but just as easily choose another brand on another occasion. Another representation of such consumers is to say that they see no meaningful differences in the brand choices available: their choice process is essentially random with respect to this product class, although it may not be with respect to others.

Segment 1 represents a small group of buyers who probably confine their purchases to other competitive brands in the class, and reject ours. In other words, our brand is not in their *consideration class* or *evoked set* of alternatives from which they make a choice, even though they are aware of it. Their negative attitudes could be based on a host of reasons, many of which are sustained by our competitors.

This viewpoint is also useful in suggesting the basic problem that a new brand faces in entering a market. In many respects, it enters at stage 4, in which most people are unaware of its existence. Attitudes toward it can subsequently develop in either a positive or negative direction. It is obvious which direction is in the advertiser's interests.

Figure 6-3 also suggests that the basic objective of advertising is to move people in the positive direction, as shown by the arrow. For positive segments, the objective will be to sustain positive attitudes. For neutral and negative segments, it will be to change these states to positive. As suggested in previous chapters, which objective becomes emphasized is heavily governed by the length of time a brand has been on the market and its market share. A well-established brand with a large market share is likely best represented by an attitude distribution skewed to the right—a high proportion of positive people relative to the total market. In such circumstances, emphasis will be placed on the sustaining function. A well-established brand with a small share of market might be represented by a distribution skewed to the left—a relatively high proportion of negative or neutral people. In these circumstances, the best strategy need not, however, be an attempt to shift such people into the market. It might rather be sensible to concentrate on the relatively small segment to which the brand is appealing and "serve it well."

In any of these situations, an argument can be made for continuing to engage in advertising to sustain or change attitudes for two fundamental reasons. First, attitudes decay over time. Just as a good friend can be forgotten when not around, so a good brand can be forgotten unless effort is expended to keep its name before the public. Longman[5] has suggested that there is in fact a market threshold of attitude below which the customer is likely not to choose the brand. The attitude objective of advertising thus can be viewed as the maintenance of a level of customer attitude above this point. The rate of decay and the number of insertions necessary to sustain the threshold level are questions to be examined in later chapters.

The second reason is that in most market situations competitors are constantly attempting to create favorable attitudes for their brands at the expense of our own.

In terms of Figure 6-3, there is in effect a constant force operating in the opposite direction, as shown by the opposing arrow, a force that attempts to pull our customers away—in attitude terms, to change their attitude for our brand from positive to negative. Again, as has been stated, many advertising objectives are thus couched in terms of competition, and use is made of advertising to prevent the inroads of competition.

The use of advertising to sustain or change attitudes is generally considered a long-run objective: to build a long-run franchise of satisfied customers generally resistant to competitive attack who will "'remember'' our brand when the purchase opportunity arises. Advertising accomplishes this goal when some meaningful and relatively stable positive attitude can be identified, supported, of course, by all other relevant components of the marketing mix—a good product, good distribution, and a good price. In such circumstances, purchases of competitive alternatives to take advantage of a price or dealing offer may be regarded as only temporary adjustments that do not change the basic attitude.

Figure 6-4 shows an eye-catching pictorial display combined with an effective headline and detailed copy in an advertisement for the Grumman Aerospace Corporation. The objectives of the campaign in which it appeared were to create a more favorable attitude toward management and company products and services among financial, business, and government audiences. Figure 6-5 provides an example from the consumer products area. The dramatic picture and headline draw attention to the brand and its sponsors by inviting the reader to consider the question of dental hygiene and the use of Crest in fighting cavities. Such advertising can reinforce current users of the brand and can facilitate generation of favorable attitudes among those who have not yet tried it.

IMPORTANCE OF ATTRIBUTES

Although an advertiser can glean much useful information from knowing the market's attitude for his or her brand, it is equally or more important to know what lies behind those attitudes. Basically, what are the strengths and weaknesses of the brand and what are the important criteria or attributes on which decision making is based? Particularly significant is the identification of the one or the few attributes used by consumers to choose between brands that are relatively similar or, as some would say, "functionally equivalent."

In most cases, copy development will focus on one or a few attributes. Competition for the consumer's attention is usually so intense that it is only possible to get one or a few ideas across, and it thus becomes crucial to identify the attribute (or the few attributes) that are most important in consumer decision making. Should a toothpaste manufacturer, for example, focus on decay prevention, bright teeth, fresh breath, or perhaps the taste of the product? Would a university be better off stressing the international reputation of its faculty, the physical environment in which it resides, or some exceptional aspect of its teaching or research programs?

Figure 6-4.   **An energy-associated advertisement by an industrial goods manufacturer**

Courtesy of Grumman Aerospace Corporation.

Many of the questions reviewed in the last chapter concerning which positioning strategy to adopt can be reduced to ''which attribute(s) is most important in a given purchasing or choice situation?'' More precisely, these questions are ones of identifying the attributes that are most important in attitude formation and change and ultimately in the purchase-choice decision itself.

Figure 6-5. **An appeal to the importance of dental hygiene for a consumer goods product**

Teeth don't die a natural death. You kill them.

©1983, The Procter & Gamble Company

Chances are, when you lose a tooth, it's because you killed it with neglect. By not eating the right foods, or seeing the dentist often enough, or brushing properly.

Such neglect can lead to cavities, and cavities can lead to tooth loss.

In fact, the average person loses 6 to 9 teeth in a lifetime *simply* due to cavities.

Crest with fluoride fights cavities. So, besides seeing your dentist and watching treats, make sure you brush with Crest.

Because the more you fight cavities, the less your teeth have to fight for their lives.

Fighting cavities is the whole idea behind Crest.

"Crest has been shown to be an effective decay-preventive dentifrice that can be of significant value when used in a conscientiously applied program of oral hygiene and regular professional care." Council on Dental Therapeutics, American Dental Association.

Courtesy of Procter & Gamble Company.

Every product, service, or choice situation has associated with it a set of attributes on which the choices are made. In the case of choosing betwen Coke and Pepsi, for example, taste is likely to be very important. On the other hand, taste will not be important in choosing between brands of fishing rods. Attributes can be psychological rather than physical (size) or sensory (taste). Thus, where two brands are very similar on physical or sensory attributes, more attention may have to be put on less tangible characteristics such as creating a "warm feeling" for the brand, or associating it with desirable people, and these become the important attributes. What is fundamental is that there is an important or *salient* set of attributes for every choice situation, and the identification of this set is the advertiser's first task. The size of the set is likely to vary with the complexity of the product and the importance of the decision involved. Because of limits on human information processing, it is unlikely that over seven attributes are used in most decision making. In other terms, people tend to compare alternatives using a relatively small set of characteristics, attributes, or benefits as the basis for comparison.

An important attribute is one that is considered an important benefit toward the satisfaction of needs and wants that the product is to fulfill. Obviously, some attributes within the target set will be more important than others. However, an attribute may be important, but buyers may perceive all brands to be virtually identical with respect to that attribute and thus the attribute does not affect decision making. A buyer, for example, may consider power steering to be an important and essential requirement in the next car purchase, but if all the cars being considered at the time the decision is made have power steering, this feature could really not be considered a cause of the final choice. Airline safety is another example. Safety may be the most important airline characteristic, but all major airlines are perceived to be equally safe (or unsafe). Attributes on which product offerings are perceived to differ and which are considered important are called *determinant attributes* because they will often be determinant in final choice decisions. Thus, the identification of important attributes is a necessary step, but the advertiser should be sensitive to the possibility that an important attribute may not be determinant.

IDENTIFYING IMPORTANT ATTRIBUTES

A great many methods, approaches, and techniques have been developed to identify and determine the relative importance of the set of attributes on which brands are perceived and evaluated. In some cases, the relevant set of attributes will be known from past experience with the product category or past research with similar brands. In others, the first task will be to conduct research designed to reveal the attribute set itself. Once this set has been found, other procedures for developing specific measures or *importance weights* on each attribute can be used.

Suppose an advertiser faces a situation in which very little is known about how buyers choose among alternatives. How can the relevant attribute set be identified? Procedures such as the Kelly repertory grid[6] and factor analysis, reviewed in

Chapter 5, can be used. Jacoby and others[7] developed an extension of the repertory grid that uses an information display board. Analysis procedures have been developed that allow the ordering of the attributes identified in this way on the basis of their importance.[8]

Once the set of attributes has been identified, the problem of identifying which of them are more or less important can be addressed. In particular, the advertiser needs a specific measure of the importance of each attribute in the set. Various forms of attribute rating and ranking instruments can be used to obtain judgments about the attributes themselves. Also, methods called *conjoint analysis,* which give respondents *levels* of each attribute to consider, are employed. Examples of these various approaches are presented in the next sections.

Rating and Ranking

Attributes, rather than brands or objects, can be the focus of research, and procedures similar to those used for measuring overall attitude given earlier applied to measure attribute importance. The most straightforward ranking approach is simply to ask consumers to rank a list of attributes in order of importance. This is much like voting data in political elections, and the attributes that receive the most "votes" are considered to be the most important.

The most straightforward rating method, which has the advantage of ease of understanding and administration, is to present the attributes as a list with a Very Important-Very Unimportant scale alongside each. The consumer simply checks the appropriate scale position in each case according to how important the particular attribute is in the purchase decision. A modification of this procedure is to use a Likert scale. In this case, statements such as "It would be very important for me to know whether the next tire I purchased was steel-belted or nylon-belted" are developed. The respondents are asked to record the degree to which they Agree or Disagree with each such statement.

The direct rating and ranking methods, particularly those which ask in a straightforward way the degree of importance of each attribute, are comparatively inexpensive and easy to administer. The argument is that, if some attributes are included that are unimportant, this will simply show up in the final data analysis. A problem, of course, is that consumers are prone to want "everything" and tend to reflect these desires by rating everything as important. Most products are in effect trade-offs of desirable attributes, and the direct methods tend not to uncover these trade-offs. What the advertiser really wants to know is the degree to which consumers are willing to trade off one desirable feature in favor of another.

Another problem with the direct methods is that they do not specify what really is meant by "more" or "less" of an attribute. The respondent is presented with the attribute only, and not *levels* of the attribute. Much interest has thus been generated in methods designed to *recover* importance weights from data generated by presenting respondents with combinations of attribute levels. As a group, these procedures are known as conjoint analysis or conjoint measurement. The next section reviews some of the major types of conjoint analysis and how importance weights are derived using this approach.

Conjoint Analysis

The goal of conjoint analysis is to derive importance weights of the attributes and attribute levels; this is similar to that of the ranking-rating methods, but the procedures differ in how the data are collected and analyzed. In all versions of the technique, the consumer is asked to make trade-offs between various attributes, all of which may be seen as desirable. The two major approaches are called *trade-off analysis* and the *full-profile approach.*

Figure 6-6 gives an example of a stimulus card used in each approach for a study of automobile tires in which five attributes, brand, tread life, sidewall, price, and type of belting, were involved.

In the trade-off approach, the consumer would be asked to fill in 10 cards, like the one shown to the left, for each pair of attributes and levels taken two at a time. The task is to rank the preferred combinations (in this case Goodyear and 50,000 miles) from most to least preferred. The trade-offs really take place in the middle rankings. Here, for example, tread life is very important because the consumer prefers to have the same high amount of tread life and is willing to switch to other brands to get it, rather than choose as second place Goodyear at a lower tread life.

Figure 6-6. **Examples of stimulus cards used in trade-off and full-profile approaches of conjoint analysis**

I. Trade-Off Approach

	TREAD LIFE		
BRAND	30,000 Miles	40,000 Miles	50,000 Miles
Goodyear	8	4	1*
Goodrich	12	9	5
Michelin	11	7	3
Brand X	10	6	2

1* Denotes best-liked combination

II. Full-Profile Approach

Brand: Brand X
Tread Life: 50,000 Miles
Sidewall: White on Black
Price: $55
Type of Belt: Steel Belted Radial

Respondent Rating?

7

Least Liked								Most Liked
1	2	3	4	5	6	7	8	9

Scale Board

Source: Patrick J. Robinson, "Applications of Conjoint Analysis to Pricing Problems," in David B. Montgomery and Dick R. Wittink, eds., *Market Measurement and Analysis* (Cambridge, Mass.: Marketing Science Institute, 1980), p. 185.

In the full-profile approach shown to the right, the rater sees all the attributes at once rather than two at a time. The difference between cards in this case is between the levels of the attributes being considered.

Various computer analysis routines can be used to derive importance weights from the data generated by either procedure. Figure 6-7 shows the first type of result. In this study, for example, respondents valued long tread wear (80,000 miles) and low price ($40) very highly in comparison with whether sidewalls were a particular color or even the tire brand. Also, as can be seen, whether the tire is steel-belted or fiberglass appears to make a significant difference. Respondents value steel-belted much more than fiberglass.

The overall importance of each attribute can be derived from such data. Figure 6-8 shows the results in this study. As can be seen, price and tread life are the most important attributes in the set of five attributes tested, whereas type of belt, brand, and sidewalls follow in that order.

A significant advantage of conjoint measurement is that new combinations of attributes, and hence judgments about the relative attractiveness of new "products" can be derived from the data. By knowing how important each level of an attribute is, the researcher can combine various levels and derive the overall value of the new combination. Obviously, the most important level of each attribute will generate the best overall product, but this may not be economically feasible to produce. The real question is what combination is both feasible and desirable. Table 6-1 shows examples of this extension for the tire study. As can be seen, a Goodrich, white on black, steel-belted tire that will last 50,000 miles and cost about $70 is the preferred alternative. It has more *total utility* for respondents in this study than a much lower-priced Michelin with fiberglass belts and a 30,000-mile tread life.

Ranking, rating, and conjoint analysis procedures are most useful for deriving importance weights on a set of attributes as well as providing the advertiser with many additional insights into feasible brand and product combinations. Whether such attributes do in fact determine attitudes and ultimate brand purchases is the subject of the next section.

Leverage and Determinant Attributes

Are the attributes identified by consumers as important really the ones that affect their attitudes and brand choices? This is the question of research in the area of leverage and determinant attributes. We want to know whether the attributes derived in any of the ways just described really make a difference when it comes to overall brand attitudes, preferences, and choices.

An attribute that has high leverage is one that has a high degree of influence on overall attitude. Its influence may derive from its importance to individuals in their attitude structure, the attribute weight. However, its influence may not be totally reflected by the importance weight. It is not unlikely that one attribute affects another in a cognitive structure. Thus, a communication that affects perception or

Figure 6-7.   **Importance of attribute levels in a study of automobile tires**

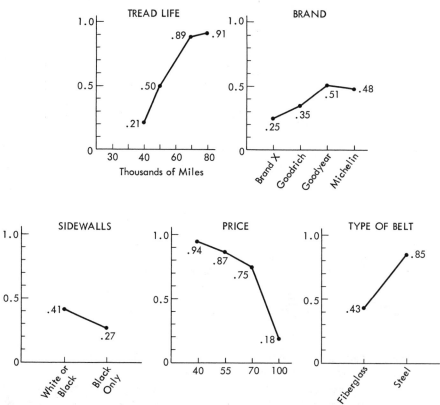

Source: Patrick J. Robinson, "Applications of Conjoint Analysis," in David B. Montgomery and Dick R. Wittink, eds., *Market Measurement and Analysis* (Cambridge, Mass.: Marketing Science Institute, 1980), p. 186.

belief along one attribute might have a significant indirect effect on other attributes and thus on the attitude structure. For example, an attribute like styling may have high leverage not only because the consumer values it highly (and by itself) with respect to a product class, but also because it may affect evaluations on other attributes like performance and convenience. Thus a change in brand perception on the styling dimension may affect perception with respect to performance and convenience, and therefore have a stronger influence on attitude than might at first be suspected. If styling is, for some reason, the foundation for performance and convenience, a change in either of the latter may not have a similar effect on styling.

The concept of leverage is similar to the question of what are really the keys to the success of a football team. One might be the highly visible quarterback or halfback who is an outstanding athlete. Another might be the unnoticed captain of the special teams (kickoff squad, punt-return unit), or an interior lineman. Such an

Figure 6-8.   **Overall attribute importance in the automobile tires study**

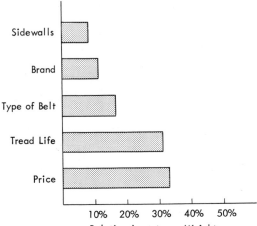

Relative Importance Weights

Source: Patrick J. Robinson, "Applications of Conjoint Analysis," in David B. Montgomery and Dick R.
Wittink, eds., *Market Measurement and Analysis*
(Cambridge, Mass.: Marketing Science Institute,
1980), p. 186.

individual by himself may not have an obvious or well-publicized influence on the
team's fortunes, but he may have a decisive impact due to his influence on others.
In our context the practical question is, how does one move an individual with
respect to an intervening variable called attitude? Are there one or perhaps two
attributes on which the entire cognitive structure rests that, if changed, result in the
most significant change in overall attitude? The concept of leverage is really an

Table 6-1.   **Relative Utility Scores of Possible Product Configurations**

	TIRE 1	*TIRE 2*	*TIRE 3*
Sidewalls	(0.41) White on black	(0.41) White on black	(0.41) White on black
Brand	(0.48) Michelin	(0.35) Goodrich	(0.51) Goodyear
Construction	(0.43) Fiberglass belted	(0.85) Steel-belted	(0.85) Steel-belted
Tread life	(0.21) 30,000 miles	(0.89) 50,000 miles	(0.91) 70,000 miles
Price	(0.94) $40	(0.75) $70	(0.18) $100
Total utility	2.47	3.25	2.86

Source: Patrick J. Robinson, "Applications of Conjoint Analysis," in David B. Montgomery and Dick
R. Wittink, eds., *Market Measurement and Analysis* (Cambridge, Mass.: Marketing Science Institute,
1980), p. 187.

untested hypothesis at this point, which has potential for providing significant insight for creative strategy.[9]

One approach to measuring leverage might be to measure the strength of the cognitive link between one attribute and others. An attribute that is independent and not "connected" to other attributes might be considered to have no influence beyond that represented by its importance weights. Another attribute that seemed closely intertwined with other attributes (tends to have strong cognitive association) might have more leverage than is reflected by its importance weights. Research is needed to operationally define cognitive links and how they can be measured.

Another more direct approach to measuring leverage might be to systematically alter the perception of a brand on a dimension and observe the change on the overall attitude scale. Attributes that had the greatest impact on overall attitude would be those with the highest leverage.

Another approach is to obtain evaluative beliefs on a set of attributes and correlate these with brand attitude scores or buying intentions. The attributes with the highest correlations are considered to have the highest amount of leverage and are called *determinant attributes*.

Myers and Alpert[10] examined correlations of five attributes of a snack mix with a measure of overall attitude and buying intention. The new snack food was placed in 200 homes in the Los Angeles area, and homemakers were asked to serve it to families and friends. After serving, they were asked to rate the snack food in terms of color, appearance, taste, strength of flavor, and spiciness. Overall opinion (attitude) and buying intention measures were also obtained. The correlations (a number between -0.1 and $+0.1$ that indicates the degree of association) between these scales are given in Table 6-2. Of the five product attributes, taste has a much higher positive correlation with buying intention. Not only was taste by far the best predictor of buying intention, but it was a better predictor than overall attitude. Taste is obviously important in judging a snack food, but it may not be a useful criterion for distinguishing one brand of snack food from another.[11]

The Grey Advertising Agency has applied a similar conceptual approach by using different data collection and analysis procedures in well over 20 studies of attitudes and product usage over an 8-year period. Their studies have involved

Table 6-2. **Correlation Matrix of Product Ratings for Snack Mix**

	1	2	3	4	5	6	7
1. Overall opinion		0.325	0.209	0.782	-0.324	-0.313	0.609
2. Color			0.498	0.308	-0.045	-0.099	0.189
3. Appearance				0.260	0.006	-0.133	0.036
4. Taste					-0.172	-0.161	0.617
5. Strength of flavor						0.759	-0.092
6. Spiciness							-0.084
7. Buying intention							

Source: James H. Myers, "Finding Determinant Buying Attitudes," *Journal of Advertising Research,* 10, December 1970, p. 11.

relatively large (over 1,000 subjects) well-developed samples and explicit consideration of object (brand) differences, and thus have an impressive credibility. The procedure essentially begins with developing a large attribute list for the product class. For example, 40 attributes were used in a study of women's hosiery, and as many as 130 in a study of general merchandise stores. Importance weights are obtained for each attribute. The attribute list is then reduced via factor analysis to a smaller set of relevant dimensions that account for most of the variance in the data. Evaluative beliefs are then obtained for brands in the product class with respect to this set of dimensions. Respondents are also asked to express their overall feelings for each brand along a poor-to-excellent scale. The final data input is thus a set of dimension and overall attitude ratings of each brand by each respondent. Brands are selected two-at-a-time from the brand set, differences in dimension and overall ratings are calculated, and the correlation of these difference scores between dimensions and overall attitude is examined. Subsequent dimensions are then put through a similar analysis. Those dimensions that correlate most highly with overall attitude are considered to be those with the highest leverage.

Achenbaum,[12] in describing the Grey approach, points out that it has in many practical situations provided information useful for product development and packaging, as well as advertising. In general, it is a diagnostic tool for understanding why particular attitude states exist. He provides an interesting summary of general findings from many replications of the procedure:

1.   No one set of specific attributes is universally applicable to all products. Each product category has its own unique set of factors by which people evaluate the desirability of the product. They range in number from 5 to 18—the mean being 10.

2.   In every case studied, the product either provided more than one functional benefit or the functional benefit was multidimensional.

3.   Nonfunctional benefits came up in every case, many of which rarely showed up when using traditional questioning techniques.

4.   Certain factors, like safety, although relevant, rarely had competitive leverage among the major brands rated. Presumably most consumers consider the major brands to be safe to use although this may not be the case with some of the less well-known brands.

5.   Attitude factors that count with people did not always reveal themselves in terms of specific benefits. Often, some product attribute takes on such importance or provides so many diverse benefits that it is considered intrinsically desirable in itself—for example, menthol in a cigarette or whether a shampoo is a cream or a liquid.

6.   Some benefits were more likely to be stated in terms of the way the product performed than the specific benefits it provided. For example, people talked about the ease of opening, carrying, or storing a paper product, rather than the benefit of convenience, although all three performance qualities are concerned with convenience.

7.   Although considerable variation was found among products, on the basis

of one or two specific attempts to replicate the procedure using the same product category, there is considerable stability in results by time and location and by groups of consumers.[13]

The question of the connection between attributes and attitudes is further complicated by the fact that not just importance weights but also beliefs about a particular brand or object should be taken into account. A consumer, for example, may feel that the attribute MPG is very important, but that a Volvo gets very poor miles per gallon. A negative attitude for Volvo, in this case, would not result from a lack of importance of the attribute, but rather from the consumer's perception (belief) that this car did not possess the right amount of it.

Attitude models bring together the belief and importance-weight components. Also, as we will see, they draw attention to the fact that in most choice situations not only are multiattributes involved, but also multiobjects.

ATTITUDE MODELS

There are dozens of models and theories about the connection between perception and preference or attributes and attitudes. In economics, for example, a long tradition of utility theory and associated models exists that essentially deals with this question. In social psychology, they are often referred to as evaluative-belief models to emphasize that attitudes are the product of both evaluations of the attributes and beliefs about how much of the attributes are possessed by the attitude object.

Paralleling the development of evaluative-belief models and procedures has been a class of models that depend on deriving the attitude measure from a knowledge of the consumer's *ideal point*. Brands or objects that are closest to the ideal point are considered most preferred, and those farthest away, least preferred. The focus is first on locating the ideal point, and then deriving attitudes for each object as a function of the distance from this point.

In this section, the basic principles underlying each of these model classes are presented and assessed. An impressively large amount of research has been done to test their validity. Much of it has to do with the basic question of whether attributes, beliefs, and perceptions are related to attitudes and subsequent behavior.

Evaluative Belief Models

Evaluative belief models assume that overall attitudes can be derived by adding up the buyer's beliefs about each component or attribute of the brand. The respondent does not provide explicit information concerning his or her "ideal" brand. Rather, attention focuses on beliefs about the real brand alternatives under consideration. In the simplest of these models, no account is taken of the importance of each attribute. The assumption is that in revealing beliefs about the brand the respondent implicitly includes attribute importance. The beliefs are thus called *evaluative beliefs*. A good example of evaluative beliefs was presented in Chapter 5 in connection with the beer brands study reported by Mindak. Recall that brand X was rated as more relaxing, refreshing, and so on, than either brands Y or Z. The ratings in each case are measures of evaluative belief. The attitude for brand X would simply be the summation of all these scores across the nine attributes used.

We can formalize this procedure as a model of brand attitude. Let a_{iod} refer to an evaluative belief of individual (or group), i, for object, o, on attribute, d. The first model is thus

$$A_{io}^{(1)} = \frac{1}{D} \sum_{d=1}^{D} a_{iod} \tag{1}$$

where $A_{io}^{(1)}$ = attitude of individual (or group) i toward object o given attitude model 1

a_{iod} = evaluation of individual (or group) i toward object o with respect to attribute d

d = index of attributes, $d = 1, \ldots, D$

i = index of individuals or groups, $i = 1, \ldots, I$

o = index of objects, $o = 1, \ldots, o$

The superscript (1) is included to distinguish this attitude model from others that will be introduced as the discussion proceeds.

Another example of evaluative beliefs is represented in the following set of ratings for a car such as the Chevrolet Citation using a semantic differential instrument:

Good gas mileage	___:___:___:___: X :___:___	Poor gas mileage
Roomy	___: X :___:___:___:___:___	Cramped
Reliable	___:___: X :___:___:___:___	Unreliable

Scores ranging from $+3$ to -3 are then assigned. In this case, the evaluative belief scores would be

$$a_{io1} = -1$$
$$a_{io2} = 2$$
$$a_{io3} = 1$$

and the attitude for the Citation would be

$$A_{io}^{(1)} = \frac{2}{3} = 0.67$$

There are several other assumptions implicit in this attitude model. First, it is assumed that the list of attributes is relevant. This problem is illustrated by the motivation researcher's maxim, "People don't go to cocktail parties because they are thirsty.'' Sensory qualities like taste and smell may not be those most relevant to brand choice. In an industrial context the obvious attributes like speed or accuracy for an electronic counter may not be so influential on brand choice as some would assume. The determination of the relevant attribute list involves the same difficult theoretical and practical problems as those reviewed earlier.

It is further assumed that the measurement instrument used to obtain the subject's response along these attributes has an acceptable degree of validity (is it really measuring what it is supposed to and not something else?), reliability (if we repeated the experiment, would approximately the same results emerge?), and lack of reactivity (the instruments measure rather than influence the attitude structure).

Another assumption is that redundancy has been removed through factor analysis or a similar technique so that the resulting attributes are really measuring different things.

When the attitude is specified for a group rather than an individual, the attribute values, a_{iod}, are themselves averaged over those in the group. An implicit assumption is that the group is not excessively heterogeneous so that this average is representative of the total group, rather than only a small portion. The measuring instrument, even if adequate, is not going to measure an individual's evaluation along a dimension without some error. Furthermore, the individuals are by no means identical. Therefore, there will be dispersion. The assumption is that this dispersion does not dominate the results.

As suggested in the section on identifying important attributes, it is unlikely that all are equally important to all people. Assume that the relative importance of attribute d to individual or group i is known and defined as w_{id}. The w_{id} could be obtained by any of the methods presented earlier. The most widely accepted form of the weighted evaluative belief model is thus

$$A_{io}^{(2)} = \sum_{d=1}^{D} w_{id} \, a_{iod} \qquad (2)$$

where w_{id} = measure of the relative importance of attribute d to individual or group i
$A_{io}^{(2)}$ = attitude of individual (or group) i toward object o given attitude model 2[14]

The like-dislike polarity of the attributes used to measure them deserves special mention. A zero or neutral score is particularly ambiguous. Theoretically, it means that the respondent is neutral toward the brand with respect to that attribute. However, it could also mean she or he is too ill-informed to make a judgment. This possibility is related to the concept of attitude strength or stability. A value near zero on an attribute could also mean that it has zero weight. When the weighting factor is included explicitly, as it is in the second attitude model, the interpretation of the middle-scale position can be made more explicit.

A second aspect of the way the attributes are labeled is that there is an assumption that, if a little bit is good, a lot is better. Clearly, one must use care in applying such an assumption because it is easily possible to conceive of too much of certain attributes.

It might be reasonable to introduce the assumption that all individuals (or groups) in the population hold the same evaluation of the object on each attribute. Thus, the individual's (or group's) variation is restricted to the weights, w_{id}. The assumption would be that the population is heterogeneous with respect to the attributes that they consider important, but reasonably homogeneous with respect to their evaluations of the brand on each attribute. Symbolically, the assumption is

$$a_{iod} = a_{od} \qquad \text{for all } i \tag{3}$$

In a sense, the a_{iod} values might be interpreted as reflecting the perceptions that make up the brand images despite the fact that there is an evaluation present. If this is the case, the values would have to be combined with independent measures of importance weights to generate an attitude measure.

A similar assumption was discussed in Chapter 5. The perceptions of the brands, the brand images, were assumed to be the same across individuals, but the location of the ideal points was permitted to vary widely.

Other Attitude Models

There are dozens of other attitude models that are elaborations of the basic evaluative belief model. Some, such as *ideal-point models*, rely on different approaches to data collection and an assumption that a particular combination of levels on each attribute can be found that represents a person's or total market's "ideal" combination. These models involve perceptual mapping and multidimensional scaling procedures reviewed in Chapter 5.[15] Given the importance of attitude in advertising and marketing, a great deal of research attention has been given to testing various models and evaluating their performance and reliability and validity.[16]

The unweighted (model 1) and weighted (model 2) belief models are examples of *compensatory models*. A low rating on one dimension can be compensated for by a high rating on another dimension. There are also a set of noncompensatory models that might be better in certain situations. Three such models are the conjunctive, disjunctive, and lexicographic. The conjunctive model emphasizes low ratings on the various attributes. An object will be deemed acceptable if it meets a minimum standard (a minimum a_{iod}) on each attribute. This process has been shown to operate in supermarket buying decisions. In one study,[17] new grocery products were considered for stocking only if they rated at least average in quality, company reputation, sales representation, and category volume, and were less than 110 percent of the cost of the closest substitute. If they failed to meet any of these criteria, they were excluded.

The disjunctive model stresses high ratings. It regards objects as positive only when they have been rated outstanding on one or more of the relevant attributes.

The lexicographic model assumes that an individual will evaluate the brand on the most salient attribute. If two or more brands "tie" on this attribute, the evaluation will shift to the second most salient attribute. The process will continue until a brand is selected.

It is quite possible that an individual in some contexts may use more than one model. He or she could, for example, use a conjunctive model to determine a set of brands to consider and then use a compensatory model to make the final decision. Clearly, the existence of such multimodel decision processes makes model evaluation more difficult.

SEGMENTATION REVISITED

Attitude models and their components provide the advertiser with additional ways to segment markets. Variation in evaluative beliefs, for example, can be used to identify groups of buyers who perceive brands in different ways. Also, the fact that buyers will tend to have different importance weights on a set of attributes leads logically to the fact that they represent different segments to which specific brands and advertising appeals can be directed.

Benefit Segmentation

The basic idea of segmenting on the basis of important attributes has been termed *benefit segmentation* by Russell Haley.[18] He illustrates the perspective by an analysis of the toothpaste market. Four segments are hypothesized, as shown in Table 6-3. The first is the Sensory segment, which values flavor and the appearance of the package. This segment tends to be represented by children characterized by high self-involvement and hedonistic life-style. Colgate and Stripe do well in this segment. This segment should have high importance weights on a dimension reflecting flavor and appearance and tend to prefer brands whose product and advertising strategies have emphasized these dimensions.

The second segment, termed the Sociables, contains those who are interested in the brightness of their teeth. They are largely young people in their teens or early twenties who lead active lives and are very social. They have a relatively large percentage of smokers in their midst. Macleans, Plus White, and Ultra Brite are big sellers in this segment.

The benefit sought by the third segment is that of decay prevention. A high proportion of this segment has large families who tend to be heavy toothpaste users. In general, they have a conservative life-style and show concern for health and dental hygiene. Crest is disproportionately favored by this segment, which is termed the Worriers.

The fourth segment, the Independent segment, is made up of people oriented toward price and value. It tends to include men who are heavy toothpaste users.

Table 6-3. Toothpaste Market Segment Description

CHARACTERISTICS	SENSORY SEGMENT	SOCIABLES	WORRIERS	INDEPENDENT SEGMENT
Principal benefit sought	Flavor, product appearance	Brightness of teeth	Decay prevention	Price
Demographic strengths	Children	Teens, young people	Large families	Men
Special behavioral characteristics	Users of spearmint-flavored toothpaste	Smokers	Heavy users	Heavy users
Brands disproportionately favored	Colgate, Stripe	Macleans, Plus White, Ultra Brite	Crest	Brand on sale
Personality characteristics	High self-involvement	High sociability	High health	High autonomy
Life-style characteristics	Hedonistic	Active	Conservative	Value-oriented

Source: Adapted from Russell I. Haley, "Benefit Segmentation: A Decision-Oriented Research Tool," *Journal of Marketing,* 32, July 1968, p. 33.

They probably have a high degree of autonomy, are concerned with obtaining good value in all their purchases, and tend to be attracted to whatever brand is on sale.

The value of benefit segmentation for advertising is seen by considering the different advertising approaches that will be appropriate for each segment. The copy should probably be light for the Sociable or Sensory segments but more serious for the others. The setting could also be adjusted; the focus should probably be on the product for the Sensory group, on a social situation for the Sociable segment, and perhaps on a laboratory demonstration for the Independent segment. Similarly, the media to be used can be selected with the particular target segment in mind. Television might be more appropriate for the Sociables and the Sensory segment, where there is less need to communicate hard information. A serious rational argument, possibly supported by clinical evidence, might appeal to the Independent group, assuming that such an argument can demonstrate value. A long, print advertisement, therefore, might be appropriate for this segment.

Haley has speculated on the possibility of generalizing benefit segmentation across product categories. Some of the following, he suggests, may appear as market segments across almost all product and service categories, although there is no guarantee that they will, and it is the purpose of the analysis to discover them:

1. *The Status Seeker:* a group that is very much concerned with the prestige of the brand purchased.
2. *The Swinger:* a group that tries to be modern and up-to-date in all of its activities. Brand choices reflect this orientation.
3. *The Conservative:* a group that prefers to stick to large successful companies and popular brands.
4. *The Rational Man:* a group that looks for benefits such as economy, value, durability, and so forth.
5. *The Inner-Directed Man:* a group that is especially concerned with self-concept. Members consider themselves to have a sense of humor, to be independent, and/or honest.
6. *The Hedonist:* a group that is concerned primarily with sensory benefits.[19]

A NORMATIVE MODEL

A normative model is one that provides the advertising manager with a formal mechanism for choosing among alternatives. Such a model was introduced in Chapter 4. Recall that it was discussed in the context of an example involving the intervening variables of awareness, buying class, consideration class, and first choice. These variables were developed in connection with a study for one of the automotive divisions of General Motors. The issue was, in part, if these intervening variables defined market segments, which one should be the target of advertising? The model used a basic procedure that is applicable in other situations. First, the behavioral goal and its worth needed to be specified. In that example, the goal was a car purchase, and its value was the profit margin on a car. Second, the link between the intervening variable and the behavioral goal had to be specified. In the example, the impact of moving an individual from one hierarchy level to another (for example, from consideration class to first choice) on the purchase probability was developed. Third, the cost of moving the segment from one level to the next must be explicitly considered. This cost will depend on the difficulty of the communication or persuasion task—on whether people can be moved from one level to another and, if so, how efficiently it can be done.

It will be useful to illustrate these principles when an attitude model provides the intervening variable on which the advertising objectives are to be based. Suppose that the goal was to increase the positive attitude of current users of a brand of aerosol furniture cleaner. This attitude might be reflected in relatively high repeat purchase and brand loyalty patterns of an identifiable group of users. Suppose, further, that model 2 is operative and that two relevant dimensions, cleaning power and convenience, have been identified on which the mean values of the importance weights, w_{id}, for segment i are 0.5 for each dimension. Let us assume that users rate the brand slightly negative on cleaning power and quite positive on convenience. These ratings could be scaled so that $a_{io1} = 3$ and $a_{is2} = 7$ for cleaning power and convenience, respectively. Another assumption could be that the brand is sharing top rating with another aerosol brand on the convenience dimension, and is just behind two other brands of, say, nonaerosol cleaners on the cleaning power dimension. Thus, the $A_{io}^{(2)}$ value for the set of buyers is 5.0. With this background we can proceed.

The first step is to determine the value of the desired behavioral action. An increase in loyalty as measured by brand-switching patterns might reasonably be expected to result in a profit level in the one-year period following an advertising campaign of 20 percent more than the profit level would be without the increase in loyalty. The second stage is to provide a link between the desired behavior and the intervening variable, attitude. Suppose that the current loyalty level is associated with an $A_{io}^{(2)}$ value of 5.0, and it is believed that an increase in the $A_{io}^{(2)}$ value to 6.0 would generate the higher loyalty level. The economic value of accomplishing that objective would be the 20 percent increase in profits.

The problem could then reduce to a choice between alternative advertising strategies: should cleaning power or convenience, or perhaps both, be stressed? Let us further assume that it were known that through advertising the evaluative belief rating on cleaning power could be raised two points, from 3.0 to 5.0 (perhaps by using a demonstration appeal), or that the importance weight on the convenience dimension could be raised from 0.5 to 0.65 (possibly by showing how important it is to clean hard-to-reach places). In this case, the selection of the optimal strategy alternative would depend on an estimate of the cost of the campaign required to implement it. The campaign that would be least costly would be selected, assuming that its cost was less than the expected value to be achieved when the objective is reached.

To fix the procedure, another example will be considered. In this case, the behavioral objective will be to minimize the number of high school students who start smoking cigarettes. Again assume that attitude model 2 is operative, and that the probability of smoking is below 0.1 if a negative attitude of -4 is developed. If, on the other hand, the attitude score is only -2, the probability of smoking becomes 0.2, or if the attitude score is 0, the probability of smoking is 0.3. Thus, if the attitude of a sizable group of high school students can be shifted from 0 to -4, then only 10 percent of that group will start smoking instead of 30 percent. If it is shifted to -2, the percentage who would start smoking would be 20 percent. Suppose, further, that either goal could be achieved by campaigns directed at the underlying attitude structure, but that a campaign that would generate an attitude level of -4 would cost three times as much as a campaign that would generate an attitude level of -2. In this case, the selection of the appropriate objective would depend on a judgment about the "value" of the end result and the availability of money to conduct the campaign. The objective selected would be specified in terms of the underlying structure, as well as in terms of the desired attitude score. Thus the objective might be to achieve an attitude level of -2 by attempting to engender an evaluative belief on a health dimension of -5 if the health dimension were shown to have such a relationship to overall attitude.

The process will not be quite so simple as these examples may have implied. The models in this chapter have provided a link between image and certain elements of attitude structure and the overall attitude rating. However, as has been shown, even the establishment of this link involves complex conceptual and measurement problems. The problem is compounded because a decision maker must also develop the link among the advertising, its effects on the attitude value, and ultimately its effects on the desired behavior. It is important to recognize that there is a distinction between finding a good strategy and executing it. The models developed in these chapters are most useful for the first of these tasks. Questions of how attitudes can be changed and how copy and advertising programs are executed will be dealt with in subsequent chapters.

The point is that such links need to be forged, and they are often difficult to substantiate with hard empirical evidence. Even estimating the costs of the campaign to accomplish the alternative objective is a difficult task. Ideally, a specific copy and media plan would be developed to provide the basis for cost estimates. However, at the objective-setting stage of the decision process, cost estimates must be made based on very crude ideas of what it might take to achieve each alternative objective. The normative model we have discussed, however, provides the decision maker with an analytical approach that is basically both sound and rich and applicable to a wide variety of decision-making situations.

SUMMARY

Attitude is a central concept in social psychology and has become, perhaps, the most significant focus of study in the fields of advertising management and consumer behavior. The most well-accepted view is that attitude is made up of three interrelated components called cognitive, affective, and conative. There are numerous approaches to attitude measurement, but they can be broadly classified into those that involve direct measures and those that involve derived measures.

Direct measures involve questioning or observations of respondent behavior in which no explicit attribute criterion concerning the attitude object(s) is provided the respondent. Derived measures rely on assessing an attitude state by examining patterns of subject response concerning the attitude object(s) and usually involve a set of attribute criteria. Derived measures can thus be viewed as various types of attitude models, and an assessment can be made of which type of approach or model is most appropriate to use in a given market situation.

A market can be segmented on the basis of varying degrees of attitude—positive, neutral, and negative—held by customers or potential customers of a brand. Advertising objectives can then be cast in attitude terms with respect to specific segments or the market as a whole. In general, the two broad classes of objectives from this viewpoint are to attempt changes in the market from some negative or neutral to some positive position, or to sustain and to maintain a positive attitude and avoid attitude decay. Competition in this context is a force attempting to shift attitudes in the opposite direction.

Although knowing the overall market attitude for his or her brand is very useful for the advertiser, it is equally significant to identify the reasons for the attitude. In other terms, the advertiser needs to know what attributes are important in the product-market situation, and in particular which of them are determinant in brand choice. In many situations, the first task will be to identify the relevant set of attributes. Several procedures for doing this have been developed. Specific importance weights on each attribute can then be derived by rating, ranking, and conjoint analysis methods. Leverage and determinant attribute research can be used to identify the attributes that appear to have the greatest leverage in affecting an attitude structure or are most closely related to brand choice and behavior.

Attributes, perceptions, and beliefs and their relation to overall attitudes have been formally studied in the context of attitude models. Two of the most well-known perspectives involved are the evaluative-belief and the ideal-point models. Such models are motivated both by the desirability of attempting to improve the methods for measuring attitude and by the needs of a strategist to know why a particular attitude state exists. The first two models depend on measures of a respondent's evaluative beliefs about the attitude object. Ratings of the strengths and weaknesses of various brands on a number of attributes are the basic input. The number and nature of the attributes thus become crucial points of focus in these two models. The first model simply states that the attitude of individual or group i toward object o is the average of all the positive and negative ratings made about it.

Model 2 extends this perspective by introducing attribute weights. A particular important or salient attribute might override other positive and negative evaluations. A respondent might be highly negative about a particular feature of a brand, for example, but if the feature is not important to him or her, this judgment should not dominate his or her overall attitude toward it. An implicit assumption is that if a little of the attribute is good, a lot is better. Considerable work has been done to evaluate these models, or variations of them, along a number of criteria.

It is possible to focus on the two central constructs of an attitude model, evaluative beliefs and importance weights, and perform a segmentation analysis useful for diagnostic purposes. Each construct provides a criterion for classifying consumers into different market segments that have important strategy implications. The term *benefit segmentation* has been used to refer to identifying market segments based on the differential importance that people place on the relative benefits offered by a product.

An advertising decision maker must be concerned with the predictive as well as the diagnostic utility of attitude models in setting objectives. She or he needs a normative perspective that assesses the economic value to the firm of an attitude shift. This includes considering both the long-run revenues that such a shift will generate and the advertising costs of accomplishing the shift. In the next chapter this perspective will be extended to the case in which the objective is to precipitate some type of explicit behavioral action.

DISCUSSION QUESTIONS

1. Discuss the strategy implications of a bimodal (two-humped) distribution of brand attitude rather than the distribution shown in Figure 6-3.

2. Day recommends the following seven-point scale for obtaining direct measures of brand attitude:
   1. This brand is the best that is available.
   2. I like this brand very much—but there's another just as good.
   3. I like this brand—but other brands are better.
   4. This brand is acceptable—but most other brands are better.
   5. I neither like nor dislike this brand—it doesn't have any particular merits.
   6. I don't like this brand very much—although it is not as bad as some.
   7. I don't like this brand at all—it is one of the worst available.

   Administer this scale to 20 to 30 friends using 5 to 10 brands in an appropriate product class. What are the shapes of the resulting distributions? What explanation could you offer for the shapes?

3. Discuss ways in which you could assess the strength (sometimes called the "valence") of an attitude. Is it true that a highly valenced attitude is always more stable than a weak one?

4. Compare and contrast the several methods used for identifying important attributes.

5. What fundamental assumption about belief-attitude relations underlies the "leverage" approaches to assessing the relative worth of alternative

attributes? Why might an attribute be regarded as important but have low leverage? How might leverage be determined?

6. If in model 1, the $1/D$ term were removed, the model would be a "summation" model instead of an "averaging" model. What rationale might there be for a summation model?

7. Conduct a small-scale study in which an averaging model is tested against a summation model using a direct attitude measure as the criterion variable.

8. Extend the study in question 7 to compare the utility of including "importance weights" in the model and a behavioral measure as a criterion variable.

9. Assume the following information is available to you concerning the locations of four cereal brands on the two attributes of sweetness and crunchiness:

	SWEETNESS	CRUNCHINESS
Brand A	2	-3
Brand B	-1	-2
Brand C	-4	5
Brand D	3	2

Calculate the segment's attitude for each brand using attitude model 1 given in the chapter. Rank the brands on this basis. Suppose that the importance weight for Sweetness was found to be 0.80 and for Crunchiness, 0.20, and calculate attitude using attitude model 2. How would this change the rankings? Assume that you are the manager of brand B. Discuss the implications of these results for product and advertising strategy.

10. Think of a product category that you can meaningfully relate to, perhaps something you have contemplated buying but have not gotten around to. What comes to mind first as you contemplate the purchase, the attributes you would like to have satisfied, or the brands that are available to satisfy them? Will all people tend to follow this processing sequence? If so, why? If not, why not?

11. Concerning the product category in Question 9, write down the attributes that are meaningful to you and assign importance weights to each. Compare your results with two or three friends doing the same exercise. What problems occur in developing "importance weights" in this fashion?

12. Concerning the exercise in Question 10, expand your discussion by considering the possibilities of a "step-function," a hurdle or boundary that exists within which the brand must lie for it to be considered a reasonable alternative. What impact, if any, is likely to arise from

postulating differences among people in the size of the evoked set of brands? At what point on a distance measure of brand attitude does the attitude turn from positive to negative, from predispositions to "approach" versus predispositions to "avoid," and so on? What is the meaning and/or location of the neutral point on such a scale?

NOTES

1. Gordon W. Allport, "Attitudes," in C. Murchison, ed., *Handbook of Social Psychology*, (Worcester, Mass.: Clark University Press, 1935). Reprinted in Martin Fishbein, ed., *Readings in Attitude Theory and Measurement* (New York: Wiley, 1967), p. 3.

2. George S. Day, *Buyer Attitudes and Brand Choice Behavior* (New York: Free Press, 1970), p. 160.

3. Alvin A. Achenbaum, "Knowledge Is a Thing Called Measurement," in Lee Adler and Irving Crespi, eds., *Attitude Research at Sea* (Chicago: American Marketing Association, 1966), pp. 111–126.

4. Ibid, p. 114.

5. Kenneth A. Longman, *Advertising* (New York: Harcourt Brace Jovanovich, 1971).

6. W. A. K. Frost and R. L. Braine, "The Application of the Repertory Grid Technique to Problems in Market Research," *Commentary*, 9, July 1967, pp. 161–175; and G. A. Kelly, *Psychology of Personal Constructs*, Vols. I and II (New York: W. W. Norton, 1955).

7. Jacob Jacoby, George J. Szybillo, and J. Busato-Schach, "Information-Acquisition Behavior in Brand Choice Situations," *Journal of Consumer Research*, 3, March 1977, pp. 209–216.

8. John A. Quelch, "Behavioral Measurement of the Relative Importance of Product Attributes: Process Methodology and Pilot Application," Working Paper 180R (London, Canada: School of Business Administration, University of Western Ontario, 1978).

9. John G. Myers and Francesco M. Nicosia, "Cognitive Structures, Latent Class Models, and the Leverage Index," paper presented at the Annual Meetings of the American Association for Public Opinion Research, Western Division, Santa Barbara, Calif., May 1968.

10. James H. Myers and Mark I. Alpert, "Determinant Buying Attitudes: Meaning and Measurement," *Journal of Marketing*, 32, October 1968, pp. 13–20.

11. Mark I. Alpert, "Identification of Determinant Attitudes: A Comparison of Methods," *Journal of Marketing Research*, 8, May 1971, pp. 184–191.

12. Achenbaum, "Knowledge Is a Thing Called Measurement."

13. Ibid., pp. 123–124.

14. The term 1/D has been absorbed by the w_{id} term. It could have been retained, but there is no benefit in doing so. This model corresponds to influential theories of attitude developed by Rosenberg and Fishbein. The basic postulate of these theories is that an attitude toward an object is a composite of the perceived instrumentality of that object to a person's goals, weighted by his or her evaluation of those goals. For discussions of these theories, see Milton J. Rosenberg, "Cognitive Structures and Attitudinal Affect," *Journal of Abnormal and Social Psychology*, 53, 1956, pp. 367–372; Martin Fishbein, "Attitude and the Prediction of Behavior," in Martin Fishbein, ed., *Readings in Attitude Theory and Measurement* (New York: Wiley, 1967), pp. 477–492; Martin Fishbein and B. H. Raven, "The A-B Scales; An Operational Definition of Belief and Attitude," *Human Relations*, 15, 1962, pp. 35–44; and Lynn R. Anderson and Martin Fishbein, "Prediction of Attitude from the Number, Strength, and Evaluative Aspect of Beliefs about the Attitude Object: A Comparison of Summation and Congruity Theories," *Journal of Personality and Social Psychology*, 3, 1965, pp. 437–443. An interesting marketing application can be found in Peter Sampson and Paul Harris, "A User's Guide to Fishbein," *Journal of the Market Research Society*, 12, July 1970, pp. 145–166.

15. For some classic papers on the foundations of the work in advertising, see Ledyard R. Tucker, "Intra-individual and Inter-individual Multidimensionality," in H. Gulliksen and S. Messick, eds., *Psychological Scaling: Theory and Applications* (New York: Wiley, 1960); C. H. Coombs, "Psychological Scaling without a Unit of Measurement," *Psychological Review*, 57, 1950, pp. 148–158; and J. F. Bennett and W. L. Hays, "Multidimensional Unfolding: Determining the Dimensionality of Ranked Preference Data," *Psychometrika*, 25, 1960, pp. 27–43.

16. Many of the evaluation issues are reviewed in William L. Wilkie and Edgar A. Pessemier, "Issues in Marketing's Use of Multi-attribute Attitude Models," *Journal of Marketing Research,* 10, November 1973, pp. 428–441.

17. David B. Montgomery, "New Product Distribution—An Analysis of Supermarket Buyer Decision," *Journal of Marketing Research,* 12, August 1975, pp. 255–264.

18. Russell I. Haley, "Benefit Segmentation: A Decision-Oriented Research Tool," *Journal of Marketing,* 32, July 1968, pp. 30–35.

19. Ibid., p. 35. For a follow-up study, see R. I. Haley, "Beyond Benefit Segmentation," *Journal of Advertising Research,* 11, August 1971, pp. 3–8.

7

Precipitating Action: Behavioral Objectives

The five basic rules for making advertising:
1. Make it clear (what the proposition is).
2. Make it complete (what the promise is).
3. Make it important.
4. Make it personal (who is the promise important to?).
5. Make it demanding (that some action be taken). (Fairfax Cone, Foote, Cone & Belding)

Advertising is a communication tool and in most cases it is advantageous to set objectives and measure results in terms of intervening variables like brand awareness, brand image, or attitude. However, these communication tasks are ultimately expected to create a behavioral response to the marketplace. This behavior could be a first purchase of a brand, a visit to a retailer's showroom, or simply the act of continuing to buy the brand. Without the ultimate behavioral response, advertising can become simply good or bad entertainment. Chapters 5 and 6 have discussed the link between communication goals and behavior. In this chapter the focus is on behavior. It is useful to examine behavior in more detail because it provides additional insight into the nature of the link between communication goals and behavior and because there are circumstances in which behavioral measures are appropriate bases for primary or secondary advertising objectives. These circumstances are particularly common in advertising involving retailing, direct mail, industrial contexts, and sales promotion. Our discussion of objectives is thus completed in this chapter by focusing on advertising's role in influencing behavior and how behavior can become a useful basis for setting objectives in special market situations.

SHORT-TERM SALES OR MARKET SHARE AS AN OBJECTIVE

In Chapter 4, it was argued that immediate sales or market share is a behavioral measure that is usually inappropriate for measuring advertising effectiveness and therefore is an inappropriate criterion for setting advertising objectives. There are two primary reasons.

1. Advertising is usually only one of many marketing and nonmarketing variables that contribute to sales. An advertising campaign may be effective in building brand awareness but may contribute nothing to generating sales if the brand is priced too high or has not gained distribution.

2. Sales data gathered immediately after a campaign has been run usually will not reflect the full impact of the campaign. Those sales generated by advertising during the campaign period by getting consumers to try a brand, for example, may continue on into the future with no incremental advertising expenditures. If consumers are satisfied with a product's performance, having been induced to try it by an advertising message, there is a strong possibility that they will continue to buy for a period of time even though the campaign stops. The result is significant future sales that are not reflected in immediate sales statistics. Furthermore, there will be some potential consumers exposed to the campaign who could be influenced to buy sometime in the future, but who did not buy during the campaign or immediate postcampaign period. The future sales represented by these people, traceable to the influence of advertising, are also not reflected in short-run sales statistics.

The preceding discussion, of course, applies to market-share measures as well as sales. Market share and sales have the same two potential problems. When the product class is well defined, planners will in fact use market share instead of sales, because market share tends to be a more sensitive and appropriate indicator of the impact of the marketing program and the competitive situation. It is not affected by product class sales fluctuations caused by seasonal or economic factors. Thus, planners will often talk of gaining a share point or of using advertising or a sales promotion to "buy" a share point. The value of a share point is usually just as easy to determine as the value of a sales increment.

Despite the two potential problems associated with sales and market-share objectives, there are situations in which sales or market share will become appropriate measures on which to base objectives. These situations will tend to have two characteristics. First, advertising will be the primary cause of immediate sales or share. The sales or share will not be affected to any substantial extent by any other types of marketing variables, nor will they be meaningfully affected by external events or actions that can be identified. Second, there will tend to be little carryover effect. Sales will be generated primarily by current advertising. Past advertising will have little relevance to the buying decision, and current advertising will have relatively little impact on future sales. Discussions follow of situations that have these characteristics to a greater or lesser extent.

Direct Mail

The cleanest example of such a situation is a one-time mail-order campaign introducing a product for a firm that is not concerned with establishing its name or drawing on a previously established name. This hypothesized mail-order campaign would attempt to precipitate a buying decision. In this case, factors like store location, shelf display, and other marketing variables are not involved. The mail-order advertisement could be assumed to be the principal force in precipitating a purchase decision. Furthermore, there would be no carry-over effect, assuming that the impact of that one exposure does not induce purchasing on future occasions. In this instance an advertising objective based on a sales measure becomes highly appropriate and operational. Decisions regarding copy and audience can indeed be made, using short-term sales as a criterion. Furthermore, the results can be measured and compared against the objective. Direct-mail campaigns can have similar characteristics.

Figure 7-1 shows an advertisement from a very successful mail-order campaign. Although the advertisement is not a one-time effort but part of a continuing campaign, its primary goal is intended to precipitate immediate response and its effectiveness can properly be measured by this response.

Mail-order advertising has long been recognized as being perhaps the only area in advertising in which immediate sales are a reliable indication of advertising performance. As a result, advertising professionals look to the experience of mail-order advertisers to learn what works and what doesn't. In 1923 Claude Hopkins, one of the great creative people in advertising, wrote a book called *Scientific Advertising* in which he made this point. In his words,

> The severest test of an advertising man is in selling goods by mail. But that is a school from which he must graduate before he can hope for success. There cost and result are immediately apparent. False theories melt away like snowflakes in the sun. The advertising is profitable or it is not, clearly on the face of returns. Figures which do not lie tell one at once the merits of an ad.
>
> This puts men on their mettle. All guesswork is eliminated. Every mistake is conspicuous. One quickly loses his conceit by learning how often his judgment errs—often nine times in ten.
>
> There one learns that advertising must be done on a scientific basis to have any fair chance at success. And he learns how every wasted dollar adds to the cost of results.
>
> Here he is taught efficiency and economy under a master who can't be fooled. Then,

Figure 7-1.   **A successful mail-order advertisement**

Courtesy of Book-of-the-Month Club, Inc.

and only then, is he apt to apply the same principles and keys to all advertising. . . .
A study of mail order advertising reveals many things worth learning. . . . Study those
ads with respect. There is proved advertising, not theoretical. It will not deceive you.
The lessons it teaches are principles which wise men apply to all advertising.[1]

Retail Advertising

Another example of a situation that comes close to meeting the two criteria is the
advertising of retailers. There is probably little carryover effect of advertising of a
storewide sale, for example, especially when the advertisements cover product lines
with which a store is already associated. Furthermore, although shopping trips are
influenced by a host of variables, there are situations in which advertising can have
an important and immediate impact on store traffic and sales. David Ogilvy, in fact,
has pointed out that, next to direct-mail advertising, the

most valuable source of information as to what makes some techniques succeed and
others fail is the experience of department stores. The day after they run an advertisement they can count the sales it has produced. That is why I am so attentive to the
advertising practices of Sears, Roebuck, who are the most knowing of all retailers.[2]

Cooperative Advertising

A closely related situation is cooperative advertising, in which a manufacturer offers
retailers an advertising program for the latter to run.[3] The program may include
suggested advertising formats, materials to be used to create actual advertisements,
and money to pay a portion of the cost. It also often includes requests that the
retailer stock certain merchandise quantities and perhaps use certain displays.
The intent of cooperative advertising, in part, is often to stimulate short-term sales.
The advertising is well suited to this task because it is usually specific as to the
product, the place at which it can be purchased, and the price. Figure 7-2 illustrates
with a Marshall Field advertisement.

Reminder Advertising

Sometimes the primary role of advertising is to act as a reminder to buy and use the
brand. The brand may be established and have a relatively solid, stable image.
Reminder advertising then serves to stimulate immediate purchase and/or use to
counter the inroads of competition. A good example is the Budweiser advertisement
shown in Figure 7-3. Because the primary impact of advertising is thus immediate
and because other factors such as distribution and price are likely to be fairly stable,
sales or market share become appropriate measures of advertising.

Reminder advertising can work in several ways. First, it can enhance the
top-of-mind awareness of the brand, thus increasing the probability that the brand

Figure 7-2. **A cooperative advertisement**

POP INTO OUR NEW COCA-COLA® SHOP

What's as American as a grand slam, videomania, the penny loafer revisited? The extravaganza opening of our new Coca-Cola® Shop. It's funwear with lots of fizz for juniors and young guys that's sweeping the nation in logo laden shirts, shorts, pants and jeans. Tops that pop with color. Striped and solid separates. Cleverly constructed classics. Check it out—the new Coca-Cola® Shop for carefree clothes with style, selection and overall cool.

Junior's collection in sizes S,M,L and 3 to 13. 18.00 to 46.00. Young Men's collection in sizes S to XL. 16.00 to 44.00. Coca-Cola® Shop, First Floor, State Street (North Wabash) and Oakbrook. Selections also available in J.R.'s, at all stores except Evanston, Oak Park, Park Forest, Lake Forest, CherryVale, Spring Hill and Louis Joliet. Young Men's available at all stores except Lake Forest.

Marshall Field's

Courtesy of Marshall Field's.

Figure 7-3.   **A reminder advertisement**

Courtesy of Anheuser-Busch, Inc.

gets included on the shopping list or gets purchased as an impulse item. Second, it can increase the motivation for the use of the product class. In this context the advertising may tend to simply increase the purchase and use of the product class and thus work to the advantage of the leading brand. Thus, reminder advertising for Royal Crown Cola may tend to increase purchases of other colas to the advantage of Coke and Pepsi. Similarly, Campbell soup is the soup brand that is in the best position to conduct reminder advertising.

Evaluation over a Long Period

Sales or market share may be quite appropriate as a bottom-line measure of advertising over a period long enough to absorb the carryover effects of advertising, a period that usually will need to exceed one year. Such a circumstance is particularly likely when advertising is a key, if not the dominant, marketing variable.

An example is the case of Winston cigarettes. An agency obtained the Winston account in 1974, at which time it was the largest selling brand in the United States.

During the fourth quarter of 1975, Marlboro passed Winston. This market share decline continued until the end of 1979 when the account was removed from the agency. The loss of share points, particularly relative to its key competitor, Marlboro, was the reason for the decision.

Another example involved a new Union Carbide product in what is called the "wrap market," plastic or paper products used for the storage of foods and disposal of garbage. Manufacturers in this category, such as Dow Chemical, Union Carbide, Crown-Zellerbach, Colgate-Palmolive, and Mobil, generate a total revenue figure that is the base value for the category. Union Carbide was one of the late entries into this market at a time when it was dominated by Saran Wrap, a Dow Chemical product, and several manufacturers of waxed paper products.

Working closely with their advertising agency, Leo Burnett, Union Carbide first decided to position their product between Saran Wrap and waxed paper. Research had reported that many consumers thought Saran Wrap difficult to handle. In contrast, waxed paper products were regarded by consumers as easy to handle but not as effective in sealing products or otherwise protecting them from the air. In developing the campaign, Leo Burnett devised the idea of a character, the "Man from Glad," and the product line that eventually included bags for storage, garbage, and related uses became known as Glad Bags. Within three years, Glad Bags became the market leader in that product category with more than 35 percent of the market share and, in the process, considerably expanded the product category itself. Thus, their share was not only greater than that of the leading competitors, but was a share of an increasingly larger base. This market share achievement reflected upon advertising, an important marketing variable. Again, market share was a useful measure of advertising even in this new-product context, partly because market share was monitored over a period of several years.

Short- and Long-run Objectives

It is sometimes possible to specify both short- and long-run objectives for the same advertising message or campaign and relate short-run sales increments to one aspect of the message. For example, a food company will attempt to create a long-run sustaining positive image for its products by using trustworthy and competent people to demonstrate product advantages. The idea is to build a reputation of quality for the company over the long run. At the same time, the message could be designed to make consumers aware of a forthcoming cents-off sale or a promotion. The contribution of advertising to the success of the promotion in the short run can be assessed even though there is likely to be a longer-run carryover effect as well.

In one study, a short-term sales response from a single advertisement was identified.[4] The study involved interviews with more than 2,000 housewives in six test cities. The interviews took place approximately 30 hours after the housewives received a morning newspaper that contained several test advertisements. In the interviews, a determination was made of the purchases of the test brands during the preceding 30-hour period. Each test advertisement was exposed to half the sample.

In the aggregate, it was found that the group exposed to an advertisement bought 14 percent more of the advertised brand than the control group (a difference that would occur by chance only one in eight times). Since just a single exposure of a single advertisement was involved in this study, it was a rather convincing demonstration that a short-term sales effort can be isolated.

It is necessary to determine when the short-term effect of advertising is meaningful enough to include it in the analysis of a campaign that has primarily a long-run sales objective. In making such a judgment, a careful distinction should be made between incremental short-term sales that are "borrowed" from the future and short-term sales increases that really represent immediate incremental profits. It is of little value to alter by a few weeks purchases that would have been made of your brand anyway. Furthermore, it is important that a company, in attempting to capture short-run sales or market shares, does not develop advertising that is detrimental to the long-run image or reputation of the brand, which could endanger long-run sales. A brand image can be tarnished or cheapened by too hasty reactions to competitive activity, constant price cutting, or promotional deals.

BEHAVIORAL MEASURES, REFINING THE SALES MEASURE

For a well-established brand, most purchases, and therefore the bulk of sales, are in the category of habitual decision making. Only a small portion of total sales is represented by decisions to try the brand for the first time or to try the brand in a new application. Thus, total sales in the short run are usually an extremely insensitive measure because they are dominated by habitual purchasing decisions. Advertising, of course, can play a role in sustaining these habitual purchasing decisions by reminding people of the brand's existence.

The portion of immediate sales that reflects decisions significant to a brand, decisions that will result in a sales flow over time, can be appropriate bases for setting objectives. Two such examples are the decision to try the advertised product for the first time or to try the product in a new application. Such disaggregative measures can avoid the problems associated with overall sales measures and can provide the basis for operational objectives.

Suppose that the objective of advertising is to induce a certain number of families to try a product for the first time or to use the product in a new application. The advertising may attempt to precipitate the consumer decision directly. For example, it could ask the consumer, "Have you tried brand A?" In that case, there could be a direct link between advertising and the decision to try the brand, the behavioral objective:

$$\text{Advertising} \longrightarrow \text{Behavior (tried brand A)}$$

The advertising may attempt to precipitate behavior by communicating persuasive information that would tend to lead to the desired behavior. For example, advertising might suggest that the consumer ''Try the new product because it smells like lime.'' In that case, the operative model would be

$$\text{Advertising} \longrightarrow \text{Brand comprehension} \longrightarrow \text{Behavior}$$

In this case the advertising objective could be couched in behavioral terms since the brand comprehension (the brand smells like lime) and the behavior might be expected to be achieved within a very short time span.

The Clairol advertisement shown in Figure 7-4 is designed to generate action, to get women to color their hair. It does attempt to generate brand comprehension by communicating the fact that Clairol Balsam Color leaves hair shiny and more manageable. However, the comprehension is designed to help stimulate or trigger immediate behavior. It is not primarily designed to provide a cognitive change that could result in an action months or years in the future.

The time lag between the advertising and the behavior is most relevant. For behavior to be an appropriate measure, the time lag should be short. It should be anticipated that the advertising would be capable of generating a change in behavior immediately. If it is necessary to build up brand comprehension with several exposures spread over a period of months or years, then the behavioral measure will be less appropriate. The utility of a behavioral objective is also increased if advertising will be a dominant cause of the induced behavior. Again, if advertising is to be held accountable for a behavioral objective, it should be capable of effecting that objective by itself. When a specific decision, like the decision to try a different brand is involved, in some situations it may be reasonable to assign to advertising the task of precipitating that decision. Such a task, of course, is considerably different in content from that of increasing or maintaining overall sales.

One aspect of the carryover effect of advertising is worth emphasizing again at this point. Assume that the objective is to attract new customers to a product. Then the number of first purchases of the brand will not by itself reflect the value of the advertising campaign to the advertiser. In fact, these purchases will represent only a small part of the value of the campaign, since they reflect consumer decisions that will generate a future sales stream of considerable value to the firm. To evaluate objectives of this type, to establish the advertising budget, and to measure results, it is necessary to estimate the net value to a firm of such a campaign.

The Value of a New-Trier Group*

Assume that a three-month advertising campaign has been run to attract a group of new triers to a brand called Dream, which is competing for market share in an established product class—detergents. A new trier is someone who has not previously bought the brand (Dream), or who made the previous purchase sufficiently long ago that it has been effectively forgotten. The purchase in either case will tend to precipitate some kind of evaluation with respect to Dream that will affect future

*The next four sections can be bypassed without loss of continuity.

Figure 7-4.   **An advertisement designed to precipitate action**

buying decisions. The worth of such a group of new triers will certainly depend on their product class buying potential, the brand's profitability, their acceptance of the brand, and some discount factor reflecting future uncertainties. More specifically, the group's value can be represented by the following expression:

$$W = \sum_{n=0}^{\infty} Nvmg^nP = \frac{NvmP}{1 - g} \tag{1}$$

where W = long-run value of a group of new triers attracted by an advertising campaign

n = index of a time period of analysis (that is, one year)

N = number of new triers in the group

v = average per capita product-class purchasing volume per time period of the new-trier group

m = gross margin of the brand

g = discount factor representing the cost of capital and the risks of the market

P = factor representing the brand's long-run share of the group's purchasing volume

The first term, N, indicates the number of new triers of Dream attracted by the advertising campaign. It could be estimated by a survey of consumers or by monitoring a panel of consumers such as the IRI Behavior Scan panel. In either case, unless the brand was new, it would have to be determined that any previous purchase of the brand occurred a sufficiently long time ago to be effectively forgotten. One study showed that if the previous purchase was made over 15 months ago, a consumer evaluated it in the same manner as she or he would evaluate a new brand.[5] The term N should not include those new triers who would have appeared during this period or shortly thereafter in the absence of the advertising campaign. Methods to estimate these categories of new triers have been developed by Parfitt and Collins.[6] In most cases, however, such consumers can be neglected, particularly if there is a strong link between the advertising and the decision to try the brand.

The second term, v, represents the buying potential of the new-trier group, the average product-class purchasing volume in the future. It reflects the fact that those who consume more of the product (heavy users) are more worthwhile than those who consume less (light users). If the time period of analysis is one year, the product class used (that is, the amount of detergent used) during the year would be the relevant statistic for the individual new trier.

The third term, m, represents the profit contribution of the brand. Clearly, the brand's profit contribution should be explicitly considered in an evaluation of advertising aimed at attracting new customers. If the brand is very profitable on a per-unit basis, it will be easier to justify a campaign aimed at increasing those buying the brand.

The discount factor, g, reflects the fact that profits during the coming year are more certain to occur than profits in future years. If a new trier makes a positive decision with respect to Dream, the person is likely to give it all or part of his or her subsequent detergent purchases. If he or she buys a box every month, then Dream can expect sales from these purchases for some time. However, in future years new products and new advertising for existing products will appear and may entice the Dream user away. Therefore, it is prudent to discount sales in future years. The discount factor should normally be fairly large, perhaps 25 percent a year, since it is absorbing the uncertainties of the market.

The term P is a summary of the brand's ability to gain acceptance. If all new triers dislike the brand, it would be zero. If they all liked it well enough to decide to buy it exclusively in the future, it would be 1. The appropriate statistics to estimate P are the repeat-purchase statistics. The first repeat-purchase statistic is obtained by asking a sample of new triers whether they repurchased the brand (Dream) the next time they bought the product (detergent). Suppose that 40 percent of the new triers repurchased the brand the next time they bought the product. This number would be an indication of P. If the second and perhaps other repeat-purchase statistics were obtained, the estimate of P would become more reliable. Suppose that 20 percent of the new-trier group repurchased Dream on their second purchase occasion after their trial purchase (the second repeat-purchase statistic). Suppose, further, that the third and fourth repeat-purchase statistics were both 15 percent. It might then be assumed that Dream will be bought 15 percent of the time by the new-trier group into the indefinite future. This estimate could be still further refined by applying one of the models that has been specifically designed to represent the decision process following the first purchase of a brand and to project this process for a group of new triers.[7]

Lacking a Well-Defined Product Class

Equation (1) will still apply if the advertising campaign is designed to attract new triers of a product or service that is not competing in a well-defined product class. A product like granola bars, for example, may not be included in a well-defined product class. In that case, the relevant question is to predict the eventual product purchasing rate that will be obtained from the new triers. In essence, the product will constitute its own unique class, and the problem will be to estimate a number comparable to NvP. The relevant statistic is the interpurchase time, the time between subsequent purchases. For example, it might be determined that 25 percent of the new triers repurchased the product within 2 weeks after their first purchase, 40 percent repurchased it within 4 weeks, 50 percent within 6 weeks, 52 percent within 8 weeks, and 53 percent within 10 weeks. These data might suggest that eventually 60 percent of the new triers will rebuy the product once. Similar data can be obtained on those who rebought it twice. Suppose that it was estimated that 80 percent of those rebuying the product would buy it a third time, and that all those buying it three times would continue buying it. The market for the product would then be N, the number of new triers, times the product of 0.60, 0.80, and 1.00 (or 0.48N) times the average usage rate of the new product.

New Product Uses

An alternative objective is to increase sales by getting existing customers to use the product in new ways. For example, Arm & Hammer baking soda ran a campaign to get housewives to use the product in the refrigerator to absorb odors. In another case, cranberry producers attempted to encourage consumers to substitute or supplement orange juice with cranberry juice. An objective of the campaign could have been to introduce a new product application. In this case, equation (1) would be modified somewhat. The term N would be the number of customers who tried the product in the new way. The term v would be the increased product-class usage volume that would be expected, given the new usage.

Increasing Brand Loyalty

It may be worthwhile to attempt to increase the brand loyalty of existing customers. Brand loyalty could be measured simply by the number of purchases that a brand obtained in a certain number of purchase occasions. More sophisticated measures are also available that involve models (for example, the Markov or linear learning model) that examine the pattern of purchases one brand receives versus another. They would distinguish, for example, between the case of buying Dream every other purchase and buying another brand three times and then buying Dream three times. In the former case, a buyer would seem to share purchases between the two brands in a rather random way, whereas in the latter case there might be evidence of an increase in loyalty toward Dream.

When an increase in loyalty is the objective, copy might be directed at the postpurchase experience, attempting to reinforce a positive experience or to neutralize or help avoid a negative experience. It might also be directed at stimulating interest. Some products, like cereals, experience a "fad and fatigue" purchasing cycle. People are very loyal about purchasing one particular brand for a period of time. Eventually, however, they get tired and bored with it and switch to another brand. The switch does not mean that they dislike the brand (they are likely to return to it), but simply that they want to try something new. A job of advertising might then be to maintain interest in the brand to fight fatigue or to stimulate interest to reduce the period between times in which the brand enjoys high loyalty.

OTHER BEHAVIORAL MEASURES

A variety of other behavioral measures can be used productively as a basis for setting advertising objectives. Each has a relatively direct link to advertising and can be justified in terms of its value to the advertiser.

Shopping Decisions

For durable products, like large appliances and automobiles, an appropriate behavioral objective might be to entice customers to visit a dealer's showroom. For large-ticket consumer items, the final phases of the selling process are usually best handled by a person-to-person sales effort, with advertising used appropriately to draw people to the showroom. With any behavioral measure, it is important, for purposes of budgeting and performance evaluation, to estimate the value of the behavioral action. Thus, the value of a visit to an automobile showroom should be estimated. What percentage of those visiting a showroom eventually buy an automobile? Is this percentage different for those attracted by the advertising?

Similarly, retailers and shopping centers often have as the primary objective of advertising the generation of store traffic. Thus, a count of shoppers (or a surrogate measure such as cars entering the parking lot) might be a better measure of advertising than daily sales. One study attempted to evaluate the impact of a small sales catalog mailed directly to more than 290,000 residents of a metropolitan area.[8] The catalog contained 210 items, emphasized price, and was sent by a chain of seven large discount department stores. In-store interviews of 1,400 shoppers were conducted to determine the impact of the catalog. Of the total sample,

- 66.5 percent received the catalog.
- 57.8 percent read the catalog.
- 28.6 percent were in the store to buy something advertised in the catalog.
- 24.9 percent bought something read about in the catalog.

Such data fall short of providing the number attracted to the stores by the advertising, because it is not known how many of the 57.8 percent who read the catalog might have come to the chain store that day anyway. One approach would be to ask the respondents when they last shopped at the chain and to compare their answers to those obtained from a second, control sample. The increase in shopping frequency would allow an estimate of the extra shoppers generated by the advertising.

Industrial Marketing: Sales Leads

Industrial marketing is similar to the marketing of durables in that advertising can rarely be expected to make the sales. Rather, a salesperson is usually required to supply information and to handle the details of the transaction. Advertising, in this case, can provide the engineer or buyers with the opportunity to express interest in the product by returning a card—often called a bingo card—which is a request for additional information. The salesperson then follows up these leads by calling on the prospect and discussing his or her requirements. Thus, for industrial advertising, a useful objective is to generate bingo cards. A more refined objective would be to generate a certain number of bingo cards from certain types of prospects. Furthermore, the value of a bingo card to an industrial advertiser could be determined. A salesperson could report back on which of the bingo cards came from real prospects, which were of little value, and ultimately what sales or potential sales they represented. Figure 7-5 shows a rather dramatic industrial advertisement. The reader can get specific information by circling a number on a postcard enclosed in the magazine.

Demarketing

Some marketing programs are designed to get people to use less of a product or to discontinue the use of a product completely. In such cases, a behavioral measure will often be a useful basis for a primary or secondary advertising objective. For example, advertising campaigns have been developed that included such behavioral objectives as encouraging people

- To stop smoking.
- To reduce the temperature level in homes in the winter.
- To reduce the use of the automobile.
- To reduce the use of bridges and highways during rush hours.
- To refrain from driving while drinking

Measuring Intentions

Although not measuring purchase behavior itself, another useful variable often used as a good substitute for a direct behavioral measure is to ask a consumer her or his intentions with respect to brand purchase. Thus, people could be asked, on a 0- to 7-point scale, their likelihood of trying a brand or using it in a new context. The use of intentions measures is especially important in copy testing when it is often inconvenient to obtain direct measures of behavior.

SALES PROMOTIONS

Sales promotions are an important marketing force in many industries. They come in a variety of forms. Some are directed at the retailer in the form of price discounts that are intended to be passed on to the end consumer or to provide incentives to feature the brand in a special display. Advertising might be called on to support such promotions by generating interest in the brand during the time of the promotion. Several issues have emerged in recent years with respect to these promotions. How can a cycle of destructive price competition through these promotions be broken? How can a manufacturer make sure that the price reductions are passed through to the customer? How large and how frequent should such promotions be?

Consumer promotions usually provide a temporary price reduction directly to consumers through price-off coupons, a two-for-one sale, a free sample, or some type of premium that may have little relationship to the brand. Such promotions can

Figure 7-5.   **An industrial advertisement**

Raising the temperature 1° in Greenland would raise eyebrows in New York.

In spite of raging storms, severe cold, floods, heat waves, earthquakes, and tornados, nature is mighty even-tempered.

For it's a recognized fact that only a slight average temperature increase in polar regions would melt enough ice to raise oceans to disastrous levels.

Nature's delicate balancing act is emulated every day in industrial process plants the world over.

Take semiconductor manufacturing. If temperature inside quartz furnaces isn't repeatedly maintained to within half a degree, often at over

1400°C, specs fall off, yield is reduced, and profits degenerate.

Food processing, too. A precise time/temperature ratio is critical to balance food sterilization and quality. What any imbalance can do to tastebuds, profits and lost energy is unprintable.

Little differences in temperature, flow and pressure mean a lot.

Engineers who can't afford such situations — who can't afford anything but the best — specify data acquisition and control products from Doric.

Flexible digital indicators that measure voltage to one microvolt reso-

lution. Long-arm data loggers that scan at rates to 27 points per second. And industrial controllers that take action when temperature varies just fractions of a degree from setpoint.

For full details, contact: Doric Scientific Division, Emerson Electric Co., 3883 Ruffin Road, San Diego, CA 92123, 714/565-4415, Toll Free 800/854-2708, Telex: 695-001. In Europe: Av. Ad. Lacomble 52, 1040 Brussels, Belgium.

**WHEN A LITTLE
DIFFERENCE MAKES
A BIG DIFFERENCE.**

From single-point indicators to multi-point loggers to closed-loop controllers, Doric digital instrumentation technology has set new price/performance standards for the industry

Courtesy of Doric.

have several objectives. One is to entice people who have not used the product for some time to try it. One measure of the promotion is the extent to which it is successful at attacking a sizable new-trier group. Of course, the value of the group also depends upon the ability of the brand to gain acceptance among this group. Another objective could be simply to stimulate sales among existing customers by creating short-term interest. The problem is, of course, to avoid the promotion becoming so commonplace that it fails to attract interest.

A promotion can be used to build purchase volume and brand loyalty by stimulated multiple purchases of the brand. Thus, the Cathy Rigby exercise program, shown in Figure 7-6, is offered with four purchases of Dial soap. The frequent-flyer program offered by airlines provides free tickets to those flying a prescribed number of miles. AT&T offered a $1 discount off name-brand items and services for every $1 spent on long-distance billing exceeding $15 a month. They sent 54 million catalog sets to 22 million homes and 5 million business accounts. During the first months 1.1 million homes and businesses participated.[9]

A promotion can help zero in on a target segment. The GE ad shown in Figure 7-6, for example, is directed at those needed flash bulbs for taking pictures of their small children. If the loyalty to a bulb manufacturer is low, a premium such as the coloring book can be persuasive.

Consumer promotions do not always have to involve an effective price reduction. Apple Computer supported the introduction of its Macintosh with a "Test Drive a Macintosh" promotion, which allowed customers to leave computer showrooms with $2,400 worth of equipment.[10] The budget was $10 million, of which $8 million went to advertising and the rest supported such activities as in-store displays and carrying the inventory costs. Around 200,000 Macintoshes were test driven, at a cost of only $5 each. Federal Express sent jellybeans to nearly 200,000 customers to deliver the message that large packages such as candy are priced better by the pound.[11]

Promotions can also be used to contribute to the image of the brand. The Cathy Rigby advertisement provides association with Dial soap that would have been much more difficult without the promotion. Allstate's "Shape Up & Save" consumer sweepstakes promotion provided an association with health and fitness for the insurance company.[12] The campaign also received advertisement readership scores about 50 percent higher than those of their previous advertising, indicating that promotions can enhance advertising simply by creating interest.

Promotions can also contribute negatively to a brand image. A brand that relies on frequent price promotions or inappropriate premiums runs a real risk of damaging a brand image. Thus, it is important to consider the impact on image as well as the short-term results of a promotion.

Figure 7-6.   **Sales promotions in advertisement**

Figure 7-6. (Cont.)

Courtesy of Armour-Dial Company and General Electric Company.

SUMMARY

When there is a strong link between advertising and sales or market share and carry-over effects are small, it can be appropriate to use immediate sales or share as a basis for setting advertising objectives and measuring performance. Such a situation often exists in mail-order campaigns and sometimes exists in the advertising of retailers and in reminder advertising. Even when carry-over effects are substantial, it can be useful to have immediate sales or shares as part of a dual objective.

One reason that overall sales or share do not provide the basis for good operational objectives is that they mainly represent habitual decision making, which is largely insensitive to advertising in the short run. It is possible to consider behavioral measures that represent decisions more relevant to an advertiser, such as the decision to try a product for the first time or to try a product in a new application. In either case, the advertising goal would be to precipitate some form of new action.

In using such objectives, it is necessary, for purposes of setting budgets and evaluating performance, to determine the value of the desired behavioral response. The value of a new trier, for example, will be a function of his or her product-usage rate and brand acceptance. The brand acceptance can be estimated from repeat purchase statistics.

Other behavioral measures can also be appropriate in some situations. It could be useful to attempt to maintain or increase the loyalty of existing customers. A durable goods manufacturer may wish to precipitate visits to a showroom. An industrial advertiser may want to generate leads (bingo cards) for his or her salespeople. A demarketing campaign may want to reduce driving. For copy-testing purposes, the behavior response could be estimated by some form of intention measure. Sales promotions can be designed to create trial purchases, to stimulate short-term sales, to enhance purchase volume or brand loyalty, or to affect the brand image.

DISCUSSION QUESTIONS

1.   Suppose that you are the advertising manager of a large department store who had been asked by the president to establish a system to measure the effectiveness of advertising. How would you go about developing such a system? What measures would you use? How would you test the advertisements before they run to determine if they will be effective?

2.   What types of behavioral measures might the following consider using as the basis for advertising objectives? How would they go about determining which to select? How would they formulate the objective: establishing the number and nature of behavioral responses?

   a.   Cereal company
   b.   Pest-control company
   c.   Oil company

     d. Farm-equipment manufacturer
     e. Large bank
     f. *Time* magazine
     g. Computer company

3. Provide examples of current advertising campaigns that seem to be directed at generating behavioral response. Are they attempting to communicate information and/or change attitudes or are they concerned solely with behavior? Write a reasonable objective for each campaign that is operational. How would you measure results against that objective?

4. Evaluate the advertisements shown in Figures 7-1 through 7-6. What do you think are their objectives? What would you say are their deficiencies? How could they be improved?

5. Consider the American Airlines frequent flyer program, a free sample program for a new soap, a 25 percent off price offered to retailers by a cereal brand and two promotions that recently affected your purchasing. What were the objectives of these promotions? What role does advertising play in these promotions? What impact will these promotions have in the long-term? How would you measure that impact?

NOTES

1. Claude C. Hopkins, *My Life in Advertising/Scientific Advertising* (Chicago: Crain Books, 1966), pp. 229–230.

2. David Ogilvy, *Confessions of an Advertising Man* (New York: Atheneum, 1964), p. 92.

3. Robert F. Young, "Cooperative Advertising, Its Uses and Effectiveness: Some Preliminary Hypotheses," Marketing Science Institute Working Paper, 1979.

4. Leo Bogart, B. Stuart Tolley, and Frank Orenstein, "What One Little Ad Can Do," *Journal of Advertising Research,* 10, August 1970, pp. 3–14.

5. David A. Aaker, "The New Trier Stochastic Model of Brand Choice," *Management Science,* 17, April 1971, pp. B435–450.

6. J. H. Parfitt and B. J. K. Collins, "The Use of Consumer Panels for Brand Share Prediction," *Journal of Marketing Research,* 5, May 1968, pp. 131–146.

7. See the models reported in Aaker, "The New Trier," and Parfitt and Collins, "Consumer Panels."

8. Danny N. Bellenger and Jack R. Pingry, "Direct-Mail Advertising for Retail Stores," *Journal of Advertising Research,* 17, June 1977, pp. 35–39.

9. William A. Robinson and Kevin Brown, "Best Promotions of 1984: Back to Basics," *Advertising Age,* March 11, 1985, pp. 42–44.

10. Ibid., p. 42.

11. Ibid., p. 44.

12. Ibid., p. 42.

CASE FOR PART II

Canada Packers: Tenderflake*

In December 1979, Mr. Brian Burton, brand manager for Canada Packers' Tenderflake lard was writing the annual marketing plan for the fiscal year ending in March 1981. He had been assigned to Tenderflake one year earlier and his first action had been to initiate a basic attitude and usage study on Tenderflake and its competitors. With these data in hand, Mr. Burton was considering possible changes in brand strategy.

Background

Canada Packers Limited was incorporated in 1927 as a meat-packing company. The company had diversified into a wide variety of products, one of which was Tenderflake lard. Lard is a pork by-product produced by every major meat-packing company in Canada because it offers an opportunity to fully utilize raw materials.

Until 1970, Canada Packer's lard had been distributed in the same manner as the company's meat products. Canada Packers had divided the country into five regions, each of which had been serviced by a separate and autonomous plant. Each plant manager had set prices for his products and had operated a sales force that called on grocery stores in that region. The company had not advertised lard extensively because personal service and low price had been considered the important factors in selling to food wholesalers and supermarkets.

In 1969 top management at Canada Packers had felt that the company's packaged-goods lines were not reaching their profit potential under this decentralized approach. In 1970, they established the Grocery Products Division, and by 1973, this division marketed the company's lines of shortening, margarine, lard, canned meats, cheese, soap, pet food, peanut butter, and salted nuts. Each product had been assigned to a brand manager whose responsibility was to develop strategy and monitor the performance of the brand.

Tenderflake Brand History

Tenderflake lard had never been advertised, but it benefited from the high awareness and reputation of the Tenderflake name, the Maple Leaf family brand name, and the Canada Packers corporate name. Tenderflake lard had achieved sales of 25 million pounds in fiscal 1979, which represented 65 percent of the total lard market. This dominant share had been achieved by Canada Packers' aggressive pricing, which

* K. G. Hardy et al., *Canadian Marketing: Cases and Concepts* (Boston, MA: Allyn and Bacon, Inc., 1978).

few competitors could match. As a result the brand had generated pretax profits of only 1 cent a pound in fiscal 1978, 1.6 cents a pound in fiscal 1979, and would be fortunate to break even in fiscal 1980.

Tenderflake was distributed across Canada by the 65-person Grocery Products sales force. Each salesperson had a territory that included large and medium-sized grocery outlets and a few wholesalers who serviced the very small grocery stores. Chain retail outlets took a markup of 16 percent on their selling price. In 1979 a standard co-op advertising program was offered to retail outlets whereby Canada Packers put 1 percent of the invoice value of a customer's purchase into a fund used for advertising. Standard volume discounts amounted to another 1 percent variable cost for the brand.

The Market

Mr. Burton knew that shortening and lard were used interchangeably. Company executives estimated that 84 million pounds of lard and shortening would be sold in fiscal 1981. The combined sales of lard and shortening had been declining at about 2 percent per year.

Of the 84 million pounds of lard and shortening to be sold to consumers in fiscal 1981, approximately 60 percent would be shortening. Crisco would sell 55 percent of the shortening poundage, and Tenderflake would sell 65 percent of the lard poundage.

Shortening is white and odorless because it is made from vegetable oil or from a mixture of animal and vegetable fat. Tenderflake is white and odorless (which is not true of all lards) because Canada Packers employed a superior refining process that completely removed all odor and color from the lard. Regardless of color or odor, lard tends to produce a flaker pie crust than shortening because lard creates more layers of pastry, and most experts agreed that lard is easier to use. Major industrial consumers in the quality pastry area specified lard regardless of price.

The price of shortening appeared to influence the sales of lard. Mr. Burton had noted that whenever the price of lard was less than 7 cents below the price per pound of shortening, consumers tended to switch from lard to shortening. Retail prices of lard and shortening had traditionally fluctuated with the price of raw materials. Only Crisco had maintained stable prices and growth in sales and profits despite the general market decline. The prices of competitive products as of December 1979 were as shown in Exhibit 1.

Competition

Crisco shortening was marketed by Proctor and Gamble, and it was the only major advertised brand of lard or shortening. Mr. Burton estimated that Procter and Gamble spent approximately $550,000 per year in advertising Crisco. Their campaigns had stressed that Crisco was all vegetable, that the product was dependable,

Exhibit 1.

	RETAIL PRICE PER POUND
Lards	
Tenderflake	$0.45
Burns	0.44
Schneider	0.44
Swifts	0.45
Shortenings	
Crisco	0.56
Average of cheaper shortenings	0.50
Average of all shortenings	0.53

and that it was desirable for deep frying and pastry making. Crisco was promoted by the Procter and Gamble sales force, which sold a wide line of paper, food, and soap products to grocery outlets and a few wholesalers. Procter and Gamble's only trade incentive on Crisco was a co-op advertising plan that paid 18 cents on every 36-pound case. Crisco followed a premium price strategy that appeared to produce a profit of 8 cents per pound on the product. Exhibit 2 shows the estimated cost structures of Crisco and Tenderflake as of December 1979.

Crisco and Tenderflake both were packaged in 1-pound and 3-pound containers. Approximately 5 percent of Tenderflake's sales came from the 3-pound container, the majority of these coming from western Canada, while 39 percent of Crisco's sale came from the 3-pound size. Mr. Burton believed that Crisco had higher sales on the 3-pound size because it was priced at a lower cost per pound than the 1-pound size. Because of the low margins and a higher per pound packaging cost on the larger size, Canada Packers sold the 3-pound size at a slight premium to the 1-pound package, and Mr. Burton believed that the higher price was responsible for the low proportion of sales in the 3-pound size.

Exhibit 2.   **Estimated Cost Structure of Crisco and Tenderflake**

	CRISCO (PER POUND)	TENDERFLAKE (PER POUND)
Retail price	$0.56	$0.45
Less retail margin	0.09	0.07
Factory price	0.47	0.38
Cost of goods sold	0.31	0.31
Gross margin	0.16	0.07
Expenses (including sales force, general administration, freight, distribution, trade allowances, coop advertising, and volume discounts, but excluding media advertising)	0.06	0.06
Media advertising	0.02	
Profit	$0.08	$0.01

Exhibit 3.   **Consumer Use of Fats and Oils[a] (Percent)**

	SALAD/ COOKING OIL	BUTTER	MARGARINE	SHORTENING	LARD
Pan frying	43	6	21	13	13
Deep-fat frying	24	1	2	14	11
Salad dressing	25	—	—	—	—
Baking cakes	8	8	20	24	4
Baking cookies	3	10	24	27	13
Baking pastries	1	2	3	49	62
Spreading	—	84	53	—	—
Total ever used	90	89	85	78	58

Users of Lard and Shortening by Application (Percent)

			DUAL USERS	
Total	Lard Only	Shortening Only	Use of Lard	Use of Shortening
(1565)[b]	(287)	(609)	(669)	(669)
Pastries	60.6	49.0	61.9	28.0
Cakes	4.9	14.6	4.0	23.1
Cookies	15.0	15.9	12.6	26.0
Pan frying	11.5	10.1	10.6	10.7
Deep-fat frying	8.0	10.3	12.3	11.9

[a] Tables may not sum to 100% because of multiple mentions.

[b] Number of women responding

Consumers

Mr. Burton's first action as brand manager of Tenderflake had been to commission a consumer study to determine the usage of lard and competing products, a profile of the consumer, and the consumer's attitude toward lard and its competition. A well-known market research company had conducted interviews with a representative sample of 1,647 women across Canada, and this research had been the basis of the "Fats and Oils Study"* that Mr. Burton had received in March 1979.

Women were asked about the time of year when they baked, and this led to the development of the baking seasonality index.

Spring	132
Summer	100
Fall	161
Winter	196

* Lard, shortening, cooking oil, butter, and margarine are defined as fats and oils.

Exhibit 4. **Average Pounds of Lard and Shortening Used per Week**

	Total Users	Maritimes	Quebec	Ontario	Prairies	British Columbia
			REGION			
Lard	0.42	0.45	0.65	0.35	0.42	0.25
Shortening	0.49	0.91	0.60	0.40	0.32	0.37

	LANGUAGE		
	French Quebec		Remainder of Canada
Lard	0.70		0.37
Shortening	0.62		0.45

	CITY SIZE			
	500,000 and Over	100,000– 499,999	10,000– 99,999	Under 10,000
Lard	0.35	0.35	0.40	0.52
Shortening	0.35	0.45	0.47	0.64

	FAMILY SIZE		
	2	3–4	5 and Over
Lard	0.35	0.34	0.57
Shortening	0.33	0.44	0.70

	INCOME			
	Under $4,000	$4,000– $6,999	$7,000– $9,999	$10,0000 and Over
Lard	0.57	0.52	0.35	0.27
Shortening	0.59	0.59	0.44	0.36

	AGE			
	Under 35	35–44	45–54	55 and Over
Lard	0.42	0.44	0.39	0.43
Shortening	0.51	0.58	0.45	0.41

	HEAVINESS OF USE				
	Total Users	Heavy	Heavy Medium	Medium Light	Light	Non-respondents
	(956)[a]	(174)	(206)	(209)	(354)	(13)
Lard	0.42	1.41	0.40	0.25	0.05	
Percent consumption	100	62	21	13	4	
Shortening	(1278)[a]	(300)	(271)	(295)	(364)	(48)
Usage per week		1–2 lb	1½ lb	1 lb	1 lb	

[a] Number of women responding.

The report indicated that lard and shortening were used mainly for baking. Lard was used primarily for pastries, while shortening was used more for cakes and cookies. Exhibit 3 shows how consumers use various fats and oils; Exhibit 4 gives specific data on lard and shortening users.

The attitude toward the product itself seemed to be largely rooted in the usage role of lard and the tradition of passing this role from one generation to the next. Exhibit 5 shows the data on consumer perceptions of lard as a product, perceptions of brands, and reasons for using or not using lard.

Crisco and Tenderflake showed uniform strength across the country, but smaller brands of lard and shortening demonstrated some regional strength (Exhibit 6).

In addition to the fats and oils study, Mr. Burton had employed a commercial research firm to conduct several focused group interviews in order to obtain "soft" or qualitative data on Tenderflake and its competitors. Typically, 10 to 15 women gathered and talked freely about baking and oil products under the leadership of a

Exhibit 5.   **Perceptions of Brands of Lard[a] (Percent)**

		TOTAL USERS (956)
All brands are equally good		55
One brand is better		42
Tenderflake/Maple Leaf	21	
Burns	3	
Schneider	3	
Crisco[a]	8	
Miscellaneous	7	

[a] Crisco frequently was mistaken as a brand of lard.

Volunteered Reasons for Preferring a Particular Brand of Lard (Percent)

	CRISCO (79)	TENDERFLAKE/ MAPLE LEAF (199)	BURNS (32)
Baking end benefits			
Flaky/light/better pastry dough	32	34	38
Excellent for pies/cookies/doughnuts	13	13	6
Good/better tasting/baked product	11	13	3
Product benefits			
Easier to handle/blend	14	11	3
Less greasy/not greasy	11	6	—
Better texture	5	11	9
Smells better	4	5	3
Other reasons			
Good result	20	18	34
Always used it	5	18	9
Cheap	4	6	3
Miscellaneous	18	20	22

Perceptions of Lard and Shortening by Users (Percent)

PERCEIVED PRODUCT PERFORMANCE	LARD USERS SAID	SHORTENING USERS SAID
Best for pie shells		
Lard	62	25
Shortening	30	68
No difference	8	7
Total	100	100
Produces flakiest pastry		
Lard	54	24
Shortening	38	69
No difference	8	7
Total	100	100
Best for frying		
Lard	38	20
Shortening	35	60
No difference	27	20
Total	100	100
Cheapest		
Lard	74	62
Shortening	6	14
No difference	20	24
Total	100	100
Most tolerant		
Lard	31	9
Shortening	46	71
No difference	23	20
Total	100	100

Volunteered Reasons for Not Using Lard (Percent)

	TOTAL NONUSERS (691)
Prefer other product	
Prefer/use shortening/Crisco	26
Prefer/use oil/margarine/butter	12
Health reasons	
Too much fat/animal fat	12
Not good for heart/liver	11
Difficult for digestion/too heavy	6
Too greasy	6
Do not eat fried things/grease	2
Dislike product	
Do not like taste	7
Do not like it	6
Other reasons	
Never tried it	9
Don't see need for it	4
Don't get good results	2
Miscellaneous responses	12

[a] Tables may not add to 100% because of multiple mentions.

Exhibit 6.   **Brand of Shortening Bought Last[a] (Percent)**

Brand	Total (1278)	Maritimes (122)	Quebec (345)	Ontario (487)	Prairies (193)	British Columbia (131)
			REGION			
Crisco	52	38	64	47	42	64
Fluffo	12	24	1	15	19	7
Domestic	8	10	9	7	6	6
Others	8	20	2	6	13	11
Don't remember	20	8	24	25	20	12

Brand of Lard Bought Last (Percent)

Brand	Total (859)	Maritimes (48)	Quebec (176)	Ontario (308)	Prairies (235)	British Columbia (92)
			REGION			
Tenderflake	52	69	49	60	51	36
Burns	13	2	2	7	23	30
Swift	7	—	5	5	6	22
Schneider	5	—	1	12	1	—
Crisco	11	4	39	3	4	2
Miscellaneous	18	27	22	14	23	7

[a] Tables may not add to 100% because of multiple mentions or rounding.

skilled psychologist. Little attempt was made to generalize from these interviews because the samples were small and were not selected randomly. However, the technique produced ideas for marketing strategy and could be verified by the fats and oils study.

The focused group interviews suggested that flakiness and fear of failure were the key areas of consumer concern. For pastries, lard was perceived as a better product than shortening among lard users, and Tenderflake seemed to have a premium-quality image. Among women who used only shortening, there was a strong perception that lard was an oily, cheaper product.

Attack by Crisco

Early in 1979 Crisco aired the television advertisement shown in Exhibit 7. The commercial clearly attacked lard's major product advantage, and Mr. Burton felt that Tenderflake, as the major lard producer, might lose market share to Crisco. He saw this as the same type of approach directed at lard that Procter and Gamble had used previously to pull Crisco ahead of the cheaper shortenings. By December 1979, Mr. Burton had developed several options, and he was about to take action.

Options

Mr. Burton saw an opportunity to raise the price of Tenderflake and to begin advertising. The reasoning was that advertising could help to ensure the stability of Tenderflake volume while improving the gross margin in order to cover advertising and profit. Further decisions would be to define target audiences, brand positioning, and copy strategy for Tenderflake. Mr. Burton thought that the fats and oils study suggested a number of opportunities. In Mr. Burton's judgment an advertising budget of $350,000 probably would receive management approval provided it was well conceived and promised a financial payout.

The sales manager had pointed out that the chain-store buyers saw the main competition as other lards and that raising the price of Tenderflake would permit cheaper lards to erode Tenderflake's market share. He strongly advised that Tenderflake maintain its price position with other lards rather than "chasing after Crisco."

The most difficult task would be to estimate the probable results of whatever marketing strategy Mr. Burton chose. However, senior marketing managers at Canada Packers would expect the annual marketing plan for Tenderflake to show sales and profit projections for the next five years.

Exhibit 7. **Crisco TV Advertisement**

Product:	Crisco	
Length:	30 seconds	
Monitored:	Toronto	
	December 1978	
Frame 1:	Scene:	*Young man and woman in kitchen.*
	Woman 1:	John, you never have seconds of my pie.
	Man:	Marie, this pie crust is so flaky.
Frame 2:	Scene:	*Close-up of Crisco can on table.*
	Woman 1:	OK, Marie, how'd you make your pie crust?
	Woman 2:	With Crisco.
	Woman 1:	But isn't lard cheaper?
Frame 3:	Scene:	*Close-up of ingredients being blended in a bowl. Crisco can in background.*
	Woman 2:	Maybe . . . but Crisco's worth the difference. It's softer than lard, so blending's easier.
Frame 4:	Scene:	*Close-up of ingredients being blended in bowl. Crisco can in background.*
	Woman 2:	Even the bottom crust has such delicate flakes they blow away.
Frame 5:	Scene:	*Two women talking in kitchen.*
	Woman 2:	And Crisco's one hundred percent pure vegetable.
	Man:	Mmmm . . . . really flaky.
Frame 6:	Scene:	*Woman 1 and man in another kitchen.*
	Woman 1:	Seconds, John?
	Man:	Mmmm.
	Announcer:	Use all-vegetable Crisco instead of lard. You'll think it's worth the difference.

8

The Perception Process

I advise you to include the brand name in your headline. If you don't, 80 percent of the readers (who don't read your body copy) will never know what product you are advertising. If you are advertising a kind of product only bought by a small group of people, put a word in your headline that will flag them down, such as asthma, bedwetters, women over 35. (David Ogilvy)

The advertiser must provide vivid incentives if he is to gain the favorable attention of a person whose senses have been dulled by fatigue or relaxation. (Darrell Lucas and Steuart Britt, *Advertising Psychology and Research*)

How does advertising communicate and persuade? What happens when a viewer is exposed to a television commercial? Will it be interpreted differently than intended by the advertiser or, worse, ignored? Will the viewer change perceptions of a brand or an attitude toward it? Should an advertiser be concerned about whether the commercials are liked or about any feelings such as warmth or happiness precipitated by the commercial? Will such liking or feelings affect the impact of the advertisement? How?

These questions and others will be addressed in Part III. Answers to these and similar questions require an understanding of psychological processes such as perception, processing information, communication, persuasion, and attitude change. The goal is to introduce and discuss creative alternatives in the context of these processes and various theories associated with them. The focus now shifts from advertising strategy, the subject of Part II, to tactical issues, the development of specific campaigns and advertisements. The copy director must decide: What creative approach will be most effective? What message? Which characteristics should a spokesperson have? What mood should be created? The detailed elements of advertisement creation are both fascinating intellectually and crucial to the impact and success of advertising.

In this chapter, the perception process will be discussed. The following chapter will describe several models of how information is processed and how advertising can change attitudes by communicating information. Chapter 10 turns to feeling advertising, advertising that has an impact largely by focusing on the arousal or generation of feelings in the audience, which include the liking of the advertisement and perceptions of feelings surrounding the use experience. Chapter 11, the final chapter in this part, begins with a general model of the advertising communications system and reviews the source, message, and social factor components of the model. Issues involving the source of the advertising message, usually the spokesperson, alternative message approaches, and the social factors, which include harnessing the power of word-of-mouth advertising, are addressed.

THE PERCEPTION PROCESS

It is generally believed that before an advertising message can transfer knowledge, create or change an image, create or change an attitude, or precipitate behavior, it must enter the mind of the receiver. Perception is an important part of communication and persuasion processes and is itself a process made up of elements, flows, and forces that enhance or inhibit messages to which an individual is exposed. The balance of this chapter focuses on an understanding of the perception process.

There are two important prerequisites for a successful advertising message. First, an individual must be exposed to it and pay some attention to it. Second, he or she must interpret it in the way the advertiser intended it to be interpreted. Each represents, in some sense, a perceptual barrier through which many advertisements fail to pass. Some advertisements are not successful at stimulating sense organs in the recipient to a minimal threshold level of interest or awareness. Other advertisements have their meaning distorted by the recipient in such a way that the effect of the advertisement is quite different from what the advertiser intended.

Perception has been defined as "the process by which an individual maintains contact with his environment"[1] and elsewhere as "the process whereby an individual receives stimuli through the various senses and interprets them."[2] Stimuli here can refer to sets of advertisements, to a single advertisement, or to a portion of an advertisement. The process, as conceptualized in Figure 8-1, includes two stages—attention and interpretation. Both play a role in helping an individual cope with the infinite quantity of accessible stimuli, a quantity that would be impossible to process.

The first stage is the attention filter. An individual, overtly or accidentally, avoids exposure to stimuli. He or she reads only certain publications, sees only selected television programs, and never drives near some billboards. Furthermore, most stimuli to which a person is exposed are screened out because she or he considers them uninteresting and irrelevant. Thus, only a small fraction of all advertisements are exposed to a given person. Also, only a portion of those advertisements to which an individual is exposed will get through the attention filter. The second stage is the interpretation process. An individual organizes the stimulus content into his or her own models of reality, models that may be very different from those of other individuals or of the sender. In doing so, the person often simplifies, distorts, organizes, and even "creates" stimuli.[3] The output of this process is a cognitive awareness and interpretation of the stimulus—a cognition.

There are two principal types of variables that influence the process. The first is the input to the process—the *stimulus*. Its size, intensity, message, novelty, position, and context will affect both stages of the process. Later we will examine these stimulus characteristics to see how they exert an influence. The second class of variables is termed *audience conditions,* or variables reflecting individual differences. The process is not identical across people, even for the same stimulus. On the contrary, there are extreme differences among people in terms of their exposure, to what they are attracted, and how they interpret information. A most important aspect of the study of the perceptual process is to determine what variables explain these differences. Among those to be considered are information needs, attitudes, values, interests, confidence, social context, and cognitive style.

Figure 8-1.   **The perception process**

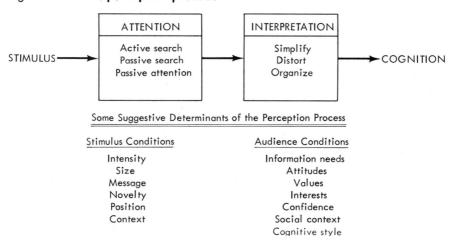

Stimulus Conditions	Audience Conditions
Intensity	Information needs
Size	Attitudes
Message	Values
Novelty	Interests
Position	Confidence
Context	Social context
	Cognitive style

In the balance of the chapter we will consider, in turn, attention and interpretation. In Chapter 16, methods for measuring attention will be presented and will be related to several precise definitions of advertisement exposure and readership.

ATTENTION

Attention can be viewed as an information filter—a screening mechanism that controls the quantity and nature of information any individual receives. The fact is that there are an infinite number of stimuli to which an individual could be exposed and an infinite variety of parts or components of a stimulus to which he or she might attend. Clearly, it is possible for an individual to absorb only a small fraction of the available stimuli.

At least two studies have attempted to estimate the average number of advertisements to which a person is exposed in a normal working day. One study concluded that it was more than 560, whereas the other found approximately 300.[4] Whatever the number, the set of advertisements to which a person is exposed is certainly nonrandom. It reflects the person's interests, reading habits, information needs, life-style, and so on. Such predictors of exposure are naturally of interest to advertisers; without exposure there can be no communication.

Only a small percentage of the exposed advertisements get through the attention filter—are actually "seen" or "attended to." In one study, Raymond Bauer and Stephen A. Greyser had a set of subjects use a small hand counter to determine the number of advertisements they saw during the course of a day. They were told to depress the counter every time they saw or heard an advertisement. Of course, there are biases inherent in this method. People will be sensitized to advertisements merely by the fact of having the counter in hand. They might also miss advertisements if they are not conscientious. However, it is a rather well-defined measure. The average adult in the sample reported seeing 76 advertisements a day.[5] Even if one quarrels with the counter methodology, it seems clear that a large number of advertisements to which an individual has the opportunity to be exposed are never seen.

The attention filter operates at various levels of effort and consciousness. At one extreme is the process of *active search* wherein a receiver actually seeks information. He or she might solicit opinions of friends or search through magazines not normally read. Another level could be termed *passive search*. A receiver searches for information only from sources to which he or she is exposed during the normal course of events. The final level might be called *passive attention*. Here a receiver has little immediate need for the information and makes no conscious effort to obtain it, but some information may nevertheless enter the system.

At all three levels it is appropriate to discuss why a person obtains information. There are, of course, as many reasons as there are situations and individuals. However, it is instructive to examine four general motives for attending to informative stimuli. In a sense, these are audience conditions influencing attention. One motive is to obtain information that will have a high level of utility for a person. In an advertising context, an individual will obtain product information that will help make better purchase decisions. Second, people may be motivated to expose themselves to information that supports their opinions—supportive exposure—and to avoid "discrepant" information. Third, there is a desire to be exposed to information that stimulates. Finally, people are motivated to find stimuli that are interesting to them. These motives will be examined in turn. We will then consider some stimulus characteristics that influence attention.

Information of Practical Value

It might seem more than slightly redundant to mention that advertising does, in fact, inform and that people do use such information in making decisions. Although advertising practitioners and behavioral scientists search for subtle and often-disguised explanations for why some advertisements register and others do not, it is too easy to overlook the obvious and principal role of advertising as a mechanism for informing. Indeed, psychologists cite studies that demonstrate that people do expose themselves to information that has practical value to them. By now, the reader should not require such evidence. Clearly, there is a practical need for product information and effective advertisements tend to fulfill this need.

The Shell Company advertisement shown in Figure 8-2 is an example of an advertisement that offers to the reader some practical information, the availability of one of their "answer series" booklets. A measure of the success of the campaign was the fact that 600 million of these booklets were distributed during the first three years of the campaign. Clearly, the offered information was regarded as useful. Incidentally, the Shell campaign was effective in affecting the Shell image. One image scale concerned people's perception of Shell as a company that provides useful information for consumers.[6] Shell went from 31 in January 1977 to 43 in May 1978, while their closest competitor fell from 26 to 12 in the same period.

Burnkrant applies a general theory of motivation that the behavioral tendency to process information is based upon three factors.[7] The first is the need for information about some topic. Obviously, audience members will have more information need for some products than others. For example, products that are costly, complex, or somewhat unknown because they are new or for some other reason will have associated with them an information need. The second is the expectancy that processing a particular stimulus will lead to relevant information exposure. It would be scaled as a probability. The third would be a measure of the value of the message as a source of relevant information. It is measured in terms of the goodness or badness of the message as an information source. This structure provides an approach to determine the extent to which a person might be motivated to process information. A more detailed discussion of motivation to process information is given in Chapter 9.

Figure 8-2.   **An advertisement offering practical information**

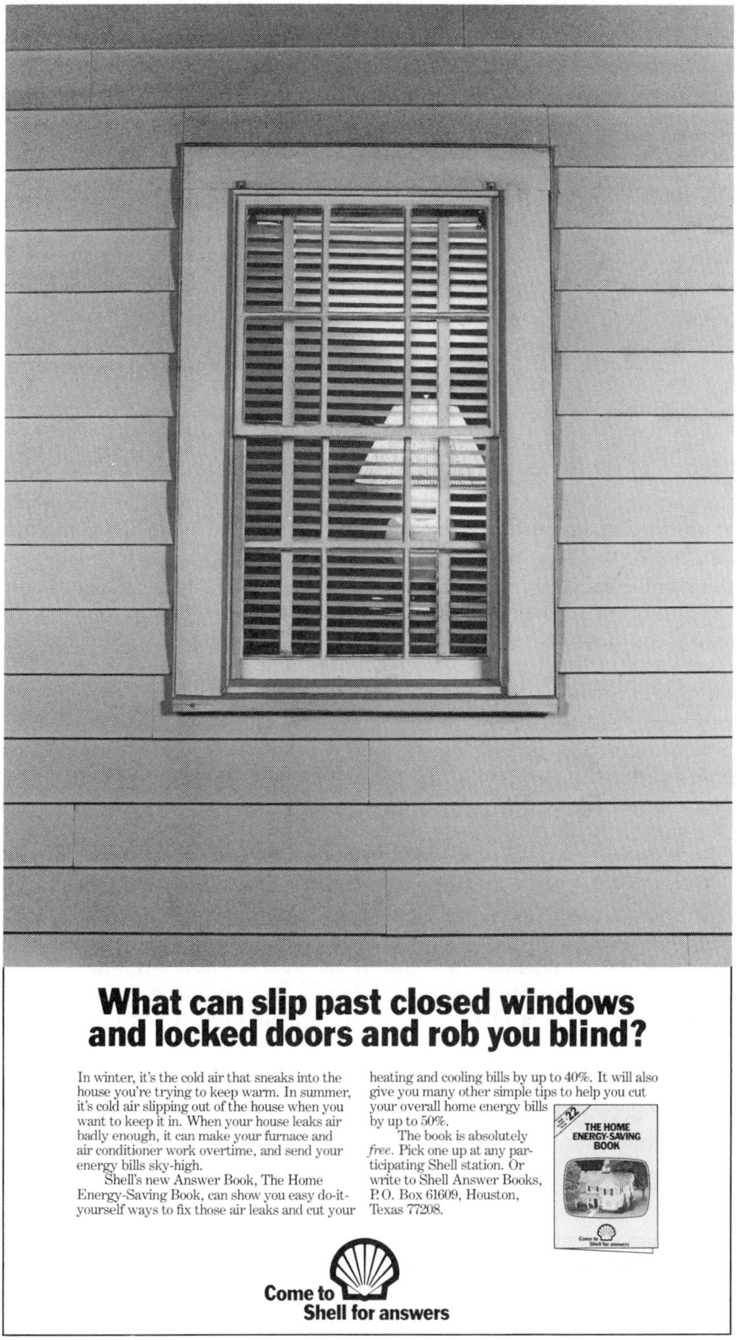

What can slip past closed windows and locked doors and rob you blind?

In winter, it's the cold air that sneaks into the house you're trying to keep warm. In summer, it's cold air slipping out of the house when you want to keep it in. When your house leaks air badly enough, it can make your furnace and air conditioner work overtime, and send your energy bills sky-high.

Shell's new Answer Book, The Home Energy-Saving Book, can show you easy do-it-yourself ways to fix those air leaks and cut your heating and cooling bills by up to 40%. It will also give you many other simple tips to help you cut your overall home energy bills by up to 50%.

The book is absolutely *free*. Pick one up at any participating Shell station. Or write to Shell Answer Books, P.O. Box 61609, Houston, Texas 77208.

Come to Shell for answers

Courtesy of Shell.

Long Copy.   An advertisement with short copy can be informative. A new brand or model in an established product class with strikingly different features may require no copy at all. However, in many situations a truly informative advertisement requires rather long copy. The use of long copy and, consequently, the development of advertising with high informative content is inhibited by a widely accepted "rule" of the advertising business. This rule stipulates that copy must be short and punchy to be read. The concept is that readers will turn away from formidable lengthy copy.

Although such a rule may indeed apply for some products in some situations, it is by no means universally true. If a reader has a real use for the information and the information is well packaged, she or he can be induced to read long copy. Furthermore, it is often a small sacrifice to lose readership among those who do not need the information and thus are not motivated to read it. David Ogilvy, head of the Ogilvy and Mather Advertising Agency, makes the case for long copy, illustrating his point by his own print advertising.

> How long should your copy be? It depends on the product. If you are advertising chewing gum, there isn't much to tell, so make your copy short. If, on the other hand, you are advertising a product which has a great many different qualities to recommend it, write long copy: the more you tell, the more you sell.
>
> There is a universal belief in lay circles that people won't read long copy. Nothing could be farther from the truth. Claude Hopkins (a great copy writer in the first part of the century) once wrote five pages of solid text for Schlitz beer. In a few months, Schlitz moved up from fifth place to first. I once wrote a page of solid text for Good Luck Margarine, with most gratifying results.
>
> Research shows that readership falls off rapidly up to fifty words of copy, but drops very little between fifty and 500 words. In my first Rolls-Royce advertisement I used 719 words—piling up one fascinating fact on another. In the last paragraph I wrote, "People who feel diffident about driving a Rolls-Royce can buy a Bentley." Judging from the number of motorists who picked up the word "diffident" and bandied it about, I concluded that the advertisement was thoroughly read. In the next one I used 1400 words.
>
> In my first advertisement for Puerto Rico's Operation Bootstrap, I used 961 words. . . . Fourteen thousand readers clipped the coupon from this advertisement and scores of them later established factories in Puerto Rico. . . . We have even been able to get people to read long copy about gasoline. One of our Shell advertisements contained 617 words, and 22 percent of male readers read more than half of them.[8]

Active Search.   There are situations in which buyers will not obtain adequate information for decision making from sources to which they are normally exposed. In such cases they may actively seek out information from advertising in special-interest magazines, by soliciting opinions from others, or by reading technical reports.

Active search generates exposures that are extremely important because of the salience of the information to the receiver. Such exposures will be more likely to affect product knowledge and attitude structure than those not associated with effort. Furthermore, the receiver is apt to be close to a purchase and the chances of forgetting the message are therefore lower. Also, the effort that went into the search process tends to enhance and legitimize the information source. *Playboy* may be regarded as a reliable source of information on men's fashions by someone seeking such knowledge, but the magazine's status is still further enhanced as soon as an issue is purchased. The act of purchase represents a commitment to the magazine as a reliable source. Despite the strong impact resulting from the exposure associated with active search, it is uncommon for advertisers or media to make any effort to measure this type of audience characteristic.

Active search is more likely to occur when risk and uncertainty are high—with major purchases, products involving relatively high involvement, and products that are new. The need for information will be highest for new products and lowest for brands with which a buyer is very familiar. As buyers develop brand loyalty, for example, their need for product information will be reduced. Evans found that automobile buyers who repurchased the same make are less likely to shop than those who switched from one make to another.[9]

Future Reference.   A purchase need not necessarily be imminent for a person to collect product information. It is reasonable to acquire such information for future use, using processes we have described as passive search or passive attention. It costs time and effort to engage in active search, but such costs can be avoided or reduced if an individual keeps informed about a product class. In particular, a boy may keep informed about motorcycles, or a woman about fashions, to prepare themselves for the time when they make a purchase. Of course, there will likely be other motivations as well. Howard and Sheth mention the need "to be a well-informed buyer in fulfilling a social role, in maintaining a social position. One is valued according to how much he knows with regard to the availability and value of products."[10]

Information That Supports: The Consistency Theories

A natural and intuitively appealing hypothesis is that people have a psychological preference for supportive information. It follows that they therefore tend to avoid nonsupportive or discrepant information. This latter tendency is illustrated by a line attributed to comedian Dick Gregory: "I have been reading so much about cigarettes and cancer that I quit reading." The term *selective exposure* has been applied to these twin drives.

Selective exposure can be explained by the consistency theories, such as dissonance theory, which suggest that people have a cognitive drive to develop consistent cognitions and behaviors about objects. Dissonance theory predicts that cognitive dissonance, the existence of conflicting cognitive elements, is discomforting and that people will try to reduce it. One mechanism for reducing dissonance is selective exposure—to obtain supportive information and to avoid discrepant information.

Efforts to confirm the selective exposure hypothesis in psychology have not been definitive. In part, this has been due to the difficulty of disentangling selective exposure from the other motives to process information, particularly information utility and interest factors. However, the evidence in contexts more relevant to advertising is much more positive.

Ehrlich and other psychologists, showed recent car buyers eight envelopes allegedly containing advertisements for different makes of cars. Over 80 percent of the respondents chose the advertisements for their own cars—advertisements that would presumably be supportive.[11] Engel interviewed two matched samples, one of which had purchased a new Chevrolet (a later replication used Volkswagens) a short time before (from one day to two weeks). New-car owners seemed to have greater recall and interest in Chevrolet advertising.[12] Mills found that, after controlling for differences in product desirability, a positive interest for advertisements of chosen products existed although there was no negative interest in advertisements for rejected products.[13]

Involuntary Exposure.   Selective exposure should tend to increase when an individual's position is threatened by involuntary exposure to nonsupportive information. Consider a person who has a stable attitude and is loyal to one or several automobile models. Suppose that he or she is told of a rumored government report suggesting that one of the models he or she prefers has a characteristic that makes it tend to develop transmission difficulties. The person might then be sensitive to information that would support his or her position—that the model is actually quite reliable. An advertiser might therefore stand ready to respond immediately to any negative information his customers are likely to receive. Such a campaign would capitalize on selectivity and could be very effective. Its target would be existing customers, even loyal buyers, instead of those not now buying the brand.

Combating Selective Exposure.   How does an advertiser combat selective exposure—be it overt or de facto? He or she can use rewards, contests, or premiums to get people to read the material. Users of direct-mail advertisements have had great success with using contests to break through the selective-exposure barrier. An alternative is to not even try to reach certain segments directly, but to try to do it indirectly by a two-step flow of information: that is, reach opinion leaders and rely on word of mouth to reach others. Another approach is to broaden the media used, even if some of the additional media seem rather inefficient in terms of conventional measures, such as cost per thousand. A sophisticated media model properly used will naturally put forth such suggestions (as will be seen in Chapter 15).

Information That Stimulates: The Complexity Theories

There is a set of theories termed complexity theories that consistently make inconsistent predictions than the consistency theories. The most dramatic position among the complexity theorists is held by Maddi, who puts forth his variety theory as follows:

Its essence is that novelty, unexpectedness, change, and complexity are pursued because they are inherently satisfying. The definition of novelty and unexpectedness must stress the difference between existing cognitive content and current or future perceptions, and hence, the experience of variety is very likely to also be the experience of inconsistency.[14]

Maddi's theory rests on the very reasonable assumption that people get bored and are motivated to reduce that boredom by seeking stimuli that are novel, unusual, and different. People are curious about the world around them, and this curiosity will influence exposure patterns. In particular, they may be motivated to seek out information that does not support their positions.

The complexity theories have empirical support of their own.[15] Studies of exploratory behavior have found that when a new element is introduced into the environment, individuals will attempt to learn about it. In that respect, the use of the journalistic sense for what is news and how it can be dramatized can be useful to copywriters. David Ogilvy suggested as much when he advised copywriters to inject news into their headlines. He wrote that "the two most powerful words you can use in a headline are free and new. You can seldom use free but you can always use new—if you try hard enough."[16] Other studies have indicated that variety in the form of small degrees of novelty and unexpectedness is pleasurable, whereas completely predictable events become boring. The Simmons advertisement shown in Figure 8-3 attracts attention with a scene that is unexpected and novel, to say the least. It certainly seems obvious that advertising should avoid being predictable, especially in situations wherein selectivity can easily operate to screen out advertisements. Another empirical conclusion is that variety is not only pursued and enjoyed, but is actually necessary to normal living.

A Reconciliation.   How does one reconcile consistency and complexity theories, two intuitively plausible but conflicting positions? One approach is to assume that tendencies toward consistency and variety both exist. The one that will dominate will depend on the personality and the situation involved.[17] Assume that there is a level of activation at which an individual is comfortable and effective. When the activation level is lower than desired, the individual will pursue variety to increase it. When it is high, she or he will be motivated to reduce stimulation and seek harmony such as is predicted by consistency theories. Obviously, there will be differences across people in terms of the optimal activation level. The situation will also determine behavior. If a high level of activation is required for optimal task performance, variety seeking will emerge. Thus, if a person is embarking on a major purchase, he or she may require a variety of information; if it is a routine purchase, such a drive will not tend to emerge. McGuire indicates that this reconciliation of the two theories is quite reasonable and suggests a nonmonotonic relationship between psychological tension and cognitive variety. He concludes that he "would readily agree with Maddi that the organism probably likes a little bit, but

Figure 8-3.   **Attracting attention with an unexpected scene**

not too much novelty and surprise, with this optimal point shifting predictably with personal and situational characteristics."[18]

Information That Interests

People tend to notice information that is interesting to them. In turn, they are interested in subjects with which they are involved. They are essentially interested in themselves and in various extensions of themselves. Katz summarizes and interprets some relevant empirical findings:

> Apart from the quest for support and for utility, mere interest would seem to be an important factor in selectivity. The desire to see one's self-reflection is part of this. So is the desire to keep watch over things in which one has invested one's ego. Thus, moviegoers identify with screen stars of similar age and sex: one reads in the newspaper about an event in which one personally participated; one reads advertisements for the product one purchased; political partisans immerse themselves in political communications regardless of its source; smokers choose to read material supporting the smoking-lung cancer relationship no less than material disclaiming the relationship, and much more avidly than nonsmokers; after one has been introduced to a celebrity, one notices (or "follows") his name in print even more frequently.[19]

The relationship of interest to attention can be seen by noting the difference in advertisement readership across product classes. A study in the early 1950s of nearly 8,000 one-page advertisements in *Post* and *Life* was conducted by Starch, a service that regularly reports advertising readership. It revealed that automobile advertisement readership by men, according to one of their measures, was five times as high as that for women's clothes and about twice as high as for toilet goods, insurance, and building materials. For women, the highest categories were motion pictures and women's clothing, which had twice the readership of advertisements for travel and men's clothing and four times that for liquor and machinery.[20]

Haley offers several case studies to support his opinion that people are more apt to look at and remember things in which they are interested than things in which they are not.[21] He further hypothesized that people are interested in information concerning benefits that they feel are important in a product. He thus applies benefit segmentation to the task of penetrating the attention barrier. In one on-air television test the interest in the benefit offered in the commercial was measured for each of five segments, as was the attention level achieved by the commercial. The results showed a nice relationship between interest and attention:

SEGMENT	INTEREST	ATTENTION
1	17	43
2	12	35
3	12	23
4	10	25
5	8	27

In another study reported by Haley, the target segment was preoccupied with their children's welfare. A child-oriented test advertisement received an attention level over five times that of each of the five other advertisements.

A most effective approach for gaining attention would be to run an advertisement about the person or persons to whom it is directed, mentioning him by name and discussing his activities. Max Hart (of Hart, Schaffner & Marx) reportedly scoffed at his advertising manager, George L. Dyer, when the latter offered to bet him $10 that he could compose a newspaper page of solid type that Hart would read word for word. Dyer said, "I don't have to write a line of it to prove my point. I'll only tell you the headline: THIS PAGE IS ALL ABOUT MAX HART."[22]

Such an approach is usually impossible, but advertisements can be developed with which people can readily identify. For instance, an insurance company ran a series of advertisements in which agents were presented in a most personal way. Their hobbies and life-styles were discussed in a manner that made it easy for readers to identify with them. Such advertisements, of course, were sure to have an enormous impact on the company's agents, who could easily picture themselves in them. A firm's own employees or its retailers are often an important audience, even if not the primary one.

Another approach is to present a communication involving topical issues— those in which the audience is likely to be heavily involved. Thus, in the late 1960s and early 1970s many oil companies began tying their advertising appeals to various aspects of the highly topical issues of ecology and pollution. Another example is an airline's effort to capitalize on the high interest in football. The day following a local football game in San Francisco, Lufthansa German Airlines regularly ran an advertisement in the sports section that included the game's score. A typical headline would mention the San Francisco 49ers pro football team:

49ers	36
Eagles	14
The Red Baron	1

The accompanying copy explains that Lufthansa is the one airline flying nonstop from California to Amsterdam: "Imagine! Seven thousand miles through the air in one play." Readers of the sports section will probably have an exceptional interest in the analysis of the 49ers' game and thus will be attracted by the headline. As long as the copy is handled properly, the resulting association will very likely be positive. Naturally, the advertising must guard against irritating the reader by gaining his attention through false pretenses.

Attraction versus Communication.   An advertiser should be concerned not to attract attention in a manner that diverts interest from the important points of the message. In particular, it is not useful to attract an individual with a highly interesting subject if the brand and its message get lost in the process. For example, sexually attractive models tend to generate high interest among some audience segments, but they can also divert a reader from the message. Steadman showed 60 male respondents twelve photographs, six of which were neutral (a house, a land-scape, and so on) and six that were photographs of females in various stages of undress. Below each picture was printed a well-advertised brand name. The brand was randomly assigned to the photographs, and the set of advertisements was left with the participant for 24 hours. At the end of that time, the brand names were removed and the subjects were asked to recall them. Brand recall for the sexually oriented photographs was higher than for the others, but not significantly so. How-ever, when the recall test was repeated seven days later, the nonsexual "advertise-ments" had 61 percent recall (of 360 data points) and the sexual advertisements had only 49 percent—a considerable difference. The effect was even more pronounced for those who disapproved of sexual illustrations in advertising.[23] Thus, it appears that a portion of the advertisement can dominate a reader's perception to the det-riment of the communication impact if that portion that dominates is not related to the advertisement objective.

Combating Zapping and Clutter

Only a few years ago the major concern of television advertisers was to inhibit viewers from leaving the room during the commercials. Now there is a much more serious problem—commercials can get zapped without leaving the room.[24] A viewer can turn off the sound or change channels with a remote control tuner or run fast-forward on a prerecorded program. One advertising researcher estimated that during the average commercial break there is a tune-out factor of 40 percent.

A related problem is the difficulty of gaining attention in the face of the increase in advertising clutter. The number of network commercials jumped from 1,856 per week in 1967 to 4,566 per week in 1983. This gain was caused by the dramatic increase in the use of 30-second commercials and the increase in the time allocated to commercials. The pressure toward 15-second commercials should only make the matter worse. One measure of the impact of clutter is the drop in the correct brand recall of the last commercial seen. For an average commercial, one study showed the following drop between 1965 and 1981:

1965	18 percent
1974	12 percent
1981	7 percent

An approach to combating zapping and clutter is to create commercials that are so interesting that viewers will prefer to watch them rather than zap them.[25] Ideally, viewers would look for or wait for commercials to come on. Pepsi spent $2 million on a set of Michael Jackson commercials in an effort to make them especially interesting. Several firms have tried creating movie-quality epics. Wrangler sports-wear, for example, created a 45-second commercial costing over $1 million fea-turing a young couple out of movies such as *Raiders of the Lost Ark* or *Romancing the Stone* who survive one crisis after another. After taking a huge emerald from an idol, they escape by swinging on vines over a deep chasm as the voice-over solemnly intones, "Out here people need a Wrangler style . . . because no matter what they're doing, they want to look their best. Anytime, anywhere." Data General illustrated tomorrow's technology by simulating a catapult and a medieval battle staged complete with 150 extras and an authentic medieval setting.

Perhaps the most spectacular commercial of recent times was a spot for the Apple Macintosh computer. Called "1984," it aired only once during the Super Bowl. A young woman is shown throwing a sledgehammer through a giant TV screen featuring Big Brother. The tag line was: "Apple computer will introduce Macintosh and you'll see why 1984 won't be like *1984*." The ad was enormously successful at generating interest in their computer. Apple's "Lemmings" commercial aired at the 1985 Super Bowl, however, was less successful.[26] It showed a line of people with briefcases mindlessly walking off a cliff humming "Hi-Ho, Hi-Ho, it's off to work we go." The last marcher, presumably the one not following the IBM parade, stops at the edge and the Macintosh office systems concept was announced. In a postgame telephone survey, only 54 percent of 300 viewers recalled seeing an Apple commercial, and only 10.3 percent could describe it correctly. Asked which commercial comes to mind of all those shown, only 3.3 percent mentioned the Apple commercial. In contrast, Budweiser, which ran four commercials and was the most recognized advertiser, was mentioned by 7.7 percent of the respondents.

Other advertisers combat zapping and clutter by developing standard-length commercials that try to gain and hold attention by being very unusual or entertaining. Pioneer Electronics, for example, ran a 30-second commercial that was silent for all but a few seconds. There have been a host of campaigns that have been so humorous that they take on a life of their own.

Stimulus Factors

It is useful to consider the stimulus itself and search for generalizations relating descriptors of the stimuli, such as size and shape, to attention. What stimulus characteristics will attract attention?

Adaption-Level Theory.   Helson has developed an adaption-level theory that is relevant to this discussion.[27] He suggests that it is not only the focal stimuli that determine perception, but also the contextual stimuli (background) and residual stimuli (past experience). The individual learns to associate a stimulus set with a reference point or adaption level. Attention is then created when an object deviates markedly from that level. For example, if a person has a hand in hot water for a period of time, the hand will adapt to that temperature and other water will be perceived relative to it. Thus, a dish of warm water could be perceived as cold, relative to an individual's adaption level.

In an advertising context, a humorous advertisement may attract attention if it is surrounded by more conventional copy approaches. However, if many humorous advertisements are involved, the ability of one of them to attract attention would be reduced. The residual stimuli, the culmination of past experience, also contribute to the establishment of a reference point. If past experience has suggested that most comparable advertising avoided humor in its copy, then one using humor may attract attention even if it is not unusual in its present context.

Helson studied the adaption-level construct in various contexts—among them, light intensity, colors, and lifting tasks. He found empirically that a weighted average of the logarithm of the various stimuli—focal, contextual, and residual—provided a reliable predictor for the adaption level. The set of three weights had to be estimated for each of the various situations. They will likely be different if color is the stimulus instead of sound, for instance. The inclusion of the logarithm suggests that a very intense stimulus may not dominate the adaption level to the exclusion of the others. Helson indicated that adaption levels can be found for such stimulus properties as beauty, prestige, significance, quality, and affective value. The procedure would be to develop a measurement scale and simply pool the focal, contextual, and residual stimuli by a weighted log mean formula.

Weber's Law.   A logical question is how different does the stimuli have to be from the adaption level to be perceived as different. One answer is in the form of a law, termed *Weber's law,* after a nineteenth-century researcher. Weber's law suggests that

$$\frac{\Delta I}{I} = K$$

where ΔI = smallest increase in stimulus intensity that will be perceived as different from the existing intensity (or adaption level)

I = existing stimulus intensity (or adaption level)

K = constant that varies across senses

The law states that the degree to which a stimulus will be regarded as different will depend not on the absolute stimulus change but on the percentage of change from some point of reference. Furthermore, the percentage of change that is detectable will depend on the sense. Considerable effort has been devoted to determining K for the various senses. It was established, for example, that K for pitch is much lower than K for taste. Obviously, K will vary substantially over individuals and with the exact nature of the stimuli involved.

These concepts suggest that advertisements that are sufficiently different from an audience's adaption level and expectations will attract attention. Within an advertisement, the illustration or copy may similarly stand out from the balance of the advertisement if it is sufficiently unusual or unexpected. In Gestalt terms, the figure will emerge from the ground.

Stimulus Conditions.   Many stimulus characteristics contribute to the ability of an advertisement to attract attention. The size and intensity of a stimulus will often influence attention. Advertisement readership will increase with advertisement size, although not linearly. A loud stimulus will be more likely to be perceived than one of less intensity. Color presentations will usually attract more attention than those in black and white. Position can influence attention. The left side of the page and the upper half get slightly more readership because of people's reading habits. Movement, either real or simulated (for example, the use of jagged lines), is useful. Specific measurement techniques and research findings regarding these dimensions and their effect on advertisement readership will be discussed in Chapter 16.

Effort Required.   Instead of getting people to read the advertisement, an advertiser might be resigned to the fact that an advertisement will receive only a glance or two from most readers. It may, therefore, be worthwhile to design communications that can be perceived with only this minimum attention. It is certainly true that some advertisements require more effort, in terms of eye movement, than others to communicate. Payne, an advertising researcher, studied the relationship between eye movement and learning. He used an optiscan, a device for photographing the specific point on which a subject is focusing. There was a significant correlation (0.41) between subject learning and the extent of eye movement during 10-second exposures; for a given subject, the more eye movement, the more learning. However, in the eight advertisements tested, there was a negative relationship between scanning and learning. Those advertisements that stimulated the most content recall evoked the lowest amount of scanning. Payne concluded that advertisements designed to communicate with very little eye movement will get more information across in a given time period.[28]

INTERPRETATION

The tenets of Gestalt psychology are useful in a discussion of the interpretation of stimuli.[29] During the nineteenth century, psychologists attempted to analyze consciousness by breaking it down into its most fundamental components, elementary sensations and associations. One of the pioneers of Gestalt psychology, Max Wertheimer, challenged this approach. He pointed out that when a light in one place is turned off and another nearby is turned on, movement is perceived to occur, an illusion often used in outdoor advertising. He termed this phenomenon the *phi phenomenon,* and it served to stimulate the study of the perceptual process from a different orientation. It demonstrated that an analysis of elementary associations— several lights going on and off—would be a futile way to understand what is perceived, that is, movement. The Gestalt view is that it is necessary to consider the organized whole, the system of elementary events, since the whole has a meaning distinct from its individual parts. The German word *gestalt* is roughly translated into configuration, or whole, or pattern.

Two other researchers, Kohler and Koffka, shared with Wertheimer the early development of this orientation. They enunciated two principles. The first is the concept of the organized whole, or gestalt. Stimuli are perceived not as a set of elements, but as a whole. When a person looks at a landscape, she or he does not see many blades of grass, several trees, white clouds, and a stream, but, rather, a field or total configuration. This total has a meaning of its own that is not necessarily deducible from its individual components. The second concept is that an individual has cognitive drive toward an orderly cognitive configuration or psychological field. An individual desires to make the psychological field as good as possible. A good field or gestalt is simple, familiar, regular, meaningful, consistent, and complete. The modern consistency theories, such as dissonance theory, so useful in attitude research, are outgrowths of this second tenet, which was developed in the study of the perceptual process.

In the following section, the first and basic principle of Gestalt psychology will be discussed and illustrated in an advertising context. The emergence of the organized whole from a limited set of stimuli is demonstrated by a set of classic experiments. The importance of interrelationships among stimuli is brought out. An implication of the Gestalt view is that a brand must be considered as an organized whole and not simply as the sum of independent attributes. Another is that the context is important. After these implications are considered, we turn to the concept of a cognitive drive toward a ''good'' Gestalt and to some determinants of perceptual organization.

The Organized Whole

S. E. Asch conducted a classic set of experiments, reported in 1946, that demonstrated how individuals form organized wholes and the importance of interactions among component parts.[30] A group was read a list of personal characteristics and asked to write a brief impression of the person described by the list. The list contained seven attributes: intelligent, skillful, industrious, warm, determined, practical, and cautious. A second group, with the same instructions, was read the same list except that the word ''warm'' was replaced by the word ''cold.'' The difference in the two groups' perceptions was striking. The warm person was perceived to be happier, better natured, more sociable, more altruistic, more humorous, and more imaginative. Further experiments indicated that when polite versus blunt was used instead of warm versus cold, the differences became relatively minor. Also, Asch determined that the first few terms established a context in which later terms were evaluated. Perception was affected by the order in which the terms were presented.

Asch generated several conclusions from these experiments. Even when the stimuli are incomplete, people seem to strive to form a complete impression of a person or object. Thus, advertising copy does not necessarily have to tell the whole story; an individual will naturally fill in the gaps. The studies indicated that stimuli are seen in interaction. The intelligence of a warm person is perceived differently from that of a cold person. Because of such interaction effects, the total impact of an advertising campaign needs to be considered. An appeal or an advertisement that may prove effective by itself may not be effective in the context of the whole campaign. Furthermore, the studies suggested that some attributes (warm-cold) are more central to the conceptual process than others (polite-blunt). The value of identifying dimensions that have the quality of centrality was considered in Chapter 6. Finally, the experiments indicated that the first few traits formed a set or context within which others are interpreted. Thus, an advertiser should be very concerned with first impressions. Generating trial with a big giveaway program may project a sleazy image from which a brand may never recover.

Mason Haire, in the late 1940s, used the basic Asch methodology with a shopping list as the stimuli set and 100 housewives as the sample. Half the sample was shown a shopping list that included an instant coffee. The other half was shown an identical list, except that a regular coffee was substituted for the instant. The instant coffee housewife was described as lazy, a poor planner, and even by some as a spendthrift and a bad wife. The regular coffee housewife, on the other hand, was described quite favorably. The study helped to explain the early resistance to instant coffee even among those who could not distinguish instant from regular in a blind taste test.[31] A recent replication of Haire's experiment found that the negative image of the instant coffee user had been replaced by one of a busy girl, not necessarily a bad wife.[32] Furthermore, the differences between the two diminished considerably, although the regular coffee user was still regarded as somewhat thriftier. The increased acceptance of convenience foods probably had much to do with the altered image.

A Brand Image

That stimuli are viewed as a total configuration suggests that a brand must be considered as an organized whole. Thus, the alteration of a single component may indeed affect the total configuration. In terms of a perceptual map, introduced in Chapter 5, we might see that there are interactions among the various dimensions; that is, it is not possible to operate on one independently of the others. If one dimension is affected or a new dimension added, the perception of the brand along the others may change radically to consumers, as may the relative importance of the various dimensions (or product attributes).

Martineau provides an example of how a subtle change in a product's presentation produced an entirely different image:

> When Procter & Gamble introduced Cheer with adequate advertising proclaiming it as "good for tough-job washing," it was just another detergent going no particular place in sales, according to our research. Then it was given a blue color, and in the housewife's mind it acquired a completely different character, making it seemingly capable of functional wonders totally uncalled for by anything in the mere color. Thereupon it became a tremendous national success.[33]

White provides another example and relates it to the Gestalt notion of whole:

A study of sugar-coating added to an old, well-accepted cereal told us that the new difference was not merely that of perceiving the presweetening and liking it or not liking it. The new difference meant the perception of a whole new user group behind it, the acceptance of a different style of life. The addition of a sugar-coating to cornflakes does not make the emerging product a "super cornflakes" capable of maintaining the previous market segment while adding a new one, those who like their cereals presweetened. No, add presweetening and you no longer have cornflakes at all! Thus, it is a naive assumption that product value is the sum total of product traits— even if the added product traits are "product advantages." Once again we return to an elementary perceptual axiom that the whole is greater than the sum of its parts.[34]

Relationships among Stimuli

If perception is indeed an organized whole, then the system of interrelationships among component stimuli has meaning of its own. All the stimuli could change, but if the relationships among entities remain, the perception may not be affected. If all the notes in a song were raised an octave, the song would be perceived as being fundamentally unchanged. There might be many advertisements that are variations on a single campaign theme (for example, the Marlboro country campaign). The individual advertisements might be quite different. Yet if they are perceived as part of the total campaign, then they will likely be perceived as very similar, because certain relationships within the advertisement are constant even though the models and the settings are changed.

The Context

The concept of the organized whole dictates that we cannot consider the perception of a stimulus in isolation from its context. The setting of the stimulus is part of the total field and will influence the perception. A salty expression would be perceived quite differently at a football game than it would be in the middle of a wedding ceremony.

The context of an advertisement will affect how it is perceived. It has been well documented that many advertisements have different effects on those exposed to them, depending on the vehicle in which the advertisement appeared. If the vehicle is sufficiently incompatible with the advertisement appeal, the result may be disastrous. In Chapter 16, the vehicle-source effect will be discussed in detail, and the importance of the context will be illustrated.

The context of an advertisement can be considered far broader than simply the vehicle type in which it is imbedded. The feature material in a specific edition may create a mood that will affect interpretation. Furthermore, the company involved and all its interactions with an audience member will also affect interpretation. The advertisement may stimulate associations that will further broaden the context, which will indeed influence the resulting interpretation.

Principles of Perceptual Organization

An important tenet of Gestalt psychology is that there is a cognitive drive to obtain a good Gestalt or configuration, one that is simple, familiar, regular, meaningful, consistent, and complete. The human mind is not above making minor or even major distortions of the stimuli to accomplish this purpose. The following principles are related to this cognitive drive.

Closure.   If we see a symbol that would be a square except that a small segment of one side is missing, our minds will fill in this gap and a square will be perceived. This process is called *closure*. In the Asch experiment, in which rather strong perceptions in individuals were obtained from a short list of attributes, closure was occurring. A detailed picture of an individual emerged from a sketchy list of cues.

An advertiser can use the closure process to make a campaign more efficient. A 60-second commercial can, for example, be run several times so that the content has been learned by a worthwhile percentage of the target audience. To combat forgetting, a shorter spot—maybe only 5 or 10 seconds long—could be used. A viewer of the short spot will tend to visualize the omitted material. Thus, the material contained in the 60-second commercial will have been transmitted in a much shorter time. Furthermore, the risk of boring the viewer with repeated showings is reduced.

Another use of the closure concept is leaving a well-known jingle uncompleted. Those exposed will have a strong cognitive drive to effect closure by mentally completing the jingle. For example, Salem cigarettes mounted a campaign in which they presented "You can take Salem out of the country but you can't . . ." The audience then had to provide the familiar ending "take the country out of Salem." The Hathaway shirt advertisements showing the man in a dress shirt and eyepatch ran without any mention of Hathaway. Again, the audience was expected via the closure process to insert the manufacturer's name. The "FDR sat here" advertisement shown in Figure 8-4 invites the reader to use closure to imagine the chair's occupant. Activating the closure process in this manner can get the reader involved, even to the extent of stimulating effort on his or her part. Such involvement often enhances learning.

Closely related to closure is the process of interpreting an ambiguous stimulus. Again, the interesting part of the process is the participant's involvement. The hope is that ambiguity will stimulate sufficient interest to sustain the cognitive activity necessary to "figure it out." There are several ways in which an advertisement can be made "ambiguous." Consider, for example, an advertisement made up of three principal elements—a picture, some written material, and the brand name. Ambiguity can be introduced into any of these components (and may be a way to highlight or emphasize a component) or into the relationship among components. The picture, for example, could be made ambiguous by leaving out parts of it or using some form of abstract art. The written material could contain innuendo or indirect meanings. For example, "Does she or doesn't she?" and "I'm

Figure 8-4.   **Activating the closure process**

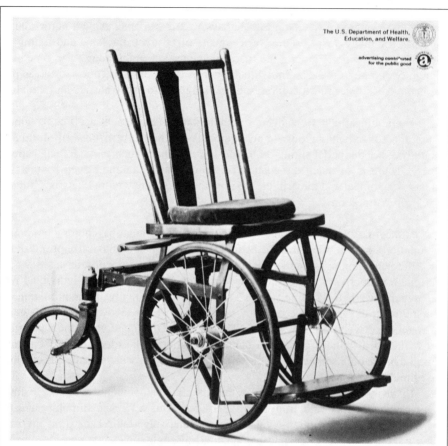

FDR sat here.

At the age of 39, Franklin Delano Roosevelt contracted polio. He went to bed one night feeling ill, and in the morning he couldn't get up. He couldn't walk.

He had a handicap. And yet, seven years later, he became governor of New York. Eleven years later, President of the United States.

He led the country out of the dark days of the depression, and still in a wheelchair, through the bitter years of a world war.

He was obviously as smart sitting down as he was standing up. And he was willing to work hard enough to prove it to himself and to the people of America.

Today, there are millions of Americans with physical and mental disabilities. Millions of people with handicaps. And they, too, realize that they have to prove themselves. But all too often, they don't get the chance.

They don't get the understanding they need to gain the confidence to ask for a break. Or they find the physical barriers to entering and leaving buildings, or to using public transportation, so discouraging that they don't even try.

And this is a tragic waste. This is the real handicap.

What can you do to help? You can take the time to think. You can take the trouble to understand. You can give these people your confidence, so they can have confidence in themselves. And you can give them the same chance you'd give anyone else.

Then, when you've given all this, you can do one final thing. You can stop thinking of them as handicapped. And start thinking of them as friends and neighbors, as people with talent and a contribution to make to the world.

Isn't it about time we stopped handicapping the handicapped?

REHABILITATION OF THE HANDICAPPED CAMPAIGN
MAGAZINE AD NO. REH-1835-73——7″ x 10″ (110 Screen)
ALSO AVAILABLE: AD NO. REH-1837-73——15″ x 10″ Spread
Volunteer Agency: Warwick & Legler, Inc. Volunteer Coordinator: Robert E. Gorman, Allstate Insurance Companies.

Sylvia—fly me to Miami'' contain other associations besides those of hair coloring and air travel. Even the brand or company name could be made relatively or completely "ambiguous," as in the Hathaway shirt example. A well-known company has for many years used advertisements of abstract diagrams and figures in which the connections among all these elements are ambiguous. The object of ambiguity can be to tease an individual's curiosity, to draw attention to the advertisement, to initiate consideration and thinking, or to motivate an individual to learn.

There are, of course, dangers in making an advertisement itself or any component thereof too ambiguous. Many examples of "bad advertising" illustrate this point. The blonde model sitting on the drill press in an industrial trade magazine is typical. There is so much discepancy between what is communicated by the two objects—the model and the drill press—that the viewer may more likely be "turned off" than "turned on."

Assimilation-Contrast.   Another principle of perceptual psychology is called assimilation-contrast. Cognitively, an individual will seek to maximize or minimize the differences among stimuli. Assimilation and contrast operate in cases where stimuli are neither very similar nor very different. In these cases, an individual will tend to perceive them as being "more" similar than they really are (assimilation) or to cognitively exaggerate the differences (contrast). Both tendencies are related to the cognitive drive to simplify stimuli. There is a certain simplicity in the perception of two identical stimuli or in two contrasting stimuli that does not exist in two stimuli that are only somewhat distinct. The perception process is made easier if one can eliminate the shades of gray.

In the advertising context, one of the stimuli to be compared is often a residual or reference stimulus built from past experience. This reference stimulus, like the residual stimulus of adaption-level theory, is relatively stable because it involves many cognitive associations and has endured through some time period. When a new stimulus is introduced by an advertisement, it is consequently the new stimulus that is cognitively adjusted to make it assimilate with or contrast to the reference stimuli. Thus, an individual when confronted with a new stimulus that is not exceptionally new or different will treat it as similar to others which she or he has learned in the past.

An advertiser can take advantage of the assimilation principle in many ways. It provides a rationale for family or umbrella brands like Kellogg's, Betty Crocker, or Westinghouse. The hope is that buyers will tend to generalize their past experiences with the brand to a new product (a cereal, a cake mix, or a dishwasher) carrying the brand name. This tendency to assimilate a new product into a family brand will be enhanced by the use of advertising styles that have come to be associated with the family brand. The assimilation principle can also be used to advantage by a relatively small advertiser who might seek to associate himself by using a similar name, for example, with a large well-regarded competitor. The Avis car advertisement "We're number 2 . . . we try harder," at least initially, was probably effective largely because the campaign served to associate Avis with Hertz.

Assimilation can also work to an advertiser's disadvantage. Thus, a new product variation may be perceived as the same as the old one unless efforts are made to guard against this reaction. Also, advertisements for similar products, like menthol cigarettes, that tend to use similar appeals run the danger of being assimilated. As a result, a smaller brand may not get much mileage out of its advertising since the audience may not distinguish it from its more widely known competitor. In such situations it is sometimes necessary to use dramatic means as Goodrich did in Figure 8-5 to ensure that "contrast" dominates "assimilation." The campaign in which the advertisement in Figure 8-5 was embedded had as one of its objectives to clear up the name confusion between Goodyear and Goodrich. The campaign was very successful. Consumer recall of the Goodrich commercials was 50 percent, five times the historical average and five times the recall of Goodyear commercials. Furthermore, the campaign established Goodrich as the number one innovator in the industry and the maker of the best radial tire.[35]

Perceptual Grouping. Wertheimer initiated the development of a number of principles about how subjects will group together or unify in a visual field stimuli to which they are exposed. Among the principles he suggested are that stimuli will be grouped together according to their similarity, their proximity in time or space, the existence of a common boundary, the tendency for the grouping to be appealing (that is, symmetrical, balanced, or orderly), the existence of a cause-and-effect relationship, past experience, or set or expectation. Since the direct or indirect purpose of advertising is usually to develop associations, these principles may be useful in suggesting effective copy aproaches.

Determinates of Perceptual Organization

The model of the perceptual process suggests that a host of audience conditions can influence interpetation. In particular, a person's needs, values, brand preferences, social situation, and cognitive style can determine how an individual interprets a given stimulus. This type of concern can be contrasted with the early classical Gestalt emphasis on stimulus factors. It recognizes that perception is the result of interaction of an active perceiver with a stimulus environment—that past experience sensitizes the individual to respond to different aspects of the stimuli and in different ways. As a result, audience characteristics need to be considered in addition to stimuli characteristics. The evolution of perceptual theory from a stimulus orientation to consideration of more complex models of the process is most natural and productive.

Needs. Bruner and Goodman showed that children from lower socioeconomic classes overestimate the size of coins, indicating that economic deprivation may affect perceptual distortion.[36] Later studies suggested that the relative subjective

Figure 8-5. **Counteracting the assimilation process**

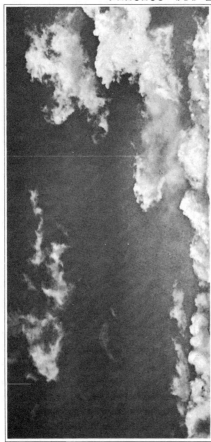

A glorious, full-color picture of the Goodrich Blimp.

What? No blimp?

Look again.

Not at the picture, the name.

Goodrich.

Not Goodyear.

Goodrich doesn't have a blimp, Goodyear does.

We haven't advertised as much as Goodyear, either. So it's not too surprising a lot of people forget our name and remember theirs.

And if you're confused about our blimps, when we don't even have one, just imagine how confused you can get about our tires.

Who knows, you might even go to Goodyear to get them. And that's too bad. You see, in 1965, Goodrich introduced the first American-made radial tire.

For five years, nationally, we've advertised nothing else.

Not because everybody wanted radials.

But because the radial tire was, and is, the most important innovation in tires in nearly a quarter century.

No conventional tire we've ever made, none, stops as fast, corners as well, and lasts as long as our Goodrich Lifesaver Steel Radial.

It's the result of our company's commitment, for ten years, to make the most advanced radial tire on the road.

Now you watch. You'll probably see Goodyear featuring a steel radial, too. Along with all their other tires.

It'll be good. But it won't be Goodrich.

And if you still get our names confused, just look up in the sky.

If you see an enormous blimp with somebody's name on it, we're the other guys.

Lifesaver® Steel Radials.
If you want Goodrich, you'll just have to remember Goodrich.

B.F.Goodrich
America's Premier Radial Tire Maker

sizes of coins of different values had a greater tendency to be distorted by poor children than the absolute sizes.

A series of early studies were concerned with the impact of food deprivation on perceptual distortion. Levine, Chein, and Murphy found that associations of an obscured stimulus with food and eating increased as the hours of food deprivation increased until it reached a maximum at 10 to 12 hours.[37] Presumably, the effect would also apply to higher-level needs as well as to basic needs such as that for food. One might speculate that advertisement exposure might be more effective if it could be precipitated at a time when the need for the object of the advertisement was most intense. An advertisement of a food product might be more effective if exposed just before dinner rather than just after dinner. Refreshing drinks might be more effectively advertised during hot summer afternoons rather than at other times. Relevant motivations are undoubtedly aroused in anticipation of national holidays such as Mother's Day or Easter. A media selection schedule could be adjusted for such possibilities.

Values. There is evidence that words that reflect a person's personal values are perceived faster than words that are less salient to an individual. In a classic experiment, Postman, Bruner, and McGinnies used a tachistoscope to expose students to a series of words.[38] The tachistoscope is a device that permits a researcher to generate exposure of a controlled length, such as 10 milliseconds. Judges chose 36 words that represented the six basic values as measured by the Allport-Vernon scale of values. The scale, which already had been applied to the subjects, measured the dominance of religious, esthetic, political, social, theoretical, and economic interests. The subjects required longer exposures to identify words associated with values that received low scores than high-value words. The high-valued words thus seem to have a lower perceptual threshold.

Preferences. Spence and Engel performed a similar experiment.[39] They used brand names and attempted to determine if brand preference was related to a perceptual threshold. They obtained a set of 53 widely known brands from five product classes. Each subject was asked to indicate brands with which he or she was not familiar. This question represented an effort to control for brand familiarity so that the effect of brand preference would be measured, not confounded, by brand familiarity. The results, when controlled for perceptual differences among age groups, did support the hypothesis that perceptual thresholds for preferred brands will occur at a lower exposure duration level than those for nonpreferred brands.

Spence and Engel suggest that there may be a kind of "perceptual defense" that inhibits the response speed to certain words or symbols and a perceptual viligance that helps an individual to perceive some things more readily. They also speculated on some practical implications of this research.

> It would appear that primary emphasis on the brand name in headline or visual elements of an advertisement may be unwise when the objective is to change preferences or switch those who are presently committed to other brands. Inhibited speed of

response may cause the individual to ignore the message completely. Other forms of attention-attraction should be used. On the other hand, dominant emphasis on the name is appropriate where the intent is to attract those who are already favorable to suggest new uses, further strengthen preference, etc.[40]

Brand preference can also contribute to perceptual distortion. Stayton and Wiener found that those who wanted to own Volkswagens tended to overestimate the size differential between it and a larger car.[41]

Group Pressure.   Stress caused by group pressure can affect perception. Asch conducted an experiment in which subjects were asked to make comparative judgments about some visual stimuli.[42] All but one of the subjects were instructed before the experiment to make an incorrect judgment even when it appeared obviously wrong. The naive subject, after hearing the judgments of the others, often yielded and conformed (32 percent of the time) to the group's judgment. When one other member of the group gave a correct answer, the tendency for the naive subject to give an incorrect answer was greatly reduced. A similar kind of self-induced pressure might be generated by a person's reference group. If a person identified with a group whom she or he believed would perceive a stimulus in a certain way, that person might be motivated to perceive it in the same way.

Cognitive Needs.   There are differences among people in their need for cognitive clarity that affect perception. A need for cognitive clarity is essentially a need to impose meaning, organization, integration, and reasonableness on one's experiences with the world. The need may develop in some people because achieving clarity may satisfy other needs, or because of demands to clarify, comprehend, and so on. Individual experiences differ according to the number of times persons are confronted with unclear, ambiguous, and poorly structured situations, and the degree to which the outcomes of these situations are unpleasant or painful. Hence, individuals differ in the degree to which they learn to be frightened of ambiguity and to become anxious or nervous when confronted with it. These differences are reflected in differences in the strength of the need for cognitive clarity. Cohen has shown that individuals with strong needs for cognitive clarity will tend to exert more effort to understand an ambiguous communication than persons whose needs for cognitive clarity are weak.[43]

Cognitive Style.   People also differ in their cognitive style. Kelman and Cohler distinguish two kinds of cognitive style called "sharpeners" (clarifiers) or "levelers" (simplifiers).[44] Sharpeners are people who emphasize unique distinguishing details, who actively look for cues that might eliminate ambiguity, and who are very receptive to available information. Levelers are people who operate with a limited set of cognitive categories. They ignore distinguishing details, simplify their environments, try to fit and even twist the content of new and distinctive experiences into familiar molds. Levelers with a strong need for cognitive clarity might be expected to react defensively in ambiguous situations. As they normally ignore particulars, they should become especially unobservant. Everything will continue to look clear and simple if they withdraw attention from whatever it is that makes the situation confusing and ignore whatever seems incongruous. Differences between levelers and sharpeners should be maximal when they have strong needs for cognitive clarity and when they find themselves in novel and unfamiliar situations. Levelers will probably be more likely to simplify the environment by activating the assimilation mechanism than will sharpeners.

Baron designed an experiment that dealt with the effects of three factors: the ambiguity of the communication, the need for cognitive clarity, and cognitive style.[45] Initially, he took measures of college students' cognitive styles and their attitudes toward advertising. In an experimental session three weeks later, they were exposed to an extremely pro-advertising communication. For half the subjects, the material was made extremely ambiguous, with its sentences and thoughts arranged in an illogical and incoherent sequence. For the other half, the communication contained identical information but was clear, logical, and orderly. Before receiving the communication, the students were given instructions designed to produce varying needs for cognitive clarity. The students' attitudes toward advertising were measured immediately after exposure to the communication and again three weeks later. Results showed that sharpeners change their attitudes more than levelers if the need for cognitive clarity is strong. If the need is weak, the effect is reversed; levelers show more attitude change than sharpeners. This effect of different needs and styles increases as the communication becomes more ambiguous.

SUMMARY

The perception process involves attention and interpretation. It is influenced by stimulus characteristics, such as copy size, intensity, and message, and by audience variables such as needs, attitudes, values, and interests.

To understand the attention filter, it is instructive to determine why people attend to advertisements. One motivation is to secure information that has practical value to them in making decisions. In some circumstances people will engage in active search for information. A second motivation is *selective exposure,* obtaining information that supports attitudes or purchase decisions and avoiding nonsupportive information. A third motivation is to obtain variety and combat boredom. Finally, people are attracted to advertisements that are interesting. Adaption-level theory suggests that attention is enhanced when the stimulus deviates markedly from the background or the context in which the advertisement appears.

Two concepts from Gestalt psychology help us to understand the interpretation process. The first is that stimuli are perceived as a whole. What is important in an advertisement interpretation is the total impression that it leaves. The second is that an individual has a cognitive drive toward an orderly cognitive configuration. Closure is an example of the cognitive drive toward a familiar, regular, and meaningful configuration. If a subject realizes that something is missing from a picture, his or her mind will add it. Assimilation-contrast, another example of this cognitive drive, is used by the audience member to remove ambiguity from a stimulus. A host of audience conditions can influence interpretation, among them needs, values, brand preferences, social situation, cognitive styles, and cognitive needs.

DISCUSSION QUESTIONS

1.   For each of the following products, indicate under what circumstances, if any, an audience member would engage in active search, passive search, or passive attention.
      a.   Automobiles
      b.   Toothpaste
      c.   Sugar
      d.   Cement mixers
      e.   Business forms
      f.   Greeting cards
      g.   Computers

2.   Under what conditions are people likely to read long copy?

3.   Consider five advertisements you have read recently. Why did you read them? What was your motivation? Does your motivation fit into one of the four categories listed in the chapter? Should other categories be added?

4.   In one study it was found that recent car purchasers tended to read advertisements for the brand they bought. How do you explain this finding? Are there explanations in addition to those that fall within the consistency-theory positions?

5.   Pick out a print and a television advertisement that you feel is informative and one of each that you feel is not informative and explain your choices. Do you feel that television advertising is informative?

6.   What are the factors that determine when a person will seek consistency and when a person will seek complexity? Suppose that you are advertising toothpaste and have identified one segment in one category and another segment in the other. How do you decide upon which segment to focus? How would the advertising campaigns for the two segments differ?

7.   How should a copy team go about balancing the need to attract attention and gain advertisement readership with the need to generate a certain kind of impact? Be specific. What procedures should be followed? Can these procedures be embedded in a formal decision model?

8.   What is adaption-level theory in the advertising context? How could one measure the environment of the advertisement quantitatively?

9. Conceive an experiment similar to the one conducted by Mason Haire in which housewives were described by a day's activities, such as prepare breakfast, play tennis, attend a luncheon, shop for a dress at———, wash clothes, prepare the evening meal, and watch television. Suppose three different stores were used for three samples, an exclusive dress shop, a department store, and a discount store. How would you expect the image of the housewives to be affected by the store used? Conduct a pilot study.

10. Recall advertisements that use the concept of closure. Were they, in your opinion, more effective because of it? Why? What is the difference between closure and contrast?

11. Give an example of an advertisement that will motivate assimilation for some and that will activate a contrast mechanism for others.

12. How might cognitive style and cognitive need be used as segmentation variables?

NOTES

1. James J. Gibson, "Perception as a Function of Stimulation," in Sigmund Koch, ed., *Psychology: A Study of a Science* (New York: McGraw-Hill, 1959), p. 457.

2. David T. Kollat, Roger D. Blackwell, and James F. Engel, *Research in Consumer Behavior* (New York: Holt, Rinehart and Winston, 1970), p. 48.

3. By creation, we refer in part to the closure process, which will be discussed later in this chapter.

4. Steuart Henderson Britt, Stephen C. Adams, and Alan S. Miller, "How Many Advertising Exposures per Day?" *Journal of Advertising Research,* 12, December 1972, pp. 3–10.

5. Raymond A. Bauer and Stephen A. Greyser, *Advertising in America: The Consumer View* (Cambridge, Mass.: Harvard University Press, 1968), pp. 173–176.

6. David A. Aaker, "Developing Corporate Consumer Information Programs," *Business Horizons,* October 1981.

7. Robert E. Burnkrant, "A Motivational Model of Information Processing Intensity," *Journal of Consumer Research,* 3, June 1976, pp. 21–30.

8. David Ogilvy, *Confessions of an Advertising Man* (New York: Atheneum, 1964), pp. 108–110.

9. Franklin B. Evans, "Psychological and Objective Factors in the Prediction of Brand Choice: Ford versus Chevrolet," *Journal of Business,* 32, October 1959, p. 363.

10. John A. Howard and Jagdish N. Sheth, *The Theory of Buyer Behavior* (New York: Wiley, 1969), pp. 164–165.

11. D. Ehrlich et al., "Post-decision Exposure to Relevant Information," *Journal of Abnormal and Social Psychology,* 54, 1957, pp. 98–102.

12. J. F. Engel, "Are Automobile Purchasers Dissonant Consumers?" *Journal of Marketing,* 27, 1963, pp. 55–58.

13. Judson Mills, "Avoidance of Dissonant Information," *Journal of Personality and Social Psychology,* 2, 1965, pp. 589–593.

14. Salvatore R. Maddi, "The Pursuit of Consistency and Variety," in R. P. Abelson et al., eds, *Theories of Cognitive Consistency* (Chicago: Rand McNally, 1968).

15. A wide variety of relevant studies are reported in D. W. Fiske and S. R. Maddi, eds., *Functions of Varied Experience* (Homewood, Ill.: Dorsey Press, 1961).

16. Ogilvy, *Confessions of an Advertising Man,* p. 105.

17. Developed in Fiske and Maddi, *Functions of Varied Experience.*

18. William J. McGuire, "Résumé and Response from the Consistency Theory Viewpoint," in Abelson et al., *Theories of Cognitive Consistency,* p. 259.

19. Elihu Katz, "On Reopening the Question of Selectivity in Exposure to Mass Communications," in Abelson et al., *Theories of Cognitive Consistency,* p. 793.

20. Daniel Starch, *Measuring Advertising Readership and Results* (New York: McGraw-Hill, 1966), p. 89.

21. Russell I. Haley, "Beyond Benefit Segmentation," *Journal of Advertising Research,* 1971.

22. This anecdote was reported by Ogilvy, *Confessions of an Advertising Man,* p. 6.

23. Major Steadman, "How Sexy Illustrations Affect Brand Recall," *Journal of Advertising Research,* 9, March 1969, pp. 15–19.

24. Felix Kessler, "In Search of Zap-Proof Commercials," *Fortune,* January 21, 1985, pp. 68–70.

25. Mark Lacter, "TV Commercial Industry Fights Back," *San Francisco Chronicle,* February 11, 1983, p. 59.

26. Joseph M. Winski, "Apple Fails to Register," *Advertising Age,* January 28, 1985, pp. 1, 98.

27. H. Helson, "Adaption Level Theory," in *Psychology: A Study of a Science: I, Sensory Perception and Physiological Formulations* (New York: McGraw-Hill, 1959).

28. Donald E. Payne, "Looking without Learning: Eye Movements When Viewing Print Advertisements," in M. S. Moyer and R. E. Vosburgh, eds., *Proceedings of the 1967 June conference of the AMA* (Chicago: American Marketing Association, 1967), pp. 78–81.

29. For an excellent introduction to Gestalt and other theories in social psychology, see Morton Deutsch and Robert M. Krauss, *Theories in Social Psychology* (New York: Basic Books, 1965).

30. S. E. Asch, "Forming Impressions of Personality," *Journal of Abnormal and Social Psychology,* 41, 1946, pp. 258–290.

31. Mason Haire, "Projective Techniques in Marketing Research," *Journal of Marketing,* 14, April 1950, pp. 649–656.

32. Frederick E. Webster, Jr., and Frederick Von Pechman, "A Replication of the 'Shopping List' Study," *Journal of Marketing,* 34, April 1970, pp. 61–65.

33. Pierre Martineau, *Motivation in Advertising* (New York: McGraw-Hill, 1957), p. 114.

34. Irving S. White, "The Perception of Value in Products," in Joseph W. Newman, ed., *On Knowing the Consumer* (New York: Wiley, 1966), p. 94.

35. *Advertising Age,* October 7, 1974, p. 64.

36. J. S. Bruner and C. C. Goodman, "Value and Need as Organizing Factors in Perception," *Journal of Abnormal and Social Psychology,* 42, 1947, pp. 33–44.

37. R. Levine, I. Chein, and G. Murphy, "The Relation of the Intensity of a Need to the Amount of Perceptual Distortion, A Preliminary Report," *Journal of Psychology,* 13, 1942, pp. 283–293.

38. L. Postman, J. S. Bruner, and E. McGinnies, "Personal Values and Selective Factors in Perception," *Journal of Abnormal and Social Psychology,* 49, 1948, pp. 142–154.

39. Homer E. Spence and James F. Engel, "The Impact of Brand Preference on the Perception of Brand Names: A Laboratory Analysis," in David T. Kollat, Roger D. Blackwell, and James F. Engel, eds., *Research in Consumer Behavior* (New York: Holt, Rinehart and Winston, 1970), pp. 61–70.

40. Ibid., p. 70.

41. Samuel E. Stayton and Morton Wiener, "Value, Magnitude, and Accentuation," *Journal of Abnormal and Social Psychology,* 62, January 1961, pp. 145–147.

42. S. E. Asch, "Effects of Group Pressure upon the Modification and Distortment of Judgment," in Dorwin Cartwright and Alvin Zander, eds., *Group Dynamics* (New York: Harper and Row, 1953), pp. 150–158.

43. A. R. Cohen, "Need for Cognition and Order of Communication as Determinants of Opinion Change," in C. I. Hovland, ed., *The Order of Presentation in Persuasion* (New Haven, Conn.: Yale University Press, 1957), pp. 79–97.

44. H. C. Kelman and Jonas Cohler, "Reactions to Persuasive Communications as a Function of Cognitive Needs and Styles," paper read at the Thirteenth Annual Meeting of the Eastern Psychological Association, Atlantic City, N.J.

45. R. M. Baron, "A Cognitive Model of Attitude Change" unpublished doctoral dissertation, New York University, 1963.

9

![grey box heading]

Information Processing and Attitude Change

Good advertising is a dialogue with people that lets them bring
something to the communication process. (Lee Clow, Creative
director, Chiat/Day)

A 60-second commercial aired during an event such as the Super Bowl can cost over
$1 million. With such investments involved, it is understandable that advertisers are
interested in the communication and persuasion process. What is the most effective
approach to a campaign? Which of two versions of an advertisement is best? Were
the commercials aired in the last Super Bowl effective? An intelligent answer to
these questions is "It depends!" In this and the next two chapters models and
theoretical explanations of advertising effectiveness will be presented which will
help address the "It depends" consideration.

The focus of this chapter will be on information processing and attitude
change. It extends the perceptual process discussion of Chapter 8. What happens to
information once it gets through the perceptual filter? How is it processed? How
does it influence attitudes and behavior? An in-depth understanding of information
processing and persuasive communication effects is perhaps the most important
thing to be learned prior to creating effective advertisements and copy. It provides
useful background for the task of generating creative strategies and selecting from
them.

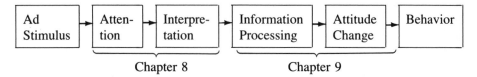

Chapter 8   Chapter 9

There is, unfortunately, no single model of information processing and attitude change that can be applied to advertising. In fact, there are a host of models or theories that propose to explain how persuasive communication works. In this chapter seven models that seem particularly relevant to the advertising context are presented. Each of these models is in some way concerned with information processing as well as attitude change. In Chapter 10, additional models of persuasion will be presented where the role of emotional reaction to advertising is central and information processing is of less concern. In Chapter 11 the impact of the source, the message, and social factors on attitude change will be presented.

The following section discusses the ELM model, which introduces two general models of information processing and attitude, the central and peripheral routes to persuasion. Five additional models of information processing and attitude change are then presented:

Cognitive response
Cognitive structure
Category-based evaluation
Consistency theory
Exposure effect

CENTRAL VERSUS PERIPHERAL ROUTES TO PERSUASION: THE ELM MODEL

A basic dimension of information processing and attitude change is the depth of information processing. At one extreme, the audience member can consciously and diligently consider the information that is relevant to the attitude position that is the target of the advertisement—that is, the attitude toward the advertised brand. Attitudes are changed or formed by careful consideration, thinking, and integration of information relevant to the product or object of the advertising. The audience member is very much an active, involved participant in the process. The exact nature of this involvement can take a variety of forms, such as the evaluation of attribute dimensions, the processing of attribute judgments, the examination of information sources, the recollection of related experiences, and the creation and testing of attitudes. This type of persuasion process is termed the central route to attitude change by the psychologists Petty and Cacioppo.[1] The resulting attitudes should be relatively strong and enduring.

In contrast, there is what Petty and Cacioppo term the peripheral route to attitude change. In the peripheral route, attitudes are formed and changed without active thinking about the object's attributes and its pros and cons. Rather, the persuasive impact occurs by associating the object with positive or negative cues, using cognitive "shortcuts." For example, rather than expressly considering the brand arguments presented in an advertisement, an audience member may accept the conclusion that the brand is superior because:

- There were numerous arguments offered.
- The source was an expert.
- The background music had the right associations.
- The commercial presented a believable result.

Conversely, a conclusion may be rejected not because of the logic of the argument but because of some surrounding cues. For example:

- The position may have been too extreme.
- The source may have been suspect.
- The magazine in which the ad appears was not respected.

Obviously, some approaches to changing attitudes will require central processing. In particular, advertisements attempting to communicate several attributes of an object will usually involve the assumption that central processing will take place. It is thus important to predict whether, in a given context, the central route is feasible—whether audience members will exert the effort involved.

Which Route?

Petty and Cacioppo have proposed the elaboration likelihood model (ELM) summarized in Figure 9-1, which predicts when the audience member will cognitively "elaborate" and follow the central route. Cognitive elaboration is issue-relevant thinking, evaluation of the claims made in the advertisement in the context of past

Figure 9-1. **The ELM Model of attitude change**

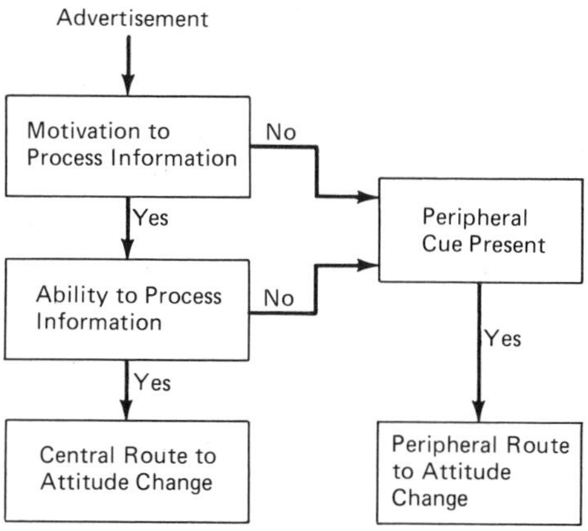

knowledge and experience. When elaboration likelihood is high, central processing tends to be present and dominate the reaction. When it is low, peripheral cues tend to determine the message reaction. The content of the message may be the same in both cases, but the method of processing will be very different.

The question is, then, when will elaboration likelihood be high and when will it be low? Two factors identified in the ELM model as significant are an audience member's motivation to process information and ability to process information.

Motivation to Process Information

Central processing requires first the motivation to process information. Information processing requires effort. Unless there is some reason to expend the energy or pay the price, the information will not be processed. Such effort will not be expended unless the audience member is involved with the product (or service or issue if the advertisement object is something other than a product) and associated purchase decision and unless the information in the advertisement is both relevant and important.

For an advertisement to be relevant, the audience member should, at a minimum, be a user or potential user of the product. A confirmed user of drip coffee will be unlikely to process information about instant coffee. For the message to be important enough to process, the involved purchase decision needs to be important or interesting. The cost of a durable such as a car could make a decision important. The appeal of a vacation alternative could stimulate enough interest to generate central processing. There may be situational factors. The choice of a wine for a special occasion will be more important than if a routine use occasion was involved. The purchase of a cosmetic for a gift may be more involving than a purchase for someone's own use.

The motivation to process centrally will be higher when an audience member is involved in the product class. This type of involvement has been studied extensively in consumer behavior. In general under a low-involvement condition there is:

- A relative lack of active information seeking about brands
- Little comparison among product attributes
- Perception of similarity among different brands
- No special preference for a particular brand[2]

When these conditions exist, the likelihood of elaboration and thus central processing occurring will be low.

Ability to Process Information

In addition to being motivated to process information centrally, the audience member must have the ability and capacity to process information. There is no point in attempting to communicate information or make an argument that the audience simply cannot process without a level of effort that is unacceptably high. For the average American, for example, an advertisement written in French or even an English dialect is less likely to lead to extensive central processing and elaboration than one in familiar English. Someone not familiar with the vocabulary and refinements of stereo systems may be unable to process a highly technical presentation of new equipment. Thus the ELM model suggests that the elaboration likelihood will decrease when the audience member is either not motivated to process information or lacks the ability to do so.

An ELM Experiment

A print ad for disposable razors was used to illustrate and test the ELM model.[3] Respondents were shown a booklet of 10 ads. A high-relevance half were told that they would be able to select a brand of razor as a gift and that the product would soon be available in their area. The low-relevance half were told they would select a free toothpaste and that the products in the booklet were being tested in another area. Half of each group were shown ads with strong arguments such as "in direct comparison tests, the Edge blade gave twice as many close shaves as its nearest competitor." The other half received weak arguments such as "designed with the bathroom in mind." Finally, the endorser was either a professional athlete or an "average" citizen of Bakersfield.

Figure 9-2 summarizes the results. The ELM model would predict that the celebrity status of the product endorsers would have a greater impact on product attitudes under low- rather than high-relevance conditions because it would then become a peripheral cue. In fact, a famous endorser did enhance attitude impact only under the low-relevance condition, where the peripheral route would be employed. Further, the impact of a strong argument is considerably less in a low-relevance condition, again where peripheral processing would tend to occur, than in the high-relevance condition.

Impact on Attitudes

Several studies have found that attitudes formed via the central route will tend to persist longer and to predict behavior better than attitudes framed by the peripheral route. Such an observation makes sense particularly if the extreme cases are considered. If a person reaches a conclusion after conscious thought and deliberation, that conclusion should be firmer than if he or she perhaps subconsciously processed a peripheral cue. Of course, that does not mean that all advertising should strive to use the central route. When people lack either the motivation or the ability to process information and both cannot be created, it would be futile to attempt a communication demanding central processing. Further, peripheral processing under conditions of heavy repetition may generate stable and strong attitudes. Research on the ELM model has usually focused on single-exposure contexts.

Figure 9-2.   **Product attitudes**

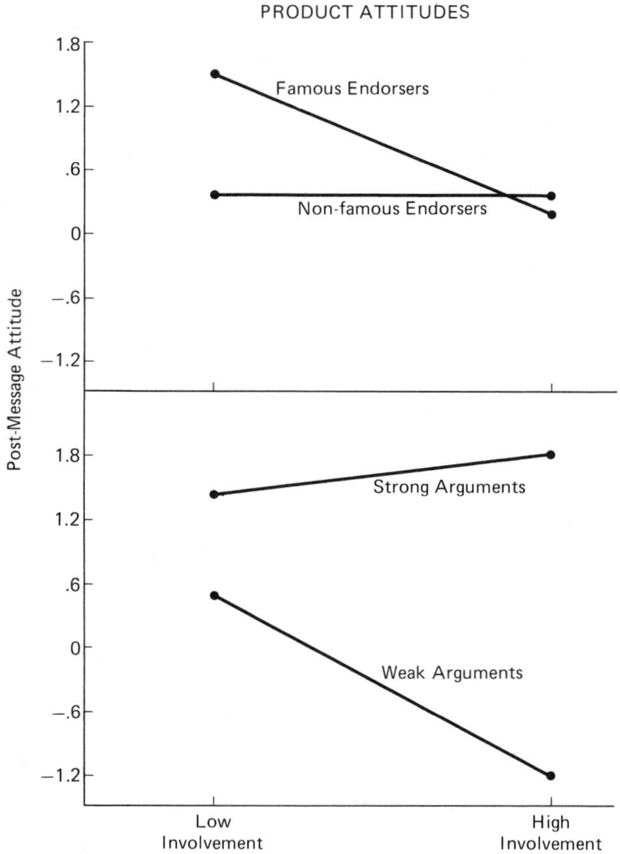

PRODUCT ATTITUDES

NOTE: Top panel shows interactive effect of involvement and endorser status on attitudes toward Edge razors. Bottom panel shows interactive effect of involvement and argument quality on attitudes toward Edge razors.

Source: Richard E. Petty, John T. Cacioppo, and David Schumann, "Central and Peripheral Routes to Advertising Effectiveness: The Moderating Role of Involvement," *Journal of Consumer Research,* 10 September 1983, p. 142.

Some Questions Raised by the ELM Model

The ELM model is a useful conceptualization of attitude change and serves to position several other models, but it is, unfortunately, not the definitive model of attitude change. It has limitations, as Bitner and Obermiller have observed, and raises several questions.[4]

How can an advertiser predict when an audience member will be motivated to process centrally and what cues will be centrally processed? One person may be motivated to process brand-relevant information centrally, while another will be less motivated, but will process background music centrally. In one study involving a shampoo, an attractive model was designed to be a peripheral cue but the subjects appeared to use "attractiveness" as a "central" evidence of the shampoo's performance. In general, audience members may be attracted to peripheral cues such as music, humor, or endorsers, and process such cues centrally.

What happens when motivation and ability are high but no central cues are available? Could audience members then rely on peripheral cues such as decor, physical features, endorsers, and so on, but not use peripheral processing?

The ELM model positions central and peripheral processing as alternatives. Could they both operate in a given context? For example, if central processing results in nearly equal preferences for alternatives, peripheral processing may be decisive. Or peripheral processing could occur first and lead to a purchase decision and use experience that later stimulates central processing. Or peripheral processing may alter motivation to process enough so that later central processing occurs.

COGNITIVE RESPONSE MODEL

The cognitive response model is a model of central processing. It assumes that the audience member is actively involved in the information process by evaluating the incoming information in the context of past knowledge and attitudes. A cognitive response is an active thought process or cognitive activity occurring during or just after a communication. In general, a cognitive response can influence the resulting attitude-change process or can even form the basis for attitudes. The basic model is:

Ad Exposure ⟶ Cognitive Response ⟶ Attitude Change

Research into cognitive response usually involves asking audience members during the ad exposure or just after it to write down all the thoughts that occurred to him or her during the exposure. These thoughts are assumed to represent all thoughts that occurred and influenced attitudes. However, a respondent may be unable or unwilling to report all the thoughts accurately, so some relevant thoughts may not get adequately transcribed.

A variety of types of cognitive responses are potentially relevant, such as curiosity statements ("I wonder if I could use the product in another application?"), thoughts about the ad ("That ad irritates me"), or thoughts connecting the ad with a person ("I'd like to visit that place"). However, two types are of particular interest, counterarguments and support arguments.

A *counterargument* (CA) occurs when the audience member argues against the attitude advocated by the ad. There are several different types of CAs. A person could disagree with the logic or content of the ad ("I don't believe the clothes are whiter''). The conclusion might be questioned (''My soap is perfectly adequate''). The context or situation might be challenged (''I don't believe that a housewife would say such a thing; it's phony''). A CA that attacks the source in some way (''He had to be paid a lot to say that'') is termed *source degradation.*

A *support argument* (SA) is a cognitive response that affirms the attitude advocated by the ad (''I could use a product that could provide whiter clothes''). It similarly could take several forms. It could involve an affirmation of the logic, the conclusion, the context, or the source, for example.

Obviously, the impact on attitude of cognitive response will depend on the nature of the cognitive response. The gross prediction is that the number of support arguments (NSA) will be positively associated with changes in beliefs, attitudes, and behavioral intentions and the number of counter arguments (NCA) will be negatively correlated. This model prediction has been generally (although not always) supported in dozens of studies in advertising and psychology.[5] Thus, it seems safe to conclude that when trying to create or change attitudes it is desirable to stimulate SAs and minimize CAs.

In any given situation, however, it may be useful to attempt to stimulate a particular type of SA or avoid a particular CA. For example, it might be useful to create enough interest to stimulate cognitive activity concerning ways to serve a new cake recipe or occasions in which a bike may be used.

How SAs and CAs Can Be Controlled

The research to date has provided some clues as to what can affect SAs and CAs.[6] Among the influences are:

- A faster-paced audio ad will generate fewer CAs among interested listeners.
- The knowledge level of the subjects—more knowledgeable people will be able to generate both SAs and CAs.
- Repetition—one study found that CAs were high initially, then fell and then rose with repetition, while SAs did the reverse.
- Discrepancy from the held position or belief—if the currently held position or belief matches the communication, SA is likely, but as the discrepancy increases, so will the CA.
- Number of arguments—there is some evidence that increasing the number of arguments may increase the number of SAs.

The Distraction Hypothesis

Probably the most useful research finding supported by numerous studies is that distraction can affect the number of CAs and thus enhance persuasion. The distraction hypothesis is that audience members can be distracted from counterarguing so that the communication will be more effective. For example, in a study by Festinger and Maccoby, a strong persuasive tape-recorded message opposing fraternities was more effective at changing attitudes among fraternity men when a silent film on modern painting was shown rather than pictures of fraternity scenes.[7] Other studies using distracting tasks, such as monitoring flashing lights while listening to an audio message, have usually found that distraction enhances attitude change. In general, distractor tasks that involve cognitive activity result in more distraction than do tasks that simply provide visual distraction or manual skills.

Bither[8] argues that distraction effects require an audience whose opinions or beliefs are opposed to the ones advocated in the communication. He designed an experiment to retest the effects of audio and visual distraction in an advertising context which showed that commitment was important in predicting the impact of distraction. In the lowest-committed groups, distraction actually produced negative attitude change results, whereas significant positive changes in attitude occurred in higher commitment groups under distraction conditions.

An advertiser interested in using distraction to break down resistance to her or his arguments is faced with the delicate task of devising something that will interfere with counterarguing but not, at the same time, interfere with the reception or learning of the message. This is a formidable task that must take into consideration all aspects of the communication and the audience. As Gardner explains,

> the critical question in defining distraction seems to be whether the process of counterarguing is interfered with. If attitude change is more apt to be induced due to interference with counterargument, then this is defined as distraction. Based on this definition, distraction takes on many dimensions. If an element in the communication is designed to add support to the message—that is, mood music, art work—this cannot be defined as distraction because it does not interfere with the counterarguing process . . . what is support in one communication could be distraction in another due to products, audiences, channels of communication, or a host of unique factors.[9]

A good example of the use of distractors in trying to communicate with a hostile audience is a campaign developed by the Standard Oil Company of California for its Chevron brand.[10] At the time, many consumers were very hostile to oil companies generally; the oil company image as a good corporate citizen was considerably tarnished. One of the first campaigns involved on-the-scene stories, showing tankers being built, explorations, and other activities. Although reasonably successful, the company subsequently developed a whimsical campaign around the theme "We're running out of dinosaurs" to encourage energy conservation. A rough mock-up of one of the commercials used is shown in Figure 9-3. The campaign not only proved effective in educating consumers about the energy situation, but most important, resulted in a significant shift in favorable attitudes for Standard Oil. In this case, executives generally agreed that it does pay to advertise to hostile audiences.

COGNITIVE STRUCTURE MODELS

A cognitive structure model assumes that a person forms an attitude toward an object by developing beliefs about that object and then combining those beliefs into a general overall attitude toward the object. The most commonly used cognitive structure model in advertising is the evaluative belief model introduced in Chapter 6, where the attitude is the sum of the evaluative beliefs each weighted by their importance:

Evaluative Belief Model

$$A_o = \Sigma w_d \, a_{od}$$

where A_o = attitude of an individual or segment toward object o

Figure 9-3. **A mock-up of the Chevron dinosaur commercial**

Dinosaur Commercial

1. Once there was a dinosaur, a pterodactyl!

2. And some other weird-looking sea creatures and plants.

3. Together, they became a layer of organic material.

4. And then . . . with a little heat and pressure, a poof of crude oil . . .

5. Which turned into 6 tanks of gas, ten thousand kilowatts and a lot more.

6. Now we're plumb out of dinosaurs, pterodactyls and the like. So when you jump in your car, don't waste 'em . . .

7. Some prehistoric creature gave his or her all for that tank of gas!

Source: Lewis C. Winters, "Should You Advertise to Hostile Audiences?" *Journal of Advertising Research,* 17, June 1977, p. 13.

a_{od} = evaluation of an individual or segment toward object o with respect to attribute or dimension d, the evaluative belief

w_d = measure of the relative importance or weight of attribute d to the individual or segment

Suppose that A_o represents the attitude for a particular model of automobile, a Ford Escort, for example, and three characteristics—size, miles per gallon, and price—are most important to a particular segment. A study of the segment revealed the following set of weights and evaluative beliefs:

$$A_o = w_1\, a_{01} + w_2 a_{02} + w_3 a_{03}$$
$$= 2\,(-2) + 5\,(+1) + 3\,(+1)$$

How could advertising improve the attitude toward the Escort? There are three routes. First, to change the weights. Advertising might attempt to decrease the importance of the size factor, for example, either by explicitly downplaying it or by ignoring it altogether and emphasizing good gas mileage instead. Second, the segment could be enticed to include new attributes, such as reliability, in their appraisal. Third, their evaluative beliefs could be altered by advertising. For example, a comparative advertisement could show that the Escort gets better mileage than its nearest competitors, and at the same time, costs less.

The model was used in Chapter 6 as a state model of a person's attitude. As such it was particularly useful as a model of a brand's status with consumers and played a useful role in objective setting. Here the model is being used as a process model. The implication is that people actually process information at least implicitly according to the model. Although the model is plausible and has been shown to correlate with attitudes, intentions, and behavior, there is little evidence that it mirrors the way people actually think.

Model Assumptions

The model includes several explicit assumptions that may not always hold. For example, it assumes that there are a limited number of known attributes with known weights. In some circumstances, a consumer may not be aware of all the attributes used. A consumer, for example, may rationalize the purchase of a small sporty convertible on the basis of gas mileage, but actually buy it on a subconscious drive to lead an exciting life. Further, the model assumes that the weighted evaluative beliefs are added when there could be interactions present. A person may want some combination of attributes and will not value the object highly unless the desired set of attributes is included.

Another assumption is that a person first obtains belief information and then uses that information to alter attitudes. However, the process could actually work the opposite way. In one clever study, the psychologists Nisbett and Willson had subjects observe an interview with a person with a European accent.[11] For one group the person spoke in an agreeable and enthusiastic manner, while for another group, the same person appeared autocratic and distrustful. The students then rated the person's likeability and three other attributes that were the same for both groups: physical appearance, mannerism, and accent. Subjects in the "warm" condition found these attributes attractive, whereas subjects in the "cold" condition found them irritating. Further, subjects in both conditions were certain that their liking of the teacher did not influence the attribute ratings, but rather, the reverse was true.

Two other cognitive structure models were discussed in Chapter 6. In the lexicographic model, a brand is evaluated only on the most important attribute. A second attribute is considered only if there is a tie on the first. In the conjunctive, an acceptable brand must meet minimal standards on all attributes. A cognitive structure model would usually involve central processing, although peripheral process could presumably affect an evaluative belief and therefore an overall attitude. The next model is more of a peripheral processing model.

CATEGORY-BASED EVALUATION STRATEGIES

The implicit assumption of cognitive structure models is that products are made up of discrete attributes and the decision makers combine these attributes to form an overall product attitude. A very different approach is "category-based evaluation" based on the premise that people often divide the world into categories. In evaluating a new stimulus, it is placed into a category and the attitude toward that category is retrieved from memory and applied to the stimulus.

For the category-based evaluation approach to operate, consumers develop a set of expectations about the product category. This expectation can be represented by either a typical example of the category, a "prototype," or by a good example of the category, an "exemplar."

The study of problem solving in such diverse fields as chess and physics shows that expertise relates to the ability to recognize patterns and categorize them. In the area of person perception, the notion of categories has been applied to explain like-dislike judgments. Reactions toward an individual can result from matching up that individual to a person category and applying the established attitudes toward that category.

The Camera Study

Sujan applied the category-based evaluation approach in an advertising experiment involving cameras.[12] Two ads were developed. One described a 35mm single-lens reflex (SLR) camera along five dimensions, including the fact that "the fine lenses permit high-quality enlargements." Another was for a 110 camera (less versatile but cheaper and easier to use than a 35mm camera) and said in part that it is engineered to fit a jacket pocket easily. In the mismatch-to-category condition the 35mm SLR description was used for the 110 camera or the 110 camera description was used for the 35mm SLR camera. The respondents were divided into expert or novice based on several questions measuring knowledge of cameras.

After being exposed to one of the four ads, the subjects were asked to report all thoughts they had while reading the ad and to indicate their overall attitude toward the product. Responses were coded into several groupings, including whether they were simple evaluative thoughts ("I like it") or attribute-oriented thoughts ("Cartridge loading is useless").

The results suggest that novice consumers tend to use category-based evaluation. They had fewer product-related or attribute-related thoughts than did experts. Further, they rated the cameras labeled 35mm SLRs higher even when the camera description did not match the type. The experts also tended to use category-based evaluation when the matched ads were shown. However, when information was discrepant from the category knowledge, the experts engaged in more product- and attribute-oriented thoughts, spent more time evaluating, and in general did not engage in category-based evaluation.

Implications

To implement ad advertising strategy based on the category-based model, the advertising focuses on positioning the brand with respect to some category exemplar. There would be no effort to communicate explicitly at the attribute level. One example is the humorous advertising for Parkay margarine which has a voice coming out of a box saying "butter." The advertising serves to position margarine with butter.

Another good example are the ads for the Yugo, the new, boxy Yugoslavian car that was introduced into the U.S. market at a base price under $5,000. The goal is to communicate that it is not only small and inexpensive but also dependable and reliable. The solution was to associate it with the Volkswagen Bug. A TV commercial opens with a Bug sitting in a white one-car garage with a voice-over saying: "The beloved Beetle. Once the lowest-priced car in America. Dependable. Basic transportation. But homely. And then it went away. Leaving an emptiness in the hearts of America." A Yugo print ad is shown in Figure 9-4.

CONSISTENCY THEORIES

An important group of attitude-change theories rests on the assumption that attitude change results by exploiting a person's drive for consistency among the facts associated with an object. For example, an audience member may have a negative opinion about a brand but a positive opinion about a person who is endorsing the brand in an advertisement as illustrated in the figure on page 263. The inconsistency should create a tension and a drive to reduce that tension.

There are three obvious routes to the reduction of tension in this context. First, it can be assumed that the endorser is not really enthusiastic about the brand.

Figure 9-4.   **Positioning a brand with respect to a category**

Courtesy of Yugo-America.

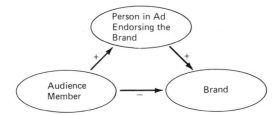

Second, the positive opinion of the endorser can be altered to one less positive. Third, the attitude toward the brand can be changed to one more positive. If the advertising can select an endorser for which audiences have strong positive attitudes and link the endorser strongly to the brand, there will be a tendency to engage in brand attitude change. To maximize the likelihood of attitude change, it's useful for the source not only to be well liked but also relevant and credible with respect to the product class involved. Otherwise, the audience member can resolve the inconsistency by observing that the endorser's opinion about the product is not relevant because the endorser is not knowledgeable about the product or that the endorser's experience will not apply to others. Chapter 11 will explore the source impact in more detail.

Suppose, for example, that Bill Cosby is well liked and is advocating increased milk consumption. If attitudes toward Bill Cosby are strong and he strongly recommends increased milk consumption, attitudes toward milk consumption will probably be influenced.

Consistency theory can also work with respect to evaluative beliefs. Suppose that research has shown that taste is the most important attribute in selecting catsup. However, communicating good taste is difficult. One solution is to focus on other evaluative beliefs about the catsup brand, the attractiveness or convenience of the package, the freshness of the ingredients, or even the public spirit of the firm. The logic would be that if positive evaluative beliefs can be developed for several attributes, the drive for consistency will help encourage the consumer to develop positive evaluative beliefs on attributes such as taste that are not mentioned in the advertising. In fact, research has shown that there is a tendency for evaluative beliefs to be consistently negative or consistently positive.

There are several types of consistency, including balance theory (which emphasizes the role of an endorser), congruity theory (which predicts the size of attitude change knowing the strengths of existing attitudes and the size of the advocated change), and dissonance theory (which considers the drive to make attitudes consistent with behavior). They all focus attention on tension created by cognitive inconsistency that can be resolved by changing beliefs and attitudes. The basic model is:

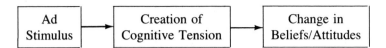

The difficulty in applying the model is not only to predict the context in which it will apply but to determine how to create tension such that it will result in the desired belief or attitude change. The task is complicated by the fact that audience members will differ in the nature and strength of prior beliefs and attitudes. The advertising must decide on the source of the tension, the endorser, evaluative belief, context, product application, or other source. Then some kind of discrepancy to currently held beliefs must be generated. Care must be taken to ensure that the discrepancy is adequate to create tension and is not so excessive as to be ignored or to irritate. Consideration will need to be given to the structure and strength of currently held beliefs and attitudes but also to their dynamics, their potential to change.

THE EXPOSURE EFFECT

Some ads have very low information content and yet seem to be effective at affecting attitudes, particularly with repetition. Why? Some answers will be provided in Chapter 10 and in Chapter 16, when repetition is discussed. However, one explanation considered here is that mere exposure affects liking. Such a model is at a polar extreme from cognitive response models.

Mere Exposure

The most extreme and controversial version of the exposure effect has been advanced by a prominent psychologist, Zajonc, who hypothesizes that preference is created simply from exposure with no associated cognitive activity.[13] For example, preferences have been developed for a variety of objects such as nonsense syllables, faces, Chinese ideographs, and melodies that have been exposed more than alternative objects. Such preferences have been demonstrated even when the subjects have no recognition memory that they had previously been exposed to the object.

In one study, for example, Kunst-Wilson and Zajonc presented subjects with a series of polygons.[14] They then exposed the subjects to pairs of polygons, asking which one they had seen previously and which one was new, and which they preferred. The previously exposed polygons were preferred even though there was no recognition above chance levels as to which they had seen previously.

A finding of interest in this stream of research is that subjects verbalize reasons for their choice that have nothing to do with exposure and repetition. They offer rational explanations such as that they like the sound or the shape had some attractive quality.

There is some question as to whether there is a complete absence of cognitive activity in these studies, and if so, how the liking develops.[15] Perhaps the activity occurs and is forgotten or occurs at a subconscious level. Further, it is not clear how studies involving new abstract concepts, although intriguing, will help us shed light on the impact of advertising repetition.

The "Familiar Model"

Another view of the exposure effect suggests that exposure creates a familiarity which causes liking. The concept is that familiar, known objects are evaluated more highly than are unknown objects with associated uncertainty. Perhaps uncertainty creates a tension, which is undesirable. Or familiarity may create positive feelings of comfort, security, ownership, or intimacy. Certainly all have experienced such a phenomenon with a poem, a song, a food, or a brand name. Liking emerges as the object becomes more familiar. Although the "familiar model" does not involve any in-depth cognitive activity, there is cognition change that can be measured by recognition tests. This model would explain why people develop positive attitudes toward brands and advertisements that are recognizable, even if they cannot provide any facts about them.

A study conducted by Obermiller supported the familiarity hypothesis over the "exposure without cognition" model.[16] Using random melodies, he found that liking was related to repetition for those melodies that had become familiar (the subject thought that he or she had heard it before) but not for those not familiar.

Krugman's Low-Involvement Learning

Still another variant of the mere exposure effect is Herbert Krugman's classic model of television advertising, low-involvement learning, first offered in 1965.[17] Krugman observes that most products advertised on television tend to be low-involvement types and that television itself tends to be a low-involvement medium. In a study comparing cognitive responses of TV ads with print ads, Krugman found fewer responses linking the ad to a person's own life for the TV ads. Under extremely low involvement, there is no resistant attitude to overcome and perceptual defenses are low or nonexistent.

Low-involvement learning becomes a very subtle process. Krugman compares the exposures to peripheral vision. The viewer looks but really does not see in the sense that the viewer is not really paying attention to or even being aware of what he or she is looking at. The viewer may be capable of recognizing that the ad was seen but often could not recall the contents.

The exposures result in shifts in the cognitive structure that fall short of attitude change. The prominence of the brand name may increase or the salience of an attribute may change. Thus, a brand might be considered primarily "reliable" instead of being primarily "modern." The brand may be seen as just as modern as before and no more reliable. However, repeated exposure to a reliable message altered the viewer's frame of reference and now gives reliability the primary role in organizing the concept of the brand.

This subtle change in cognitive structure provides the potential to see a brand differently and can trigger a behavioral event such as an in-store purchase of the brand. This behavioral event can generate an attitude change or adjustment that is more consistent with the shift in perceptual structure. Thus, if the brand is purchased, the new way of seeing it may then for the first time be expressed in words to explain why it was selected.

Without this behavioral completion, there is an unstable condition that is characterized by a shift in perceptual structure without a corresponding shift in attitudinal structure. For low-involvement products, product adoption can be characterized in Krugman's terms as occurring through gradual shifts in perceptual structure, aided by repetitive advertising in a low-involvement medium such as television, activated by behavioral choice situations, and followed at some time by a change in attitude. The implied model is:

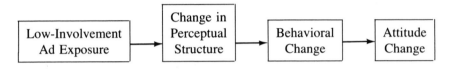

Recognition versus Recall Measures

These exposure models are reasonable and help explain how much of advertising, particularly television advertising, works. However, the exact process is unclear. In essence, the explanation of attitude change without cognition, the familiarity link to attitudes and learning without involvement, undoubtedly happens, but the explanation of how it happens is sketchy. Further, the models help justify some types of advertising but provide little guidance on how to develop or refine it. There is general agreement that recall measures (What do you recall about the ad?) are not relevant and that recognition measures (Did you see this ad?) will be more useful.

SUMMARY

This chapter discusses seven models of information processing and attitude change. The first model, termed the central route to persuasion by Petty and Cacioppo, describes an active, conscious, in-depth processing of information and adjustment of attitudes. The second, termed the peripheral route, models contexts in which peripheral cues such as the credibility of the source influence attitudes with little active thinking about the object. The central route will be employed only when the audience member is motivated to process information and has the ability to do so. For motivation to be present, the audience member needs to be involved with the product, and the information in the ad needs to be relevant and important. A problem is to determine exactly what will be processed as a peripheral cue and exactly how it will affect attitudes.

During or just after being exposed to a communication, the audience can engage in cognitive responses such as counterarguing or support arguing. In the cognitive response model this activity is assumed to affect attitudes. By this model advertising can increase its effectiveness by encouraging support arguing and by inhibiting, perhaps via distraction, counterarguing.

A cognitive structure model, such as the evaluative belief model, assumes that a person forms an attitude toward an object by developing beliefs about that object and then combining those beliefs into a general overall attitude toward the object. Attitude change is accomplished by changing the structure, that is, by changing the attributes, the attribute weights, or the evaluative beliefs.

A category-based evaluation model hypothesizes that people divide the world into categories and that an object is evaluated similarly to the other objects in its category. Consumers are assumed to develop a set of expectations about the product category represented by a ''prototype'' or by an ''exemplar.'' The model implies that advertising should attempt to position a brand with respect to a category, such as Parkay and butter.

Consistency theory hypothesizes that attitude change results by exploiting a person's drive for consistency among the facts associated with an object. Thus, a person may alter a brand attitude to be consistent with a positive attitude toward an endorser of a brand. Advertising could work by creating cognitive tension by creating sets of attitudes that are inconsistent and can be relieved only by altering beliefs or attitudes.

The most extreme version of the exposure effect hypothesizes that liking can be created simply from exposure with no cognitive activity at all. Such a phenomenon has been demonstrated for nonsense syllables and could provide insights as to how repetition affects the impact of advertising. The ''familiar model'' suggests that people like objects with which they are familiar. Krugman's low-involvement learning postulates that television advertising, operating under low involvement and perceptual defenses, creates changes in perceptual structure that can trigger a behavioral act which in turn affects attitude.

DISCUSSION QUESTIONS

1. Contrast the central and the peripheral routes to persuasion. Categorize the other five models covered in the chapter as to whether they follow the central or peripheral route.

2. Bring in a print ad that provides an example of a peripheral cue and another with an example of a central cue. Consider the Yugo ad in Figure 9-4. Is there a peripheral cue here?

3. Provide an example of a case when a reader of a print ad would not be motivated to process information and an example when a reader would not be able to process the information in the ad.

4. What other types of cognitive responses are there besides support and counterarguments? How could they be useful in predicting and managing response to advertising?

5. Why might the number of CAs start high, then recede, and then increase with repetition? What else might you predict about cognitive response over repetition?

6. What exactly is distraction in advertising? What is its purpose? What provided the distraction in the Chevron advertisements? Provide other examples of distraction in advertising.

7. The evaluative belief model is one cognitive structure model. Develop another cognitive structure model and discuss its implications for the problem of changing attitudes.

8. Do people first form beliefs and then attitudes, or the reverse? Do people change attitudes before changing behavior?

9. Pick a product category and give an example of a "prototype" and an "exemplar."

10. What types of people would tend to use the category-based evaluation strategy?

11. Develop a consistency model of attitude change that would predict the changed attitude toward a brand knowing the existing attitude on a -5 (strongly dislike) to zero (neutral) to $+5$ (strongly like) scale; the existing attitude toward the proposed source, also on a -5 to $+5$ scale; and the link between the source and the brand on a 0 (weak link) to $+5$ (strong link) scale.

12. What is cognitive tension? Recall an instance in which you experienced it. How would you measure cognitive tension?

13. In proposing that liking can occur without any cognitive activity, Zajonc suggests that the acquisition of tastes for very hot spices in Mexico (spices that others would dislike intensely) need not involve any rational decision or cognitive activity but might involve parental reinforcement, social conformity pressures, identification with a group machismo, and so on. Do you agree that no cognitive activity is involved in the development of such tastes?

14. Subliminal advertising is that in which a message such as "Drink Coke" is flashed during a movie so fast that it is not visible but still influences behavior. Such stimuli have been shown to activate drives such as hunger, but the consensus among advertisers is that it simply does not work in the advertising context. (See Chapter 17.) Relate subliminal advertising to the exposure effect.

15.   Contrast the three types of exposure effects. How would you measure involvement? Could there be high involvement in the advertisement but low involvement in the product message?

NOTES

1. See Richard E. Petty and John T. Cacioppo, "Central and Peripheral Routes to Persuasion: Application to Advertising," in Larry Percy and Arch Woodside, eds., *Advertising and Consumer Psychology* (Lexington, Mass.: Lexington Books, 1983), pp. 3–23; and Richard E. Petty, John T. Cacioppo, and David Schumann, "Central and Peripheral Routes to Advertising Effectiveness: The Moderating Role of Involvement," *Journal of Consumer Research,* 10, September 1983, pp. 135–146.

2. Judith Lynne Zaichkowsky, "Measuring the Involvement Construct," *Journal of Consumer Research,* 12, December 1985, pp. 341–352.

3. Petty, Cacioppo, and Schumann, "Central and Peripheral Routes to Advertising Effectiveness."

4. Mary J. Bitner and Carl Obermiller, "The Elaboration Likelihood Model: Limitations and Extensions in Marketing," Proceedings of the ACR Conference, 1984.

5. See a review by Peter Wright, "Message-Evoked Thoughts: Persuasion Research Using Thought Verbalizations," *Journal of Consumer Research,* 7, September 1980, pp. 151–175.

6. Ibid., pp. 166–171.

7. L. Festinger and N. Maccoby, "On Resistance to Persuasive Communications," *Journal of Abnormal and Social Psychology,* 68, 1964, pp. 359–367.

8. Stewart W. Bither, "Comments on Venkatesan and Haaland's Test of the Festinger-Maccoby Divided Attention Hypothesis," *Journal of Marketing Research,* 6, May 1969, pp. 237–238.

9. David M. Gardner, "The Distraction Hypothesis in Marketing," *Journal of Marketing Research,* 10, December 1970, pp. 25–30.

10. Lewis C. Winters, "Should You Advertise to Hostile Audiences?" *Journal of Advertising Research,* 17, June 1977, pp. 7–15.

11. Richard E. Nisbett and Timothy D. Wilson, "Telling More Than We Can Know: Verbal Reports on Mental Processes," *Psychological Review,* 84, May 1977, pp. 231–259.

12. Mita Sujan, "Consumer Knowledge: Effects on Evaluation Strategies Mediating Consumer Judgments," *Journal of Consumer Research,* 12, June 1985, pp. 31–46.

13. R. B. Zajonc, "Feeling and Thinking: Preferences Need No Inferences," *American Psychologist,* 35, 1980, pp. 151–175; and R. B. Zajonc and H. Markus, "Affective and Cognitive Factors in Preferences," *Journal of Consumer Research,* 9, September 1982, pp. 123–131.

14. William R. Knunst-Wilson and Robert B. Zajonc, "Affective Discrimination of Stimuli That Can Not Be Recognized," *Science,* 207, February 1980, pp. 557–558.

15. Yehoshua Tsal, "On the Relationship between Cognitive and Affective Processes: A Critique of Zajonc and Markus," *Journal of Consumer Research,* 12, December 1985, pp. 358–362.

16. Carl Obermiller, "Varieties of Mere Exposure: The Effects of Processing Style and Repetition on Affective Response," *Journal of Consumer Research,* 12, June 1985, pp. 17–31.

17. Herbert E. Krugman, "The Impact of Television Advertising: Learning Without Involvement," *Public Opinion Quarterly,* 29, 1965, p. 353.

10

Feeling Response to Advertising

Advertising that works is advertising that makes somebody feel something. . . . All advertising has some emotion. Some advertising is all emotion. (Hal Riney, Creative Director, Hal Riney & Associates)

In Chapters 8 and 9 the focus has been on the thinking or cognitive response to advertising. The audience member processes information which potentially can change beliefs, attitudes, and behavior. This response often involves a logical, rational, thinking process. As a result of the advertising, the audience member often learns relevant facts about the brand. Thus, the audience learns that a toothpaste cleans better or that Pepsi won a taste test. Advertising that attempts predominately to communicate or inform and thus activate the thinking process is termed "thinking" advertising.

Advertising can also work by creating feelings that can ultimately influence attitudes and behavior. Thus, a commercial could portray active teenagers playing volleyball at the beach and enjoying 7-Up. A feeling of energy, vitality, fun, and belonging could be created that gets associated with the brand and thereby affects brand attitudes and behavior. In this chapter the focus turns to the feeling side of advertising. Since these feeling responses usually are considered positive (liked) or negative (disliked), they are also termed affective responses.

"Feeling" *advertising* is used here to describe advertising for which audience feeling response is of primary importance, and usually (but not always) little or no information content is involved. It usually is very much execution-focused, as opposed to message-focused, and relies on the establishment of a feeling, emotion, or mood and the association of this feeling, emotion, or mood with the brand. Feeling advertising is also termed execution-focused, emotional, end-benefit-oriented, mood, experiential, image, or associational advertising.

It should be clear that all commercials, even the most logical and informative, can develop feeling or affective responses. Similarly, some argue that even the most emotional commercials, seemingly without information content, can evoke some type of thinking and cognitive activity. A person will be able to recall its content and even the feelings it evoked, for example. Thus, there is a spectrum between pure "feeling" and pure "thinking" advertising according to the relative importance of the thinking response as opposed to the affective or feeling response. *Thinking response* refers to any thinking activity about the advertisement or brand, usually with the potential to change beliefs.

In fact, the Marschalk Company believes that an effective advertisement should communicate at both the rational and emotional levels, using what they term the "emotional hard sell."[1] The idea is that it is necessary to arouse an emotional response, but the advertising needs that rational hook—the tangible end benefits that the product will fulfill.

MODELING THE FEELING RESPONSE TO ADVERTISING

In Chapters 8 and 9 we have discussed a variety of models and approaches that were most relevant to understanding the thinking response to advertising. Most of these models are relatively well developed and accepted. In contrast, remarkably little is known about the feeling or affective response to advertising and how it works. Models of feeling advertising are just beginning to emerge.

Emerging models of feeling or affective response tend to introduce one or more of four constructs. The first are the feelings that are engendered by the advertisement, feelings such as warmth, excitement, fear, and amusement. The second is the attitude toward the advertisement, the degree to which an audience member likes or enjoys the advertisement. The third is the transformation of the use experience, where attributes that may be intangible are effectively added to the brand. The fourth is the process, usually considered the classical conditioning process, by which the feelings, the attitude toward the advertisement, or the transformed use experience get associated with the brand.

Figure 10-1 provides one model of how feeling or affective response works.

Figure 10-1.   **A model of the feeling response to advertising**

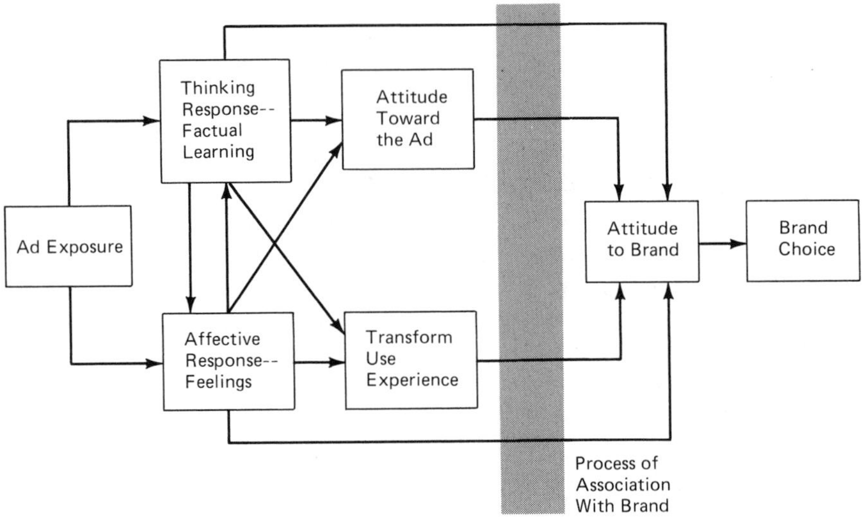

The advertisement exposure, shown at the left, can have two responses. One is the thinking response, which usually involves factual learning. The second is the affective response, the feelings that are created or aroused by the advertising. Feelings can be positive, such as feeling warm, cheerful, happy, energetic, active, or giving. Or they could be negative, such as feeling afraid, depressed, guilty, anxious, or irritated. Feelings are not as extreme or pronounced as emotions, although they have been described as mild emotions, and we will sometimes use the two terms interchangeably.

Feelings are shown in Figure 10-1 having four possible impacts. First they can affect the thinking response. For example, if a person's feelings match the exposed material, he or she will be more likely to recall it than if they do not.[2] Further, positive feelings may promote support arguments, and extreme negative feelings may distract, thereby inhibiting counterarguments.

Second, these feelings can become associated with the brand, perhaps through a process such as classical conditioning as shown by the shaded area in Figure 10-1. The result of this association could be an effect on the brand attitude or brand choice or both. For example, the Lowenbrau "Good friends" campaign contained some extremely warm commercials. The feelings of warmth that the audience experienced when being exposed could, over time, become associated with Lowenbrau, and this association could affect the attitude toward the brand and purchase behavior. This impact would occur simply because of the association formed between the feeling and the brand through many repetitions.

Third, Figure 10-1 shows that feelings can also work by creating a positive attitude toward the advertisement. Thus, the Lowenbrau commercial tends to be well liked, perhaps in part because of the warm feeling it engenders. The model suggests that this attitude toward the advertisement then becomes associated with or transferred to the brand. Thus, the liking of the advertisement can become an important objective because of the potential to affect brand attitudes directly and because it can reflect the ability of the advertising to create the right feeling.

Finally, feelings can also work by transforming the use experience. The theory is as follows. After many exposures to a McDonald's commercial showing a happy, family scene, a family's experience at McDonald's will actually be different because of the exposure to the advertising. The advertising exposures make their visit to McDonald's warmer and happier than it would otherwise be. Their McDonald's experience is transformed into one more closely matching that shown in the advertising.

The feelings, the attitude toward the advertisement, and the use transformation can also be affected by the thinking activity:

- An audience member could stimulate a feeling by mentally interpreting the scene recalling relevant personal experiences.
- Prior beliefs (for example, that it is offensive to advertise hemorrhoid products on TV) could influence an attitude toward an advertisement (for example, a hemorrhoid advertisement). Also, the advertisement could be liked because it is informative, even when it essentially generates no feelings at all.
- An advertisement could communicate the fact that Lowenbrau beer is served at special occasions when friends gather and that friends will consider the beverage as a symbol of the occasion being special.

The Association Process

Note the central role that the association process plays in the model. In particular, the positive feelings or positive attitudes toward the advertisement or the transformed use experience created by the advertisement need to be associated with brand. Advertising history is full of examples of campaigns that have been extremely entertaining and well liked but had no impact in part because the ads did not get associated with the brand. Audience viewers could recall much of the ad but not the brand advertised. The association is enhanced when the brand is made the hero of the ad.

A very successful Dr. Pepper campaign, for example, had people search for an unusual and exciting ("out of the ordinary") drink option.[3] The main character would voice dissatisfaction with ordinary drinks. There would be a certain anger and tension even though the total setting was bizarre and the commercial as a whole was humorous. The solution, as illustrated in Figure 10-2, was Dr. Pepper. The brand was an integral part of the ad, the hero. It would be impossible to recall the ad without recalling its hero, Dr. Pepper.

Theory and research from psychology can provide insights into how this

Figure 10-2. **The brand as hero—Sugar-Free Dr. Pepper**

YOUNG & RUBICAM NEW YORK

CLIENT: DR PEPPER
PRODUCT: SUGAR FREE DR PEPPER
TITLE: "QUEEN OF HEARTS"

LENGTH: 30 SECONDS
COMM. NO.: DPYT-4603
DATE: 3/18/85

(MUSIC UNDER) NARRATOR (VO): Once upon a time,

a beautiful queen got thirsty.

(VOICE LIKE A QUEEN): "Jaaack . . . I'm parched," she said.

NARRATOR (VO): The Jack . . .

knowing she watched her figure along with everyone else . . .

offered her an ordinary diet drink.

(VOICE LIKE A QUEEN): "Diet cola?"

"Have this man shuffled," she said.

NARRATOR (VO): Fortunately a young girl . . .

had an ace up her sleeve.

(LITTLE GIRL VOICE): One of a kind, of course.

CHORUS: HOLD OUT . . . HOLD OUT . . .

FOR THE OUT OF THE ORDINARY . . .

SUGAR FREE DR PEPPER.

NARRATOR (VO): And so folds . . .

the card fable.

Courtesy of Dr. Pepper Company.

association is created. One such theory, the exposure effect, was discussed in Chapter 9. Another, classical conditioning, will first be presented. In the balance of this chapter the various components of the Figure 10-1 model will be explored. A discussion of the attitude toward the advertisement will be followed by a presentation of a theory that advertising can transform the use experience. The focus will then turn to feelings. After an overview of some feelings that may be employed in advertising, several feelings—humor, warmth, and fear—are considered in more detail. Conditions under which feelings will emerge or be enhanced will be explored.

THE ROLE OF CLASSICAL CONDITIONING[4]

One explanation as to how feeling advertising works draws on the theory of classical conditioning, which is based on Pavlov's work in the 1920s. Pavlov exposed a neutral stimulus, a metronome, termed a conditioned stimulus (CS), to a hungry dog. The conditioned stimulus was followed by another stimulus, the unconditioned stimulus (US), namely food. The food automatically evoked a response, called the unconditioned response (UR), namely salivation. As a result of the pairing of the two stimuli, the metronome (CS) and the food (US), the dog eventually salivated even when only the metronome stimulus was present, a response which is called the conditioned response (CR)—the dog became conditioned to it. Diagrammatically:

UNCONDITIONED STIMULUS (US)→UNCONDITIONED RESPONSE (UR)

Food   Salivation
Commercial   Positive attitude or feelings

CONDITIONED STIMULUS (CS) ⟶ CONDITIONED RESPONSE (CR)

Metronome   Salivation
Brand or brand use   Positive attitude or feelings

Notice that there is no reinforcement present. The conditioned response does not occur because the subject has been rewarded or reinforced. It is simply due to the fact that the conditioned and unconditioned stimuli are contiguous and became associated. In our context, there is a commercial with actors and a scene that represents the unconditioned stimulus (US). The positive attitude toward the ad or the positive feelings are the unconditioned response (UR). The idea is to pair the brand or use of the brand, which is the neutral or conditioned stimulus (CS), with the commercial content, the unconditioned stimuli (US). The goal is to have the unconditioned response become the conditioned response—that is, the brand or use of the brand should precipitate the same positive attitude or feelings that the commercial did.

The classical conditioning theory has rarely been applied to affect (liking) in humans. Thus, there is a good deal of controversy as to whether it can be used to explain the use of advertising, particularly feeling advertising, to create positive attitudes. Three influential studies addressing this very point have provided encouragement.

Three Conditioning Experiments

In a pioneering experiment, Gorn showed that background music (UC) could be associated with a colored pen (CS).[5] Two hundred students heard music played while watching a slide containing a print ad with little information for an inexpensive pen costing 49 cents. Half the group heard a known "liked" 1-minute segment of music from a popular musical. The ad showed a beige pen for half of this group and a light blue pen for the other half. The other half heard classical Indian music, known to be disliked. All subjects later were invited to select one of the two colored pens. A total of 79 percent picked the color associated with the liked music. When asked why, 62 percent said they had a reason. Most said they had a color preference and no one mentioned the music.[6]

Another study, by Bierley et al., exposed 100 subjects to four sets of three colored arbitrary geometric stimuli.[7] In the first two sets, red stimuli were always followed by well-liked music and yellow was never followed by this music. In the second set the colors were changed. In the third, continuous music was in the background, and in the fourth, no music was present. The preference for a stimulus was higher when it predicted music than when it did not for both colors.

Finally, Kroeber-Riel paired a model brand name with emotion-loaded pictures in slide advertisements.[8] The pictures conveyed emotional events concerned with eroticism, social happiness, and exotic landscapes. A day after the conditioning the name alone aroused significant emotional reactions. Interestingly, the conditioning worked only after 30 five-second exposures (20 was inadequate) and only if the stronger of two emotional scenes was used.

Some Relevant Classical Conditioning Findings

There has been an enormous amount of classical conditioning research conducted over the past five decades, and many of the findings have relevance to advertising. In particular, consider the following:

1. *Acquisition.* The strength of the conditioned response increases as a function of the number of pairings of the US and the CS. However, each pairing results in a smaller increase in strength than the previous one until, after many pairings, the strength of the CR does not increase meaningfully. Thus, advertisers should plan to use enough repetitions to create the necessary associations. The speed of acquisition of the CR will depend on the salience of the US—how interesting and important it is to the audience. Therefore, it is important to involve strong US (the advertisement should make an impact), and CS (the brand or its use) needs to be prominent and strongly linked to the US.

2. *Extinction.* Classical conditioned behavior will disappear if the relationship between the US and the CS is broken because, for example, a new advertising campaign does not maintain the same US. Suppose that a jingle (US) which generates a positive, upbeat feeling (UR) has been

associated with a soft drink (CS). If the soft-drink advertising is presented without the jingle, the CR will also disappear. Note that extinction is different from forgetting. The jingle may still be recalled, but the association will not be there.

3. *Generalization.* Generalization occurs when a new conditioned stimulus (CS_2) resembles the original conditioned stimulus (CS_1) and thus generates the same conditioned response. The color preferences generated in the Bierley et al. experiment generalized to colored shapes different from those used in the experiment. Thus, product extensions such as new varieties of a breakfast cereal might be presented in such a way as to create generalization.

The discrimination/generalization phenomenon is particularly important when competitive advertising is considered. There is always the possibility that your brand could be generalized to a competitive brand, a development that could have a positive as well as a negative impact. For example, COMPAQ makes a computer compatible with the IBM PC. It may be very helpful for COMPAQ to have generalization occur. They could then actually benefit from IBM's advertising.

ATTITUDE TOWARD THE ADVERTISEMENT

Perhaps the simplest explanation of how a feeling advertisement works is that people like it or dislike it and this attitude gets transformed to or associated with the brand. There is thus the potential for direct causal link between the attitude toward an advertisement and attitude and behavior toward a brand. As noted in Figure 10-1, feelings engendered by an ad can create or influence an attitude toward the ad. Thus, an indirect way to evaluate the impact of feelings is to study and measure the attitude toward the ad.

Mitchell and Olson demonstrated that the attitude toward an ad provided an impact over and above any ability of the ad to communicate attribute information.[9] They created four print ads for facial tissue, one with an explicit softness claim, another with a picture of a kitten, a third with a sunset picture, and a fourth with an abstract painting. Subjects were exposed to each ad either two, four, six, or eight times in a single setting. A significant amount of the brand attitude created could be explained by beliefs as to the tissue's softness, absorbency, and other attributes. However, a substantial additional amount of the brand attitude was caused by the attitude toward the ad.

Ray and Batra have suggested that attitudes toward a brand have two components, an evaluative component that is influenced by beliefs about the brand and a brand-specific "liking" component that cannot be explained by knowledge about beliefs.[10] This "liking" component is based on the attitude toward the ad as well as by exposure effects. The relative importance or "percentage contribution" of "liking" will be high when the amount of brand attribute information and associated processing effort are low.

Other Effects of the Attitude toward an Advertisement

A positive attitude toward an advertisement, in addition to creating positive associations with the brand via a process such as classical conditioning, can affect
advertising impact in a variety of ways. In particular, as suggested in the perception
chapter, a well-liked advertisement could improve attention by providing entertainment value. Further, it could actually improve information processing, in that
evidence suggests that a positive attitude toward the ad can[11]

- Affect the level of information processing by creating arousal and acti-
  vation[12]
- Lead to more positive judgments of the advertised message
- Improve the recall of the advertised material

Further, there is an argument that disliked commercials can be effective and
that, in fact, it is much better to be disliked than to be ignored. There is no shortage
of anecdotal evidence that irritating commercials have been effective. The classic
example is the strong Rosser Reeves campaigns of past decades featuring his Unique
Selling Propositions for Anacin, in which a hammer hitting a head was shown again
and again and again.

There are three explanations as to why a disliked ad can be effective.[13] First,
in some contexts, attention and processing could be stimulated without the negative
reaction being transferred to the product. Second, brand familiarity is created which,
particularly for low-involvement products, may increase liking of the brand via the
exposure effect. This exposure effect is most likely to be effective if, over time, the
negative ad becomes disassociated with the brand (termed the "sleeper effect").
Thus, the impact of the negative feelings on the brand attribute information declines
over time. Third, irritation could distract viewers from counterarguing with the
message, therefore enhancing persuasion.

How to Create Well-Liked Commercials

One problem with the attitude toward ad-focused research is that there has been little
effort to make distinctions between different execution strategies. For example,
three equally liked commercials, one using slapstick humor, another employing
serious informative copy, and a third with warm, sentimental copy, may impact in
completely different ways, as could two equally disliked commercials, one that is
considered boring and the other irritating. Further, there has been little research
attempting to determine what it is that makes some commercials liked and how the
liking level is affected by repetition.

One study by Aaker and Bruzzone did explore the copy characteristics that
distinguished irritating commercials.[14] They located 18 pairs of commercials for the
same product (10 had a common brand and five had common copy) with significantly different irritation levels. They found that the ads with higher irritation levels

tended to portray an unbelievable situation, a "put-down" person, a threatened relationship, graphic physical discomfort, tension, an unattractive or unsympathetic character, a suggestive scene, poor casting, or a sensitive product with a product focused message. Irritation levels were lowered when the commercial included or conveyed a happy mood, a warm mood, a credible spokesman, humor, or useful information.

Of interest was the level of irritation that crept in when a person was "put down" or an important relationship such as that of a mother and daughter or a wife and husband was threatened. For example, in one Head and Shoulders commercial, a wife, who is positioned as a hair expert, smiles as she tells her husband about his dandruff problem and about Head and Shoulders. In contrast, in the companion commercial that had virtually identical copy, a husband is serious when voicing the key line, "I've got something to tell you." In this case, the wife seemed much more vulnerable and threatened. Apparently, it was irritating to see the husband being so judgmental about the woman's appearance and perhaps even her acceptability.

ADVERTISING THAT TRANSFORMS THE USE EXPERIENCE

Transformational advertising, a concept associated with William Wells of Needham, Harper and Steers, involves developing associations with the brand or brand use such that the experience of using the brand is transformed or changed into something quite different.[15] Puto and Wells note that transformational advertising contains the following characteristics:[16]

1. It must make the experience of using the product richer, warmer, more exciting, and/or more enjoyable than that obtained solely from an objective description of the advertised brand.
2. It must connect the experience of the advertisement so tightly with the experience of using the brand that consumers cannot remember the brand without recalling the experience generated by the advertisement.

How Transformational Advertising Works

There are several theoretical explanations as to how transformational advertising might work. One is that the feeling engendered during the commercial gets transferred to the use experience. The audience understands and relates so closely with the actors in the advertisement that the experience portrayed corresponds to actually having the experience. They key, then, would be for the commercial to be empathetic, believable, and meaningful, perhaps reminding the audience of experiences they have had in their lives. Thus, when the use occasion occurs, the experience and associated feeling are simply repeated. The use experience then makes the feeling experience stimulated by the next commercial exposure even stronger.

Another explanation is that the audience perceives the strong feeling response from the actors toward the use of the brand.[17] Over time and with repetition the audience will eventually associate the feeling response to the brand just as the actors did. In essence, over repetitions of the advertising and use experience, the vicarious experience becomes a real experience.

A third explanation is based on the generalized emotion concept of Clynes.[18] Transformational advertising may facilitate the recall of past experiences associated with the feeling engendered by the advertising. The recall is effortless and the focus is on drawing on similar feelings from past experiences rather than the recall of the actual experiences. Further, the audience may create new fantasies that will then be associated with the feeling. They may, in effect, embellish the scene in the commercial to make it more relevant to them. Puto and Wells note that this fantasy creation is illustrated by the Marlboro Country advertising, where "viewers were free to overlay their own feelings and fantasies onto the scene, and these feelings and fantasies then become permanently associated with the experience of smoking the advertised brand of cigarette."[19]

Wells has suggested that a successful transformational advertising campaign must be able to make and maintain the necessary associations, and it must put forth a positive campaign that rings true.[20]

Creating and Maintaining Associations

Transformational advertising involves two types of associations. Creating and maintaining both are crucial to its success. The first are the associations with the use experience. It may be desired to associate with the use experience feelings (the use of Grandma's Cookies generates "motherly" feelings) or the type of user (active, stylish people wear Levi's jeans). A Lowenbrau campaign, for example, may try to associate warm feelings and relaxed camaraderie with the Lowenbrau use experience. The second is the association between the use experience that has to be created and the brand.

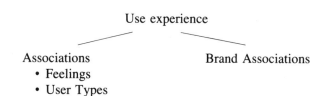

To achieve these associations it is necessary to:

• have a substantial media budget
• maintain consistency over time
• closely connect the brand with the advertising

Adequate Budget.   Informational advertising can sometimes work with a single exposure. However, transformational feeling advertising requires heavy repetition to build the associations. Thus, a media budget and schedule delivering frequent exposure are necessary. Further, advertising testing must also adjust to the reality that the advertising impact is based on many exposures. Thus, single-exposure tests will probably understate the impact and may actually have little relevance in the evaluation of a commercial's ultimate performance in a transformational campaign.

Consistency.   To obtain and retain the desired associations, transformation advertising must be consistent over time. The thrust of the campaign cannot be allowed to change frequently. It might be desirable or even necessary to be consistent for decades. That does not mean that the advertising needs to be repetitive. Rather, it means that it needs to be cohesive, supporting the same associations.

Links to the Brand.   The advertising needs to connect the use experience that is being created to the brand so tightly that people cannot recall one without thinking of the other. What will be ineffective is to establish the right use experience but not the association with the brand. Wells notes that a series of soap ads used the lines:[21]

- "New blouse?" "No, new bleach"
- "New dress?" "No, new bleach"
- "New shirt?" "No, new bleach"

Almost everyone remembered the line but almost no one remembered the advertiser. The link between the advertiser and the use experience requires constant reinforcement. If Marlboro were to stop advertising, someone else could occupy Marlboro country.

A Positive Campaign that Rings True

Effective transformational advertising should be positive. It should make the experience richer, warmer, and more enjoyable. An implication is that transformational advertising may be inappropriate for some products. It will be difficult to turn scrubbing the floor, cleaning the oven, or taking a laxative into fun, upbeat experience. However, transformational advertising has been used to mitigate an unpleasant experience. For example, some of the transformational airline advertising has probably helped some face the anxieties of flying. The "People Use Our Money to Make the Most Out of Life" campaign for HFC may have reduced the unpleasantness of applying for a loan.

Transformational advertising must also ring true. It will not be effective if it is disconfirmed by real-life experiences with the product. No amount of "ride the friendly rails" would transform the experience of riding the New York subway.

FEELINGS EXPERIENCED BY AUDIENCE MEMBERS

Undoubtedly, there are countless numbers of feelings and combinations of feelings that could potentially be precipitated by advertising. The fact is that we not only know little about how such feelings affect the persuasion process, but we do not even really know which feelings are the most relevant. There do exist many lists of feelings, emotions, and moods that may be helpful.

The psychologist Plutchik, for example, developed a list of 40 emotion words, including[22]

Defiant	Adventurous	Disgusted
Surprised	Inquisitive	Expectant
Enthusiastic	Affectionate	Curious
Receptive	Shy	Hopeless
Unhappy	Perplexed	Hesitant
Afraid	Bewildered	Annoyed
Hesitant	Sad	Cheerful
Joyful	Elated	Hostile

Any of these could be important to a given advertisement. Sadness would be aroused by a commercial showing an older woman reflecting on the loss of a mate or by an advertisement attempting to gain support for resources for a famine-stricken country such as Biafra by portraying an undernourished child. Enthusiasm and joy might be created by commercials showing people playing volleyball at a beach with upbeat, active music in the background.

Some ads can create a feeling of excitement, adventure, action, and danger. A good example is a 30-second spot for Pepsi Free which used the tag line "Because life is stimulating enough" to communicate the message that life does not need the stimulant caffeine in cola.[23] After watching the 16 seconds of a pair of policemen chasing a motorcycle maniac, the viewer might agree. After they lose the cyclist they stop for a Pepsi Free only to see the maniac flippantly riding his cycle on the roof of their car. The scene in Figure 10-3 provides a flavor of the ad.

Other ads can create feelings of elegance. A perfume ad showed a sophisticated woman preparing for a ball. A BMW ad showed a stylish, elegant woman slowly entering a car. Both ads surely engendered feelings of elegance, style, and class for some audience members.

Among the feelings that have been studied in the advertising context in some depth are warmth, humor, and fear.

Warmth in Advertising

When audiences are asked to describe advertisements, one dimension that is used can be interpreted as perceived warmth. The Aaker and Bruzzone study found a warmth dimension associated with commercials that utilized sentimental/family–kids/friends–feelings/feel good about yourself creative approaches.[24] Wells et al.

Figure 10.3.   **A daredevil motorcyclist eludes two policemen from a Pepsi Free 30 second action commercial**

included adjectives such as gentle, tender, soothing, serene, and lovely into a dimension they termed sensuousness.[25] Schlinger found an "empathy factor" associated with commercials involving affectionate couples, warm relationships, mother-child interactions, attractive products, vacation settings, or appealing characters such as Pillsbury's soft and cuddly doughboy.[26] The warmth construct emerging from these dissimilar studies, although certainly complex, has some consistent characteristics and associations.

The Warmth Construct.   The warmth construct has been defined by Aaker, Stayman, and Hagerty to be "a positive, mild, transitory emotion involving physiological response and precipitated by experiencing directly or vicariously a love, family or friendship relationship."[27] A detached expression of love or friendship without concurrent involvement and physiological arousal would not generate warmth. On the other hand, a relationship experience in which the involvement, depth of feeling, and physiological arousal were extremely high would be too intense to be warm. Warmth is thus positioned as moderate in terms of involvement, depth of feeling, and physiological arousal. It is short term in duration—capable of being created or changed in seconds or minutes rather than hours or days.

A notable aspect of the definition is the suggestion that the direct or vicarious experience of a love, family, or friendship relationship is involved. Thus, it follows in the tradition of Charles Darwin, who did pioneering work on emotions in humans and animals, and many modern psychologists who view emotions in a social context. Averill, for example, defines emotions as transitory social roles.[28] Thus, a social object such as a person or persons, animal, organization (for example, fraternity, team, or club), or institution (for example, country) will usually be involved. Further, this social object will usually be linked to another social object in a relationship that involves emotions such as love, pride, acceptance, joy, sentimentality, tenderness, or happiness.

In the advertising context, warmth can be experienced vicariously when one or more characters in a commercial are experiencing warmth. For example, a happy dinner scene in a Lowenbrau commercial between a proud father and a son who just passed his bar exam shows feelings of warmth in both characters. The viewer could become involved enough to share the emotional experience vicariously with one or perhaps both. An advertisement could also involve a relationship between the audience member and a character in the commercial. The commercial character might be the object of pride or love. For example, an audience member might be proud of an elderly person seen accomplishing a difficult task or an athlete winning an Olympic gold medal. Finally, a viewer might be reminded of a prior warm experience by a commercial and be stimulated to relive it. For example, a Christmas scene could recall warm family moments.

A Warmth Experiment.   One series of experiments concluded the following about the warmth construct:[29]

1. A "warmth monitor," where respondents continuously recorded their felt warmth by moving a pencil down a paper that was scaled from "emotional, moist eyes" to "warmhearted, tender" to "neutral" to "absence of warmth," was used to show that commercials are capable of altering felt warmth levels substantially with even the first portion of a 30-second commercial.

2. Warmth was accompanied by physiological arousal. The warm level was correlated (the correlation averaged 0.67 across six warm commercials) with galvanic skin response (GSR), one of the commonly used measures of physiological arousal.

3. Warm commercials were clearly more effective in terms of postexposure measures such as liking of the ad, copy recall, and purchase intention when they followed a humorous or irritating commercial rather than another warm commercial, even when the humorous commercial was equally well-liked. The probable explanation from adaption theory is that a warm commercial will appear warmer when the audience becomes used to the warmth level of a very different type of commercial.

4. A strong relationship between warmth levels and the change in warmth throughout the commercial and the postexposure commercial impact was found, which suggests that warmth does indeed contribute to a commercial's impact.

Humor

As noted previously, humor appeals can potentially affect information processing in a variety of ways such as attracting attention, improving memory of copy points, and distracting the audience from counterarguing. The concern here is with the feeling that accompanies humor in advertising and the associated laughter. In terms of the list above, it probably involves feelings such as cheer, joy, and happiness. The potential exists, of course, for the feelings engendered by this humor to become associated with the brand, thereby affecting the attitude toward the brand and perhaps its image/beliefs as well. Clearly, a humor-based appeal is complex and much is yet to be learned about it.

Of course, even a casual observer of humor in advertising will note that there are very different types. For example, some humorous advertising is very warm, such as a charming old couple teasing one another. Other humor efforts are very sophisticated and clever, such as a series in which James Garner bantered with a wife about Polaroid. Then there is the heavy slapstick commercials such as those for Dorito Corn Chips, in which characters are knocked over by the sound of a loud crunch. Consider also the boisterous, silly commercials for Miller Lite Beer. Clearly, each of these approaches will involve different sets of feelings.

One of the difficulties in working with humor is that what strikes one person as humorous, another will simply consider silly and irritating. Thus, it is particularly important with humor to have a good concept of the target audience. Further, the tendency for humor to irritate undoubtedly will increase with repetition. Since feeling advertising requires repetition to build associations, the tendency for some to become irritated is enhanced. The use of many executions for the same campaign will reduce the problem but it still will remain.

A U.S. campaign for Kronenbourg beer which used a heavy dose of British humor was disliked by the managers of the French parent firm.[30] The campaign would have been killed had it not been so successful. Sales increased 22.5 percent during the year, while imports were up only 14 percent. One radio spot described the brew's slogan "better, not bitter" as the "current No. 1 advertising disaster" and that the beer is a "terrific beer that doesn't taste as if it had a dead rat in it."[31] Later spots begged the audience to try the beer, as "it is the leading bottle of beer in the whole of Europe—it's not going to kill you."[32]

Fear Appeals

Fear, a very different type of feeling than warmth or humor, has been used in a variety of contexts.[33] The most obvious are those involving a product designed to protect a person from loss of property (automobile or home insurance) or health (life insurance or antismoking campaigns). Advertising for seat belts and against smoking have both focused on the fear of losing one's life. There are also more subtle fears associated with social and psychological motivations—the loss of friends, status, or job or a sense of failure to be a good parent or homemaker. Such fears are relevant to personal-care products (mouthwash, toothpaste) and homemaking products (foods and appliances).

Fear appeals engender the emotional response of fear as well as related feelings such as fright, disgust, and discomfort. However, one well-accepted theory of fear appeals, the "parallel response model" of the psychologist Leventhal, suggests that a cognitive response, the belief that harm is likely to occur, is evoked in addition to the emotional response.[34] Both responses need to be considered in attempting to predict the reaction of audience members. The preferred audience reaction is to comply with the communication and change attitudes or behavior accordingly. The alternative is to engage in defensive processes such as to deny vulnerability, counterargue, become irritated at something in the ad, or ignore it.

For the preferred "comply" reaction to occur, the fear needs to be at just the right level. If it is too low, the emotional response will not be forthcoming and the ad will not be successful at creating attention and interest in the basic problem. If it is too high, the audience member will attempt to activate some defense mechanism to avoid facing the problem. Clearly, the level will be sensitive to the target audience. Strong fear appeals for campaigns such as antismoking should probably be directed at teens who do not now smoke. If they were directed at smokers already concerned, a strong appeal may result in an avoidance strategy. For low-involvement products such as mouthwash, the problem may be to generate a strong enough appeal to break through the perceptual filter.

Equally important to the fear level is to provide an acceptable solution to the problem, one that the audience member feels that he or she is capable of pursuing. Without some reassurance that the solution is feasible, the audience member will tend to "turn off" the message. Thus, there needs to be a cognitive element. At the outset of the chapter we discussed the Marschalk philosophy of "emotional hard sell," where an emotional appeal is coupled with a rational hook. Fear appeals usually need such a rational hook.

Figure 10-4 shows a fairly mild fear appeal. There might be an issue as to whether it is arousing enough. The solution is to obtain a booklet to tell how to cope with the problem drinker.

What Affects the Intensity of Feelings

The intensity of feelings or emotions precipitated by the advertising will depend on many factors. Although research is still preliminary, it seems likely that an advertisement attempting to generate an emotional response should be believable and engender empathy.[35]

Believability.   If a person is to share an emotional experience vicariously or to be stimulated to relive a prior emotional experience, it may be necessary for there to

Figure 10-4.   **A National Highway Traffic Safety Administration advertisement**

TODAY
YOUR FRIENDLY NEIGHBOR
MAY KILL YOU.

The guy next door is probably a nice guy. Wife. Kids. House. Job. Car. And, for all you know, a drinking problem.

No matter how nice he is, if he drives when he's drunk, he's a potential killer. Last year, problem drinkers killed 19,000 people in car accidents.

They all live next door to somebody, and most of them wouldn't hurt a butterfly on purpose. But they didn't do it on purpose. They did it because they didn't

know what they were doing.

Most of them were very, very drunk. Like eight drinks in two hours. Like scotch for breakfast. And lunch. And dinner.

The problem drinker is the problem. And we have to get him off the road because he can't get himself off.

There are many things that can be done to help him and to help us. Stricter drunk driving laws, stricter law enforcement, scientific breath tests and court

supervised treatment among them. There's a huge national highway safety project just beginning that needs you to understand and to help. Help.

```
┌─────────────────────────────┐
│ DRUNK DRIVER              10 │
│ BOX 1969                     │
│ WASHINGTON, D.C. 20013       │
│ I want to help. Please tell me how. │
│ My name is_____  │
│ Address_____    │
│ City_____State____Zip___ │
└─────────────────────────────┘
```

GET THE PROBLEM DRINKER OFF THE ROAD. FOR HIS SAKE. AND YOURS.

U.S. DEPARTMENT OF TRANSPORTATION   NATIONAL HIGHWAY TRAFFIC SAFETY ADMINISTRATION.

Courtesy of the National Highway Traffic Safety Administration and Grey Advertising, Inc.

be literal believability. If the scene is not realistic, if it could not happen in real life, it will be more difficult to generate a meaningful emotional response.

For any emotional response to occur, it seems evident that the advertisement must have verisimilitude—the appearance of truth or the depiction of realism, as in the theater or literature. The scene may not be literally true, but the commercial generates a willing suspension of disbelief. It has a ring of truth—if paper towels could speak, they would speak that way. There is no distracting thought that the scene is phony, contrived, or silly. For example, the introduction of a mouthwash solution to a social situation might be so contrived as to disrupt the verisimilitude and prevent the desired emotion from emerging. Thus, believability can act as a block to and/or an enhancer of an emotional response.

Empathy.   Here we refer to cognitive empathy, which is the understanding of the situation of others, as opposed to emotional empathy involving a vicarious emotional experience. If empathy is high and thus the understanding of another's situation is deeper, the emotional response should be more likely and more intense. Empathy will tend to be higher if the characters in the commercial are similar to the audience member and the settings are familiar. It will also tend to be higher when the audience member has had an experience identical or similar to that shown in the advertisement. The expectation is that a prior experience should make it easier to experience another's feelings vicariously. If a viewer has experienced the exultation of winning a tennis championship, he or she may be more likely to share vicariously the emotions of a commercial character who is clearly experiencing such emotions.

The role of feelings in advertising is most obvious for commercials that contain little or no product information for which feelings obviously play an important role. However, the presence of feeling responses for commercials that are informative, stressing product attributes, should not be overlooked. For example, one commercial was classified as very informative because its thrust was to communicate the effectiveness of a mosquito repellant. The commercial recruited a person to test the product by placing an arm in a container of mosquitoes. The shock and horror of the participant was extremely emotional, and this emotion unquestionably affected the commercial's impact.

SUMMARY

In addition to communicating information, advertising can generate feelings such as warmth, happiness, fear, or irritation. Such feelings can influence attitudes and behavior directly or indirectly by helping to create positive attitudes toward the advertisement or by transforming the use experience.

Classical conditioning provides one explanation for how feeling responses become associated with the brand. The feeling response (UR) is associated with the commercial (US). The commercial is then associated with the brand (CS). Finally, exposure to the brand even without the commercial stimulates the same feeling response (CR). The strength of the association between the feeling and the brand or brand use will depend on several factors, such as the number of repetitions, the time since the last exposure, and how close the brand is linked to the commercial.

Research has shown that a positive attitude toward the advertisement can affect the brand over and above any communication effect. Because the attitude toward the advertisement can apply to a wide variety of feelings, it becomes a potentially important way to conceptualize and measure feeling advertisements. There has been little systematic research on how to create a well-liked ad, but there is evidence on what makes an ad disliked. Irritating television commercials tend to portray an unbelievable situation, a "put-down" person, a threatened relationship, graphic physical discomfort, tension, an unattractive or unsympathetic character, or a sensitive product with a product-focused message.

Transformational advertising transforms the use experience by associating feelings with it. It makes the experience richer, warmer, more exciting, and/or more enjoyable. For transformational advertising to work, it must be positive and ring true and the associations (between the feelings and the use experience and between the brand and the use experience) must be created and maintained with heavy repetition.

There are many feelings and combinations of feelings that have potential relevance to advertising, including warmth, humor, and fear. Warmth has been shown to be very volatile, changing in a matter of seconds, yet capable of stimulating a physiological response (as measured by GSR). It is precipitated by experiencing directly or vicariously a love, family, or friendship relationship. A fear appeal in a context such as insurance advertising creates an emotional response and also a cognitive awareness of a problem. The ad should attempt to generate the optimal level of emotional response and provide a feasible solution to the problem. With humor, care is needed to ensure that some people are not irritated instead of entertained, especially over repetition.

DISCUSSION QUESTIONS

1. Identify a feeling television commercial or print advertisement. Analyze exactly how it works. What feelings might be engendered by it? How will those feelings help the brand? Did the ad do well in creating an association between the brand and the feelings? How would you change the ad?

2. Analyze Figure 10-1. How would you change the model? What characteristics of the ad will affect the feeling response? To what extent is it important to have cognitive empathy—that is, the audience understanding the characters or literal believability?

3. What characteristics of the audience will be relevant in predicting the feeling response of the ad? What characteristics of the context in which the exposure is embedded will affect the emotional response?

4. Using an example of an actual commercial, explain to a friend how classical conditioning works. How does it differ from the exposure effect? Illustrate generalization. In the Bierley experiment, why was a group included that just heard the music and a group that saw the stimuli but heard no music?

5. What implications for advertising do you see for the three classical conditioning experiments that were reported? What problems do you see in applying them to the "real" world? Do the first two indicate that you do not need many repetitions?

6. What are some ads that you liked? Why? What makes an ad well-liked?

7. Under what circumstances will an ad be effective even if it is disliked?

8. What is transformational advertising? How does it work? What are some examples? When should it be used? "If Marlboro ever left Marlboro country (stopped the Marlboro Country campaign), someone else could move right in." Comment.

9. A transformational ad must "ring true." Must it have literal believability? You should not use transformation advertising for avoidance products such as oven cleaners. Do you agree?

10. What is warmth in advertising? Must a social relationship be involved? Can a sunset generate a feeling of warmth? Give some examples of warm advertising. How did the "warmth" help? Would a warm ad be more effective if it followed a humorous ad, a warm ad, or an irritating ad? Why? What would you predict would be the response to a warm ad over repetition?

11. How does humor work in advertising? Give some examples. What about fear? What other feelings can you identify as being present in advertising?

12. The chapter talks of believability, both literal and "verisimilitude." What is verisimilitude? Give some examples from current advertising. In your example, what emotional response is likely?

13. Classify products such as cars, jewelry, cigarettes, food, candy, house furnishings, and motorcycles as to whether they should use thinking or feeling advertising. Within each class divide them into high- and low-involvement products.

NOTES

1. Stuart J. Agres, "Cognitive and Emotional Elements in Persuasion and Advertising," Working Paper, The Marschalk Company, undated.

2. For an excellent review of the impact of mood states on communication see Meryl Paula Gardner, "Mood States and Consumer Behavior: A Critical Review," *Journal of Consumer Research,* 12, December 1985, pp. 281–300. A classic reference is Gordon Bower, "Mood and Memory," *American Psychologist,* 36, no. 2, 1981, pp. 129–148.

3. Sid Hecker, "The Reality of Fantasy," presented at the American Marketing Winter Conference, Phoenix, Ariz., 1985.

4. For an overview, see Frances K. McSweeney and Calvin Bierley, "Recent Developments in Classical Conditioning," *Journal of Consumer Research,* 11, September 1984, pp. 619–631.

5. Gerald J. Gorn, "The Effects of Music in Advertising on Choice Behavior: A Classical Conditioning Approach," *Journal of Marketing,* 1, Winter 1982, pp. 94–101.

6. A study similar to Gorn's failed to find the same effect. However, the study used humor, a relatively complex stimulus, instead of music and had only 60 subjects, 15 to each cell. See Chris T. Allen and Thomas J. Madden, "A Closer Look at Classical Conditioning," *Journal of Consumer Research,* 12, December 1985, pp. 301–315.

7. Calvin Bierley, Frances K. McSweeney, and Renee Vannieuwkerk, "Classical Conditioning of Preferences for Stimuli," *Journal of Consumer Research,* 12, December 1985, pp. 316–323.

8. Werner Kroeber-Riel, "Emotional Product Differentiation by Classical Conditioning," in Thomas C. Kinnear, ed., *Advances in Consumer Research,* Vol. XI (Ann Arbor, Mich.: Association for Consumer Research, 1983), pp. 538–543.

9. Andrew A. Mitchell and Jerry C. Olson, "Are Product Attribute Beliefs the Only Mediator of Advertising Effects on Brand Attitude?" *Journal of Marketing Research,* 18, August 1982, pp. 318–332. See also Meryl Paula Gardner, "Does Attitude toward the Ad Affect Brand Attitude under a Brand Evaluation 'Set'?", *Journal of Marketing Research,* 22, 1985; and Richard J. Lutz, Scott B. MacKenzie, and George Belch, "Attitude toward the Ad as a Mediator of Advertising Effectiveness: Determinants and Consequences," in Richard Bagozzi and Alice Tybout, eds., *Advances in Consumer Research,* Vol. 10 (Ann Arbor, Mich.: Association for Consumer Research, 1983), pp. 532–539.

10. Michael L. Ray and Rajeev Batra, "Emotion and Persuasion in Advertising: What We Do and Don't Know about Affect," in Richard P. Bagozzi and Alice M. Tybout, eds., *Advances in Consumer Research* (Ann Arbor, Mich.: Association for Consumer Research, 1983), pp. 543–547.

11. See Meryl Paula Gardner, "Mood States"; and Terence Shimp, "Attitude toward the Ad as a Mediator of Consumer Brand Choice," *Journal of Advertising,* 10, 1981, pp. 9–15.

12. Werner Kroeber-Riel, "Activation Research: Psychological Approaches in Consumer Research," *Journal of Consumer Research,* 5, 1979, pp. 240–250.

13. Alvin J. Silk and Terrence G. Vavra, "The Influence of Advertising's Affective Qualities on Consumer Responses," in G. D. Hughes and M. L. Ray, eds., *Consumer Information Processing* (Chapel Hill, N.C.: University of North Carolina Press, 1974), pp. 157–186.

14. David A. Aaker and Donald E. Bruzzone, "What Causes Irritation in Television Advertising?" *Journal of Marketing,* Summer 1985.

15. William D. Wells, "How Advertising Works," unpublished paper, 1980; and Christopher P. Puto and William D. Wells, "Informational and Transformation Advertising: The Differential Effects of Time," in Thomas C. Kinnear, ed., *Advances in Consumer Research,* Vol. XI (Ann Arbor, Mich.: Association for Consumer Research, 1983), pp. 638–643.

16. Ibid., p. 638.

17. Richard E. Petty and John T. Cacioppo, *Attitudes and Persuasion: Classic and Contemporary Approaches* (Dubuque, Iowa: Wm. C. Brown, 1981).

18. Manfred Clynes, "The Communication of Emotion: Theory of Sentics," in Robert Plutchik and Henry Kellerman, eds., *Emotion: Theory, Research, and Experience* (New York: Academic Press, 1980), pp. 271–301.

19. Puto and Wells, 1984, "Informational and Transformation Advertising," p. 639.

20. Wells, "How Advertising Works."

21. Ibid.

22. Robert Plutchik, "A General Psychoevolutionary Theory of Emotion," in Robert Plutchik and Henry Kellerman, eds., *Emotion: Theory, Research, and Experience* (New York: Academic Press, 1980), p. 18.

23. Lisa Phillips, "Pepsi Free Claims Life Needs No Stimulants," *Advertising Age,* April 4, 1985, p. 4.

24. David A. Aaker and Donald E. Bruzzone, "Viewer Perceptions of Prime-Time Television Advertising," *Journal of Advertising Research,* October 1981, pp. 15–23.

25. William D. Wells, Clark Leavitt, and Maureen McConville, "A Reaction Profile for TV Commercials," *Journal of Advertising Research,* December 1971, pp. 11–15.

26. Mary Jane Schlinger, "A Profile of Responses to Commercials," *Journal of Advertising Research,* 1979, pp. 37–46.

27. David A. Aaker, Douglas M. Stayman, and Michael R. Hagerty, "Warmth in Advertising:

Measurement, Impact, and Sequence Effects," *Journal of Consumer Research,* 12, March 1986, pp. 365–381.

28. James R. Averill, "A Constructivist View of Emotion," in Robert Plutchik and Henry Kellerman, eds., *Emotion: Theory, Research, and Experience* (New York: Academic Press, 1980), p. 305, Clynes, op. cit. p. 276.

29. Aaker, Stayman, and Hagerty, "Warmth in Advertising."

30. "Dry Humor Is Building a Thirst for Kronenbourg," *Business Week,* March 11, 1985, p. 120.

31. Ibid.

32. Ibid.

33. Michael L. Ray and William L. Wilkie, "Fear: The Potential of an Appeal Neglected by Marketing," *Journal of Marketing,* 32, January 1970, pp. 54–62.

34. T. John Rosen, Nathaniel S. Terry, and Howard Leventhal, "The Role of Esteem and Coping in Response to a Threat Communication," *Journal of Research in Personality,* 16, Spring 1983, pp. 90–110.

35. David A. Aaker and Douglas M. Stayman, "What Mediates the Emotional Response to Advertising? The Case of Warmth," Proceedings of the 1985 Advertising and Consumer Psychology Conference, Chicago, 1986, Pat Caferata and Alice Tybout, eds.

11

The Source, the Message, and Social Factors

We despise no source that can pay us a pleasing attention. (Mark Twain)

This last chapter in Part III will focus on the source, message, and social factors involved in advertising communication. In Chapters 8, 9, and 10 in-depth analyses of the perception process, information processing and attitude change, and the affective or feeling dimension of advertising were presented. In this final chapter, we begin with an overview model of advertising communication in which the source, message, and social factors are shown as part of an overall system of advertising communication, and then discuss each of these major components of the system.

MODEL OF THE ADVERTISING COMMUNICATION SYSTEM

Figure 11-1 shows a simple model of the advertising communication system. Advertising communication always involves a perception process and four of the elements shown in the model: the source, a message, a communication channel, and a receiver. In addition, the receiver will sometimes become a source of information

Figure 11-1.   **Model of the advertising communication system**

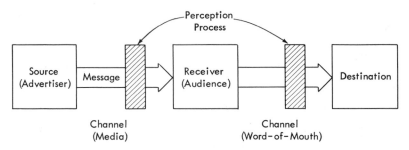

by talking to friends or associates. This type of communication is termed *word-of-mouth* communication, involves *social* interactions between two or more people, and the important ideas of *personal influence* and the *diffusion of information.*

Source.   The source of a message in the advertising communication system is where the message originates. There are many types of "sources" in the context of advertising, such as the company offering the product, the particular brand, or the spokesperson used. A model on source factors is developed in the following section to show the various source components of advertising copy and the dimensions of source components such as the credibility and attractiveness of the source.

Message.   The message refers to both the content and execution of the advertisement. It is the totality of what enters the receiver's perception process. The message execution can be described in a great variety of ways, such as the use of humor and fear appeals discussed in the preceding chapters. In later chapters, specific types of television commercials will be discussed and can also be considered ways to think about the advertising message. In this chapter, particular attention is given to two-sided messages, comparative advertising, and advertising directed to building resistant attitudes.

Channel.   The message is transmitted through some channel from the source to the receiver. The channel in an advertising communication system consists of the media, such as radio, television, newspapers, magazines, billboards, point-of-purchase displays, and so on. The impact of the communication can be different for different media. For example, an advertisement exposure in *Vogue* magazine can have quite a different effect than exposure to the same advertisement in *Good Housekeeping.* In Chapter 16, this channel effect will be considered in more detail.

Word-of-mouth communication represents another channel that is of special interest because it can sometimes play a key role in an advertising campaign.

It should be noted that a communication usually has a channel capacity. There is only so much that a receiver will be motivated and capable of processing. Furthermore, there is a physical limit to the number of advertisements that can be shown on prime time. For example, shortages of available advertising time can be a real problem.

Receiver. The receiver in an advertising communication system is the target audience. Thus, the receiver can be described in terms of audience segmentation variables, life-style, benefits sought, demographics, and so on. A particular interest can be the involvement in the product and the extent to which the receiver is willing to search for and/or process information. These receiver characteristics and others have been explored in earlier chapters. It is characteristics of the receiver, demographic, psychological, and social that are, of course, the basis of understanding communications, persuasion, and market processes.

The communication can have a variety of effects upon the receiver, as the past chapters have made clear. In particular, it can

Create awareness
Communicate information
Develop or change an image
Create or change an attitude
Precipitate behavior

Destination. The communication model in Figure 11-1 does not stop at the receiver but allows for the possibility that the initial receiver might engage in word-of-mouth communication to the ultimate destination of the message. The receiver then becomes an interim source and the destination becomes a receiver. Word-of-mouth can be a critical part resulting from an advertising program. The reality is that for some products the absence of word-of-mouth communication can be fatal, because it is only the word-of-mouth communication that has the credibility, comprehensiveness, and impact to affect ultimate behavior of a portion of the audience. Furthermore, advertising can actually stimulate word-of-mouth activity. Even when it cannot stimulate it, a knowledge of its appropriateness and power can be very helpful. The final section of this chapter on social factors will discuss word-of-mouth communication and related concepts of opinion leadership and personal influence.

SOURCE FACTORS

Source factors play an important role in persuasive communication. Research on source factors and their influence on persuasion has a long history in social psychology and mass communication and can provide some insight into this aspect of copy information and how it works. In advertising, the idea of the "source" of the message is complicated because many types of sources can be involved within any particular advertisement or commercial. For example, the endorser or spokesperson chosen in a testimonial advertisement for a particular brand of shoes is one type of source. How the receiver perceives this person can affect the persuasive impact of the advertisement. All such perceptions are usually referred to as the *credibility* of the source, and it is on this aspect of mass communication information that much basic research focuses.

But, in advertising, the credibility of other components of copy information must also be considered. For example, it has been shown that the credibility of the manufacturer of the product or, in general, the sponsor of the advertising is a factor that affects persuasive impact. And it is easy to appreciate that the product itself (the object of the advertising) can be considered by receivers to have higher or lower amounts of "credibility." Another factor on which source credibility comes into play is the vehicle in which the advertisement appears. Different magazines, for example, have been shown to have different credibility ratings.

To complicate matters further, not only are there multiple-source components of advertising on which credibility judgments can be assessed, but source credibility itself is a complicated multidimensional construct. On what criteria can the credibility of a particular advertising component be judged? As we shall see, any particular component can be considered highly credible on one dimension of credibility and have low credibility on another dimension.

Research has shown that the influence of source credibility factors must explicitly take into account the attitudes and behaviors of the audience to whom the advertising is targeted. In particular, source credibility factors play a different role depending on whether the audience is positive, neutral, or negative with respect to the object of the advertising. To keep things straight, we next present a model of source factors in advertising.

A Model of Source Factors in Advertising

Figure 11-2 shows various factors of source on which research has focused and about which creative copy decisions must be made. The central idea is the *credibility of a source component*. Research on source credibility can be divided into (1) studies concerned with the impact of credibility on social influence, and (2) research on the underlying dimensions of credibility.[1] In the former, a general conclusion is that the more credible the source, the more persuasive he or she is likely to be. In the latter, attention focuses on how an audience judges the credibility of the source. The three dimensions of trustworthiness, expertise, and likeability were most often used in early research.

More recently, researchers have recognized that some judgments concern a cognitive dimension and others an affective dimension. The cognitive dimension includes judgments about the power, prestige, competence (expertise) of the source, and the affective judgments about trustworthiness, attractiveness, and dynamism.[2] Other constructs, such as unbiasedness, similarity (between the source and receiver), and physical attractiveness, have been the focus of research. All such constructs are considered to be dimensions on which the credibility of a source component can be measured. A source can be high on one dimension and low on another. Consider the competence and unbiasedness dimensions. A doctor could be

Figure 11-2. **A model of the source dimensions of copy information**

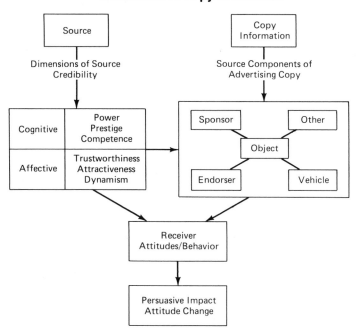

considered very competent (an expert) in recommending a drug product, but he or she would have less persuasive influence if listeners or viewers considered the recommendations to be biased by money payments given the doctor for making the commercial. Similarly, many politicians, although considered expert in their field, are also considered biased in their viewpoints.

Shown to the right in Figure 11-2 are various source components of advertising copy. At the center is the *object* of the advertising. This can be a brand, product, service, idea, political candidate, corporation, and so on. The credibility of the object of the advertising is often crucial to understanding source effects. For example, Zanot and Maddox[3] studied the credibility of the Mark Eden Developer and Bustline Contouring course among groups of college and noncollege women. The questions were phrased in terms of the companies' advertisements, such as "Do you think the Mark Eden ads are honest?" As might be expected, a large majority of female respondents (from 79 to 94 percent) judged the ads to be dishonest, in poor taste, and unbelievable. Although credibility judgments of noncollege women were slightly higher, both groups were very skeptical of claims being made for this particular service.

The *sponsor* is another source component of advertising copy about which credibility judgments are made. A famous study by Levitt,[4] for example, tested whether the effects of salespeople representing a prestigious company (Monsanto Chemical), a medium-credible company (Denver Chemical), and an anonymous company had a differential impact on purchasing agents. It was found that the better the company's reputation, the better were the salespeople's chances of getting a first hearing for a new product and early adoption of the product. Company source effect declined, however, with the riskiness of the decision. For high-risk decisions, the nature of the sales presentation and other factors were more important than the "source effect."

A third source component is called the *endorser*. The endorser in an advertisement is the person, celebrity, spokesman, announcer, and so on, who endorses or who demonstrates the product. Not all advertisements have an endorser as a copy component, but many of them do. Most of the work on source credibility in advertising has focused on this component and we shall discuss findings and implications later.

A fourth is the *vehicle*. This source component has also been shown to have an impact and is called the vehicle source effect. The same advertisement appearing in *Ladies Home Journal,* for example, can have a different impact than if it appeared in *Playboy* magazine. We will discuss this source component in later chapters dealing with media decisions, but you should recognize here that it is also an important source factor in advertising.

Another component is included in the Figure 11-2 model, called *other*. A range of execution elements in advertising can be considered from the source credibility viewpoint. Caricatures such as Superman, the Green Giant, the Marlboro Man, or General Foods doughboy are examples. Even brand names—Jaguar, Fox, Rabbit, Cougar, and so on—can be evaluated as source components. Music, whether classical, pop, rock, or western, is often included in radio or television advertising and its appropriateness judged on the basis of source credibility dimensions. As noted above, the advertisement itself can be considered the "source" and evaluated for its "credibility." Some researchers have considered the claims or "information" in the advertisement to be a source component that varies on credibility dimensions. As you can see, source credibility is a subject of far-reaching implications and importance in advertising.

The next part of the model recognizes the importance of existing receiver attitudes and behavior in understanding source effects. How the receiver perceives a particular source component is crucial. Sources that are highly credible to some audiences (for example, teenagers) will be less credible to others (for example, adults). Also, research has shown that the receiver's existing attitude toward the object, whether negative, neutral, or positive, has a great deal to do with source credibility effects.

Finally, the last part of the model suggests that a source effect can be analyzed in terms of its persuasive impact on the receiver/audience. Such effects can be identified as changes in beliefs about the object, changes in the affect (feelings) for the object, or changes in the intentions to purchase, use or behave (vote) toward the object in some way. Obviously, behavior itself (purchasing, voting, information search, and so on) can also be used in assessing several source credibility impacts.

Source Credibility Research

In terms of the Figure 11-2 model, this section presents a brief review of some research on source credibility which focuses on the endorser component. Interest in this area has increased because of the costs in copy creation and production of using celebrities as endorsers. Advertisers spent more than $25 billion for product endorsements by celebrities in 1977. Polaroid is reputed to have paid James Garner $3 million to appear in advertisements for Polaroid, and John Wayne received $350,000 a year for appearing in television commercials for Great Western Savings and Loan. An article in *Business Week* estimated that 33 percent of all television commercials contained celebrities in 1976.[5] Experts and typical consumers who are not celebrities are also widely used as endorsers, but there are costs associated with using these elements as well. Testimonial advertising is representative of this kind of advertising and is widely used by all kinds of advertisers in all kinds of media. Why is the endorser strategy so popular, and what does research show about the relative value of using high versus low credible sources?

Research has been reported that shows testimonials enhance readership scores.[6] Testimonials have also been shown to increase awareness and induce positive attitude change toward a company and its products.[7] In general, the more credible a source, the more persuasive that source is likely to be. It has also been found that celebrities can be overused, and may lose their effectiveness if they serve as endorsers for too many products.[8] Other research shows that the effectiveness of an endorser is related to the type of product being endorsed. There must be a reasonable match between the celebrity chosen and the product being advertised. In an experiment comparing the impact of using an expert rather than a typical consumer or celebrity in advertising a low-priced but fairly technical product (electronic calculator), it was found that the expert was more effective than either a typical consumer or a celebrity. Good reviews of the source credibility literature are available.[9]

A source can be used to attract attention even if there is high risk of the perceived credibility of the source. The reason is called the *sleeper effect*. The sleeper effect refers to the case where the persuasive impact of a message actually increases rather than decreases over time. Advertisers would, of course, like to have this happen in airing any particular commercial or in showing a print advertisement. One theory of why persuasive impact increases is that at the time of viewing or reading, some cue, such as the source, is negative or "discounting," and with the passage of time, the association of this negative cue with the message breaks down. The result is an increase in the overall impact of the message over time. Another explanation focuses on the information that is available at the time of exposure. This theory emphasizes the cognitive *elaboration* idea discussed in Chapter 9. If elaboration can be focused on the message rather than the cue, and these elaborations are more "support arguments" than they are "counterarguments," persuasion increases with time because the discounting cues are again lost or suppressed. Although the idea is intuitively appealing, there are surprisingly few studies that have demonstrated the presence of a "sleeper effect," even though dozens of experiments have been done on the subject.[10]

Recall from the review of congruity theory in Chapter 9 that the proposition that highly credible sources will lead to an increase in positive attitude for the object must be qualified somewhat. Congruity theory predicts that although a low-credible product should gain from the association with a high-credible source, the source will tend to lose some credibility from the association. The predictions of relative gains and losses of each component are functions of the initial credibility positions of each before the association occurs.

Conditions under which the basic proposition that "high-credible sources lead to higher persuasion" breaks down have been the focus of recent studies.[11] There are situations where a low-credible source is about *equal* in effectiveness to a high-credible source. Even more interesting are those situations where a low-credible source is *more* effective than a high one.

Low-credible sources are about equal in effectiveness to high-credible sources where:

1. The message is incongruous with the source's best interests or the source justifies the position advocated with unfamiliar arguments.
2. The audience is highly authoritarian or highly involved in the product.
3. The message is in some way threatening.

There are at least two situations in which it might be preferable to choose a low-credible source over a high one. In other words, a low-credible source can be *more* effective. First, it has been found that when receivers feel their behavior is being controlled, negative reactions can be increased if the source is highly credible. In effect, they are more likely to attribute the reasons for the behavior to a highly credible source than to a low one. The second case occurs in situations where receivers have a strong initial positive attitude about the brand or product. Such people tend to generate more support arguments during exposure if the source has low credibility rather than high. The reason is that they are more highly motivated to assure themselves that the position with which they agree is the right one. In sum, low-credible sources generate more support arguing and less counterarguing among people with strong positive initial attitudes. Research has also shown that for people who have neutral attitudes, there is no real difference between using high- or low-credible soures, whereas those who have strong negative attitudes initially tend to generate more counterarguments. In this latter case, using a highly credible source would make sense.

The choice of a source to be included in an advertisement must therefore be done very carefully. If the strategy is to try to increase positive attitudes, high-credible sources should be used. However, if the strategy is to induce behavior such as product trial directly, it is possible that using a highly credible source can undermine the formation of positive attitudes and reduce the incidence of repeat purchases and brand loyalty.

Klebba and Unger[12] in a field study examined the relationship between negative and positive information about the object and its impact on source credibility. The source in this experiment was Lee Iacocca, chairman and advertising spokesperson for the Chrysler Corporation. Negative information consisted of his prior association with the development of the Pinto while at Ford, and a law suit concerning the Pinto at the time of the experiment. Positive information concerned the Ford Mustang, with which he was also associated. Three hypotheses were tested in this research:

1. Subjects who possess negative information will rate the source lower on all dimensions of credibility than subjects who do not possess negative information.

2. Subjects who possess only positive information will rate the source higher on all dimensions than subjects who possess only negative information, both positive and negative information, or either positive or negative information.

3. All dimensions of credibility will be positively related to perceptions of the Chrysler Corporation and its products.

Although some directional suppport was shown for these hypotheses, it was generally not statistically significant. The authors conclude, however, that when an audience is exposed to negative source information, this information may more strongly influence perceptions of trustworthiness and likeability than perceptions of expertise or power. In general, affective dimensions have been found more strongly related to overall credibility than cognitive dimensions, and affective dimensions should be emphasized. The authors also advocate the alternative of delivering a message partially contrary to the source's own interests as a way to increase perceived trustworthiness in a low-credibility source.

Source credibility research highlights the importance of two basic principles for copy design: (1) source credibility is a *multidimensional* construct in which both cognitive and affective judgments are involved; and (2) although in general there exists a main effects impact (high-credibility sources lead to greater persuasion), potential interaction effects must be considered in any particular advertising planning situation. Factors such as endorser-product compatibility, audience attitudes toward the product, and the stimulation or suppression of counterarguing are examples.

Creating Source-Oriented Advertising

The advertisement for Maytag dishwashers shown in Figure 11-3 illustrates the use of a source in a testimonial-type format that is likely to be credible to readers on both cognitive and affective dimensions. The copy describes Mrs. Carlton's experiences, adds other features of the product, and invites the reader to send in for an illustrated booklet.

There are four primary endorser types from which a copy writer must choose in selecting an endorser for situations like this one: (1) a celebrity, (2) an expert, (3)

Figure 11-3.   **A testimonial advertisement for Maytag Dishwashers**

"I bought my Maytag Dishwasher sight unseen," writes Mrs. Carlton.

"John and I wouldn't have anything but. Not after the way our other Maytags have gone three rugged years without needing a single repair"

THE MAYTAG COMPANY, NEWTON, IOWA. WASHERS, DRYERS, PORTABLE WASHERS AND DRYERS, DISHWASHERS, DISPOSERS.

"We both work, so the last thing we need at home is troublesome appliances," says Mrs. John Carlton, Ontario, California.

"That's why the first time we saw an ad for Maytag Dishwashers, we decided to buy one. I didn't even have to go to the store to see it first.

"One thing I especially like about my Maytag Dishwasher is all the bother it saves. I put even heavily-soiled dishes right in, without rinsing them off. And they come out cleaner than my previous dishwasher ever got them."

Thanks for noticing, Mrs. Carlton. That's because Maytag has the Micro-Mesh™ Filter that traps even the tiniest food particles. And Maytag also has a full-size spray-arm *on top*, as well as one below, for extra cleaning power.

Giant capacity is another Maytag convenience. A Maytag does dinner dishes for a big family in *one load*. It's the only dishwasher that takes 10-inch plates in both racks.

See Maytag Built-In and Portable Dishwashers, and also Maytag Food Waste Disposers, at your Maytag Dealer's now. He's in the Yellow Pages.

We don't say that Mrs. Carlton's dishwasher will equal the record of her washer and dryer, but dependability is what we aim to build into every Maytag. No matter what job it's made for.

MAYTAG
THE DEPENDABILITY PEOPLE

Courtesy of the Maytag Company.

a typical satisfied customer, and (4) an announcer. Using a celebrity has the advantage of the publicity and attention-getting power of the celebrity virtually regardless of the product type. Large segments of the audience can instantly recognize and identify with the famous person, and the attraction and goodwill associated with the celebrity can be transferred to the product. Local celebrities or actors and actresses who are not so well known can often be used in local or regional market situations to good effect. On the negative side, this type of copy strategy will often be the most expensive and risky. Celebrities not only cost a lot, but are hard to get, and if they are already being used by other advertisers, they may be losing credibility at the time they are chosen. Also, as noted earlier, in cases where the audience is already very supportive of the product, the highly credible source can result in less persuasive impact than one which has lesser power and prestige.

An expert is likely to be the best choice where the product is technical or consumers need to be reassured that the product is safe to consume. An expert can allay fears in the audience concerning the product whether those fears arise from not knowing how something works, concern about side effects, concern about fulfilling a role such as father, mother, housewife, and so on, or health-related concerns about product use. Doctors, dentists, lawyers, engineers, and other kinds of experts can be chosen and at considerably less cost than a national celebrity.

A typical satisfied consumer such as Mrs. Carlton is often the best choice, particularly where it can be anticipated that there will be strong audience identification with the role involved, the person is "like" many members of the audience, and attributes of sincerity and trustworthiness are likely to come through. To maximize the naturalness of the situation, it is often useful to use a hidden camera and capture the consumer's real-world reactions to using the product in a situation with which the audience can identify. The choice might be a child rather than an adult, or an animal, such as an enthusiastic dog for a dog food commercial.

The national or local "talk show" in television, and a great deal of local radio advertising, typifies the choice of the announcer format. Johnny Carson and Ed McMahon are classic examples of using an announcer spokesperson as the essential source component. The choice in this case is really determined by the availability of the show and the particular announcer associated with that show. The actual copy generation process is often less expensive because only the script and, in television, some simple props must be provided. This does not imply that the media buy will be less expensive, but the trade-off is really deciding to put more money into the media buy than into copy production. The addition of props or ways to have the announcer do more than simply sit behind a desk and talk about the product can often enhance the persuasive impact considerably.

Three dimensions of source credibility are particularly important in advertising. These are discussed next.

Prestige.   Prestige derives from past achievements, reputation, wealth, political power, and the visibility of a person in some reference group—from a circle of friends to a nationally prominent reference group such as movie stars or athletic heros. A research firm, Marketing Evaluations, annually determines a familiarity and evaluative rating of top male and female personalities based on a mail questionnaire survey of television viewers. The basic rating is obtained by dividing the number who rated the personality as "one of my favorites" by those who indicated that they were "totally familiar" with the personality. In 1981, for example, Alan Alda and Carol Burnett were the top personalities and Howard Cosell and Rona Barret aroused the strongest negative feelings.

Similarity.   The source, instead of being admired or envied, could be effective by being liked and by having the audience member strongly identify with it. A source that is presented as being similar to the audience member in terms of attitudes, opinions, activities, background, social status, or life-style could achieve both liking and identification. There are many situations in which people will tend to like people with whom they have things in common. At the extreme, an audience member would like to see himself or herself in a commercial. The next best thing could be to see someone like him or herself. In addition, it should be easier to establish empathy and identification with sources that exhibit some similarity. Obviously, in most circumstances, prestige versus similarity present two very distinct alternatives.

Physical Attractiveness.   The research on physical attractiveness tends to show that "what is beautiful is good." All other things being equal, the stronger the physical attraction of the source, the greater the liking will be, and the stronger will be the persuasive impact. One study showed that attractive female models resulted in greater intention to buy perfume among males than when unattractive models were used. However, when the product was coffee, endorsement by the unattractive models led to a greater intention to buy. Significant attention has been given to the sexuality dimension. Although research suggests that sexually appealing sources are generally more persuasive, extreme or exotic poses can distract. Advertisements using nude models, for example, have been shown to be significantly less appealing than those where the model is clothed seductively.

Like the design of any advertising, source-oriented advertising needs to attend to the *compatibility of components* at the creation and design stage. This is perhaps the premiere lesson of source credibility research. Such advertising should strive for impact while remaining believable and combining elements that lead to a persuasive and realistic impression in the minds of the audience. Also, like any advertising, the decision as to which of thousands of alternative elements to choose should largely be governed by copy research. In other words, source-oriented copy should be tested for its impact using representative samples of an audience to whom it will be directed. Because of the complexity of advertising copy, it can never really be known how consumers will react until they are exposed to the copy itself (or at least the central ideas involved). The importance of copy testing and the various types of procedures involved will be presented in Chapter 14. We turn now to the second major set of factors involved in advertising copy information—the message factors.

MESSAGE FACTORS

In advertising, consideration of message factors and message-oriented advertising concern the claims, arguments, and the essential attribute information of the object that the advertising is trying to convey. Although not restricted to attribute information about the central object of the advertising, it is this aspect on which we focus in this section. Issues such as how much attribute information to include (should the copy be "long" or "short"), what attributes to focus on, what kinds of arguments are most effective in particular situations, and so on, are the focus of attention in discussing message factors.

For example, a message can be designed to focus a receiver's attention on the source. Such messages are said to appeal to *ethos*. An alternative is to concentrate on generating emotional reactions such as a pleasant mood, bolstering the ego, or appealing to a person's dreams, wishes, and fantasies. This approach essentially emphasizes *pathos*. Finally, a receiver's attention can be directed mainly to the claim being made. The appeal is to logic and to the receiver's capacity to think and reason logically. This approach is often referred to as appealing to *logos* or logic.

Another general issue is whether conclusions and arguments should be spelled out explicitly in the advertisement or whether the receiver should be left to draw his or her own conclusions. It is often advantageous to leave something out of a message. The closure principle discussed in Chapter 8 comes in here. Leaving something out can stimulate curiosity and motivation to seek additional information about the brand. Much depends on whether curiosity is indeed aroused. Also, there is some risk in assuming that a receiver will "draw his own conclusions." Research suggests that conclusions should be stated explicitly when there is a significant chance that the audience will not be motivated to draw their own conclusions, or when there are real risks of having them draw the wrong conclusions.

Comparative Advertising

Comparative advertising is a form of advertising in which two or more specifically named or recognizable brands of the same product class are compared and the comparison is made in terms of one or more specific product attributes.[13] It is interesting that prior to about 1970, comparative advertising was illegal and could not be used. It is now perfectly legal, however, and is used quite widely. One estimate is that as of 1977, from 7 to 25 percent of all advertising in major media was comparative advertising.[14] A great deal of research has also been done on comparative advertising, and there are 25 to 30 published studies on the subject in advertising and consumer behavior literature. Examples are given in Figures 11-4 and 11-5.

Is a comparative advertisement more effective than a noncomparative one? Much of the research has focused on this question. Consumer advocates and the Federal Trade Commission, which legalized comparative advertising in the 1970s,

Figure 11-4.   **A storyboard for the Schick Flexamatic Commercial**

DANCER · FITZGERALD · SAMPLE, INC.

Client: SCHICK ELECTRIC INC.	Title: "B·V.I.P." (DIMMITT)
Product: FLEXAMATIC	Commercial No.: SKMS2347
As Filmed/Recorded: COLOR	Date: 12/26/72 Length: 30 SECONDS

1. ANNCR: (VO) This man has just shaved with   2. the Norelco VIP.   3. Now he is trying a second shave   4. with the Schick Flexamatic.

5. Will it get any more beard?   6. Look ... the Flexamatic gets the stubble Norelco left behind.   7. Reverse the order and Norelco can't match this amount.   8. Tests prove the Schick Flexamatic shaves closer than Norelco, or Remington's leading sellers.

9. Closer because the head is super thin ...   10. comfortable because it's soft.   11. Get the Schick Flexamatic.   12. DIMMITT: (DV) Definitely closer.

Courtesy of Schick Incorporated.

have argued that the increased information should be beneficial to consumers and increase the chances for better decision making. Some researchers have, however, found that comparative advertising can lead to greater consumer confusion, and people may consider it offensive, less credible, and less informative. Some studies have shown that comparative advertising appears to stimulate more elaboration and counterarguing.[15]

Recent studies shed some light on under what conditions comparative advertising might be the better way to go. Swinyard[16] argues that the relative effectiveness of comparative advertising relates to the degree of counterarguing it evokes and whether the message is "one-sided" or "two-sided." A message is one-sided if it presents only positive arguments or attributes, and two-sided if some qualifications are presented. Figure 11-6 shows some of the results of an experimental field study in which consumers were exposed to comparative and noncomparative versions of retail advertising.

As can be seen in the upper left panel, the comparative version resulted in a higher percentage of people who engaged in counterarguing than the noncomparative version. Counterarguing declines however in the case of two-sided claims, and

Figure 11-5.   **A comparative advertisement**

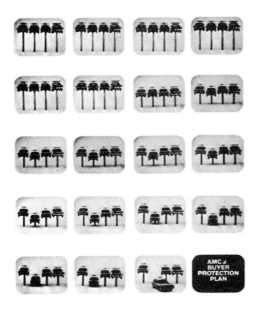

relatively more counterarguing occurs if only one-sided claims are presented. The center panel shows that comparative ads were also perceived as less truthful, and also that the claims were perceived as less truthful. The final panel shows an interesting interaction effect. Acceptance of the key claim increases dramatically when two sides are presented in the comparative advertisement rather than just one side. The nature of the claim does not, on the other hand, appear to have a significant effect in the noncomparative case.

Gorn and Weinberg[17] point out that although many research studies appear to show that comparative advertising is no more effective than noncomparative advertising, advertisers are making increasing use of comparative advertising. The risks of using comparative advertising are that the competitive brand is explicitly exposed, and the audience may not believe the comparative claims. A leading brand might therefore *not* want to engage in comparative advertising, whereas a challenger brand might gain from associating itself with the leader. As one senior marketing executive puts it, ''Comparative ads are good when you're new, but when you're the standard, it just gives a lot of free publicity to your competitors.''[18] The authors conducted an interesting experiment to see if a challenger brand gains by using comparative advertising.

The study involved exposing students to comparative and noncomparative versions of ads for brands of toothpaste, cigarettes, and golf balls. One condition was exposure of the challenger ads with the leader ad versus exposure to the

Figure 11-6.   **Interactions between comparative advertising and copy claims**

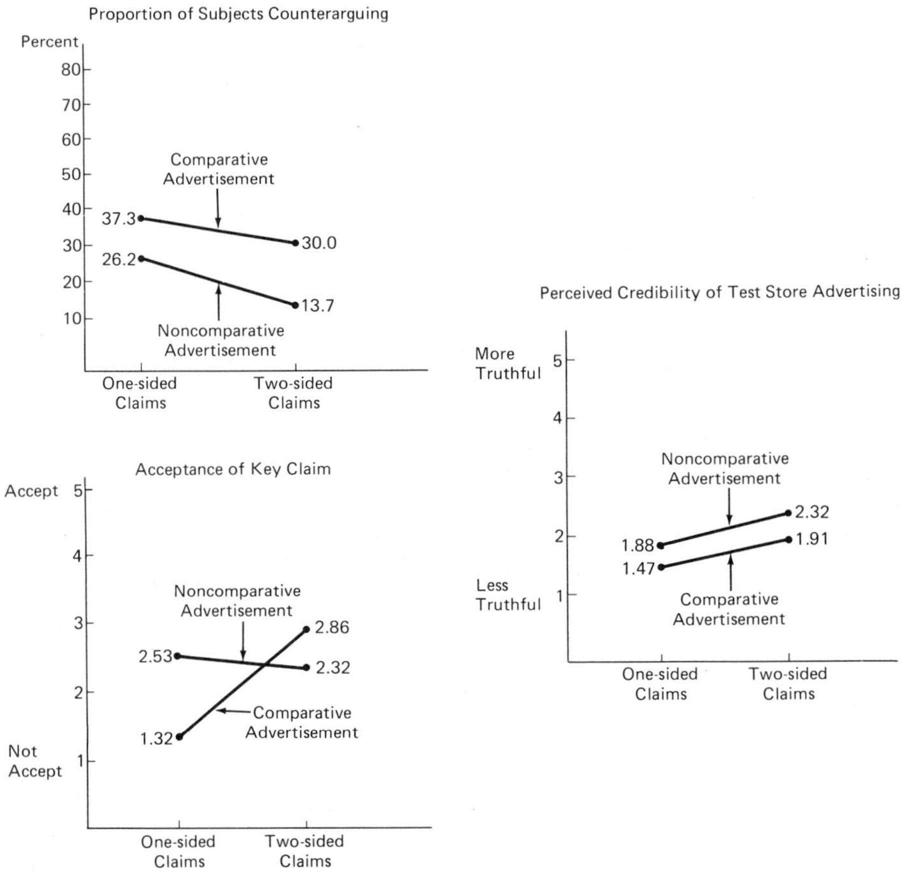

Source: William R. Swinyard, "The Interaction between Comparative Advertising and Copy Claim Variation," *Journal of Marketing Research,* 18, May 1981, pp. 175–186. Published by the American Marketing Association.

challenger ad without the leader present. As expected, it was found that comparative ads evoked more counterarguing. Also, it was found that a relatively greater degree of counterarguing occurred when the leader ad was absent than when it was present. Table 11-1 shows a count of the number of counter, support, and other types of arguments and responses in each condition.

Although counterarguments were greater for comparative ads, comparative advertising was found to be much more effective than noncomparative in increasing perceived *similarity* of the challenger and leader brands. This was particularly true in the leader-present condition. This study thus lends support to the idea that comparative advertising by new brands or challenger brands makes sense. Obviously, the attributes chosen as the basis for comparison should be chosen with care, and the claims made should be believable (legally, they should be capable of being

Table 11-1. Cognitive Responses to Challenger Ad: Number and Percentage of Cognitive Responses by Experimental Condition[a]

| | NONCOMPARATIVE | | | | COMPARATIVE | | | |
| | Leader absent | | Leader present | | Leader absent | | Leader present | |
	Number	Percent	Number	Percent	Number	Percent	Number	Percent
Specific counter	9	15	2	4	7	18	6	13
General counter	7	12	1	2	4	10	1	2
Source derogation	7	12	11	19	10	25	10	22
Negative responses	23	39	14	25	21	52	17	37
Specific support	4	7	4	7	2	5	6	13
General support	2	3	2	4	1	2	2	4
Source enhancement	8	14	13	23	0	0	2	4
Positive responses	14	24	19	33	3	8	10	22
Other responses	16	27	21	37	13	32	12	26
Blank	6	10	3	5	3	8	7	15
Total responses	59		57		40		46	
Total respondents	41		39		29		32	

[a] Percent totals may not add up due to rounding.

Source: Gerald J. Gorn and Charles B. Weinberg, "The Impact of Comparative Advertising on Perception and Attitude: Some Positive Findings," *Journal of Consumer Research*, 11, September 1984, pp. 719–727.

supported by research evidence). There is, nevertheless, always the basic trade-off to be made between the risks of stimulating more counterarguing and careful scrutiny versus the benefits of associating with a leading brand and gaining instant recognition.

Building Resistant Attitudes

Can a person be made to resist attempts by competitors or outside influences to change his or her attitudes? A great deal of advertising activity is associated with this goal. Given that we have developed favorable patronage—have a good share of market, for example—how can it be sustained? In attitude theory terms, how can we induce those currently loyal to our brand to remain loyal?

There are several ways to think of this goal. First, in purchase-cycle terms, it is a formal way of stating what advertising people mean when they speak of "extending the length of the fad" and "reducing the length of the fatigue," where the focus is on keeping purchasers in rather than out of a market. Second, it can be related to the concept of brand switching. The goal would be to reduce the probability of switching to competitive brands. Third, it can be cast in terms of the product life cycle. As Bither and his associates[19] have pointed out, it amounts to extending the profitable portion (usually the maturity phase) of the life cycle as long as possible. The assumption is that during introduction, growth, and maturity, consumers develop favorable attitudes toward a brand. In later stages, consumers are changing their attitudes and beginning to buy competing brands, brands that may be neither significantly different nor better. Marketers need to investigate methods to make a consumer's favorable attitudes more resistant to change.

A consumer can be made more resistant to competitive appeals either by attempting to make a brand offering more attractive or by attempting to train the consumer to withstand the persuasive efforts of competitors. From the first viewpoint, for example, one strategy would be to anchor beliefs about the brand to other beliefs that the consumer values highly. The brand might be shown to be significant in maintaining one's self-esteem or in otherwise enhancing the ego in various ways. Or the risks involved in not using the brand might be emphasized or the brand might be otherwise positioned as a means of ego defense. The goal of such approaches would be to try to increase the degree to which the consumer made a private commitment to continue using the brand. Furthermore, the degree to which such a commitment can be made public has also been shown to be effective in increasing resistance to competitive attacks. For an advertiser, this amounts to stimulating word-of-mouth activity, social interactions in which the brand is involved, or otherwise emphasizing its use as an indicator of social position, status, or role. Word-of-mouth activity can be stimulated by emphasizing the importance of seeking out opinions about the brand from other people.

The alternative of attempting to train a consumer to withstand competitive attacks has been the subject of some empirical work in marketing. The diffusion of advertising messages can be thought of as similar to the diffusion of germs in the spread of a disease through a population. If individuals are given weakened doses of the germs, they can build defenses to withstand the more potent ones, and thus be made resistant to the disease when exposed to it. The medical or biological analogy is, of course, the notion of inoculating an individual with a weakened dosage, and for this reason it has been called the "inoculation approach."[20]

The biological analogy is a good one. Disease resistance can be enhanced by pre-exposing a person to a weakened dose of the attacking material that is strong enough to stimulate his or her defenses, but not strong enough to overcome them.

It has been demonstrated that pre-exposure to weakened forms of counterargument (arguments counter to the position or object being defended) is more effective in building up resistance to strong subsequent attacks than is prior presentation of supportive arguments. Bither and his colleagues tested the proposition that "a portion of the subpopulation exposed to an immunization message designed to induce resistance to persuasion will show less change in belief level following an attack on the belief than will those subjects who were not exposed to the immunization prior to the attack."[21] The belief chosen was that there would be little or no censorship of movies. Support for the immunization argument in this experiment was provided by "high-prestige" sources. High-prestige sources seemed capable of immunizing subjects by a sequence of counterarguments followed by refuting arguments.

Refutational Approach.   Another term closely related to inoculation is "refutation." It refers to the process of explicitly or implicitly stating competitive appeals and then refuting them. Unlike the usual advertisements that deal exclusively with brand benefits, refutational advertisements deal with competitor claims and then refute them. Ray[22] has shown that, although advertising only the advantages of a brand may appear to be more effective in the usual before-after commercial test situation, these situations do not take into account the longer-run impact of advertising nor the competitive environment in which most advertisements are read. Refutational advertisements may be superior when these two elements are taken into account. Some examples in an advertising context will help fix the ideas.

Consider the benefits of regular toothbrushing. The positive benefits of brighter teeth, less decay, better health, and so on, could be stressed. This is often referred to as the supportive approach to advertising. If competitive claims are taken into account, a competitive claim might be mentioned and then refuted. For example, the charge that too frequent toothbrushing pits the teeth could be refuted by evidence that this is not true. This is called the refutational approach. Hertz and Avis advertising are examples of both the refutational and supportive approaches. Hertz for many years used a supportive approach, the many benefits of renting a Hertz car. Avis, on the other hand, refuted the implicit claim that "No. 1 equals the best," by suggesting that "No. 2 tries harder." The advertisement for British Caledonian Airways shown in Figure 11-7 is an interesting version of refutational advertising. "Fiona MacIntosh" is referred to as "the world's most hated stewardess" in

Figure 11-7. An advertisement for British Caledonian Airways

Courtesy of British Caledonian Airways Limited.

obvious contrast to her picture, which shows her with a happy child clinging to her. The theme is carried out by the reference to British Caledonian as "the airline airlines hate." Ray provides the following examples of refutational advertising:

Mutual of New York refutes the idea that people would be better off putting less money in life insurance and more in stocks and bonds as follows:

> MONY HEADLINE: I'm in stocks and bonds. I'll take them over life insurance. But a MONY man gave me a new look at life insurance. As an investment cornerstone it would protect my family . . . and build cash, too!

In the headache remedy area, Bayer refutes the claim that various products are stronger or better than aspirin as follows:

> BAYER HEADLINES: (1) Tower of Babble. (2) Does buffering it, squaring it, squeezing it, fizzing it, flavoring it, flattening it, gumming it or adding to it improve aspirin?

Perhaps the classic case of refutational advertising is Volkswagen. Like any small car, the main counterclaim is small size. VW meets this claim squarely: "So if you're 7'1" tall like Wilt our car is not for you. But maybe you're a mere 6'7"." Or, "Anybody for half a station wagon?"

It is possible to overrefute or misguide a viewer. The following is an example for Renault advertising:

> RENAULT HEADLINES: (1) "I won't buy a Renault no matter how good it is." (2) "It's not German. How good could it be?" (3) "Sure they save money, but I wouldn't take a long trip in one."

As Ray states,

> although refutational messages are superior to supportive in almost all studies of inducing resistance to persuasion, it was found in one study that people are more interested in reading supportive than refutational essays or articles . . . in order for a refutational ad to be read and to be effective, the headline should include some supportive aspects and should not be as ambiguous and possibly threatening as the Renault headlines are.[23] He cites three reasons why refutational messages appear to work:

1. They are more stimulating than supportive messages. They underline conflict and get people concerned about an area. This motivating factor alone can be quite effective, since refutational defenses can work even if they deal with claims other than those that appear in subsequent attacks.
2. They refute counter-claims and thus make the competitive attacks appear less credible when they appear. This refutation is probably quite satisfying. Statements of counter-claims can arouse dissonance or imbalance. The refutation can restore balance.
3. Refutational messages do contain some supportive information, even though less than supportive messages.[24]

Like all social psychological laboratory-oriented research findings, there is the question of whether the principles of refutation developed in laboratory situations are appropriate to field advertising situations. Ray mentions, for example, that, unlike most designs involving laboratory experiments on the effects of refutational messages, when respondents are given the choice of what they can read (for example, in actual field situations), the advantage of refutation is muted. One disadvantage of refutational messages is that they provide a viewer with information about a competitor's product and thus might enhance rather than defend against competitive alternatives. It is, nevertheless, a preferred approach to market situations in which the goal of an advertiser is to build resistance to attitude change and defend against competitive attack. Chivas scotch has for many years built its distinctive image on the notion of paying more rather than less for its product. The following ad appeared in the September 18, 1972 issue of *Time* magazine. The copy was positioned in the center of a full page against a white background:

> If money were no object, which scotch would you be drinking? Well, Chivas only costs a few dollars more than regular scotch.

We now turn to a discussion of social factors.

SOCIAL FACTORS

In addition to source and message factors, social factors must also be considered in designing advertising. This section focuses on such factors, particularly on the interplay between advertising and personal influence. Personal influence refers to the influence on brand choice and purchasing that flows from a consumer's friends and associates and is sometimes called *word-of-mouth advertising*. A related concept is *diffusion*. Diffusion refers to the spread of an advertising message through a market segment by word-of-mouth. Thus, an advertising message can reach a person even though he or she has not been directly exposed to it via word-of-mouth.

Diffusion and personal influence are important topics for an advertiser for several reasons.[25] First, great advertising campaigns and many apparently worthwhile products have floundered because of a failure to stimulate diffusion and word-of-mouth communication to support the product or service advertised. Some campaigns, on the other hand, have achieved great success, primarily because of the word-of-mouth communication that they stimulated. Second, there are significant reasons why, in many product categories, the relative influence of face-to-face communications greatly surpasses the influence of advertising in stimulating or determining brand choice. Third, segmentation strategies must take into account the fact that a target segment may have an important influence on the attitudes and behaviors of other groups not included within it.

It is first important to know the degree to which personal influence is likely to play a major or minor role in the consumer decision-making process. If personal influence plays a major role, then strategy, tactics, and many aspects of the advertising program can be adjusted accordingly. On the other hand, if personal influence is relatively unimportant in the decision-making process, other kinds of strategy and tactics will be needed. Every advertiser, including those from the nonprofit sector, should examine and assess the product being advertised from this viewpoint—the degree to which personal influence is operating in the purchase or exchange situation.

The Personal Influence Audit

It is well known that consumers differ with respect to the extent of their susceptibility to personal influence. Some people are simply more ''persuadable'' than others, more extroverted or introverted, more likely to engage in social interactions, and more affected in their decisions by the opinions of friends, neighbors, role models, and so on. This heterogeneity can be found within any particular market target. In terms of diffusion concepts, some part of the market target will contain opinion leaders and some part followers. It is also well known that the degree to which such social influence processes operate is affected by the nature of the product, service, or idea in question. It is this latter perspective on which we will focus: what is it about the nature of the product or the decisions involved with it that makes for more or less personal influence?

There are two kinds of personal influence: (1) external and explicit, and (2) internal and implicit. By external we mean the likelihood that decision making involves explicit social interactions such as a situation in which two or more people (for example, a husband, wife, and children) are involved. The consumer might search out friends and neighbors in the decision-making process or otherwise refer to the product in the course of conversations and social interactions. An industrial buyer might seek advice or information from associates. This is often called *word-of-mouth* advertising to distinguish this kind of communication from *mass communication* advertising.

Internal personal influence refers to the likelihood that decision making is affected by mental processes that involve people or groups. Thus, for example, many products are purchased as gifts for someone else where no interaction takes place with the intended recipient. Others are purchased primarily for their symbolic role. They may symbolize a particular social class position or status. Still others, particularly in the clothing and fashion industry, are heavily influenced by the decision-maker's judgment of ''what other people might think'' or ''how I will look to the Joneses'' and so on. Many products are purchased so as to be ''first with the latest thing.'' In all these instances, personal influence is operating but may involve little or no explicit social interaction or specific conversation between the consumer and someone else. Fishbein has extended the basic evaluative belief attitude models reviewed in Chapter 6 to include an explicit measure of this type of personal influence referred to as the *subjective norms* associated with the choice object. A personal influence audit focuses the manager's attention on the uses of his or her product from this point of view, as well as cases where personal influence is more explicit.

In conducting such an audit, the first thing to consider is the nature of the decision-making unit with respect to the product or object in question. Does the purchase or exchange decision tend to involve one, two, or many people?

Decision-Making Unit

The purchase of a package of gum, a breath mint, or numerous other types of consumer products, particularly in the "impulse" category, is predominantly an individual-oriented decision. The decision-making unit (DMU) tends to be one individual, and such purchases are unlikely to involve a group decision. In contrast, many major purchases in the consumer products area, such as a home or an automobile, and a large number of industrial product decisions are group decisions. At least two, and often several people will be involved, and it is a better understanding of this group decision-making process that advertisers in these product categories must acquire. In other terms, explicit personal influence is much more likely to be involved in the latter case than in the former, and the advertiser must take into account the fact that the target in the latter case is really a group rather than one individual.

An implicit personal influence process takes place in many purchase decisions. Many purchases that appear to be made for the self are in fact being made with some other individual or reference group in mind. Thus, the homemaker, for example, in buying provisions for the household, is often more concerned with what others in the household will want, use, and eat than with his or her own personal consumption. The distinction between the "consumer" and the "customer" in each situation must be clearly understood. The consumer of men's socks is in the majority of cases men. The customer for men's socks, however, is often a woman. All products given as gifts fall into this category, and it is of fundamental importance to assess the nature of the thing being advertised from this viewpoint. Many additional insights will be generated from such analysis. It is obvious, for example, that the principal consumers of baby foods are babies, and the principal customers for this product are mothers. But much baby food is purchased by elderly people for their own personal consumption. In the latter case, the consumer and customer are the same thing. Dogs are the primary consumer of dog foods, but it is really the dog owner who is the customer and to whom advertising messages must be addressed.

Information Acquisition and Processing

Recall from Chapter 9 that information acquisition and processing need to be understood in creating any form of advertising. Here we emphasize their importance in conducting a personal influence audit.

A basic question is the degree to which personal influence or word-of-mouth advertising plays a role in the information-acquisition process. Although there are no definitive conclusions, researchers have found that personal influence will be more likely to operate in situations where large rather than small amounts of money are involved, when the decision is *riskier,* and when the consumer is more *involved* in the choice. Thus, consumers are likely to seek out and acquire information of all kinds, including the advice and opinion of friends, family, and experts, where the financial and emotional investment is high. Where risk and high involvement are present, personal influence will also be likely to occur at the decision and postdecision stages of the process. Thus a salesperson plays a more important role with some products than with others, and the opinion of friends may be actively sought out after the decision has been made. These conditions are most likely for products such as large appliances, television sets, home computers, automobiles, and furniture.

Internal personal influence, from the information-processing perspective, involves the memory structure of the consumer. A stored information bit for Mrs. Jones in considering a purchase may be "What Mrs. Smith thinks."

The *situation* for which the purchase is made is another factor that has been intensively studied and shown to affect product attitudes and choice. Personal influence is often the major distinguishing characteristic between one situation and the next. Purchasing beer or wine to drink by oneself can differ from the situation of purchasing these products for an important social occasion. The advertiser must appreciate that his or her product may be locked into a particular situational use for which personal influence will operate to a greater or lesser degree. Judgments about the situational effects surrounding purchase are another important consideration in a personal influence audit.

Family decision making obviously involves personal influence, and the advertiser should make a determination of the existing and potential uses of the product in the consumption system of the family and the likely relative influence of various family members. Does the wife tend to carry most weight in choosing a brand for this product? The husband? Are children likely to be a significant influence?

Characteristics of the Innovation

In the case of new products or, more generally, *innovations,* an assessment should be made concerning the degree to which the innovation is easy to buy, use, and understand, and whether it involves relatively simple or more complicated aspects. Five concepts[26] are useful in making such an assessment:

1. *Relative advantage* (RA): the degree to which the new product is perceived as superior to the one it replaces or to existing products with which it will compete.
2. *Compatibility* (CO): the degree of consistency between the current set of alternatives used by the consumer to satisfy needs and the new product.

3. *Complexity* (CM): the degree of difficulty the consumer has in understanding or using the product.
4. *Divisibility* (DV): the degree to which the new product or samples of it can be tried out with a minimum of financial or time investment. Can the consumer easily reverse the decision in the sense of choosing not to adopt the product without at the same time losing or risking a great deal?
5. *Communicability* (CN): how difficult is it to communicate information about the new product?

All these factors will affect the degree to which information about the new product is passed along and the extent of word-of-mouth advertising that takes place. RA, CO, DV, and CN are essentially supportive factors in the diffusion and personal influence process, whereas CM will tend to retard the process.

A recent extension of these ideas is to consider the risk and habit factors associated with an innovation.[27] The basic argument is that reception of a new product will hinge on the degree of risk associated with its purchase and the prior entrenchment of consumer purchase habits in the product class.

Motivational Characteristics

Another useful dimension of the personal influence audit is to ask what motivates people to talk about a product and what motivates them to listen to a recommendation and to act on the recommendation of another person. The advertiser needs to make an assessment *before* a campaign is launched of the nature of her or his product and the consumer motivations that will lead to "talking and listening" about it.

Dichter[28] argued that for talking to take place there must exist some material interest: there must be satisfaction or reward associated with the behavior. In other words, a speaker will choose products, listeners, and words that are most likely to serve basic needs and goals. In a study of product talking and listening behavior, he found that talking motivations tended to fall into four categories, each associated with various kinds of involvement.

The first is *product involvement.* People have a tendency to want to talk about distinctly pleasurable or unpleasurable things. Talk can serve to relive the pleasure the speaker has obtained and dissipate the excitement aroused by the use of a product or the experience of having shopped for and purchased it. Talk can confirm ownership of it for the speaker in many subtle ways.

The second is *self-involvement.* The speaker essentially seeks confirmation of the wisdom of the decision from his or her peers and as a way to reduce dissonance. Self-confirmation behavior is engaged in to gain attention, show connoisseurship, and to enhance feelings of being first with something, having inside information, suggesting status, spreading the gospel, seeking confirmation of one's own judgment, and asserting superiority. The point is that a product or advertising object can be the central focus of conversations engaged in for these kinds of goals and motivations.

The third is *other involvement* in which the major motivation is the need and intent to help other persons and share with and enjoy the benefits of the product. Products can serve to express sentiments of neighborliness, care, friendship, and love. The fourth motivation for speaking about products is called *message involvement* and derives from the nature of advertising itself. Advertising, for many reasons, can stimulate word-of-mouth communications and often itself becomes the focus of such conversations.

Motivations for listening also require that the listener receive some satisfaction or reward from the interaction. Dichter found two conditions particularly important: (1) that the person who recommends something is interested in the listener and his or her well-being, and (2) that the speaker's experience with and knowledge about the product are convincing. Obviously, basic questions of the trust the listener-receiver has in the speaker-sender are involved and the credibility of the source of the communications. Seven kinds of sources were found to be particularly important and potentially successful in their influence attempts: commercial authorities, celebrities, connoisseurs, sharers of interest, intimates, people of goodwill, and bearers of tangible evidence.

Reference Group Influence

A final and related dimension on which the personal influence potential of a product can be assessed is called reference group influence. Whether or not a product is socially conspicuous is probably the most general attribute bearing on its susceptibility to reference group influence. The product must be conspicuous in the most obvious sense that it can be seen and identified by others, and it must be conspicuous in the sense of standing out and being noticed. No matter how visible a product is, if virtually everyone owns it, it is not conspicuous in the second sense.

Shibutani[29] has defined a reference group as "that group whose outlook is used by the actor as the frame of reference in the organization of his perceptual field." He identifies three types of reference group: (1) a group that serves as a *comparison point* for an individual, (2) a group to which an individual *aspires,* and (3) a group *whose perspective* is assumed by an individual. They need not be the groups in which the individual participates, although they sometimes are, but can be large social groupings—social class, ethnic group, subculture, or even imaginary groups such as those that motivate a genius working for "the good of humanity." The important feature of the reference-group concept is that an individual does not have to be a member of the group for the influence to occur. Thus, a student's behaviors and life-style can be heavily determined by emulation of the people in a group to which he or she aspires to belong.

This type of influence is particularly important and relevant with new products. In many cases, the mere fact that the product is new and other people do not yet have it is the crucial motivation for buying. New products that are significant breakthroughs at the time of their introduction such as television sets, hand-held calculators, air conditioners, home computers, and so on, are particularly likely to be affected by reference-group influence. However, even established products and brands vary in the degree to which reference-group influence operates, and this variation extends to differences that occur across market segments. Staples such as salt, sugar, and pepper are not likely to be affected, whereas clothing items, particularly in the area of fashion, will be. Radios are socially very important among teenagers. Furniture and automobiles serve important social as well as functional needs and are much affected by reference-group influence.

The personal influence audit could be extended in a variety of ways. The closely related concept of *social class* should be considered in the analysis. Is the product or brand used as a symbol of social-class position, aspiration, or mobility? Do all social classes use the product (for example, Coca-Cola) or is its use largely confined to one social class? The question of *culture* should be considered. Is the product bound to a particular ethnic group such as kosher foods, or does the ethnic background of the consumer play little or no role? Does ownership signify membership in a particular subculture, which may exclude it from the more general market? The *family life cycle* should be considered.[30] Is the product suitable to the "empty nest" family, the young couple just starting out, or some other stage of the family life? All these questions have ultimately to do with personal or social influence.

Figure 11-8 shows an example of how a particular product to be advertised could be assessed in terms of personal influence potential. Six factors are shown, each of which would require a judgment on the standing of the product with respect to the factor. The assessment could be extended and made more complicated by judging the product on other more specific factors that could enter into an overall value on any particular dimension. Data would be obtained either from the experience of executives and researchers familiar with the product category, or perhaps by explicit consumer influence studies that focused on measures of the personal influence construct.

Receivers and Opinion Leadership

The concept of the receiver as an opinion leader has been a central focus for much empirical research in sociology and marketing.[31] It is interesting to recall how Katz and Lazarsfeld first defined the concept:

> What we shall call opinion leadership, if we may call it leadership at all, is leadership at its simplest. It is casually exercised, sometimes unwittingly and unbeknown, within the smallest grouping of friends, family members, and neighbors. It is not leadership on the high level of a Churchill, nor of a local politico, nor even of a local social elite. It is at quite the opposite extreme; it is the almost invisible, certainly inconspicuous form of leadership at the person-to-person level of ordinary, intimate, informal, everyday contact.[32]

In their pioneering study, four types of opinion leaders were identified: marketing, fashion, movie, and public affairs leaders. Marketing leaders were found to

Figure 11-8.   **Personal influence product assessment form**

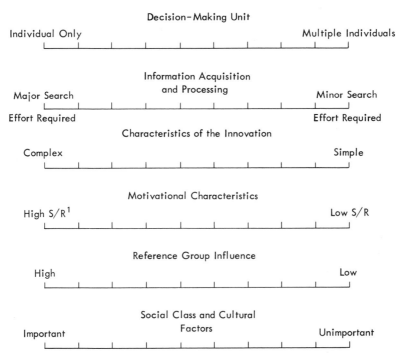

1 S/R signifies sending-receiving potential. Are there high or low motivations in the product-choice situation for trying to convince others (sending) to buy the product or for seeking out information from others (receiving) about the product?

be married women with comparatively large families, gregarious, and not concentrated at any particular social-status level. In contrast to the influence of immediate family members (for example, husband and child), the authors stressed the importance of extrafamilial influence in many consumer product situations.

Since the publication of this study, a great deal of research attention has been devoted to the concept of opinion leadership, both in marketing and in other disciplines. Myers,[33] for example, found in the case of the adoption of new frozen-food products, in which the new products were given to "positive" and "negative" opinion leaders, that group opinions toward the new products tended to follow those of the opinion leader in both positive and negative cases. One of the first questions that needs to be asked is whether opinion leadership is a general or a specific phenomenon. For example, does an opinion leader in one product class also tend to be an opinion leader in another?

Montgomery and Silk[34] tested the notion of overlap in opinion leadership as being more likely to occur where interests overlap. The data were drawn from a study of media habits and attitudes. Cluster analysis was used to examine the degree to which opinion leadership overlap and interest overlap were synonymous, and the authors conclude that this effect does in fact occur. In their terms, "Topic groupings for shared interests resemble those for which the same persons tend to designate themselves as influentials." It is reasonable to conclude that opinion leadership does overlap *within* product categories, but overlap *among* product categories is likely to occur much less often.

There are some important strategy implications of the overlap question. An advertiser can profitably investigate the degree to which overlap occurs in his or her product class. Particularly for companies that have lines of several related products or brands, it is significant to know the degree to which one set of people tends to be opinion leaders for all of them or whether opinion leadership tends to be specific for each.

From an advertiser's viewpoint, another important question is the degree to which opinion leaders are differentially responsive to advertising appeals. Without the establishment of this fact, many of the basic postulates of a two-step flow of mass communications break down. It is ultimately a question of the connection, or lack of connection, between the formal mass media channel and the informal channels of interpersonal communication and influence. Do individuals play different roles in introducing advertising communications into a social network? Not only is this important in understanding an advertising communication process, but it leads to a different interpretation of the decoding process—whether the "source" of the advertising information is consistently "direct" for some people and consistently "indirect" for others.

In an important book on the subject, Rogers[35] argued that at the time of introduction of an innovation, the population can be divided into five groups (segments) made up of *innovators, opinion leaders, early majority, late majority,* and *laggards.* He further argued that the distribution of these groups approximated a normal curve: the early and late majority groups would tend to be much larger than those at the tails, innovators and laggards. Second, he redefined the process of diffusion and adoption as involving five stages: *awareness, interest, evaluation, trial,* and *adoption.* The argument is that all people go through this process on the way to adoption (or rejection) of an innovation. Mass media and impersonal sources of influence tend to be most important at the early stages of awareness and interest, and word-of-mouth and personal influence tend to be most important in the later stages of evaluation, trial, and adoption.

Researchers have focused attention on the degree to which the five types of market segments exist during new-product introductions. The results are mixed and depend heavily on the nature of the new product and the competitive and other conditions at the time of entry. The concept of "innovator" has received particular attention. It is useful to consider the innovator concept for several reasons. First, it can be a useful segmentation variable. An advertiser may want to reach an innovator if a new product is involved simply because innovators may represent the most attractive segment, especially at the onset. Second, an innovator may, by example, influence others. Noninnovators tend to wait until innovators have acted. Therefore, it is reasonable to look first at the innovator segment. Finally, much research has gone into describing innovators in marketing. Since there is evidence of an overlap between innovators and opinion leaders, this research should also be relevant to those who would attempt to identify opinion leaders.

Strategy and Tactics

Following the personal influence audit and an analysis of the diffusion process, the advertiser should develop specific strategies and tactics. A recognition of the role and significance of personal influence should enter into the specification or elaboration of advertising objectives, specific strategies designed to achieve those objectives, and copy and media tactics used to carry them out.

The most straightforward strategy implication is that the advertiser can attempt to single out the crucial innovator and opinion leadership segments and target promotion and advertising messages to them. This strategy has not been followed as often as it might seem. Because of the costs of attempting to identify innovators in many product or market situations and the inherent spillover effects of mass media like television, it is often more efficient to segment on the basis of other criteria such as age, income, education, and so on.

There are, however, many ways in which advertising can be designed so as to appeal to innovators and/or otherwise enhance the diffusion and personal influence process. It is possible to directly *simulate* personal influence in the content of the advertisement itself. This is effectively used in "slice-of-life" advertising, which shows a group of people discussing the product. Normally, one of the individuals takes the role of spokesperson for the product and demonstrates or persuades the other or others to use it. Robertson[36] has argued that the advertiser can essentially seek to "simulate," "stimulate," "monitor," or "retard" personal influence. Concerning simulation, for example, advertising can be used as a replacement for personal influence. An advertising message can show people similar to the viewer who are buying and using the product and, in this sense, act as a "personal influence." Advertisements should be pretested for their conversational impact in reference to the stimulation function. This testing should include attention to an assessment of the degree to which an advertisement tends to diffuse positive information as well. An advertisement should use the language of the viewer and provide enough information to allow him or her to answer questions from friends about the product.

Advertisements can stimulate either information giving or information receiving. The giver of information is most likely to be a recent purchaser. He or she is likely to be in dissonance, and advertising information or direct-mail programs should supply information that can readily be passed along to others. A seeker of information is most likely to be someone considering a purchase. Advertising here should encourage themes like "Ask the man who owns one" to stimulate personal influence. A good example is the advertisement for Sony television sets shown in Figure 11-9.

Figure 11-9.   **An advertisement for Sony Color Television**

Photographed in the Press Gallery after a typical session.

What sets did the press bring to Miami Beach?

If anyone ever needed a bright, sharp color TV picture, it was the newsmen covering the political conventions.

A picture so sharp, they could make out who that was, at the center of all the attention, in the V.I.P. Box.

A set so reliable, it wouldn't conk out in the middle of a crucial roll call.

In short, a Sony Trinitron. The news media brought more Sony TV's to the conventions than all other makes put together.

We know because we counted them. At a typical session, we counted 102 Sony sets out of a total of 199.

In the press galleries. In the glass booths of the TV newscasters. In the control rooms and work areas behind the scenes.

And don't think that, in order to do this ad, we gave away a single Sony. The news media *bought* them from our dealers, the same way you do.

One of the big TV networks, alone, bought 29 of our Trinitron® color sets.

Why Sony, when they could have had any TV in the world? It must be our bright, sharp, reliable Trinitron picture. No one else has the same picture, because no one else has our Trinitron all-solid-state system.

Did you know it now comes in 9, 12, 15, and 17-inch-diagonal screen sizes?

At the conventions, you probably watched your favorite TV anchorman watching a Sony.

At the elections, watch a Sony yourself.

SONY. Ask anyone.

* Sony Corp. of America. Visit our Showroom, 714 Fifth Ave., New York, N.Y.

Courtesy of Sony Corporation.

The purpose of monitoring personal influence is to identify what attributes of the product are being discussed, what product use is being emphasized, what product weaknesses are a point of focus, and the overall attitude toward the product. Such information may indicate, for example, that the features being stressed in advertising are not those being talked about in face-to-face conversations. Advertisements can be used to reinforce positive things being said or to combat negative attitudes that could well be developing toward minor product features.

It may be desirable to retard diffusion and the flow of personal influence in some instances. For new and complicated products, it is particularly important to provide extensive factual information and product demonstrations to avoid the possibility of consumer confusion and negative information flow. Also, as we discussed in the Resisting Attitude Change section, it may be advantageous to design campaigns to build resistance to competitive appeals, particularly among opinion leaders.

Media can also be chosen to encourage or, in one way or another, take advantage of the flow of personal influence. In some cases, it may be appropriate to single out opinion leaders, and, through selective magazines or journals (for example, *Engineering News, Golf Digest*) or through direct-mail campaigns, to appeal to them directly. This type of strategy is particularly appropriate in industrial marketing. Direct mail possibly can make the communication more personal and give the recipient a feeling that she or he is part of a select group.

There are dangers in assuming that singling out opinion leaders and appealing directly to them can be used to reduce advertising costs. It is doubtful that any opinion leader group could ever be considered to act truly as a company "sales agent." And in appealing only to them, there is always the risk of turning off nonleaders.

Other Promotional Tactics.   A wide variety of other sales and promotional devices have been used to stimulate word-of-mouth activity and to take advantage of personal influence.[37] Block parties are often used to promote china and silverware sales. In-store demonstrations give the consumer an opportunity to use the product without buying it. House-to-house sampling puts the product physically into the hands of both leaders and nonleaders and can result in source- or recipient-initiated conversations about it. The Ford Motor Company used a number of programs in introducing the Mustang. Disc jockeys, college newspaper editors, and airline stewardesses were loaned Mustangs on the theory that they were likely to influence other people. Upon evaluation, the airline stewardess program was felt to have been unsuccessful since stewardesses were not looked upon as a source of information about automobiles. The other programs were considered successful. Automobile companies, in general, attempt to stimulate adoption and interpersonal information flows through the medium of rent-a-cars. It is a way in which the consumer or potential consumer has the opportunity to use the product without actually purchasing it.

In the case of new products or product modification, a major advertising strategy concern will be with attempting to predict adoption rates. The rate of adoption of a new product is affected by factors over which an advertiser has some control, as well as by factors over which he or she has little or no control. The controllable factors are essentially components of the marketing mix that can be altered and combined in various ways. The uncontrollables, of course, are consumer, competitive, and environmental factors, which should be carefully monitored.

The advertiser should recognize that decisions made across the total marketing mix have an impact on personal influence and affect the diffusion and adoption rate. Pricing, distribution, packaging, and many other aspects of the total marketing mix, in addition to the product and advertising, both affect, and are affected by, the process of diffusion and personal influence.

SUMMARY

Looking at creativity and the development of advertising from the perspective of source, message, and social factors completes the picture of Part III and a better understanding of communications, persuasion, and market processes.

The source concept is a crucial focal point for thinking about copy and copy development because many elements within the advertisement can be considered a "source" and because the choice among those elements often involves significant commitments of time and money. Choosing a celebrity for a testimonial, for example, will be more expensive than choosing an ordinary citizen, but the celebrity may result in many more impressions and greater impact. This principle is true for special effects, the choice of the vehicle in which the copy will appear, and issues such as how much attention should be given to the brand being advertised versus the company or sponsor of the brand. A model of the source dimensions of copy information shows these types of source components and the various dimensions of source credibility on which they can be evaluated.

Source credibility has thus become an important topic for research and for understanding under what conditions particular effects are most likely to occur. Studies have focused on cognitive dimensions such as the expertness or unbiasedness of a source, and on affective dimensions such as the attractiveness, similarity, or the amount of prestige associated with the source. The premiere lesson from this research is that interaction effects are important, and advertisers are cautioned against assuming that, for example, highly credible sources are always to be preferred in all circumstances.

Message factors generally focus attention on how and what to say about the object of the advertising, in many cases the particular brand being advertised: whether the copy should be "long" or "short," what attributes should be highlighted, what kinds of arguments are most effective, whether two-sided or one-sided arguments should be used, and so on. Much attention has been focused on comparative advertising and whether it is more or less effective than noncomparative advertising. A general conclusion from many studies is that, for leading brands, comparative advertising does not appear to offer significant advantages. For new brands or challenger brands, however, the brand may gain significantly if an association with the leader can be established and the better features of the challenger brand made believable. Another kind of message factor concerns refutational advertising and the conditions under which it should be used. The rationale for refutational advertising is the biological analogy of inoculation. Consumers may be made more resistant to competitive attack by inoculating them with small doses of the competitor's arguments. The most noteworthy example attesting to the effectiveness of refutational advertising is Volkswagen. Calling your product a "lemon" is certainly not consistent with the argument that only positive attributes should be featured in advertising. But few will deny that this was very effective strategy in the case of Volkswagen advertising.

Social factors must be taken into account because personal influence can have much more persuasive impact on purchase than advertising, and because "word-of-mouth" is considered a form of advertising. In designing copy or in marketing a product in general, a personal influence audit can provide valuable insights into how much and in what forms personal influence is operating. Are advertising messages more or less likely to be passed along? Is the purchase decision essentially being made for an individual or does it involve a group—a decision-making unit? Judgments about these and similar social factor questions can do much to guide creativity and copy development. Particular attention should be given to whether or not opinion leadership is important in the situation, or whether for new products there is a pattern of early adopters, early majority, and laggards that might be specifically targeted with different campaigns or messages. As presented in the chapter, advertising can play a role in stimulating diffusion and the spread of information, in simulating the process such as in the typical slice-of-life commercial, or in retarding diffusion.

DISCUSSION QUESTIONS

1. Choose two testimonial advertisements. Assess their relative persuasiveness using the source factors model in Figure 11-2.
2. Discuss the desirability of using a doctor instead of a dentist as a spokesperson in a toothpaste commercial. Assume that the same advertising objectives and the same type of target audience are involved in each case.
3. Develop an advertisement for Pabst Blue Ribbon beer that is based on the refutational approach. Discuss the degree to which it would be likely to build resistant attitudes among current Pabst drinkers versus the degree to which it might attract new drinkers to the brand.

4. Consider advertising by utility companies to reduce energy consumption and encourage energy conservation attitudes. Is distraction a useful approach in this case? Why or why not?

5. Conduct a personal influence audit for a laundry detergent, electric car, home computer, university, and women's fashion jeans.

6. For the products in Question 5, assign a score based on each of the six factors shown on the assessment form (Figure 11-8). Are there any differences in the overall scores for these products? What about scores on the individual characteristics?

7. Analyze your own motivations for sending and receiving information regarding purchasing behavior and television commercials. Compare these with the ideas of Dichter given in the chapter.

8. Design an advertisement specifically directed to stimulate a diffusion process. What are its characteristics? Why did you choose particular elements and components?

9. Find a case example of a successful and unsuccessful new-product introduction. Analyze the advertising campaigns in each case from the viewpoint of the concepts and models given in the chapter.

10. Most of us think that advertising almost never persuades us to do anything. Consider your own purchasing behavior. In which cases do you think advertising may have had some influence? Where, in your judgment, would you say that advertising has had no influence, or possibly a negative influence?

NOTES

1. Joahne M. Klebba and Lynette S. Unger, "The Impact of Negative and Positive Information on Source Credibility in Field Settings," in Richard P. Bagozzi and Alice M. Tybout, eds., *Advances in Consumer Research,* Vol. 10 (Ann Arbor, Mich.: Association for Consumer Research, 1982), pp. 11–16.

2. Galen R. Rarick, "Effects of Two Components of Communicator Prestige," unpublished doctoral dissertation, Stanford University, 1963.

3. Eric J. Zanot and Lynda M. Maddox, "An Empirical Study of the Credibility of Bust Developer Advertisements among Young Women," in James Leigh and Claude R. Martin, Jr., eds., *Current Issues and Research in Advertising 1978* (Ann Arbor, Mich.: Division of Research, Graduate School of Business Administration, University of Michigan, 1978), pp. 53–62.

4. Theodore Levitt, *Industrial Purchasing Behavior* (Boston: Harvard Graduate School of Business Administration, 1965).

5. "The Big New Celebrity Boom," *Business Week,* 1978, pp. 77–80.

6. See W. Freeman, *The Big Name* (New York: Printer's Ink, 1957); and H. Rudolph, *Attention and Interest Factors in Advertising* (New York: Printer's Ink, 1947).

7. R. B. Fireworker and H. H. Friedman, "The Effects of Endorsements on Product Evaluation," *Decision Sciences,* 8, 1977, pp. 576–583; and Joseph M. Kamen et al., "What a Spokesman Does for a Sponsor," *Journal of Advertising Research,* 15, 1975, pp. 17–24.

8. John C. Mowen and Stephen W. Brown, "On Explaining and Predicting the Effectiveness of Celebrity Endorsers," in Kent B. Monroe, ed., *Advances in Consumer Research,* Vol. III (Ann Arbor,

Mich.: Association for Consumer Research, 1981). For recent studies, see Lynn R. Kahle, "Physical Attractiveness of the Celebrity Endorser: A Social Adaptation Perspective," *Journal of Consumer Research*, 11, March 1985, pp. 954–961; and John L. Swasy and James M. Munch, "Examining the Target Receiver Elaborations: Rhetorical Question Effects on Source Processing and Persuasion," *Journal of Consumer Research*, 11, March 1985, pp. 877–886.

9. See Hershey H. Friedman and Linda Friedman, "Endorser Effectiveness by Product Type," *Journal of Advertising Research*, 19, October 1979, pp. 63–71. For reviews of literature, see W. Benoy Joseph, "The Credibility of Physically Attractive Communicators: A Review," *Journal of Advertising*, 11, 1982, pp. 15–24; and Brian Sternthal, Lynn W. Phillips, and Ruby Dholakia, "The Persuasive Effect of Source Credibility: A Situational Analysis," *Public Opinion Quarterly*, 42, Fall 1978, pp. 285–314.

10. Darlene B. Hannah and Brian Sternthal, "Detecting and Explaining the Sleeper Effect," *Journal of Consumer Research*, 11, September 1984, pp. 632–642.

11. Ruby Roy Dholakia and Brian Sternthal, "Highly Credible Sources: Persuasive Facilitators or Persuasive Liabilities?" *Journal of Consumer Research*, 3, March 1977, pp. 223–232. See also, Brian Sternthal, Ruby Dholakia, and Clark Leavitt, "The Persuasive Effect of Source Credibility: Tests of Cognitive Response," *Journal of Consumer Research*, 4, March 1978, pp. 252–260."

12. Klebba and Unger, "The Impact of Negative and Positive Information."

13. William L. Wilkie and Paul Farris, "Comparison Advertising: Problems and Potential," *Journal of Marketing*, 39, October 1975, pp. 7–15.

14. Gordon H. C. McDougall, "Comparative Advertising: Consumer Issues and Attitudes," in B. A. Greenberg and D. N. Bellenger, eds., *Contemporary Marketing Thought* (Chicago: American Marketing Association, 1977), pp. 286–291.

15. For recent work in the marketing area, see Albert J. Della Bitta, Kent B. Monroe, and John M. McGinnis, "Consumer Perceptions of Comparative Price Advertisements," *Journal of Marketing Research*, 18, November 1981, pp. 416–427; Michael Etgar and Stephen A. Goodwin, "One-Sided versus Two-Sided Comparative Message Appeals for New Brand Introductions," *Journal of Consumer Research*, 8, March 1982, pp. 460–465; Z. S. Demirdjian, "Sales Effectiveness of Comparative Advertising: An Experimental Field Investigation," *Journal of Consumer Research*, 10, December 1983, pp. 362–364; and Roobina O. Tashchian and Mark E. Slama, "Involvement and the Effectiveness of Comparative Advertising," in J. H. Leigh and C. R. Martin, Jr., eds., *Current Issues and Research in Advertising, 1984* (Ann Arbor, Mich.: Graduate School of Business Administration, University of Michigan, 1984), pp. 79–92.

16. William R. Swinyard, "The Interaction between Comparative Advertising and Copy Claim Variation," *Journal of Marketing Research*, 18, May 1981, pp. 175–186.

17. Gerald J. Gorn and Charles B. Weinberg, "The Impact of Comparative Advertising on Perception and Attitude: Some Positive Findings," *Journal of Consumer Research*, 11, September 1984, pp. 719–727.

18. "Creating a Mass Market for Wine," *Business Week*, March 15, 1982, pp. 102–118.

19. Stewart W. Bither, Ira J. Dolich, and Elaine B. Nell, "The Application of Attitude Immunization Techniques in Marketing," *Journal of Marketing Research*, 8, February 1971, pp. 56–61.

20. William J. McGuire, "The Nature of Attitude and Attitude Change," in *The Handbook of Social Psychology*, Vol. 3, edited by G. Lindzey and E. Aronson (Reading, Mass.: Addison-Wesley, 1969), p. 263.

21. Bither, Dolich, and Nell, "The Application of Attitude Immunization Techniques in Marketing," p. 57.

22. Michael L. Ray, "The Refutational Approach in Advertising," paper presented to the Advertising Division, Association for Education in Journalism, Boulder, Colo., 1967.

23. Ibid., p. 7.

24. Ibid., p. 8.

25. For recent articles on diffusion research and opinion leadership, see Hubert Gatignon and Thomas S. Robertson, "A Propositional Inventory of New Diffusion Research," *Journal of Consumer Research*, 11, March 1985, pp. 849–867, and Dorothy Leonard-Barton, "Experts as Negative Opinion Leaders in the Diffusion of a Technological Innovation," *Journal of Consumer Research*, 11, March 1985, pp. 914–926.

26. Everett M. Rogers, *Diffusion of Innovations* (New York: Free Press, 1962).

27. Jagdish N. Sheth, "Psychology of Innovation Resistance: The Less Developed Concept (LDC) in Diffusion Research," Working Paper No. 622, College of Commerce and Business Administration, University of Illinois, October 1979.

28. Ernest Dichter, "How Word-of-Mouth Advertising Works," *Harvard Business Review,* 44, November–December 1966, pp. 147–166.

29. Tamotsu Shibutani, "Reference Groups as Perspectives," *American Journal of Sociology,* 60, May 1955, pp. 562–569.

30. William D. Wells and G. Gubar, "Life Cycle Concept in Marketing Research," *Journal of Marketing Research,* 3, November 1966, pp. 355–363.

31. The earliest and best-known follow-up studies to Katz and Lazarsfeld's *Personal Influence* (see note 32) were done on physician drug adoptions. See Herbert Menzel and Elihu Katz, "Social Relations and Innovation in the Medical Profession: The Epidemiology of a New Drug," *Public Opinion Quarterly,* 19, Winter 1956, pp. 337–352. For a fully developed treatment of the two-step flow model, see Elihu Katz, "The Two-Step Flow of Communication: An Up-to-Date Report on an Hypothesis," *Public Opinion Quarterly,* 21, Spring 1957, pp. 61–78.

32. Elihu Katz and Paul F. Lazarsfeld, *Personal Influence* (New York: Free Press, 1955), p. 138.

33. John G. Myers, "Patterns of Interpersonal Influence in the Adoptions of New Products," Raymond M. Hass, ed., *Proceedings of the American Marketing Association* (Chicago: American Marketing Association, 1966), pp. 750–757.

34. David B. Montgomery and Alvin J. Silk, "Clusters of Consumer Interests and Opinion Leaders' Spheres of Influence," *Journal of Marketing Research,* 8, August 1971, pp. 317–321.

35. Everett M. Rogers, *Diffusion of Innovations.*

36. Thomas S. Robertson, *Innovative Behavior and Communication* (New York: Holt, Rinehart and Winston, 1971), 210–223.

37. Mancuso, for example, reports on a study in which high school students selected for their opinion leadership potential were given the new product (a new rock and roll record) and encouraged to use and develop positive opinions for the record among fellow classmates. See Joseph R. Mancuso, "Why Not Create Opinion Leaders for New Product Introductions?" *Journal of Marketing,* 33, July 1969, pp. 20–25.

CASE FOR PART III

Perdue Food*

"It Takes A Tough Man to Make a Tender Chicken" was the theme of the advertising campaign developed for Perdue Foods, Inc., of Salisbury, Maryland, by its New York–based agency, Scali, McCabe, Sloves, Inc. The campaign often featured Mr. Frank Perdue, president of Perdue Foods, who had become something of a celebrity as a result in the New York market and elsewhere where the print and radio and TV ad campaign had been run. From an obscure position as one of several hundred companies raising broilers in 1968, Perdue Foods had become by the end of 1972 the largest producer of branded broilers in the United States, killing about 1.5 million birds each week, almost twice as many as when the new agency had acquired the account in 1971.

Such visibility attracted competitors as well as customers, and in February of 1973 a major competitor, Maryland Chicken Processors, Inc., launched a direct frontal attack on Perdue Chickens with ads in the New England trade press carrying the headline:

Read how Otis Esham's Buddy Boy chicken is going to beat the pants off the other guy's chicken.

The "other guy," of course, was Frank Perdue, and the Buddy Boy trade ad even featured a back-of-the-head picture of Frank Perdue with the caption "the other guy." It was a no-holds-barred approach which made direct and frequent reference to Perdue Chickens. For example, the trade ad began:

The other guy has been a friend and neighbor of ours for years, as well as a competitor.

To be truthful about it, our hat's off to him. In the past year or so, he's probably done more for the chicken business than any other guy we know.

With his help and the help of his fine New York advertising agency, the consumer is now beginning to realize that it's worth paying a few more pennies a pound to get the kind of fine, plump, golden-yellow chicken we produce down here on the Eastern Shore of Maryland.

What this means is that the days of footballing the price of chicken all over the lot are probably numbered.

The new name of the game is Profits, and that's not just profits for the chicken business but profits for you, too.

So, as far as we are concerned, that other guy is doing a real good job.

But he's vulnerable.

---

* This case was prepared as a basis for classroom discussion by Frederick E. Webster, Jr. Copyright © 1973 by the Trustees of Dartmouth College.

The other guy is a spunky little guy (no offense intended, Frank) who loves to go on television and the radio and tell folks about the fine kind of chicken we produce down home.

You think those commercials are going to hurt us?

Uh-uh. They can't do anything but *help* us.

What those commercials are doing is making the consumer aware that a chicken that's good enough to carry the brand name of a proud producer is going to be a *better* chicken than the one that is only good enough to be acceptable to the U.S. government.

Well, the actual truth is, those commercials could just as well be talking about Otis Esham's fresh Buddy Boy chicken. Because Otis's methods of raising and processing chicken are just about identical to the other guy's.

Except for one very important thing and here's where we get to the part about how the other guy is vulnerable.

That was only the first of four columns in a double-page spread. The ad went on to say that "the other guy's" chickens are packed and shipped in ice and that as the ice melts "your chicken is going to begin to get all water-logged," whereas Buddy Boy chickens are quick-chilled to 30° F and shipped in refrigerated trucks. The ad reported that Purity Supreme, a major New England chain, had taken on the Buddy Boy product and that a "hot" Boston-based ad agency, Pearson and MacDonald, had been given the Buddy Boy account. The ad also featured pictures of Otis Esham (whose position was not disclosed*), Jack Ackerman, head meat buyer for Purity Supreme (with the caption "Jack Ackerman of Purity Supreme, a 'tough bird' "), Pearson and MacDonald, and a crate of dressed broilers showing the "old-fashioned 'ice-packed' method." The ad went on to explain that "By the time you're reading this, Otis Esham will be on the major Boston radio stations telling your customers about how his fresh Buddy Boy chicken is a better chicken because it's a chilled chicken." More information about media plans was given and readers were given a telephone number to call collect in Parsonsburg, Maryland, to talk with "Bubba Shelton, Otis Esham's right-hand man for sales."

An executive at Scali, McCabe, Sloves called this "one of the most blatant frontal assaults I have ever seen in advertising" as the account executive and top agency personnel began to talk about their response. Three classes of action were being considered. Some favored simply ignoring the Buddy Boy campaign because "it can't hurt us, it can only help us." Others wanted to respond directly, with trade and consumer ads, to the charge that ice-packing was an inferior method and that chickens became "water-logged," because this was not true. A third group suggested that now was the time for an entirely new Perdue campaign to take the initiative away from Buddy Boy and go after entirely new segments.

* In point of fact, Esham was President of Maryland Chicken Processors, a family-owned business. Esham and Perdue had known each other all their lives; at one time they had owned abutting properties.

Growth of Perdue Foods, Inc.

An article in *Esquire* magazine in April 1973 described chicken farming as "about the last free-enterprise industry in America. Chicken is produced in a no-holds-barred, rags-to-riches, no-control system, at the fascinating confluence of all the commercial strains in the land: the chicken is where the most volatile elements of the assembly line, of the farm and the field, and bid-and-ask all come together." Until 1968, Perdue was raising chickens for resale to other processors. In 1967, sales had been about $35 million, mainly from selling live birds, but the business also included one of the East Coast's largest grain storage and poultry feed milling operations, soybean processing mulch plants, a hatchery, and 600 farmers raising broilers under contract to Perdue.

A buyer's market existed in 1967, which had squeezed chicken profits. More and more processors were lining up their own contract growers and cutting out Perdue and other middlemen. As Frank Perdue noted, "The situation was good for processors. As in all commodities, profit depends on high volume and small margins. A processor's normal profit on chickens runs ¼ to ½ cent per pound. But in 1967's market, processors were paying us 10 cents a pound for what cost us 14 cents to produce and their profits were as much as 7 cents per pound."

As a result of these conditions, Frank Perdue decided to redesign his business to coordinate egg hatching, chick delivery and feeding, broiler processing, and overnight delivery to market, and to develop his own brand. The aim was to develop a quality chicken that could demand premium prices. Special attention was devoted to development of exact feeding formulas which would optimize the chickens' growth rate and give the chicken a golden-colored skin preferred by consumers.

Over the next three years, Perdue began consumer advertising on a limited basis. Distribution was concentrated in New York, with a small percentage of other East Coast cities and as far west as Cleveland. The Perdue brand was identified by a tag on the wing of the processed chicken. Distribution was concentrated in butcher shops and smaller chain food outlets.

Perdue Advertising

As the new strategy of integrated production and product differentiation began to prove itself in the form of increased sales and profit margins, Frank Perdue became increasingly concerned with the quality of his advertising. After a period of intensive reading on the subject and interviews with almost 50 agencies, Perdue selected Scali, McCabe, Sloves, Inc., in April 1971. The agency immediately began to prepare for a major campaign to be launched in New York City in July. Over Frank Perdue's initial objections, the agency developed a campaign featuring him as the spokesman for the product.

The campaign focused on the quality of Perdue's product, often using subtle

Exhibit 1. Perdue Foods, Inc.

SCALI, McCABE, SLOVES INC.

CLIENT: PERDUE FOODS INC.

PRODUCT: PERDUE CHICKENS

TITLE: "MY CHICKENS EAT BETTER THAN PEOPLE"

LENGTH: 30 SECONDS

COMMERCIAL NO.: TV-PD-30-2C

1. FRANK PERDUE: A chicken is what it eats. And my chickens eat better than . . .

2. people do. I store my own grain and mix my own feed.

3. And give my Perdue chickens nothing but pure well water to drink.

4. That's why my chickens always have that healthy golden-yellow color.

5. If you want to eat as good as my chickens, you'll just have to eat my chickens.

IT TAKES
A TOUGH MAN
TO MAKE
A TENDER CHICKEN.

PERDUE

6. That's really good.

Exhibit 2. Perdue Foods, Inc.

SCALI, McCABE, SLOVES, INC.
CLIENT: PERDUE FARMS
PRODUCT: CHICKEN

TITLE: "BUTCHER SHOP"
LENGTH: 10 SECONDS
COMM'L. NO.: TV-PD-10-9

1. FRANK PERDUE: I don't allow my superior chickens in just any store.

2. That's why you can only buy Perdue chickens in butcher shops and better markets.

3. I don't want to give my name a bad name.

humor to make the point. The direction of the campaign is indicated in Exhibits 1 to 4, photo boards of four TV commercials. Radio and newspaper advertising was also planned. A new wing tag was designed featuring the company name and a money-back guarantee of quality. In an early 60-second TV commercial, Frank Perdue made the following comments:

> When people ask me about my chickens, two questions invariably come up. The first is "Perdue, your chickens have such a great golden-yellow color it's almost unnatural. Do you dye them?" Honestly, there's absolutely nothing artificial about the color of my chickens. If you had a chicken and fed it good yellow corn, alfalfa, corn gluten, and marigold petals, it would just naturally be yellow. You can't go around dyeing chickens. They wouldn't stand for it.
>
> The other question is "Perdue, your chickens are so plump and juicy, do you give them hormone injections?" This one really gets my hackles up. I do nothing of the kind. When chickens eat and live as well as mine do, you don't have to resort to artificial techniques. . . .

In the first year with the new agency, all advertising expenditures were aimed at the consumer. Only after consumer awareness and preference had been created was trade advertising begun. By the end of the first year, Perdue had achieved distribution in more than half of all New York butcher shops and small retail food outlets. Consumer surveys showed well over 50 percent awareness of the Perdue brand. While financial information was not publicly available, Perdue said "you have to assume it paid off." Competitors estimated that Perdue's costs increased between 2 and 4 cents per pound due to promotional expenses. At the retail level, Perdue chickens were able to command a premium of 5 to 10 cents per pound. One out of every six chickens sold in the New York market carried the Perdue brand. Similar campaigns were launched in Hartford, Connecticut (March 1972) and Baltimore (April 1972). Sales in 1972 exceeded $80,000,000.

Perdue advertising attracted a good deal of public attention, partly due to the distinctiveness of Frank Perdue's presentation, which was described by one commentator as having the sincerity and fervor of a Southern preacher. Stories about the company and its advertising appeared in *Business Week* (September 16, 1972), *Newsweek* (October 16, 1972), and *Esquire* (April 1973), among other places.

The Boston Campaign

Perdue's Boston campaign was launched in December 1972, following the basic pattern now established. The Boston market was somewhat different from New York in that a high percentage of chicken sales occurred through chain store supermarkets, whereas in New York the majority was sold through butcher shops and independent food outlets.

Shortly thereafter, Otis Esham publicized his plans to advertise in Boston and even gave the exact dates on which consumer advertising would break. Perdue's immediate response had been to triple GRP TV and radio coverage and to contract

Exhibit 3.   Perdue Foods, Inc.

SCALI, McCABE, SLOVES INC.

CLIENT: PERDUE FOODS INC.

PRODUCT: PERDUE CHICKENS

TITLE: "CLEAN LIVIN'"

LENGTH: 30 SECONDS

COMMERCIAL NO.: TV-PD-30-3C

1. FRANK PERDUE: Nobody gets near my chickens unless they wear this fancy get-up.

2. This is not to protect people from my chickens.

3. It's to protect my chickens from people.

4. My competitors think I'm nuts to go through all this.

5. But why do you suppose my chickens always have that healthy golden-yellow color . . .

6. instead of a pale one. I'll tell you why. Clean livin'.

IT TAKES
A TOUGH MAN
TO MAKE
A TENDER CHICKEN.

PERDUE

7. (SILENT)

Exhibit 4. **Perdue Foods, Inc.**

SCALI, McCABE, SLOVES INC.

CLIENT: PERDUE FOODS INC.

PRODUCT: PERDUE CHICKENS

TITLE: "COMPETITION"

LENGTH: 30 SECONDS

COMMERCIAL NO.: TV-PD-30-5C

3. We put them through the same rigid inspection that our own Perdue chickens have to . . .

6. How're we doing? Did we win yet?

2. So every week I have my people go out and buy cases of my competitors' birds.

5. It's the only way I have of knowing that I'm ahead of these guys.

1. FRANK PERDUE: Knowing how good my chickens are isn't good enough for me.

4. go through. It costs me a lot of money. But it's worth it.

for additional newspaper coverage on heavy food-buying days, in anticipation of Buddy Boy's campaign. Perdue's first radio ads ran on December 18 and TV ads began on January 15.

Now that Buddy Boy's first trade advertising had appeared early in February, executives at Scali, McCabe, Sloves were wondering what steps to take next. Esham was planning radio for the second week of February and TV was scheduled for the beginning of April. It would be possible for Scali, McCabe, Sloves to prepare television ads within 72 hours to refute the points about "water-logged" chickens in the Buddy Boy advertising.

A principal of Buddy Boy's agency, Terry MacDonald, was quoted as saying "We're going to kill them. They have brilliant advertising. But we have the product advantage."

DISCUSSION QUESTION

1. What action should Scali, McCabe, Sloves recommend to Frank Perdue?

12

Creative Styles

"The cat sat on the mat" is not a story. "The cat sat on the dog's mat," now that's a story. (Gerry Miller, Creative Director, Dentsu)

Advertising is a little like art and painting. Two artists viewing the same scene may paint it quite differently, but both can produce high-quality paintings and "effective" products. In this chapter, several of the creative giants of advertising and examples of their work are presented. An important factor that tends to distinguish them is the nature of the product or market situation. As will be seen, however, there are points of emphasis and style that tend to characterize the approach and make it recognizable. Just as an art critic can distinguish a Picasso from a Monet, so an experienced copy director can distinguish the work of a David Ogilvy from that of a Leo Burnett. The styles of creative giants in advertising have, over time, become exaggerated to the point of caricature. Furthermore, right or wrong, their approaches become associated with a considerable amount of advertising of the agency with which they are associated. Thus, any description of their creative style may tend to be exaggerated. Such an exaggeration is useful for our purposes, however, because it helps to illustrate the diversity among creative teams in the advertising profession.

The first set of examples profiles the works of David Ogilvy, William

Bernbach, Rosser Reeves, and Leo Burnett. These creative giants have had major impacts on advertising over the years and it is useful to study their styles and classic examples of their work. This is followed by five copy directors who have achieved prominence and recognition in recent years: Philip Dusenberry, Alexander Kroll, Jim Patterson, Bob Levenson, and Lee Clow. Each has had a major impact on the creative output of the advertising agencies with which they are associated and, in many respects, represent the "state of the art" in advertising in the mid-1980s.

DAVID OGILVY: THE BRAND IMAGE

David Ogilvy is most concerned with the brand image. Due in part to the nature of the products with which he works, this usually means that he is concerned with developing and retaining a prestige image. He argues that, in the long run, it pays to protect a favorable image even if some appealing short-run programs are sacrificed in the process. In his words,

> Every advertisement should be thought of as a contribution to the complex symbol which is the brand image. If you take that long view, a great many day-to-day problems solve themselves. . . . Most of the manufacturers who find it expedient to change the image of their brand want it changed upward. Often it has acquired a bargain-basement image, a useful asset in time of economic scarcity, but a grave embarrassment in boom days, when the majority of consumers are on their way up the social ladder. It isn't easy to perform a face-lifting operation on an old bargain-basement brand. In many cases it would be easier to start again, with a fresh new brand. . . . A steady diet of price-off promotions lowers the esteem in which the consumer holds the product; can anything which is always sold at a discount be desirable?[1]

Ogilvy goes on to say that the personality of the brand is particularly important if brands are similar:

> The greater the similarity between brands, the less part reason plays in brand selection. There isn't any significant difference between the various brands of whiskey, or cigarettes, or beer. They are all about the same. And so are the cake mixes and the detergents, and the margarines. The manufacturer who dedicates his advertising to building the most sharply defined personality for his brand will get the largest share of the market at the highest profit. By the same token, the manufacturers who will find themselves up the creek are those shortsighted opportunists who siphon off their advertising funds for promotions.[2]

When Ogilvy obtained the Puerto Rico account, he indicated that what was needed was to "substitute a lovely image of Puerto Rico for the squalid image which now exists in the minds of most mainlanders."[3]

One of the most distinctive aspects of many of Ogilvy's most well-known campaigns is the use of prestigious individuals to convey the desired image for the product. In two cases he actually used clients to represent their own products: Commander Whitehead for Schweppes Tonic and Helena Rubinstein for her line of cosmetics. One of the original advertisements for the Schweppes campaign is shown in Figure 12-1. Others he ''created'' or developed from individuals or ideas not explicitly part of the original company. One of the most successful was the campaign for Hathaway shirts in which a male character with an eye patch was featured. Ogilvy tells how the campaign evolved, for a product with an initial advertising budget of only $30,000.

> I concocted eighteen different ways to inject this magic ingredient of ''story appeal.'' The eighteenth was the eye patch. At first we rejected it in favor of a more obvious idea, but on the way to the studio I ducked into a drugstore and bought an eye patch for $1.50. Exactly why it turned out to be so successful, I shall never know. It put Hathaway on the map after 116 years of relative obscurity. Seldom, if ever, has a national brand been created so fast, or at such low cost. . . . As the campaign developed, I showed the model in a series of situations in which I would have liked to find myself: conducting the New York Philharmonic at Carnegie Hall, playing the oboe, copying a Goya at the Metropolitan Museum, driving a tractor, fencing, sailing, buying a Renoir, and so forth.[4]

Ogilvy will, when possible, obtain testimonials from celebrities. Usually their fee will go to their favorite charity. Thus, Ogilvy has used Queen Elizabeth and Winston Churchill in ''Come to Britain'' advertisements, and Mrs. Franklin Roosevelt saying that Good Luck margarine really tastes delicious. Charge accounts for Sears, Roebuck were advertised by reproducing the credit card of Ted Williams, ''recently traded by Boston to Sears.'' A campaign for the *Reader's Digest* featured many national figures explaining that they relied on such a magazine because of their busy schedules.

Ogilvy, in addition to being a very creative person, is also research oriented. He looks to the experiences of direct-mail advertisers and the various advertising readership services for possible generalizations. He also looks to his colleagues and competitors for insights. From these sources he puts forth various guides, rules, and commandments for the creation of advertising by his staff. The following are his 11 commandments for creating advertising campaigns:[5]

1. What you say is more important than how you say it. Two hundred years ago Dr. Johnson said, ''Promise, large promise is the soul of an advertisement.'' When he auctioned off the contents of the Anchor Brewery he made the following promise: ''We are not here to sell boilers and vats, but the potentiality of growing rich beyond the dreams of avarice.''

2. Unless your campaign is built around a great idea, it will flop.

3. Give the facts.
   The consumer isn't a moron; she is your wife. You insult her intelligence if you assume that a mere slogan and a few vapid adjectives will persuade her to buy anything. She wants all the information you can give her.

Figure 12-1.   **An early advertisement for Schweppes**

The man from Schweppes is here

MEET Commander Edward Whitehead, Schweppesman Extraordinary from London, England, where the House of Schweppes has been a great institution since 1794.

The Commander has come to these United States to make sure that every drop of Schweppes Quinine Water bottled over here has the original bittersweet flavor essential for an authentic Gin-and-Tonic.

He imports the original Schweppes elixir and the secret of Schweppes unique carbonation is securely locked in his brief case. "Schweppervescence," says the Commander, *"lasts the whole drink through."*

Schweppes Quinine Water makes your favorite drink a truly patrician potion—and Schweppes is now available at popular prices throughout Greater New York.

Courtesy of Schweppes U.S.A. Limited.

4. You cannot bore people into buying.
    We make advertisements that people want to read. You can't save souls in an empty church.

5. Be well-mannered, but don't clown.

6. Make your advertising contemporary.

7. Committees can criticize advertisements, but they cannot write them.

8. If you are lucky enough to write a good advertisement, repeat it until it stops pulling.
    Sterling Getchel's famous advertisement for Plymouth ("Look at All Three") appeared only once, and was succeeded by a series of inferior variations which were quickly forgotten. But the Sherwin Cody School of English ran the same advertisement ("Do You Make These Mistakes in English?") for forty-two years, changing only the type face and the color of Mr. Cody's beard.

9. Never write an advertisement which you wouldn't want your own family to read.
    Good products can be sold by honest advertising. If you don't think the product is good, you have no business to be advertising it. If you tell lies, or weasel, you do your client a disservice, you increase your load of guilt, and you fan the flames of public resentment against the whole business of advertising.

10. The image and the brand.
    It is the total personality of a brand rather than any trivial product difference which decides its ultimate position in the market.

11. Don't be a copy cat.
    Nobody has ever built a brand by imitating somebody else's advertising. Imitation may be the "sincerest form of plagiarism," but it is also the mark of an inferior person.

WILLIAM BERNBACH: EXECUTION

Perhaps the most exciting agency in the past few decades has been the one William Bernbach established in 1949, Doyle Dane Bernbach. It has been enormously successful although apparently violating several well-established dictums of the advertising business. One of the most sacred laws in evaluating an advertisement is to determine if it really communicates a persuasive message or if it is merely clever or memorable. The primary job of an advertisement is to sell—to communicate a persuasive message. David Ogilvy's first rule for copywriters is "What you say is more important than how you say it." Bernbach replies that "execution can become content, it can be just as important as what you say . . . a sick guy can utter some words and nothing happens; a healthy vital guy says them and they rock the world."[6] In the Bernbach style, the execution dominates.

To say that Bernbach emphasizes execution is, of course, a rather incomplete description of his style. What kind of execution? Although it is difficult to verbalize such an approach because it does not lend itself to rules, there are certain characteristics that can be identified. First, Bernbach does not talk down to an audience. An audience is respected. As Jerry Della Femina, a colorful advertising executive, put it: "Doyle Dane's advertisement has that feeling that the consumer is bright enough to understand what the advertising is saying, that the consumer isn't a lunkhead who has to be treated like a twelve year old."[7] The copy is honest. Puffery is avoided, as are clichés and heavy repetition. The advertising demands attention and has something to say. Second, the approach is clean and direct. Bernbach has pointed out that "you must be as simple, and as swift and as penetrating as possible. . . . What you must do, by the most economical and creative means possible, is attract people and sell them."[8] Third, the advertisement should stand out from others. It should have its own character. In Bernbach's words:

> Why should anyone look at your ad? The reader doesn't buy his magazine or tune in his radio and TV to see and hear what you have to say. . . . What is the use of saying all the right things in the world if nobody is going to read them? And, believe me, nobody is going to read them if they are not said with freshness, originality and imagination . . . if they are not, if you will, different.[9]

Finally, the often repeated rule that humor does not sell is ignored. Doyle Dane Bernbach frequently uses humor to gain attention and to provide a positive reward to an advertisement reader. Robert Fine, one of Bernbach's copywriters, said:

> We recognize that an advertisement is an intrusion. People don't necessarily like advertisements, and avoid them if possible. Therefore, to do a good advertisement you're obligated, really, to reward the reader for his time and patience in allowing you to interrupt the editorial content, which is what he bought the magazine for in the first place. This is not defensive. It just takes into account the fact that an advertisement pushes its way uninvited into somebody's mind. So entertainment is sort of repayment.[10]

Doyle Dane Bernbach deemphasizes research, believing that it tends to generate advertisements too similar to those of competitors. The assumptions are that others are doing the same type of research, interpreting it the same way, and generating the same policy implications. In Bernbach's words:

> One of the disadvantages of doing everything mathematically, by research, is that after a while, everybody does it the same way. . . . If you take the attitude that once you have found out what to say, your job is done, then what you're doing is saying it the same way as everybody is saying it, and you've lost your impact completely.[11]

One of Bernbach's first accounts in 1949 was Levy's bread, a relatively unknown New York bread. Bernbach developed radio spots that featured an unruly child asking his mother for "Wevy's Cimmanon Waison Bwead" and getting his pronunciation corrected. In addition, subway posters were used. One showed three slices of bread, one uneaten, one with a few bites gone, and the third with only the crust remaining. The copy read simply "New York Is Eating It Up! Levy's Real Jewish Rye." Without using a single product claim, Levy's bread reportedly became one of the best-known brands in town.[12]

Doyle Dane Bernbach generated the now-classic Avis campaign.[13] The "We're Number 2, We Try Harder" campaign was effective for various reasons. It dared to admit that a firm was indeed in second place. At the same time, it turned this fact to advantage by indicating that a customer could expect better because Number 2 would naturally tend to try harder. It was the perfect application of two-sided communication: state the opposing position first (Hertz is the largest), and then rebut it (We Try Harder). The campaign was supported by red "We Try Harder" buttons and by a real effort to improve the Avis service. The service was affected, in part, owing to the impact of the campaign on Avis employees. Ironically, despite the fact that the campaign was directed at the giant Hertz, the impact fell primarily on Avis's other competitors. When the campaign began, Avis and National were neck and neck and Hertz was ahead. The campaign made the rent-a-car industry seem to be a two-firm affair. As a result, National and the other competitors were damaged much more than Hertz. In fact, because primary demand was stimulated, Hertz probably benefited from the Avis advertisements. The campaign received an impetus when Hertz decided to reply directly. This reply, which was a controversial strategy, was perhaps the first time the top dog actually recognized a competitor publicly. The strategy was triggered in part by a need to boost the morale of Hertz employees. This whole situation is a good example of how advertising has an impact on employees, which usually is not considered in campaign planning. The Mary Wells TWA campaign, in which $1 million was given to employees nominated by customers, is another case in which the firm's employees turned out to be affected by the advertising.

It was the Volkswagen campaign that really established the Bernbach approach. As Jerry Della Femina said, "In the beginning there was Volkswagen."[14] It ushered in a decade of the hot, creative agencies that attempted to duplicate the Doyle Dane Bernbach success. The Volkswagen advertisements, like many Doyle Dane Bernbach advertisements, almost always had a large photograph of the product in a setting with a headline and copy below. The headline was usually provocative and tempted readers to continue to the copy. One advertisement showed steam coming out of a nonexistent radiator with the caption "Impossible." A headline under a picture of a flat tire read "Nobody's Perfect." Several advantages of the car were listed under the headline "Ugly is only skin-deep." The two real classics were the lines "Think Small" and "Lemon."

The Lemon advertisement was particularly noteworthy. Many of the advertisements directly disparaged the product, an approach that was frowned on in many circles and never used to the extent it was in the Volkswagen campaign. Even for the Volkswagen campaign, Lemon was extreme and was approved by the Volkswagen management only after some tribulation. The copy went on to identify a defect caught by one of 3,389 inspectors and discussed the elaborate quality assurance program of the firm.

The campaign eventually moved into television. One of the early television advertisements was described as follows:

> The camera looks through the windshield of a car traveling on a dark, snowcovered country road. Heavy loads of fresh snow bend down pine and fir branches. No announcer's voice is heard; the only sound is that of an engine prosaically purring along. In shot after shot the headlights illuminate the falling snow ahead, piling up deeper on the winding, climbing, untracked road. Robert Frost's haunting lines about the woods on a snowy night are inevitably evoked. Curiosity and a measure of suspense are created: Who is driving and where? What errand has taken him out on such a night? Finally the headlights swing off by a large dark building and are switched off. A high door opens and a powerful snowplow rolls past as the announcer's voice begins, "Have you ever wondered how the man who drives the snowplow drives to the snowplow? This one drives a Volkswagen. So you can stop wondering."[15]

The Volkswagen advertising was particularly fresh when contrasted with the competition. Most Detroit advertising, for example, tended to use drawings rather than photographs so that the impression of elegance could be enhanced. Their copy tended to be rather predictable and bland. The Volkswagen use of photographs, which very realistically set forth the product in all its commonness, and its copy with a tendency to laugh at itself, had to be refreshing.

The campaign was by any measure a phenomenal success. Sales climbed impressively, even when the domestic compacts were introduced, and other foreign cars were severely hurt. The advertising undoubtedly contributed to sales performance. The advertisements were consistently well read, even on occasion substantially outscoring cover stories and editorial features.[16] They were talked about by the man in the street and won all sorts of creative awards in the profession. The Volkswagen story is a good illustration of the Bernbach approach to copywriting. Figures 12-2 and 12-3 show later versions in which the appeal is tied in with problems of rising meat prices and gasoline shortages that were of major public interest and concern at the time they were run.

ROSSER REEVES: THE USP

Especially under the scrutiny of advertising critics, it is considerably easier to justify or explain advertising that is clever, tasteful, and entertaining than advertising that is not so described. In that regard, the approaches of Ogilvy or Bernbach are somewhat easier to defend than the style attributed to Rosser Reeves of the Ted Bates agency. Reeves does not, of course, try to produce advertising that is not tasteful, but he does make it clear that he writes not for esthetic appeal but to create sales. He challenges the "artsy, craftsy crowd" by observing, "I'm not saying that

Figure 12-2.   **A Volkswagen advertisement comparing the car's price to that of a pound of meat**

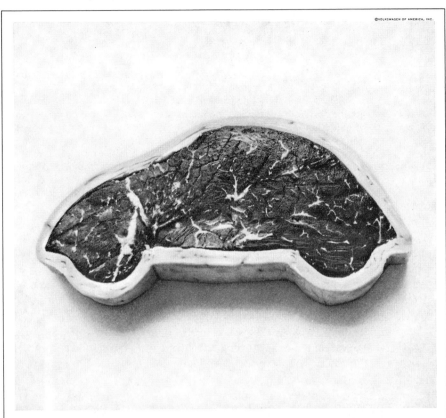

Can you still get prime quality for $1.26 a pound?

A pound of Volkswagen isn't cheap compared to other cars. But what you pay for is the quality. Prime quality.

Just look at what you get for your money:

13 pounds of paint, some of it in places you can't even see. (So you can leave a Volkswagen out overnight and it won't spoil.)

A watertight, airtight, sealed steel bottom that protects against rocks, rain, rust and rot.

Over 1,000 inspections per one Beetle.

1,014 inspectors who are so finicky that they reject parts you could easily ride around with and not even detect there was anything wrong.

Electronic Diagnosis that tells you what's right and wrong with important parts of your car.

A 1600 cc aluminum-magnesium engine that gets 25* miles to a gallon of regular gasoline.

Volkswagen's traditionally high resale value.

Over 22,000 changes and improvements on a car that was well built to begin with.

What with all the care we take in building every single Volkswagen, we'd like to call it a filet mignon of a car. Only one problem. It's too tough. **Few things in life work as well as a Volkswagen.**

*DIN 70030

Dealer Name
33-11-38660

AUTHORIZED
DEALER

Courtesy of Volkswagen of America, Inc.

Figure 12-3. **Volkswagen advertising that ties to Alka-Seltzer and the energy crisis**

Courtesy of Volkswagen of America, Inc.

charming, witty and warm copy won't sell. I'm just saying that I've seen thousands of charming, witty campaigns that didn't sell."[17]

His conception of the appropriate role of advertising is illustrated in the following questions he poses:

> Let's say you have $1,000,000 tied up in your little company and suddenly, for reasons unknown to you, your advertising isn't working and your sales are going down. And everything depends on it, your family's future depends on it, other people's families depend on it. And you walk in this office and talk to me, and you sit in that chair. Now, what do you want out of me? Fine writing? Do you want masterpieces? Do you want glowing things that can be framed by copywriters? Or do you want to see the . . . sales curve stop moving down and start moving up? What do you want?[18]

Reeves is particularly critical of approaches in which the copy is so clever that it distracts from the message.

Reeves has proposed that each product develop its own unique selling proposition (USP) and use whatever repetition is necessary to communicate the USP to the audience. There are three guidelines to the development of a USP. First, the proposition needs to involve a specific product benefit. Second, it must be unique, one that competing firms are not using. Third, it must sell. It therefore must be important enough to the consumer to influence the decision process. The most successful USPs such as "M&M candies melt in your mouth instead of your hand" result from identifying real inherent product advantages. The determination of a USP generally requires research on the product and on consumer use of the product. When a good USP is found, the development of the actual advertisement is a relatively easy process. Among Ted Bates' USPs are "Colgate cleans your breath as it cleans your teeth," "Viceroys have 20,000 filter traps," and "Better skin from Palmolive."

Reeves relies heavily on product research to support specific claims. This support often takes the form of rather elaborate experiments. The research tends to be reliable in the sense that others, if they wished, could replicate it and generate similar conclusions. In one case, Ted Bates and Colgate spent $300,000 to prove that washing the face thoroughly (for a full minute) with Palmolive soap would improve the skin.[19] The concern over support of claims is, of course, a useful precaution to avoid FTC action. Reeves does not obtain the documentation only for legal purposes. The fact is that good research can be used to help make the claim more credible.

Once an effective USP is found, Reeves believes that it should be retained practically indefinitely. Such a philosophy requires vigorous defending, especially when a client gets tired of a campaign, which usually happens before the campaign even starts. One client asked Reeves, "You have seven hundred people in that office of yours, and you've been running the same advertisement for me for the last eleven years. What I want to know is, what are those seven hundred people supposed to be doing?" Reeves replied, "They're keeping your advertising department from changing your advertisement.''[20] According to Reeves, Anacin spent over $85 million in a 10-year period on one advertising commercial. Reeves pointed out that the commercial "cost $8,200 to produce and it made more money than 'Gone With the Wind.' ''[21] The psychological learning theories with their emphasis on habit formation via repetition provide some theoretical support for the use of heavy repetition in advertising.

The Reeves approach is undoubtedly successful. The Ted Bates agency, which Reeves helped organize in 1940, was the fourth largest United States agency in 1970, with worldwide billings of $414 million. It has a remarkable record of retaining clients. However, the approach is highly controversial. People object to the style and to the repetition. The use of a USP is particularly troublesome in political campaigns, when many feel that a more thorough discussion of issues is appropriate. In 1952 the Reeves approach was applied to the Eisenhower campaign.[22] Reeves made a set of 20-second spot commercials for Eisenhower. They all started with the statement "Eisenhower Answers the Nation." Then an ordinary citizen would ask a question such as, "What about the high cost of living?" Eisenhower would then reply. To the cost-of-living question, he said, "My wife, Mamie, worries about the same thing. I tell her its our job to change that on November fourth." Such advertisements may have been effective, but they created a storm of controversy about the nature of political advertising campaigns that still exists to this day.

LEO BURNETT: THE COMMON TOUCH

The Leo Burnett agency differs from other larger agencies in that it is not located in New York, but rather, in Chicago. Perhaps partially because of that, it is associated with the common touch. Burnett often used plain ordinary people in his advertisements. The Schlitz campaign featured a neighborhood bartender. A Maytag advertisement showed a grandmother with 13 grandchildren and a vintage Maytag. In that respect he contrasts rather vividly with David Ogilvy. Burnett put it this way:

> As I have observed it, great advertising writing either in print or television, is always deceptively and disarmingly simple. It has the common touch without being or sounding patronizing. If you are writing about baloney, don't try to make it sound like Cornish hen, because that is the worst kind of baloney there is. Just make it darned good baloney.
>
> Not only is great copy "deceptively simple"—but so are great ideas. And if it takes a rationale to explain an ad or a commercial—then it's too complicated for that "dumb public" to understand.
>
> I'm afraid too many advertising people blame the public's inability to sort out commercial messages or advertisements in magazines on stupidity. What a lousy stupid attitude to have! I believe the public is unable to sort out messages, not just because of the sheer flood of messages assaulting it every day, but because of *sheer boredom!*
>
> If the public is bored today—then let's blame it on the fact that it is being handed boring messages created by bored advertising people. In a world where nobody seems

to know what's going to happen next, the only thing to do to keep from going completely nuts from frustration is plain old-fashioned work! Having worked many, many years for peanuts and in obscurity, I think I know how a lot of writers feel today and I sympathize with them, but I also wonder if a lot of writers aren't downright spoiled.[23]

Burnett further described his orientation by indicating that the best copywriters have "a flair for expression, putting known and believable things into new relationships. . . . We [the Chicago school of advertising] try to be more straightforward without being flatfooted. We try to be warm without being mawkish."[24] The key words are warm and believable. The approach aims for believability with warmth.

In the spirit of providing a common touch, Burnett looks for the "inherent drama" of a product—the characteristic that made the manufacturer make it, that makes the people buy it. The objective is to capture the inherent drama and make it "arresting itself rather than relying upon tricks."[25] Burnett is impatient with a dull factual recitation or a cleverness with words or a "highfaluting rhapsody of plain bombast."[26] The preferable approach is to dig out the inherent drama and present it in a warm, realistic manner. The inherent drama is "often hard to find, but it is always there, and once found it is the most interesting and believable of all advertising appeals."[27]

The Green Giant company has been with Burnett since the agency was established in 1935. One early advertisement illustrates the use of the inherent drama concept. Burnett wanted to communicate the fact that Green Giant peas were of good quality and fresh. He used a picture of a night harvest with the caption "Harvested in the Moonlight" and included an insert of the giant holding a pod of peas. As Burnett states, "It would have been easy to say, 'Packed Fresh' in the headline, but 'Harvested in the Moonlight' had both news value and romance, and connoted a special kind of care which was unusual to find in a can of peas."[28] A series of four advertisements that featured paintings by Norman Rockwell also were used in early campaigns. One showed a farm kitchen with a boy enjoying a platter of corn on the cob. Jerry Della Femina comments on the Green Giant campaign:

Burnett even tells people what a corny agency he has, but he's not corny. He is a very brilliant man. . . . That Jolly Green Giant is fantastic. He sells beans, corn, peas, everything. When you watch the Jolly Green Giant, you know it's fantasy and yet you buy the product. Do you know what Libby does? I don't. Most food advertising is like gone by the boards, you don't even see it. But the Jolly Green Giant, it's been automatic success when he's on the screen.[29]

The Pillsbury account arrived in 1945. One series of advertisements was termed the Pillsbury "big cake campaign." A large picture of a cake with several slices removed dominated the advertisements, another example of "inherent drama" letting an appetizing picture do the selling. The Marlboro campaign started in the mid-1950s. The Marlboro cowboy, the tattoo, the Marlboro country approach is still going strong and is probably considered one of the classic campaigns. The country flavor and the use of the tattoo provided the common touch. Another early product that used the common touch was Kellogg's cereal. For example, in the campaign for Kellogg's corn flakes, the headline "the best to you each morning" was used in conjunction with an appealing human interest photo (see Figure 12-4).

In what follows, several creative directors who have achieved prominence in recent years are profiled and some of the well-known agency styles are discussed. It is interesting and useful to compare and contrast them with David Ogilvy, William Bernbach, Rosser Reeves, and Leo Burnett. We will also provide some insights into their life-styles, their particular approaches to creating advertising, and the agencies with which they are associated.

PHILIP DUSENBERRY, BBDO

Producing television commercials can be dangerous! During the shooting of a commercial for Pepsi-Cola in 1984, the central figure, the well-known rock star Michael Jackson, was injured when his hair caught on fire. Although obviously unplanned, it became a national news event. Philip Dusenberry, vice-chairman and executive creative director of Batten, Barton, Durstine & Osborn was the person responsible for development of this famous campaign. Another Dusenberry-BBDO effort was an 18-minute film of President Reagan shown at the Republican Convention in the summer of 1984 before the President's acceptance speech. It also became national news when the networks refused to air it. The criticism was that it did not address the issues and lacked balance.

Dusenberry has been described as a quiet man who doesn't mind the attention.[30] Indeed, largely under his direction, BBDO won the coveted "Agency of the Year" award in 1984. This award, given annually by Crain Communications and *Advertising Age,* is based on an evaluation of the total creative product of the agency in any particular year. This includes evaluations of copy, creative strategies, merchandising, media planning, and research. BBDO was judged the best agency based on this total creative product.

Dusenberry advocates flexibility and "shunning of the familiar" as basic tenets for good creative strategy. "Don't get too happy too soon with the first idea that comes into your head." BBDO abandoned the familiar theme song and life-style approach for soft-drink advertising in its Pepsi-Cola campaign, and replaced the usual suffering faces in cold-remedy advertising with more upbeat themes. Flexibility includes not just production techniques for their own sake, but tying them into strong creative strategies. For example, in developing ads for Dodge, which had a rather staid image, Dusenberry and the creative people at BBDO had cars drive up the sides of buildings. Fragmented close-ups and intimate dialogue were used to help Diet Pepsi target the sophisticated low-calorie-cola user. Intense, zoom-in shots were used to capture the muscle of the heritage of Black and Decker tools.

Another characteristic of this style is to "elevate people above the product," and to use people in lively and engaging situations. In the Pepsi campaign, the

Figure 12-4.   **A Kellogg's Corn Flakes advertisement**

"All us men eat Kellogg's Corn Flakes."

"The best to you each morning"

Best liked (*World's favorite*)
... Best flavor (*Kellogg's secret*)
...Worst to run out of

Kellogg's CORN FLAKES

© 1958 by Kellogg Company

Courtesy of the Kellogg Company.

emphasis is on "Pepsi people," for example. A similar thrust was used in the President Reagan film. The film shows people, all presumably Reagan supporters, getting married, eating ice cream cones, delivering newspapers, and generally feeling "proud to be an American." According to Dusenberry, too much mention of issues is simply "boring." The film was intended to appeal to the viewer's sense of pride and the needs for developing feelings of patriotism and loyalty.

Dusenberry has been described as a "rabid baseball fan" and one-time aspiring big league catcher. Among his many other accomplishments is a screenplay he wrote called *The Natural*. It met nothing but rejections before catching the eye of the actor-director Robert Redford. Redford directed and played a starring role in the film, which became a box-office hit and a popular videocassette. As we will see, many of the creative giants in advertising have made similar impressive creative contributions outside the field of advertising.

For many years, BBDO was considered a rather conservative agency and the Pepsi campaign emphasizing "Choice of a New Generation" was a significant break with traditional styles. As stated by one reviewer, "the long Coke versus Pepsi battle over which one could sing a better jingle or portray people having more fun at picnics finally came to an end, or at least entered a lull."[31] The attempt was to reach out to the younger generation in their own language, not just through a single campaign format. In addition to Michael Jackson, takeoffs on popular science fiction movies at the time, such as *E.T.* and *Close Encounters of the Third Kind*, were used. Much of this turnaround in style is attributed to Allen Rosenshine, BBDO's chairman, chief executive officer, and former creative director. According to Rosenshine:

> When parity products develop creative strategies, they all come out the same. Using line extensions and market segmentation to differentiate only adds to the problem. All aimed to be authoritative, assertive, competitive, and convincing about why one product was better than the other. For BBDO, it became clear that the way to go was to leave the rational sell behind. We are far more devoted now to the concept that advertising is a consumer experience with the brand. We are more sensitive too and careful that the experience is enjoyable, pleasant, human, warm and emotional, while no less relevant from the sales strategy viewpoint.[32]

ALEXANDER KROLL, Y & R

Alexander Kroll, chief executive officer of Young & Rubicam, has been a major creative force at the agency and was responsible for memorable campaigns for products such as Mercury, Dr. Pepper, Dentyne chewing gum, Metropolitan Life insurance, and many others. The agency has had a long-standing relationship with General Foods and has developed the advertising for GF brands, including Sanka and GF International coffee, Tang, Orange Plus, Awake, and Postum beverages, all Jell-O products, Birds-Eye vegetables, and Quick Thaw fruits. Kroll has described the agency's creative philosophy as "It must have the right strategy, be believable, have drama, make the product a hero, make a friend, and build on and be consistent with the basic personality of the product."[33] Recall the discussion of the Dr. Pepper ad in Chapter 10 and the product-as-hero idea.

The agency's creative accomplishments are very impressive. In 1984, they were the "runner-up" to BBDO in the Agency of the Year award. They were the finalist in 1983, and cowinner with N. W. Ayer in 1978. Kroll has overseen development of a 90-page catalog of ad awards garnered by Y & R affiliates around the world. The list includes 13 citations from the International Advertising Film Festival at Cannes, France. In the forward, Kroll states:

> While we do not measure our success by awards . . . they tell us whether our creative product is near, or at the leading edge of inventiveness. . . . They show us where we stand on the "art" of commercial communications, which is at least half the business.[34]

Young & Rubicam has been a very successful advertising agency and moved up to first place in world billings in 1979, for the first time surpassing the long-standing leadership position of J. Walter Thompson. A recent example of their advertising is the Metropolitan Life Insurance Company advertisement shown in Figure 12-5. In this campaign, widely known and recognized characters from the comic strip "Peanuts" are used to capture attention and stimulate interest in the company's products.

A basic thrust of Young & Rubicam advertising is to take everything known about the product category, define the problem the advertising must solve, and list all mandatory information about the product or service. In the case of their Kentucky Fried Chicken account, for example, the guidelines resulted in the idea of a "guilt-free" fast food and the "perfect meal for any occasion." The campaign theme, "It's nice to feel so good about a meal," meshed well with the industry trend to focus on nutrition and good food.

For the Pabst Brewing Company, a macho image and a "homey" approach, with such tunes as "Pabst Blue Ribbon on my mind," were developed. The General Foods Jell-O campaign featuring Bill Cosby in scenes with children is another good example. The resulting soft sell plays up fun and family warmth at meals, and makes the most out of Cosby's style and empathy with kids. In one version, Cosby tries to convince a "small person" that a "big person" with no dessert ought to have a serving of Jell-O pudding. For Dr. Pepper soft drink, the advertising focused on the drink's difference—"most misunderstood, most unusual soft drink." Sugar-free Dr. Pepper was positioned as "It tastes too good to be true." The famous "bullish on America" campaign for Merrill Lynch and many others (Oil of Olay, Eastman Kodak cameras, Keds shoes, Excedrin PM, Eastern Air Lines, Security Pacific Bank) are good examples of the Young & Rubicam style.

Figure 12-5. **Metropolitan Life Insurance advertising using "Peanuts" characters**

Courtesy of Metropolitan Life Insurance Company and United Feature Syndicate, Inc.

JIM PATTERSON, J. WALTER THOMPSON

According to one reporter, "Jim Patterson looks all the world like the tall, unsmiling hero of one of his own best-selling novels. An intensely private, almost shy man, he talks as he writes—weighing his words carefully, doling out his life, like his fiction, in neat exacting measures."[35]

Patterson is executive vice-president and creative director of J. Walter Thompson. At age 38, he is responsible for the creative efforts behind millions of dollars of advertising on accounts such as Burger King hamburgers, Kodak cameras, Toys R Us, and Miller High Life beer. Concerning advertising for Burger King, he states: "We tried to see it realistically. It's a hamburger. It's not life and death, as some see it. So we always try to serve it up with a certain amount of humor." The advertisement for Kodak film in Figure 12-6 shows two delightful children in a shot that few parents could resist.

Patterson is a good representative of the change in attitudes toward creativity at J. Walter Thompson. Under the leadership of chairman Burt Manning, a new attitude that focused attention on creativity and the importance of producing a high-quality creative product took hold at the agency. Manning states of Patterson: "I have great admiration for him. From the beginning, Patterson exhibited an astonishing grasp of what advertising really is. I don't know of anyone more powerful than him when it comes to television. He has an instinct for what is the most powerful appeal. He has a very loyal creative department; morale is really very high."[36]

Like other creative giants in advertising, he has also had a successful career in other pursuits. A graduate of Vanderbilt University, he considered becoming an English professor and two years after joining JWT wrote his first novel *The Thomas Berry Number.* He is reported to have completed this project by writing between 6:00 and 8:30 every morning! The novel, a murder mystery, was published in 1976 and won the Edgar Allan Poe award for the best American mystery book. Many more novels followed. His most successful, a book called *Virgin,* about the rebirth of Christ in the 1980s, sold more than 400,000 copies in the United States. According to his agent, Patterson is among the top 15 percent fiction writers in the United States, is an excellent story teller, has original ideas, and can follow them through into readable prose. It is no mystery that he has become such an effective creative director in advertising.

A major accomplishment was winning the Miller High Life account, a brand with a spectacular history of success and subsequent loss in market share. Patterson sees the product's problems as analogous to a good actor stuck with the wrong role. As he states:

> The brand has to be reestablished. . . . It has to stand for something. If the beer wasn't good, it would be different. But it's a premium beer. We hope we'll turn it around. . . . I don't think we're capable of producing something stupid. If we produce something stupid, then obviously the campaign will fail. But it's our reputation too. We'll fight the client who wants to produce something stupid.[37]

Figure 12-6.   **A Kodak advertisement**

Courtesy of J. Walter Thompson USA.

Patterson is an important contributor to an agency that has consistently been one of the largest in the world and has won many awards. For example, in late 1984, a survey of advertising directors judged JWT the agency that "provides the best overall services and products." JWT's reputation is distinguished by its across-the-board strengths and in this study was ranked first in top-of-the-mind awareness as the agency that "comes first to mind."

BOB LEVENSON, SAATCHI & SAATCHI COMPTON

Bob Levenson is vice-chairman and chief creative officer at Saatchi & Saatchi Compton. Before joining S&SC, he had been the creative director at Doyle Dane Bernbach, and was associated with DDB over a span of 26 years. Recall the discussion of the Bernbach style earlier. Levenson has been described as "Bernbach's real son," and as a "warm-hearted, sentimental guy." According to one colleague, the key to understanding his joking personality is to remember that he is the nephew of the late humorist Sam Levenson.[38] If you have ever wondered who created the line, "Have you ever wondered how the man who drives a snowplow drives to the snowplow?", you can stop wondering—it was Bob Levenson. In fact, the history of Volkswagen advertising is very much intertwined with Bernbach, Levenson, and the Doyle Dane Bernbach agency.

Other campaigns with which he is associated include Mobil Oil's "We want you to live," in which a car is tossed off a 10-story building to demonstrate the impact of a crash, the famous line "Nobody Doesn't Like Sara Lee" for Sara Lee products, and campaigns for Polaroid cameras, Clairol hair products, and Parker Pen. It is for print advertising that he is best known.

In discussing his creative style, Levenson makes it clear that persuasion is the name of the game. "You are not right if in your ad you stand a man on his head just to get attention. You are right if you have him on his head to show how your product keeps things from falling out of his pockets." And he agrees with Bernbach that

> merely to let your imagination run riot, to dream unrelated dreams, to indulge in graphic acrobatics and verbal gymnastics, is not being creative. The creative person has harnessed his imagination. He has disciplined it so that every thought, every idea, every word he puts down, every line he draws, every light and shadow in every photograph he takes, makes more vivid, more believable, more persuasive the original theme or product advantage he has decided he must convey.[39]

Levenson's first job in advertising was with DDB and he stayed with this agency for 26 years. A graduate of New York University, he had intended to become a college professor of English. Some of his colorful background includes selling encyclopedias door-to-door and working as a used-car salesman and as an interviewer for the Starch research firm. As one reporter relates:

> Mr. Levenson's career as a used car salesman consisted of selling one car, a 1954 Mercury, to himself. . . . One day in October 1959, when Cay Gibson, who headed

the DDB promotion department, asked if anybody knew about cars, Mr. Levenson was able to raise his hand. He had, after all, sold cars. It became his entry into the Volkswagen account.[40]

Levenson is clearly one of the recent creative giants in advertising and has made enormous contributions to advertising creativity. As stated in reflecting on his years at DDB: "No account ever came into an ad agency as a plum. In 1959, when Volkswagen came into Doyle Dane Bernbach, it was not unique. There were two cars in the market, the Renault Dauphine and the Fiat 600, that were almost as ugly, that had air-cooled engines in the rear. It's what you do with it!"[41]

LEE CLOW, CHIAT/DAY

Clow has been identified as "the force behind some of the most remarkable U.S. ad campaigns of recent years."[42] Among his major accomplishments was a 60-second minimovie for Apple Computer's Macintosh, showing a clubwielding symbol of freedom smashing the 1984 Orwellian nightmare. Although aired only once, it generated enormous publicity. Although its successor, a commercial called "Lemmings," was not as successful, it nevertheless established an irreverent style that has become Apple's trademark in advertising. The creative genius behind these commercials was Lee Clow, executive vice-president and creative director of Chiat/Day, a Los Angeles-based agency.

Other major campaigns with which he has been associated are for products such as Nike brand sports apparel, PepsiCo's Pizza Hut, and Porsche automobiles. In one famous billboard campaign for Nike, he had unidentified Olympic hopefuls in striking poses, such as clearing hurdles at the track, displayed on massive outdoor billboards and the sides of buildings, with only the smallest mention of the sponsor, Nike. He has been described as having a unique ability to spot an idea and know if it will work. In discussing his creative style, Clow argues for the need to generate confidence and to take the lead in sticking to an idea.

If you don't act sure of yourself, it's very easy for other people's faith in your product to get shaky. Apple's 1984 commercial, for example, was an idea that was very easy to get nervous about. If it seems that you have some misgivings or second thoughts about something, it's easy for people who are less tuned into creative communication to get nervous about it. Most ideas are a bit scary, and if an idea isn't scary, it's not an idea at all.[43]

The adopted son of an aerospace worker in the Los Angeles area, Clow is reported to lead a surprisingly traditional life, and to be an avid television watcher. It is interesting that Clow attributes to DDB and Volkswagen advertising much of his inspiration for getting into advertising, and has described this campaign as the "single greatest advertising work in the history of the business." Volkswagen advertising was launched during the so-called creative revolution of the 1960s, and Clow acknowledges creative artists such as the Beatles, Andy Warhol, and major events during the period, such as the assassinations of President Kennedy and Martin Luther King, Jr., and going to the moon, as having a major impact on his creative development. The fact that he works in advertising, the antithesis of many of the values espoused during this period, doesn't seem to bother him.

In the survey of advertising agency reputations mentioned earlier, Chiat/Day was identified as the "hottest" agency of the year. Although Clow reputedly does not actually draw many ads, he is a major force in developing the concepts on which many famous Chiat/Day campaigns are based. His style is designed to create impact and he emphasizes the need for an honest dialogue with the consumer and respect for consumer intelligence.

> If you think you have a better mousetrap or car, or shirt, or whatever, you've got to tell people, and I don't think that has to be done with trickery, or insults, or by talking down to people. I think it can be an honest dialog with the consumer. Good advertising is a dialog with people. . . . The smartest advertising is the advertising that communicates the best and respects the consumer's intelligence. It's advertising that lets them bring something to the communication process, as opposed to some of the more validly criticized work in our profession in which they try to grind the benefits of a soap or cake mix into a poor housewife's head by repeating it 37 times in 30 seconds.[44]

OTHER CREATIVE APPROACHES AND STYLES

There are, of course, many other advertising agencies and many other creative approaches and styles that could be presented and discussed. Those reviewed in this chapter are, however, fairly representative of the range of creative output, at least in the very large, leading agencies. Two of the top 10 agencies, McCann-Erickson and Foote, Cone & Belding, are not represented in these profiles and, of course, there are dozens of other creative people associated with highly successful agencies and creative output that could be reviewed. Previous winners of Agency of the Year awards, such as N. W. Ayer, Cunningham & Walsh, Scali, McCabe, Sloves, DKG Advertising, and Needham, Harper & Steers, are notable for their creative output and the styles of their creative people.

SUMMARY

Like art, two or more creative people can look at the same problem and develop advertising that is quite different. These differences are differences in the creative style of the individual or agency. Even though different, the advertising and the campaigns that evolve can be "successful." For example, the styles of William Bernbach and Rosser Reeves are very different in terms of philosophy and execution, but each has been associated with highly successful advertising. It is also true, of course, that regardless of creative style, campaigns may fail if the product is weak, economic or social conditions change, a superior competitive product enters the picture, or the creative style does not mesh well with all the other factors involved in marketing the product.

Nine profiles of leading creative people in advertising and the agencies with which they are associated were presented and discussed. The first four, David Ogilvy, William Bernbach, Rosser Reeves, and Leo Burnett, are notable for setting the standards of creative style in the early 1950s and 1960s. The next four, Philip Dusenberry, Alexander Kroll, Jim Patterson, and Bob Levenson, represent current leaders in an analogous set of leading advertising agencies. The final profile on Lee Clow provides a snapshot of an emerging new style and a smaller, rapidly growing, and "hot" advertising agency.

Although descriptions of creative styles are difficult and tend to become exaggerated and stereotypical, it is nevertheless useful to compare and contrast them and to analyze where they appear to be similar and different. In the more recent profiles, some additional information is provided on the background and other activities of the person to provide insights into who creative people are and where they come from.

DISCUSSION QUESTIONS

1. Ogilvy, Bernbach, Reeves, and Burnett are all creative giants in advertising who have retired or passed on. Compare and contrast their styles with those of Dusenberry, Kroll, Patterson, and Levenson, who are current leaders in top 10 agencies. Who is more like whom? Why?

2. The creative styles of Bernbach and Reeves are probably two ends of a continuum, yet both are associated with highly successful agencies and campaigns. One could conclude that creative style makes no difference. Do you agree or disagree? Why or why not?

3. In what ways is the Lee Clow style "different" from all the rest? How would you explain the phenomenal growth of this young agency, Chiat/Day?

4. To what extent do the following models explain why some of the creative styles profiled work or do not work?
    a. Exposure effect
    b. Peripheral processing
    c. Cognitive response
    d. Classical conditioning
    e. Word-of-mouth advertising

5. Drawing on the concepts of Chapters 8 through 12, to what extent do you feel the nine advertisers profiled would like their advertising to be characterized in general as:
    a. Having empathy
    b. Being believable
    c. Being informative

      d. Being interesting

      e. Generating emotional response

      f. Using sources who are expert, prestigious, or unbiased

6. Suppose that you were chairman of a billion-dollar agency and were having to choose among three candidates for the position of creative director. Discuss the qualities you would look for in filling the position. What are the characteristics of a top-quality creative person?

7. Choose a word or phrase that would best characterize the creative styles of Dusenberry, Kroll, Patterson, and Clow analogous to those for Ogilvy, Bernbach, Reeves, and Burnett. Explain your decisions.

NOTES

1. David Ogilvy, *Confessions of an Advertising Man* (New York: Atheneum, 1964), pp. 100–102.

2. Ibid., p. 102.

3. Ibid., p. 51.

4. Ibid., pp. 116–117.

5. Ibid., pp. 93–103.

6. Martin Mayer, *Madison Avenue, U.S.A.* (New York: Pocket Books, 1958), p. 64.

7. Jerry Della Femina, with Charles Spokin, ed., *From Those Wonderful Folks Who Gave You Pearl Harbor* (New York: Simon and Schuster, 1970), p. 29.

8. Denis Higgens, ed., *The Art of Writing Advertising* (Chicago: Crain Books, 1965), pp. 117–118.

9. Mayer, *Madison Avenue, U.S.A.*, p. 66.

10. Frank Rowsome, Jr., *Think Small* (New York: Ballatine Books, 1970), p. 81.

11. Ibid., p. 12.

12. Mayer, *Madison Avenue, U.S.A.*, p. 65.

13. For an interpretation of this campaign from which these comments were drawn, see Femina, *From Those Wonderful Folks*, pp. 38–39.

14. Ibid., p. 26.

15. Rowsome, *Think Small*, p. 116.

16. Ibid., p. 117.

17. Higgens, *The Art of Writing Advertising*, p. 120.

18. Ibid., pp. 117–118.

19. Mayer, *Madison Avenue, U.S.A.*, pp. 59–61.

20. Ibid., p. 52.

21. Higgens, *The Art of Writing Advertising*, p. 124.

22. Described in Mayer, *Madison Avenue, U.S.A.*, p. 300.

23. Leo Burnett, "Keep Listening to That Wee, Small Voice," in *Communications of an Advertising Man,* Copyright 1961 by Leo Burnett Company, Inc., from a speech given before the Chicago Copywriters Club, October 4, 1960.

24. Higgens, *The Art of Writing Advertising*, p. 17.

25. Ibid., p. 44.

26. Burnett, "Keep Listening," p. 154.

27. Mayer, *Madison Avenue, U.S.A.*, p. 70.

28. Higgens, *The Art of Writing Advertising*, p. 45.

29. Femina, *From Those Wonderful Folks*, p. 141.

30. *Advertising Age,* August 27, 1984, p. 1.

31. Stewart Alter, "Ad Age Honors BBDO as Agency of Year," *Advertising Age,* March 28, 1985, p. 3ff.

32. Ibid., p. 4.

33. *Advertising Age,* March 14, 1979, p. 1.

34. *Advertising Age,* March 28, 1985, p. 40.

35. Ann Cooper, "Patterson's Write-On Approach," *Advertising Age,* February 21, 1985, p. 37ff.

36. Ibid., p. 37.

37. Ibid., p. 37.

38. Stewart Alter, "Bob Levenson, Creative Boost for Saatchi's Compton Unit," *Advertising Age,* May 9, 1985, p. 5.

39. Quoted in Alter, ibid.

40. Ibid., p. 9.

41. Ibid.

42. Jennifer Pendleton, "Bringing New Clow-T to Ads, Chiat's Unlikely Creative," *Advertising Age,* February 7, 1985, p. 1ff.

43. Ibid., p. 5.

44. Ibid.

13

Creating and Producing Copy

Nobody Doesn't Like Sara Lee

Where's the beef?

Reach out and touch someone

The creation and production of advertising is a process involving many people, much time, and signficant expenditures of money. Although the major components of this process can be described, it is very difficult to explain precisely how effective copy is actually created. It is like asking an artist to explain how to create and produce a great painting. Although we might recognize greatness in the final output of the process, it is difficult to set up a creation and production system that will always guarantee such greatness. Behind any print advertisement or television commercial lie hundreds of decisions involving artistic and other judgments by teams of people inside and outside the agency. The process of creating and producing copy is very like the process of creating and producing the product itself.

Copy decisions are important because all the investment on research and development for a new product or maintaining sales levels of an established product is at stake. Copy is the means through which advertising objectives are carried out and strategy is executed. All the attention to careful specification of objectives can be ruined by poor copy. And copy is expensive. Creating, producing, and the research done on one television commercial, for example, can involve hundreds of thousands of dollars. Although media costs will be even more expensive (on average media costs represent about 85 percent of a total advertising budget), they too ultimately depend on copy and copy decisions.

This chapter reviews the copy creation and production process. A general model is first presented which traces the various stages and activities involved in the overall process. The creation stage part of the model is then presented in detail. It includes a discussion of creativity and the creative process, and specific activities such as copywriting, illustrating, layout, client approval, and supplier selection. This is followed by a review of activities at the production stage. Production differs according to whether copy is being produced for print media or for broadcast media. In print media, the important components concern typography and engraving, whereas in broadcast, filming and editing are of central importance. Finally, a review of types of television commercials is presented and discussed. A vital, though neglected managerial decision is how many copy alternatives to create and how much of the advertising budget should go into the creative process. The Appendix addresses this topic.

What are the basic tasks involved in creating and producing an advertisement? Who does what at which stage? What are the important ways of generating ideas and carrying them forward into final production? What should an advertising manager know about the creation and production process?

A MODEL OF THE CREATION AND PRODUCTION PROCESS

Figure 13-1 presents a model of the creation and production process. Note that two basic stages are involved, *creation* and *production*. The distinction is somewhat artificial because creative activities can take place at any point throughout the entire process, but it is a convenient distinction for several reasons. First, the activities associated with the creation stage take place largely within the confines of the advertising agency. Those associated with production are usually done by outside suppliers to the agency. Second, creation activities are in many ways similar for either print or broadcast advertising. In most cases the generation of words (copywriting) and the generation of pictures (illustrating) are involved whether the end result is a print advertisement or a broadcast commercial. A preliminary print advertisement ready to be shipped out for production is called a *layout*. In the case of a prospective television commercial, the layout is called a *storyboard,* but the creative activities involved in the generation of each are in many ways similar. Finally, production activities by external suppliers do differ in significant respects for print production or broadcast production. Print production involves the graphic arts and specialists in typography, engraving, printing, and so on. Broadcast production, particularly in television, involves audiovisual studios, production houses, and the basic tasks of filming and editing, which are very similar to the production

Figure 13-1.   **Model of the creation and production process**

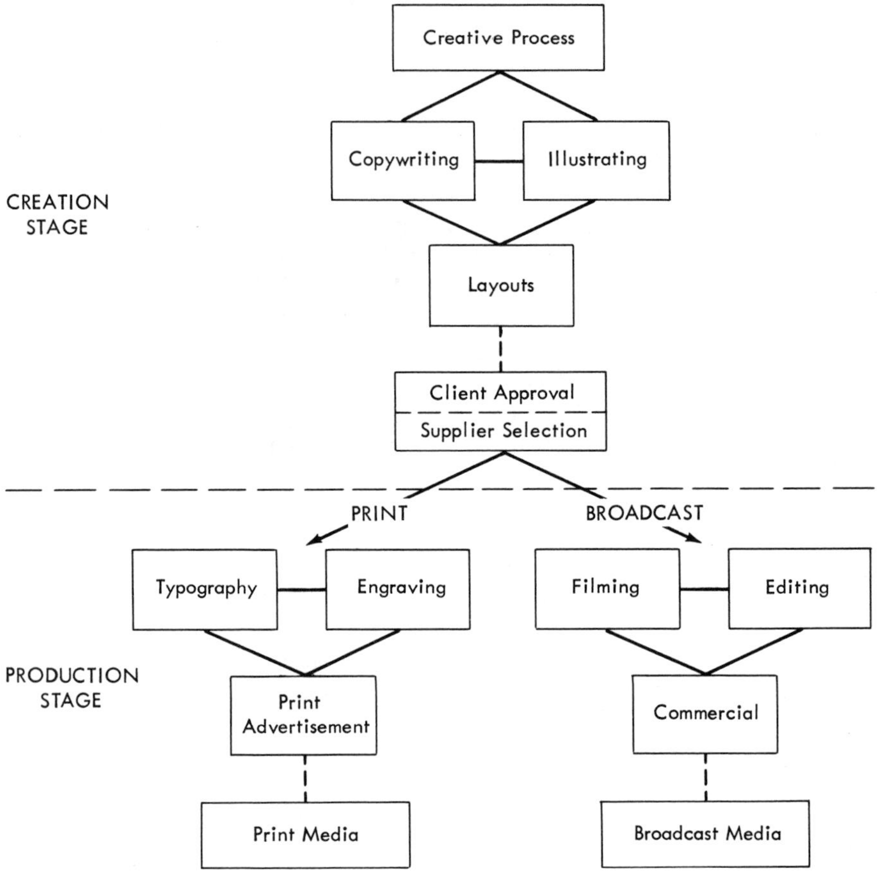

of a movie. In sum, different types of external suppliers are involved for print and broadcast at the production stage.

The important input to the generation of advertising is referred to as the *creative process* in the model. Much attention has been given to ways of improving this process and generating ideas. Following the generation of a layout, the creative director and the agency account executive will next seek the client's approval for the layout and the general nature of the advertising to be produced. An important decision at this point is the selection of suppliers to actually produce the finished advertisements. These tasks are noted in the model as *client approval* and *supplier selection*.

Following production, the final print advertisements or broadcast commercials are distributed to the appropriate newspapers, magazines, radio, or broadcast stations (media) for printing and airing. This step completes the *copy-decision* aspects of advertising management insofar as the basic messages are created and produced. Copy-testing research, the subject of Chapter 14, can be done at the layout stage or on the final print advertisement or commercial generated by the suppliers. We will examine various alternatives for copy testing in Chapter 14 and how this task enters the overall picture.

CREATION STAGE

Although much advertising, particularly local advertising, is created by someone at the client and media level without the inputs of an advertising agency, most national advertising involves an agency. It is the job of the creative department of the agency to generate alternative advertising ideas and ultimately to pick one or a few that will go forward into production. The creative department is made up of copywriters who have the main responsibility for creating the advertising and artists who are expert at creating or otherwise introducing illustration and pictorial materials. These people are generally under the supervision of a creative director, and a team of such people are involved in developing the advertising to be used on any one campaign. An individual copywriter will, however, be the person responsible for generating the layout associated with a particular print advertisement or commercial storyboard. The creative team also must work closely with and coordinate its activities with the traffic department and a production supervisor. People in traffic work on scheduling the process and making sure that deadlines are met and that finished advertising reaches media at the times specified in the contract.

The creation stage encompasses the creative process, the generation of written copy (copywriting), artwork of various kinds (illustrating), and a preliminary or comprehensive version of the advertisement (layout). As suggested in the Figure 13-1 model, client approval and supplier selection are also important activities that must be done before final production can begin. First, we consider the creative process.

Creative Process

The creative process has interested many different types of people for some time. One of the pioneers in studying creativity, Alex Osborn, was, interestingly, a founder or Batten, Barton, Durstine & Osborn, one of the largest agencies. Osborn saw the creative process as starting with the following.[1]

1. Fact-finding
   a. Problem-definition: picking out and pointing up the problem.
   b. Preparation: gathering and analyzing the pertinent data.
2. Idea-finding
   a. Idea-production: thinking up tentative ideas as possible leads.
   b. Idea-development: selecting from resultant ideas, adding others, and re-processing by means of modification, combination, et cetera.

The process begins with fact finding—picking out and identifying the problem and gathering and analyzing pertinent data. The raw material for ideas is information—information from all sources. Burnett once said, "Curiosity about life in all of its aspects, I think, is still the secret of great creative people."[2] Of course, some information is more useful than others. In particular, the creative team should become immersed in as much factual information about the company, the product, competition, and the target audience (their language, needs, motivations, desires) as possible. Obviously, they should have access to the available consumer research. Sometimes it is worthwhile to get firsthand knowledge of the consumer. Claude Hopkins, whom we met in Chapter 1, would always go out and discuss products with housewives. One of the top agency executives today still makes it a point to regularly visit supermarkets and ask shoppers why they make certain shopping decisions. Leo Burnett believes in

> depth-interviewing where I come realistically face to face with the people I am trying to sell. I try to get a picture in my mind of the kind of people they are—how they use this product, and what it is—they don't often tell you in so many words—but what it is that actually motivates them to buy something or to interest them in something.[3]

Focus group interviewing is another approach that tends to generate useful ideas and appropriate words and phrases for use in developing copy.

Fact-finding should include a careful discussion of the advertising objectives. The objectives provide the point of departure for the creative process while, at the same time, constraining it. The creative team might properly challenge the constraints implied by the objectives, at least in the early stages of campaign development. In doing so they might open the way for worthwhile alternatives and provide their own input to formulating objectives. Some solutions to tough problems come only when the focus of the problem is broadened. Thus, the objective need not be viewed as a unilateral, rigid set of constraints, but rather as a flexible, dynamic guide that is the result of creativity as well as empirical research and managerial experience.

Fact finding should include a digestion and incubation time. The various facts need to be absorbed or "digested," and usually the best ideas emerge only after a period of incubation.

Idea generation, after the information has been digested, is the heart of the creative process. The key is to generate a large quantity of ideas—to avoid inhibiting the process. Evaluating a set of alternatives is a relatively trivial problem next to that of obtaining good alternatives to evaluate. It is somewhat ironic that in refining decision theory very sophisticated methods have been developed to choose among alternatives although we still have only the crudest notion of how to generate alternatives.

Osborn tells of a successful copywriter at BBDO who starts a job by clearing his mind and sitting down at a typewriter and simply writing everything that comes to mind.[4] He even includes silly, worthless phrases with the thought that they will block others if they are not included. In some cases, a piece of copy will be generated on the first try, but, more typically, hundreds of possible ideas will be created before several reasonable alternatives are generated.

There are certain questions that, when posed, can suggest ideas, as shown in Table 13-1. One of the most fertile is the suggestion to combine various concepts. There have been several systematic approaches proposed to aid the process. One such approach is termed HIT, or the heuristic ideation technique.[5] Several relevant dimensions of a problem area are identified. For a citrus drink we might consider the context in which it is used (snack, breakfast, or parties), the benefit it provides (nutrition, preparation ease, color), and the personalities that could endorse it (an athlete, a popular singer, a nutritionist). Then the total set of ideas is the set of all possible combinations of these concepts. Techniques similar to this one have been successful at stimulating new product ideas. One can readily see that products such as toaster waffles, breakfast milkshakes, canned whiskey sours, and aerosol hair sprays could have been conceived with such methods. In a similar vein, some agencies have developed computer-aided name generators. Various words or combinations of letters are systematically combined to provide alternative names for new products.

For some, idea generation comes easier in a group, where more information and associations are collectively available. The difficulty here is to overcome the inhibiting aspects of group behavior. One technique to encourage the free flow of ideas is *brainstorming*.[6] Developed by Osborn and used regularly at BBDO, it features a group of six to ten people who focus on a problem. The cardinal rule is that criticism is prohibited. All evaluation is withheld until later. The wilder the idea

Table 13-1. Questions That Spur Ideas for New and Improved Products

Put to other uses?	New ways to use as is? Other uses if modified?
Adapt?	What else is this like? What other ideas does this suggest? Does past offer parallel? What could I emulate?
Modify?	New twist? Changing meaning, color, motion, sound, odor, form, shape? Other changes?
Magnify?	What to add? More time? Greater frequency? Stronger? Higher? Longer? Thicker? Extra value? Plus ingredient? Duplicate? Multiply? Exaggerate?
Minify?	What to subtract? Smaller? Condensed? Miniature? Lower? Shorter? Lighter? Omit? Streamline? Split up? Understate?
Substitute?	Who else instead? What else instead? Other ingredients? Other material? Other process? Other power? Other place? Other approach? Other tone of voice?
Rearrange?	Interchange components? Other pattern? Other layout? Other sequence? Transpose cause and effect? Change pace? Change schedule?
Reverse?	Transpose positive and negative? How about opposites? Turn it backward? Turn it upside down? Reverse roles? Change shoes? Turn tables? Turn other cheek?
Combine?	How about a blend, an alloy, an assortment, an ensemble? Combine units? Combine purposes? Combine appeals? Combine ideas?

Source: Philip Kotler, *Marketing Management: Analysis, Planning and Control* (Englewood Cliffs, N.J.: Prentice-Hall, 1967), p. 247; adapted from Alex F. Osborn, *Applied Imagination,* 3rd rev. ed. (New York: Scribner's, 1963), pp. 286–287.

that survives, the better, for it may stimulate a new association that will trigger a more useful idea. The participants are encouraged to build on ideas that appear, combining and improving them. The atmosphere is positive. The objective is quantity. Osborn reported that one such session generated 144 ideas on how to sell blankets.

A related technique, called *synectics,* was developed by William J. J. Gordon.[7] It differs from brainstorming in that it does not focus on a clearly specified problem. Rather, a discussion is stimulated around a general idea that is related to the ultimate specific problem. Instead of being concerned with marketing a citrus beverage, the group might discuss drinking. When a variety of ideas is exposed, the leader starts directing the discussion toward the specific problem. The sessions tend to last longer than the 60- or 90-minute brainstorming sessions, based on a belief that fatigue tends to remove inhibitions.

John Keil,[8] in a book on creativity, argues that there are several myths about creativity and creative people, none of which are really supported by the facts. Keil's six myths of creative people are as follows:

1. Creative people are sophisticated and worldly. They are cultured, well read, and snobbish.
2. Creative people are more intelligent than others.
3. Creative people are disorganized.
4. Creative people are witty and seldom boring.
5. Creative people are more involved with liquor and drugs than others are.
6. Drugs and alcohol stimulate creative thinking.

Like the social stereotypes of any profession, Keil essentially cautions against such stereotyping and argues that creative people have a wide variety of habits, styles, and values. There are boring creative people, as well as witty ones. The incidence of alcoholism and drug abuse in this profession appears no greater than in others, such as law or medicine.

The creative process culminates in the specific activities of writing copy, illustrating, and layout. Each of these activities is briefly described in the next sections.

Copywriting

Copywriting, illustrating, and layout are different activities associated with the creative stage of advertising development and are usually done by different people who specialize in one or the other. Copywriting in print is the activity of actually putting words to paper, particularly those contained in the main body of the text (the main arguments and appeals used), but also including attendant by-lines and headlines. In broadcast, the copywriter is in effect a ''script'' writer who develops the scenario or script to be used in a radio or television medium. Illustrating is usually the work of an artist in the case of television. Layout generally refers to the activity of bringing all the pieces together and, as will be seen, differs in the case of print and broadcast.

John Caples is a member of the Advertising Hall of Fame. He retired in 1981 after 54 years at Batten, Barton, Durstine & Osborn, the last 40 years as vice-president. Caples was one of the giants contributing to the success of BBDO. In 1984, BBDO International was the sixth largest agency with worldwide billings of $2,275,000,000. A classic direct-mail advertisement created by Caples is shown in Figure 13-2. Caples states that the best ads are "written from the heart." "Write down every idea that comes into your head—every selling phrase, every key word. Write down the good ideas and the wild ideas. Don't try to edit your ideas at the start. Don't put a brake on your imagination."[9] In his book, he develops a checklist of important guidelines for copywriting:

1. Cash in on your personal experience.
2. Organize your experience.
3. Write from the heart.
4. Learn from the experience of others.
5. Talk with the manufacturer.
6. Study the product.
7. Review previous advertising for the product.
8. Study competitors' ads.
9. Study testimonials from customers.
10. Solve the prospect's problem.
11. Put your subconscious mind to work.
12. "Ring the changes" on a successful idea.

Following these rules is good advice in creating copy. The idea of "ring the changes" is particularly useful and interesting. Once a successful idea has been found, it should be used repeatedly with variations on the central theme. For example, an insurance company found that ads featuring retirement annuities brought the most coupon replies. So all the ad headlines featured retirement. However, the appearance of the ads was varied by using different illustrations such as: Man fishing . . . a couple sitting on the beach under a palm tree . . . an elderly couple embarking on a cruise ship. As Caples says:

> Once you have found a winning sales idea, don't change it. Your client may tire of it after a year or two. He sees all the ads from layout stage to proof stage to publication stage. Explain to him that when he is tired of the campaign, it is just beginning to take hold of the public.[10]

Many of the insights and rules outlined in the preceding section on the creative process apply to copywriting and will not be repeated here. Copywriting obviously becomes more important in the case of long copy, as illustrated in the Bell Telephone advertisement (Figure 13-3), and less important in the case where few words are included.

Figure 13-2.   **A famous direct-mail advertisement of John Caples**

"Can he really play?" a girl whispered.
"Heavens no!" Arthur exclaimed. "He
never played a note in his life."

They Laughed When I Sat Down
At the Piano
But When I Started to Play!~

ARTHUR had just played "The Rosary." The room rang with applause. I decided that this would be a dramatic moment for me to make my debut. To the amazement of all my friends, I strode confidently over to the piano and sat down.

"Jack is up to his old tricks," somebody chuckled. The crowd laughed. They were all certain that I couldn't play a single note.

"Can he really play?" I heard a girl whisper to Arthur.

"Heavens, no!" Arthur exclaimed. "He never played a note in all his life. . . But just you watch him. This is going to be good."

I decided to make the most of the situation. With mock dignity I drew out a silk handkerchief and lightly dusted off the piano keys. Then I rose and gave the revolving piano stool a quarter of a turn, just as I had seen an imitator of Paderewski do in a vaudeville sketch.

"What do you think of it!" Arthur called a voice from the rear.

"We're in favor of it!" came back the answer, and the crowd rocked with laughter.

Then I Started to Play

Instantly a tense silence fell on the guests. The laughter died on their lips as if by magic. I played through the first few bars of Beethoven's immortal Moonlight Sonata. I heard gasps of amazement. My friends sat breathless—spellbound!

I played on and as I played I forgot the people around me. I forgot the hour, the place, the breathless listeners. The little world I lived in seemed to fade—seemed to grow dim—unreal. Only the music was real. Only the music and visions it brought me. Visions as beautiful and as changing as the wind blown clouds and drifting moonlight that long ago inspired the master composer. It seemed as if the master

musician himself were speaking to me—speaking through the medium of music—not in words but in chords. Not in sentences but in exquisite melodies!

A Complete Triumph!

As the last notes of the Moonlight Sonata died away, the room resounded with a sudden roar of applause. I found myself surrounded by excited faces. How my friends carried on! Men shook my hand—wildly congratulated me—pounded me on the back in their enthusiasm! Everybody was exclaiming with delight—plying me with rapid questions. . . . "Jack! Why didn't you tell us you could play like that?". . . "Where did you learn?"—"How long have you studied?"—"Who was your teacher?"

"I have never even seen my teacher," I replied. "And just a short while ago I couldn't play a note.",

"Quit your kidding," laughed Arthur, himself an accomplished pianist. "You've been studying for years. I can tell."

"I have been studying only a short while," I insisted. "I decided to keep it a secret so that I could surprise all you folks."

Then I told them the whole story.

"Have you ever heard of the U. S. School of Music?" I asked.

A few of my friends nodded. "That's a correspondence school, isn't it?" they exclaimed.

"Exactly," I replied. "They have a new simplified method that can teach you to play any instrument by mail in just a few months."

How I Learned to Play Without a Teacher

And then I explained how for years I had longed to play the piano.

"A few months ago," I continued, "I saw an interesting ad for the U. S. School of Music—a new method of learning to play which only cost a few cents a day! The ad told how a woman had mastered the piano in her spare time at home—and *without a teacher!* Best of all, the wonderful new method she used, required no laborious scales—no heartless exercises—no tiresome practising. It sounded so convincing that I filled out the coupon requesting the Free Demonstration Lesson.

"The free book arrived promptly and I started in that very night to study the Demonstration Lesson. I was amazed to see how easy it was to play this new way. Then I sent for the course.

"When the course arrived I found it was just as the ad said — as easy as A.B.C! And, as

the lessons continued they got easier and easier. Before I knew it I was playing all the pieces I liked best. Nothing stopped me. I could play ballads or classical numbers or jazz, all with equal ease! And I never did have any special talent for music!"

Play Any Instrument

You too, can now *teach yourself* to be an accomplished musician—right at home—in half the usual time. You can't go wrong with this simple new method which has already shown 350,000 people how to play their favorite instruments. Forget that old-fashioned idea that you need special "talent." Just read the list of instruments in the panel, decide which one you want to play and the U. S. School will do the rest. And bear in mind no matter which instrument you choose, the cost in each case will be the same—just a few cents a day. No matter whether you are a mere beginner or already a good performer, you will be interested in learning about this new and wonderful method.

Send for Our Free Booklet and Demonstration Lesson

Thousands of successful students never dreamed they possessed musical ability until it was revealed to them by a remarkable "Musical Ability Test" which we send entirely without cost with our interesting free booklet.

If you are in earnest about wanting to play your favorite instrument—if you really want to gain happiness and increase your popularity—send at once for the free booklet and Demonstration Lesson. No cost — no obligation. Right now we are making a Special offer for a limited number of new students. Sign and send the convenient coupon now — before it's too late to gain the benefits of this offer. Instruments supplied when needed, cash or credit. U. S. School of Music, 1031 Brunswick Bldg., New York City.

Pick Your Instrument

Piano	'Cello
Organ	Harmony and
Violin	Composition
Drums and	Sight Singing
Traps	Ukulele
Banjo	Guitar
Tenor	Hawaiian
Banjo	Steel Guitar
Mandolin	Harp
Clarinet	Cornet
Flute	Piccolo
Saxophone	Trombone
Voice and Speech Culture	
Automatic Finger Control	
Piano Accordion	

U. S. School of Music,
1031 Brunswick Bldg., New York City.

Please send me your free book, "Music Lessons in Your Own Home", with introduction by Dr. Frank Crane, Demonstration Lesson and particulars of your Special Offer. I am interested in the following course:

....

Have you above instrument?.....................

Name...
(Please write plainly)

Address......................................

City........................... State...........

Source: Advertising Age, August 1, 1983, p. M50.

Figure 13-3.   Long copy used in a Bell System advertisement

Bell helping you to manage your business better #2

DON'T TURN YOUR BACK ON WATS BECAUSE YOU THINK IT'S ONLY FOR THE BIGGIES.

If you think WATS lines are only for the big boys, it's time to take another look. Because you don't have to be one of the Fortune 500 to make WATS a profitable addition to your business. If you deal with out-of-town customers, WATS could be for you.

WATS works because you can choose a Long Distance calling area as close as your own state and those that adjoin it. And as your business area grows, you can add contiguous WATS calling areas to coincide with the locations of your customers and sources.

What's WATS

WATS stands for Wide Area Telecommunications Service. It's a way to tailor Long Distance to your special needs. You buy a specific area, and a specific number of hours, at a monthly fee. You can use those hours whenever you choose. Within that area, and within those hours, you make as many Long Distance calls as you wish.

This means you can limit your Long Distance costs without limiting your Long Distance calls.

Why WATS

Imagine the ways a WATS line can power-pack your business effort. WATS helps you beef up business to those tempting smaller accounts that might otherwise be too far out of the way. Sell 'em by phone, and save costly travel expenses!

How about collecting overdue accounts? Use WATS to improve your cash flow and operating expense positions. Unlimited phone contact also helps you avoid the high costs of inventory outages, and it's a boon to your customer service efforts.

Can WATS help your business? You bet it can!

Choose your area of coverage

It's simple. If your company's market takes in the region surrounding your home state, make that your

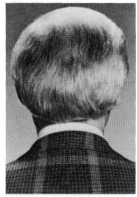

WATS calling area. Is your market more extensive? Then add additional, contiguous calling areas until your market coverage is complete.

Are you trying to expand your market? Don't plod blindly into that field. Make phone forays first. We can add adjoining regions into your WATS calling area any time, helping you to eliminate a lot of expense in a new business drive.

The big boys might need a calling area that includes all fifty states. You can choose the states that suit your business best!

Choose the time volume you need

You can also choose *when* to call!

If your needs are small, select our WATS 10 (Measured Time) plan: up to 10 hours of unlimited calling per month. Want more? Then WATS 240 (Full Business Day) is for you: up to 240 hours of unlimited calling per month. Need overtime? You've got it! And it's billed at a lower rate than the monthly charge.

Anything else? There's the usual one-time installation charge.

And that's the whole ball of wax.

30-day trial

Want to test the WATS waters before you jump? Give WATS a 30-day try. Buy a month of WATS, and see for yourself just how much it will help your business. All types of businesses use WATS to solve all types of business problems. Let a WATS line help you!

Here's more help

In addition to WATS, Bell has all these programs to help you manage your business better.

#1 800 Service. Generate direct response leads using the toll-free 800 number. Improve service, speed orders to wholesalers, retailers. Expand market area, answer consumer questions, conduct product research, improve company image.

#3 Remote Call Forwarding (RCF). Customers dial a local number, reach you in a distant city. You have a local "presence" without the expense of a local office. Lets you open new markets, test out those new markets and give better service.

#4 Selling Smaller Accounts. Instead of visiting distant accounts, sell by Long Distance. Reduce the cost of making the sale. Sell more accounts. Reach customers at the point where lowered inventory prompts them to buy.

#5 Improving Credit Management. It's the key to cash flow—programs that expand your market, develop customers, build profits. Helps you check the customer's ability to pay, calculate marginal risk, and collect overdue accounts.

#6 Opening New Accounts. A tested, practical way to do it by Long Distance. Total program covers everything from building a list and screening a prospect's interest to closing the sale.

Courtesy of AT&T Corporation.

Illustrating

The activity of illustrating is of crucial importance for many consumer nondurable products where pictures or photographs are used to convey a central idea, and there is little or no need for long explanations or a recitation of copy points. Normally, an artist will be involved in selecting materials, or will actually draw original pictures for the advertising. Artwork is equally if not more important than writing copy, particularly where the goals of the advertising are attention getting or building awareness. As in writing copy, pictorial materials should be developed that are tied into the self-interest and understanding of the audience, are relevant to the product and copy theme, and accurate and plausible in the context of the selling message. Another popular rule is to include pictures of at least some or all of the product.

Illustrating also involves decisions as to what "identification marks" to include. These fall into one of three categories: company or trade name, brand name, and trademarks. In family-branding strategy, the company name, such as Del Monte or Levi Strauss, will obviously play a major role. In other cases, the company name may not even be mentioned or deemphasized, as in many of the detergent brand advertisements of Proctor & Gamble. The decision regarding brand name will probably have been made prior to actual copywriting, but it may not. A great deal of time and research effort may be required to arrive at the right brand name. Trademarks, service marks, and certification marks like the *Good Housekeeping* seal of approval must also be considered for inclusion in the visual materials. Often a caricature or identifying symbol such as the Pillsbury doughboy, the Green Giant, or Mr. Peanut will be included, and decisions as to how they will be positioned will be required. The visual content, color, artwork, and identification mark decisions are a crucial aspect of print advertising, and choices will heavily determine the effectiveness of the final result.

The United States Trademark Association lists the following as desirable characteristics of a trademark: brevity, easy to remember, easily readable and speakable, easily adapted to any media, no unpleasant connotations, suitable for export, lends itself to pictorialization, and subtlety.

Guest provided one of the few studies that examined the differential effect of color.[11] He asked respondents to evaluate companies after being exposed to advertisements. Half the respondents saw a color version of the advertisements and the other half saw a black-and-white version. The ones in color consistently did better across advertisements and years (the study was replicated three times), but the differences were small and usually not statistically significant. Guest concludes that "these studies do not support the contention that companies sponsoring colored advertisements receive a bonus of greater prestige as a consequence of color only."[12] It seems clear that more research is needed in this area, particularly research that would use multiple-criterion measures and would carefully control for the nature of the appeal and for the degree to which surrounding advertisements were also in color.

Many of the same kinds of decisions must be made with respect to the video portion of a television commercial. Here, however, the emphasis is on action and the dynamics of each scene. The director must take into account how one scene will blend into the next, how video materials will serve to enhance and reinforce the audio message, which will be mainly attention getters, and which will carry the copy points, and so on. The task is further complicated in television by the addition of music or sound effects other than voice.

Layout

The layout activity involves bringing all the pieces together before the advertising is sent out for production. A layout can be in relatively unfinished form, a *preliminary* layout, or can be a very detailed specification of all aspects of the production requirements, a *comprehensive* layout. The decision as to how detailed the layout is to be will rest on the agency's trust in the supplier firms. Many agencies choose to send on only preliminary layouts to allow room for a significant amount of creativity in the production process.

Layout involves decisions as to how the various components of headline, illustration, copy, and identification marks are to be arranged and positioned on the page. The size of the advertisement will obviously have an effect on this decision. There are five considerations to take into account in developing print layout:

1. *Balance:* the arrangement of elements to achieve a pleasing distribution or visual impression.
2. *Contrast:* using different sizes, shapes, densities, and colors to enhance attention value and readability.
3. *Proportion:* the relation of objects to the background in which they appear and to each other.
4. *Gaze-motion:* the headline, illustration, copy, and identification marks in that order will usually provide the most logical sequence for gaze-motion (in some cases, however, it may be useful to alter this typical pattern).
5. *Unity:* the qualities of balance, contrast, proportion, and gaze-motion should be combined to develop unity of thought, appearance, and design in the layout. Coupons, for example, should not be placed at the beginning of an advertisement unless the copy theme is built around the idea of clipping the coupon. Unity is best achieved by keeping the layout simple and uncluttered and to ease the reader's task in comprehending the advertisement. Simplicity can be carried forward in many instances by judicious use of "white space" in which most of a large part of the advertisement shows nothing.

Concerning layout, Stephen Baker, an art director, draws a distinction between "arranging elements on a page" and "visualizing an idea." He states:

The former is a designer's (or layout man's) feat; his innate sense of composition, balance, color is brought fully into play. On the other hand, presenting the clearest visual interpretation requires a strong desire to communicate with the audience, a flair for the dramatic, the ability to think in pictorial terms (usually referred to as "visual sense") and, probably most significant, a firm understanding of the advertiser's goal.[13]

The rules of balance, contrast, proportion, gaze-motion, and unity should be considered in a good layout.

The layout of a television commercial is the storyboard. Figure 13-4 shows an example of a storyboard of the finished commercial for Union Oil. Here, again, it can be generated in a relatively primitive form, in which only artist sketches and suggestive copy are included, or in a more comprehensive form that details more precisely what actors are to say, how scenes will blend in, and the precise location of identification marks, background music, special effects, and so on.

Client Approval and Supplier Selection

Following the creation of the layout, the creative director and account executive usually get client approval of the advertising prior to production. There is always the danger at this point that the client will evaluate it subjectively and get involved in the creative process. When that happens, the result is usually a creative effort that is compromised. Rather, the focus of discussion should be on the advertising objectives and the relationship of the proposed copy to those objectives. The client could, properly, discuss copy testing that has been considered or planned to demonstrate that the advertising will be effective in achieving those objectives.

Suppliers (typographers, engravers, and printers in the case of print and production houses, sound studios and many others in the case of broadcast) must be selected at this stage. In print, it is usual for an agency to have a group of suppliers that it has come to know and trust and for which print production activities are carried out. In broadcast, particularly television, it is more usual to "put the production out to bid." Often, this involves obtaining bids from three different production studios who will use the storyboard as a basis for bidding. Television commercials in this sense are like other supplies the corporation buys, and getting them produced is treated as a bidding process in much the same way.

PRODUCTION STAGE

Production of advertising generally involves a great number of external outside supplier firms and individuals. Although we have not stressed this component of the overall advertising system presented in Chapter 1, it is indeed interesting and represents a "fifth" level or institution that depends heavily on advertising. Print advertising production differs in significant respects from broadcast production, and we have stressed this fact in the Figure 13-1 model. In print, firms specialized in type and typesetting called typographers will be involved. Others specialized in graphic materials, engravers, may be necessary. Some large printers include these

Figure 13-4. **Example of a completed storyboard for a Union Oil commercial**

LEO BURNETT COMPANY, INC. UNION 76 DIVISION
AS FILMED AND RECORDED (4/80) "Junk Trunk" :30 UOCV3670

1. NICK: Whatcha doin', Jake?

2. JAKE: I'm going to check the air in my spare, Nick.

3. Y'know, proper tire inflation helps conserve gas.

4. NICK: Jake, for you conservation should start right here. (Indicating trunk)

5. JAKE: Huh?

6. NICK: Get the junk outa your trunk!

7. JAKE: Junk? NICK: Sure, you're carryin' around all this extra weight.

8. Makes your engine work harder... cuts down the gas mileage.

9. GUY: Ok Nick. I'll get rid of this junk. In fact...

10. ...how'd you like to buy...

11. ...my old exercise set?

12. NICK: Oh sure.

13. SONG: Go with the spirit...

14. NICK: Oooooooo! Murph!!

15. SONG:...the Spirit of 76.

Courtesy of Union Oil Company.

services as part of their offerings. The choice of whether to use specialists or one large printer is another decision facing the creative team.

Concerning broadcast, many other kinds of specialists are needed. These can include a producer, director, set designer, film editor, actors and actresses, composers, musicians, talent scouts, casting directors, music arrangers, camera crews, video and audio equipment supply companies, and many others. Many of these people freelance, and the process of producing a television commercial may require considerable effort in bringing a team together. Often production is channeled through a production house that will contain a sound studio and most of what is necessary to get the job done.

Production is a process that takes a considerable amount of time; from 6 to 8 weeks can be involved. In what follows, we provide a brief sketch of the major activities involved in print and broadcast production. The advertising manager should not hope to become an expert in the graphic arts, but decision making can be enhanced once the basics are known.

Print Production

The most important components of print production deal with the art and science of typography and engraving. Each is a fast-evolving field that has been affected greatly in recent years by computerization.

Typography is done by a specialist in type and typesetting. What the advertiser needs to know is that there are thousands of different type styles and forms from which choices must be made for a specific print advertisement and many ways of composing type. Typography is a complex field in itself that takes significant skill and experience to master. It should be appreciated that there is a range of alternatives from which to choose, and the creative director must be prepared to question and oversee those choices. Figure 13-5 gives some valuable lessons on typography from an article by David Ogilvy.

The second major activity in producing a print advertisement is *engraving*. Engraving basically deals with the generation and reproduction of pictures, photographs, and the visual elements of the advertisement. Photoengraving is the process using photography to create a printing surface. Through the photoengraving process, artwork (line charts, drawings, photographs) and paste-up of type can be transferred to a negative photochemically, and the image on the negative transferred to a metal plate for printing. Photoengraving is most commonly used to reproduce artwork, but is also used to reproduce combinations of illustration and type.

Actual printing of the advertisement involves yet another process and more alternatives. Printing can be done by letterpress, gravure, lithography, or silk screening. The first three are processes associated with basic ways of photoengraving. In each case, some type of plate or ''mat'' is developed from which copies are run.

Figure 13-5.   **Some principles of typography**

Typography—"the eye is a creature of habit"

Good typography *helps* people read your copy, while bad typography prevents them from doing so.

Advertising agencies usually set their headlines in capital letters. This is a mistake. Professor Tinker of Stanford has established that capitals retard reading. They have no ascenders or descenders to help you recognize words, and tend to be read *letter by letter*.

The eye is a creature of habit. People are accustomed to reading books, magazines and newspapers in *lower case*.

Another way to make headlines hard to read is to superimpose them on your illustration.

Another mistake is to put a period at the end of headlines. Periods are also called full stops, because they stop the reader dead in his tracks. You will find no full stops at the end of headlines in newspapers.

Yet another common mistake is to set copy in a measure too wide or too narrow to be legible. People are accustomed to reading newspapers, which are set about 40 characters wide.

Which typefaces are easiest to read? Those that people are *accustomed* to reading, like the Century family, Caslon, Baskerville and Jenson. The more outlandish the typeface, the harder it is to read. The drama belongs in what you say, not in the typeface.

Sanserif faces like this are particularly difficult to read. Says John Updike, "Serifs exist for a purpose. They help the eye to pick up the shape of the letter. Piquant in little amounts, sanserif in page-size sheets repels readership as wax paper repels water; it has a sleazy, cloudy look."

Some art directors use copy as the raw material for designing queer shapes, thus making it illegible.

In a recent issue of a magazine I found 47 ads with the copy set in *reverse*—white type on a black background. It is almost impossible to read.

If you have to set *very long* copy, there are some typographical devices that increase its readership:

1. A subhead of two lines, between your headline and your body copy, heightens the reader's appetite for the feast to come.

2. If you start your body copy with a drop-initial, you increase readership by an average of 13 percent.

3. Limit your opening paragraph to a maximum of 11 words.

4. After two or three inches of copy, insert a crosshead, and thereafter throughout. Cross-heads keep the reader marching forward. Make some of them interrogative, to excite curiosity in the next run of copy.

5. When I was a boy, it was common practice to *square up* paragraphs. It is now known that widows—short lines—increase readership.

6. Set key paragraphs in bold face or italic.

7. Help the reader into your paragraphs with arrowheads, bullets, asterisks and marginal marks.

8. If you have a lot of unrelated facts to recite, don't use cumbersome connectives. Simply *number* them—as I am doing here.

Figure 13.5. (Cont.)

9. What size type should you use?

This is 5-point, and too small to read.

This is 14-point, and too big.
This is 11-point, and about right.

10. If you use leading (line-spacing) between paragraphs, you increase readership by an average of 12 percent.

You may think that I exaggerate the importance of good typography. You may ask if I have ever heard a housewife say that she bought a new detergent because the ad was set in Caslon. No. But do you think an ad can sell if nobody can read it? You can't save souls in an empty church.

As Mies van der Rohe said of architecture, "God is in the details."

Source: Adapted from "Ogilvy on Advertising, Wanted: A Renaissance in Print Advertising," *"Advertising Age,* August 1, 1983, p. M4ff. See also the book, *Ogilvy on Advertising* (New York: Crown Publishers, 1983), by the same author.

Broadcast Production

In explaining the basic elements of broadcast production, we focus on television commercial production. Many of the elements of radio commercial production are analogous to the audio portion of television commercials and involve audiotapes rather than videotapes or films. Much radio commercial production is very uncomplicated, consisting of "live commercials" in which written copy is simply provided to a disc jockey or news commentator who reads the copy at the appropriate time slot (with appropriate emphasis, voice delivery, and so on).

Producing one television commercial can, on the other hand, involve 100 or more people, and cost $50,000 or more. As suggested earlier, it begins with one person—the copywriter—but can involve significant creative inputs at the production stage as well. The two major tasks in television commercial production are filming and editing.

Filming generally is based on a storyboard and a list of specifications supplied by the advertising agency; a production house is the usual type of company involved in television commercial production. These are centered in large metropolitan areas such as New York and Los Angeles, and many specialize in the business of producing television commercials.

Filming begins after all the necessary ingredients have been brought together. A director and/or producer will be assigned. A talent scout may be hired to interface with professional actors or actresses to be included in the commercial. A composer may be hired to develop an original score and musicians and singers to carry it out. The inclusion of a "jingle" in the commercial invariably leads to finding and using this type of talent.

The filming may be done in a fixed location studio. Often, however, it is necessary to move people and equipment to a location site where particular background scenes are called for—a forest, seaside cliffs, and so on. Filming is done in pieces and parts and later put together and edited at the editing stage. The Green Giant commercial, for example, was made by building a Styrofoam model of a "valley," superimposing animated characters, and then filming the feet and legs of a male model (the giant) standing over the whole thing.

In sum, producing a filmed (or videotaped) television commercial is a major complicated process. Even before filming starts, the producer using the storyboard guide and production notes (announcer preference, set sketches, ideas for props, musical requirements, and so on) gets involved in many activities. These include casting sessions to select the actors and/or announcer, set design sessions to work out exactly how the background will look, location discussions or trips to decide where the commercial will be shot, prop sessions to decide on various articles to be used, and arranging shooting schedules, recording sessions, and completion dates. All this must be done before filming begins. Filming of individual scenes is usually not done in the sequence in which they appear in the final commercial. Also visual and sound tracks are usually not recorded at the same time.

Editing is required because much more footage is generated than is finally used. Several different camera angles will be shot, for example, to give the director some choice of the best possible ones to use. After the shooting begins, the film is quickly developed, often overnight, to provide rushes or dailies, which are hurried prints of inferior quality. These are used by the director to screen the preceding day's work, to select the best shots, and to decide whether further retakes are necessary before the set is torn down and the cast disbanded.

After the sound track is completed and the picture cut and edited, the two are combined into an answer print. There are usually several sound tracks, including the voice and music tracks, and often special sound effects tracks. A sound cutter "lays in" these tracks so they can be mixed. An audio engineer is then brought in to weave the various tracks together. An equally complicated series of editing operations takes place on the picture part of the track. When complete, it is brought together with the master sound track to produce the answer print. The whole process from storyboard to answer print usually takes 7 to 8 weeks. The answer print is used primarily to get agency and client approval. From it an appropriate number of release prints are generated and shipped to the networks and/or individual stations for broadcast. The release print is what is commonly referred to as the finished commercial. It is not uncommon to produce it in several versions, such as 10 seconds, 30 seconds, or 60 seconds, depending upon the media scheduling decisions. It is the release prints that are shipped to the broadcast media and aired.

The following article discusses the development of a new television commercial for American Express. The issues and complexities of television commercial production are nicely illustrated in this story. Note the importance given to minute details such as what the actor wears, the subleties required in the father-son relationship, the 43 takes plus "dozens without sound" and the great stakes involved.

Behind the Scenes
at an American Express Commercial*

The marketing executives from American Express Co. are unhappy. After months of research, prepreproduction meetings, preproduction meetings, casting sessions, budget audits, and other preparations for this moment, they arrive on location for filming of their television commercial—only to find the leading man wearing the wrong jacket.

In a big national ad campaign, little things like this count. "We believe that advertising is important enough that you want to get it right," says Diane Shaib, vice-president for consumer marketing at American Express. For this commercial, getting it right is especially urgent: Both the client and its agency, Ogilvy & Mather, have a lot riding on the outcome. American Express is eager to get more men in their 20s and 30s to sign up for its plastic charge card. Ogilvy needs to come up with a successful commercial after the failure of a recent string of American Express ads that the client pulled off the air. Both nervously await reaction to the 30-second ad, which cost about $100,000 and is now hitting the national airwaves.

Wardrobe Chaos.   Just days before the filming, the American Express marketers discuss the wardrobe with the agency. What will look more universal, they wonder—a blue blazer or a corduroy jacket? They are still pondering the question and leaning toward the blazer when they walk onto the set and find the actor wearing a dark corduroy jacket. Some of the scenes have already been shot, and the budget clock is ticking. Amid the controlled chaos of a commercial shoot, exasperation is rising behind polite smiles, urgent conflabulations are held in corners, and higher authorities are summoned.

For more than 10 years, American Express has been running its "Do you know me?" commercials, aimed at its traditional market: successful, older businessmen. Three years ago, however, AmEx decided to pursue the large number of younger women entering the work force and launched its "Interesting Lives" series. The first commercial, its "New Card" spot, showed a young woman taking her husband out to dinner to celebrate the arrival of her card, and it scored big. Women applied in droves. By last year, they held 27% of all AmEx green cards, up from 10% in the 1970s. The spot won awards and lavish praise for showing a strong, successful woman.

While that reaction startled American Express, subsequent audience research surprised the company even more. Instead of offending young men by showing a woman taking a man out to dinner, the commercial actually attracted them. "We're talking about three years ago—and markets outside of New York," says Shaib. "That's a bit shocking."

That's also when the trouble started. The company and its agency decided to extend the "Interesting Lives" campaign to attract young men by intention rather

* Mark N. Vamos. Reprinted from the May 20, 1985 issue of *Business Week* by special permission, © 1985 by McGraw-Hill, Inc.

than by accident—in effect, to turn it into an all-purpose yuppie campaign. "The mission is to tweak their awareness of the card's appropriateness for them," says Shaib. Over the next three years, the company shot six new ads, but the only things they seemed to tweak were noses. One by one, as audience reaction arrived, AmEx pulled the ads. Two were so troublesome that they never even made it past the test-marketing stage. One showed a woman paying for dinner on a first date, the other a husband accompanying his wife on her business trip. Audience reactions included words such as "abrasive" and "castrating"—not exactly the message American Express wanted to convey. "It's very difficult these days to do ads with men and women as equals," sighs Kathleen O'Shaughnessy, a manager of marketing research at AmEx.

Early this year, the client and the agency agreed to try again, and Ogilvy wrote five new commercials. This time, however, AmEx decided to test the spots in rough form before any were produced, something it had not done before. Each ad was translated into color sketches that were transferred onto slides. Actors recorded the accompanying dialogue. With the roughs in hand, AmEx and Ogilvy headed into the field.

One-way Mirror. At 8 o'clock one evening in late February, nine men and a moderator sit around a gray conference table in midtown Manhattan. They are the targets of the campaign—young men who are eligible for an American Express card but haven't applied. Each will receive $50 for participating in this focus group, the last of 11 such sessions held nationwide. Observing them from a darkened room behind a one-way mirror are 11 staffers from AmEx and Ogilvy, including account managers, researchers, and copywriters. Surprisingly, in a commercial aimed at men, all the observers are women.

Eugene Shore, a psychologist and president of Business Information Analysis Corp., a Pennsylvania research firm, shows the five rough commercials. He asks the focus group for comments and suggestions after each. Some win raves, others are panned. After one rough is shown, someone says, "If I saw this on TV, I'd just say, 'Boy, this is another one of those dumb commercials that make no sense.' "

Working with comments like these, the marketers have already narrowed the choice to two or three strong candidates, one of which is known as "Young Lawyer." It opens with father and son seated at a restaurant table. The dialogue concerns the son's career and how disappointed the father was when he didn't join the family law firm. But now that the son is "Mr. District Attorney," the father is proud of him. The son objects, saying he's only "an assistant to an assistant." He places his American Express card on the tray that the waiter puts on the table with the check. The father laughs, saying: "The pay must be getting better over at City Hall."

The lights come up, and Shore asks for reactions. "I feel this is pointed at the business community, because you have to be successful to have this card," says Stephen, an accountant. Tim, who works for a menswear designer, disagrees: "He says he's an assistant to an assistant. So maybe I can qualify." The women behind the mirror smile at this response. The line is a crucial one. To attract new cardholders, the commercial must convey accessibility—but not too much. The American Express card is prestige plastic. The ad can't make it seem as easy to get as MasterCard or Visa, which AmEx staffers contemptuously refer to as "shoppers' cards." As O'Shaughnessy, the market researcher, later puts it, "It's very difficult to communicate eligibility and at the same time maintain prestige. We're sort of talking out of both sides of our mouth."

'Too Northeast'.   Over the next few weeks, Ogilvy staffers begin scouting locations for "Young Lawyer." They also hunt for a director with a flair for filming realistic dialogue. "This ad lives and dies on being able to cast two people who have believable rapport," says Ann Curry Marcato, the Ogilvy vice-president responsible for producing the spot. And, Shore warns at the session, the father and son risk "coming across as WASP, bank-club, Harvard."

It is late March when the account-management team from Ogilvy and two executives from American Express hold a preproduction meeting to go over the casting, wardrobe, location, and production schedule. That's when the problem of the corduroy jacket first surfaces. The feedback we've been getting from the research is that the Midwest and West Coast don't respond because they read it as too Northeast," says K. Shelly Porges, director of special markets at AmEx. "Can we do something more cross-country?" Ogilvy's Marcato replies that the agency is aware of the problem, and the discussion moves to other topics.

Ed Bianchi, Marcato's choice for director, who once shot a Dr. Pepper extravaganza set on a giant pinball machine, outlines his notion of how the commercial should unfold. He plans to open with a wide shot, showing diners and waiters, and then cut to a close-up of the father and son. "We pick them out through the crowd so you really have the feeling of eavesdropping on them," he says.

Porges objects to opening with a wide shot crowded with 14 extras. "What makes this an interesting life, anyway? The quality of a relationship. What will a long shot add to that?" she asks. Paul Pracilio, a vice-president and associate creative director at Ogilvy, replies: "We have 30 seconds to reach out of that tube and grab someone by the necktie. By cutting in to see them, it's a damn sight more exciting piece of film."

Happy Medium.   The discussion moves to the waiter who will bring the check. Since the ad must make the card seem upscale but still accessible, the waiter can't look as if he works at too ritzy a restaurant. "It must be above Brew Burger but below the 21 Club," says Porges. Director Bianchi suggests that the waiter appear early in the commercial, as the son is saying he's only an assistant to an assistant district attorney. "The action of the waiter bringing the check is a subtle hint of what this commercial is going to be about," he says. Porges objects again. "Because of the 'assistant to an assistant' line, the focus groups said, 'Gee, maybe I could get this card,' " she says. "Getting that part garbled would be disastrous to us."

Three days later, the film crew has converted Jerry's Restaurant in Manhattan into a madhouse. The sidewalk is a jumble of cables, reflecting panels, and tripods. In the dining room, 25 crew members mill about, carrying equipment and shouting. The father-and-son team sits at a table, repeating their lines. The entire commercial will be reshot from several angles, Bianchi explains, to give the editor the option of cutting from one perspective to another.

Representatives from Ogilvy and AmEx are at the back of the room, watching and making suggestions. Still more staffers are in another room, watching a video monitor. Director Bianchi calls for take after take. Frequently, a telephone rings or a bus rumbles past on 23rd Street, ruining the shot. For most of the takes, Bianchi sits next to the camera, his face pressed against the lens so he can see what it is seeing, and grins at the actors.

After 43 takes involving dialogue—and dozens more without sound—Bianchi is satisfied. But suddenly, he insists on one more close-up of the son pulling the charge card from his wallet. The executives from Ogilvy and American Express are crowded around a video monitor, staring intently as the image of the wallet fills the screen. The son's hand reaches over, pulls out the card, and pauses. It's a Visa card. Everyone laughs and goes home.

Tense Tryout.   A week later, the preliminary version of the commercial is ready. A dozen client and agency people sit in red bucket chairs in an eighth-floor screening room at Ogilvy & Mather's New York office. Tension is in the air—not least because, after all the discussion of wide shots and extras, those scenes wound up on the cutting-room floor. "We were thrilled to find so much of the personality of the son and father coming through," Marcato explains as she introduces the commercial. "We thought that it would be strongest to stay up tight." The commercial is run several times. The ad seems a bit choppy, jumping from close-ups of the son to the father to the check to the wallet and, finally, to the card. The Ogilvy team waits for a reaction.

"I think you've captured them just as I always envisioned them," says Shaib, the AmEx marketing vice-president. "But because of the number of cuts back and forth, I never feel like I'm intimate with them." She also points out that, with all the close-ups, the commercial never shows the father and son together. After some discussion, the Ogilvy representatives agree to reedit the commercial to include the wide shot that American Express had initially argued against.

AmEx executives say they are pleased with the final version, which includes the wide shot. All the research was worthwhile, they say, because it helped them avoid some pitfalls, such as making the father too stern or the son too wimpy. The father's line about his son's pay getting better, for example, was ultimately given to the son because some viewers saw it as a subtle put-down. Now, the marketers say, the father is distinguished but warm, and the son is the kind of likable but independent character with whom the target market can identify.

The ad, which first appeared on May 6, will run for six to eight weeks, after which American Express will assess its impact. The company thinks it has a winner, but there's one little thing that still bothers it a bit: The son is wearing a corduroy jacket.

TYPES OF TELEVISION COMMERCIALS

Audio and visual elements can be combined to produce several types of television commercials, just as a story can be told in many different ways. Emphasis can be placed on the story itself, the problem to be solved, the central character such as in a testimonial, or on special human emotions or storytelling techniques such as satire, humor, fantasy, and so on. Book and Cary[14] provide a useful classification of the possible alternatives, based on the point of emphasis, focus, or style adopted. Each is referred to as a particular kind of commercial structure to emphasize that a commercial is other than an unrelated jumble of ideas and techniques. The 13 types of structure identified by them follow:

1. *Story line:* a commercial that tells a story; a clear, step-by-step unfolding of a message that has a definite beginning, middle, and end.

2. *Problem-solution:* presents the viewer with a problem to be solved and the sponsor's product as the solution to that problem. Probably the most widely used and generally accepted example of a TV commercial.

3. *Chronology:* delivers the message through a series of related scenes, each one growing out of the one before. Facts and events are presented sequentially as they occurred.

4. *Special effects;* no strong structural pattern. Strives for and often achieves memorability through the use of some striking device, for example, an unusual musical sound or pictorial technique.

5. *Testimonial:* also called "word-of-mouth" advertising, it uses well-known figures or an unknown "man in the street" to provide product testimonials.

6. *Satire:* a commercial that uses sophisticated wit to point out human foibles, generally produced in an exaggerated style. Parodies on James Bond movies, "Bonnie and Clyde," "Hair," and the like.

7. *Spokesperson:* the use of an on-camera announcer who basically "talks." Talk may be fast and hard sell or more personal, intimate sell.

8. *Demonstration:* uses some physical apparatus to demonstrate a product's effectiveness. Analgesic, watch, and tire commercials employ this approach heavily.

9. *Suspense:* somewhat similar to story-line or problem-solution structures, but the buildup of curiosity and suspense to the final resolution is given a heightened sense of drama.

10. *Slice-of-life:* a variation on problem solution. Begins with a person at the point of, and just before the discovery of, an answer to a problem. Heavily used by detergent manufacturers.

11. *Analogy:* offers an extraneous example, then attempts to relate it to the product message. Instead of delivering a message simply and directly,

an analogy uses one example to explain another by comparison or implication. "Just as vitamins tone up your body, our product tones up your car's engine."

12. *Fantasy:* uses caricatures or special effects to create fantasy surrounding product and product use: "Jolly Green Giant," "White Knight," "White Tornado," "the washing machine that becomes ten feet tall."

13. *Personality:* a technical variation of the spokesperson or announcer-on-camera, straight-sell structure. Relies on an actor or actress rather than an announcer to deliver the message. Uses a setting rather than the background of a studio. The actor plays a character who talks about the product, reacts to its use, or demonstrates its use or enjoyment directly to the camera.

These structures are, of course, not mutually exclusive, but rather serve to provide points of focus for analysis, copy production, and research. For example, in testimonials and, perhaps, in spokesperson and demonstration commercials, the credibility of source and/or the mode of presentation are likely to be most important. Customer reactions to source could receive special attention, utilizing the ideas on source credibility given earlier. In story line, problem solution, and perhaps the chronology and analogy structures, focus would tend to center more on the type of argument (for example, one- versus two-sided or refutation) or the order of argument (primacy-recency, stating a conclusion) dimensions. A researcher would be particularly interested, for instance, in whether the problem conveyed and the solution presented in the commercial were perceived as such by a sample of potential customers. Each of these seven types of commercials also tends to be more factual in orientation. The appeal is to ethos or logos, rather than to pathos.

The remaining six types all are more emotional in orientation and can be distinguished on the basis of whether the emotion-arousing capacity or the *characterization* being used relates to source or message. The personality and slice-of-life structures, for example, are likely to be more source oriented. The choice of the personality to be used or the characters who will play the role in the slice-of-life situation are emphasized. Source effects would also tend to be the point of focus, but specific attention might be devoted to the *attractiveness* component of source and whether the respondents tended to identify readily with the personality or characters involved. In this sense, the overriding concern with commercials of this type may be the emotions and interest aroused and what the consequences of that arousal process are.

The special effects, fantasy, satire, and suspense structures are all fundamentally emotional in orientation. Special effects, for example, might be used to arouse emotions with respect to fear, sex, or status. Attention here would not focus so much on the people in the advertisement as on the special effects—the type of humor used, whether a particular form of background music achieved the desired mood, whether the satire was indeed satirical, and so on. In other words, *message* rather than *source* would be the focus. Once again, however, the principal objective would be emotional arousal, and interest would center on whether the particular emotion was manifested in the test group (for example, laughter, anxiety) and what the consequences of the arousal process were for the object being advertised.

One overriding rule for developing copy is to keep the format simple, uncluttered, and straightforward. Whether in print or in broadcast, the tendency for including too much information or for complicating the television commercial with too many scene changes, or scenes that are not well integrated, should be avoided. This principle of simplicity extends to the language used as well. Like cluttered format, complicated language is unlikely to induce people to spend the time to ''figure it out.'' Furthermore, it is very important to recognize that the advertisements are being created for someone and are not just descriptions of the brand. The message should always be true to the product. Claims should be substantiable, and the style should not be radically altered over the life cycle of the product.[15]

In the appendix, a mathematical model concerning copy and copy decisions is presented and discussed. The basic question is how many copy alternatives to generate given that each new alternative adds to cost but that adding alternatives increases the likelihood of maximizing profits. This is a classic model which also introduces basic questions of copy-test reliability and validity, topics which are addressed again in Chapter 14.

SUMMARY

Creating and producing copy is a vital part of advertising management. The skills that are brought to bear during this stage of campaign development are often the deciding factors in distinguishing great from mediocre or poor advertising. Copy decisions are important because the investment of the total advertising campaign rests on decisions made at this point, because copy is the means by which objectives are carried out and strategy is executed, and because considerable financial investments and many people and organizations are involved. The advertising manager needs to know what kinds of copy alternatives can be generated, how the creation and production process works, and how many copy alternatives to generate.

Creative people are, on the one hand, constrained in their activities by the physical time and space limitations of the media in which advertising can appear and, on the other, have a virtually limitless number of creative elements that can be brought together to make up a finished advertisement. A basic understanding of these constraints and opportunities for each of the major media, as well as those imposed by external government and other forces, is the key to identifying the range of alternatives that can be created.

The creation and production process involves two major stages and differs at the production stage for print and broadcast. The creation stage begins with the creative process in which ideas are generated and developed. Idea generation really begins with fact finding and the immersion of the creative team in all the relevant information surrounding the company, product, competition, and consumers. Brainstorming and synectics are two procedures used for maximizing the likelihood of generating worthwhile ideas. Copywriting, illustrating, and layout are tasks to be done at the creation stage. The copywriter will generate the words and copy points to be used, whereas an artist is usually involved with the pictorial materials. Layout involves bringing all the pieces together in a form that can be used to guide production. Before production begins, the client must usually approve the print layouts or storyboards involved, and production supplier companies must be selected.

The production stage generally involves outside suppliers. In print, this means the contracting of typographers, engravers, and printers to produce the finished advertisements. In broadcast, production studios and a wide range of additional organizations and individuals will ordinarily be involved. Print production is characterized by the graphic arts and the activities of typography and engraving. Broadcast production is characterized by the basic activities of filming (or videotaping) and editing.

Television contains the full spectrum of audiovisual possibilities. There are 13 types of television commercials, each of which focuses on a particular kind of presentation or technique. An important rule in both print and broadcast is to keep the format simple, uncluttered, and straightforward. The tendency to include too much information and for including words or language that is too complicated for the target audience should be avoided.

DISCUSSION QUESTIONS

1. Analyze the model of the creation and production process presented in the chapter. The production stage is viewed as different for print and broadcast production, whereas the creation stage is considered essentially similar for both. Do you agree or disagree? Discuss.

2. Compare and contrast the HIT method of generating advertising ideas with brainstorming. What are the essential similarities and differences? Organize a small group to conduct a brainstorming session and a synectics session regarding some product of service. Which produced the greatest number of ideas? Which produced the best ideas?

3. What, in your opinion, distinguishes a more creative person from a less creative person?

4. Caples argues that advertisers should "ring the changes." What are the pros and cons of this idea? Under what conditions might it be better to not do so.

5. What are the differences between "illustrating" and "layout"?

6. Discuss some of the factors that you would consider in selecting a production house for a television commercial.

7. Compare and contrast Ogilvy's ideas on typography presented in this chapter with the ideas of "source effects" in earlier chapters.

8. Read the material on producing a television commercial for American Express. What are the major steps in the process? To what degree is a lot of "creativity" taking place at the production stage? Discuss.

9. Pick six examples of recent television commercials that you know of that represent six of the 12 types described in the chapter.

10. Contact an account executive in a local advertising agency and write a brief paper on the client approval and supplier selection process used by the agency.

APPENDIX

How Many Copy Alternatives to Generate*

In the development of an advertising campaign, the advertising manager is faced with the decision of how many copy alternatives to generate. Is one enough, or should two, three, four, or more alternatives be generated? Advertisers generally follow one of two different strategies regarding this problem as outlined in the following two scenarios:

1. Create, produce, and test one alternative. The argument is that a single advertisement is like a new product and bringing it into being involves a long process and many complicated steps. It is improved, tested, and made as good as possible along the way. The role of pretesting is to assure that no major errors have been made. Expenses are minimized. Shorter and/or longer versions of this one alternative may be developed for use throughout the campaign, and different print and broadcast versions developed for a multimedia campaign. The focus, however, is on generating and testing one alternative.

2. Create, produce, and test several alternatives involving very different copy approaches. The argument is that there is potentially wide variability in the effectiveness of the alternatives. One alternative can generate a stream of profits that is significantly better or worse than another. Finding the best alternative should be done by choosing from a pool of different advertisements. The role of pretesting is to help decide which of them to choose. A commitment is made to invest more in the process, and expenses are consequently greater.

Although most advertising practice today appears to follow the first of these strategies, there are good economic arguments to be made for the second. Irwin Gross, marketing research director of the Du Pont Company, has developed a model of budgeting the creative and testing process based on the second type of reason-

* This appendix can be bypassed without loss of continuity.

ing.[1] Gross argues that not enough of the advertising budget goes into creativity and testing. What the manager really needs to know is how many alternatives to generate. Costs will rise as more are generated, but the likely payoffs of the alternative chosen will also rise. What should be the correct number of alternatives?

Gross first points out that different creative approaches should be considered. A commercial based on an image campaign or a testimonial might be more effective than one based on a demonstration approach. An assumption of the model is that the following procedure is carried out by an advertising manager. He or she obtains n advertising campaigns. Each campaign could be generated by different advertising agencies, by different creative teams within the same agency, or even by the same creative team. The manager then decides on a copy test and applies the same preselected test to each alternative. Let the score of campaign alternative i from the test be S_i. The campaign alternative that has received the highest S_i test score is the one selected. The advertising media budget is then spent on running that campaign alternative.

Suppose, for example, that for a line of cookingware the manager obtained the services of three agencies, each of which generated a campaign and at least one television commercial representing that campaign. Suppose, further, that the copy test chosen was a service in which commercials are shown to a theater audience and they are asked before and after exposure to the commercial to select a brand they would want if they were to win a lottery. The difference in the percentage who choose the advertised brand, with respect to some established norms, provides the basis for the copy-test score. A manager could thus test the commercial of each campaign. Assume that the image commercial received the highest score. The manager would then spend the advertising media budget running advertisements based on the image campaign.

The principal question to which the Gross model is addressed is: What n should a manager use? To utilize the model, she or he must provide estimates of several model parameters. Essentially, the manager needs an estimate of the dispersion in quality of alternative advertising campaigns, the validity and reliability of the copy test to be used, and the costs of generating and testing the objective function that reflects the profit expected when n campaign alternatives are involved.

Model Objective Function

When different campaigns are generated, whether by different creative groups or by the same group, it is reasonable to suppose that they will vary in both approach and effectiveness. There may be a brilliant campaign among them and, perhaps, a sure loser—and probably some in between. To fix the concept, it is useful to conceptualize a measure of campaign effectiveness (as was done several times in Part II). Let us assume that, in the absence of advertising, a known stream of profits will be generated over time. Furthermore, assume that each campaign will generate a known incremental profit stream higher than one that would be realized without advertising. The present value of this incremental profit stream associated with campaign alternative i will be its effectiveness. The term E_i will represent the effectiveness of campaign i, relative to a campaign with average effectiveness. If a campaign is average in effectiveness, it would have a relative effectiveness value of zero. If it were better than average, it would have a positive relative value and, if less, a negative relative effectiveness value. The frequency or probability distribution of the relative effectiveness, E_i, could be shown as in Figure A-1. Let us call σ_E the variance of E_i. A high variance would indicate that there is a high degree of variation in the quality of the advertising campaign alternatives as measured in this manner.

A manager generates n campaigns and selects the one with the highest copy-test score. The relevant question here is what is the expected relative effectiveness, or the expected E_i, for the alternative that will emerge from the process. This expected relative effectiveness will be termed V_n. It can be conceptualized as the average E_i that would be obtained if the process involving n campaigns were repeated thousands of times. Gross determined that V_n is equal to the product of four terms:

$$V_n = E_n \sigma_E \rho R \qquad n > 1$$

where V_n = expected relative effectiveness. E_i, of the campaign receiving the highest copy-test score among n alternative advertising campaigns

E_n = expected value of the largest number in an independent sample of the size n from a normal distribution with zero mean and variance of 1.0

σ_E = variance of E_i

ρ = validity of the copy test

R = reliability of the copy test

The first term, E_n, reflects the fact that, as n gets larger, the selected alternative, the one with the highest copy-test score, is likely to be a better-quality

Figure A-1.   **Probability distribution of E_i**

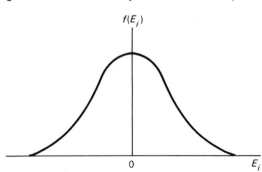

campaign; it is likely to have a higher E_i value. That is, from this factor's contribution, it would pay to have more rather than fewer alternatives to consider. The act
of drawing n numbers from any distribution and selecting the largest can be conceived. The expected value of this number is the value that would be obtained if the
drawing were repeated many times. The term E_n is the expected value of the
outcome when the distribution happens to be a normal distribution with a mean
equal to zero and variance equal to 1.

The remaining three terms are among the model input parameters that need to
be estimated from other empirically based or subjective data. A discussion of
estimation procedures will follow the presentation of the model.

The second term, σ_E, reflects the fact that the distribution involved does not
have a variance of 1, but rather a variance of σ_E. If the variation among the quality
of the generated campaigns is high, the chances are that the E_i of the selected
alternative will also be high. If the quality of all the campaigns is about the same,
however, they will all have close to an average impact, and the E_i of the one that
received the highest copy-test score will also be close to average.

The third term, p, is a measure of the validity of the copy test. Validity refers
to the copy test's ability to predict the actual effectiveness of the campaign when it
is run. Some copy tests will forecast more accurately than others the success or
failure of an advertising campaign, measured in terms of the present value of the
incremental profit stream, E_i. Of course, the more valid copy tests will probably
also be more expensive. More formally, the validity of the copy test is assumed to
be the correlation between the S_i scores of the copy test and the E_i values of the
campaigns being tested.

The final term, R, is a measure of the reliability of the copy test. It reflects
variation of test scores over repeated use. If R were 1.0, a copy test of a given
campaign alternative would generate the same score every time. However, most
copy tests are not completely reliable because of several sources of variation. The
population sample used in the test could differ. The setting used to expose the
subject to the advertisement could vary owing to differences in room temperature or
lighting. In the model, of course, a manager runs the copy test only once for each
alternative campaign. If, however, it were applied several times to the same campaign alternative, different S_i scores would probably result. Thus, if a manager had
run the reason-why advertisement through the in-theater copy-testing system three
separate times (on different evenings and with different people), he or she might
well have gotten different scores each time. The fact is that there is a certain random
component in the S_i scores that reflects experimental conditions. The reliability, R,
is a measure of the size of the random variation.[2] R is constrained here to be
between 0 and 1.0. If this random variation is large, R will approach zero. If there
is little random variation, the reliability will be close to 1.0.

From the expected value, V_n, we must now subtract the cost of generating and
testing the campaign alternatives to obtain the model's objective function. We will
then select the n that will optimize this objective function. Let g be the cost of
creating a campaign alternative, assuming that at least one campaign has been

generated. We assume that one campaign will be created. The issue is whether two or more should be generated. Thus, the cost of generating the first campaign does not have to be explicitly introduced into the model but, rather, can be assumed to be included in the relative effectiveness term. The fixed cost of setting up the copy test will be denoted by f. The marginal screening copy-test cost per campaign alternative will be denoted by s. For some copy tests, the setup costs may be very significant; for others they may be small.

The expected relative profit contribution from generating and testing n advertising campaigns instead of one, termed P_n, is thus

$$P_n = V_n - g\,(n - 1) - f - sn \qquad n > 1$$

where P_n = expected relative profit contribution from generating and testing n advertising campaigns instead of just one

g = cost of generating each advertising campaign beyond the first one

f = fixed costs of the copy test

s = marginal copy-test costs per alternative campaign

n = number of alternative campaigns

Selecting the Optimal n

A decision model can now be developed. Clearly, as more campaign alternatives are developed, the expected E_i of the one chosen will increase. However, at some point, the marginal gain of one additional alternative will not exceed the costs involved, and the optimal number of alternatives will already have been developed. In essence, we select the n that will maximize P_n, the objective function. If all values of P_n are negative, then the optimal n is 1.[3]

An Application of the Model

Gross provided some crude estimates of the model parameters to determine the optimal number of campaign alternatives that should be developed. Since somewhere around 5 percent of media expenditures are spent on creative activities (15 percent, less 10 percent of overhead and other costs) he assumed that the creation and copy testing of one campaign alternative was 5 percent of the total media budget. If we assume that f is negligible, it would be reasonable to assume that

$$g = 0.04B$$
$$s = 0.01B$$
$$f = 0.0$$

where B is the size of the media budget.

To determine σ_E, Gross assumed that an outstanding campaign, the best that might be expected in 30 years of creating one campaign per year, will exceed the profits of an average campaign by an amount equal to the media budget. The normal distribution can be employed to translate this assumption to $2\sigma_E$ equals B, the media budget, or that

$$\sigma_E = \tfrac{1}{2} B$$

The validity of the copy test, p, was assumed to be 0.63 and the reliability, R, was set at 0.71.

Table A-1 provides the values of e_n, V_n, and P_n for n between 1 and 8. Clearly, the maximum value of the objective function, p_n, occurs at an n equal to 3. Therefore, the optimal n in this case is 3. Notice that e_1 (and thus V_1) is equal to zero for one campaign. If one campaign is developed, the expectation would be that it would be average. Recall that the E_1 of an average campaign is zero.

If it can be supported, this finding has significant implications for the advertising industry, where, typically, something under 5 percent of the advertising budget is spent on creativity and testing. It suggests that the size of this expenditure should be increased rather dramatically. Clearly, the 15 percent agency commission arrangement would have to be replaced if such a change were to be implemented. A more flexible fee arrangement would be required. Agencies and advertisers have experimented with various fee arrangements, although these arrangements are usually not motivated by a desire to increase the creative effort. Indeed, they are often designed to reduce agency services received by some advertisers. To evaluate this suggestion more carefully and to understand the model more completely, we now turn to an examination of the underlying assumptions and the measurement issues.

Variation in Advertising Campaigns

A critical parameter of the model is σ_E. It reflects the different degrees of effectiveness achieved by different campaigns. Different copy approaches will have very

Table A-1.   **Model Application**

n	e_n[a]	V_n	P_n
1	0.00	0	0
2	0.56	0.125B	0.065B
3	0.85	0.190B	0.080B
4	1.03	0.230B	0.070B
5	1.16	0.260B	0.050B
6	1.27	0.284B	0.024B
7	1.35	0.302B	−0.008B
8	1.42	0.316B	−0.041B

[a] From Ronald A. Fisher and Frank Yates, *Statistical Tables* (New York: Hafner Press, 1963), p. 94.

different levels of effectiveness. In this model we are now asked to quantify the extent of this variation.

One practical example concerns a test of five different advertising themes for Campbell soups. Despite the fact that all five alternatives appeared quite acceptable to management before the test was run, considerable variation was obtained in the criterion variable of increased sales. The σ_E was 72 percent of the average sales' increment achieved. If we assume that the average advertisement was worth the media cost, then σ_E would be 0.72 of the media budget, considerably more than Gross used in his example.

It is reassuring to have hard data to calculate a parameter such as σ_E. However, even in the absence of such information, the analysis can proceed with subjective estimates obtained from knowledgeable managers. Gross has obtained estimates of the value of σ_E by asking managers to guess the incremental profitability in terms of media expenditures of outstanding campaigns (the top 2 or 3 percent) compared with an average campaign. He obtained estimates of σ_E ranging from two to ten times the media budget. This indicates that the above empirically based measure might be conservative.

Naturally, the estimate appropriate to a given situation will depend on the circumstances: the product involved, its stage in the product life cycle, the segments to be reached, competitive factors, and so on. It will usually not be realistic to borrow an estimate of σ_E from another context.

The parameter estimate will depend on how the alternative campaigns are generated. At one extreme, if different creative groups in different agencies should be generating the alternatives, σ_E would be maximized. In earlier sections, the creative style that often permeates an agency was illustrated. Two creative groups working within the same agency might operate with lower σ_E simply because of agency style, the effects of social interaction, and so on. At the other extreme, a single person or creative team might generate different alternative campaigns that bear little resemblance to one another. In fact, during the creative process, campaign ideas and alternatives are continually being proposed and refined. Usually, the creative group will settle on one or two, but the group nevertheless does consider various alternatives. The question is, how independently are such campaigns generated? The level of independence is undoubtedly lower than when different groups, even from the same agency, are involved.

Gross cites an example of a mail-order test conducted by Time, Inc. In the test, nine copy alternatives were created by the same person and another five people each created a single alternative. Each of the fourteen alternatives was tested with a mail sample of 90,000. The mean responses to the two sets of alternatives were about the same, but the variances were significantly different (at the 0.05 level). The standard deviation of the five individuals was approximately twice that of the single person, which suggests that the σ_E value is indeed sensitive to the level of independence involved.

Copy-Test Reliability

The same advertisement can be subjected to a copy test many times, and the variation in the resulting scores can be used to estimate the reliability. Gross used data by the Schwerin Research Corporation to estimate reliability for a product class in which the reliability was thought to be low. A total of 106 advertisements for brands in the product class had been tested over an 8-year period. Several of the advertisements had been tested several times, providing estimates of the reliability. Based on these data, R turned out to be 0.81.[4] Gross concludes that reliability will rarely be a limiting problem. If this does seem worrisome, a researcher, by increasing the sample size (and the copy-test cost), can improve its reliability.

Copy-Test Validity

Validity is a key parameter in the model and a very difficult one to measure. What is the correlation of the S_t values generated by a certain copy test and E_i, the actual effectiveness of the advertising being tested? Gross suggests the use of subjective estimates of p. For example, he would ask a manager to assess the probability that the best of 10 campaigns would be rated among the top three by a given pretest. From this type of information, an estimate of p can be obtained. Of course, it would be reassuring to measure p empirically.

Whether one is using subjective or objective measures, the basic problem is that it is extremely difficult, if not impossible, to determine or to know E_i for the different alternatives. One might conceive of measuring E_i with an elaborate and expensive controlled market test employing several campaign alternatives. The output of such a test would then be related to various copy-test scores. But even in such a circumstance, problems remain. All the interpretive difficulties of test markets exist—variations in consumer characteristics, competitive activity, and so forth—which can contaminate the results.[5] Furthermore, can validity measures so obtained be applied to new situations wherein the environment, product, and copy approach may differ?

One effort to measure p was presented in Chapter 3, where the score from the Schwerin pretest was used as one of the independent variables in a regression model in which change in market share was the dependent variable. The other independent variables used included the amount of advertising employed and a measure of market momentum. In this study, the copy test involved performed well. The dependent variable, market share change, was used as a surrogate for E_i. Although market share change is probably correlated with E_i, it is a less-than-perfect representation since it does not include important factors such as carryover effects.

An intervening variable on which the advertising objective is based can be used in lieu of E_i. With operational advertising objectives, the relationship of the test output, S_i, to these objectives is the focus of attention, instead of the correlation between S_i and E_i. What is suggested is the inclusion of an intervening variable between E_i and S_i, just as an intervening variable between advertising expenditures and sales was inserted when advertising objectives were established. We must, of course, be convinced that there is, in turn, a high correlation between the intervening variable (for example, attitude) and E_i if the ultimate goal is to influence brand choice. However, the advertising objective has presumably already been justified by such an argument so that aspects of the problem can be bypassed (although certainly not ignored).

There still remains the problem of determining the correlation between copy-test scores and the intervening variable inserted between S_i and E_i. Although it may be less difficult to determine, either subjectively or objectively, the relationship between a pretest score and the probable effect of an advertising campaign on a communication measure is by no means a trivial problem.

The validity parameter, p, being a correlation, reflects the ability of the pretest to make relative, not absolute, judgments about an advertising alternative. Thus a copy test is not expected in this context to predict the sales or awareness level that will be generated by an advertising alternative. It is simply expected to predict the performance of an alternative *relative* to another alternative or set of alternatives. If absolute judgments were expected, the task would be infinitely more difficult.

The Gross model provides a structure within which the creative budget decision and the question of how many copy alternatives to generate can be addressed. The model, with some crude but reasonable parameter estimates, suggests that substantially more money should be allocated to the creative activity than is the present practice and that more than one alternative should be developed. The effectiveness of an advertising campaign is considered by the model to be determined by the number of campaign alternatives generated, the variation in effectiveness among the different campaigns, and the quality of the copy test—its validity and reliability.

Advertisements versus Campaigns

The Gross model is designed to determine how many different advertising campaigns should be developed and tested to determine how much money should be spent on the creative effort. The model structure will apply equally well to the problem of how many individual advertisements should be developed to support a single advertising campaign. The parameters, σ_E and g, would be expected to be significantly smaller in this context than when campaign alternatives are involved. The variation in the effectiveness, E_i, of various advertisements within the same campaign should be much smaller than the variation of advertisements drawn from different campaigns. The cost of generating different advertisements from the same campaign will also be lower. If the variation from advertisement to advertisement is small, the cost of generating them will also be small.[6] The model illustrates the need to select a copy test that has a balance between cost (f and s) and validity and reliability.

It is probably unrealistic to say that every advertiser should generate a specific number of alternatives in every situation. What is important, however, is that in most situations more expenditure is warranted than the generation of just one alternative, as is the dominant industry practice. In several tests of his model, Gross generally argues that the magic number is 3. In a great many cases, profits can be improved if three alternatives are used to initiate and guide the process. The really important consequence of this strategy is that the advertising budget gets reallocated so that more money is put into this end of the process and comparatively less is spent on media costs. The economic justification for this strategy is of course contained in all the arguments presented in the model.

SUMMARY

The creative budget involves expenses associated with the creation and production of individual advertisements and the costs of the copy testing used to decide which of several possible alternatives should be chosen. The Gross model provides a rigorous, analytical approach toward determining the size of the creative budget and the question of how many copy alternatives to generate. The key assumptions in the model are that not all creative effort will generate outputs having the same degree of effectiveness and that it is possible to develop copy-testing methods that can measure the quality of creative effort reliably and validly.

The model assumes that a manager has several advertising campaigns generated, tests each one with a specific copy test, and chooses the one with the highest test score. The question the model addresses is how many advertising campaigns should be generated, given this decision procedure.

The model inputs are estimates of the variation in the quality of the advertising campaigns, the validity and reliability of the copy test, the costs of generating a campaign, and the costs of running a campaign through a test. Validity of a copy test is measured by it ability to predict the true effectiveness of the advertising campaign. Three major factors must be considered with respect to copy-test validity. First, there must be an operational objective. Second, subjects in the test should be representative of the target population. Third, reactions of the subjects to the testing situation that might bias the results should be minimized. Reliability is measured by its ability to generate the same test scores, given differences in people and testing situations. It refers to the variation in copy-test scores caused by random experimental variations in the sample or setting. The output of the model is the optimal number of campaign alternatives to generate.

DISCUSSION QUESTIONS

1. Discuss possible measures of the effectiveness construct, E_i, in the Gross model.

2. Develop an example in which six commercials were involved. Discuss the meaning of the terms e_n, σ_E, and R with respect to the example.

3. Using the Gross model, determine the optimal n when

$$\sigma_E = 0.50B$$
$$\rho = 0.70$$
$$R = 0.80$$
$$g = 0.04B$$
$$s = 0.01B$$
$$f = 0$$

a. Repeat the determination when g is equal to $0.01B$, $0.02B$, $0.06B$.

b. Repeat the determination when σ_E is equal to $0.20B$, $0.40B$, $0.60B$, $0.80B$, $1.20B$.

c. Repeat the determination with ρ equal to 0.30, 0.50, 0.80, 1.00.

d. Repeat the determination with R equal to 0.40, 0.60, 1.00.

e. What can you say about the relative importance of these terms?

4. Give five reasons why one commercial might be expected to vary from another in effectiveness, assuming that two creative groups had been assigned the task of creating the commercial and that each group knew the product situation and the objectives of the campaign.

Notes to Appendix

1. Irwin Gross, "The Creative Aspects of Advertising," *Sloan Management Review*, Fall 1972, pp. 83–109.

2. The S_i test score could be divided into two components, One, t_i, would be the random component reflecting experimental conditions. The other, termed T_i, would be the "true" copy-test score. If we repeated a copy test of the same alternative thousands of times, the average S_i score would be T_i. Gross actually defines R to be

$$R = \left(\frac{\sigma^2}{\sigma^2 + \sigma^2} \right)^{1/2}$$

3. If P_2 is positive, successive campaigns will be justified as long as

$$P_n > P_{n-1} \qquad n > 2$$

or

$$V_n - g(n-1) - f - sn > V_{n-1} - g(n-2) - f - s(n-1)$$

or

$$V_n - V_{n-1} - g - s > 0$$

or

$$(e_n - e_{n-1})\sigma_E \, \rho \, R > g + s$$

or

$$e_n - e_{n-1} > \frac{g+s}{\sigma_E \, \rho \, R} \qquad n > 2$$

4. Using the formula introduced in footnote 2.

5. The problem, of course, is similar to the one discussed at length in Chapters 3 and 4: there are many factors that affect sales besides advertising, and it is extremely difficult to isolate the contribution of advertising in actual market situations.

6. In this formulation of the Gross model, g is the cost of creating any additional advertisement, assuming that the campaign has been conceived and at least one advertisement has been developed.

NOTES

1. Alex F. Osborn, *Applied Imagination,* 3rd rev. ed. (New York: Scribner, 1963), p. 11.

2. Leo Burnett, "Keep Listening to That Wee, Small Voice," in *Communications of an Advertising Man,* Copyright 1961 by Leo Burnett Company, Inc., from a speech given before the Chicago Copywriters Club, October 4, 1960, p. 160.

3. Denis Higgens, ed., *The Art of Writing Advertising* (Chicago: Crain Books, 1965), p. 43.

4. Alex F. Osborn, *Your Creative Power* (New York: Dell, 1948), p. 135.

5. Edward M. Tauber, "HIT: Heuristic Ideation Technique—A Systematic Procedure for New Product Search," *Journal of Marketing,* 36, January 1972, pp. 58–61.

6. Osborn, *Your Creative Power,* p. 294.

7. Discussed in Philip Kotler, *Marketing Management: Analysis, Planning and Control* (Englewood Cliffs, N.J.: Prentice-Hall, 1967), p. 256.

8. John M. Keil, *The Creative Mystique: How to Manage It, Nurture It, and Make It Pay* (New York: Wiley, 1985). See also, "Popular Myths about Creativity Debunked," *Advertising Age,* May 6, 1985, p. 48.

9. John Caples, *How to Make Your Advertising Make Money* (Englewood Cliffs, N.J.: Prentice-Hall, 1983).

10. John Caples, "A Dozen Ways to Develop Advertising Ideas," *Advertising Age,* November 14, 1983, p. M-4ff.

11. Lester Guest, "Status Enhancement as a Function of Color in Advertising," *Journal of Advertising Research,* 6, June 1966, pp. 40–44.

12. Ibid., p. 44.

13. Stephen Baker, *Advertising Layout and Art Direction* (New York: McGraw-Hill, 1959), p. 3.

14. Albert C. Book and Norman D. Cary, *The Television Commercial: Creativity and Craftsmanship* (New York: Decker Communication, 1970).

15. For an interesting book on the subject of making television commercials, see Michael J. Arlen, *Thirty Seconds* (New York: Farrar, Straus & Giroux, 1980).

14

Copy Testing

Most of our research tools, strategic disciplines, and the marketing process, however, overlook the critical ingredient—human emotion. (Joseph T. Plummer, Young & Rubicam)

Will a proposed copy theme be effective at achieving advertising objectives? Does the set of advertisements that makes up an advertising campaign create the desired interest level and image? Will an individual advertisement attract the attention of the audience? Such questions are addressed in copy testing.

Copy testing is an important part of advertising management and also an interesting subject from the professional and scientific points of view. Professionally, there are now hundreds of companies who offer services having to do with assessing the effectiveness of print advertisements or broadcast commercials. A significant industry has evolved in the United States and increasingly in other countries made up of companies in the business of supplying this kind of service.[1] From the scientific viewpoint, advertising research reflects the applications of theories and methodologies that derive from psychology, sociology, and economics and, more specifically, from various branches of each of these disciplines.

The chapter begins with a section on copy-testing strategy. Four widely used criteria in copy testing and examples of related services are then presented and discussed. This is followed by a review of other tests. A final section is devoted to evaluating copy tests.

COPY TESTING STRATEGY

There are three factors that have to be addressed in copy testing: (1) whether or not to test, (2) what and when to test, and (3) what criteria or test to use. Every advertising manager must consider these factors in the context of the overall advertising plan. Copy testing implies that funds will be allocated to *research* on consumer reactions to the advertising before the final campaign is launched. The first decision is really whether or not to spend more money on research.

It is interesting that in terms of total advertising volume, the usual decision is "no." Most local advertising is not tested, and there are many cases in national advertising where copy is used without formal copy testing of any kind. Not only are there money costs involved in testing, but there are time costs as well. Copy testing can mean weeks or months of delay in launching a campaign. On the other hand, if you are managing a new product entry involving a $20 million advertising budget, investing in copy testing makes sense. Relying solely on the judgments of a creative team, your own experience, or somebody's intuition is very risky when so much is at stake. What is needed is a test of how potential *consumers* will react, that is, copy testing.

What and when to test? Copy testing can be done at (1) the beginning of the creative process, (2) the end of the creative process (at the layout stage), (3) the end of the production stage, and/or (4) after the campaign has been launched. In general, tests at the first three stages are called *pretests* and those at the final stage are called *posttests.*[2] Various types of tests can be used at any of the four stages, and will differ by whether broadcast or print advertising is involved. Testing at the beginning of the creative process often involves qualitative research, such as focus group interviews to get reactions to copy ideas. At stage two, rough mock-ups of the finished copy or, in television, partially complete commercials are tested because of the lower expenses involved. In fact, stage 3 is often bypassed, particularly in cases where the advertising has been shown or aired several times and the new copy is not radically different. A basic issue is whether to develop and test just one version of the advertising, or whether two or more versions should be developed and tested. It is logical, but also expensive, to have alternatives to test. In general, it is more expensive to test at the third and fourth stages. When there is much at stake, when millions of dollars of media time and expensive creative and production effort are involved, a substantial investment in copy testing at all stages is easily justified.

What criteria or copy test should be used? Copy-testing services can be distinguished by the nature of the response variable used in the test. Although many other factors enter into the choice of a copy test, the criterion (dependent) variable is probably the most important thing on which to focus. What does a particular test measure? How accurate or valid are these measures? These are some of the considerations of copy-test strategy that must be addressed. The next section reviews four criteria widely used in copy testing and gives examples of copy-testing services based on them.

FOUR CRITERIA USED IN COPY TESTING

Why is one advertisement effective and another a dud? Much depends on the criteria used to measure effectiveness. The criteria will, of course, depend on the brand involved and its advertising objectives. There are four basic criteria or categories of response that are widely used in advertising research. The first is advertisement recognition. The second, used heavily in television, is recall of the commercial and its contents. The third is persuasion. How persuasive is a commercial, for example? Finally, the criterion of purchase behavior is used. In many cases, this is most important. Does the advertisement or the advertising campaign have an effect on purchase behavior?

Each criterion and the measures and service associated with them will be illustrated and discussed in what follows. Concerning the copy strategy question of which is used where, some will be seen to be more suitable for posttesting of running advertisements, and others for pretesting. Most can be adapted to either pre- or posttesting, however.

Recognition

Recognition refers to whether a respondent can recognize an advertisement as one he or she has seen before. An example of recognition testing is the Bruzzone Research Company (BRC) tests of television commercials. These tests are done by mail survey in which questionnaires, such as the one shown in Figure 14-1, are mailed to 1,000 households. The sample is drawn from a specially prepared mailing list of households that have either a registered automobile or a listed telephone number. Interest in the task and a dollar bill enclosed with the questionnaire usually generates a return sample of about 500. The recognition question is shown at the top. At the bottom is the brand association question, a critical dimension of most campaigns. On average, 60 percent will recognize a commercial, and 73 percent of these can correctly select the right brand from a list of three alternatives.[3] Test-retest correlations of 0.98 have been reported.

Communicus is another company that uses recognition measures for either television or radio commercial tests. In television, respondents are shown brief (10-second) edited portions of the commercial, excluding advertiser identification. They are asked if they have seen or heard it before, to identify the advertiser, and to play back other identifying copy points. Some research has shown that there is a drop-off in the percentage of people who can identify a sponsor, falling from an average of 59 percent in 1974 to about 50 percent in 1980, perhaps because of increased clutter.[4]

Figure 14-1. Advertising campaign effectiveness survey

Please look over these pictures and words from a TV commercial and answer the questions on the right.

(Boy #1) What's this stuff?

(Boy #2) Some cereal. Supposed to be good for you.

(Boy #1) Did you try it?

(Boy #2) I'm not going to try it. You try it.

(Boy #1) I'm not going to try it.

(Boy #2) Let's get Mikey.

(Boy #1) Yeah.

(Boy #2) He won't eat it. He hates everything.

He likes it! Hey, Mikey!

(Announcer) When you bring brand name home, * don't tell the kids it's one of those nutritional cereals you've been try-ing to get them to eat. You're the only one who has to know.

Do you remember seeing this commercial on TV?

₅₉·□ Yes   ·□ No   ·□ Not sure—I may have

How interested are you in what this commercial is trying to tell you or show you about the product?

₆₀·□ Very   ·□ Somewhat   ·□ Not
     interested   ·□ interested   ·□ interested

How does it make you feel about the product?

₆₄·□ It's good ·□ It's OK ·□ It's bad ·□ Not sure

Please check any of the following if you feel they describe this commercial.

₆₅·□ Amusing   ₇₄·□ Familiar   ₈₃·□ Pointless
 ·□ Appealing   ·□ Fast moving   ·□ Seen a lot
 ·□ Believable   ·□ Gentle   ·□ Sensitive
 ·□ Clever   ·□ Imaginative   ·□ Silly
 ·□ Confusing   ·□ Informative   ·□ True to life
 ·□ Convincing   ·□ Irritating   ·□ Warm
 ·□ Dull   ·□ Lively   ·□ Well done
 ·□ Easy to forget   ·□ Original   ·□ Worn out
 ·□ Effective   ·□ Phony   ·□ Worth remembering

Thinking about the commercial as a whole would you say you:

₉₄·□ Liked it a lot   ·□ Disliked it somewhat
 ·□ Liked it somewhat   ·□ Disliked it a lot
 ·□ Felt neutral about it

* We have blocked out the name   Does anyone in your
  Do you remember which brand   household use this
  was being advertised?   type of product?

₉₅·□ Life   ₉₈·□ Regularly
 ·□ Total   ·□ Occasionally
 ·□ Special K   ·□ Seldom or never
 ·□ Don't know

Courtesy of Bruzzone Research Company.

The most widely known service in measuring print advertising recognition is Starch INRA Hooper. This service began in 1923. In a typical Starch test, respondents are taken through a magazine and for each advertisement, asked if they saw it in the issue. Three measures are generated for each advertisement in the magazine called *noted, seen associated,* and *read most.* Each is a percentage derived as follows:

- Noted: the percent of readers of the issue who remember having seen the advertisement.
- Seen associated: the percent who saw any part of the advertisement that clearly indicates the brand, service, or advertisement.
- Read most: the percent who read half or more of the copy.

Studies using Starch data show that recognition depends on the product class, the involvement of the segment in the product class, and on variables such as size, color, position, copy approach, and the nature of the magazine or media. Although Starch scores are highly reliable in a test-retest sense, there is concern about validity. The respondent can claim readership where none exists to please or impress the interviewer or because of confusion with prior advertising for the brand. Further, this bias can be difficult to predict for a particular advertisement.

Recognition is a necessary condition for effective advertising. If the advertisement cannot pass this minimal test, it probably will not be effective. In one study of inquiries received by an advertiser of electronic instrumentation, those with low Starch scores were also low in inquiries received. Of course, high recognition does not guarantee effectiveness.

Recall

Recall refers to measures of the proportion of a sample audience that can recall an advertisement. There are two kinds of recall, *aided recall* and *unaided recall.* In aided recall, the respondent is prompted by showing a picture of the advertisement with the sponsor or brand name blanked out. In unaided recall, only the product or service name may be given. The best known recall method in television, interviewing viewers within 24 to 30 hours after the commercial is aired, is called the day-after-recall method.

Day-After-Recall. The day-after-recall (DAR) measure of a television commercial, first used in the early 1940s by George Gallup, then with Young & Rubican, is closely associated with Burke Marketing Research.[5] "How did the ad Burke out?" is a common question. The procedure is to telephone 150 to 300 program viewers the day after a television commercial appears. They are asked if they can recall any commercials the previous day in a product category (such as soap). If they cannot identify the brand correctly, they are then given the product category and brand and asked if they recalled the commercial. They are then asked for anything they can recall about the commercial, what was said, what was shown, and what the main idea was. DAR is the percent of those in the commercial audience (who were watching the show before and after the commercial was shown) who recalled something specific about the commercial, such as the sales message, the story line, the plot, or some visual or audio element.

The DAR is an ''on-air'' test in that the commercial exposure occurs in a natural, realistic in-home setting. It is well established and has developed extensive norms over the years. The average DAR is 24. One-fourth of all commercials score under 15 and one-fourth score over 31. It also provides diagnostic information about which elements of the commercial are having an impact and which are not. Gallup & Robinson and Mapes & Ross provide a similar measure for print media. They place a magazine with 150 regular readers of that magazine and ask that it be read in a normal manner. The next day readers are asked to describe ads for any brands of interest.

Recall measures have generated controversy over the years and as a result, are not as influential as they once were. One concern is that they are an inappropriate measure of emotional commercials. Foote, Cone & Belding measured both masked recognition (where the brand name is blocked out) and DAR for three ''feeling'' commercials and three ''thinking'' commercials.[6] The DAR was much lower for the feeling commercials (19 versus 31) whereas the recognition scores were only marginally lower (32 versus 37). The conclusion was that recognition is a better measure of the ability of a feeling commercial's memorability than DAR, which requires the verbalization of the content.

A more basic concern with DAR is that it simply is not a valid measure of anything useful.[7] First, its reliability is suspect. Extremely low test/retest correlations (below 0.30) have been found when commercials from the same product class have been studied. Second, DAR scores are unduly affected by the liking and nature of the program. For example, DAR scores of commercials in new programs average 25 percent or more below commercials in other shows. Third, and most compelling, of eight relevant studies, seven found practically no association between recall and measures of persuasion. Neither is there evidence of a positive association between recall and sales. In contrast, there is substantial evidence linking persuasion measures with sales. Thus, copy-test interest has turned toward persuasion.

Persuasion

Forced-Exposure Brand-Preference Change.   Theater testing, pioneered by Horace Schwerin and Paul Lazarsfeld in the 1950s, is now done by McCollum/Spielman, ASI, and ARS.[8]

The McCollum/Spielman test uses a 450-person sample spread over four graphically dispersed locations.[9] The respondents are recruited by telephone to come to a central location to preview television programing. Seated in groups of 25 in front of television monitors, they respond to a set of demographic and brand/product usage questions that appear on the screen. The respondents view a half-hour variety program featuring four professional performers. In the midpoint, seven commercials, including four test commercials, are shown.

Performer A	Performer B	T 1	C	T 2	C	T 3	C	T 4	Performer C	Performer D

C = Constant Commercials   T = Test Commercial

After audience reactions to the program are obtained, an unaided brand-name-recall question is asked that forms the basis of the clutter/awareness score (the percent who recalled that the brand was advertised). The clutter/awareness (C/A) score for 30-second commercials averages 56 percent for established brands and 40 percent for new brands.[10] The four test commercials are then exposed a second time surrounded by program material:

Program Intro.	T 1	Program	T 2	Program	T 3	Program	T 4	Program

T = Test Commercial

An attitude shift (AS) measure is obtained. For frequently purchased package goods such as toiletries, the preexposure designation of brand purchased most often is compared with the postexposure brand selection in a market basket award situation. The respondents are asked to select brands they would like included if they were winners of a $25 basket of products. In product fields with multiple-brand usage, such as soft drinks, a constant sum measure (10 points to be allocated to brands proportional to how they are preferred) is employed before and after exposure. For durables and services, the pre- and post-preference is measured by determining:

• The favorite brand
• The next preferred alternative
• Those brands that would not be considered
• Those brands that are neither preferred not rejected

An important element of the test is the use of two exposures. McCollum/Spielman and many advertisers argue that fewer than two exposures represents an artificial and invalid test of most advertising.

Finally, diagnostic questions are asked. Some of the areas that are frquently explored include:

• Comprehension of message/slogan
• Communication of secondary copy ideas
• Evaluation of demonstrations, spokesperson, message

- Perception of brand uniqueness/brand differentiation
- Irritating/confusing elements
- Viewer involvement

In a rare copy-test validity check, McCollum/Spielman asked advertisers of 412 campaigns (some campaigns consisted of several commercials) that were tested over a three-year period whether the brand had exceeded marketing objectives during the time that the campaign was being aired.[11] These advertising campaigns were then divided into four groups:

- High AS (attitude shift) and high A/C (awareness/communication)
- High AS and low A/C
- Low AS and high A/C
- Low AS and low A/C

The results are shown in Figure 14-2. Clearly, the AS persuasion measure was a good predictor of campaign success. The A/C recall measure, on the other hand, may have diagnostic value but it had little relationship to campaign success.

The ARS approach is similar except that their proven recall measure is the percent of respondents that 72 hours later claim having seen the advertisement and can give some playback of it.[12]

ARS obtained a correlation of 0.78 with their proven recall measure and the unaided brand awareness level achieved by 24 new brands in test markets. Their pre-post-persuasion measure had a correlation of 0.85 with the trial rate of 26 new

Figure 14-2. **The percentage of campaigns exceeding marketing objectives by their performance in the McCollum/Spielman test**

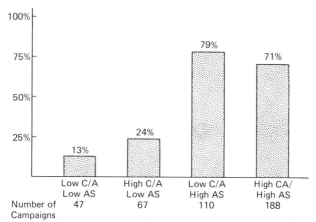

| Number of Campaigns | Low C/A Low AS 47 | High C/A Low AS 67 | Low C/A High AS 110 | High CA/ High AS 188 |

Source: Adapted from Peter R. Klein and Melvin Tainter, "Copy Research Validation: The Advertiser's Perspective," *Journal of Advertising Research*, 23, October–November 1983, pp. 9–18. Copyright © 1983 by the Advertising Research Foundation.

brands in test markets. Further, the ARS persuasion score correctly predicted which of two commercials would achieve higher test market sales. ASI, which uses a central Los Angeles location, relies on a pre-/postmeasure of brand selection in a prize-drawing context. Reliability studies across 100 commercials in 15 product categories yielded test-retest reliability correlations of from 0.81 to 0.88. Fifteen hundred commercials per year are tested by ASI, so well developed and current norms are available.[13]

The Buy Test design of the Sherman Group does not involve a central location. The respondents are often recruited and exposed to advertising in shopping malls.[14] A series of unaided questions on advertisement and copy recall identify those in the "recall/understand" group. The advertising "involvement" group are those who had a favorable emotional response, who believed that the brand positioning fit the execution, and who felt that the advertisement was worth looking at (or reading). The "buying urgency" group is identified in part by intentions to buy, improved product opinion, and the motivation to tell someone something about it. A basic measure, the BUY score, is the percent of those exposed who become part of all three groups. In 75 percent of 50 cases, the BUY score generated different outcomes from other persuasion measurements. In 20 test-retest contexts the average difference of the BUY score was within three percentage points.

On-Air Tests: Brand-Preference Change.   In a Mapes & Ross test, commercials are aired in a preselected prime-time position on a UHF station in each of three major markets. Prior to the test, a sample of 200 viewers (150 if it is an all-male target audience) are contacted by phone and invited to participate in a survey and cash award drawing that requires viewing the test program. Respondents provide unaided brand-name awareness and are questioned about their brand preferences for a number of different product categories. The day following the commercial exposure, the respondents again answer brand preference as well as DAR questions. The key Mapes & Ross measure is pre and post brand-preference change.

A Mapes & Ross study involved 142 commercials from 55 product categories and 2,241 respondents who were recontacted two weeks after participating in a test. Among those who bought the product category, purchases of the test brand were 3.3 times higher among those who changed their preference than among those who did not change.[15]

The ASI Apex system differs from the Mapes & Ross approach in several important ways.[16] First, before exposure, brand preference is measured by determining the brand bought most often and the brand most likely to be bought next. Thus, people who both use the brand and plan to buy it next are distinguished from those who answer only one or none of those questions positively. The impact of sample composition with respect to brand usage is thus potentially controlled (although the test samples of size 200 are limiting in this respect). Second, the after-exposure brand-preference measure, based on the brand to be selected if the respondent won a drawing and the brands they would consider if their preferred brand were unavailable, differs from the before measure. The use of different before-after measures reduces the likelihood that the before measure will influence the after measure. Third, the results are compared to a control group of 600 who go through the complete procedure but do not see the test advertisements. Thus, the impact of the procedure itself on brand preference for a given product class can be determined.

Customized Measures of Communication/Attitude.   Standardized copy-test measures are useful because they come with norms sometimes based on thousands of past tests. Thus, the interpretation of the test becomes more meaningful. Some objectives, particularly communication objectives, are necessarily unique to a brand and may require questions tailored to that brand. For example, Chevron ran a series of 12 print ads in 1980, such as the one shown in Figure 14-3, mostly telling people that Chevron made a lot less profit than people thought.[17] A posttest sample of 380 respondents were interviewed. Belief change was measured on the item "Chevron makes too much profit" for those aware of the advertising. The ads had a small effect, as those agreeing fell from 81 percent to 72 percent.

Interestingly, however, data from the same study showed that people seeing these print ads and the very positive "Energy Frontier" television campaign actually had less attitude change toward Chevron than did those seeing only the television ads. Thus, the print ads (20 percent of the budget) actually reduced the impact on the attitude toward the firm. Creating a positive attitude obviously had a positive impact on all belief dimensions. Calling attention to a source of irritation— oil company profits—tended to counteract the positive attitude change. The Chevron experience graphically illustrates the risk of measuring a part of a campaign in isolation.

Purchase Behavior

The fourth criterion is actual brand choice in an in-store, real-world setting. These tests focus on the effects of exposure to shifts in actual purchase behavior. Two well-known tests are those using coupons to stimulate purchasing and those involving split-cable testing.

Coupon Stimulated Purchasing.   In the Tele-Research approach, 600 shoppers are intercepted in a shopping center location, usually in Los Angeles, and randomly assigned to test or control groups. The test group is exposed to five television or radio commercials or six print ads. Around 250 subjects in the test group complete a questionnaire on the commercial. Both groups are given a customer code number and packets of coupons, including one for the test brand, which can be redeemed in a nearby cooperating drugstore or supermarket. The selling effectiveness score is the ratio of purchases by viewer shoppers divided by the rate of purchases by control shoppers. Purchases are tracked by scanner data. Although the exposure context is

Figure 14-3.   **A Chevron "profit" print advertisement**

Chevron energy report:

Compared to all U.S. industry—

Chevron's nickel profit makes us just average.

The average profit for all major U.S. industries last year was 5.5¢ on a sales dollar.

By comparison, in 1979 Chevron made about 5.1¢ on each sales dollar of U.S. petroleum sales—a little less than the average of U.S. Industry.

Even on our worldwide sales, we still made less on a sales dollar than the average of all U.S. industries.

Like most companies, we reinvest most of our worldwide profits after dividends plus cash from operations (including depreciation). In 1980, Chevron's reinvestment in energy development in the U.S. will be a <u>record</u> for us—more than <u>twice</u> our '79 U.S. profit.

Investment in U.S. energy development is the best way to help move America toward energy independence. But we must all continue to conserve as much energy as possible.

CHEVRON'S PROFIT ON U.S. PETROLEUM SALES VS. ALL U.S. INDUSTRY
(per dollar of sales in 1979)

5.1¢	**5.5¢**
CHEVRON	**ALL U.S. INDUSTRY**

CHEVRON'S PROFIT ON U.S. PETROLEUM SALES VS. INDIVIDUAL U.S. INDUSTRIES.
(per dollar of sales in 1979)

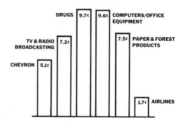

DRUGS 9.7¢   9.6¢ COMPUTERS/OFFICE EQUIPMENT

TV & RADIO BROADCASTING 7.2¢   7.5¢ PAPER & FOREST PRODUCTS

CHEVRON 5.1¢

1.7¢ AIRLINES

Chevron

(JWT) Ad No. 100062—
Time, Newsweek, Spts. Ill., U.S. News—4/14, 4/21, 1980

Courtesy of J. Walter Thompson USA.

highly artificial, the purchase choice is relatively realistic in that real money is spent in a real store.

Split-Cable Testing.   Split-cable testing by firms such as BehaviorScan was described in Chapter 3. A panel of around 3,000 households is recruited in test cities. An ID card presented by the panel member to the checkout stand, coupled with a computerized scanner system, allows the purchases of the member to be monitored. The in-store activity is also monitored. Further, panelists have a device connected to their TV set that allows BehaviorScan to monitor what channel is tuned, and also to substitute one advertisement. Thus, panelists can be divided into matched groups and different advertising directed at each. In Chapter 3, the use of split-cable testing to conduct advertising weight tests was discussed. They can and are also used to test one set of advertisements against another or to evaluate a host of options, such as the time of day or program in which the ad appears, the commercial length, or the bunching of exposures (versus an even distribution through time).

AT&T used the AdTel (Burke) split-cable system to test a new "Cost of Visit" campaign against the established "Reach Out" campaign.[18] Research had determined that a substantial "light user" segment had a psychological "price barrier" to calling and overestimated the cost, particularly at off-peak times.

The campaign objective was to communicate among the light users how inexpensive a 20-minute telephone visit can be and to stimulate usage during off-peak times. The "Cost of Visit" theme contained surprise (of the low cost), the appropriateness of a 20-minute visit, and the total cost of $3.33 (some believed that it would cost $20.00). One of the ads, AT & T Long Lines Residence, is shown in Figure 14-4.

Two matched AdTel panel groups of 8,000 were created. During a 15-month period the two campaigns were aired, one to each group. Each household received three exposures per week (300 gross rating points per week). Compared to the "Reach Out" campaign, the "Cost of Visit" campaign increased calls during the deep discount period by 0.6 calls per week among all households and 1.5 calls per week among light-user households. Projections indicated that the campaign would generate $100 million in extra revenue during a five-year period.

Two additional analyses are of interest. During the six months after the test ended, usage fell off but not to the level prior to the test. However, it was clear that reinforcement advertising was needed. The "Cost of Visit" campaign changed two key attitudes more than the "Reach Out" campaign, the attitude toward the value of a long-distance call and the attitude about the rates.

Split-cable testing is the ultimate in testing validity. However, it can cost from 20 to 50 times that of a forced exposure test ($100,000 to $200,000) and take six months to a year or more before the results are known. By that time, new brands or changing consumer preferences could make the results somewhat obsolete. For these reasons, most firms use the split-cable testing far less than other alternatives.

Figure 14-4.   **AT&T long lines residence**

Courtesy of AT&T Communications.

OTHER DIAGNOSTIC TESTS

An entire category of advertising research methods is designed primarily not to test the impact of a total ad but to help creative people understand how the parts of the ad contribute to its impact. Which are weak, and how do they interact? Most of these approaches can be applied to mock-ups of proposed ads as well as finished ads.

Qualitative Research

Focus groups research is widely used at the front end of the development of an advertising campaign. In one study of the techniques used by 112 (out of 150 surveyed) of the top advertisers and agencies, focus groups were used 96 percent of the time to generate ideas for advertisements, and 60 percent of the time to test reactions to rough executions.[19]

Audience Impressions of the Ad

Many copy tests add a set of open-ended questions to the procedures designed to tap the audience's impressions of what the ad was about, what ideas were presented, interest in the ideas, and so on. One goal is to detect potential misperceptions. Another is to uncover unintended associations that may have been created. If too many negative comments are elicited, there may be cause for concern. A Volkswagen commercial showing a Detroit auto worker driving a VW Rabbit because of its superior performance was killed because a substantial part of the audience disliked the company disloyalty portrayed.[20]

Adjective Checklists

The BRC mail questionnaire, shown in Figure 14-1, includes an adjective checklist that allows the advertiser to determine how warm, amusing, irritating, or informative the respondent thinks it to be. Similar checklists are used by ASI, Teleresearch, and other firms and agencies. The agencies Leo Burnett and Young & Rubicam use a similar phrase checklist extensively. Several of their phrases tap an empathy dimension. "I can see myself doing that," "I can relate to that," and so on. Some believe that unless advertisements can achieve a degree of empathy, they will not perform well.

Physiological Measures

Several kinds of instruments are used to observe reactions to advertisements. In general, they attempt to capture changes in the nervous system or emotional arousal during the exposure sequence. The first two reviewed below focus on eye movement.

Eye Camera.   This is a device that photographs eye movements, either by photographing a small spot of light reflected from the eye, or by taking a motion picture of eye movement. A device used by Burke records the point on a print advertisement or package, where the eye focuses 60 times each second. Analysis can determine what the reader saw, what he or she "returned to," and what point was "fixed upon." In package research, a respondent can be asked to find a test brand placed on a shelf of competing packages.

Pupillometrics.   Pupillometrics deals with eye dialation. Eyes dialate when something interesting or pleasant is seen, and constrict when confronted with unpleasant, distasteful, or uninteresting things. One interesting application is its use in screening new television programs.[21] Several related eye-movement devices are used, including the tachistoscope, blur meter, distance meter, illumination meter, and stereo rater.[22]

CONPAAD.   Conjugately programmed analysis of advertising (CONPAAD) has a respondent operate either a foot or hand device which controls the intensity of the audio and video channels of a television set. The viewer must exert effort to sustain the signals, which have been programmed to decay in a specific pattern. His or her effort to keep audio and video going is used as a measure of attention and interest in the advertising.[23]

Monitoring Commercial Response

A device used by respondents to register interest is part of ASI in-theater tests. It is a dial that can be turned up or down to indicate high or low interest. Data from the dial interest recorder are used to provide diagnostic information on what parts of the commerial were of high or low interest. Aaker, Stayman, and Hagerty have used a computer joystick to measure respondent reactions to feelings of warmth while viewing commercials. This procedure can also be used to monitor other feelings, such as irritation, humor, or liking.[24] MacLachlan and Myers have used the time it takes the respondent to make a choice between competing brands as a measure of the relative effectiveness of advertising. This is called "response latency" and has several other applications in advertising research.[25] Another potentially useful technique is called "facial action coding." By observing changes in facial expression during exposure, several kinds of emotional responses can be monitored.[26]

Market Facts has developed a system in which a respondent presses a button when something in the commercial strikes her or him as especially interesting or irritating. The respondent is then shown the commercial again and asked why the button was punched at each point. The result is a second-by-second understanding of audience reaction.

TRACKING STUDIES

When a campaign is running, its impact is often monitored via a tracking study. Periodic sampling of the target audience provides a time trend of measures of interest. The purpose is to evaluate and reassess the advertising campaign and perhaps also to understand why it is or is not working. Among the measures that are often tracked are advertisement awareness, awareness of elements of the advertisement, brand awareness, beliefs about brand attributes, brand image, occasions of use, and brand preference. Of particular interest is knowing how the campaign is affecting the brand, as opposed to how the advertisement is communicating.

Figure 14-5 shows the tracking of an advertising campaign directed at children for a beverage product. Personal interviews were held with children from 6 to 12 years old. They were shown visual stimuli such as pictures of brand packaging or line drawings of advertising characters. The mostly open-ended questions were consistently coded over five years. The interest was in the "main character," who was the personification of the brand and playback of the "story" of the advertising, the main creative element.[27]

The successful campaign of year 1 was expanded with additional executions which apparently did not have comparable impact. The disappointing results of year 2 led to a fresh round of copy development aimed at making it more "modern" and "relevant" for kids. However, the decline continued in year 3. An analysis of verbatim playback suggested that the predictability of the main character's actions

Figure 14-5.   **Examples of ad tracking**

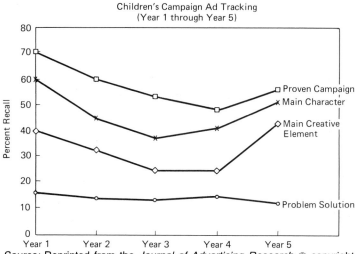

Children's Campaign Ad Tracking
(Year 1 through Year 5)

Source: Reprinted from the *Journal of Advertising Research* © copyright 1985, by the Advertising Research Foundation.

were too predictable and new ads were developed which placed it in a more heroic role, "rescuing" children in adventurous situations. In year 4 the main character measure turned up. For the next season, the campaign used situations from a child's real life to attempt to make the advertising more relevant. The result in year 5 was a dramatic increase in recall of the central creative element and an important increase in two other measures. The tracking program provided in this case actionable information over time, allowing the advertising to be adjusted around the same theme to become more effective.

The TEC Audit

The Eric Marder firm provides one approach to obtaining tracking data without doing customized studies.[28] They maintain a panel of 3,000 women from 1,000 areas. Each woman keeps a record of all television commercials she sees in the course of one randomly assigned day each month. Before watching television on her assigned day, she records her buying intention for each product category. On the assigned day she watches television normally except that she records the time, the channel, and the brand advertised from every ad she sees, and her buying intention immediately after exposure. The received messages (RMs) are defined as the total number of commercials recorded per 100 women. The persuasion rate (PR) is defined as the net percent of the RM that produces a shift in buying intention from some other brand to the advertised brand. Subscribers obtain quarterly reports of the RM and PR from all competing brands in the product class.

SELECTING COPY TESTS

A very wide range of copy-testing alternatives has been developed and is available to the advertiser. Beyond the question of whether to test copy at all lies the question of what particular test or tests should be used. The question has occupied the attention of professional and academic researchers since copy testing first began, and a great deal has been written on the subject. Much of the interest lies in assessing the validity and reliability of various types of tests. The subject is also important because considerable stakes are involved by research supplier companies who tend to offer a particular kind of testing service or rely on one testing method. The Advertising Research Foundation maintains a standing committee to monitor and encourage the development of new and better testing methods, and its annual conferences generally relate to questions of the strengths and limitations of particular methods or techniques.

The basic question in test selection is whether or not a test is valid and reliable. Does it really measure the effectiveness of advertising? More specifically, are the particular measures used in any one test true measures of the constructs involved? Is the test reliable and will it measure the same thing each time it is used?

Can one test measure everything or are multitests required? These are some of the questions of copy-test selection.

Copy-Test Validity

The first problem in assessing copy-test validity is that, if the advertisement is to be tested with respect to a communication objective and a copy test evaluated in that context, there must exist an operational objective—a measurable and useful variable that represents the objective. As Chapter 4 indicated, the development of an operational objective is no simple task. In fact, researchers must often work with a vague or ill-defined set of objectives.

Second, given that a target population can be sensibly defined, the subjects in the test should be representative of the target population. Ideally, they should be selected randomly and the sample size should be large enough so that the results are statistically valid. Of course, compromises must be made. It is often not feasible economically to obtain large random samples, especially if personal interviews are involved. The bias introduced by nonrespondents is a problem that is particularly crucial in some tests. People differ widely in their propensity to answer questions, to participate in laboratory experiments, to be subjects in physiological tests, and to be members of consumer panels. The danger is that those who refuse to participate may respond differently from those who do. Consequently, the results may not represent the population for which the sample was drawn.

Third, and perhaps most significant, is the reaction of the respondents to the test environment and the measuring instruments. This reaction can distort the results. When a respondent is in a test situation, he or she tends to act differently. The main problem in any advertising study is the tendency of respondents to act as they should act (called reactive effect, role selection, the guinea pig effect, etc.).

There are techniques to minimize the reactive effect. One is to divert respondents from the actual purpose of the experiment. Thus, a respondent may be told that she or he is evaluating television programs instead of their accompanying commercials. This technique, however, by no means eliminates all such bias. Furthermore, it has moral and ethical implications. How much deception should a respondent be subjected to without his or her consent? Another approach is to use, wherever possible, nonreactive measures. Thus, one might unobtrusively observe store traffic or sales. Direct-mail tests can usually be conducted with little reactive effect since a nonreactive response measure to the direct-mail advertisement is usually available.

These are some of the considerations that need to be taken into account in assessing test validity. Equally important are the constructs being measured. If two or more are involved, how can we know if they represent different kinds of response?

Figure 14-6 provides an overview of some of the important ways in which copy tests can differ. Each dimension involves validity issues and trade-offs with

Figure 14–6. **Alternative methods of copy testing**

The Advertisement Used

- Mock-Up
- Finished Advertisement

Frequency of Exposure

- Single exposure test
- Multiple exposure test

How It's Shown

- Isolated
- In a clutter
- In a program or magazine

Where the Exposure Occurs

- In a shopping center facility
- At home on TV
- At home through the mail
- In a theater

How Respondents are Obtained

- Prerecruited forced exposure
- Not prerecruited/natural exposure

Geographic Scope

- One city
- Several cities
- Nationwide

Alternative Measures of Persuasion

- Pre/post measures of attitudes or behavioral that is, pre/post attitude shifts
- Multiple measures that is, recall/involvement/buying commitment
- After only questions to measure persuasion that is, constant sum brand preference
- Test market sales measures that is, using scanner panels

Bases of Comparison and Evaluation

- Comparing test results to norms
- Using a control group

---

cost. There follows a discussion of several important considerations involved in evaluating validity.

Measuring Response.   There is a concern with the reactive effect of the study. The respondent may behave differently because he or she knows that actions and opinions are being recorded. There is evidence that this problem is minor in a system such as BehaviorScan when the panel member becomes acclimated to the system. However, it is of greatest concern in systems which demand that the respondent give an attitude response. Is the respondent willing and able to respond accurately?

The Stimuli.   One issue is whether a rough mock-up or a finished ad is used. Several copy-test firms have reported high correlations with mock-up measures and finished copy measures. The seriousness of the problem will depend on the difference between the mock-up and the finished commercial and the impact of this difference on audience response. For example, it is very difficult to test humor in rough form.

Another issue is the frequency of response. To what extent can a copy test predict the response to a campaign that will involve dozens or even hundreds of exposures? Can a single exposure provide meaningful results, or should a minimum of two or three be used?

Still another is the context in which the test advertisement is embedded. The use of a cluster of advertisements embedded in a program or magazine is the most realistic but adds complexity and is possibly confounding.

The Exposure.   Such approaches as the theater tests or mall intercept exposure contexts are termed forced exposure tests because the setting is artificial and the respondent is required to watch. The others, such as the BehaviorScan split-cable testing, are termed ''on-air'' tests because the exposure is a natural home setting in the context of watching a show. Approaches such as the ASI Apex method are on-air but the respondents realize they are in a test and are not watching a show they would watch at a time they would normally watch it. Thus, there is still concern that the exposure context may affect the results.

The Sample.   The sample should be representative of the target population. In all copy-test approaches the biggest concern is with the bias introduced by nonresponse. The danger is that those who refuse to participate may respond differently from those who do agree to respond. In addition, mall intercept methods obviously access only mall shoppers, and cable-based tests miss those not connected to a cable. There is also a question as to whether one or even three or four cities can provide a representative sample.

Appropriateness of the Response Measure.   Obviously, copy-test validity will depend on the advertising response that is desired. A campaign that is designed to gain awareness may not best be measured by a test that focuses on immediate behavioral response. A campaign that attempts to create an image or an association with a feeling such as warmth might require many repetitions and a subtle measurement method, perhaps asking some questions directed at the use experience. A single exposure test with a coupon-redemption measure may not be appropriate at all. Thus, the usefulness of the various criteria used in testing needs to be evaluated in the context of the advertising objectives involved.

Natural versus Artificial.   Running through the validity considerations is a spectrum from artificial to natural. At one extreme would be forced exposure to a commercial mock-up with a paper-and-pencil response using a convenience mall intercept sample. At the other would be the BehaviorScan system, where the audience member realizes that he or she is in a panel but otherwise everything is completely natural, including multiple exposures over time.

Copy-Test Reliability

Copy-test selection must also take into account the reliability of a particular test. Will it measure the same thing each time it is used? Some work has also been done on this question. In a study by Clancy and Ostlund, for example, a second measure taken at a later time was developed for 106 on-air recall tested commercials. The authors report reliability coefficients (the correlation of scores taken at one time with those taken at another time) of 0.67 (and when product category effects were removed) of 0.29.[29] These are comparatively low, and on this basis the authors challenge the reliability of on-air tests. Silk[30] has pointed out some of the dangers of using the test-retest approach to reliability assessment. It is important that test-retest conditions be equivalent. If, for example, consumers have been exposed to the advertising in different contexts between the two testing occasions or to competitive advertising, the testing conditions may not be equivalent, and a low correlation may not signify low reliability. It is indeed difficult to make straightforward assessments of copy-test reliability using the test-retest procedure because of such factors.

Other Considerations

Copy-test selection should take into account several other considerations concerning the nature of a particular test or supplier providing the test. In addition to reliability and validity, for example, Plummer[31] recommends that tests be assessed on five other criteria:

1. *Sensitivity:* The test should be able to discriminate between different commercials within brand groups.
2. *Independence of measures:* The different test measures should have little interrelationship across many testing experiences.

3. *Comprehensiveness:* It should provide, in addition to basic evaluative scores, some information that will indicate the reason for the levels of the evaluative scores.

4. *Relationships to other tests:* It should provide similar results for the same stimuli tested by a similar but different measurement system.

5. *Acceptability:* It must have some acceptance by those responsible for decisions in terms of a commitment to work with the test findings.

In choosing a supplier, obviously the reputation of the company, such as its service and delivery record, availability of norms, and stature in the industry, will be important. Things like geographic location and costs of the service relative to competitive offerings also come into play. There are suppliers in each of the three major categories of copy-testing research: laboratory tests, simulated natural environment tests, and market tests. In television, laboratory and simulated natural environment tests involve forced exposure, whereas market tests tend to be on-air recall tests. A study of advertiser and agency executive opinion on preferences between different versions of on-air and forced-exposure tests[32] revealed the most preferred to be single-exposure, multiple-market tests in the on-air case (rather than single exposure, single market; multiple exposure, single market; or multiple exposure, multiple market). In the forced-exposure case, in-theater and laboratory tests were preferred to mobile trailer and in-home forced-exposure tests. These data of course indicate overall general preference, and test choices should be made on the basis of the particular situation involved.

The choice of a copy test should be guided by the riskiness of the decision involved. To begin a major new campaign involving strategic departure is a high-risk decision that requires a total evaluation of all the constructs mentioned earlier. It is also important to assess whether the copy appears to antagonize respondents in any way. A total evaluation should also involve enough diagnostic information about consumer reactions to the execution so that the decision could be based on all the evaluative and diagnostic measures. It is possible to get high awareness but negative reactions. Total evaluation is not always economically practical or necessary. Extensions of existing campaigns are low-risk decisions requiring only *partial* evaluation. In particular evaluations, persuasiveness or attitude change will sometimes be the issue and attention will be of little concern. Sometimes clarity of communication will be the issue, and a subjective judgment of its persuasiveness will suffice. Sometimes the major concern will be focused on possible negatives in execution. In each case, the objectives of the copy test will differ.

One overriding problem with attempting to assess the costs and benefits of copy testing is that effects on sales or any other criterion variable also are likely to be influenced by the media decision. Planning a campaign and any research activity to be associated with it therefore requires explicit consideration of the media choice as well. An argument can be made that, once a target group has been identified and objectives set in either communicative or behavioral terms, the first decision to be made is what media should be chosen to reach them. The important overall criterion for decision making among media and copy alternatives thus becomes the choice of media and copy that will maximize the present value of the projected profit stream. The following two chapters extend this viewpoint by concentrating on media decisions.

SUMMARY

During and after the creation and production process, the advertiser must decide whether to invest in copy-testing research and what kinds of tests to use. An industry of research supplier companies has evolved to supply copy-testing services. There are hundreds of methods used to test copy. Much advertising is placed without formal copy testing, particularly by local advertisers for whom the investment in advertising does not warrant the extra expense. Copy testing tends to be done by national advertisers where the risks and investments are much higher.

Copy testing can be done at the beginning of the creation process, at the end (layout) stage of the creation process, at the end of the production stage, and after the campaign is launched. Tests at the first three stages are called pretests, whereas those at the fourth stage are posttests. Numerous types of criteria and constructs are used to guide copy-testing research. Many tests are associated with attention, recognition, and recall constructs. The argument is that if these objectives are accomplished the advertising will at least achieve the essential steps in communication. The full array of constructs involved in the hierarchy of response model can, however, be used. In this case, several types of tests will be needed and expenses will increase accordingly,

Criteria used in copy testing can be usefully grouped into four types: recognition, recall, persuasion, and behavior. BRC uses mail questionnaires to measure television commercial recognition and brand-name association; Communicus for television and Starch for print use personal interviews. Day-after-recall is widely used but controversial because of its inability to predict persuasion or behavior, especially for emotional appeals. Persuasion has been measured in forced exposure or on-air contexts, by change in brand preference after an exposure to an ad on a UHF station, by change in prize-list brand preference in a theater test, by comparison of the effect on brand preference with a nonexposed control group, measures of advertising involvement and brand commitment, and by measures tailored to particular advertising objectives. Behavior measures include coupon-stimulated buying after a forced exposure to an ad and scanner-based monitoring of panelists in a split-cable testing operation.

Diagnostic testing, to evaluate the advertisement content at all stages of the process, includes qualitative research, audience ad impressions, adjective checklists, eye movement, and the monitoring of audience response during the commercial.

Within the laboratory-physiological methods group, measuring devices such as the eye camera, polygraphs, tachistoscopes, pupillometers, and computer-assisted effort measurement are the major alternatives. Recent developments in this area include response latency and face-coding methods. Simulated natural environment tests include those based on intercept research and mobile trailers, fixed facility research, and in-home interviewing. Many of the recognition, rather than the recall, methods fit into this category. Services provided by M/S/C, ASI, Starch INRA Hooper, and Bruzzone Research are representative of these kinds of tests.

A tracking study provides measures of advertising impact over time by taking periodic (monthly, quarterly, or yearly) surveys of audience response. Awareness of the advertising or of specific claims or elements of the advertising is often included, but any measure relevant to the objectives can be used.

Given the vast array of alternative methods and commercial services for copy testing, the question becomes how to choose sensibly among them. The basic question is whether a particular test is valid and reliable. Three major factors must be considered with respect to validity. First, there must be an operational objective. Second, subjects in the test should be representative of the target population. Third, reactions of the subjects to the testing situation that might bias the results should be minimized. Copy-test validity concerns usually focus on the appropriateness of the response measure, the reactive (or guinea pig) effect of being in an experiment (especially when the exposure setting is not natural and when an attitude measure is required), the use of mock-ups, and the representativeness of the sample.

Generally, it has been found that no one test or method is sufficient to satisfy all the needs of copy research, but that tests designed to measure different constructs can indeed do so. Which tests are better, particularly whether recognition or recall tests are better for testing television commercials, is a continuing debate in the industry. Test reliability must also be considered. Here, again, because of the difficulties of measuring reliability, there are no definitive answers. The norms developed by suppliers over years of testing remain the advertiser's best guide to this question.

Many other practical considerations about the supplier (reputation, service, location, costs, and so on) and the service or test (sensitivity, independence, comprehensiveness, relationships to other tests, and acceptability) should be included in the selection process. The overriding considerations in this decision are that the test or tests chosen should be governed by the objectives of the advertising, the amount of investment involved, and the extent to which there is little or no past experience on which to guide decision making in a particular product or market situation.

DISCUSSION QUESTIONS

1. Make a list of the factors you would consider in deciding whether to invest in copy-testing research at each of the four stages of testing given in the chapter.

2. Why measure recognition anyway? Why would it ever be of value to have an audience member recognize an ad when he or she could not

recall it without being prompted and could not recall its content? Why not just measure recall?

3.   Compare the BRC recognition method with the Cumminicus method. What are the relative strengths and weaknesses?

4.   DAR is widely used. Why? Would you use it if you were the product manager for Lowenbrau? For American Express? Under what circumstances would you use it?

5.   Review the validity problems inherent in the McCollum-Spielman theater testing approach discussed in Chapter 4. Compare these to:

   a. The Mapes & Ross method.

   b. The Apex method.

   c. The Tele-Research approach

   d. The Behavior Scan approach

6.   Why conduct tracking studies? Why not just observe sales?

7.   How will adjective checklists help a creative group? What about eye movement data?

8.   Suppose that the advertising objective is to entice people to try a new brand. Predictive validity is whether recall predicts purchase, whether memorability predicts purchase, whether arousal and interest predict purchase, or whether attitudes predict purchase. From what has been reviewed in previous chapters, discuss the validity question at each of these levels.

9.   The various methods of copy research are representative of the various methods of research in social science, particularly psychological and sociological research methods. Give an example in which the methods used by psychoanalytic (Freudian) or clinical psychologists, stimulus-response (behavior) psychologists, multidimensional scalers, attitude researchers, and sociologists are employed in copy research.

10.   Laboratory methods are often criticized for their "artificiality" in copy-testing research. Are there any counterarguments? Discuss.

11.   Discuss the advantages and disadvantages of an in-theater method compared to a market test, and a recall method versus a recognition method.

12.   Design an ideal test of copy effectiveness. Assuming the measures would be made in a natural environment, critically examine the difficulties involved.

NOTES

1. One estimate is that as much as $75 million was spent on copy testing in 1976. Robert Mayer of Young & Rubicam advertising agency suggests that there are "33,000 ways" to test advertising copy. Basal skin response, brain waves, eye movement, pupil dilation, physical effort, aided and unaided

noting and recall, copy-point recall, visual and slogan recall, interest and attitude toward the advertisement, knowledge and attitude toward brand product attributes and benefits, buying intentions, coupon redemption and simulated sales response are some of the measures used. Copy-testing designs include prepost or post-only studies, single versus multiple exposure, projectable versus nonprojectable samples, natural exposure versus forced exposure. Other alternatives include where the exposure should take place (in-home, in-theater, mobile trailer, shopping-center intercept, fixed facility), whether the testing is done in groups (such as the family) or individually, and whether the exposure should attempt to simulate the natural setting by introducing distraction or competitive advertising?

2. Readers should refer to the materials in Chapter 13 on the creation and production process for a better understanding of where testing "fits in."

3. Donald E. Bruzzone, "The Case for Testing Commercials by Mail," presented at the 25th Annual Conference of the Advertising Research Foundation, New York, October 23, 1979.

4. Lewis C. Winters, "Comparing Pretesting and Posttesting of Corporate Advertising," *Journal of Advertising Research,* 23, February–March 1983, pp. 25–32.

5. Benjamin Lipstein, "An Historical Perspective of Copy Research," *Journal of Advertising Research,* 24, December 1984, pp. 11–15.

6. Hubert A. Zielske, "Does Day-After-Recall Penalize 'Feeling' Ads?" *Journal of Advertising Research,* 22, February–March 1982, pp. 19–22.

7. Lawrence D. Gibson, "Not Recall," *Journal of Advertising Research,* 23, February–March 1983, pp. 39–46.

8. Lipstein, "An Historical Perspective."

9. AC-T Advertising Control for Television, undated publication of McCollum/Spielman Research.

10. Ibid.

11. Lipstein, "An Historical Perspective."

12. "Advertising Quality Deserves More Weight!", Research Systems Corporation, August 1983.

13. ASI Laboratory Methodology, ASI Market Research, Inc., New York, undated.

14. Milton Sherman, "The BUY Test," presented to The Market Research Society, Manchester, England, May 20, 1982.

15. Descriptive material from Mapes & Ross.

16. APEX, ASI Market Research Inc., New York, March 1984, p. 46.

17. Winters, "Comparing Pretesting and Posttesting," p. 28.

18. Alan P. Kuritsky, John D. C. Little, Alvin J. Silk, and Emily S. Bassman, "The Development, Testing, and Execution of a New Marketing Strategy at AT&T Long Lines," *Interfaces,* 12, December 1982, pp. 22–37.

19. Benjamin Lipstein and James P. Neelankavil, "Television Advertising Copy Research: A Critical Review of the State of the Art," *Journal of Advertising Research,* 24, April–May 1984, pp. 19–25.

20. "VW Has Some Clinkers among Classics," *Advertising Age,* September 9, 1985, p. 48.

21. Eckhard H. Hess, "Pupillometrics," in F. M. Bass, C. W. King, and E. A. Pessemier, eds., *Applications of the Sciences in Marketing Management* (New York: Wiley, 1968), pp. 431–453.

22. A variation introduced by Haug Associates of Los Angeles utilizes a modified portable tachistoscope device that is taken into the home and allows testing in the in-home environment. Respondents are shown the first few seconds of a commercial and asked if they know what it is and, if so, to reconstruct the copy points.

23. See, for example, Ogden R. Lindsley, "A Behavioral Measure of Television Viewing," *Journal of Advertising Research,* 2, September 1962, pp. 2–12; and Lewis C. Winters and Wallace H. Wallace, "On Operant Conditioning Techniques," *Journal of Advertising Research,* 5, October 1970, pp. 39–45. Associates for Research in Behavior in Philadelphia provides a copy-testing service based on CONPAAD.

24. David A. Aaker, Douglas Stayman, and Michael Hagerty, "Warmth in Advertising," Working Paper, University of California, Berkeley, 1985.

25. James M. MacLachlan and John G. Myers, "Using Response Latency to Identify Commercials That Motivate," *Journal of Advertising Research,* 23, October–November 1983, pp. 51–57. For a book on the subject, see James M. MacLachlan, *Response Latency: New Measure of Advertising* (New York: Advertising Research Foundation, 1977).

26. John G. Myers, "Response Latency and Facial Action Coding Research in Advertising," *American Marketing Association Doctoral Consortium*, University of Chicago, 1978. See also John L. Graham, "A New System for Measuring Nonverbal Responses to Marketing Appeals," American Marketing Association Proceedings, 1980.

27. Douglas F. Haley, "Advertising Tracking Studies: Packaged-Goods Case Histories," *Journal of Advertising Research*, 25, February–March 1985, pp. 45–50.

28. The TEC Audit, TEC Measures, Inc., New York.

29. Kevin J. Clancy and Lyman E. Ostlund, "Commercial Effectiveness Measures," *Journal of Advertising Research*, 16, February 1976, pp. 29–34. See also, Derek Bloom, Andrea Jay, and Tony Twyman, "The Validity of Advertising Pretests," *Journal of Advertising Research*, 17, April 1977, pp. 7–16; and Richard P. Bagozzi and Alvin J. Silk, "Recall, Recognition, and the Measurement of Memory for Print Advertisements," *Marketing Science*, 2, Spring 1983, pp. 95–134.

30. Alvin J. Silk, "Test-Retest Correlations and the Reliability of Copy Testing," *Journal of Marketing Research*, 14, November 1977, pp. 476–486.

31. Joseph T. Plummer, "Evaluating TV Commercial Tests," *Journal of Advertising Research*, 12, October 1972, pp. 21–27.

32. Lyman E. Ostlund, Rakesh Sapra, and Kevin Clancy, "Copy Testing Methods and Measures Favored by Top Ad Agency and Advertising Executives," Working Paper, Graduate School of Business, University of Arizona, 1978.

APPENDIX
NOTES ON FOUR COPY-TESTING SERVICES

Burke Marketing Research: Day-After-Recall (DAR)

Methodology

- *Prime-time spots are purchased in three markets. The spots are to be within a program (other than news) that does not have a low rating among the target audience.*
- Using the telephone directory as a sampling base, 200 *program viewers are called.*
- They are asked if they can recall any commercials the previous day in a product category (*like soap*). *If they cannot identify the brand correctly, they are then given the product category and brand and asked if they recalled the commercial.*
- *They are then asked for anything they can recall about the commercial, what was said, what was shown, and what the main idea was.*
- *All respondents are asked if they can recall specific incidents in the program that occurred just before and just after the commercial.*
- *DAR is the percent of those in the commercial audience who recalled something specific about the commercial, such as the sales message, the story line, the plot, or some visual or audio element. The commercial audience is all those who saw the program and were not distracted or changing channels when the commercial was on or who correctly recalled the program segment that occurred just before and just after the commercial or who saw the commercial.*

- *Approximate cost: $4,600 plus media cost.*
- *Rough commercial testing is available for approximately $2,200 including media for female audiences and approximately $4,000 for male audiences including media costs. The approach is the same except that the respondents are recruited by calling them prior to the program and asking them to watch and evaluate a particular program. The program is a daytime show in a certain city (for men the program is an early afternoon Sunday program).*

Discussion

Burke's DAR has two salient attributes. First, it provides the commercial exposure in a natural, realistic in-home setting. Second, it is well established and has developed extensive norms over the years. The average DAR is 24. One-fourth of all commercials score under 15 and one-fourth score over 31.

Mapes & Ross

Methodology

- *Commercials are aired in a preselected prime-time position on a UHF or independent station in each of three major markets.*
- *Prior to the test, a sample of 200 viewers (150 if it is an all-male target audience) are contacted by telephone and invited to participate in a survey that requires viewing the test program (a drawing for three cash awards is an incentive). Appointments are set up to interview the respondents the day after the program is aired. Respondents are questioned about their brand preferences for a number of different product categories. Respondents provide brand names on an unaided basis.*
- *The day following the airing of the test program those who watched the program are asked on an unaided basis their brand preferences for a number of product categories.*
- *The respondents are then asked on an aided basis about recall of six commercials that appeared within the program. Open-ended questions pertaining to what the commercial was about, what ideas were presented, interest in the ideas, and reactions to the commercial are asked of all respondents claiming recall.*
- *As an option, respondents can be asked to provide ratings on a 10-point scale on statements about the test brand or test commercial.*
- *Demographic and brand bought last questions complete the interview.*
- *Approximate cost per commercial: $3,500 plus air time of approximately $700.*

Discussion

The key measure provided by Mapes & Ross is pre and post brand-preference change. A 1979 study by Mapes & Ross in which they related recall and brand-preference change to purchase behavior is instructive. They recontacted 2,241 respondents 2 weeks after they had participated in a standard Mapes & Ross test. A total of 142 commercials from 55 product categories were represented. They were questioned about their purchases in the 2-week period. Among those who bought the product category, purchases of the test brand were 3.3 times higher among those who changed their preference than among those who did not change. Proven recallers exhibited somewhat higher brand buying levels than nonproven recallers. However, this higher buying level can be attributed in large measure to those within the proven recall group who also changed their preference toward the test brand. Those who did prove recall, but who did not change their preference toward the test brand, exhibited a purchase level only slightly higher than those who neither proved recall nor changed their preference. A total of 7,283 product category purchases were involved, 758 of which represented a switch to the test brand.

ASI Market Research, Inc.

Methodology

- *A sample of 410 respondents are recruited by telephone or from shopping centers. Of this group, 250 are selected to match a standard audience profile, which may be augmented to reflect some target group specification.*
- *The respondents come to a Los Angeles theater, 200 seats of which are equipped with dial interest recorders that allow the respondents to continuously dial their interest in the material. The information from 150 seats that are active at any one time is monitored by a computer and presented graphically as continuous-line charts. Respondents who forget or refuse the dials are switched to "inactive" status.*
- *The audience completes a classification questionnaire and a preexposure brand preference measure presented in the form of a prize list.*
- *The audience is then exposed to a control cartoon, a television pilot, a control commercial, and a set of four noncompeting test commercials.*
- *If desired, ten respondents are pulled out of the audience and asked to participate in a group discussion.*
- *Respondents are apologetically told by the moderator that the prize list was incomplete—one product cateogry was omitted—so they will have to complete a corrected sheet from which the drawing will be made.*
- *After viewing another control cartoon and an entertainment segment, the respondents are asked to write down brands and product categories of commercials together with anything they could remember seeing or hearing in them. Door prizes are then awarded.*

- *An option is to then reexpose the audience to the test commercials and to administer a customized questionnaire that can contain up to three open-ended questions.*
- *Among the outputs are interest and involvement in the commercial obtained from the dial interest recorders, communication recall achieved, the pre and post brand preference measure, and optionally the diagnostic information from the discussion group and the refocus exposure questionnaire.*
- *Approximate cost: $3,025, plus $925 for the refocus exposure, plus $300 to $900 for the group discussion (depending on the length and depth).*

Discussion

ASI checks the representativeness of each audience by measuring demographics, product usage patterns, television viewing patterns, audience reactions to control material, and preference changes obtained in a product category for which no commercials were run. If the audience is judged abnormal, it is discarded. Reliability studies across 100 commercials in 15 product categories yielded test-retest reliability correlations of from 0.81 to 0.88.

Tele-Research, Inc.

Methodology

- *Six hundred shoppers are intercepted in a shopping center location in Los Angeles (other markets are available at higher cost) and randomly assigned to test or control groups.*
- *A short brand usage and demographic interview is followed by exposure to five commercials (television or radio.) One commercial is a control and the others are noncompetitive test commercials. When print is used, six advertisements are used instead of five. The test group sees the test commercial and the control group does not.*
- *One hundred subjects in the test group complete a self-administered questionnaire, which includes questions on the main point, likes, dislikes, believability, influence on attitudes (increase versus decrease in interest in the brand), and an adjective checklist (clever, informative, silly, stale, and so on).*
- *Both groups are given packets of coupons, including one for the test brand, which can be redeemed in a nearby cooperating drugstore or supermarket.*
- *Selling effectiveness score is the ratio of purchases by viewer shoppers divided by the rate of purchases by control shoppers. A percentile ranking is obtained by comparing to category norms.*
- *Delayed telephone recall based upon 150 of the 200 viewers who did not participate in the postexposure questionnaire has an approximate additional cost of $2,000.*
- *Approximate cost: $3,000 per commercial.*

Discussion

A prime selling point of Tele-Research is that they provide a behavioral response measure that is based on the highly realistic context of a shopper spending their own money in a real store. Some early 1960s research by Tele-Research is relevant. They compared day-after-recall scores with their selling effectiveness scores for 300 commercials. Those commercials that had DAR scores in the lowest quartile tended to have low selling effectiveness scores. However, there was little correlation between DAR and selling effectiveness among the balance of the commercials. In the same study the Tele-Research forced-exposure DAR was compared with that of non-forced-exposure (in-home) DAR for 182 commercials. The correlation between the two was approximately 0.80, but the recall levels were much higher for the forced-exposure conditions.

There is a problem in applying the Tele-Research methodology directly to products like clothing. A clothing store familiar to the respondents may not be at the shopping center. More serious is the fact that the purchase cycle is relatively long and many of the respondents may not be in the market for clothing. One approach to adapt would be to offer subjects a $5-off coupon for an item of clothing and ask their first and second choice brand. They would then be told that all coupons for those brands not available are not available and given $5 in cash instead.

CASE FOR PART IV

Levi Strauss & Co.*

Sue Swenson, a member of the research group at Foote, Cone & Belding/Honig, a San Francisco advertising agency, was reviewing four copy-testing techniques described in the appendix to Chapter 14. A meeting was scheduled with the Levi Strauss account group the next day to decide on which copy tests to employ on two new Levi's campaigns. The following week a similar meeting was scheduled involving a campaign for a new bar soap for another client. In each case the task was to determine which testing approach would be used to help make the final selection of which commercials to use in the campaigns. Sue knew that she would be expected to contribute to the discussion by pointing out the strengths and limitations of each test and to make her own recommendation.

Levi Strauss & Co. had grown from a firm serving the needs of miners in the Gold Rush era of the mid-1800s to a large sophisticated clothing company. In 1979 it had sales of over $2 billion drawn from an international and domestic operation. The domestic company, Levi Strauss USA, included six divisions: Jeanswear, Sportswear, Womenswear, Youthwear, Activewear, and Accessories. In 1979,

* Courtesy of Levi Strauss.

Levi Strauss was among the 100 largest advertisers, with expenditures of $38.5 million, primarily on television.

Concerning the Levi's campaigns, Swenson recognized that two very different campaigns were involved. The first was a corporate image campaign. The overall objective was to build and maintain Levi's brand image. The approach was to build around the concepts of "Quality" and "Heritage," the most meaningful, believable, and universal aspects of the Levi's corporate personality. Unlike competitors who claim quality as a product feature, Levi's 128-year heritage advertisements had an important additional dimension. More specifically, the advertising involved the following strategy:

1. Heritage-quality: communicate to male and female consumers, ages 12 to 49, that Levi's makes a wide variety of apparel products, all of which share in the company's 128-year commitment to quality.
2. Variety-quality: Communicate to male and female consumers, ages 12 to 49, that Levi's makes a wide variety of quality apparel products for the entire family.

Exhibit 1 shows one of the commercials from the pool that was to be tested for the corporate campaign.

The second campaign was for Levi's Action suits. In 1979, the Sportswear division responsible for Action suits spent approximately $6 million on network television commercials and coop newspaper ads to introduce Actionwear slacks, which topped the sales of both leading brands of men's slacks, Haggar and Farah, in that year. The primary segment was middle-age males who often suffer from middle-age spread. Actionwear slacks, a blend of polyester and other fabrics with a stretchable waistline, were presented as a solution to the problem. The advertising objectives for the new campaign were guided by the following:

Focus: Levi's Action garments are comfortable dress clothes.

Benefits: Primary—comfortable
Secondary—attractive, good looking well made, long wearing

Reasons Why:

1. Levi's Action slacks are comfortable because they have a hidden stretch waistband and expandable shell fabric.
2. Levi's Action suit jacket is comfortable because it has hidden stretch panels that let you move freely without binding.
3. The Levi's name implies quality and well-made clothes.

Brand character: Levi's Action clothing is sensible, good-value menswear manufactured by Levi Strauss & Co., a company dedicated to quality.

Exhibit 2 shows a commercial from the pool for the Levi Action campaign.

Swenson also knew that previous Levi's commercials had proved exceptionally memorable and effective, owing to their distinctive creative approach. In part,

Exhibit 1. **A corporate commercial**

LEVI'S® "ROUNDUP"

(Music) Yessir, this drive started over a hundred years ago, back in California.

Just a few head of Levi's Blue Jeans, and a lot of hard miles.

Across country that would've killed ordinary pants.

But Levi's? They <u>thrived</u> on it! If anything, the herd got stronger —and bigger.

First there was <u>kid's</u> Levi's. Ornery little critters…seems like nothing stops 'em.

Then there was <u>gal's</u> pants, and tops, and skirts. Purtiest things you ever set eyes on.

And just to prove they could make it in the big city, the herd bred a new strain called Levi's Sportswear.

Jackets, shirts, slacks… a bit fancy for this job, I reckon, but I do admire the way they're made.

Fact is, pride is why we put our name on everything in this herd.

Tells folks, "This here's <u>ours</u>!" If you like what you got, then c'mon back!

We'll be here. You see, fashions may change…

…but quality <u>never</u> goes out of style!

Courtesy of Levi Strauss & Co., Two Embarcadero Center, San Francisco, California 94106.

their appeal lies in their ability to challenge the viewer's imagination. The advertising assumes that viewers are thoughtful and appreciate advertising that respects their judgments.

In preparing for the next day's meeting with the Levi account group, she decided to carefully review the notes on four copy-testing services prepared by a staff assistant at FCB/H (see appendix). The immediate problem was to decide which of the services to recommend for testing commercials from the two Levi's campaigns. She knew that similar issues would be raised in discussions with another of the agency's clients the following week concerning a national campaign for a bar-soap line extension. Positioning for the bar soap essentially involved a dual cleanliness-fragrance theme and a demonstration commercial focusing on these two copy points.

DISCUSSION QUESTIONS

1. What copy-testing service or services should Sue Swenson recommend for testing the two Levi Strauss commercials?
2. What service or services should she recommend for testing the bar-soap commercial?

Exhibit 2. **An Action Suit commercial**

TV. 30 Sec.
Title: "Action Suit/Bus"

ANNCR: If a man's suit jacket fits
like a straight jacket . . .
WIFE: Hold on, Joe!
JOE: I can't raise my arms.

ANNCR: If his pants fit their worst
around his waist,
WIFE: Sit down.
JOE: I can't—these pants are too
tight.

ANNCR: Then he needs Levi's*
Action Suit . . . perhaps
the most comfortable suit
a man can wear.

ANNCR: The waistband strrrr-
retches to give more room
when you need it.

JOE: Comfortable.
ANNCR: The jacket lets you
move your arms without
binding.

JOE: I can sit.
OLD LADY: Hmmmmmmph!

JOE: I can stand, too.

ANNCR: Levi's Action Suit from
Levi's Sportswear.

Courtesy of Levi Strauss & Co., Two Embarcadero Center, San Francisco, California 94106.

15

Developing the Media Plan

But do the people in Maine have anything to say to the people in Texas? (Mark Twain when informed that the telegraph cable had been stretched all the way from Maine to Texas.)

Should we advertise in *Cosmopolitan* or *Vogue* or both? Should a two-page advertisement be used or would a single-page advertisement be better? Should our television spot be in prime time or during daytime programming? Should it be 30 seconds or 60 seconds? Such questions need to be addressed in the development of the media plan. This and the following chapter focus upon the media plan, the media component of the advertising plan.

The media plan identifies and details the media schedule that is to be used. A media schedule specifies how the media budget is to be spent. Although the level of detail of a media schedule can vary, it can include the specification of up to four types of media factors:

1. *Media class:* a type of medium, such as television, radio, newspapers, magazines, billboards, and direct mail.
2. *Media vehicles:* provides the immediate environment for the advertisement. For example, with the media class of television there are various vehicles, such as NBC News and Wide World of Sports, and within the media class of magazines there are *Playboy, Time,* and *Vogue.*

3. *Media option:* a detailed description of an advertisement's characteristics other than the copy and the artwork used. It specifies in addition to the media vehicle such advertisement characteristics as size (full page or half page), length (30 second or 60 second), color (black and white or four color), or location (inside front cover or interior location).

4. *Timing:* how media options are scheduled over time. Among the strategy alternatives are (a) *flighting,* periods of total inactivity, (b) *continuous,* advertising spread evenly through time, and (c) *pulsing,* a continuous base augmented by intermittent bursts of heavy advertising. Timing decisions include the selection of specific issues (the August 17 issue of *Time*) or time slots (the second World Series Game).

The media schedule will at a minimum specify the number of planned insertions in each media vehicle. A more detailed media schedule also specifies the other details of a media option, such as size or length and the timing of the advertisement insertions. For example, one media schedule might include ten network commercials on daytime television and two advertisements in *Time, Women's Day,* and *Newsweek* all in the first quarter of the year. A more detailed media schedule might specify 60-second commercials and two-page advertisements and that all the advertising was to be placed during the first week in February.

Even for small media budgets there can be literally thousands, even millions, of possible media schedules from which to choose. The task is to select a media plan from this set that will be relatively effective. In making this selection the media planner will usually first select a limited set of media options. From this set the planner will then attempt to develop and evaluate a limited number of media schedules. A media model like those described at the end of this chapter can be very helpful in this stage of the process.

SELECTING THE PLAN—FOUR CRITERIA

The selection of the most effective media schedule is based in large part upon four considerations or criteria. The first is *exposures.* How many advertisement exposures are created by the media schedule? The remaining considerations represent qualifications or refinements of the quantity of exposures obtained. The second is the *segmentation effect.* Who is exposed? What percentage of the audience represents target segments? The third is the *media-option source effect.* Does an exposure obtained in one vehicle have any more impact than an exposure obtained in another? How much more impact does a 60-second commercial have than one of 30 seconds? The fourth is the *repetition effect.* Suppose one media schedule generates more exposures to the same audience members than another. What is the relative impact of successive exposures to the same person? Is the second exposure as worthwhile as the first? What about the ninth? What forgetting occurs between exposures? What is the nature of this decay?

The exposures and segmentation effect will be discussed and then illustrated in the context of a media plan of The Broiler. The media option source effect and the repetition effect will then be presented. A description of two media models wil follow. Each will provide a way to integrate the four media decision considerations into a formal mechanism to help the advertiser make the very complex decision as to which media schedule to use. They represent a class of models that have practical utility and, in addition, serve to structure the media decision area. The chapter will conclude by discussing the possibility of merging the media decision with the budget and copy decisions. In the next chapter, several areas of measurement associated with media decisions will be explored.

COUNTING EXPOSURES

The first considerations in making a media decision is simply the number of exposures that can be obtained. Perhaps too often it is essentially the only consideration used.

Table 15-1 shows the type of information used by the media planners at the J. Walter Thompson agency in selecting magazines. The first column is the unit cost of a full-page color advertisement. The second column shows the total audience in millions obtained by the magazine. Note that the total audience is much higher than the circulation because of the substantial numbers who read a magazine that someone else bought. The third column is the basic counting statistic, cost per thousand or CPM. It is the cost per thousand audience members. Thus, the CPM for *Good Housekeeping* is $1.20, which means that it cost $1.20 to reach 1,000 members of the *Good Housekeeping* audience. The circulation trend figure allows media planners to project the CPM number into the future. As a practical matter, there is a lag of several months and perhaps even a year between the media decision and the placement of the advertisements, so such trends can be significant. However, magazines will often guarantee a certain circulation level and will refund part of the payment if the circulation does not achieve the guaranteed level.

It is, of course, of no value to obtain audience members if they are not exposed to the advertisements or the media options. It is advertisement exposures that are of ultimate interest, not vehicle exposures. If there is reason to believe that advertisement readership among some vehicles is higher than others, the basic CPM figures should be adjusted accordingly. In Table 15-1, the fourth column is an effort to measure page exposure. It is based upon the survey question, "How many pages out of 10 did you open in this particular copy of the magazine?" The result is a crude indicator of page exposure as opposed to vehicle exposure. Sometimes a subjective opinion as to how seriously audience members look at the advertisements is helpful. Some magazines, for example, are actually bought by some because their advertisements provide information about home decorating, fashion, instrumentation technology, or some other specialized area of interest.

In buying television, the basic unit of counting is the gross rating point or GRP. A commercial's rating is the percent of the audience that are tuned in to the commercial. If the commercial is associated with a program, its rating would be the

Table 15-1. Selecting Magazines

	Unit Cost ($1,000s)	Total Audience (millions)	Cost per Thousand CPM[a]	Percent Mag. Exposed	Circulation Present	Circulation Trend	Target Segment %	Target Segment millions	Target Segment CPM[a]	In Home % Aud.	In Home CPM[a]	Target Concern Index	Compact Pages	Reader Opinion	Other Considerations
Good Housekeeping	$27.9	23.2	$1.20	62	5.6	+ 1%	21[b]	10.1[c]	2.74	57[d]	4.87[e]	123[f]	14[g]	91	Seal of Approval
Glamour	11.3	5.6	2.02	54	1.7	+ 4	6	2.9	3.88	41	9.46	NA	5	63	Pers. card
Cosmopolitan	13.0	7.5	1.73	63	1.9	+14	7	3.3	3.92	41	9.56	NA	NA	74	Singles aud.
Family Circle	36.0	18.9	1.90	66	8.3	+ 8	18	9.0	4.00	69	5.80	121	4	56	Practical
Woman's Day	34.9	19.2	1.82	67	7.9	+ 5	16	7.9	4.43	63	7.03	118	6	60	Practical
Redbook	26.2	13.7	1.91	66	4.8	– 1	11	5.5	4.79	58	8.26	136	0	79	Mommas aud.
Mademoiselle	7.5	3.0	2.50	58	.8	+ 1	3	1.5	4.95	35	14.14	NA	1	67	Pers. card
Parents	17.4	5.5	3.16	46	2.0	+ 1	5	2.4	7.25	60	12.08	130	10	74	Environment

Source: Adapted from "Numbers Aren't Everything," *Media Decisions*, 10, June 1975, p. 69.

[a] Cost per thousand.
[b] The percent of the target segment covered by the magazine.
[c] The number of the target segment covered by the magazine.
[d] The percent of the magazine's audience exposed in the home.
[e] Cost per thousand considering only the in-home audience.
[f] The extent to which the editorial content reaches out to the target segment.
[g] Compatible pages—the number of editorial pages devoted during the past year to the relevant subject.

rating of the program. If it is not associated with a program, it would be the average rating during that time period. The highest rated period is prime time, followed by the period just prior to prime time, termed the early fringe. To obtain total gross rating points for a media schedule, the ratings of the commercials are summed. For example, the following schedule in which a commercial is run 17 times in a one-week period yields 142 GRP.

$$
\begin{array}{lr}
3 \text{ showings in a time slot with a 12 rating } = & 36 \text{ GRP} \\
4 \text{ showings in a time slot with a 4 rating } = & 16 \text{ GRP} \\
10 \text{ showings in a time slot with a 9 rating } = & 90 \text{ GRP} \\
\text{Total for the week} & 142 \text{ GRP}
\end{array}
$$

Thus, the average member of the audience will be exposed 1.42 times, although many, of course, will not be exposed at all and others will be exposed up to 17 times since there are 17 potential opportunities to be exposed. For a national buy, the audience could be all U.S. homes with television. However, the concept will apply for audiences defined by region (the Los Angeles area) or by any other means (for example, adults from 18 to 35).

One measure of the efficiency of a given program or time slot will be the cost per rating point (CPRP).

$$
\text{Cost per rating point } = \text{CPRP} = \frac{\text{cost of a commercial}}{\text{GRP of the commercial}}
$$

Another would be the CPM or the commercial cost divided by the audience delivered by the commercial.

THE SEGMENTATION EFFECT

The first refinement of the counting-exposures approach is to consider the types of people being exposed. A primary issue in developing advertising objectives is to specify the target segment or segments. It will be of little value to deliver an audience containing people not in a target segment.

In Table 15-1, the seventh column shows the percent of the target audience that is covered by the magazine. The eighth column is the total target audience reached by the magazine, and the ninth is the CPM, only including the target audience. *Good Housekeeping* is still the most efficient magazine, but now *Glamour's* cost looks better relative to the other alternatives than it did when the total audience was considered.

In Chapter 2 the various alternative segmentation variables were discussed. Recall that product usage is often useful. The heavy user of cosmetics, for example, might be an attractive segment for a cosmetics company. In such a case, vehicle audiences would be desired that included a higher percentage of heavy cosmetic users. Another segmentation variable often useful is life-style. Recall the Charlie cosmetics line that was designed around a life-style profile. Thus a life-style profile of vehicle audiences would be helpful to a media planner with such a target segment.

In Chapter 16, the available media data will be discussed in more detail. It turns out that data such as product usage and life-style profiles are available, but that demographic data on vehicle audiences is much more complete, convenient, and inexpensive. Thus, if a target segment is defined in terms of demographics, the task of matching the target segment to a vehicle audience is much easier. For example, an automobile firm may be targeting on the young adult market or on the senior citizen market. When other segmentation variables are employed, it is usually possible to describe the target segment, for example, heavy users of credit cards, in terms of demographics so that the media demographic information can be employed. One study, however, showed that such an indirect approach sacrificed considerable efficiency.[1]

When several target segments are involved it might be useful to formally weight each as to its relative value. Thus a computer component manufacturer might have as a primary segment design engineers and maintenance engineers, and buyers might represent secondary segments. A quantification of this might be as follows:

SEGMENT	RELATIVE VALUE
Design engineeers	1.0
Maintenance engineers	0.6
Buyers	0.4

THE MEDIA PLAN FOR "THE BROILER"

A simulated television plan for one of the leading fast food chains "The Broiler" is shown in Figure 15-1. The total advertising and promotional budget is around $250 million, of which well over one-half is earmarked for television. The television plan illustrates a segmentation strategy and several types of scheduling alternatives.

The children segment, including teens, is an important market. The Broiler has always lagged McDonald's with respect to children but has made inroads with the St. Bernard advertising spokesman. The St. Bernard's campaign with additional characters and a "fun" theme is planned. As the Figure indicates, national buys of 140 GRP per week will be supported by 300 GRP's per week on local television. Six Saturday Morning pulses were planned during the year. In such a pulse, 30 second commercials would appear every half-hour from 8:30 A.M. to the conclusion of children's Saturday programming.

The young adult market, the 18- to 34-year-olds is another important segment for The Broiler. Research showed that within this segment, it was leading on the product quality dimension. For example, in terms of having hot and tasty food, The Broiler received a 88 percent rating about 20 to 30 points above its rivals. Ratings for "value" were much weaker. The strategy was to lead from strength by

Figure 15-1.   National television media plan for The Broiler

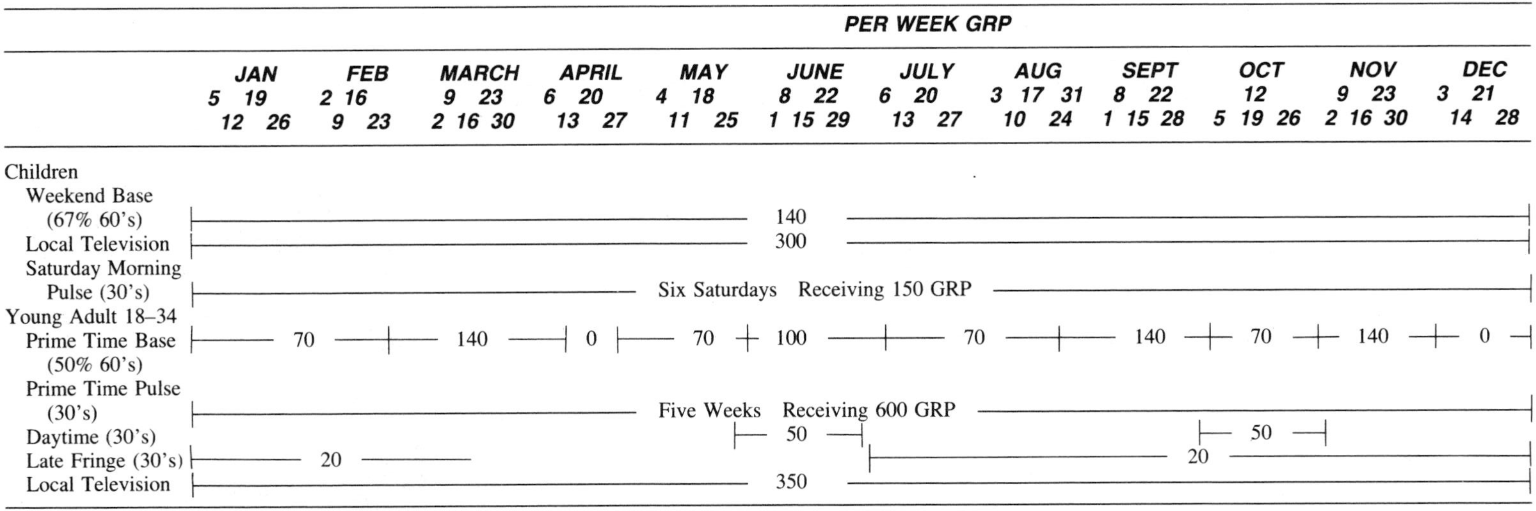

PER WEEK GRP

	JAN	FEB	MARCH	APRIL	MAY	JUNE	JULY	AUG	SEPT	OCT	NOV	DEC
	5 19	2 16	9 23	6 20	4 18	8 22	6 20	3 17 31	8 22	12	9 23	3 21
	12 26	9 23	2 16 30	13 27	11 25	1 15 29	13 27	10 24	1 15 28	5 19 26	2 16 30	14 28

Children
  Weekend Base
    (67% 60's)   140
  Local Television   300
  Saturday Morning
    Pulse (30's)   Six Saturdays   Receiving 150 GRP
Young Adult 18–34
  Prime Time Base   70 ——— 140 ——— 0 ——— 70 ——— 100 ——— 70 ——— 140 ——— 70 ——— 140 ——— 0
    (50% 60's)
  Prime Time Pulse   Five Weeks   Receiving 600 GRP
    (30's)   50
  Daytime (30's)   50
  Late Fringe (30's) 20   20
  Local Television   350

[1] Late fringe is the two hour period following prime time.

focusing upon the product quality dimension. To attract this segment, the media plan suggested 500 to 600 GRP's per week for the adult segment. Five adult pulses were planned, each of which will translate into a 30-second spot every 30 minutes on each network during prime time.

The plan called for advertising to focus upon certain themes for relatively long periods and to be linked to simple, tested promotions. For example, a hamburger theme was to be used in January and February. In March and April, the emphasis was to be on breakfasts, supported by a breakfast promotion.

Research indicated that The Broiler had not penetrated the heavy user group sufficiently, the group that accounts for 50% of the total market. Thus, more attention was focused upon the heavy user segment, especially blacks, Hispanics, and the 10- to 17-year-old set. The prime time adult schedule included spots featuring blacks. The effort toward blacks also included *Ebony* and *Jet* magazines and black radio. The Hispanic thrust used Spanish television.

Women were to be reached not only by the daytime national media effort, but by a $2 million campaign in *Family Circle, Good Housekeeping,* and *People.*[2]

THE MEDIA OPTION SOURCE EFFECT

The media option source effect is a meausre of the qualitative value of the media option. There are actually three types of media option source effects. One is the *media class source effect.* It may be that an exposure to a television commercial will have more or less impact than an exposure to a magazine advertisement. Another type of media option source effect relates to the *media option characteristics* of advertisement size (full or half page), length (30 or 60 second), color (black and white or color), or location. A two-page advertisement might be a more effective communicator to an exposed reader than a one-page presentation. A 60-second commercial may have more impact than a 30-second version. A four-color advertisement may have more effect than single color. Impact does not here refer to an ability to attract a certain kind of audience member; rather, it refers to the differential impact on an audience member already exposed to the advertisement.

The third type of media option source effect is the *vehicle source effect.* The concept is that an exposure in one vehicle might have more impact than an exposure of the same advertisement in another vehicle. For example, an advertisement for a women's dress line in *Vogue* might make more of an impact on those exposed than the same advertisement in *True Confessions,* even if the audiences were the same. Similarly, it is claimed that *Esquire* provides an above-average vehicle for men's fashions because it is an appropriate environment for this type of advertising. The differential impact could be caused by editorial environment, physical reproduction qualities, or audience involvement.

In Table 15-1 several approaches to the measurement of the vehicle source effect are illustrated. The target concentration index reflects the degree to which the editorial product reaches out to the target segment, people who have traveled overseas for example. Each magazine is scored subjectively on this basis. The concept is that if the editorial content is involving, the advertisement will be read with more intensity. A more objective measure is the number of compatible pages, the editorial pages that the magazine has devoted during the last year to the subject in question, such as foreign travel. The reader opinion column is based upon the number of readers who indicate that the magazine is "very important in my life" or is "one of my favorites" or "find considerable interest in its advertising pages." The Table 15-1 in-home columns indicate the percent of the magazine's audience who read the magazine in their home. It may be that the in-home reader is less distracted and more likely to read an advertisement more thoroughly than an out-of-home reader.

The determination of media option source effects is of course linked to advertising objectives. If the campaign is intended to develop or change a brand image, the media option source effects should be considered in that context. Will the vehicle contribute to or detract from the advertisement's ability to affect the brand's image? In Chapter 16, a more detailed examination of the media option source effect and its measurement will be presented.

REPETITION

The exposure-counting approach to media decisions implicitly assumes that all exposures to an individual will have equal impact. Thus ten exposures to one individual is as desirable as two exposures to each of five people or one exposure to each of 10 people. Clearly, the value of successive exposure will eventually diminish, at least within some time period. If the number of exposures is excessive, the audience can become annoyed and the impact of future exposures may actually be negative.

Reach and Frequency

The first step to move beyond total exposures is to determine the reach and frequency. The reach is simply the number of people exposed to one or more of the vehicles in the media schedule, the unduplicated audience. *Cumulative audience* is a more restrictive term commonly used to designate the reach of two or more issues of a given vehicle. Similarly, *net coverage* designates the reach of a combination of single issues of two or more vehicles.

Frequency is the average number of vehicle exposures each person will receive from a given media schedule. A measure of reach and frequency are usually calculated for a proposed media schedule. For example, The Broilers adult advertising pulse involving 600 GRP during a three-day period was estimated to have achieved a reach of 85 percent of the 18- to 34-year-old adults and a frequency of seven.

Total exposures is simply reach times frequency. Similarly, GRP can be obtained from a knowledge of reach and frequency with the formula

$$GRP = \frac{reach}{total\ audience} \times frequency$$

A very basic question for the media planner is the trade-off between reach and frequency. For some campaigns, reach will be critical. For example, a campaign to gain awareness of a new product may need to reach a substantial portion of the market to be successful. Furthermore, a punchy awareness advertisement may not require many repetitions. Another campaign involving a series of advertisements designed to communicate product details may require many exposures, as may an image campaign. In that case the frequency could be a very important characteristic of a proposed media schedule.

Frequency Distribution

The reach and frequency of a proposed media schedule is really a crude indication of the frequency distribution, which specifies the number of people exposed once, twice, three times, four times, and so on The following is a frequency distribution for a media insertion schedule involving two insertions in each of three magazines:

NUMBER OF EXPOSURES	FREQUENCY DISTRIBUTION	AUDIENCE
0	0.22	198,000
1	0.15	135,000
2	0.25	225,000
3	0.18	162,000
4	0.10	90,000
5	0.02	18,000
6	0.08	72,000
Total	1.00	900,000

The frequency distribution provides a much more detailed portrayal than reach and frequency. A variety of frequency distributions can generate the same reach and frequency values. The noticeable bulge at 0 and 6 is actually characteristic of many frequency distributions. They essentially reflect those who tend not to read many magazines and those who tend to read many.

The estimation of the frequency distribution is more complex than the estimation of the reach and frequency, but there are still a variety of approaches available. One of the fastest and most inexpensive was first suggested by Metheringham and is usually termed the Metheringham method.[3] The inputs required are the reach of each of the vehicles, the duplication between each pair of vehicles and the duplication between two insertions in the same vehicle. The output is a frequency distribution. The key assumption is essentially that all vehicles are identical with respect to reach and duplication with other vehicles. Thus, the method essentially averages all the input reach data and the duplication data. The method works quite well when only one vehicle is involved or when, for example, only daytime television spots are involved. However, it works much less well when a more realistic schedule involving several different vehicles is to be evaluated. In that case it is usually desirable to use a more realistic model, such as those contained in the two media models to be described shortly.

Value of Successive Exposures

The implicit assumption behind the consideration of reach, frequency, and frequency distributions is that the number of exposures that an individual receives matters. It is often helpful to make that assumption explicit by specifying the value of successive exposures. Some illustrative alternatives are shown in Table 15-2. Set A implies that the reach is the only value of a media schedule of interest. It indicates the need is to expose audience members once, and anything more is of no value. Set B implies that all exposures have equal value. Set C suggests that exposures will have equal impact until three exposures are obtained, and then they will have no value. The remaining sets have different assumptions. Such explicit assumptions will be needed for the two media models to be discussed.

The development of assumptions regarding the value of successive exposures must consider the timing of the exposures, because forgetting can occur between them. It is further complicated because of the differences among people appeals, the month of the year, product characteristics, and other factors. Some people require more exposures than others. Some campaigns wear well, and others tend to obtain maximum impact rapidly. The measure of the effect of repetition and forgetting will be considered in more detail in the next chapter.

Clearly, making media decision can be difficult. There are usually a huge number of alternative feasible schedules. The four considerations all add complex-

Table 15-2.   **Value of Successive Exposures**

Exposure	RELATIVE VALUE					
	A	B	C	D	E	F
0						
1	1	1	1	0	1	1
2	0	1	1	0	1	0.9
3	0	1	1	1	0.7	0.8
4	0	1	0	1	0.5	0.7
5	0	1	0	1	0.3	0.5
6	0	1	0	1	0	0.5
7	0	1	0	1	0	0.5
8	0	1	0	0	0	0.2
9	0	1	0	0	0	0.2
10	0	1	0	0	0	0

ity. It is no wonder that simple CPM measures are relied on. One solution is to use a formal media model that will integrate all four considerations and use a computer to search for the best media schedule. In the following sections, two media models, MEDIAC and ADMOD, are described in detail. The selection of these particular models for discussion is basically made on pedagogical grounds. Drawing on different assumptions of the advertising process, they provide an interesting contrast. One basically relies on a link between advertising expenditures and sales. The other focuses on a link between advertising and some result like the decision to try a brand or a change in attitudes. Together they provide the reader with a good insight to approaching the media decision through a formal model and with a set of structures into which much of what has been discussed in this book can be integrated. There are, of course, other models that are of historical interest and still others that compete vigorously in approach and thoroughness with these two. For a more comprehensive review, the reader is referred elsewhere.[4]

After the models are presented, a discussion of how they might be expanded to include the budget decision and the copy decision will be presented. The reader who is not interested in the specifics of the media models may wish to move directly to this material.

MEDIAC*[5]

There are three elements of a media model. The objective function assigns a value to a particular insertion schedule. It receives as inputs the specification of a schedule and outputs a value. It does not select a schedule. The heuristic has the task of searching systematically through various schedules until one is found that has a relatively high value in terms of the objective function and will not violate one of the constraints. As the MEDIAC objective function is discussed, the reader should remember that the discussion is predicated on the assumption that the schedule has been specified and the task of the objective function is to attach a value to that schedule. Finally, the constraints, such as the budget constraint, limit the alternatives that can be considered.

MEDIAC Objective Function

The MEDIAC objective function is based on a particular view or model of the advertising process, which is summarized by Little and Lodish, the developers of MEDIAC, as follows:

> The population is divided into "market segments." Each segment has its own sales potential and media habits. . . . A media schedule consists of insertions in "media vehicles." . . . An insertion brings about exposures in the various market segments. The exposures serve to increase what we shall call "exposure value" in the market

---

* This section can be bypassed without loss of continuity.

segments. However, people are subject to "forgetting," and so the retained exposure level decays with time in the absence of new exposures. The "anticipated sales" to a market segment increases with exposure level but with diminishing returns.[6]

Thus, advertising exposures build up mental states or exposure values that directly, although not necessarily linearly, influence sales. The exposure value is, however, continually being eroded by forgetting. This view of the advertising process might be crudely represented by considering sales to a segment as being supported by the weight of liquid in a big container that is being fed liquid by advertising and is losing liquid by forgetting. Such a model may be very appropriate, for example, when advertising is attempting to maintain loyalty levels by "reminder" advertising.

Advertising Exposures. To develop the model more formally, it will be necessary to introduce some notation. Let

j = index of the media options and the vehicles associated with them; $j = 1,2,$ $\ldots, J$

s = index of the market segments; $s = 1,2, \ldots, S$

t = index of the time period; $t = 1,2, \ldots, T$

d_{sjt} = exposure efficiency, the expected number of exposures per person produced in market segment s by an insertion in media option j in the time period t (exposure/person/time period)

The term d_{sjt} is the expected number of exposures per person obtained in segment s from media option j at time period t. It is a product of three terms:

$$d_{sjt} = h_j t_{sj} k_{jt}$$

where h_j = probability of exposure to media option j, given that a person is in the audience of vehicle j

g_{sj} = fraction of people in market segment s who are in the audience of vehicle j (the vehicle of media option j) on the average

k_{jt} = seasonal index of audience size for vehicle j

The term g_{sj} represents the fraction of people in the audience of vehicle j who are in segment s. Vehicle j is the vehicle associated with media option j. The term k_{jt} adjusts g_{sj} for seasonal reading or viewing patterns. The introduction of time makes it natural to refine the exposure to take into account changes in people's reading and viewing habits that can be associated with a time of the year. The term h_j represents a conditional probability that media option j will be exposed, given that vehicle j is exposed. It is assumed to be the same for all segments, although if the evidence suggested that important differences existed, it would not be conceptually or technically difficult to allow it to be different for different market segments. All three terms could be affected by the copy approach used.

Exposure Value. MEDIAC uses a construct called the exposure value per capita in segment s in time period t, y_{st}. It is not observable, although something closely related to it could conceivably be productively measured. Included in this measure is the media option effect, e_j. In each time period, the measure is increased by the sum of the contributions from each advertisement run in that time period:

$$\sum_j e_j d_{sjt} x_{jt}$$

where e_j = media option source effect

x_{jt} = number of insertions in media option j in time period t

However, it is also assumed that the effect of the advertising wears off over time. More specifically, it is assumed to decline geometrically at a rate of α Thus

$$y_{st} = \alpha y_{s(t-1)} + \sum_j e_j d_{sjt} x_{jt}$$

where y_{st} = exposure value per capita in segment s in time period t

α = fraction of y_{st} retained from one time period to the next

The basic forgetting assumption is that a fixed percentage of exposure value is lost or forgotten each time period. The percentage does not change over time. Thus, if 30 percent is forgotten during the first time period ($\alpha = 0.70$), then 30 percent of the balance is forgotten during the second. If the y_{st} level went from 1.00 to 0.70 after one period, it would go to $(0.70)^2$, or 0.49 after the second. The exact value of α will depend on the length of the time period. If an α of 0.49 is applied to four-week periods, the appropriate α for two-week periods would be 0.70. If the time period becomes very short (a day, or even an hour), the decay rate approaches an exponential curve, ae^{-bt}. The basic assumption, however, remains: a fixed percentage is forgotten in each period. Consequently, if the exponential curve materializes in an experimental situation, we can feel comfortable about this forgetting assumption of the MEDIAC model. Of course, the assumption could be relaxed by letting α change, but it would be desirable to avoid such a complication.

Figure 15-2 shows how y_{st} might change over time. The sharp increases represent the impact of an insertion. The decay between the insertions reflects the forgetting process, portrayed here as an exponential.

Figure 15-2.   A typical time pattern of y_{st}

Sales Response.   The next assumption is that the sales response of a market segment is some nonlinear function of y_{st}. The nature of the function should reflect the diminishing returns of advertising. Let

m_{st} = average per person sales potential of market segment s in time t (dollars/person/time period)

$q(y_{st})$ = average percentage of sales potential in market segment s in time t achieved when the exposure value per capita is y_{st}

The $q(y_{st})$ function could appear as in Figure 15-3. The term m_{st} reflects the relative value of segment s, the segment effect. The product $m_{st} q(y_{st})$ then represents the sales rate that will be obtained at the given level of y_{st}. Furthermore,

$N_s m_{st} q(y_{st})$ = sales to be achieved in segment s during time period t, given y_{st}

where N_s is the number of people in market segment s.

Insertion Schedule's Value.   To determine the total sales anticipated in the time horizon considered, it is necessary to sum over time periods and over market segments. The final MEDIAC program can be stated as follows:

Find x_{jt} and y_{st} to maximize

$$\sum_s \sum_t N_s m_{st} q(y_{st}) \tag{1}$$

subject to

$$y_{st} = \alpha y_{s\,(t-1)} + \sum_j d_{sit} e_j x_{jt}$$

$$l_{jt} \le x_{jt} \le u_{jt}$$

$$\sum_t \sum_j c_{jt} x_{jt} \le B$$

where l_{jt} = minimum number of insertions in media option j in time period t

u_{jt} = maximum number of insertions in media option j in time period t

c_{jt} = cost of media option j in time period t

B = budget constraint

Expression (1) is the final objective function. It provides a value for any given insertion schedule.

The Constraints

The budget constraint prevents the heuristic from selecting an insertion schedule that will exceed the predetermined budget level. The lower insertion constraint will force a media option into the solution if there are reasons why it is desirable that the model does not reflect. If the model involves a consumer product, a particular insertion may be desired to influence retailers, for example. The upper bound could reflect a physical constraint. A magazine appears only a certain times, and it may

Figure 15-3.   **Consumer response**

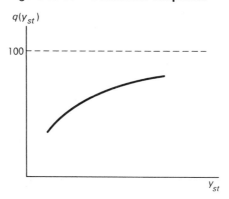

be desirable to restrict the program to the placement of one advertisement in each issue. Other constraints could be added, of course.

Selection Heuristic

The objective function will assign a value based on expression (1) to a given insertion schedule. It is the task of the heuristic to search through the schedules to determine which schedule to select.[7]

Summary

MEDIAC relies on an intuitively plausible, if simplified, model of how the advertising process works. Exposures to advertisements build up mental states, y_{st}. The population of interest will forget if they are not regularly exposed to advertising; that is, the mental state defined by y_{st} will decline. The concept of diminishing returns is introduced by the $q(y_{st})$ function that links the mental state with purchasing decisions. It indicates that after y_{st} is at a certain level there is little value in increasing it further. The model is thus based on an indirect link between advertising expenditures and immediate sales. When such a link is plausible, the model will be more appropriate than in situations when it is not plausible (recall the discussion in Chapter 7).

The introduction of real time into the model admits the scheduling of media options through time, certainly an important part of the media decision, and makes it natural to include the forgetting phenomenon. It also allows the introduction to seasonal patterns of the exposures to vehicles.

The limitation of MEDIAC is that the exposures are accumulated and forgotten only in an aggregate sense. For a given schedule, this aggregation could hide the fact that one person gets five exposures and another in the segment gets none. An aggregative approach, however, has the advantage of being efficient and able to use more readily available data sources. Little and Lodish have refined and extended the version of MEDIAC presented here.[8] One extension involves distributing y_{st} across those in segment s, using the moments of a probability distribution. In the objective function, expectations with respect to this distribution are employed. Conceptualizing a probability distribution for y_{st} undoubtedly reduces the distortion of aggregation. ADMOD, the next model to be described, takes a disaggregative approach by analyzing advertising impact at the level of individuals.

ADMOD*[9]

The Objective Function

ADMOD differs from MEDIAC and most other models in two respects. First, it draws on a different operational conception of the advertising process. Second, it considers exposure probabilities at the level of individuals without resorting to simulation.

Most media models, including MEDIAC, rely on a model of advertising that suggests that advertising creates an advertising exposure (or similar construct), which in turn creates sales. The advertising exposure level will dissipate over time but can be maintained or built up by more advertising. The heart of the model, then, is an aggregate response curve that relates exposure levels to sales or perhaps advertising expenditure levels to sales directly. ADMOD, on the other hand, focuses on specific consumer cognitive changes or decisions that advertising is attempting to precipitate and that have long-run implications for a firm. For example, advertising may be directed toward inducing a consumer to try a brand for the first time, to try a brand in a new way, to change a brand attitude, or to become aware of a brand. Such results tend to generate a future sales or profit stream that has a certain present value to a firm. ADMOD attempts to select a schedule that will maximize the total present value generated by a campaign of a prespecified length. The concern of advertising is then with some indicator that will reveal the probability of a consumer's changing cognitions in the desired way or taking the desired action. Presumably, this probability will be affected by advertising exposures.

The focus of the ADMOD objective function is not on the aggregate vehicle audience but on sample populations selected from the various segments. In evaluating a schedule, ADMOD examines its likely impact on every individual in the sample. The impact will depend on the net value of the decision or cognition change involved, the number and source of exposures to an individual created by the schedule, and the impact of the exposures on the probability of obtaining the desired cognition change or decision. Using appropriate scaling factors, the result is projected to the real population, providing the total expected profit generated by that media schedule. Recall that the objective function assigns a value to an insertion

---

* This section can be bypassed without loss of continuity.

schedule. It is, of course, the task of the heuristic to search through various insertion schedules until one is found that has a relatively high value in terms of the objective function.

A sample is thus required from each segment. The proportion of people in the sample from a certain segment need not equal the proportion of the population contained in that segment. The only requirement is that a reasonable number of people from each segment, 100 to 200, for example, be part of the sample. Of course, the sample should be representative of each segment. Ideally, each member of the segment should have an equal chance of being selected. The sample size from segment s is termed n_s. The total size of segment s is termed N_s.

Segment Effect.   The assumed objective of an advertiser is to precipitate a cognitive change or decision. The long-term value to the firm of obtaining such a result from a member of segment s is termed w_s. It will be the present value of the projected sales and profits that result from the change in cognition or buyer behavior. Model components such as the repetition function and media option source effects are then developed using operational measures that are linked to the objectives. This concept of an advertising objective is, of course, compatible with the material in Part II on setting objectives. To fix the concept in this context, several examples will be presented.

Suppose that the goal is to generate a trial purchase by a segment member. The long-term value to the firm of obtaining a trial purchase will reflect the gross margin of the brand, a discount factor reflecting the cost of capital and the uncertainties of the market, the segment member's product class purchasing volume, and the degree of brand acceptance the brand is likely to enjoy after it is used. An estimate of the brand acceptance can be obtained by various survey approaches or by simply observing the frequency with which brand purchases are repeated by "new triers." The situation is similar if the goal is to entice a customer to use the product in a new application. In that context, an important determining factor of w_s will be in acceptance of the new application after he or she is induced to try it. Again, recall the discussion in Chapter 7.

The objective could be to change a brand image. In that case the intention could be to maintain the loyalty of existing customers, to make them less vulnerable to attacks from competing brands. With the existing image, customers may exhibit a projected purchasing pattern that reflects a decline in purchases of the advertised brand. It may be that a new image will be associated with a more stable projection of purchasing patterns. The present value of the difference would then be w_s. This concept was also discussed in Chapter 7.

Exposure Probabilities.   For each member of the sample, individual i, the probability that he or she will be exposed to each vehicle, vehicle j, under consideration is derived. This probability is b_{ij}. Vehicle j is the vehicle associated with media option j. The conditional probability that media option j is exposed to an individual exposed to vehicle j is termed h_j. Thus, the probability that individual i reads a particular issue of *Good Housekeeping* would be b_{ij}, and the probability that the individual sees a particular advertisement in it if he or she reads the issue would be h_j. It might be useful to condition h_j according to the type of individual, the segment, or the copy approach. However, the notation is already cumbersome and such extensions should be obvious. The product of these two terms, $b_{ij} h_j$, reflect the probability that individual i will be exposed to media option j. Let

$$p_{ij} = b_{ij} h_j$$

where p_{ij} = probability that individual i is exposed to media option j

   b_{ij} = probability that individual i is exposed to vehicle j where vehicle j is the vehicle associated with media option j

   h_j = probability that anyone exposed to vehicle j will be exposed to media option j

Let z_i be a random variable reflecting the number of exposures received by individual i in a given insertion schedule being considered by the objective function. The value of z_i cannot be established for sure, but knowing the exposure probabilities, it is a straightforward task to derive $f(z_i)$, the probability distribution for z_i, given the insertion schedule under consideration. The distribution can be calculated exactly by making certain independence assumptions and applying probability theory. For example, if there were only two insertions under consideration, media option 5 and media option 7, the probability of zero exposures for individual i would be $(1-p_{i5})(1-p_{i7})$, the probability of one exposure would be $p_{i5}(1-p_{i7}) + p_{i7}(1-p_{i5})$, and the probability of two exposures would be $p_{i5} p_{i7}$. Similar calculations can be made for schedules of any size. However, with large schedules, the calculations can become costly, and it is reasonable to consider using the raw probabilities to estimate the parameters of a probability distribution such as the binomial, which would then become $f(z_i)$.[10] Such a distribution would be less accurate than the use of direct probabilities, but it would also be less costly.

Repetition Function and Forgetting.   ADMOD assumes that an advertising campaign of a specified duration is attempting to change cognitions or precipitate decisions. The result of the campaign will be a probability that it was successful with respect to a segment member. Let us term that probability a'_s; the subscript s indicates that the probability will be different in general for each segment, but identical for each segment member. The prime superscript indicates that all exposures are associated with the maximum vehicle source effect, e_j. This assumption will shortly be relaxed. The probability will depend on the number of exposures that the insertion schedule was able to generate for any given segment member, z_i. Thus, making the probability a function of the number of exposures, we have $a'_s(z_i)$, the repetition function.

In ADMOD there is no explicit conceptualization of forgetting, as there was in MEDIAC. However, the development of the repetition function necessarily takes into account the length of the campaign and, therefore, the length of the time between exposures. Possible repetition curves are shown in Figure 15-4. Figure 15-4 illustrated another way to conceptualize repetition functions. Curve B, for example, suggests that too few exposures will suffer from forgetting between them.

An implicit assumption in ADMOD is that a campaign is totally forgotten at its conclusion. The concept is that advertising is likely to generate the desired change in cognitions or decision in a rather limited time period or not at all. Those individuals who withstand a concentrated effort for a relatively short time will probably withstand the same campaign if it is prolonged. Therefore, this forgetting assumption of the model may not be so extreme in this context as it may first appear. It would be relatively easy to relax this assumption. It could be assumed, for example, that the average probability of a trial purchase during a subsequent time period would be a fixed fraction of its value in the time period of immediate interest. The objective function would then have a value component from two time periods.

Media Option Source Effect.   In this context the media option source effect will reflect a vertical adjustment in the repetition function. The repetition function is developed under the assumption that all exposures will be associated with the optimal environment. The magazine or television programs creating the exposures are assumed to enhance the advertisement to the maximum extent possible because of their audience involvement, prestige, and other factors. All media option source effects are assumed to be 1.0 on a 0 to 1.0 scale. Actually, media option source effects will take on values between 0 and 1.0, reflecting their relative ability to enhance or detract from the impact of the advertisement exposure on the likelihood of generating the desired decision or cognitive change.

In ADMOD the number of exposures an individual receives from a given insertion schedule is known probabilistically. However, it is not known exactly

Figure 15-4.   **ADMOD repetition function**

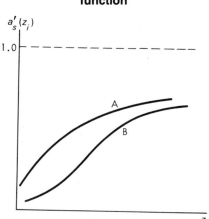

which insertion options in the schedule are creating the exposures. The solution is to compress the repetition function by an amount determined by the expected value of the media option source effect, which is simply a weighted average, with those media options that have a higher probability of creating exposures having the higher weights. The repetition function adjusted for media option source effects is denoted as $a_s(z_i)$. Notice the absence of the prime superscript.

$$a_s(z_i) = a_s'(z_i)\left[\sum_s e_j p_{ij}\left(1/\sum_j p_{ij}\right)\right]$$

Insertion Schedule's Value.   The purpose of the objective function is to attach a value to a media insertion schedule. The value to an advertiser of the campaign directed at individual i in segment s is the value of the desired result, w_s, times the probability that the advertising will stimulate the result, $a_s(z_i)$. If the number of exposures were known exactly, the expected value for segment member i would be $w_s a_s(z_i)$. The problem is that the exact number of exposures that an individual will receive, given an insertion schedule, is not known. What is known is the probability distribution of the number of exposures, $f(z_i)$. Thus the appropriate procedure is to determine the expectation over z_i of $w_s a_s(z_i)$, which yields the expected value from individual i:

$$\sum_{z_i=0}^{\infty} w_s a_s(z_i)f(z_i)$$

The total expected value received from the sample from market segment s is obtained by summing over all individuals in the sample who belong to market segment s: $i \in s$. The addition of the factor N_s/n_s explicitly scales the results to the segment size. In effect, the term $1/n_s$ provides the average expected value for each sample member from segment s and when multiplied by N_s generates an estimate of the expected value for the whole segment. Finally, all segments are summed, $\sum_s$, to arrive at the total expected value generated by the insertion schedule, the value of the model's objective function. Adding appropriate constraints, the model can be summarized as follows: Find a set of x_j terms to maximize

$$V = \sum_s \frac{N_s}{n_s}\sum_{i \in s}\sum_{z_i} w_s a_s(z_i)f(z_i)$$

subject to

$$\sum c_j x_j \le B, \textit{ budget constraint}$$
$$l_j \le x_j \le u_j$$

where c_j = cost of an insertion in vehicle j
   x_j = number of insertions in media option j
   B = budget size
   l_j = minimum number of insertions in media option j
   u_j = maximum number of insertions in media option j

Constraints and Heuristic

The constraints are the same as those introduced in the MEDIAC discussion. The capacity to set lower and upper limits on the number of insertions to any media option is included. A heuristic is required that will search systematically through various schedules.

DETERMINING THE BUDGET CONSTRAINT*

It has been assumed in the discussion of MEDIAC and ADMOD that the budget constraint is imposed on the media model. It is very possible to use the media model to determine simultaneously the budget level and make the allocation decision. A natural output of any media model is the additional increment in the objective function that would be obtained by relaxing the budget constraint slightly. For ADMOD this increment would normally be in terms of profit. For MEDIAC the increment could be converted to profit. The models could attempt to maximize the objective function less the schedule cost. The heuristic would keep adding insertions until the incremental value added by the last insertion did not exceed the insertion cost. The budget level, the cost of that final insertion schedule, is thus a model output instead of an input. It is optimal (within the limitations of the search heuristic) in that either an increase or a decrease in the budget level would reduce the net value of the advertising campaign to a firm. In essence, the approach is identical to that described in Chapter 3. The difference is that the response function is more comprehensive and hopefully more valid than those postulated in Chapter 3 (involving advertising expenditures and immediate sales).

If the model is used to make the budget decision, the measurement problems become more demanding. The repetition function and the media option source effect terms need to be established with absolute rather than relative validity. It is much easier to generate parameters that are adequately valid in a relative sense than in an absolute sense.

THE COPY DECISION*

Throughout this chapter we have assumed that the advertising campaign was set, the copy decisions made, and the advertisements, in fact, prepared. The problem was simply to place the advertisements in the available media. We have mentioned in passing that the relevant parameters could depend on the campaign involved. However, the campaign itself has been regarded as fixed.

It is possible to consider expanding the media model to include the copy decision. Thus, the model would be charged with simultaneously making the copy decision and allocating the advertisements to the media. Suppose that we let c index

---

* This section assumes that either the MEDIAC or the ADMOD section was read.

our copy alternatives and that there were two. The first ($c = 1$) could be an awareness campaign announcing a new car. The second ($c = 2$) could be an attitude campaign emphasizing a safety feature. Then, in terms of MEDIAC, we would want to select the x_{cjt} that will optimize the objective function. The inclusion of $x_{126} = 1$ in the final decision set would indicate that copy approach 1, the awareness campaign, will appear in vehicle 2 during time period 6.

The parameters will similarly include the c index, and the variations related to the copy approach will thus be introduced. The media option exposure probability (conditional on vehicle exposure, now h_{cj}) will very likely depend on the copy strategy. Some copy will certainly be much more apt to gain attention than others. The h_{cj} term will vary considerably over the copy alternatives. Similarly, the repetition function will be affected. The awareness campaign may well use an attention-grabbing advertisement, whereas the attitude-change campaign could very well avoid such an approach. Thus, we would have a $q_c(y_{st})$ or $a_{cs}(z_i)$ function. The forgetting function would also depend on the copy and the objective of the campaign. Awareness copy may be quickly forgotten. However, attitude change may likely be associated with more cognitive ties and thus may be more stable and less quickly forgotten. The forgetting parameter in MEDIAC would become α_c. The media option source effect will also vary, of course, with the copy used. An image campaign might benefit from a prestigious source, whereas a brand-comprehension campaign might do better with a source associated with a high level of expertise. Thus, an e_{cj} term would be needed.

The solution might be constrained to include only one campaign. Such a constraint would be equivalent to running the media model separately for each campaign to determine which generated the largest discounted profit flow. The most useful model would permit both campaigns to run simultaneously. The most difficult measurement problems that would then be introduced involve repetition and forgetting functions. These functions would probably depend not only on the number of exposures, but which exposures—that is, which campaigns were involved—and the order in which they occurred.

TOWARD A MORE COMPREHENSIVE MODEL

There are basically three technical advertising decisions: the copy decision, the budget decision, and the media allocation decision. Previous research into these decision areas has been remarkably isolated. Budget-setting models have generally used experimental design or statistical models, usually ignoring copy considerations or media placement. Media models normally consider the budget to be fixed and similarly ignore copy decisions. The copy decision has generally involved different research traditions.

That interdependencies exist hardly needs demonstration. Clearly, the optimal budget level will depend on the creative effort. For ineffective advertising, the optimal level will be zero. One type of copy approach will require a different level of exposure intensity than another. Similarly, the budget level will depend on the type of media used and how effectively the target segments can be reached. In Chapter 16 the interactions of exposure probabilities, repetition and forgetting functions, and media option source effects with copy approaches will be detailed.

There are, of course, good reasons why these interactions have been largely ignored in the past. First, the three areas are usually the responsibility of different decision makers. Company managers set the budget, agency media specialists allocate the budget to media alternatives, and creative people make the copy decisions. There was, therefore, little pressure to integrate. Instead, a demand existed for independent efforts to aid these decision makers. Second, there have been technical and conceptual problems in the development of the machinery oriented toward media allocation and copy decisions, even when they are considered independently. It, therefore, has been productive to make advances in these areas. Indeed, it is questionable whether any real effort toward an integrative approach would be feasible without the advances that have been achieved to date in media models, copy testing, and related techniques. Finally, when media allocation or the copy decision is considered separately, the measures need be only relatively valid, since alternative choice is the goal. When budget decisions are introduced, a measure with absolute validity is necessary and new demands are imposed on researchers.

It is now appropriate to address the budget, the media, and the copy decision in concert. The introduction of modern information systems supported by on-line computers and model banks are effectively breaking down the isolation of the different decision makers. The media model technology is at the point where it has achieved acceptance and demonstrated considerable validity. Progress has been made in understanding the communication process, in setting objectives, and in testing copy against these objectives. With barriers reduced, it is useful to push the field in the direction of more ambitious models.[11]

SUMMARY

The selection of the most effective media schedule is based upon four considerations or criteria. The first is how many exposures will a media vehicle or option of a media schedule (a set of media options) generate? The media vehicle cost is introduced to create the CPM measure. The second is the segmentation issue: to what extent will the vehicle audience cover the target segments involved? The media plan for The Broiler illustrates how television buys are planned using the GRP per week measure of advertising intensity and how segmentation interacts with media planning. The qualitative value of a media option, the media option source effect, is the third consideration. The final consideration is repetition. What will be the relative impact of successive exposures? What reach and frequency will a media schedule deliver? A media model provides a structure and a computer-assisted mechanism to make media decisions that will reflect all four considerations.

The MEDIAC model is based on a particular view of the advertising process. Advertising exposures build up mental states or exposure values among target segments. These exposure values are directly linked, although not necessarily linearly, to sales. The exposure value is, however, continually being eroded by forgetting. Such a model may be reasonable, for example, when advertising is attempting to maintain loyalty levels by "reminder" advertising. MEDIAC not only selects media options but schedules them over time. The inclusion of real time makes it natural to include formally the forgetting function and seasonal adjustments of patterns of vehicle exposures. A limitation of MEDIAC is that the exposures are accumulated and forgotten only in an aggregate sense.

ADMOD, on the other hand, focuses on specific consumer cognition changes or decisions that advertising is attempting to precipitate, such as gaining brand awareness or a decision to try a brand for the first time. The long-term value to a firm of obtaining the desired result from a segment member is the potential value of that member to the firm, w_s. The focus of advertising is then on some indicator that will express the probability of a consumer's changing cognitions in the desired way or taking the desired action. The repetition function, adjusted for media option source effects, relates this probability to the number of exposures of individuals within the segment. ADMOD utilizes a sample population selected from the various segments. In evaluating a schedule, ADMOD examines its likely impact on every individual in the sample. The impact will depend on the net value of the decision or cognition change involved, the number and source of exposures to the individual created by the schedule, and the impact of the exposures on the probability of obtaining the desired cognition change or decision. Using appropriate scaling factors, the result is projected to the real population. It is useful to consider extending the media model to include both the budget decision and the copy decision, in addition to the budget allocation decision.

DISCUSSION QUESTIONS

1. A basic component of a media model objective function involves counting exposures generated by an insertion schedule. The remaining components introduced in this chapter attempt to qualify the exposures, the potential worth of the audience member, the vehicle associated with the exposure and so on. How else might you want to qualify exposures? What other components could be added to the list? How might the existing components be further qualified?

2. Would the media class decision be more difficult to make than the media vehicle decision? Why or why not? What will be the relative roles of the different media classes in Chevrolet's multi-media introduction of a new line of cars.

3. Under what circumstances would it be effective to pulse advertising

rather than spreading it out evenly? Evaluate the strategy of The Broiler to engage in ten or so television pulse campaigns during the year.

4. Suppose you had a $55,000 budget. Given the data in Table 15-1, which magazines would you buy? What additional information would be helpful to you?

5. Construct an objective function for a media model using the information in Table 15-1. What types of constraints would you have?

6. Comment on the media plan for The Broiler. What would the "value of successive exposure" function look like? How would you go about deciding upon the mix of 60- and 30-second commercials?

7. You are an advertising manager for a new line of package-marking devices for use by retail food stores. Your advertising is designed to create awareness among chain-store managers. Two schedules with equal cost are proposed. One uses many trade journals and will reach 10,000 store managers with a frequency of 1.1. The other uses fewer journals and will reach 4,000 with a frequency of 5.4. Which of the alternatives would be optimal given this information? What other factors should be considered?

8. Compare and contrast ADMOD and MEDIAC. In what situations would MEDIAC be most appropriate and in what situations would you rather recommend the use of ADMOD? When would the use of gross rating points be superior to both?

9. What is MEDIAC's most critical and vulnerable assumption? What constraints might you add? How would you extend it? Answer the same questions for ADMOD. How might you combine the best features of ADMOD and MEDIAC?

10. Modify MEDIAC or ADMOD so that it will make the budget and copy decisions as well as the media allocation decision.

11. Suppose that you run MEDIAC with your best judgments concerning the media option source effect. When you set all the e_j values equal to 1.0, you get the same schedule. Does that mean that you should forget about the media option source effect?

12. How might you go about generating a repetition function? What information would you need and how would you go about getting it? Consider the same question for media option source effects.

13. Recall the concepts of self-selection and controlled coverage strategy from Chapter 2. Explain them, using the vocabulary of the media model.

14. Table 16-2 provides for 40 magazines an estimate of the audience size of three demographically defined segments and five segments defined by buying style. Table 16-2 also provides one page cost for black-and-white and four-color insertions. Using the four-color cost:

a   Compare the CPM of the following sets of magazines for all adults, females, high income and ecologist segments.

- *Bon Appetit* and *Gourmet*
- *Car and Driver* and *Road and Track*
- *Time* and *Newsweek*
- *Playboy* and *Playgirl*
- *TV Guide, Reader's Digest,* and *People*
- *Gun & Ammo, Ms., Golf,* and *Gourmet*

Explain any differences that you find. Under what conditions would you conclude in the media plan an alternative with a higher CPM?

b   Using the all-adult, female, style-conscious, ecologist and planner segments, compare the CPM of the following magazines:

Better Homes	*Ms.*	*Time*
Family Health	*The New Yorker*	*True Story*
Gourmet	*People*	*Vogue*
House & Garden	*Playgirl*	*Woman's Day*
McCall's	*Reader's Digest*	*Working Women*

c   Assume that you were developing a media schedule for Charlie perfume and you needed to provide and rank order a set of five magazines from which alternative schedules were to be developed. Which five of the 15 magazines in part (b) would you select? Assume that the target segment was style-conscious females.

d   Again pick and rank order five magazines, now assuming that the product was a microwave oven that had a series of new, somewhat complex cooking features to communicate. First assume that a "energy saving" appeal targeted to the ecologist segment. Then assume that the planner segment is the target and the use of a microwave to help plan meals is the appeal.

NOTES

1. Henry Assael and Hugh Cannon, "Do Demographics Help in Media Selection?" *Journal of Advertising Research,* 19, December 1979, pp. 7–11.

2. For a similar plan, see "McDonald's 1979 Plan: Beat Back the Competition," *Advertising Age,* February 19, 1979, p. 1.

3. R. A. Metheringham, "Measuring the Net Cumulative Coverage of a Print Campaign," *Journal of Advertising Research,* December 1969, pp. 23–28.

4. Dennis Gensch, *Advertising Planning* (New York: Elsevier, 1978).

5. For a complete explanation of the version of MEDIAC described here, see John D. C. Little and Leonard M. Lodish, "A Media Selection Model and Its Optimization by Dynamic Programming," *Industrial Management Review,* 8, Fall 1966, pp. 15–23. A more complex version appears in MEDIAC: John D. C. Little and Leonard M. Lodish, "A Media Planning Calculus," *Operations Research,* 17, January–February 1969, pp. 1–35.

6. Little and Lodish, "A Media Selection Model," p. 17.

7. For a comparative discussion of media heuristics, see Allan D. Shocker, "Limitations of Incremental Search in Media Selection," *Journal of Marketing Research,* 8, February 1970, pp. 101–103.

8. Little and Lodish, "A Media Planning Calculus," pp. 1–35.

9. David A. Aaker, "ADMOD: An Advertising Decision Model," in *Journal of Marketing Research,* 13, February 1975.

10. For a given schedule, the expected number of exposures, the mean of $f(z_i)$, that individual i will receive is

$$\sum_j p_{ij} x_j$$

where x_j is the number of insertions in media option j. The variance can also be calculated easily:

$$\sum_j p_{ij}(1 - p_{ij})x_j$$

11. One version of ADMOD does in fact include formally the budget decision and the copy decision. See Aaker, "ADMOD: An Advertising Decision Model."

16

Media Research

The "new media"—cable, videodiscs, video tape recorders, and satellite transmissions—make it increasingly possible to reach smaller and smaller segments of the market with special interests or special needs. The term "narrowcasting" has been coined to describe the kinds of segmentation potential offered by these media. (Russell I. Haley, Developer of benefit segmentation)

In Chapter 15, the audience size, the segment involved, the various elements of media option source effect and the implication of repetition and forgetting all were shown to be potentially relevant in developing a media plan. The relative importance of each of these considerations will depend upon the nature of the communication task and upon an understanding of the communication process involved.

In this chapter the data and measurement issues that underlie each of these media decision considerations will be addressed. The first section will focus upon estimation of the audience size. How can valid and reliable measures of the audience delivered by a vehicle be estimated? How are readership and advertisement exposure measured? The second section will explore the media-option source effect. Have media-option source effects been demonstrated? Why do they exist?

How can they be estimated? Finally, repetition and forgetting will be examined. What is the relative impact of successive exposures? What forgetting patterns are operating?

MEASURING EXPOSURE

The first job of an advertisement is to be seen, to gain exposure. If there is no opportunity for a segment member to see an advertisement, it matters little what copy approach was employed.

Measuring Print Vehicle Audiences

Print vehicle circulation data neglect pass-along readers both inside and outside the home. Thus, to measure a vehicle's audience, it is necessary to apply approaches such as recent reading, reading habit, and through-the-book to a randomly selected population sample.

In recent reading, respondents are asked whether they looked at a copy within the past week for a weekly publication or during the last month if it was a monthly publication. One problem is that the survey is unlikely to represent an "average" week, so there is a seasonality factor to consider. Also, a reader could read several issues in one week and be incorrectly reported as not being a reader in another week. Another concern is the tendency to exaggerate readership of prestige magazines and to minimize readership of vehicles that do not match people's self-image. Still another is the forgetting factor. One study found that 50 of 166 people who were observed reading magazines in a doctor's office said they had never read the magazine they had been observed reading.[1]

The reading-habit method, which asks respondents how many issues out of the last four they personally read or looked into, is also sensitive to memory difficulties. In particular, it is difficult to discriminate between reading the same issue several times from reading several issues.

The through-the-book approach attempts to reduce the memory factor. Respondents are shown a copy of a specific issue of a magazine that he or she reads and asked whether several articles were read and if they were interesting. The respondent is then asked if he or she read that issue. The approach, which requires an expensive personal interview, is sensitive to the issue age. A too-recent issue will miss later readers. A too-old issue risks forgetting.

The two major audience-measuring services are Mediamark, which relies on the recent-reading method and surveys 140 magazines, and Simmons.[2] Simmons, which interviews over 15,000 people each year, uses the through-the-book approach for 44 major magazines and estimates another 81 using the reading-habit approach (downward adjusting the resulting reading-habit estimates).[3] Differences between the two have sparked sharp controversy through the years. A 1974 recent-reading estimate showed a decline in the *Time* audience relative to *Newsweek* even though circulation had not fallen off. One explanation was that *Newsweek* does better at out-of-home readership, which is detected more easily by the recent-reading methodology. *Time,* in contrast, might get more serious, thorough readership, which is best measured by the through-the-book approach of Simmons. Table 16-1 shows a comparison of the audience estimates based on the two techniques.

Both Simmons and Mediamark obtain a variety of other information from the survey respondents in addition to vehicle exposure. For example, in addition to media exposure Simmons obtains the following:

1. Household and/or personal consumption rates and brand usage for over 500 product categories.
2. Information on 24 demographics, such as age, income, sex, and occupation.
3. Psychographic information. Respondents are asked if they agree or disagree with a set of 20 personality adjectives, such as funny, kind, and sociable and 10 buying-style adjectives such as ecologist, impulsive, and planner.

Thus audience size estimates can be obtained for segments defined by product-class usage or other segment-defining variables. Table 16-2 illustrates the type of information that is available. The audience size of 40 magazines is given in total and for eight segments. Contrast the audience profile for *Playboy* and *Playgirl*. *Playboy* has relatively fewer female readers, but is the buying-style profile very different from the *Playgirl* reader? For both magazines, for example, 25 percent of the audience regards itself as "brand loyal" consumers. What about *Time* versus *Newsweek* or *Sport* versus *Sports Afield?*

Multiple-issue exposures may be very useful. Furthermore, audience exposure estimates may underestimate the impact of a magazine like *TV Guide,* which is probably read many times by the average reader. A more appropriate measure might be the total issue exposures rather than the total audience.[4]

Table 16.1.   **Total Adult Readers Comparison**

MAGAZINE	*MEDIAMARK*	*SIMMONS*
Time	25,701,000	20,035,000
Newsweek	23,640,000	16,453,000
U.S. News	11,586,000	8,733,000
Family Circle	32,143,000	18,255,000
McCall's	24,641,000	17,287,000
Ladies' Home Journal	21,920,000	12,971,000
Haper's Bazaar	3,574,000	3,301,000
Playboy	21,401,000	15,584,000

Source: Adapted from Leah Rozen, "Reader Data Still Don't Jibe," *Advertising Age,* October 6, 1980, p. 118.

Table 16-2. **Magazine Readership as Reported by Simmons**[a]

Magazine	COST PER PAGE[c] (1000s)		AUDIENCE IN 1,000s[b]				Buying Style				
	B&W	4-Color	Adults	Female	Age 18–34	Household Income over 25,000	Brand Loyal	Ecologist	Economy Minded	Planner	Style Conscious
Total adults (millions)			155.8	81.1	63.1	41.3	40.2	43.5	60.2	67.7	36.0
1. American Baby	$15.7	$21.7	2,308	1,963	1,902	575	636	659	918	880	701
2. Better Homes	51.9	62.8	21,579	16,684	7,815	7,123	6,340	6,439	9,318	10,243	6,399
3. Bon Appetit	11.0	15.7	3,000	2,306	1,206	1,610	941	801	1,074	1,413	1,145
4. Business Week	17.4	26.1	4,147	913	1,770	2,557	1,291	815	1,465	1,878	1,012
5. Car and Driver	13.9	21.3	2,720	539	1,961	1,159	748	767	1,158	1,461	778
6. Ebony	12.9	19.9	6,925	3,639	4,029	1,461	1,716	2,020	2,678	3,036	2,034
7. Family Health	6.2	8.7	3,325	2,281	1,205	1,035	1,016	1,028	1,465	1,690	938
8. Fortune	17.9	27.3	2,190	583	889	1,541	688	425	609	904	486
9. Golf	10.3	15.5	2,283	628	902	1,266	686	568	839	996	794
10. Gourmet	7.0	12.5	2,263	1,573	670	1,126	639	725	773	1,006	773
11. Guns & Ammo	5.3	8.6	2,898	299	1,815	975	797	1,092	1,313	1,478	684
12. House & Garden	14.8	21.8	7,917	6,061	3,071	2,998	2,624	2,374	3,383	3,643	2,792
13. Mademoiselle	8.8	12.8	3,620	3,415	2,180	1,332	1,065	1,111	1,657	1,832	1,656
14. McCall's	42.5	52.2	18,372	16,266	7,143	5,753	5,131	5,577	7,930	8,672	6,023
15. Money Mag.	11.4	17.9	3,691	1,663	1,768	1,927	1,040	958	1,395	1,900	1,001
16. Motor Trend	12.4	19.8	3,358	422	1,926	1,159	823	834	1,303	1,554	721
17. Ms.	6.5	8.7	1,375	1,211	991	360	317	486	475	712	425
18. Nat'l. Lampoon	6.7	9.9	3,348	759	2,845	1,377	995	912	785	1,225	737
19. Newsweek	33.2	51.7	17,197	6,893	8,827	7,370	5,046	4,422	5,713	7,855	4,582
20. New Yorker	8.3	13.2	3,008	1,412	1,433	1,509	1,078	863	1,099	1,490	855
21. Outdoor Life	14.8	21.4	5,438	1,133	2,784	1,748	1,448	1,937	2,410	2,640	1,236
22. People	23.0	29.5	18,138	10,641	10,992	6,162	4,888	5,296	6,228	8,112	5,230
23. Playboy	36.2	50.6	13,932	2,749	9,596	4,910	3,523	3,729	4,713	5,965	3,334
24. Playgirl	6.6	8.8	2,110	1,253	1,384	546	526	613	786	1,007	513
25. Reader's Digest	74.6	89.6	39,283	22,303	12,942	12,769	11,360	10,802	15,618	17,937	9,611

26. Road & Track	10.7	16.8	2,454	405	1,761	1,098	589	657	752	1,264	474
27. Rolling Stone	9.1	13.7	2,780	943	2,552	911	663	834	910	1,249	621
28. Seventeen	10.5	15.2	5,259	4,484	3,230	1,573	1,132	1,607	2,266	2,492	1,849
29. Smithsonian	17.5	21.9	4,952	2,404	1,665	2,730	1,630	1,475	1,420	2,321	1,083
30. Sport	13.3	19.4	6,116	1,231	3,816	1,890	1,552	1,488	2,115	2,908	1,722
31. Sports Afield	7.0	10.0	5,318	1,137	2,330	1,982	1,818	1,491	2,193	2,451	1,079
32. Sunset	14.2	19.7	5,227	3,446	1,778	2,317	1,585	1,441	1,827	2,509	1,163
33. Time	45.1	70.3	20,180	8,269	9,854	8,782	5,786	5,192	6,606	9,049	5,032
34. Travel/Holiday	5.9	8.4	1,139	570	299	471	365	397	479	599	332
35. True Story	9.8	12.8	5,925	5,294	3,297	801	1,565	1,946	2,865	2,538	1,665
36. TV Guide	58.8	69.5	42,236	23,389	20,984	11,223	11,130	12,532	16,249	18,818	10,695
37. U.S. News	21.9	34.6	8,635	2,724	3,288	4,112	2,563	2,119	3,310	4,343	2,267
38. Vogue	10.4	15.2	5,755	5,192	2,825	2,194	1,775	1,970	2,495	2,824	2,367
39. Woman's Day	49.9	59.8	18,225	16,606	7,008	5,523	5,121	5,427	7,746	8,876	5,835
40. Working Woman	5.2	7.4	974	941	518	437	756	288	320	597	313

[a] The numbers here will differ from those of Table 16-1 since a different time period is involved.

[b] Source: "The 1979 Study of Media and Markets—Multi-Media Audiences: Adults," Simmons Market Research Bureau, 1979.

[c] Source: Consumer Magazine and Farm Publication Rates and Data, Standard Rate & Data Service, November 27, 1980. Shown are the costs of a one-page single-insertion advertisement.

Measuring Print Advertisement Exposure

The media planner is really concerned with advertisement audience size rather than vehicle audience size. One measurement approach is to use average Starch scores or Starch ad norms. In the Starch survey, respondents are taken through a magazine and, for each advertisement, are asked if they saw it in the issue. The *noted* score is the percentage who answer affirmatively. Two companion measures are *seen-associated* (note the name of the advertiser) and *read-most* (read more than 50 percent of the copy). The Starch measure dates back to 1923 and has been applied consistently since that early start. One indication of advertisement exposure for a vehicle would be the average Starch noted scores for the full-page advertisements contained in it.

Studies using the Starch data indicate that advertisement exposure will depend on the product class, the involvement of the segment in the product class, and on such media-option variables as the size and color of the advertisement, position, and copy approach.

Advertisement Size and Color.   Troldahl and Jones determined that the size determines 40 percent of the variation in advertisement readership.[5] Since doubling the advertisement size falls short of doubling the readership, the use of larger advertisements needs to be justified on impact rather than audience-size grounds. Starch has concluded that readership scores of full-page advertisements using four colors are about 85 percent higher than scores of half-page advertisements using four colors.[6] However, the use of four colors only generates about 50 percent more readership than black and white for one-page and two-page advertisements.

Advertisement Location.   Starch has concluded that advertisements on the back of a magazine will attract about 65 percent more readers than those toward the middle.[7] Advertisements on the inside front and back covers will attract about 30 percent more readers.

Copy Execution.   Starch found that advertisements very similar to the editorial matter of a magazine suffer somewhat in the noted score but gain 50 percent in terms of the read-most measure.[8] Similarly, the use of comic-continuity advertising—the use of panels like a comic strip—receive slightly less noted scores but substantially better read-most scores.[9]

Measuring Broadcast Vehicle Audience

The principal methods of obtaining audience data for broadcast media are the audimeter and the diary. The audimeter is attached to a television set and monitors the set's activity 24 hours a day, recording any change or activity that lasts over 30 seconds. The familiar Nielsen national television ratings, the average number of households tuned to a given program as a percent of all television homes, are based upon 1,200 Neilsen audimeter homes, 1,000 of which are providing data at a given time. In addition, Nielsen meters New York, Los Angeles, and Chicago to provide local ratings in these areas on a next-day basis. Nielsen also reports HUT, the percent of all television homes whose set is in use.

The audimeter provides an objective measure of television viewer activity with no burdensome record keeping. To avoid self-consciousness, the meter is placed out of view and a metered family is not used until several weeks of acclimation have passed. The major problem with the audimeter is its cost and the fact that it cannot provide information as to who is doing the viewing. Thus, the audimeter cannot provide information as to the age composition of the audience, for example.

Nielsen, in its national ratings estimates, supplements the audimeter with a matched sample, diary panel. A diary household notes the viewing activity, including who is doing the watching. Thus, audience estimates can be broken down by age, sex, and geographic area. A clocklike meter keeps track of how long the set is on so that Nielsen can make sure that the diary is complete.

The diary provides the basic data-gathering instrument for local television ratings. Nielsen and Arbitron, its competitor, both monitor over 200 local markets. The sample size of the Nielsen effort ranges from 2,200 households in New York to several hundred in the smallest markets. Monthly reports are provided from three to eight times a year depending on the size of the market. During three ''sweep'' months of November, February, and May, over 200 markets are covered by both Nielsen and Arbitron. Over the course of a year's time, over 800,000 households will be involved in a television diary panel for one of the two services.

Simmons also runs a two-week diary panel to supplement its media data service. Mediamark, in contrast, relies upon the recent-reading approach to generate television viewing estimates which are thus much higher.

The quality of diary data can vary. Some respondents do not fill it out during the day but try to recall viewing activity. As a result, fringe programming generally does not fare as well from the diary as it does from the audimeter. Another problem is that the homemaker is often the one who fills it out, and is often not conversant with kid shows and lesser known programs. There are thus efforts to create an audimeter extension that would monitor who is watching by, for example, having each family member assigned to a switch they would activate when entering a TV room. The major diary problem is probably nonresponse bias. It has been suggested that the diary panel tends to understate the younger audience. The cooperation rate among the 18- to 24-year-old group is especially low.[10]

MEDIA-OPTION SOURCE EFFECT

It is important to be precise when discussing the media-option source effect, for the phrase is easily misinterpreted. The media-option source effect is not a measure of a vehicle's capacity to attract readers (the audience size) nor is it the quality of the audience (the segment effect). Neither is it the quality affecting a reader's tendency to read a vehicle's advertising (more properly a refinement of the audience size). It is, rather, the differential impact that the advertisement exposure will have on the same audience member if the exposure occurs in one media option rather than another.

Types of Media-Option Source Effects

A media option is a detailed description of an advertisement's characteristics other than the copy and artwork employed. Thus, it specifies the media class used, the vehicle within the media type, plus such advertisement characteristics as size or length, color, and position. The most important media-option source effect is that attributed to different vehicles, the vehicle source effect. The concept is that the advertising environment contributed by the vehicle can have a substantial effect on the nature of the resulting communication. The vehicle source effect will be considered in some detail.

The effect of the media class could be termed the media class source effect. Television, because it can show action using both audio and visual, can make an impact that simply is not possible in other media. For some types of advertising this type of impact can be critical to the copy approach. On the other hand, television is a passive medium. Radio can involve the listener by getting him or her to use imagination to visualize stimuli. Print is more suitable for long and complex messages. Because of their association with news stories, newspapers could have a sense of objectivity and a spirit of being current that could rub off on the advertisements in the right context.

In addition to the source effect due to media type and the vehicle, there are other characteristics of the media option that can contribute to the media-option source effect. It is often believed, for example, that an exposure to a four-color advertisement will have more impact than an exposure to a black-and-white one.

The size of the advertisement might contribute to the media-option source effect. It may be that those exposed to a two-page spread may respond quite differently from the way they would respond if they were exposed to a single-page advertisement. Again, this type of argument is often employed to justify large advertisements whose marginal readership does not warrant their extra cost. Of course, media-option characteristics such as size and color are not additive in their impact. There are interactions involved.

Vehicle Source Effects

There is general agreement that there does exist a vehicle source effect. As early as 1962, the Alfred Politz research organization demonstrated that an advertisement in *McCall's* would generate higher "quality" image and brand preference ratings than identical ads placed in general readership magazines.[11] Blair, a media executive, surveyed over 100 media professionals and found strong agreement (4.4 on a 5-point scale) to the statement:[12] "The attitudes of readers toward a magazine can greatly influence their reaction to advertisements in it."

The determination of the vehicle source effect will obviously depend on the campaign objectives. An awareness objective will involve different source-effect considerations than communication or image-oriented objectives. However, there are at least five vehicle attributes that are often relevant considerations: unbiasedness, expertness, prestige, mood created, and involvement.

Unbiasedness.   The degree of unbiasedness, which in other contexts was often the most important characteristic of the source, will probably be less relevant to vehicle source effects. Vehicles tend to be rather uniformly impartial with respect to the advertising they contain. They simply rarely develop representations that relate directly to consumption issues. However, if advertising concerned with political or social issues is considered, the position of the vehicle may indeed affect the communications. For example, an advertisement opposing gun control in the publication of an organization such as the National Rifle Association may be more likely to appear biased than if the same advertisement appeared in another vehicle. The qualities of expertness and prestige, however, are more often highly relevant to the vehicle source effect.

Expertness.   Advertisements can usually be expected to reflect the degree of expertise associated with the area of interest of the vehicle in which they appear. Thus, the magazine *World Tennis* is seen by its readers as a reliable source of information regarding new product developments in tennis, new playing techniques, new types of tennis court surfaces, and so on. The editors and writers are recognized authorities in competitive and instructive tennis. A reader, therefore, comes to the magazine willing to accept information from this source. The concept is that the reader's mental set does not change when he or she moves from an article in *World Tennis* to an advertisement describing a new racket used by Boris Becker. Some of the reliability and authority attributed to *World Tennis* rubs off onto its advertisements, just as a professor on the Harvard faculty gains from whatever Harvard means to the world. The tenets of the consistency theories would support such a hypothesis. The perception of an advertisement incompatible in content and style to the authorative vehicle in which it appears could well generate some cognitive uneasiness in a reader.

The expertness effect should be expected to be enhanced if an advertisement's format is very similar to that of the vehicle articles. At times, advertisements have been so similar to the vehicle's regular articles in format that publishers were obliged to add the phrase, "This is an advertisement." The effect should also be expected to be high when a product advertised is very similar to the products associated with the vehicle. For instance, a tennis racket advertisement in *World Tennis* would be expected to benefit more than one for a sports car in the same magazine. Some vehicles will obviously have a much higher aura of authority than others. If such a dimension is to be relied on, it is, of course, appropriate to obtain empirical evidence confirming judgment in this regard.

Prestige.   A vehicle's prestige is a third attribute commonly considered to be important for some product. The *New Yorker* has an exclusiveness and aloofness that might be expected to generate a similar feeling toward products advertised in it. Thus, if a product is endeavoring to build a status image, it may well be useful to advertise it in a high-status vehicle. In addition to the immediate influence of a vehicle's prestige on advertisement impact, there is the possibility of a longer-term association developing. This possibility is certainly enhanced if a product is advertised consistently in one vehicle—especially if it appears in the same location in each issue and if it appears infrequently elsewhere.

A study by Gert Assmus provides an interesting approach toward identifying the components of the vehicle source effect and demonstrates the relevance of the prestige dimension.[13] In his study, 125 people associated with media planning in the medical field rated six medical journals as to the journal's vehicle source effect and as to the extent to which the journals were perceived to have each of 16 attributes. He found substantial differences in the vehicle source effect ratings. Furthermore, the three attributes that were the strongest predictors of the overall vehicle source effect rating were useful editorial content, prestige, and reference value. A knowledge of these elements could be of value in attempting to assign vehicle source weights in the medical context.

Mood Created.   The influence of a vehicle's prestige may be viewed as working through the mood it creates among its readers. The concept is that a vehicle-induced mood will affect the impact of a commercial communication. Axelrod, an agency research executive, provided indirect support for such a hypothesis by linking moods to attitudes.[14] He suggested that moods actually become goals. Thus, "a person not only feels happy but one of his goals is to make himself happy. He may smoke to feel calm, go to a Western movie for excitement, or drink to relieve depression."[15] A person might also read *Playboy* or *Viva* for sexual excitement, watch the Johnny Carson Show for relaxation, and listen to news reports to learn. He assumed, furthermore, that when a person is in a certain mood, that mood will be regarded as a worthwhile goal, at least for the moment. When a person is in a library, he will value concentration highly. When he is at a basketball game, he will value excitement. A third assumption was that different products have perceived association with moods. These associations are a form of beliefs about a product. Thus, if a mood changes (often due to a change in setting), the mood goal of an individual will also change; those products with a low association with the previous moods but a high association with the new ones will be regarded more favorably.

In our context, if we were advertising a Daiquiri mix, we would like to know what mood is associated with a positive attitude toward this product. Then an attempt would be made to determine which vehicles tend to provide such a mood. If any media or vehicles uniquely provided such a mood, they might well also provide more effective exposure than other vehicles. Such an argument could lead to the use of women's glamour magazines for lipsticks, powders, and perfumes, *Family Health* for nutrition-oriented advertisements, and *Sports Illustrated* for advertisements that relate to sports and exercise.

A concept related to mood is that a vehicle should harmonize with the product. Crane reported that depth interviews conducted by one advertiser

> suggest that men's products are best advertised on Westerns and with "assertive" commercials, whereas food products call for commercials using emotional appeals and appearing on situation comedies. Although these findings may reflect respondents' knowledge of current practices rather than any more basic tendencies, Schwerin's findings tend to support these conclusions. Food commercials, Schwerin reports, fit well with situation comedies but do poorly in a mystery, adventure, or Western context. Analgesics do well both in adult Westerns and situation comedies.[16]

Audience Involvement.   An involving vehicle should generate a superior commercial exposure than a vehicle that is not very interesting to the audience. Agency executives Barclay, Doub, and McMurtrey found that in daytime programming, commercials in serial programs generated more recall and attentiveness than other program types, and situation comedies fared least well. However, Soldow and Principe, in a forced-exposure lab setting, compared commercials in a low-involving program (Brady Bunch, a situation comedy) with the same commercials in a high-involving program (Baretta, an action program).[17] The low-involving environment was actually superior with respect to buying intentions and brand and sales-message recall. Their findings suggest that a program can be so suspenseful and involving that it detracts from the advertising impact.

Other Dimensions.   Wolfe and his associates reported on an advertising agency that studied vehicle effects and concluded that three factors should be "included within a qualitative publication index: competitive advertising volume (defined as number of pages), editorial content (defined as percentage of space devoted to subjects pertaining to the product), and editorial quality (defined as the ratio of editorial pages to total pages)."[18] They also discussed the methodology of a major image study involving over 3,000 respondents conducted by the Bolger Corporation.[19] The study attempted to determine the image of 11 large-circulation magazines in terms of 10 dimensions: dynamic, informational, entertainment, cultural, intelligence, influence, format, scope, moral, and goodwill.

Vehicle Source Effects and Copy Approaches

A study by Aaker and Brown illustrates that the nature of vehicle source effects will depend on the copy approach used.[20] Four print advertisements represented two copy approaches—image and reason why. One image advertisement for dinnerware had almost no copy but used a picture of a bride and groom with a headline indicating that the Queen of England had used similar dinnerware on her wedding table. The reason-why advertisement for comparably priced dinnerware, shown in Figure 16-1, used copy indicating that the product was durable, ovenproof, and safe in a dishwasher. A second product category, spices, also contributed an image and a reason-why advertisement. The reason-why spice advertisement included a recipe, noted the unique bottle shape, and included a coupon for a spice rack. The image spice advertisement showed a noted cookbook author who stressed the importance of using top-rated spices.

A survey of 30 housewives rated 18 magazines as to their prestigious and expertness with respect to cooking, foods, and kitchenware. Two magazines, *Vogue* and the *New Yorker,* were rated as prestigious and ranked low on the expert scale. Two others, *Better Homes and Gardens* and *Sunset,* were considered as expert but not prestigious.

Another sample of 64 housewives was shown a series of four folders, each with a cover page from one of the four test magazines. Each folder included three advertisements, including one of the test advertisements. Among the questions asked of the respondent about each advertisement were questions concerning perceived product price, product quality, and product reliability, all of which were expected to measure the ability of the image advertisements to affect perceived quality.

The hypothesis was that the image advertisements would perform better in prestige magazines than in expert magazines with respect to these image-oriented measures, but that the reverse would occur with reason-why advertisements. The results are summarized in Figure 16-2 for nonusers of the advertised brand who are more sensitive to the advertising. Clearly the hypotheses are confirmed. The study indicates clearly that the vehicle source effects are sensitive to the type of advertising used.

Vehicle Source Effects and Television

There has been very little research conducted on vehicle source effects in television. Thus a major field experiment with this focus conducted by J. Walter Thompson agency is of considerable interest.[21] The experiment included:

- Six products
- Three-hour-long action (police/detective) shows
- Three pairs of half-hour situation comedies
- Several commercial performance measures, including brand recall, attitude and buying intention, commercial element playback
- Two markets
- 1,200-respondent survey

The respondents were called and asked to watch the test programs. They were then called after the programs were shown and interviewed.

One remarkable finding was that there were only modest differences overall between the two types of programs. The conventional wisdom was that the types

Figure 16-1.   **A reason-why advertisement**

Figure 16-2.   **Ratings of product quality (nonusers of advertised brand)**

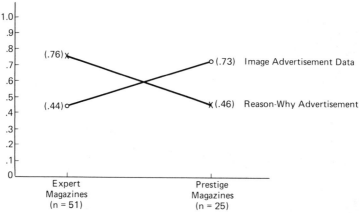

had very different effects and in fact that the action types were better vehicles. However, there were considerable differences among the specific programs within a program type. These differences consistently appeared across products and commercial performance measures. This observation suggests the hypothesis that even different episodes of the same program could have different effects on commercial performance. The action shows, although no better overall, did perform better for three of the brands and for several audience subgroups: men, lower-income viewers, parents of teen-agers, heavy television viewers, and viewers who did not object to violent programming. In contrast, no subgroups were identified in which situation comedies consistently yielded superior commercial performance.

This experiment, like the others reported, illustrates that is usually futile to demonstrate that grand generalities exist, because they usually do not. Legitimate, useful answers usually require the qualification "it depends"! In essence, a model is required. In this case, we saw that the result seemed to depend on the product or copy approach employed.

REPETITION

A crucial and basic media decision is how much media weight or budget to put behind a campaign. The issue is how many exposures over what time period is required to achieve the objective.

How Many Exposures?

Naples, then president of the Advertising Research Foundation, conducted an extensive review of industry studies of repetition and concluded that, in general, around three exposures within a purchase cycle are all that are needed to induce the desired attitudinal and behavioral change.[22]

Herbert Krugman, a General Electric manager and prominent advertising theorist, suggests that insights into repetition can be gained by considering the difference between the first, second, and third exposures.[23] In his conceptualization there is no such thing as a fourth exposure.

The first exposure elicits a "What is it?" type of response. The audience member tries to understand the nature of the communication and, if possible, categorizes it as being of no further interest.

The second exposure, if not blocked out, produces several effects. One, particularly in television or radio advertising, is a continuation of the "What is it?" response. The first exposure may not have been adequate to gain an understanding of what it was. (In fact, some television copy-testing systems require at least two exposures for this very reason). Another response is an evaluative "What of it?" response. The audience member will attempt to determine if it is relevant and convincing. The message will be evaluated. Associated with both responses could be an "Aha, I've seen this before" reaction.

The third exposure is basically a reminder in case the audience member has not yet acted on the message. Any additional exposure is another third exposure, replicating the third-exposure experience. Thus, Krugman implies that only three exposures are required. However, it is not quite that simple, because some audience segments may, after the first exposure, screen the advertisement out until they are ready to process another exposure. This phenomenon is particularly prevalent in television advertising where there is low involvement. A potential purchase or a use experience may stimulate an audience member to be receptive to a second-exposure experience. As a result, several actual exposures might be needed before a "second exposure" experience occurs. The effect of multiple exposures is not to generate a cumulative impact on an individual audience member, but to capture more second- and third-exposure experiences.

As a practical suggestion to General Electric managers, Krugman advises that they start with an objective of exposing two-thirds of their target audience at least twice and not more than four times per month. This advice is compatible with the concept that at least two exposures are needed and that any exposure over four is wasted since the second-exposure experience will have occurred for most of the audience.

Wear-out

Wear-out occurs when successive exposures no longer have a positive impact on the audience. Indeed, the marginal impact can turn negative. The determination of the optimal frequency thus involves an understanding and an ability to predict when wear-out will occur.

One of the first psychologists to study learning empirically was Ebbinghaus.[24] In a series of experiments reported in 1902, he related retention to repetition. He had a single subject (himself) learn a series of nonsense syllables by oral repetition. He found that diminishing returns set in as the number of repetitions increased. Since that time wear-out has been documented in a variety of field and laboratory studies by psychologists and advertising researchers. As repetitions build, advertising researchers have found that attention to the commercial, recall of the copy points, awareness of the advertised brand, brand attitude, and purchase intention will build, then level off and ultimately decline.

One explanation for the wear-out phenomenon is that the audience stops attending to the advertising.[25] They may feel that they have already absorbed the information, or they may become bored. One study found that exposure repetition ultimately generated a significant decline in brand-name recall, but that this decline could be reversed when attention to the advertisement was experimentally induced.[26]

Another explanation is that excessive exposure generates irritation. The audience, which accepts advertisements as a necessary part of print or broadcast media, may resent being exposed to the same advertisement many times. Psychologists Cacioppo and Petty monitored people's verbalized response to a persuasive written communication.[27] They found that the production of supporting arguments increased and then decreased with exposure. The number of negative thoughts, however, declined after the first few exposures but then increased as repetitions mounted. To combat wear-out, then, it is necessary to attempt to reduce inattention/boredom and irritation. One approach is to provide advertisements that reward the audience in some way. Information that is valued (features of a personal computer) could be provided. Humor can stimulate attention and liking. Entertainment value can also come from creative approaches using music, dancing, action, or drama. Conversely, advertisements that are irritating will not wear well. In Chapter 10 we discussed several causes of irritation, such as graphic displays of discomfort (stomach commercials) or the put-down of central characters.

Wear-out can also be combated by spacing commercial exposures over time and by running multiple executions of the same campaign theme. Another one of the findings of Ebbinghaus was that spaced repetitions were more effective than the same number massed together.[28] Calder and Sternthal conducted an experiment involving three commercial exposures embedded in a one-hour adventure show in up to six sessions.[29] The pronounced wear-out found was substantially reduced when the advertising consisted of three commercials rather than a single one. When multiple media are used, variety is naturally introduced, which will allow a higher level of repetition.

When Is More Frequency Needed?

Clearly, the number of exposures needed will depend on a host of considerations. In particular, advertising that aims to develop associations between the brand and feelings, activities, or people will require more repetition than advertising that is designed to communicate information. Transformational advertising (advertising to transform the use experience discussed in Chapter 10), for example, can require heavy repetition that continues over years or even decades. Such advertising fortunately is often entertaining and/or well liked, and thus heavy repetition involving multiple campaign executions and variations can be tolerated.

The complexity and size of the communication and persuasion task will affect the repetitions needed. For example, a task that involves establishing a new brand name and communicating a complex new service will undoubtedly require heavy repetition as well as multiple executions. Another of the classic Ebbinghaus findings was that as the number of items to be communicated increased, the number of repetitions necessary to attain a certain level of learning also increased.[30]

Ostrow, a senior advertising executive with Young & Rubicam, suggested that heavier repetition would be required when:[31]

- A new brand is involved.
- A smaller, less well-known brand is involved. A dominant brand will need less frequency because it will already have a high level of recognition and acceptance.
- A low level of brand loyalty has been achieved. A brand with a high level of purchase loyalty and attitude commitment will require less repetition.
- The purchase and use cycle is relatively long. Products with short purchase and use cycles generally need more repetition.
- When the target audience is less involved and less motivated to process the information or when it has less ability to process it (because a lack of background information or because of a lack of mental skills).
- When there exists a great deal of clutter to break through. Of particular importance is the level of competitive advertising. It may be necessary to increase repetition to break through the presence of competitor advertising.

Descriptions of two specific repetition experiments will provide a feeling for the methodologies that can be employed and deeper insights into the types of findings that emerge.

The Ray-Sawyer Study

Stanford researchers Ray and Sawyer gave 168 adult female shoppers a mobile-unit "demonstration" of a futuristic shopping system.[32] The 10-minute demonstration included exposure to a set of print advertisements projected onto a futuristic screen. Half the respondents saw advertisements for nine "convenience" goods, such as soaps or soups. The other half saw advertisements for "shopping" goods, such as washing machines or portable television sets. There were six repetition conditions of one to six exposures.

There were four basic measures of response obtained in the questionnaire for each of the products. A recall item asked respondents to play back anything they could remember about the advertising. An attitude scale with six positions reflected whether the brand was judged best, one of the best, acceptable, don't know, unacceptable, or one of the worst. A purchase-intention question asked which brand the respondents would buy if shopping for the product. Finally, the respondents were given coupon booklets for purchasing the three convenience-goods products.

Overall, the results did produce highly significant (0.001 level) repetition effects with respect to recall. As expected, repetition has a smaller effect on the other measures. The main interest, however, was on how the repetition effect interacts with the product classification and the audience and advertisement characteristics. In fact, there was a significant difference (0.05 level) for both recall and purchase intention for the product classification of convenience versus shopping goods.

The results supported the Ray-Sawyer hypothesis that the curve for shopping goods would soon level off; convenience goods would benefit more from repetition. As expected, repetition had almost no effect on purchase intentions for shopping goods and had a very positive effect on convenience goods. For recall, the impact of the advertisements reached the saturation point after four exposures for shopping goods, whereas for convenience goods the advertisements still had impact after six exposures.

Five characteristics of the advertisements were identified to see if the repetition function depended on the type of advertisement employed. These characteristics were (1) color or black and white, (2) long or short copy, (3) well-known or lesser-known brands, (4) brand emphasized or not, and (5) "grabber" or not. The last two were determined by three judges associated with the study. Two of the five characteristics—the "well-known" and "grabber" dimensions—produced significant interaction, with repetition at the 0.05 level or better.

The different repetition functions for "grabber" versus "nongrabber" advertisements are shown in Figure 16-3; Ray and Sawyer explain:

> Grabber ads were defined by three judges as different enough in format to attract attention and accomplish some communication in a single exposure. Aside from this strong single-exposure performance, however, the grabber ad was hypothesized to do relatively poorly over repetition. Its intrusive uniqueness was not expected to last in repeated exposures. The grabber and nongrabber distinction might be compared to the hard-sell and soft-sell distinction often mentioned in advertising. . . .[33]

This hypothesis is supported by the results. The purchase-intention curves showed that the grabber advertisements did poorly with repetition, whereas the nongrabbers "wore well." Notice, however, that the reverse was true to some extent on the recall measure, although these differences were not large. This is an example of reversals in results across measures and should emphasize the importance of being cognizant of the appropriate measure with which a particular advertisement should be judged. Thus, it might well be that, for the same brand, a different repetition effect is appropriate if awareness is the goal rather than if the objective is to generate purchase intentions.

The reversal effect is pronounced when Ivory and Phase III soap advertisements are compared. The Phase III advertisement shown in Figure 16-4 was judged

Figure 16.3.   **"Grabber" and "nongrabber" ad results**

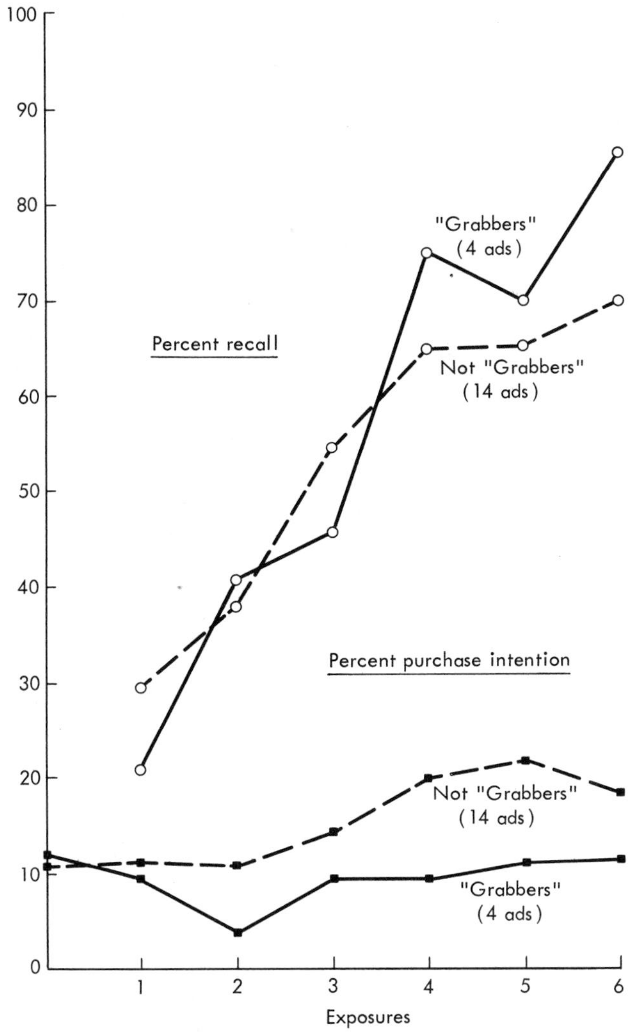

*56 and 196 responses, respectively, per condition

Source: Michael L. Ray and Alan G. Sawyer, "Repetition in Media Models: A Laboratory Technique," *Journal of Marketing Research*, 8, February 1971, p. 27.

a grabber, because of its bold claim and unusual illustration. The Ivory advertisement, also shown in Figure 16-4, was definitely a nongrabber. The Phase III advertising did much better with repetition than the Ivory advertisement, with respect to building recall. However, Ivory did significantly (0.05 level) better with respect to attitude and purchase intention. As Ray and Sawyer point out,

> This reversal . . . is quite logical considering the different communication goals for well known and lesser known products. A product like Phase III must concentrate on building awareness and so must use grabber-type advertising. A well established product like Ivory can capitalize on its past reputation with rather ordinary ads that result in adequate persuasion even at relatively low levels of exposure.[34]

A Television Repetition Study

A major 2½-year study of nine television commercials in six product categories by the New York agency of McCollum/Spielman provides additional insights.[35] They found that brand awareness steadily snowballed during a year's repetition and then stopped at a plateau. Communication of key sales messages (measured by unaided recall) gained slowly and then declined, possibly because the commercials became familiar and viewers blocked out their content. Attitude (persuasive influence) gained only slightly during the first year, then dropped sharply. One implication is that measures of attitude should be monitored to detect advertising wear-out. The authors of the study also concluded:

- Of two equally effective commercials, a well-liked one will last longer.
- A humorous or off-beat commercial will wear out faster than a straight selling one.
- The use of slight variations of a basic commercial will extend its effective life.
- Competitive advertising will affect wear-out, a competitor's hard-hitting commercials resulting in a drop in the attitude measure.
- The type of presentation, the product category activity, and the status of the presenter all affect the repetition effect.

It is clear that a host of considerations enter into the determination of repetition and forgetting, such as the criterion measure, the copy approach, the product type, the segment and competition.

FORGETTING

A host of studies, including the Ebbinghaus experiments, have confirmed the commonsense notion that recall declines over time and that this decline is greatest at the outset and diminishes over time. Lodish, one of the developers of MEDIAC, estimated the forgetting function using data from a study of advertising retention in five magazines by W. R. Simmons.[36] The retention measured was the ability of

Figure 16-4. A "grabber" and a "nongrabber" advertisement

Can you compete with your daughter's "Little Girl Look"?

Mrs. John Marino does.
She keeps her complexion young-looking with pure, mild Ivory...

The same purity and mildness daughter Christa needs is important to help grown-up skin look young; more important than extra ingredients in other soaps. More doctors recommend Ivory, 99⁴⁴⁄₁₀₀% pure.* It floats! The big girl's soap for complexions with that little girl look.

Lever Brothers' new **Phase III** has the mildness that's missing from deodorant bars and the protection that's missing from cream bars.

You'd have to bolt a deodorant bar and a cream bar together to get the deodorant and cream that's in one bar of Phase III.

Courtesy of The Procter & Gamble Company.

readers of a specific issue to distinguish among advertisements that appeared in that issue and ones that did not. Lodish found that the retention measure fell by 25 percent each week. (In terms of the MEDIAC model, the parameter would be 0.75.)

Zielske and Henry examined 17 tracking studies involving six established products.[37] A tracking study is a repeated survey over time to track a measure such as awareness. Unaided recall of advertising copy was the measure in this case. The recall level varied from 10 to 16 percent and the weekly GRP ranged from 40 to 200. A regression analysis yielded the following model:

$$\Delta A_t = 0.30W_t - 0.10A_{t-1}$$

where ΔA_t = percentage-point change in unaided recall in week t
W_t = gross rating points received in week t
A_{t-1} = unaided recall level in week t–1

The first term indicates, for example, that 100 GRP per week will, on the average, produce three percentage points of unaided recall. The second term in the formula, $-.10A_{t-1}$, represents the average forgetting rate. For example, if recall in the prior week had been at the 15 percent level, then in the absence of further advertising recall would be expected to drop to 13.5 percent. Thus, from one week to the next, just 10 percent would be forgotten. That, of course, is less than the 25 percent found by Lodish in the other context. Clearly, these functions will be unique to the situation involved. The point of these efforts to estimate parameters is not so much to indicate specific "universal" parameter values but rather to illustrate approaches that can be taken to estimate functions in given contexts.

Agency researcher Zielske conducted a field experiment that is regarded as a classic study of repetition and forgetting.[38] Two groups of women, randomly selected from a telephone directory, were mailed 13 different advertisements from the same newspaper advertising campaign for an ingredient food. One group received an advertisement weekly for 13 weeks. The other group received the same 13 mailings but at intervals of four weeks during the year. Throughout the year, aided only by mention of the product class, recall was measured by telephone interviews. No single person was interviewed in person more than once. A person can become sensitized to the advertisement after an interview; if a person has been interviewed twice, the second interview would usually be biased. The results of the study are shown in Figure 16-5 with the learning and forgetting process graphically displayed.

SUMMARY

There are three basic approaches toward estimating the audience of print vehicles; recent reading (did you read it last week?), reading habit (how many of the last four issues did you read?), and through-the-book. The first two suffer from memory problems but are more economical and efficient than the through-the-book approach. The Starch noted score is one way to determine levels of advertising exposure within a magazine. Research has shown that the Starch noted level is sensitive to advertisement size, position, and the use of color.

Figure 16-5.   **The 1958 repetition study**

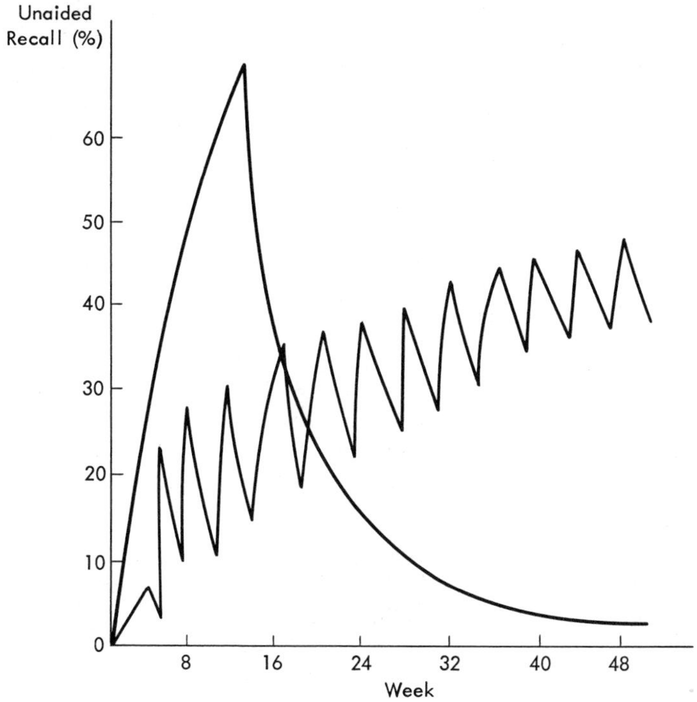

Source: Adapted from Hubert A. Zielske, "The Remembering and Forgetting of Advertising," *Journal of Marketing,* American Marketing Association, 23, January 1959, pp. 239–243.

Nielsen and Arbitron use television audimeters and panel diaries to estimate
the audience size of television programs. The diary suffers from the relative difficulty of getting cooperation of some groups, such as the 18 to 24 age group and
from inaccuracies in completing the diary.

The media-option source effect is not a measure of a vehicle's capacity to
attract readers nor the quality of the audience nor the ability of the vehicle to
generate advertisement readership. Rather, it is the differential impact that the
advertisement exposure will have on the same audience member if the exposure
occurs in one media option rather than another.

One important type of media option source effect is the vehicle source effect.
A vehicle source will tend to enhance an advertisement to the extent that it is
regarded as being impartial, expert, and prestigious, able to create the correct mood,
or involving. For example, the *New Yorker* has an exclusiveness and aloofness that
might be expected to help an advertiser who is trying to build a status image.
However, one study showed that vehicle source effects will depend on such factors
as the advertising objectives and the copy approach used.

The impact of advertising eventually declines and even turns negative with
repetition because audience members become bored or irritated. Thus, in some

contexts it may be desirable to aim for only a few exposures. Krugman postulates that three exposures are enough. More repetition is appropriate when associations are being created or maintained with ''mood'' advertising, when a complex communication task is involved, when the subject is a new brand, when brand loyalty is low, when the purchase cycle is short, when the target audience is uninvolved, when a great deal of clutter exists, with a ''nongrabber'' ad, or when the advertising is well liked. The amount of forgetting similarly declines over time, as illustrated by Figure 16-5.

DISCUSSION QUESTIONS

1. What is the relationship of the perception process to the definition of a media option exposure? Define a media-option exposure for a magazine advertisement and a radio advertisement in operational terms, that is, include a method to measure it. What does the attention filter and the interpretation process from Chapter 8 have to do with your definition?

2. In a survey of housewives, the readership of *Harper's* was exaggerated and the readership of *Modern Romance* seemed much less than circulation figures indicated. Why would respondents incorrectly report their readership in this manner? Can you think of any measure, perhaps an unobtrusive measure, to avoid this bias?

3. Compare the recent-reading and reading-habit approaches to estimating audience size. Which would be more accurate in your view? Identify any biases that might tend to inflate readership. Would you prefer the through-the-book approach used by Simmons? What are the trade-offs? Analyze Table 16-1.

4. Suppose that you are a brand manager of a line of new electronic calculators that are coming out at a price 30 percent under competition. Which of the three Starch measures would you use to compare the advertisement differences in advertisement readership across available magazines? (In the media model context, how would you estimate the h_j term?). Would your answer be the same if you were attempting to communicate the features of eastern Kentucky as a factory site to exectutives?

5. Starch claimed that if an advertisement reached $X\%$ of a magazine's audience, then doubling the advertisement would reach $X\%$ of those who would not be reached with the original-sized advertisement. For example, say the original-sized advertisement reached 40% of the audience. Then an advertisement with twice the size would reach the original 40% plus 40% of the other 60%, or a total of 64%. What assumptions are implied by this theory?

6. What are the limitations of the audimeter? What alternatives to the diary might be used to overcome these limitations? What are the weaknesses of the diary approach?

7. The *Ladies Home Journal* claims that its vehicle source effect for kitchen products is high because of the high percentage of its readership who are homemakers interested in cooking. *Esquire* claims that its vehicle source effect is high for men's clothing advertisements because its readers tend to read the advertisements. The *Journal of the American Medical Association* believes that its prestige merits a high vehicle source rating for pharmaceutical advertising. Do you agree with all of these claims?

8. Assume that you are hired as a consultant for *Tennis World* magazine. It believes that advertisements for tennis goods have greater impact in their magazine than in general sports magazines like *Sports Illustrated*. You are to design an experiment to support this claim. How would you proceed?

9. Generate vehicle source effect values for a set of magazines or television programs using your own subjective judgment, assuming a product and an advertising objective. For example, suppose that a product-effectiveness advertisement was generated for an electric frypan and the magazine alternatives were *Women's Day, TV Guide, Vogue, American Home, Ladies Home Journal,* and *Time.* Justify your set of values.

10. A study attempted to determine the relative credibility of news reporting in the various media. Nearly 50 percent of the respondents said that if they got conflicting reports of the same news story from radio, television, magazines, and newspapers, they would be most inclined to believe the one from television; 20 percent named newspapers, 10 percent named radio, 9 percent named magazines, and 12 percent did not answer. What relevance does this study have to assessing media-class source effects?

11. How should the brand manager described in Question 4 determine the repetition function?

12. Suppose that you are attempting to get housewives to try your new gourmet vegetable dish and have divided housewives into two groups— those interested in kitchens and those not so interested. Using your own subjective reasoning, estimate the probability of each group's trying the product after 0, 1, 3, 5, and 10 advertising exposures during a three-month period.

13. How might the repetition function be affected by whether the advertisement was in color, whether it used long or short copy, whether it involved well-known brands, whether the audience were brand users, and in what vehicle the advertisement appeared?

14. Explain why it was found that the vehicle source effect did not differ between action television programs and situation comedies, but did differ substantially between action shows. Illustrate your answer with sepcific programs and products.

15. What are the factors that should contribute to wear-out? Illustrate your answer with specific examples of commercials that you can recall. What are some campaigns that you have not tired of even though you might have seen 50 or more commercials? Why? Identify some factors that should be associated with the need for more repetition. Try to list some that were not discussed in the chapter.

NOTES

1. William S. Blair, "Observed vs. Reported Behavior in Magazine Reading: An Investigation of the Editorial Interest Method," *Proceedings of the 12th Annual Conference of the Advertising Research Foundation,* 1967.

2. "New Simmons Report May Stir Research War," *Advertising Age,* September 8, 1980, pp. 20, 75. Leah Rozen, "Reader Data Still Don't Jibe," *Advertising Age,* October 6, 1980, pp. 2, 118.

3. The total audience figures for the Simmons reading-habit approach is the total of the following percentages of those saying they have read the magazine in the last six months: 9% of those who claim to have read less than one out of four issues; 15% of those reading one out of four issues; 36% of the two of four group; 63% of the three of four issues group; and 73% of the all four issues group.

4. Jack Z. Sissors, "Vehicle Exposure Measurements and Beyond," *Current Issues and Research in Advertising,* University of Michigan, 1978, pp. 107–120.

5. Verling Troldahl and Robert Jones, "Predictors of Newspaper Advertising Readership," *Journal of Advertising Research,* 5, March 1965, pp. 23–27.

6. Daniel Starch, *Measuring Advertising Readership and Results* (New York: McGraw-Hill, 1966) p. 61.

7. Starch, *Measuring Advertising Readership,* pp. 51–56.

8. Ibid., p. 101.

9. Ibid., p. 108.

10. "ARB and NSI Defend Their TV Diaries," *Media Decisions,* October 1973, pp. 72–74.

11. *A Measurement of Advertising Effectiveness: The Influence of Audience Selectivity and Editorial Environment,* report by Alfred Politz Research, Inc., November 1962.

12. William S. Blair, "Attitude Research and the Qualitative Value of Magazines," in Lee Adler and Irving Crespi, eds., *Attitude Research at Sea* (Chicago: American Marketing Association, 1966), pp. 153–162.

13. Gert Assmus, "An Empirical Investigation into the Perception of Vehicle Source Effects," *Journal of Advertising,* Winter 1978, pp. 4–10.

14. Joel N. Axelrod, "Induced Moods and Attitudes Toward Products," *Journal of Advertising Research,* 3, June 1963, pp. 19–24.

15. Ibid., p. 20.

16. Lauren E. Crane, "How Product, Appeal and Program Affect Attitudes toward Commercials," *Journal of Advertising Research,* 4, March 1964, p. 15 © 1964 by the Advertising Research Foundation.

17. Gary F. Soldow and Victor Principe, "Response to Commercials as a Function of Program Context," *Journal of Advertising Research,* 21, April 1981, pp. 59–64.

18. Harry D. Wolfe, James K. Brown, G. Clark Thompson, and Steven H. Greenberg, *Evaluating Media* (New York: National Industrial Conference Board, 1966), p. 85.

19. Ibid., p. 72.

20. David A. Aaker and Philip K. Brown, "Evaluating Vehicle Source Effects," *Journal of Advertising Research,* 12, August 1972, pp. 11–16.

21. Sonia Yuspeh, "On-Air: Are We Testing the Message or the Medium?" Delivered to J. Walter Thompson Research Conference, New York, November 1977.

22. Michael J. Naples, *Effective Frequency: The Relationship between Frequency and Advertising Effectiveness* (New York: Association of National Advertisers, 1979), p. 79.

23. Herbert E. Krugman, "What Makes Advertising Effective?" *Harvard Business Review,* March–April 1975, pp. 96–103.

24. Hermann Ebbinghaus, *Grundzuge der Psychologie* (Leipzig: Viet, 1902).

25. Bobby J. Calder and Brian Sternthal, "Television Commercial Wearout: An Information Processing View," *Journal of Marketing Research,* 17, May 1980, pp. 173–186.

26. Charles S. Craig, Brian Sternthal, and Clark Leavitt, "Advertising Wearout: An Experimental Analysis," *Journal of Marketing Research,* 13, November 1976, pp. 365–372.

27. James Cacioppo and Richard Petty, "Effects of Message Repetition and Position on Cognitive Response, Recall and Persuasion," *Journal of Personality and Social Psychology,* 37, January 1979, pp. 97–109.

28. Ebbinghaus, *Grundzuge der Psychologie.*

29. Calder and Sternthal, "Television Commercial Wearout."

30. Ebbinghaus, *Grundzuge der Psychologie.*

31. Joseph W. Ostrow, "Setting Frequency Levels: An Art or a Science?" *Journal of Advertising Research,* 24, August–September 1984, pp. I-9 to I-11.

32. Michael L. Ray and Alan G. Sawyer, "Repetition in Media Models: A Laboratory Technique," *Journal of Marketing Research,* 8, February 1971, pp. 20–29.

33. Ibid., p. 26.

34. Ibid., pp. 27–28.

35. "Repeating TV Ads Makes 2 Factors Snowball, 1 Factor Wear-out," *Marketing News,* April 7, 1978, p. 1.

36. Leonard M. Lodish, "Empirical Studies on Individual Responses to Exposure Patterns," *Journal of Marketing Research,* 8, May 1971, pp. 214–216.

37. Hubert A. Zielske and Walter A. Henry, "Remembering and Forgetting Television Ads," *Journal of Advertising Research,* 20, April 1980, pp. 7–13.

38. Herbert A. Zielske, "The Remembering and Forgetting of Advertising," *Journal of Marketing,* 23, March 1959, pp. 239–243.

CASE FOR PART V

Conn-Crest Company*

The marketing manager and the advertising manager of the Conn-Crest Company in Hartford, Connecticut, were considering recommendations made by an advertising agency concerning the company's advertising effort. Involved were higher expenditures and new media.

Conn-Crest's Operations

Conn-Crest manufacturers bonded abrasive products, grinding wheels, mounted points (wheels mounted on shafts for internal and die grinding), sharpening stones, and honing sticks.

---

* Copyright © 1953 by the President and Fellows of Harvard College. Reproduced by permission. This case was set in the late 1960s. If the dollar figures were multiplied by about three they would reflect the realities of the 1980s. The reader should know that the house organ is conceived to be a sales promotion device with a format much like a trade magazine. It would contain technical articles and aimed at customers and potential customers.

In this particular industrial segment (bonded abrasives), Conn-Crest ranked third in market share—probably about 10 percent—with annual sales of some $25 million. Two larger competitors, the Acton Company and the Bensington Company, accounted for an estimated 60 percent of sales of this type of product (Acton around 35 percent, Bensington around 25 percent). But Acton and Bensington were both much larger companies; Acton, which also sold machine tools and refractory materials, had annual sales of some $500 million, and Bensington, which also sold a wide range of ceramic products, had sales of around $400 million.

In addition, there were some 30 other competitors, for the most part large companies for whom abrasives were only a small part of their product line. None of these accounted for more than 2 or 3 percent of the abrasives market. Typical were the Delta Corporation, which also sold saws, files, and other cutting tools, with annual sales of over $100 million, and the Eureka Company, which sold a wide range of adhesives, films, tools, metal products, and so on, with total sales of more than $1 billion per year.

In the past 10 years, Conn-Crest's sales had increased 15 times, while industry sales rose only 5 times, and sales of the metalworking industry (the industry's chief customer) increased only 2 times.

Conn-Crest's Product Line.   Conn-Crest's product line was about as complete as that of any of its competitors. Virtually all its products were manufactured on a job-order basis because of the great variation in specifications requested by customers. The basic vitrified manufacturing process was to mix abrasive grains, a bonding agent, water, and a filler; compress these into the required shape and size with molds and hydraulic presses; dry and then fire the product under high temperatures in kilns; and finally grind the product to the accuracy required in the size and shape specifications.

Conn-Crest's Sales Force.   From Hartford and four district offices, Chicago, Pittsburgh, Detroit, and Cleveland, about 50 Conn-Crest salespeople sold direct to customers and worked with distributors' salespeople. At each district office a salesperson functioned as a local sales manager. Acton, the largest seller of grinding wheels, was estimated to have a sales force of about 250 people. The cost of maintaining a salesperson in the field, including salary, commissions, and expenses, averaged about $30,000. Most of the 50 salespeople had been added during the last 10 years. While approximately a year was required to train a person to sell effectively, about 3 years were required before a salesperson could be considered fully productive.

Sales Engineering.   The importance of trial runs and engineering service and development work with customers meant that Conn-Crest had to maintain a special service group. This group, known as Sales Engineering, consisted of 15 engineers. Of this number, one specialized on trial orders, a second on resinoid products, a third on diamond wheels, a fourth on returned materials, and a fifth on sales manuals and bulletins; the others were available to solve customers' engineering problems at the request of the regular salespeople.

Conn-Crest's Advertising Program

Conn-Crest's advertising was designed to "pave the way" for salespeople and distributors. The elements of the advertising program were: (1) full-page, two-color advertisements run regularly in major metalworking magazines; (2) direct mail to toolroom foremen, superintendents, purchasing agents, grinding department foremen, and others; (3) two motion pictures, one concerned with abrasives manufacture and the other with the construction and uses of reinforced resinoid products; (4) stereoscopic color slides of product manufacture and use; (5) product catalogues and technical literature; (6) sales manuals; (7) souvenirs and sales aids of miscellaneous types; and (8) classified telephone directory advertisements for distributors, the cost of which was shared on a 50-50 basis by Conn-Crest.

Advertising Appropriation. Conn-Crest's advertising manager typically planned advertising expenditures as a given percentage of projected sales volume. Once the marketing manager made his forecast and decided upon the percentage to be allocated to advertising, the advertising manager went to work. The percentage typically used was about 2 percent of sales, which was about average for the stone, clay, and glass industry. Conn-Crest's total selling expense, including advertising, averaged about 18 percent of net sales. The advertising percentage was arrived at subjectively by reviewing past sales, budgets, and percentage relationships, and by looking ahead to see whether, in view of sales possibilities, advertising expenditures should be expanded or curtailed.

Last Year's Advertising Effort. In the preceding year, increased demand for grinding wheels and abrasives had been expected by the Conn-Crest management. It was decided to guide this increase into those production departments which were in the best position to increase production. Study of production facilities indicated that the company's resinoid line of abrasive products was the most desirable product line on which to concentrate. This line of products had its own brand name, "Conn-Cut."

The best market for these products was generally the foundry industry, and in foundries the "cleaning room" was the point at which such products were used. With key foundry personnel as the target, the objectives of the advertising effort were (1) making Conn-Crest's name synonymous with performance; (2) pointing to Conn-Crest's complete line of foundry abrasives; and (3) offering Conn-Crest's engineering service. Conn-Crest's foundry product line was then divided into six groupings, each to be emphasized separately: snagging wheels, inserted-nut and plate-mounted disks, cut-off wheels, mounted points, cup wheels and cones, and reinforced disk wheels. (A seventh line, core files, which had limited use, was not to be featured.)

The initial two-advertisement was a double-spread, two-color advertisement appearing in the April issue of *Foundry* magazine. Reprints of the advertisement, with a letter on Conn-Crest's stationery signed by one of the company's abrasives engineers, were sent to about 6,000 foundry superintendents whose names were on the mailing lists of the Penton Publishing Company. These mailings preceded by two weeks the appearance of the advertisement. During this period, Conn-Crest's sales department was informing its salespeople and distributors about the project and cross-checking company contact lists for special addressing. The subsequent six advertisements featured a large blowup of one of the basic groupings with a montage of reduced-size photographs of the remaining groups. In the advertisements, which appeared in six successive issues, a consistent style was maintained. Each mailing piece was sent so that it would arrive at approximately the time *Foundry* magazine would arrive. During the six-month period, revisions were made in the mailing list where returned inquiry cards indicated new names and titles.

The results of this advertising effort pleased the Conn-Crest management. Sales of foundry grinding wheels increased 50 percent over the corresponding six-month period the year before. Compared to Conn-Crest's sales of all products, the gain in foundry sales was 12.5 percent greater during the calendar year.

Record of Inquiries.   Conn-Crest's advertising manager kept a record of inquiries resulting from its publication advertising and tabulated them by product advertised, advertisement, publication, and month of issue. A summary of the inquiries received during the calendar year is contained in Exhibit 1. The cost of the business paper space used was $255,000; advertisement production expense came to $35,000.

Inquiries also resulted from direct-mail efforts. During the previous year, the company had sent out over 400,000 mailings at a cost of $60,000. In addition to reprints of magazine advertising, as described, these utilized letters, self-mailing folders, and specially prepared four-page brochures; in all cases the themes of the magazine advertising were followed, with the emphasis on the Conn-Cut line but also mentioning other products. Some 1,900 inquiries resulted from these efforts during the year.

Advertising Manager's Philosophy

The advertising manager did not believe that inquiries gave a direct indication of the value of particular business magazines. Some, he believed, by their format, editorial content, and circulation would inevitably produce more inquiries than others. He put emphasis on the importance of advertising's contribution in making buyers aware that Conn-Crest had a "better mousetrap" and in proving this claim.

In his opinion, greater advertising effort was needed in view of competitors' actions. For instance, while Conn-Crest ranked third in sales, it ranked fourth in the abrasives industry in the amount of paid advertising space used the previous two years (Delta was third). Over this two-year period, Bensington had increased its space advertising 173 percent in comparison with Conn-Crest's 54 percent. Acton,

Exhibit 1.   **Summary of Inquiries Resulting from Advertising of Conn-Cut during One Year**

	CONN-CUT	OTHER PRODUCTS	TOTAL INQUIRIES	COST PER INQUIRY
American Machinist	30	18	48	$ 275
Canadian Industrial Equipment News	—	18	18	333
Canadian Metals	—	—	—	—
Foundry	—	34	34	254
Industrial Canada	—	—	—	—
Industrial Distribution	—	—	—	—
Industrial Equipment News	52	188	240	14
Ingeneria Internacional Industria	1	—	1	905
Iron Age	—	—	—	—
Machine & Tool Blue Book	2	—	2	3,480
Machinery	—	—	—	—
Mill & Factory	60	28	88	211
Modern Machine Shop	33	94	127	54
New Equipment Digest	76	142	218	16
New Equipment News	—	34	34	99
Purchasing	2	—	2	3,725
Revista Industrial	—	—	—	—
Southern Power & Industry	—	—	—	—
Steel	—	18	18	865
Tool & Manufacturing Engineer	52	130	182	55
Tooling & Gaging	39	8	47	77
Tooling & Production	16	122	138	69
Welding Design & Fabrication	303	168	471	19
Western Manufacturing	—	6	6	900
Total	666	1,008	1,674	

the dominant company, had increased such expenditures only 8 percent, but its expenditures were already relatively large. At the same time, a survey of product acceptance among buyers had shown that, when considering buying grinding wheels, 73 percent had indicated they would turn to Acton, 57 percent to Bensington, and 29 percent to Conn-Crest.

The Agency's Recommendation

Conn-Crest's decision to retain an advertising agency, Auburn & Camass, to evaluate its advertising program was not in any way a reflection of executive dissatisfaction with Conn-Crest's advertising department or the advertising agency currently serving Conn-Crest. The decision to have the study made was based solely on the desire to have an "outsider" look at what Conn-Crest was doing with its advertising dollars. Auburn & Camass, with encouragement from Conn-Crest, decided to make an extensive survey of the company's market as a preliminary to making any recommendations. Since the survey was so extensive, Conn-Crest agreed to pay Auburn & Camass a fee for doing the job. The final report submitted by the agency

Exhibit 2.   **Questionnaire to Conn-Cut Distributors**

Please rate and discuss the outstanding factors in making sales to important users of grinding wheels, such as those named below. (Indicate the most important one, in your judgment, by the number "1," and so on down the line).

(A) General reputation of Conn-Crest
(B) Performance of trial wheels
(C) Good relations of salesperson with plant operating personnel
(D) Technical assistance of Conn-Crest's abrasive specialist to the user
(E) Conn-Crest advertising
(F) Price
(G) Past experience of user with Conn-Crest wheels
(H) Effect of friendly relations of your company with purchasing agent
(I) Prompt delivery
(J) Other factors (not tabulated)

Rating	FACTORS RATED								
	A	B	C	D	E	F	G	H	I
1st	7	20	26	5	0	2	2	6	3
2nd	2	12	15	15	1	2	4	11	2
3rd	9	11	9	7	0	1	3	12	5
4th	8	10	6	10	3	1	5	7	10
5th	9	5	2	7	9	0	7	10	6
6th	10	2	2	3	7	1	10	6	11
7th	6	—	—	7	11	5	7	3	6
8th	3	1	—	5	15	8	10	1	3
9th	1	—	—	1	7	21	3	—	1
10th	—	—	—	—	1	8	1	—	1
Total ratings	55	61	60	60	54	49	52	56	48
Median rating	4th	2nd	1st	3rd	7th	8th	6th	3rd	5th

covered more than 100 pages. Typical of the material presented are the tabulations in Exhibits 2 and 3. (In Exhibit 3, for example, 69 purchasing agents said they had seen an Acton ad shown to them with the name masked out, and 92.8 percent of these correctly recalled that it was an Acton ad.)

On the basis of its study, Auburn & Camass, in submitting its report, defined Conn-Crest's advertising tasks to be as follows: (1) to drive home to customers and potential customers that the company had become a mature supplier; (2) to promote acceptance of Conn-Crest products among operators and foremen by overcoming traditional preferences for products of its two largest competitors; (3) to attract strong and active distributors; (4) to promote new product developments; (5) to attract able sales personnel; and (6) to make existing engineering bulletins more effective sales literature. To accomplish these tasks, the agency recommended the

Exhibit 3. **Field Study of Recall of Magazine Advertising by Function and Manufacturer (500 interviews)**

MANUFACTURER	PURCHASING AGENTS	ADMINISTRATIVE AND EXECUTIVE	TOOL ENGINEERING	TOOL ROOM SUPERVISORS	GRINDING ROOM AND MACHINERY
Action					
Respondents (100%)	69	36	69	70	37
% Adtg. recall	92.8	97.2	89.9	91.4	97.3
Bensington					
Respondents (100%)	61	35	63	60	35
% Adtg. recall	78.7	88.6	81.0	81.7	65.7
Conn-Crest					
Respondents (100%)	46	26	54	50	23
% Adtg. Recall	65.6	66.3	71.4	60.0	70.9
Delta					
Respondents (100%)	23	19	24	28	12
% Adtg. recall	61.5	88.9	47.4	69.6	57.1
Eureka					
Respondents (100%)	13	6	14	16	6
% Adtg. recall	61.5	33.3	50.0	56.3	66.7
Other companies					
Respondents (100%)	56	49	67	75	53
% Adtg. Recall	25.8	40.0	53.1	15.2	33.3

expenditures shown in Exhibit 4 (an increase over current expenditures of a little more than 25 percent). The agency's report included both a recognition that sales-people and not advertising "sold" bonded abrasive products, and an admonition that advertising must be viewed as a long-range investment. Perhaps the sum of the

Exhibit 4.   **Advertising Agency's Proposal**

BUSINESS PAPER SPACE		
(ALL TWO-COLOR UNLESS OTHERWISE NOTED)		
Metalworking		
American Machinist—13 pages	$ 14,300	
Iron Age—13 pages	16,600	
Machine & Tool Blue Book—12 pages	7,000	
Machinery—12 pages	11,400	
Modern Machine Shop—12 pages	6,800	
Steel—13 pages	16,600	
Foundry—12 pages	10,600	
Purchasing		
Purchasing—13 pages	16,100	
Distributors		
Industrial Distribution—12 pages	9,700	
Specialties		
Welding Design & Fabrication—12 pages	6,100	
Automotive		
Automotive Industries—12 pages	12,400	
Executive		
Business Week—13 pages	93,400	
Fortune—6 pages	47,300	
Mill & Factory—12 pages	17,200	
Factory—12 pages	17,900	
Total space		$303,400
Note: Bleed pages, is used, are approximately 10% over above figures.		
Advertisement Production		
Estimated Sales Promotion		40,000
House organ—30,000 circulation, 12 issues per year		
8 pages plus cover at $15,000. Includes printed envelopes but not mailing and postage.	$180,000	
Trade shows (estimated)	40,000	
Literature (estimated)	70,000	
Total sales promotion		290,000
Publicity		
Fee at $1,500 per month	$ 18,000	
Expenses—mimeographing, mailing, photography, etc. (estimated)	6,000	
Total publicity		24,000
Grand total		$657,400

agency's view was that advertising could make more productive the selling time of Conn-Crest's salespeople and the salespeople of distributors.

The agency, in its report, extended its recommendations beyond advertising, and these should be noted. These suggestions were, in general, that Conn-Crest should handle large customers on an increasing scale by direct sales, and distributors' sales to medium and small customers should be increased. The former meant larger sales at lower cost to Conn-Crest; the latter meant more satisifed distributors because of the higher margins obtainable, as well as the building of a less vulnerable sales base for Conn-Crest.

To achieve these objectives, the agency proposed continuation of a program of building the Conn-Crest sales force; increasing the number of specialized distributors as opportunity arose; continuing new product leadership; and the building of distributor sales with emphasis on staple products used in small tool and die shops. In connection with the last of these, the agency urged further emphasis on a training program for distributors and their salespeople; development of branch warehouses and distributor inventories; and an advertising program aimed at foremen and toolroom personnel. A final recommendation was the expansion of the headquarters sales organization to include a person to handle distributor relations, including distributor training, and a second person to direct sales promotional effort, coordinate sales and advertising, and develop sales and distributors' manuals, motion pictures, and slide films, and trade shows. Finally, the agency noted that since Conn-Crest's sales were expected to grow by 20 percent the following year, advertising expenditures should be increased by at least that amount.

DISCUSSION QUESTIONS

1. What should the advertising objectives be? Evaluate the advertising to date. Address the media class decision.
2. What relative weight should be given to personal selling, the house organ, direct mail, trade shows, and media advertising?
3. How would you allocate the media budget?
4. What additional information would you want to help make the media allocation decision and how would you go about getting it?

17

Social and Economic Effects

Nine-tenths and more of advertising is largely competitive wrangling as to the relative merits of two undistinguishable compounds. In a truly functional society, 90 percent of people employed by advertising would be able to engage in "productive occupations." (Stuart Chase, *Tragedy of Waste,* 1925)

Advertising is more than advertisements alone. It is an institutional part of our society, a social force affecting and affected by our style of life. (Raymond Bauer and Stephen Greyser, *Advertising in America*)

For decades, indeed centuries, broad social and economic issues have been raised concerning the role of advertising in society. In 1759, Dr. Samuel Johnson suggested that advertisers had moral and social questions to consider:

> The trade of advertising is now so near to perfection, it is not easy to propose any improvement. But as every art ought to be exercised in due subordination to the publick good, I cannot but propose it as a moral question to these matters of the publick ear. Whether they do not sometimes play too wantonly with our passions.[1]

Since then advertising has been studied, analyzed, defended, and attacked by individuals representing a wide spectrum of professional interests, including economists, sociologists, politicians, businessmen, novelists, and historians.

The role of advertising in society is a controversial one, largely because opinions associated with it are heavily interwoven with more fundamental values and beliefs about how a society does and should operate. Some will view a product advance as making an important contribution to a valued life-style, increasing the range of choice and standard of living. Others who prefer a different life-style will view the same product as adding to product clutter and decreasing the quality of life. Supporters of advertising argue that it is a form of "speech," analogous to the news and entertainment components of mass media and that it should be kept entirely free of government interference. Critics often argue that government should be involved to protect the "public interest," to keep consumers from being duped by the power of advertising, and to protect the interests of competitive firms whose performance or existence could be affected by unfair advertising practices. There is little agreement about whether or not advertising has the power to "manipulate" an unwilling consumer. Since people can be influenced to a considerably different degree, there is undoubtedly some truth in both sides of the argument regarding the persuasive power of advertising. Because value judgments and basic assumptions are involved and much depends on the perspective of a particular consumer, the debate is often highly subjective.

A STRUCTURING OF THE ISSUES

A discussion of the social and economic issues of advertising can be divided into four categories, as depicted in Figure 17-1. The first category represents the nature and content of the advertising to which people are exposed. Is advertising performing an informative role or a deceptive one? Are appeals used that manipulate consumers against their will? There are a variety of issues associated with taste. Is advertising too repetitious, too silly, too preoccupied with sex? Does it irritate or offend the audience member? Finally, there are questions about the fairness of

Figure 17-1. **Structuring the issues**

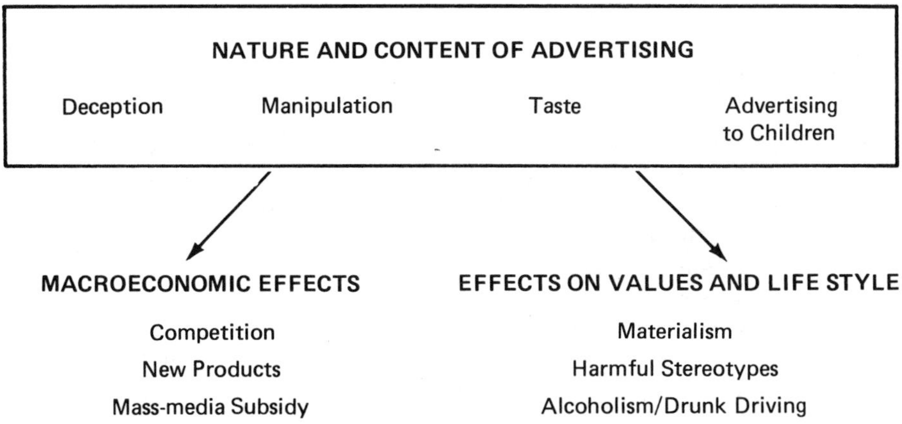

NATURE AND CONTENT OF ADVERTISING

| Deception | Manipulation | Taste | Advertising to Children |

MACROECONOMIC EFFECTS

Competition
New Products
Mass-media Subsidy

EFFECTS ON VALUES AND LIFE STYLE

Materialism
Harmful Stereotypes
Alcoholism/Drunk Driving

advertising to children, especially when the sugar products involved could adversely affect their health. In essence, this category, the nature and intent of advertising, considers the means rather than the ends of advertising, the means being the copy and media tactics used.

The remaining two categories represent the aggregate effects of advertising on society as a whole. One of these is the effect on society's values and life-styles. There are those who believe that advertising competes with or dominates such other socialization agents as literature, plays, music, the church, the home, and the school; that it fosters materialism at the expense of other basic values; that it may serve to reinforce sexual or racial discrimination, or that it promotes alcoholism and drunk driving. The second is the effect of advertising on society's economic well-being and on the efficiency of the operation of the economic system. To what extent can the power of advertising lead to the control of the market by a few firms, which will weaken competition and raise consumer prices? What is the economic value of advertising as an efficient mechanism for communicating the existence of new products? To what extent does it subsidize mass media? Because the analysis is concerned with the economic health of the economy as a whole, as opposed to that of individual consumers, it focuses on the macroeconomic rather than microeconomic effects of advertising.

NATURE AND CONTENT OF ADVERTISING

Deception

A primary concern with the content of advertising is the question of the degree to which the advertisement is deceptive in conveying the selling message. Because this area has been well developed in the law and because of its importance to the advertising decision maker and regulator, the following chapter will treat the subject in greater depth. The problems of definition and measurement of deception are closely tied to an understanding of the perception process. Such problems are also implicit in many of the issues to be raised in this chapter.

Does Advertising Manipulate?

Perhaps the essence of a free marketplace and a free society is the freedom to make decisions of various kinds, or in this context, the freedom to select or not select a particular brand. There are those who fear that this freedom is circumscribed by the "power" of advertising—that advertising is so effective it can manipulate a buyer into making a decision against his or her will or at least against his or her best interests in allocating his financial resources.

The argument takes several forms. First, there is concern with the use of motivation research, the appeal to motives at the subconscious level. Second, there is the use of indirect emotional appeals. Finally, there is the more general claim of the power of scientific advertising to persuade—to make people believe things and behave in ways that are not in their own or society's best interests.

In each of the three forms there are simple misconceptions of how advertising decisions are made, how the communication process works, and the role of advertising in the total marketing program and the consumer buying process. There also exist, however, serious questions of fact and judgment that legitimately need to be raised.

Motivation Research.   Motivation research is an approach that draws on the Freudian psychoanalytic model of consumer decision making. It assumes that important buying motives are subconscious in that a respondent cannot elucidate them when asked an opinion of a brand or a product class. Thus, a person may dislike prunes because of a subconscious association of prunes with old age or parental authority but may not consciously realize the existence of this association and its relevance to purchasing decisions. A consumer may actually prefer a cake mix that requires the addition of an egg because it subconsciously satisfies the need to contribute to the baking process, although she or he consciously believes that the only reason is that a fresh egg adds quality.

Motivation research made a strong impact on marketing in the 1950s; many saw it as a decisive and powerful marketing tool. Furthermore, it received widespread attention beyond marketing professionals by such books as Vance Packard's *The Hidden Persuaders.*[2] The result was a feeling that advertising could indeed identify subconscious motives and, by playing on these motives, influence an unsuspecting public. The result was an Orwellian spector of the consumer's subconscious being exposed and manipulated without his or her knowledge. Packard discusses

> the large-scale efforts being made, often with impressive success, to channel our unthinking habits, our purchasing decisions, and our thought processes by the use of insights gleaned from psychiatry and the social sciences. Typically these efforts take place beneath our level of awareness, so that the appeals which move us are often, in a sense, "hidden." The result is that many of us are being influenced and manipulated, far more than we realize, in the patterns of our everyday lives.[3]

The concept of the consumer being manipulated at the subconscious level reached its zenith with a subliminal 1956 advertising experiment by James Vicary. In a movie theater, he flashed the phrases, "Drink Coke" and "Hungry, Eat popcorn" on the screen every 5 seconds.[4] The phrases were exposed for 1/3,000 of a second, well below threshold levels. The tests, which covered a 6-week period, were reported to have increased cola sales by 57 percent and popcorn sales by 18 percent. The concept of subliminal advertising operating at the subconscious level really suggested manipulation. However, this test lacked even rudimentary controls and has not been replicated. Furthermore, many other tests of subliminal communication in an advertising context have had negative results. There is therefore an overwhelming consensus among the advertising professional community that subliminal perception simply does not work.

Saegert,[5] however, has suggested that perhaps this conclusion might be premature. One marketing study did generate significantly greater ''thirst ratings'' by subjects exposed subliminally to the word ''COKE'' than other subjects exposed to a nonsense syllable word. Furthermore, psychologists have been able to increase indications of existing traits like depression, homosexuality, and stuttering by subliminal stimuli but only where these traits already existed in the subjects.[6] Clearly, these studies only raise the possibility that subliminal comunication might be able to bring unconscious motives to the surface, not that it could create or change motives.

We now know that motivation research, for better or worse, was oversold, and that motivation research knowledge does not give an advertiser anything approaching total control over an audience. There are fundamental difficulties in applying the technique. It usually involves some kind of relatively lengthy, unstructured interview. Thus the interview itself is necessarily subjective and highly dependent on the interviewer. The analysis is even more subjective. It is not uncommon for two motivation research groups to address the same situation and arrive at widely different conclusions. Furthermore, controlled experimentation is usually precluded because of the small samples. Thus it is difficult to place much confidence in the result. Finally, the implementation of the conclusions, whatever they may be, is almost never obvious.

On the contrary, implementation can also take a variety of directions, and the nature of the conclusions usually provide no guidance in selecting among these directions. How does one reach a person, for example, who dislikes prunes because of an association with parental authority? Furthermore, any approach can be neutralized by competitors and other forces acting on brand choice.

Motivation research does have a role to play in developing effective advertisements, however. It has been particularly useful in providing insight, in suggesting copy alternatives, and in helping creative people avoid approaches that will precipitate undesirable reactions. However, as suggested earlier, the power of advertisers to manipulate consumers by using motivation research has been vastly overstated. Most people probably make choices most of the time for reasons they are aware of, particularly in situations in which real economic risk is involved. Unlike the situation of having the receiver totally under the control of the persuader, popularized in brainwashing experiments, advertising does not control a receiver's options. Although marketing professionals have accepted the reduced scope of motivation research, the layman is still haunted by the spector of the ''hidden persuaders.''

Although it does seem clear that the motivation research user does not have absolute power over consumers, there are still ethical questions associated with its use—indeed, with the use of many forms of market research—that are most relevant. Is the practice of conducting depth interviews to attempt to isolate hidden motives acceptable? It is one thing to probe in an analyst's office for medical reasons but another to do so in the home or laboratory for commercial reasons. Can interviewers be sure that such an experience will not do psychological harm? And what about the common situation wherein a respondent is not told the actual purpose of the interview? These issues really focus on the research effort itself. The concern with using the results brings to the surface issues that are raised in the following section wherein emotional appeals are discussed.

Emotional Appeals.   The communication of factual information about a product's primary function is usually accepted as being of value to the consumer. However, when advertising utilizes appeals or associations that go beyond such a basic communication task, the charge of manipulation via "emotional appeals" is raised. Scitovsky declared:

> To the extent that it [advertising] provides information about the existence of available [buyer] alternatives, advertising always renders the market more perfect. If advertising is mainly suggestive and confined to emotional appeal, however, it is likely to impede rational comparison and choice, thus rendering the market less perfect.[7]

The implication is that consumers will be led to make less than optimal decisions by such emotional appeals.

The FTC reviewed several hundred proposed television commercials. FTC Commissioner Mary Gardiner Jones observed:

> A typical theme running through these commercials is to hold the product out as the pathway to success and happiness and the antidote to what is otherwise a drab, boring or lonely life. Thus dishwashing liquids are advertised as sweeping away the dullness of life. They are the housewife's pathroad to beauty and romantic excitement. Their use will make the whole world soft and gentle. Bath soaps have a similar rejuvenating capacity. Use of these products is associated with cool sophistication, weddings, traveling and entertainment—enjoyment of life at its unhampered best. Some bath soap advertisers stress the sensual success which will immediately accrue to the user, others the ability of the product to resolve all husband and wife crises and still others the health and exuberance or the happy family do-it-togetherness which will be engendered by the product.[8]

These observations are related to issues of deception. The line between artistic license and deception is something hard to draw. Is an advertisement an innocent, entertaining exaggeration that few will take seriously, or is it really capable of deceiving? The next chapter will explore this issue and others that are related. Jones's observations also involve some definitional issues. How should such basic concepts as product, needs, rationality, and information be defined? Bauer and Greyser have noted that different advertising spokesmen, for convenience labeled businessmen and business critics, have radically different perceptions of these key concepts.[9]

Consider the word *product*. The critic views a product as an entity with only one primary identifiable function. Thus, an automobile is a transportation device. The businessman is concerned with a product's secondary function, because it may represent the dimensions upon which the product differentiation rests. The automobile's appearance might provide a mechanism by which the individual can express his or her personality. High horsepower and superior handling may provide an outlet for an individual's desire for excitement.

Another key concept is *need*. The critic sees consumer needs as corresponding to a product's primary function. Thus, there is a need for transportation, nutrition, and recreation. The businessman, on the other hand, takes a much broader view of consumer needs, considering any product attribute or appeal on which real product differentiation can be based as reflecting legitimate needs—needs that are strong enough to affect purchase decisions.

Two other central concepts are *rationality* and *information*. The critic sees any decision that results in an efficient matching of product to needs, as he or she defines these terms, as rational. Information that serves to enhance rational decision making is good information. The businessman contends that any decision a consumer makes to serve his or her own perceived self-interest is rational. Information, then, is any data or argument that will truthfully put forth the attractiveness of a product in the context of a consumer's own buying criteria.

In part, the resolution of these different perspectives will inevitably involve value judgments and honest differences in premises. To some extent, however, they involve assumptions about consumer decision making and utility theory that should be amenable to research. The challenge is to identify clearly, using a common vocabulary, the value judgments that are required and to isolate precisely the empirical questions.

Another relevant question is, given a decision to restrict the use of emotional appeals, how might such restrictions be formulated? Exactly what emotional appeals should be banned? How could codes be adopted so that the communication of factual information is not also inhibited? Should all animation, for example, be prohibited? The question of implementation, too often ignored, can crystallize basic issues and aid the analysis process.

Power of Modern Advertising.   There also exists a somewhat more general claim that advertisers have the raw power to manipulate consumers. Many companies have the capacity to obtain large numbers of advertisement exposures. Furthermore, some observers believe that these companies can utilize highly sophisticated, scientific techniques to make such advertising effective.

This book has, in fact, attempted to marshal scientific knowledge from theory and practice. The reader should by now be painfully aware of the limitations of the most sophisticated approaches available. The fact is that consumer-choice behavior is determined by many factors in addition to advertising—the advice of friends, decisions and life-styles of family members, news stories, prices, distribution variables, and on and on. Advertising is but one of many variables, and it has a limited role. It can communicate the existence of a new automobile and perhaps induce a visit to a dealer, but it can rarely make the final sale. It can explain the advantages of a toothpaste and perhaps be influential in getting some people to try the brand, but it has little impact on their decision to repurchase it. There is an inexhaustible number of examples of huge promotional efforts for products that failed. If advertising had the power that some attribute to it, many of these products would still be with us.

Taste

Some critics feel that advertising is objectionable because the creative effort behind it is not in good taste. This type of objection was explored in a massive study conducted in the mid-1960s.[10] More than 1,500 people were asked to list those advertisements that they found annoying, enjoyable, informative, or offensive. Of the more than 9,000 advertisements involved, 23 percent were labeled as annoying and 5 percent as offensive.[11] Although a portion of these advertisements irritated respondents because they considered deceptive, the majority were so categorized for reasons related to questions of taste.

Advertising may not be omnipotent, but many contend that it is too omnipresent or intrusive. More than 42 percent of the annoying advertisements in the foregoing study were considered too loud, too long, too repetitious, or involved unpleasant voices, music, or people.[12] Another 31 percent had content that was considered silly, unreal, boring, or depressing.[13] Nearly one-fourth of the offensive advertisements were considered inappropriate for children. More than one-fourth of the offensive advertisements involved such products as liquor or cigarettes.[14] A more recent study by Aaker and Bruzzone found of 524 prime time television commercials the top eight most irritating commercials were the eight commercials for feminine hygiene products like tampons.[15] Commercials for women's undergarments and hemorrhoid products were close behind. Clearly there is a strong product class effect with respect to irritation with television advertising.

The Appeal.   In an open letter to the *Detroit News* entitled, "You Dirty Old Ad Men Make Me Sick," a reader took issue with the use of sex in advertising. In making her case, she described several advertisements:

> A love goddess runs down the beach, waves nibbling at her toes, her blond streaked hair sweeping back behind wide, expectant eyes. A flimsy garment clings to every supple curve. She runs faster, arms open, until finally she throws herself breathlessly into HIS arms. . . .
> Where's this scene? Right in your living room, that's where.
> Wild and passionately aroused, she can't stop herself. She runs her fingers through his hair, knocks his glasses off, and kisses him and kisses him again. . . .
> Who's watching? Your nine-year-old daughter as she sits on her stuffed panda bear and wipes jelly off her face.[16]

The letter received considerable response from advertising professionals. Some argued that advertisements, as long as they are not obscene, reflect society and its collective life-styles. They observed that nudity and the risqué are part of the contemporary world in which advertising is embedded. Others agreed that sex is overused and suggested that effective advertising can be created without titillating.

One problem is that television commercials have to create attention and communicate a message—and accomplish all this in 60 or even 30 seconds—a demanding task, indeed. Another problem is that television reaches large, broad audiences. It is one thing to use a risqué approach in *Playboy* magazine and quite another to use it on prime-time television when the likelihood of offending is much greater.

Fear appeals have also been criticized. The intent of the fear appeal is to create anxiety that can supposedly be alleviated by an available product (insurance against a fire or a safe tire to prevent accidents) or action (stop smoking). There exists the possibility that such appeals may create emotional disturbances or a long-run anxiety condition in some audience members. The cumulative effects of such advertising may be highly undesirable to some, although it can also be argued that they quickly cease to have any significant degree of emotional impact, and the audience soon becomes immune to the messages.

Intrusiveness.   To some people, advertising, especially television advertising, is often like a visitor who has overstayed his welcome. It becomes an intrusion. Greyser postulates a life cycle wherein an advertising campaign moves with repetition from a period of effectiveness, and presumably audience acceptance, to a period of irritation.[17] The cycle contains the following stages:

1. Exposure to the message on several occasions prior to serious attention (given some basic interest in the product)
2. Interest in the advertisement on either substantive (informative) or stimulus (enjoyment) grounds
3. Continued but declining attention to the advertisement on such grounds
4. Mental tune-out of the advertisement on grounds of familiarity
5. Increasing re-awareness of the advertisement, now as a negative stimulus (an irritant)
6. Growing irritation

The number of exposures between the start of a campaign and the stage of growing irritation is obviously a key variable. On what factors will it depend? An important factor, of course, is the intensity of the campaign itself. Bursts of advertising that generate many exposures over a short time period will undoubtedly run a high risk of irritation. A second factor involves other advertising to which the audience is exposed. The cycle will be shorter if different brands and even different product classes use similar approaches. Advertisements involving similar demonstrations, spokespeople, jingles, or animation may be difficult to separate in the mind of an audience member. Campaigns for beer, soda, and menthol cigarettes, for example, have been perceived as being highly similar.

Product usage and brand preferences are two additional factors affecting the cycle time period. Greyser noted that consumers dislike only 21 percent of the advertisements for products used (19 percent annoying, 2 percent offensive), whereas they dislike 37 percent of advertisements for products they don't use (29 percent annoying, 8 percent offensive). For brand preferrers the tendency is even more marked: only 7 percent of advertisements for one's favorite brand are disliked compared with 76 percent of the advertisments for "brands I wouldn't buy" (only product users included).[18]

Still another factor is the entertainment value of the advertisement. Campaigns using advertisements with high entertainment value have demonstrated their ability to survive heavy repetition. An important issue is the determination of the link between liking and effectiveness. There is some evidence that the very pleasant and the very unpleasant advertisements are more effective than those in between. A disliked commercial may attract attention and communicate better than a bland commercial. Further, the negative feeling toward the ad may not get attached to the brand. The nature of the relationship will undoubtedly depend on the audience, the product, and other variables. Furthermore, there are several definitional and measurement problems involved.

One difficulty is that advertisements tend to be evaluated by advertisers in isolation, whereas the audience reacts to the totality of the advertising to which they are exposed. This reaction, when it is negative, therefore tends to apply to some extent to all advertising. The result is a decrease in the long-run effectiveness of advertising. It is in the best interests of advertisers to be concerned not only with the irritation caused by specific campaigns, but also with that caused by the impression of advertising in general. Twenty- or thirty-second television spots may be cost-effective for the brand but less so when the total impression of a cluttered media is considered.

Advertising to Children[19]

In 1977 the FTC was stimulated to examine television advertising to children. A FTC staff report recommended that:

- All television advertising be banned for any product which is directed to or seen by audiences composed of a significant proportion of children who are too young to understand the selling purpose of the advertising.
- Either balance televised advertising for sugared food products directed to or seen by audiences composed of a significant proportion of older children with nutritional and/or health disclosures funded by advertisers, or ban it completely.

These proposals, which were intensely debated, were ultimately defeated in part because of changes in the political environment in the early 1980s. However, the issues remain and parent and consumer groups are still concerned and active.

The proposals were based upon several facts and judgments. First, children between the ages of 2 and 11 spend about 25 hours per week watching television and see approximately 20,000 ads per year. About 7,000 of these ads are for highly sugared products. Second, there is evidence that some preschool children cannot differentiate between commercials and programming, cannot understand the selling intent of commercials, and cannot distinguish between fantasy and reality.[20] Third, children between the ages of 7 and 12 have difficulty balancing appeals of highly sugared products with long-term health risks—by age 2 about one-half of children have diseased gums and decayed teeth. Fourth, there are no counter-ads for fruit and vegetables. Fifth, much of children's advertising is deceptive in that it omits significant information, such as the complexity and safety of operating toys.

Opposition to the proposals marshaled their own facts and judgments. First, banning television advertising to protect those children who do not understand the selling intent of commercials will deny advertisers the right of free speech to communicate with other audience members, who, in fact, constitute the great majority of the audience for most children's programs. Second, the FTC does not have the professional competence to serve as a "national nanny" deciding to what children should not be exposed. Parents are generally both more competent and involved to help children interpret information and make decisions. Third, there is no evidence of a relationship between television exposure and the incidence of tooth decay. Further, there is very little evidence that eating the most heavily advertised products will cause tooth decay. Fourth, there is evidence that children are aware that fruits and vegetables are more nutritious than highly sugared foods.

EFFECTS OF VALUES AND LIFE-STYLES

Advertising by its very nature receives wide exposure. Furthermore, it presumably has an effect on what people buy and thus on their activities. Because of this exposure and because of its role as a persuasive vehicle, it is argued that it has an impact on the values and life-styles of society and that this impact has its negative as well as positive side. The key issues are what values and life-styles are to be encouraged as healthy, which are to be avoided, and what relative impact or influence advertising has on them. Clearly, there are many sources of social influences that have a casual impact on the nature of a culture, such as literature, plays and other entertainment forms, the church, the home, and the school. Both issues are most difficult to resolve. The first involves highly subjective and individualistic judgments and the second an almost impossible problem of causal inference. Despite their difficulty and their relationship to deep philosophical questions, they are well worth addressing to illuminate judgments and assumptions about our market system and society that are too often glossed over.[21]

Many concerns are raised in this context. Some observers feel, for example, that advertising raises the expectations of economically deprived segments of our society to their disadvantage. Others think that advertising tends to create an oppressive conformity of thought and action.

Three issues that have attracted particular attention are the relationship of advertising to materialism, the role that advertising has played in creating harmful stereotypes of women and ethnic minorities, and the possible contribution of advertising to the problem of alcohol abuse.

Materialism

Materialism is defined as the tendency to give undue importance to material interests. Presumably there is a corresponding lessening of importance to nonmaterial interests such as love, freedom, and intellectual pursuits. In 1949, Bishop wrote:

> It is common ground among the writers that the crisis of today is largely a moral crisis; and not a few of them find its essence in the loss of a sense of social purpose, and the replacement of such a sense of purpose by an acquisitive ideology in which the satisfaction of material desires is held up as the sole or principal end for the individual and the group. They point to the advertiser as the high priest of this false religion and to the all-pervading influence of modern advertising as the main obstacle in the way of those who would guide humanity into a better way of life. [22]

Bauer and Greyser argue, however, that although people do spend their resources on material things, they do so in the pursuit of nonmaterial goals. [23] They buy camping equipment to achieve a communion with nature, music systems to understand the classic composers, and an automobile for social status. The distinctive aspect of our society is not the possession of material goods, but the extent to which material goods are used to attain nonmaterial goals. Bauer and Greyser thus raise the issue of whether material goods are a means to an end rather than an end in themselves. In making such an evaluation it is useful to consider how people in other cultures fulfill nonmaterial goals. The leader in a primitive culture may satisfy a need for status in a different way from someone in our culture, but is the means used really that relevant?

Assuming that materialism does exist as an undesirable phenomenon, there still remains the issue of whether advertising creates or fosters it or merely reflects values and attitudes that are created by more significant sociological forces. Mary Gardiner Jones develops the argument that advertising, especially television advertising, is a contributing force:

> The conscious appeal in the television commercial . . . is essentially materialistic. Central to the message of the television commercial is the premise that it is the acquisition of *things* which will gratify our basic and inner needs and aspirations. It is the message of the commercial that all of the major problems confronting an individual can be instantly eliminated by the application of some external force—the use of a product. Externally derived solutions are thus made the prescription for life's difficulties. Television gives no recognition to the individual's essential responsibility for at least a part of his condition or to the importance to the individual of proving his own capacity to deal with life's problems. In the world of the television commercial all of life's problems and difficulties, all of our individual yearnings, hopes—and fears—can yield instantly to a *material* solution and one which can work instantly without any effort, skill or trouble on our part. [24]

Associating advertising with materialism, of course, does not demonstrate a causal link, as Commissioner Jones would be the first to recognize. In fact, such a link is impossible to prove or disprove. It is true that advertising and the products advertised are a part of our culture and thus contribute to it in some way. It is also true, however, that advertising does not have the power to dominate other forces (family, church, literature, and so on) that contribute to the values of society. Recall the conclusion in Chapter 6 that advertising is probably more effective at creating an image than changing an image, and that it is most difficult to alter the criteria on which people evaluate brands. Surely, affecting society's values is considerably more difficult than any of those tasks.

It is quite possible to change an individual's cognitions, and even his or her attitudes, but nearly impossible to change, via communication techniques, personality, because personality represents the accumulation of years of experience. Similarly, the values of society have evolved over centuries and have been influenced by philosophers, poets, statesmen, and others. It is unrealistic to expect advertising to have a dominant impact on them.

Promoting Stereotypes

The accusation that advertising has contributed to the role stereotyping of women and ethnic minorities has been supported by several studies. In 729 advertisements appearing in 1970, none showed women in a professional capacity, whereas 35 of them so portrayed men.[25] The authors concluded that the advertisements reflected the stereotype that women do not do important things, are dependent on men, are regarded by men primarily as sex objects, and should be in the home. Kassarjian, a UCLA psychologist, examined print advertising in 1946, 1956, and 1965 and found that only one-third of 1 percent of the advertisements contained blacks, that the blacks in the ads of the 1940s were in a low-status role, that the blacks of the 1960s tended to be entertainers, and that the appearance of blacks as true peers was sparse.[26]

A host of questions are raised. Does role stereotyping continue in advertising? What negative impact does advertising have in creating stereotypes, or what positive force does it have in breaking them down? In the absence of definitive answers to these questions, what should the advertisers' position be? Should countering role stereotypes be one objective of advertising?

Advertising Alcoholic Beverages

There is a national concern with the problems of alcoholism and drunk driving.[27] Local legislators have increased taxes to around 45 percent of total alcohol sales and toughened drunk driving laws. Happy Hours have been banned in several states. Twenty-three states have complied with a federal law to increase the drinking age to 21 or lose highway funds.

Attention has turned to the over $700 million of broadcast advertising for wine and beer. A group calling itself SMART (Stop Merchandising Alcohol on Radio and Television) has proposed a ban on wine and beer advertising. There have been other less severe proposals as well. Some have suggested counter-ads which would dramatically "advertise" the health disadvantages of drinking. Similar ads against cigarettes were effective and led to the banning of cigarette advertising on television. Others have proposed that beer advertising (like wine advertising) stop using sports figures in their advertising. There is already a ban on the use of active athletes and actual drinking in beer commercials.

The basic argument is that alcohol, like cigarettes, is unhealthy for the individual and is indirectly responsible for injuries and deaths resulting from drunk drivers. Why encourage people to use alcohol via advertising? Michael Jacobson, director of the Center for Science in the Public Interest (CSPI), argues that "Americans are angered by the incessant advertising for alcoholic beverages. Children see thousands of ads for beer and wine long before they are old enough to drink."[28] The use of Mickey Mantle and other former sports stars whom kids admire suggests that alcohol is not only harmless but that it is associated with fun-loving, healthy people.

There are a variety of counterarguments. First, there is no evidence that advertising, which is geared toward brand choice rather than increasing consumption, affects alcohol consumption.[29] Across-country studies do not indicate that those countries, such as Finland and Norway, which already ban alcohol advertising on television have lower consumption than other countries, such as the United Kingdom, which do not. Over time, observations are similar. Beer advertising has increased substantially in the first half of the 1980s, while sales dropped around 12 percent in the same time period. On the other hand, per capita alcohol consumption has risen during the past 30 years at the same rate as in Western Europe, without, of course, any advertising. In addition to this basic counterargument, there is also the suggestion that:

- A ban of advertising would prohibit product innovation that may be helpful. For example, firms have introduced products such as the enormously successful wine coolers and the low-alcohol beers.
- The real goal is to return to alcohol prohibition, which did not work—it only created a revenue source for gangsters and made lawbreakers of the rank and file of America.
- Many other products could be criticized on similar grounds. Should advertising for automobiles be banned when high performance and sportiness is stressed since they could contribute to reckless driving?

ECONOMIC EFFECTS OF ADVERTISING[30]

It is unreasonable to separate the economic and social impact of advertising. The social issues, by themselves, tend to focus on the negative aspects of advertising— its intrusiveness, content that is in bad taste, and the possibly undesirable impact on values and life-styles. If advertising were regarded solely on these grounds, it would be difficult to defend, despite the fact that much advertising is entertaining, some may even be of real artistic value, and some is directed toward supporting causes that are universally praised. Advertising is basically an economic institution. It performs an economic function for an advertiser, affects economic decisions of the audience, and is an integral part of the whole economic system. Thus an economic evaluation should accompany other types of appraisal of advertising.

Ideally, an economic balance sheet should be developed in which there are clearly defined dimensions on which advertising could be appraised. If a dollar value could be associated with advertising along each dimension, a net number could be obtained that would represent the economic value of advertising. Such an analysis, if feasible, might be conducted for different industries (or media) to identify subsets of the advertising industry that are not generating a net positive value and to stimulate proposals to alter these subsets. Such an effort is impossible, of course. It is most difficult for a firm to determine the value of its own advertising even to itself. Determining the value of *all* advertising to the *whole* economy is naturally considerably more difficult.

Although an economic balance sheet may not be feasible, it is possible to identify several appropriate dimensions of analysis. They include the value of information to buyers, the role of new-product development, the support of media, the impact on distribution costs, the effect on the business cycle, the role in creating brand identification, and the development of brand utility. These dimensions will be examined in turn. The analysis will then turn to the relationship of advertising to competition. To what extent does advertising create or contribute to oligopolistic market power that, some argue, results in high prices and reduced competition.

Providing Informational Utility

Advertising that distributes information to consumers that can help them make better economic decisions than they would in the absence of that information provides a positive economic service. Of course, any advertising that, by deception or any other means, induces consumers to make suboptimal decisions provides a corresponding negative economic service. Some advertising is of more value than others along this dimension. Classified advertising, advertising for retail stores, catalog advertising, and much of industrial advertising are usually sought out because of their informational value. Other types are not so frequently sought out, and their information value is therefore less obvious.

A study by Aaker and Norris of 524 prime-time television commercials suggests that even television advertising is perceived as informative by substantial groups of people.[31] On the average 18.1% of respondents (approximately 500 per commercial) checked the word informative from a list of 20 adjectives when asked to describe the commercial. The percentage was over 20 when snack and beverage items were excluded.

Advertising and Brand Names

Advertising plays an important role in establishing and maintaining brand names.[32] A brand name identifies the source of a product and provides a construct by which a buyer can store information about that source. Such a construct is of little consequence in product lines like screws or shoelaces, wherein the perceived differences among brands are minor, or in products like greeting cards, which can be evaluated relatively competently by the buyer. For products like automobiles, appliances, or men's shirts, however, which have relatively high levels of perceived quality differences among brands and which are difficult to evaluate by inspection, the brand name plays an important role in the buying process. A buyer can reasonably assume that a manufacturer willing to risk large sums of money to tell about a product is not likely to let poor product quality damage the investment. The economic value of a brand name is evidenced by the fact that they have been introduced into socialistic countries with centrally planned economies, which theoretically have little need for such concepts.

Media Support

Advertising provides more than 60 percent of the cost of periodicals, more than 70 percent of the cost of newspapers, and nearly 100 percent of the cost of radio and television.[33] For their support of the commercial television stations, advertisers receive approximately 15 percent of the air time.[34] Of course, a pay television system could be developed or public funds could be used, but either alternative would cost the consumer something in direct cash outlays or increased taxes. Consumers probably pay something for television now through higher prices for some products, but would very probably involve some net cost.

Distribution Costs

Advertising is part of a total marketing program; it does not operate in isolation. Its function is usually to communicate to large audiences, and it often performs this function very efficiently. Without advertising, the communication function would still remain but would probably have to be accomplished in some other way by retailers, salespeople, and so on. The alternative in many situations could cost significantly more.

In 1964, cookie companies spent only 2.2 percent of sales on advertising, whereas cereal companies spent 14.9 percent.[35] However, the cookie companies spent 22.1 percent of sales on other selling and distribution costs, compared with 12.1 percent of sales for cereal companies. Cookie companies employed routemen to deliver goods and service the shelves. Cereal companies, however, had created sufficient consumer demand so that the retailer found it worthwhile to monitor the stock, and the firms were relieved of this marketing expense. In this instance, then, it can be argued that cookie companies shifted marketing cost from advertising to other marketing activities and that an evaluation of their advertising expenses in isolation would be deceptive.

Effect on Business Cycles

Advertising could theoretically be a tool to alleviate the extremes of the business cycle. A knowledgeable businessman, anticipating a booming economy and capacity production, should reduce advertising expenditures. Conversely, when the economy is weak and orders are needed, many firms should increase their advertising. Since the extremes of a business cycle cause inflation or unemployment, any mechanism to stabilize conditions would be an economic benefit. The problem is that many advertisers, especially those who tend to set their advertising budgets at a fixed percentage of sales, actually increase advertising when times are good and decrease it when sales are weak. These firms may thus actually increase the extremes of the business cycle instead of decreasing them. Simon reviewed the literature and concluded that this tendency actually dominates—advertising expenditures generally follow the same course as the business cycle.[36] He also concluded that the potential of advertising to affect the business cycle is small, since decisions such as inventory investment are much stronger determinants of the nature of economic cycles. Advertising may be capable of dampening economic swings for some firms and even for some industries, but the evidence to date, with respect to the whole economy, is that advertising has a negative though small impact in reducing the extremes of the business cycle.

Providing Product Utility

Advertising, by generating associations between products and moods, life-styles, and activities, can add to the utility a buyer receives from the product. Most people do not buy cars solely to move from one point to another, but to achieve a feeling of independence, to express a personality, or to establish a certain mood or feeling. Evaluating the amount of utility, if any, that advertising adds to a product returns us to the fundamental issue raised earlier of the definition of such terms as "need" and "product."

Encouraging New Products

Advertising encourages product development by providing an economical way to inform potential buyers of the resulting new products or product improvements. In many situations, innovation requires large research and development expenditures and substantial investments in production facilities that might be difficult to justify if advertising could not be efficiently employed to communicate the existence of the innovation. In this respect, advertising encourages product competition.

The development of new products and the improvement of existing products can mean an expanding economy with more jobs and investment opportunities and a buyer selection that is continually improving in breadth and quality. However, as Borden stated in his classic study of the economic effects of advertising, published in 1942, an expanding set of product options can be disadvantageous for the buyer, especially when they reflect minor differentiation of existing products that add little real utility.[37] In such situations, Borden suggests that the larger number of brands could increase distribution costs and make consumer buying more complex. A central question is whether the value to consumers of the product option expansion exceeds the associated costs. These and related issues will be considered in more detail in the following section, which examines the relationship of advertising to competition.

ADVERTISING AND COMPETITION

The existence of vigorous competition is important to a market economy. Competitive forces lead to real product innovation, the efficient distribution of goods, and the absence of inflated prices. The question is, what impact does advertising have on competition? There have been hypotheses put forth indicating that advertising can actually decrease the level of competition. For example, it is argued that heavy advertising expenditures in many industries generate strong brand loyalty that tends to create barriers to potential competitors. The hypothesized result is fewer competitors, less competition, and higher prices. Fortunately, these hypotheses have been examined theoretically and empirically by economists and, although few definitive conclusions are yet available, it is now possible to structure the argument, identify some key issues, and marshall some empirical studies that bear on these issues.

A Measure of Competition

One measure of competition within an industry is the degree to which the sales of the industry are concentrated in the hands of a few firms. The specific construct is the concentration ratio—the share of the industry sales held by the four largest firms. When the concentration ratio exceeds 50%, price competition is theorized to be less vigorous and high prices result. Among the many industries that would qualify under this criterion are automobiles, aircraft, electric lamps, flat glass, primary aluminum, and household refrigerators and freezers.[38]

The concentration ratio as an indicator of market concentration and competition has intuitive appeal and is convenient, but conceptual and theoretical problems are associated with it. The main problem is in defining the industry meaningfully. Theoretically, an industry should include all brands from which buyer choice is made. Such a judgment is not easy to make. Does the cereal industry include instant breakfast, breakfast squares, and pop tarts? Do aluminum companies compete only with one another or do they also compete with copper and steel companies? Should import competition be included? What about industries in which regional brands are important such as the cement industry which has a low concentration nationally but a high concentration in regional markets. The definitional problem is compounded by the fact that most empirical studies are based on the Standard Industry Classification (SIC) of the United States Census Bureau whose categories are somewhat arbitrary. Another problem with the four-firm concentration ratio is that it does not reflect the distribution of market shares among firms. It is thus now largely replaced with HHI (the Hefindahl-Hirschman Index), which is the sum of the squares of the market shares of all the competitors. For example, the HHI of a four-firm industry would be 2500 if all had 25% shares but would be twice as much if one firm had a 70% market share.

A Causal Model

Figure 17-2 provides a simplified causal model that summarizes various hypotheses suggesting that advertising contributes to a reduction of competition in the marketplace. The model introduces several crucial constructs such as market concentration, barriers to entry, and product differentiation. The arrows represent hypothesized causal relationships among these constructs. After presenting these hypotheses, some counterarguments will be raised and several relevant empirical studies will be examined.

The central construct in the model is market concentration. The basic argument is that when concentration exists, there is little incentive to engage in vigorous price competition since any price decrease would be immediately neutralized by a

Figure 17-2.   **Market concentration: some hypothesized causes and effects**

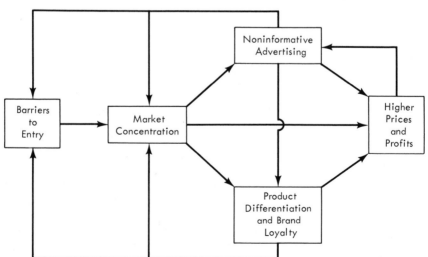

similar price change by the other major competitors. A direct result, therefore, is higher prices and profits.

With price competition inhibited, there is a hypothesized incentive to advertise heavily, since a competitor will not be likely to duplicate an advertising campaign. An advertising campaign that duplicates a competitor's is rarely successful. Thus, one result of concentration is thought to be heavy, noninformative advertising, the cost of which is passed on to the buyer in the form of higher prices. The reduced price of private-label brands is cited as evidence of such higher prices.

Another hypothesized effect of concentration is the attempt, by advertising and minor product changes, to differentiate products that are essentially identical with respect to their primary function. Differentiated products can generate brand loyalty and thus escape vigorous price competition. The result is another link to higher prices and profits. Product differentiation can be a highly desirable response to diverse market needs and wants and is not bad per se. As Scherer points out:

> The relevant question for economic analysis is not . . . whether product differentiation is a good thing but rather, how much product differentiation there should be, and whether certain market conditions might lead to excessive or inadequate differentiation. . . . Product differentiation activities most often singled out for a vote of public disapproval include image differentiation created or reinforced through intensive advertising.[39]

The higher profits are not considered earned rewards of product innovation but the result of market power. The issue of the definition of a product is, of course, central (recall the earlier discussion on the definition of product and related terms).

Concentration is said to be perpetuated and increased by the existence of barriers to entry that prevent or at least discourage potential competitors from entering the market. Advertising is thought by some to generate entry barriers directly and through the product differentiation it generates. The purpose of product differentiation is presumably to develop a reason for a buyer to buy one brand over another, to generate brand loyalty. This brand loyalty is hypothesized to be a barrier to entry. It is argued that a potential new competitor finds it difficult to compete against established products. He or she must attract the attention of habitual and satisfied consumers and motivate them to change loyalties, and must also convince retailers to remove from their shelves established products to make room for the new entries.

Advertising is also hypothesized to generate entry barriers by providing the larger advertiser in some industries with two kinds of advantages over a smaller competitor. First, the large advertiser is thought to receive preferential treatment by the media with respect to the cost and selection of advertising space. Second, a threshold level of advertising is hypothesized to exist, below which advertising would be ineffective simply because the exposure frequency would be too low to communicate. When this threshold level is high, the cost of entering a market—and thus the risk—becomes excessive. Scanlon argues that by and large it is only the very largest firms in an industry that can afford either the high cost of say TV network or the high risk inherent in gambling such large sums of money on these high-cost advertising campaigns. The result is that in industries where intensive advertising is the rule, concentration tends to be very high, with the smaller firms being effectively barred from serious growth (and small outside firms from entry) by the high-cost, high-risk nature of that kind of promotion. High-volume advertising tends to increase concentration still further, then, continuously widening the gap between the large and small, the established firm and the potential entrant.[40]

Notice that, to the extent that advertising and product differentiation place the small competitor at a disadvantage, it not only represents a barrier to entry of new competitors, but could also impede the growth of existing ones, thereby increasing the level of concentrations. If existing competitors weaken and perhaps disappear, the concentration, and thus the market power, of those remaining could be increased.

One additional feature of Figure 17-2 should be emphasized. The existence of higher prices and margins tends to generate advertising since it "pays" to advertise high-margin products. Thus, the feedback from higher prices to advertising. The result is that an ever-increasing cycle of concentration-profitability-advertising-concentration, and so on, is created.

Advertising, then, is not only considered an effect of concentration generating economic waste, it is also an important cause. The argument is that it helps create "artificial" product differentiation that, in turn, creates brand loyalty—a major entry barrier. Furthermore, it has the potential of discouraging a small competitor by increasing the market risk and by placing him at a cost disadvantage.

The Cereal Industry

The cereal industry provides a good vehicle to illustrate the argument further, as it has frequently been used as an example by those observers concerned with concentration. Scanlon summarized the case against the cereal industry.[41] He pointed out that the three largest firms in the industry, Kellogg, General Foods, and General Mills, account for about 85 percent of industry sales, and all but about 2 percent of the balance is held by the next three largest firms. Thus, the concentration level is indeed high. Scanlon further suggested that the concentration is caused by advertising levels that have operated at approximately 15 percent of sales for the three largest firms. Turning to market performance, he observed that the industry profits are high and that product quality is low, as evidenced by the nutritional shortcomings of breakfast cereal, particularly of the more popular, heavily advertised brands. Scanlon estimated that cereal prices were 25 percent higher than they would be if the industry were not concentrated. He claimed that there were no natural production scale economies to justify the concentration, that a brand volume of 1 percent of industry sales would represent an efficient production level.

These arguments have not gone unchallenged. Stern and Dunfee found that the four largest cereal brands (as opposed to firms) controlled only 29.7 percent of the market in 1964, down from 37.5 percent in 1954.[42] These statistics could indicate the existence of significant interbrand competition that may (or may not) provide a similar market situation as more interfirm competition. They also pointed out that two other indexes of competition had increased over time. One, total cereal consumption, increased 10 percent between 1960 and 1970, despite rises in cereal prices that exceeded the inflation rate. The other was new-product introductions. Of course, a question arises whether the new brands represented real consumer benefits or whether they were instead only minor variations of existing products designed to replace competitive brands.[43]

Concentration and Prices

A viable level of competition and relatively low prices might exist with high levels of concentration in at least two situations. The first is when it is feasible to enter the market on a local or regional scale. Brands that dominate the market nationally may be vulnerable in a local market where buyer tastes and needs may be somewhat unique. Furthermore, while the cost of a national entry may be large, the cost of reaching a small geographic segment may be more modest.

The second type of situation is where there exists what Galbraith termed countervailing power on the buyer side.[44] If concentration exists on the buyer side, it can counter the market power of a few sellers. Thus, Sears, Roebuck, Montgomery Ward, and the major automobile companies can extract price concessions from the tire companies. A & P, Safeway, and the other large grocery chains are in a position to gain price reductions from grocery manufacturers.

Empirical Studies

Several of the hypotheses imbedded in the model represented in Figure 17-2 have been explored empirically. Some associations have been found but the associations often have alternative explanations. Several of the relevant studies will be examined. The intent is to suggest generalizations where they emerge and to illuminate the issues further.

Advertising and Prices.   A very basic question is what impact advertising has upon prices. Buzzell and Farris found that firms with higher relative prices advertise their products more intensively than do those with lower prices.[45] They controlled for product quality by using judgments of perceived quality made by the managers of the involved products. Farris and Albion review this study and several others and conclude that there is a relationship between advertising and pricing.[46] However, they caution that several factors need to be considered in making interpretations. First, a higher price could simply reflect higher quality and the controls for quality are difficult to make. Second, consumers would probably demand lower prices for a non-advertised product as it is not obvious how unadvertised products could compete in the same market with a lack of advertising being their sole distinguishing feature. Finally, the relative prices of advertised and unadvertised brands are less important than the absolute or average price level of a product category that would prevail in the absence of advertising. It is by no means clear that the average price is higher when some brands are heavily advertised. The argument that advertising can support the entry of new "low cost" brands is supported by research on eyeglass retailing. Benham found that eyeglass prices were 25 to 30 percent higher in states with total advertising bans presumably because the entry of high-volume, low priced retailers is inhibited.[47]

Advertising and Profitability.   The evidence of an association between advertising and profitability is stronger. Economists Comanor and Wilson, in an influential study, attempted to explain interindustry differences in profit rates.[48] They examined the return on equity after taxes of 41 consumer-goods industries, using both the A/S ratio and the average advertising expenditures of the major firms as indicators of advertising intensity. Although they did not find high correlation (only 0.10) between four-firm concentration ratios and the A/S ratio, they did determine, using a regression model, that both advertising measures were significantly related to profitability. They concluded that industries with high advertising outlays earned approximately 50 percent more than other industries. They further attributed much of the profitability differential to entry barriers created by advertising expenditures, arguing that such a cross-sectional study (as contrasted with a time-series study) tends to emphasize the long-run difference among industries and thus should reflect basic structural characteristics like concentration. At least for manufacturing industries, this basic finding has been consistently found in several studies using different samples and measures.[49]

However, such speculation on causal explanations for the association is naturally less than definitive. Other explanations might be just as convincing. It may be, for example, that there are industry characteristics that could jointly cause profits and a tendency to rely on advertising. Or it may be that advertising in some industries is often a more economically efficient means of marketing than any other marketing alternative. From this perspective, the finding that firms in an industry who use advertising compared with those that do not (or use it less) are more profitable is not surprising. In such instances, the nature of the causal link might be quite different from what is implied by Comanor and Wilson.

Advertising and Brand Stability.   Brand loyalty, created in part by advertising, is hypothesized to be a barrier to entry and thus to competition. If such a hypothesis holds, relatively stable brand shares might be expected in industries with extensive advertising. Telser, however, examined the leading brands of various product categories in 1948 and 1959 and found an inverse relationship between product class advertising intensity and the stability of the market share of the leading brands.[50] He suggested that the advertising helped to encourage new brand introductions, which, in turn, contributed to the lack of brand stability.[51]

Remedies

The problem of the relation of advertising to concentration and competition has been studied in some detail. Yet it is still far from clear whether advertising has any independent causal effect on concentration. However, even if it is assumed to have an effect, the question remains of what remedy might be useful in altering the effect. The issue, in part, is if the argument represented by Figure 17-2 is accepted, what should be done about it? In particular, are additional restrictions on advertising appropriate?

Assume, for example, that some advertising actually does encourage concentration and results in anticompetitive effects and that therefore some restraints could be justified. The problem is "which part of whose advertising results in anticompetitive effects?" Should restrictions be placed on the cereal industry or only on its largest firms? Or should any restraints apply to the entire food industry? What kinds of restraints? Should advertising actually be banned in some industries? What impact would that have on new-product development?

There are restraints on some advertising now. Certain services like legal and medical services are restricted in the way they can be advertised. In most states, the prices of prescription drugs cannot be advertised. There are restraints with respect to certain media. Liquor and cigarettes cannot be advertised on television. It is instructive to review these situations and to consider whether the reasons for the restrictions are defensible and whether they have had undesirable, unanticipated consequences. To what extent, for example, will television advertising expenditures for cigarettes simply be directed into other media? Furthermore, what impact will the ban on television advertising and the threat of a total ban on all cigarette advertising have on industry efforts to produce safer cigarettes? Proposals to restrict advertising selectively because of a concern with industry competition should be similarly evaluated, both in terms of rationale in a specific context and the likely consequences.

It might be possible for the government to restrict advertising levels in certain industries. This restriction could take the form of mandatory controls on the rates at which firms could increase their advertising budgets. It could even include a provision for firms to decrease their level of advertising. A problem with any such proposal is that it would work to the disadvantage of the small, vigorous firm that is trying to compete with larger organizations and of the innovative firm that must announce new-product developments. If the absolute level of advertising were controlled, the smaller firms would not be inhibited, but the large firms would be penalized simply because of their size. Furthermore, there is the sticky issue of determining the exact level of advertising expenditures that would be desirable in any given context. There is precedent for such a move, however. In 1966, the Monopolies Commission in Great Britain recommended a 40 percent cut in advertising expenditures of the leading detergent companies and a 20 percent reduction in wholesale prices. However, partly because of threats to move some of their operations to the European continent, an alternative proposal was adopted. The two involved companies agreed to introduce new, less promoted detergents, priced 20 percent below existing brands.[52]

There have been proposals made to place a tax on advertising or to reduce the tax deduction allowed for advertising over a certain amount. It presumably would not affect the small competitor who would not be advertising at the affected level. Of course, the determination of the amount of reduction and the level at which the reduction would be applicable would be difficult to fix, Furthermore, companies could alter their marketing mix in ways to shift the advertising dollar to other forms of promotion that might have an impact similar to that of advertising. Also, any such plan would discriminate against those companies that tend to rely on advertising in favor of companies like Avon, for example, that rely mainly on direct selling.

The practical question of the nature of the remedy and how it should be implemented needs to be more formally introduced into the analysis. It is tempting to propose a remedy that will seem to rectify obvious problems. However, in many cases, the remedy can be worse than the original problem.[53]

SUMMARY

A discussion of the social and economic issues of advertising can be divided into three categories. Two of these represent the aggregate effects of advertising on society's value and life-styles and on society's economic well-being. The third category represents the nature and content of advertising. It involves issues of deception (which will be examined in the following chapter), manipulation, and taste, issues that are magnified when the audience is children.

The argument that advertising manipulates consumers takes several forms. First, there is concern that advertisers, using subconscious motives uncovered by motivation research, can manipulate an unwilling consumer. Although it is now recognized by professionals that the power of motivation research is limited, some ethical questions about its use still remain. Second, there is a concern with the use of "emotional" appeals. The key issue here is the definition of a product. Is a product an entity with one or more primary functions or does it involve any dimension relevant to the consumer when she or he makes a purchase decision? Finally, there is the more general concern with the power represented by the volume of advertising and the skill of the people who create it.

Some advertising is criticized on the basis of taste—that it uses appeals that are offensive, that the content is annoying, or that it is simply too intrusive. Some critics object to the use of sex, especially when children may be exposed to it. Others are concerned with the use of fear appeals. The irritation life cycle is conceptualized to help understand the intrusive quality of advertising. An FTC proposal to ban all television advertising to preschool children and all sugar-product television advertising to older children was seriously and vigorously debated.

It is argued that advertising has a negative impact on values and life-styles of society. The key issues are what values and life-styles are to be avoided and what relative impact or influence does advertising have on them. What is materialism and is it bad or is it merely a means to various goals? What role does (and should) advertising have in promoting or combating stereotypes? Does beer and wine television advertising promote alcoholism and drunk driving? Should it be banned from television and radio?

It is unreasonable to separate the economic and social impact of advertising. Advertising is basically an economic institution, and any overall appraisal of advertising should include an analysis of its economic impact. Advertising provides economic value to society in many ways. It enhances buyer decision making by providing information and by supporting brand names. It provides an efficient means for firms to communicate with their customers. Such a function is particularly important in the introduction of new products. By generating various product associations, advertising can add to the utility a buyer receives from a product. It supports the various media and has the largely unrealized potential to reduce extremes in the levels of consumer buying.

A central issue is the impact that advertising has on competition. It is argued that heavy advertising expenditures in some industries generate product differentiation among products that are essentially identical. This product differentiation provides the basis for brand loyalties that represent a significant barrier to potential competitors. It is also hypothesized that in these industries heavy advertising expenditures are needed for successful competition. Such large expenditure levels represent another barrier to entry of new competitors. With the entry of new competitors inhibited, there is a tendency for industries to become more concentrated over time—to have fewer competitors. The result is a reduction in vigorous competition, higher prices, and excessive profits. Advertising in such industries is regarded as noninformative; its role is to shift buyers around among "identical" products and is thus largely an economic waste.

The implications of these hypotheses have been studied by economists. They have found evidence of association between advertising and concentration, but, on balance, the evidence was weaker than might be expected. The evidence of association between advertising and profitability was somewhat stronger. The studies, however, must deal with such difficult methodological problems as generating definitions of concentration and making causal inferences.

The practical question of what remedies seem appropriate needs to be formally introduced into the analysis. Remedies that are defensible and will not cause more problems than they solve are not easy to develop. Among the proposed remedies are that advertising in some industries be limited or prohibited or that a tax be applied to advertising.

DISCUSSION QUESTIONS

1. Suppose that a motivation research study found that housewives disliked a certain transparent, clinging, wrapping material because of their basic dislike of cooking, which was subconsciously transferred to the material. As a result, nonkitchen uses were emphasized in the advertising. Is this manipulation? In the research, the housewives were told only that the aim of the study was to determine their attitudes toward housekeeping in general. Was such a guise ethical?

2. Define the terms "need," "product," "information," and "rationality." Does a commercial showing a group of people enjoying a cola drink communicate information? Is it an appropriate appeal? Consider other examples. Is manipulation involved?

3. Richard Avedon, a photographer and consultant to agencies and clients, helped develop for Calvin Klein jeans a very controversial set of television commercials. They featured the 15-year-old actress-model Brooke Shields in a variety of sultry, sophisticated, suggestive commercials. In one, Brooke Shields says in a suggestive manner: "Nothing comes between me and my Calvins." In another controversial television commercial for a men's fragrance, a man wearing a pajama bottom is seen getting out of bed and discussing the previous night by phone with a woman who had slept with him.
    a. Do you feel that such advertising is effective? In what way?
    b. Would you run such advertising on network television if you felt it was effective if you were an advertiser? If you were an agency whose client had insisted on it?
    c. If you were a CBS censor, would you allow it on your network?

4. Suppose you are the president of a major consumer food company. A church group claiming to represent 2.5 million members is attempting to reduce the "excessive violence, sex and profanity" on television. They have informed you that they are boycotting all products advertised on eight programs, including "Miami Vice" and "Dallas," and expect that their boycott will cost you $20 million in sales. What would your response be? Do you feel that you should have a policy concerning such programming? Would you screen episodes of such programs and selectively avoid episodes that are particularly objectionable?

5. Take a position on the FTC proposals regarding television advertising to children. What about banning the advertising of sugar products directed at children under 12? Would you prefer that food advertisers to children fund "counter-ads" geared to promote nutrition? What about cutting back Saturday morning kids' advertising to four minutes per hour? Would you alter or add to the following partial listing of the provisions of a Canadian broadcasting code for children?

    a. Product characteristics should not be exaggerated.

    b. Results from a craft or kit that an average child could not obtain should not be shown.

    c. Undue pressure to buy or to urge parents to buy should be avoided.

    d. A commercial should not be repeated during a program.

    e. Program personalities will not do commercials on their own programs.

    f. Well-known persons other than actors will not endorse products.

    g. Price information should be clear and complete.

    h. Messages must not reflect disdain for parents or casually portray undesirable family living habits.

    i. Advertising must not imply that product possession makes the owner superior.

    j. The media should contribute directly or indirectly to sound and safe habits.

6. Should there be similar codes for other society groups such as senior citizens or ethnic minorities?

7. What is materialism? It has been said that our society emphasizes the use of material goods to attain nonmaterial goals. Comment. Is America too materialistic? What is advertising's role in establishing values and life-styles? How does a nation go about changing its values?

8. Should advertisers be concerned about minority stereotypes developed in advertisements? Why? If you were an agency president, how would you develop a policy and set of procedures in this regard?

9. In your view, should beer advertisers be banned from using sports figures in their ads? What about the use of image advertising in general? Should beer and wine advertising be banned from television and radio advertising? From all advertising? What about the use of "power/sportiness" appeals in automobile advertising? Should beer advertisers stop all college and sports promotions?

10. In an open letter to the makers of Alka-Seltzer, the following questions were posed by Ries, Cappiello, Colwell, a New York advertising agency: Why did you spend $23 million to promote a product that everyone knows about? Why did you spend $23 million to promote a product that is mostly bicarbonate and aspirin? Why not put some of that money into your laboratories? Why not develop new products that are worth advertising? Comment.

11. What would be the economic effect of a ban on all advertising? Of a ban on radio and television advertising?

12. What is the definition of a market? What is the distinction between the compact car market and the automobile market? Campbell had 8 percent of the dry-soup market in 1962 versus 57 percent for Lipton and 16

percent for Wyler's. Should an analyst focus on the soup market or the dry-soup market?

13. The concentration ratio in the beer industry went from 21 percent in 1947 to 34 percent in 1963. Yet the fact that Pabst was third in 1952, ninth in 1957, and third again in 1962 indicates that the industry was far from stable. Furthermore, regional brands like Lone-Star and Pearl, two Texas brands that forced a national brand out of their market, compete very effectively with national brands and require only a regional advertising budget. Comment.

14. What is the economic impact of advertising? When will it generate lower prices? Under what conditions will it increase prices? Evaluate the causal model represented in Figure 17-2.

15. What is your judgment about the cereal industry? Should the government take action? What kind of action? Why?

16. It has been proposed by Ralph Nader that a 100 percent tax be applied on all advertising expenditures in excess of a percentage specified for different companies by the FTC. Evaluate this proposal. How else might large advertising expenditures be reduced? What would be the effect of a law outlawing advertising in the cigarette industry? In the detergent industry (in which 11 percent of sales is spent on advertising)?

NOTES

1. *The Works of Samuel Johnson, LL.D.,* IV (Oxford: Talboys and Wheeler, 1825), p. 269.

2. Vance Packard, *The Hidden Persuaders* (New York: Pocket Books, 1957).

3. Ibid., p. 1.

4. William L. Wilke, *Consumer Research* (New York: John Wiley & Sons, 1986), p. 377.

5. Joel Saegert, "Another Look at Subliminal Perception," *Journal of Advertising Research,* 19, February 1979, pp. 55–57.

6. Del Hawkins, "The Effects of Subliminal Stimulation on Drive Level and Brand Preference," *Journal of Marketing Research,* 7, August 1970, pp. 322–326.

7. Tibor Scitovsky, *Welfare and Competition* (Homewood, Ill.: Richard D. Irwin, 1951), pp. 401–402.

8. Mary Gardiner Jones, "The Cultural and Social Impact of Advertising on American Society," *Arizona State Law Journal,* 3, 1970.

9. Raymond A. Bauer and Stephen A. Greyser, "The Dialogue That Never Happens," *Harvard Business Review,* 50, January–February 1969, pp. 122–128.

10. Raymond A. Bauer and Stephen A. Greyser, *Advertising in America: The Consumer View* (Boston: Division of Research, Graduate School of Business Administration, Harvard University, 1968).

11. Ibid., p. 183.

12. Ibid., p. 217.

13. Ibid.

14. Ibid., p. 223.

15. David A. Aaker and Donald Bruzzone, "What Causes Irritation in Television Advertising," Spring 1985, pp. 47–57.

16. Kathy McMeel, "You Dirty Old Ad Men Make Me Sick," *Advertising Age,* December 1, 1969, p. 28.

17. Stephen A. Greyser, "Irritation in Advertising," *Journal of Advertising Research,* 13, February 1973, p. 8.

18. Ibid., p. 6.

19. A compact description of the issues can be found in summaries of two sets of comments made in 1978 by some of the leading participants in the debate over the FTC proposed "kid-vid" rule. Scott Ward ("Researchers Look at the 'Kid Vid' Rule") summarized remarks of two researchers, Charles K. Atken and Marvin E. Goldberg. Michael B. Mazis ("Can and Should the FTC Restrict Advertising to Children?") summarized the comments of Tracy A. Westen, Robert B. Choate, John A. Dimling, Seymour Banks, Stanley Cohen, Fletcher C. Waller, and William Van Brunt. These summaries are published in William Wilkie, ed., *Advances in Consumer Research:* 6 (Ann Arbor, Mich.: Association for Consumer Research, 1979), pp. 3–11, and in David A. Aaker and George S. Day, eds., *Consumerism* (New York: Free Press, 1982), pp. 224–237.

20. J. Blatt, L. Spencer, and S. Ward, "A Cognitive Development Study of Children's Reactions to Television Advertising," *Effects of Television on Children and Adolescents,* unpublished paper (Cambridge, Mass.: Marketing Science Institute, 1971).

21. J. G. Myers, *Social Issues in Advertising* (New York: American Association of Advertising Agencies Educational Foundation), 1972.

22. F. P. Bishop, *The Ethics of Advertising* (London: Robert Hale, 1949), p. 17.

23. Bauer and Greyser, "The Dialogue That Never Happens."

24. Jones, "The Cutlural and Social Impact of Advertising on American Society," presented to the Trade Regulation Roundtable of the Association of American Law Schools, San Francisco, December 1969, pp. 13–14.

25. Alice E. Courtney and Sarah Wernick Lockeretz, "A Woman's Place: An Analysis of the Roles Portrayed by Women in Magazine Advertisements," *Journal of Marketing Research,* 8, February 1971, pp. 92–95.

26. Harold H. Kassarjian, "The Negro and American Advertising, 1946–65," *Journal of Marketing Research,* 6, February 1969, pp. 29–39.

27. "Alcohol on the Rocks," *Newsweek,* December 31, 1984, pp. 52–54.

28. Ibid.

29. "Whole World Is Watching U.S. Alcohol Ad Debate," *Advertising Age,* February 11, 1985, p. 70.

30. The authors would like to thank Ewald T. Grether, Lee E. Preston, and Louis W. Stern for making helpful comments on this section and the one that follows.

31. David A. Aaker and Donald Norris, "Characteristics of Television Commercials Perceived as Informative," *Journal of Advertising Research,* February 1982.

32. Phillip Nelson, "Advertising as Information," *Journal of Political Economy,* 82, July/August 1974, pp. 729–754.

33. Fritz Machlup, *The Production and Distribution of Knowledge in the United States* (Princeton, N.J.: Princeton University Press, 1962), p. 265.

34. Julian L. Simon, *Issues in the Economics of Advertising* (Urbana, Ill.: University of Illinois Press, 1970), p. 276.

35. "Grocery Manufacturing," Technical Study No. 6, National Commission on Food Marketing, June 1966, p. 147.

36. Simon, *Issues in the Economics of Advertising.*

37. Neil H. Borden, *The Economic Effects of Advertising* (Homewood, Ill.: Richard D. Irwin, 1942), p. 609.

38. Frederic M. Scherer, *Industrial Market Structure and Economic Performance* (Boston: Houghton-Mifflin), 1980, p. 62.

39. Ibid., p. 375.

40. Paul D. Scanlon, "Oligopoly and 'Deceptive' Advertising: The Cereal Industry Affair," *Antitrust Law & Economics Review,* 3, Spring 1970, p. 101.

41. Ibid., pp. 99–110.

42. Louis W. Stern and Thomas W. Dunfee, "Public Policy Implications of Non-price Marketing and De-Oligopolization in the Cereal Industry," in Fred C. Allvine, ed., *Public Policy and Marketing Practices* (Chicago: American Marketing Association, 1973), pp. 271–287.

43. See also Paul N. Bloom, "The Cereal Companies: Monopolists or Super Marketers?" *MSU Business Topics,* Summer, 1978, pp. 41–49.

44. John K. Galbraith, *American Capitalism: The Concept of Countervailing Power* (Boston: Houghton Mifflin, 1956).

45. Robert D. Buzzell and Paul W. Farris, "Marketing Costs in Consumer Goods Industries," Marketing Science Institute, Report N. 76–111, August 1976.

46. Paul W. Farris and Mark S. Albion, "The Impact of Advertising on the Price of Consumer Products," *Journal of Marketing* 44, Summer 1980, pp. 17–35.

47. Lee Benham, "The Effect of Advertising on the Price of Eyeglasses," *The Journal of Law and Economics,* 15, October 1972, pp. 337–352.

48. William S. Comanor and Thomas A. Wilson, "Advertising, Market Structure and Performance," *Review of Economics and Statistics,* 49, November 1967, pp. 423–440.

49. Scherer, *Industrial Market Structure and Economic Performance,* p. 286.

50. Lester G. Telser, "Advertising and Competition," *Journal of Political Economy,* December 1964, pp. 537–562.

51. New brand introductions, of course, are far different from the entry of new competitors.

52. Scherer, *Industrial Market Structure,* p. 404.

53. Many judge the Robinson-Patman Act to be in that category. Instead of a simple tool to protect competition, it has, in the eyes of some, greatly inhibited price competition.

18

Advertising Regulation

Consumers have a considerable tolerance for exaggeration and puffery in advertising. . . . They undoubtedly expect advertisements to be biased and to present merchandise in an attractive light. (Neil Borden, 1942, Professor of advertising, Harvard)

Advertising has a large responsibility within our economic system and is a highly visible and important institution affecting many people. What role should the government play in regulating advertising? This question has occupied the attention of businessmen, politicians, and citizens for many years. The most significant question pertaining to advertising regulation concerns deceptive advertising. If the information provided is misleading or deceptive, then the responsibility of advertising in providing information for consumer decision making is not being fulfilled. The result is, in economic terms, a misallocation of resources. In more personal terms, the result is a disappointed buyer or, worse, a real economic or physical injury.

The need to avoid deception in advertising is well recognized by both industry and government leadership. The American Association of Advertising Agencies published a Creative Code in 1962 that affirmed that the members in addition to supporting and obeying the laws and legal regulations pertaining to advertising, undertake to extend and broaden the application of high ethical standards. Specifically, we will not knowingly produce advertising which contains:

1. False or misleading statements or exaggerations, visual or verbal.
2. Testimonials which do not reflect the real choice of a competent witness.
3. Price claims which are misleading.
4. Comparisons which unfairly disparage a competitive product or service.
5. Claims insufficiently supported, or which distort the true meaning or practicable application of statements made by professional or scientific authority.
6. Statements, suggestions or pictures offensive to public decency.[1]

The issue seems rather clear. Advertisers need only follow this code and no problems will arise. It is, however, not that simple. First, everyone does not agree on the definition of deception. When Blatz claims that it is "Milwaukee's finest beer" some (particularly other Milwaukee brewers) could argue that in fact another beer is superior. Is deception involved? What does "finest" mean? One advertisement claimed that a hair dye would color hair permanently. If someone exposed to the advertisement believed that the dye would hold for hair not yet grown and thus a single dye would last for decades, is the claim deceptive? How many people need to misunderstand before deception is involved? When there is disagreement about what is deception, who should decide? How can dishonest and careless advertisers be detected, prosecuted, and punished? To what extent can self-regulation be relied upon? What are appropriate remedies? These questions and others make the issue of deception a complex area for an advertiser, the media, and the government.

In the following sections, the history of regulation will be briefly sketched. The concept of deception will then be considered. Who is it that is being deceived? How does one determine what is promised by an advertisement? Various existing and proposed remedies will then be discussed. Finally, the truth in advertising legislation will be examined.

HISTORY OF FEDERAL REGULATION OF ADVERTISING

In 1914, the Federal Trade Commision Act was passed, which created the federal agency that has had the primary responsibility for the regulation of advertising. Section 5 of the FTC Act contained the prohibition: "Unfair methods of competition in commerce are hereby declared unlawful." The aim was to provide an agency that could deal with restraints of trade more effectively than had the Sherman Anti-Trust Law. The problem of deceptive advertising was not a target of the FTC Act. Millstein, a legal scholar, observes: "The most important development in the long history of the FTC's prohibition of false advertising was that the FTC concerned itself with the problem in the first place."[2] In many respects it was a fortuitous accident.

The FTC became concerned with deceptive advertising because of its effect upon competition. In the first test case in 1919 the FTC moved against Sears

Roebuck.[3] Sears had advertised that their prices for sugar and tea were lower than competitors because of their larger buying power. The claim was found to be false, but the FTC action was upheld not because of subsequent damage caused the consumer but by the fact that smaller competitors could be injured. Thus for many years advertising regulation was largely concentrated on the need to protect small firms and competitors rather than consumers themselves. The Federal Trade Commission promulgated these cases through its antitrust division. In recent years, more advertising cases go through the consumer protection division.

In 1931, in the landmark *FTC* v. *Raladam* case, the Supreme Court specifically held that the FTC could not prohibit false advertising if there is no evidence of injury to a competitor.[4] The ruling struck a decisive blow in that it stopped any movement in the direction of protecting the consuming public directly. However, it was a blessing in disguise for it helped to mobilize support for redefining the powers of the FTC. The ultimate result was the Wheeler-Lea Amendment passed in 1938, which amended Section 5 of the FTC Act to read: "Unfair methods of competition in commerce and unfair or deceptive actions or practices in commerce are hereby declared unlawful." Thus the obligation to demonstrate that injury to competition occurred was removed. The issue then was not a jurisdictional one but rather how to move forward against deceptive advertising.

A basic issue in the enforcement of these laws against deceptive advertising, to which we now turn, is how to define and identify deception.

WHAT IS DECEPTIVE ADVERTISING?

Conceptually, deception exists when an advertisement is introduced into the perceptual process of some audience and the output of that perceptual process (1) differs from the reality of the situation, and (2) affects buying behavior to the detriment of the consumer. The input itself may be determined to contain falsehoods. The more difficult and perhaps more common case, however, is when the input, the advertisement, is not obviously false, but the perceptual process generates an impression that is deceptive. A disclaimer may not pass through the attention filter or the message may be misinterpreted. Since the determination of deception is closely tied to the perceptual process, the reader should recall the material presented in Chapter 8. It will be helpful to evaluate the ground rules regarding deception that the FTC and the courts have developed. Realize, however, that the decisions supporting these ground rules have been made by lawyers who, for various reasons, have not drawn extensively on the expertise of psychologists and advertising researchers.

Legally, the definition of deception has evolved over the years since the Wheeler-Lea Amendment was passed. Refinements have been caused by the FTC in their decisions in individual cases and in their Trade Regulation Rules which cover unlawful trade practices of entire industries. The FTC positions can be appealed to the courts, which ultimately provide the legal definition of deceptive advertising.

The formal FTC position on the meaning of deception was put forward by the five commissioners in 1983. Although somewhat controversial (it was passed on a 3 to 2 vote) and untested in the courts, it does represent an important effort to define deception. It states that

". . . The Commission will find deception if there is a misrepresentation, omission or practice that is likely to mislead the consumer acting responsibly (or reasonably) in the circumstances, to the consumer's detriment . . . (that is the act or practice is) likely to affect the consumer's conduct or decision with regard to a product or service. If so the practice is material, and consumer injury is likely because consumers are likely to have chosen differently but for the deception."[5]

In the following, specific issues regarding deceptive advertising raised by the FTC and the courts will be discussed.

Who Is Deceived?

How extensive must the deception be before deception is determined to exist? If one naive person is misled, is the advertisement deceptive? Or 1 percent, or 10 percent, or 30 percent? Who is it that is to be protected? The FTC has historically taken the extreme position that essentially all are to be protected, in particular those who are naive, trusting, and of low intelligence, small though their numbers might be.

In 1944 this position was graphically illustrated by two cases. In the Charles of the Ritz case, the FTC found that the trademark "Rejuvenescence" was associated with a foundation makeup cream in a manner that promised the restoration of a youthful complexion.[6] Some, including those ignorant, unthinking, and credulous, might believe that the product could actually cause youth to be restored. In *Gelb* v. *FTC,* the FTC prohibited the claim that a hair-coloring product could color hair permanently.[7] Their position was that some might believe that even new hair would have the desired new color.

The 1955 Kirchner case provided some relief to the charge that no deception can exist.[8] It involved a swimming aid and the claim that when the device was worn under a swimming suit it was "thin and invisible." The commission decided that buyers who were not "foolish or feebleminded" would be unlikely to take this claim literally, noting:

Perhaps a few misguided would believe, for example, that all "Danish pastry" is made in Denmark. Is it, therefore, an actual deception to advertise "Danish pastry" when it is made in this country? Of course not. A representation does not become "false and deceptive" merely because it will be unreasonably misunderstood by an insignificant and unrepresentative segment of the class of persons to whom the representation is addressed.[9]

The Kirchner case also indicated that advertising aimed at particularly susceptible groups will be evaluated with respect to that group. Thus, when children are the target, deception will be evaluated with respect to them. One case was decided on the basis of the advertising impact on a "busy businessman." This refinement is interesting because it recognizes that people may perceive stimuli differently, depending on the situational context.

Despite the Kirchner case, the FTC and the courts have generally considered advertisements deceptive if only a modest percentage were deceived. In the 1972 Firestone Tire case, the advertising claimed that the Safety Champion tire was free of any defects and safe under any conditions.[10] The FTC concluded that for basis of demonstrating deception even 10 percent of the public was a substantial proportion of the public.

The demand that deception be at a zero or close to zero level is usually unrealistic and effectively means that there is no defense against a charge of deception. However, the justification of nonzero baseline levels of misperception or deception, especially in the contest of the legal history, is difficult. We shall return to this issue shortly.

Materiality of the Falsehood

For an advertisement to be deceptive, it must contain a material untruth, that is, one capable of affecting purchase decisions. It should be likely that the advertisement will cause public injury. Millstein explains:

> "Public injury" does not mean that a consumer must actually suffer damage, or that it must be shown that goods purchased are unequal to the value expended. Rather, "public injury" results if the advertisement has a tendency to induce action (such as the purchase itself) detrimental to the consumer that might not otherwise have been taken. If such action could *not* have been induced by the claim (even though false), there is no "public injury." This requirement comports with the express provision of Section 15 of the FTC Act, as amended, that the advertisement must be misleading in a material respect to be actionable.[11]

The 1964 Colgate-Palmolive case is one instance in which the court applied the materiality requirement to modify a commission decision.[12] The case involved the shaving of simulated sandpaper, sand on Plexiglas. The advertisement appeared to demonstrate the moisturizing qualities of Palmolive Rapid Shave. The commission pointed out that in fact sandpaper could only be shaved after a lengthy period of soaking and thus the advertisement was deceptive. This type of deception was material in that consumers were likely to rely upon the demonstration in making purchase decisions. However, the commission went further and stated that the use of a sand on Plexiglas mock-up would have been prohibited even if Rapid Shave could shave sandpaper as represented. The Court of Appeals rejected the sweeping language of the complaint, arguing that mock-ups are permissible if they do not affect purchase decisions. As a result, the commission revised its opinion, stating that only mock-ups and props that were intended to demonstrate visually a quality that was material to the sale of a product would be prohibited. Thus, mashed potatoes could be used in television commercials in scenes depicting ice cream consumption (ice cream will melt too rapidly under lights) if the texture and color of the prop were not emphasized as selling points ·of the product.

In 1984, the FTC narrowed its definition of deception in an important way.[13] Previously an advertisement was held to be deceptive if it "has the tendency or capacity to deceive a substantial number of consumers in a material way." However, in the Cliffdale case, the proper test for finding deception was whether the claim is "material and likely to mislead consumers acting 'reasonably' under the circumstances." The key word is "reasonably." A mail-order company, Cliffdale Associates, had advertised an automobile fuel economy device, the $12.95 BallMatic Valve, which made deceptive performance claims. The FTC concluded that consumers acting reasonably would not be materially affected.

The Entire Advertisement

An advertisement will be judged by its general impression. It may be that all claims made within an advertisement are literally true yet the total impression of the advertisement may still be deceptive. Thus, in a 1950 decision, the courts ruled that Lorillard had developed deceptive advertisements despite the fact that their claims were literally true.[14] *Reader's Digest* had run an article that indicated that all cigarettes were harmful and that the differences among them were minor. To illustrate the point, a list of cigarettes was included along with the tar and nicotine content of each. A Lorillard brand happened to have the lowest level of tar and nicotine, although by an insignificant margin. The Lorillard campaign emphasizing the *Reader's Digest* article was therefore deemed deceptive.

In another example, a television commercial for a car wax used flaming gasoline on an automobile to demonstrate that the wax could withstand intense heat.[15] However, the gasoline was only burning for a few seconds. It was extinguished before any significant heat was generated. Consequently, the advertisement was determined to be deceptive in that the claim was not actually demonstrated by the test.

Such a criterion is sound from an advertisement research viewpoint. Recall the material on perception, particularly the concept of a gestalt, which suggests that an individual's perception has a meaning of its own that cannot necessarily be deduced from the meanings of its components. An individual will complete a phrase or scene or will actually distort it in order to achieve an improved gestalt—one that is more familiar, meaningful, regular, or consistent. Thus, to determine the meaning of an advertisement with measures such as recall of specific copy points is usually less useful than a higher-order measure that reflects the total perception. Even more useful are measures linked more closely with advertising objectives and ultimate behavior, that is, measures reflecting the impact of the advertisement on brand image and consumer attitudes. The courts for various reasons rarely conceptualize at these levels of analysis.

The Ambiguous Statement

If an advertisement can be interpreted in two ways and one of them would be deceptive, the advertisement is regarded as deceptive. Thus, the use of the phrase "government supported" could be interpreted as "government approved" and was therefore challenged.[16] In another case the FTC held that a toothpaste claim that it "fights decay" could be interpreted as a claim that it provides complete protection and was therefore deceptive.[17]

Sometimes it is necessary to use the secondary meaning of a word. In those cases, the danger that the primary meaning will be incorrectly perceived by those exposed can be high unless a qualification is included. Thus, a drink may be described as an orange drink if it is artifically made to look and taste like orange despite the fact that it is not made from oranges.[18] The problem is that there may be no real substitute word that will be adequately descriptive. In such cases the term may be allowed, but the probability of misinterpretation should be reduced by suitable qualification.

If a claim is extremely vague, the alternative interpretations are not always obvious. An advertisement may claim, for example, that its product tones up muscles, or provides a lifetime guarantee, or is helpful in the treatment of a certain disease. What do these terms really mean? To an advertising researcher, the quantification of the number of interpretations and the extent to which each would emerge would not be unusually difficult or costly research task. However, the commission and the courts tend not to rely upon such techniques, for reasons that will be discussed later.

Misleading Silence

The FTC can require that a more complete disclosure be made to correct a misconception. Thus Geritol was required to indicate that the "tired feeling" it was supposed to help was possibly due to factors that the product could not treat effectively.[19] Similarly, baldness cures have been required to indicate that baldness usually is hereditary and untreatable. Toys usually are assumed to be safe. Therefore, toy manufacturers have a special responsibility to point out possible unsafe aspects of their toys.

It is interesting to consider how far pressure from the FTC for complete disclosure could go. There are a wide variety of advertised brands that differ little in substance from competitors. It is a common practice to associate a brand with an attribute of the product class. Should the brand be required to state in its advertisement that all brands are virtually identical in this respect? For example, an aspirin advertisement may emphasize the product's pain-relieving quality without mentioning that all aspirin-based brands will have a similar effect. A FTC complaint against Wonder Bread argued that Wonder Bread's claim that their brand build bodies 12 ways falsely implied that Wonder Bread was unique with respect to such a claim. Although this charge was subsequently dropped, it does illustrate one possible way in which the definition of deception could be broadened.[20] Interestingly, Hunt-Wesson Foods, soon after the Wonder Bread complaint was filed, developed a policy of avoiding advertising brands that are virtually similar to their competitors.

The argument for disclosing that all brands are similar with respect to a certain product attribute is primarily that advertising is a mechanism to communicate information that will be helpful to the consumer in making a purchasing decision and that "image" or "characterization" advertising is not helpful. If advertising content is not informative from this perspective and in fact could lead to nonoptimal brand choice decisions, it should be curtailed. However, it may be that such a rule could, at least to some extent, reduce the product-class information a consumer receives as brands lose their incentive to communicate product-class attribute information. Further, a problem associated with such a proposal is to determine if a brand really has a real differential advantage. To a researcher who has the benefit of perceptual maps and sophisticated taste tests, a brand may seem significantly different. To a consumer, and perhaps to the FTC, these differences may seem minor.

Puffery

A rather well-established rule of law is that "trade puffing" is permissible. Puffing takes two general forms. The first is a subjective statement of opinion about a product's quality, using such terms as "best or greatest." Nearly all advertisements contain some measure of puffery. "You can't get any closer" (Norelco) . . . "Try something better" (J&B Scotch) . . . "Gas gives you a better deal" (American Gas Association) . . . "Live better electrically" (Edison Electric Institution) . . . "State Farm is all you need to know about insurance" . . . "Super Shell." None of these statements has been proved to be true but neither have they been proved false. They all involve some measure of exaggeration.

The second form of puffery is an exaggeration extended to the point of outright spoof that is obviously not true. A Green Giant is obviously fictitious, and even if he were real he wouldn't be talking the way he does. Hai Karate aftershave really isn't so appealing that it arouses the beast in females.

In the 1927 Ostermoor case, the court pointed to the puffery argument in denying that a mattress company was deceptive in using an illustration appearing to depict that the inner filling of a mattress would expand to 35 inches when in fact it would expand only 3 to 6 inches.[21] The court observed:

> The statutory power to prohibit unfair methods of competition cannot be stretched to this extent; the slightest pictorial exaggeration of the qualities of an article cannot be deemed to be either a misrepresentation of an unfair method of competition. The time-honored custom of at least merely slight puffing, . . . has not come under a legal ban. . . . Concededly it is an exaggeration of the actual condition; indeed petitioner asserts that it is not and was not intended to be descriptive, but fanciful, and as such the subject matter of valid trade-marks.[22]

Later, in 1946, the court set aside the FTC ruling in the Carlay case that a weight reduction plan involving Ayds candy, which claimed to be "easy" to follow, was deceptive. The court made the following comments:

> What was said was clearly justifiable . . . under those cases recognizing that such words as "easy," "perfect," "amazing," "prime," "wonderful," "excellent," are regarded in law as mere puffing or dealer's talk upon which no charge of misrepresentation can be based.[23]

Preston and Johnson and later Preston examine the puffery issue and declare that although it is well established in law, it is at the same time somewhat vulnerable.[24] They state that over the years the puffery defense has been frequently relied on. Yet the courts have ruled in many of these cases that the claim goes beyond puffery to real deception. The question is, then, what is puffery? One answer is that the definition seems to be changing over time. A claim that would have been regarded as subjective opinion and legitimate puffery years ago might now be viewed in a different light.

In the Tanners Shoe Company case decided in 1957, the FTC denied the puffery defense, declaring that

> it was stipulated that it is not literally true that respondents' shoes will "assure" comfort or a perfect fit to all individuals. However, respondents contend that such representations constitute legitimate trade puffery and are not false representations within the meaning of the law. . . . The representation that the product provides support where it is most needed clearly carries an orthopedic or health connotation, and it is undisputed that respondents' shoes are not orthopedic . . . but are stock shoes. It would appear that such a representation is false in attributing to the product a quality which it does not possess rather than exaggerating a quality which it has.[25]

In the Colgate-Palmolive case involving the sandpaper shaving demonstration, the respondent claimed that the advertisement was merely fanciful exaggeration. The FTC decision pointed out that to term the demonstration puffery was "inconsistent with the prevalent judicial and administrative policy of restricting, rather than expanding, so-called puffing."[26]

DETERMINING DECEPTION USING ADVERTISING RESEARCH

The crucial issue in deceptive advertising is often the determination of how the advertising claims are perceived by consumers and what impact such perceptions have on consumer behavior. Since these issues are also central to copy testing and to the evaluation of an advertising campaign, it would be natural for the FTC and the courts to avail themselves of the methodologies of advertising research. Until the late 1960s, however, there was actually little consumer research employed in this context. The reasons that linger are instructive:

1. The FTC simply was not required by the courts to develop evidence. Its subjective judgment was held as adequate.

2. The use of independently commissioned survey research is somewhat inconsistent with the traditional adversary system of justice wherein each side submits arguments and evidence to support a position. To an attorney, agreeing to a carefully conceived and conducted survey might be too much like calling a prestigious witness without knowing which side his or her testimony will support.

3. There are methodological difficulties and pitfalls in any study. The population must be defined, a defensible sampling plan created, and questions designed to pass tests of unbiasedness and validity. Additional pressures on any research design are created in the legal context by opposing lawyers and experts who will try to discredit it. Some early survey efforts were extremely flawed with small, unrepresentative samples and naive questionnaires.

4. Defendants have lacked motivation to introduce survey evidence, as it would tend to be used against them. In the 1963 Benrus Watch case a survey showed that 86 percent correctly interpreted an ad, but the FTC used the fact that 14 percent had been deceived as evidence against Benrus.[27]

In the late 1960s a variety of factors combined to stimulate the use of consumer research until by the middle 1970s it became the norm. Prompted by FTC commissioner Mary Gardner Jones, the FTC in 1969 began to use research consultants full-time, typically consumer behavior professors on temporary leave. These people over the years have been extremely influential in bringing to a lawyer-dominated FTC the knowledge and expertise necessary to apply consumer research to the issues surrounding deceptive advertising. Commissioner Jones was also the force behind the 1971 hearings on modern advertising practices in which industry professionals explained to the FTC their consumer research techniques as well as the advertising creation and testing process.[28] In addition, there were advances in consumer research and evolutionary changes in the law that helped make the use of consumer research more accepted.

In the 1972 Firestone case, expert witnesses on consumer response were used for the first time.[29] In the 1974 Wonder Bread case the FTC first introduced into evidence a survey that was not conducted by the advertiser; it was a survey originally created for academic purposes.[30] The first survey commissioned by the FTC specifically to support a prosecution was in the 1974 Sun Oil case.[31] The use of consumer research did not resolve the many issues surrounding deception. In fact, it perhaps created some new ones. The same challenges that consumer research faces in the advertising management context—what should be measured and what the appropriate target levels are—reappeared although they seemed magnified in the legal context. The determination of level of deception that is unacceptable is a key question. Obviously, it is not practical to have no misperceptions. But what level is acceptable? A major study sponsored by the AAAA (American Assocation of Advertising Agencies) bears directly on this question.

The Miscomprehension of Television Advertising: The AAAA Study

The AAAA study, conducted in 1979 by Jacoby, Hoyer, and Sheluga, attempted to provide evidence as to the level of consumer miscomprehension of television advertising and how that compares to miscomprehension of excerpts of other programming.[32] Sixty different 30-second communications were selected: 25 commercial ads, 13 noncommercial ads, and 22 program excerpts. Respondents in shopping mall interviews were exposed to two of these communications and given a six-item miscomprehension quiz about each. A total of 90 respondents saw each communication.

On the average 29.6 percent of the quiz items were answered incorrectly across the 2,700 respondents. This percentage was actually slightly lower, 28.3 percent, when only commercial advertisements were considered. Although the miscomprehension ranged from 11 to 50 percent, half the communications were between 23 and 36 percent (between 22 and 34 percent for commercial advertisements). These levels did not dramatically change across age and education levels. Presumably these numbers would be even higher if the respondents had not been allowed to guess if they were not sure, and if the measures were not taken immediately after exposure. The implication is a certain level of miscomprehension should be expected in advertisements or any communication. Any reasonable standard ought to recognize that fact. ·

Because of the scope and influence of the study, its methodology and conclusions have been challenged by consumer researchers. Ford and Yalch noted that there was only a single exposure to a broad audience in an artificial situation, whereas most advertising involves multiple exposures in natural settings involving a target audience.[33] They also suggest that the quiz involved at least some questions that were ambiguous, poorly worded, or immaterial.

Mizerski's position is that other measures of miscomprehension may be more appropriate and that miscomprehension levels are extremely sensitive to the measure used.[34] A FTC test of a 30-second allegedly deceptive television commercial for a drug product involving 190 mall intercept interviews illustrates. The measure of deception with respect to one claim ranged from 6 percent (the percent naming it in unaided recall) to 16 percent (the percent naming it when asked: "what does the ad mean by saying. . . ?'') to 95 percent (who identified it as one of 10 discomforts that the brand could relieve). Another discomfort in the list, completely bogus in that it could not possibly be implied from the ad, was identified by 10 percent as a discomfort that could be relieved by the brands.

Conclusion

There is no question that miscomprehension does occur. The question is: What should the "baseline" level be in a particular context? There are several key issues. First, what, in general, is the level of miscomprehension? Is the 28 percent found by Jacoby et al. of value is establishing a baseline standard? Second, what measures should be used in establishing any standard? Obviously, as Mizerski so graphically showed, the levels can be dramatically affected by the measure selected. Naturally, this issue has to be addressed by advertisers as well, but the problem here is more severe. Third, the standard will surely depend on the context. If health and safety are involved, only very low or even zero levels of misperception might be tolerated. However, if the "danger" in buying the wrong soap or toothpaste is modest, higher levels could be tolerated.

ADVERTISING SUBSTANTIATION

In mid-1971, the FTC adopted a documentation program that, in essence, shifted the burden of proof in deceptive advertising cases by requiring an advertiser to submit proof that advertising claims are truthful—in other words, to substantiate their advertising claims.[35] It required advertisers from selected industries to submit evidence that claims made with respect to safety, performance, efficacy, quality, or comparative price be submitted to the FTC. The program also included the right of the FTC to compel advertisers to engage in tests or studies to support claims if such evidence did not already exist. Furthermore, the program allowed the FTC to make the information, "except for trade secrets, customer lists, or other financial information which may be privileged or confidential," available to the public.

The first industries affected were the automobile, air conditioner, and electric shaver industries. For example, Borg-Warner was required to provide evidence that their York room air conditioner would indeed put out air that is clean and healthful, as their advertising claimed.

After receiving documentation from numerous companies, the FTC issued a number of constant order decrees, which stopped the advertising of claims that were inadequately substantiated. For example, Firestone was ordered to stop advertising that its tires "stop 25% faster" and Fedders was told to stop calling its reserve cooling system "unique."

The substantiation concept was broadened considerably in 1972 when the FTC offered the opinion that advertisers have an obligation to substantiate advertising claims before the advertising appears. Thus, unless an advertiser has a reasonable basis for making an affirmative claim, it would be illegal to do so. Furthermore, the FTC has in various cases held responsible not only the manufacturers but the advertising agency that produced the advertisements, the retailers who run the advertisements, and even the celebrity who endorsed the product.

Clearly, there are important policy questions as to which advertisements make claims requiring substantiation and what is considered adequate substantiation. In addressing these questions the FTC considers the following:

1. Whether the claim is one that the consumer cannot evaluate for himself or herself
2. Whether the claim involves health or safety, whether a large number of consumers are likely to be influenced, and whether a vulnerable group is involved
3. Whether the claim will affect purchase decisions

Of course, such considerations really apply in any deceptive advertising case. The level of substantiation required has ranged from competent scientific tests in the case of auto tire safety and efficiency claims, to the opinion of a qualified person that competent tests or other objective data exist, which applied for denture adhesive comfort claims.

A study by Healey and Kassarjian indicated that the substantiation program did affect advertising.[36] They compared magazine advertisements in 1970 for pet food and antiperspirants, two industries for which ad substantiation was required, with those in 1976. They found that in 1976 claims were either accompanied by more verification in the ad or expressed more ambiguously, precluding the need for verification. Further, the number of claims included in advertisements may have been reduced. Advertisers appeared to be more conscientious about claims being made after being asked to provide substantiation.

REMEDIES

The FTC has a variety of remedies at its disposal. One task is to select the remedy most appropriate to the situation. Among the remedies are the cease-and-desist order, restitution, affirmative disclosure, and corrective advertising.

Cease-and-Desist Orders

The cease-and-desist order, which prohibits the respondent from engaging any more in the deceptive practice, is actually the only formal procedure established by the FTC Act for enforcing its prohibition of "deceptive acts and practices." It has been criticized as being a command to "go and sin no more," which has little practical effect. Due to procedural delays, it is not uncommon for several years to elapse between the filing of the complaint and the issuance of the order. In one extreme case, it took 16 years for the commission to get the "Liver" out of "Carter's Little Liver Pills."[37] During the delay, the advertising can go on. By the time the cease-and-desist order is issued, the advertising may have served its purpose and another campaign may be underway anyway.

Restitution

Restitution means that the consumer is compensated for any damage. For example, the FTC required a mail-order company to make restitution in the form of full refunds for their skin cream, diet plans, vitamin supplements, and other products that had advertised claims not adequately substantiated.[38] Restitution is rarely considered because of its severity.

Affirmative Disclosures

If an advertisement has provided insufficient information to the consumer, an affirmative disclosure might be issued.[39] Affirmative disclosures require "clear and conspicuous" disclosure of the omitted information. Often the involved information relates to deficiencies or limitations of the product or service possibly relating to matters of health or safety. Kenrec Sports, Inc., was ordered to disclose certain limitations to its swimming-aid, such as that the device is not a life preserver and should always be used in shallow water.[40] Medi-Hair International was required for 1 year to devote at least 15 percent of each advertisement for its baldness concealment system to the limitations and drawbacks of the system.

Corrective Advertising[41]

Corrective advertising requires advertisers to rectify past deception by making suitable statements in future commercials. The concept is illustrated by the 1971 Profile Bread case, the first case for which corrective advertising was a part of the remedy.[42] The consent order agreed to by Continental Baking specified that 25 percent of the next year's Profile Bread advertising had to support a FTC-approved correct message, such as one featuring Julia Meade which read in part:

> Hi, Julia Meade for Profile Bread. Like all mothers, I'm concerned about nutrition and balanced meals. So, I'd like to clear up any misunderstanding you may have about Profile Bread from its advertising or even its name.
>
> Does Profile have fewer calories than any other brands? No. Profile has about the same per ounce as other brands. To be exact, Profile has seven fewer calories per slice. That's because Profile is sliced thinner. But eating Profile will not cause you to lose weight. A reduction of seven calories is insignificant. It's total calories and balanced nutrition that count. And Profile can help you achieve a balanced meal because. . . .[43]

There was some evidence that the sales of Profile bread suffered as a result of the corrective advertising.

The 1975 FTC corrective advertising order against Warner-Lambert's Listerine is important because it was appealed all the way to the Supreme Court.[44] Listerine had advertised for over 50 years that gargling with Listerine mouthwash helped prevent colds and sore throats by killing germs. They were required by the courts to include the statement, "Listerine will not help prevent colds or sore throats or lessen their severity'' in $10 million of advertising, which was equal to the average annual expenditure during a prior 10-year period.

Listerine implemented the order by embedding the statement in a commercial featuring two couples, each with a husband finding himself having ''onion breath.'' One couple used Scope and the other Listerine. The wife using Scope sniffed her husband's breath and said that she didn't know that ''clinical tests prove Listerine fights onion breath better than Scope.'' The other replied, ''We always knew.'' The corrective disclosure appeared midway in the 30-second spot as follows: ''While Listerine will not help prevent colds or sore throats or lessen their severity, breath tests prove Listerine fights onion breath better than Scope.''

Three field studies basically found that the corrective advertising had a modest impact. In day-after-recall tests, only 5 percent mentioned the corrective message when asked to describe the ad; it was the fourth most recalled message in the ad.[45] Two studies focused on before-after changes in beliefs about Listerine. One, using four waves of telephone interviews, found a reduction of about 20 percent in overall deceptive beliefs about Listerine's effectiveness.[46] The other, an FTC study, consisted of seven waves of questionnaire mailings which garnered 10,000 returned questionnaires (a 70 percent response rate) from the Market Facts consumer panel.[47] Beliefs that Listerine is effective for colds and sore throats fell about 11 percent (14 percent for Listerine users). The amount of mouthwash used for colds and sore throats dropped 40 percent. Thus, a substantial level of misperception about Listerine effectiveness remained after the campaign.

The Listerine case clearly established the FTC's authority to order corrective advertising, but it also served to raise some important issues. Any remedy should be nonpunitive in nature and should be the least burdensome remedy. How do you determine whether the corrective advertising is generating damage to sales or image that would not be necessary to correcting the misperceptions? A remedy should preserve the First Amendment right to express ideas. What about those ideas that are counter to the corrective message's claims? Can an advertiser simply decide to stop advertising, thereby avoiding corrective advertising?

One problem with corrective advertising is that it has usually resulted in lawyers writing copy and insisting that it be run some arbitrary length of time. Wilkie has observed that the much more sensible approach would be to give the advertisers a communication task and let them achieve it any way that they can.[48]

Such an approach was partially applied in the Hawaiian Punch case.[49] Hawaiian Punch used a catchy jingle, ''Seven Natural Fruit Juices in Hawaiian Punch,'' together with fruit photos even though it contains only 11 to 15 percent fruit juice. Hawaiian Punch agreed to disclose the actual fruit juice content of the product (''contains not less than 11 percent natural fruit juice''). The disclosure was to run until a specified survey found that 67 percent of fruit-drink purchasers are aware that Hawaiian Punch contained less than 20 percent natural fruit juice. A series of 17 semiannual telephone surveys indicated that relevant perceptions were slow to change.[50] Over the 1974–1982 period, the proportion of consumers who believed that Hawaiian Punch had 20 percent or less fruit juice increased from 20 percent

(1974) to 40 percent (1975) to 50 percent (1982). The target was reached only after nine years of advertising.

The implementation of the communication objective approach to corrective advertising will always face difficulties. The problem of ascertaining how misperception and its effect are to be measured and the appropriate target level of misperception that should be obtained reappears in this context. Judgments on such questions are required to set communication objectives. Obviously, a zero misperception level is not generally feasible. Yet regulators and the general public to which they must answer have difficulty accepting realistic standards. A key is to know whether the advertiser is making a good faith effort toward the objective. Copy testing could logically be used to address this point, but the parties would have to agree in advance on relevant and suitable tests, a difficult prospect. Another problem is the cost of measuring deception over time. The tracking required to measure the impact of the commercials—no problem for large advertisers, who do that anyway—could be costly for smaller advertisers and may require the government to share some of the costs.

SELF-REGULATION

In 1971 an ambitious program of self-regulation was established by the advertising industry in concert with the Council of Better Business Bureaus (CBBB). The objective of the program was to establish a "self-regulatory mechanism that would respond constructively to public complaints about national advertising and would significantly improve advertising performance and credibility. It was further intended that this mechanism be flexible, efficient, respected, and reliable."[51] The program was initially established to be concerned with matters of truth and accuracy in advertising but has expanded its interests to include the broader questions of taste and social responsibility. The following discussion outlines the program.

Complaints against national advertising are investigated by the National Advertising Division (NAD), an arm of the CBBB. In evaluating a complaint, NAD normally requests that the advertiser submit substantiation for the claims made in the challenged advertisements. Following its investigation, NAD will (1) dismiss the complaint on the ground that the advertiser, in NAD's opinion, provided adequate substantiation of his claims, or it will (2) find the complaint to be justified. In the latter case, NAD will request modification or withdrawal of the challenged advertising.

Either the advertiser or the party filing the original complaint can appeal the decision of the NAD to a National Advertising Review Board (NARB). The NARB consists of a chairman and 50 members drawn from advertisers (30), agencies (10), and from outside the industry (10). In response to the appeal, the chairman at his discretion may appoint a five-member panel to review the case. If the findings of a NARB panel are in favor of the advertiser, the case is closed. If not, the advertiser will be requested to modify or discontinue the advertising under review. If the advertiser refuses to change or discontinue the challenged advertising, the case is referred by NARB to an appropriate government agency. Public disclosure is made of the findings of all NARB panels, together with any statement submitted by an advertiser who disagrees with a panel decision.

In one series of 11 rulings by the NAB, three involved claims that were substantiated.[52] For example, Revlon supplied independent research to support its claim that Colorsilk, a hair coloring product, promises color that is rich, true, and lasting, and hair that feels silkier and looks healthier.

The other eight companies either modified or discontinued their advertising. Curtis Mathes failed to mention that labor charges were not included when advertising their four-year limited warranty on their television sets. Hall of Music in television advertisements offered over 80 of the world's greatest masterpieces in a two-album collection. The NAD was concerned that the consumer might believe that he or she was getting the entire selection instead of excerpts. Louis Marx in television advertisements for Big Wheel, a ride-on toy, used the disclaimer, "assembly required." The children's unit of NAD felt that simpler wording is needed for child-directed advertisements. E. J. Brach advertised that "We still use fresh, natural ingredients, so Brach's tastes better than other candy." The NAD indicated that some clarification was required since some artificial coloring and flavoring is used.

The self-regulation effort has been markedly successful by many measures. Around 400 cases are handled each year, many of which are initiated by businessmen unhappy with the advertising tactics of competitors.[53] Cases are handled rapidly and at a fraction of the cost of processing a case through the FTC. Though the cases are publicized, the adverse publicity is much less than associated with FTC cases. A company can be completely exonerated by the courts yet suffer considerable harm because of the publicity surrounding a FTC action.[54] However, the effort is limited. The capacity of the system really prevents it from publicizing itself widely. Thus few consumers know about it. Furthermore, there is the voluntary aspect. Although there has not been a single instance where the verdict of the NAD staff or review panels was ultimately defied, the fact remains that the enforcement power is not great.

SUMMARY

Conceptually, deception exists when an advertisement is input to the perceptual process of some audience and the output of that perceptual process (1) differs from the reality of the situation and (2) affects buying behavior to the detriment of the consumer. The legal definition has developed through the years as decisions are reached by the FTC and the courts. The courts have generally held that the law is designed to protect those who are naive, trusting, and of low intelligence. For deception to occur, it must contain a material untruth, one capable of affecting purchase decisions. An advertisement is judged by its general impression. An advertisement could leave an erroneous impression even if each claim made by the advertisement were technically true. An advertisement can be regarded as deceptive if it can be interpreted in two ways and one of them would be deceptive. If important information is omitted from the advertisement, deception can result. Puffing, the subjective statement of opinion concerning a product's quality, using terms such as "best," is permissible. However, the definition of what is puffery has been narrowed over time.

Consumer research was rarely used in deception cases until the 1970s because the FTC subjective judgment was deemed adequate, legal adversaries would not be comfortable agreeing to allow a study to prove deception, of methodological difficulties, and because defendants feared that consumer research would be used against them. The AAAA study found that around 28 percent of claims made in commercials are misperceived, about the same level found in other television programming. The baseline level of misperception will depend on the measure used, however.

The FTC advertising substantiation program requires an advertiser to submit proof that advertising claims are truthful. A practical issue is what claims require substantiation and what constitutes adequate substantiation.

The FTC has several available remedies. Cease-and-desist orders prohibit the respondent from engaging further in the deceptive practice. Restitution provides compensation to those deceived. Affirmative disclosure requires that missing information be disclosed in a clear and conspicuous manner. Corrective advertising seeks to eliminate the effects of prior misleading advertising. Efforts to employ corrective advertising by requiring the insertion of some phrase in the ads generally has little impact. A more useful remedy would be to demand corrective advertising aimed at some communication objective. The difficulty is to establish that objective.

The advertising industry has developed an ambitious program of self-regulation, which rests largely on the support of the industry itself. The industry needs to be committed to the concept that improvement in advertising is desirable because it is right and because the credibility of all advertising will thereby be enhanced. An advertiser who is found to have offending advertisements has other incentives to cooperate. The program involves public disclosure of findings and referral to appropriate government agencies if a solution is not forthcoming.

DISCUSSION QUESTIONS

1. In your judgment, are the following deceptive?
   a. The Geritol case (tired blood).
   b. Wonder Bread (the implied uniqueness issue).
   c. Colgate-Palmolive case (the use of simulated sandpaper).
2. For the advertisements in Question 1, how would you use advertising research to help determine whether deception is present?

3. All advertisements have the capacity to deceive some audience members. For example, if you just showed a picture of a glass of milk, some people would believe that the advertisement was falsely implying that everyone must drink at least one glass of milk a day because that belief has been ingrained in them. Comment.

4. Evaluate the following proposals:
   a. Advertising for brands that are, for all practical purposes, identical to competitors should be eliminated.
   b. The use of live models or spokespeople should be eliminated.
   c. Only the product itself, with no background scenes, can be shown in an advertisement.

5. The FTC is concerned about the use of endorsements by celebrities or experts (as opposed to the use of spokesperson or a "slice-of life" dramatization). What guidelines would you suggest that would help ensure that such advertisements would not be deceptive? Illustrate how your guidelines would apply by considering examples.

6. If a brand is not substantially different from its competitors, should its advertisements state that fact? What would be the effect of such a rule?

7. Pornography, which is protected by free speech guarantees, is judged by whether the average person applying contemporary community standards, believes the dominant theme appeals to prurient interests. What is the standard applied to advertising? Is that appropriate? Should the rights of business to inform be specified by the FTC? What guidelines should be used in interpreting surveys designed to measure deception?

8. If the FTC holds that inadequate substantiation exists for an advertising claim, they have held responsible not only the manufacturer but also the agency preparing the advertising, the retailer running it, and the celebrity used in the advertisement to endorse the product. Comment on this policy.

9. Identify three advertisements that contain claims that should have prior substantiation.

10. In some corrective advertising proposals, a one-year period and 25 percent of advertising budgets were suggested as the extent of the corrective advertising effort. How should the percentage and the time period be determined? How should it vary with products and situation? Give examples.

11. Will the National Advertising Review Board be effective at resolving complaints concerning deceptive advertising? If its concern is broadened to include issues of taste, how do you think it will perform in that regard? How would you measure performance?

12. In a survey of 200 people, 90 percent recognized the Good Housekeeping Seal, 50 percent relied upon it for purchasing decisions, and 29

percent believed that the product met federal quality and safety standards, but no one interviewed recognized that the seal was given only to advertisers. Should such a seal be continued? What role does it have in consumer decision making?

13. Consider again Question 5 in Chapter 17 regarding an advertising code for children.

14. Some argue that comparative advertisements in which one or more competitors are explicity named are unfair to competitors and tend to be deceptive and therefore should be illegal. Such advertisements are, in fact, illegal in France, Belgium, Spain, and Italy. Comment.

15. Comment on the AAAA study of miscomprehension levels. Does 28 percent provide a benchmark level of miscomprehension to be used in deceptive advertising cases?

NOTES

1. *Creative Code* (New York: American Association of Advertising Agencies, 1962).

2. Ira M. Millstein, "The Federal Trade Commission and False Advertising," *Columbia Law Review,* 64, March 1964, p. 439.

3. *Sears, Roebuck & Co.* v. *FTC,* 258 Fed. 307 (7th Cir. 1919).

4. *FTC v Raladam Co.,* 258 U.S. 643 (1931).

5. FTC (1983) at 689–690. For an excellent analysis of this statement, see Gary T. Ford and John E. Calfee, "Recent Developments in FTC Policy on Deception," in *Journal of Marketing,* 50, July 1986, pp. 82–103.

6. *Charles of the Ritz Dist. Corp.* v. *FTC,* 143 F. 2d 676 (2d Cir. 1944).

7. *Gelb* v. *FTC,* 144 F. 2d 580 (2d Cir. 1944).

8. Trade Reg. Rep. 16664 (FTC, Nov. 7, 1963).

9. Ibid., at 21539–40.

10. Firestone Tire, 81 FTC Decisions 298, 1972.

11. Millstein, "False Advertising," p. 438.

12. *Colgate-Palmolive Co.* v. *FTC,* 310 F. 2d 89 (1st Cir. 1962).

13. Richard L. Gordon, "FTC Vote Jettisons Former Deception Policy," *Advertising Age,* April 2, 1984, p. 6.

14. *P. Lorillard Co.* v. *FTC,* 186 F. 2d 52 (4th Cir. 1950).

15. Hutchinson Chem. Corp., 55 FTC 1942 (1959).

16. *FTC* v. *Sterling Drug, Inc.,* 215 F. Supp. 327, 330 (S.D.N.Y.) aff'd. 317 F. 2d 699 (2d Cir. 1963).

17. Bristol-Myers Co., 46 FTC 162 (1949) aff'd. 185 F. 2d 58 (4th Cir. 1950).

18. *FTC* v. *Morrissey,* 47 F. 2d 101, 103 (7th Cir. 1931).

19. J. B. Williams Co., 3 Trade Reg. Rep. 17. 339 (FTC Dkt. No. 8547, 1965), appeal docketed, No. 16, 969 (6th Cir. Dec. 3 1965).

20. "FTC to Issue Consent in Wonder Case," *Advertising Age,* November 5, 1973, p. 1.

21. *Ostermoor & Co.* v. *FTC,* 16 F. 2d 962 (2d. Cir. 1927).

22. Ibid., p. 962.

23. *Carlay* v. *FTC,* 153 F. 2d 493, 496 (1946).

24. Ivan L. Preston and Ralph H. Johnson, "Puffery: A Vulnerable (?) Feature of Advertising," paper presented at the annual convention of the Association for Education in Journalism, University of South Carolina, August 1971; Ivan L. Preston, "The FTC's Handling of Puffery and Other Selling Claims Made 'By Implication,' " *Journal of Business Research,* June 1977, pp. 155–181.

25. Tanners Shoe Company, 53 FTC Decisions 1137 (1957).

26. *Colgate-Palmolive Co.* v. *FTC,* footnote 24, p. 1452.

27. Benrus Watch Co., 3 Trade Reg. Rep. 16541 (FTC, July 31, 1963).

28. Ivan L. Preston, "A Review of the Literature on Advertising Regulation," in James H. Leigh and Claude R. Martin, Jr., eds., *Current Issues & Research in Advertising* (Ann Arbor Mich.: University of Michigan, 1983), p. 4.

29. Firestone Tire, 81 FTC Decisions 398 (1972).

30. ITT Continental Baking, 83 FTC Decisions 865 (1973); modified, 83 FTC 1105 (1973), 532 F. 2d 207 (2d cir. 1976), 90 FTC 181 (1977).

31. Sun Oil, 84 FTC Decisions 247 (1974).

32. Jacob Jacoby, Wayne D. Hoyer, and David A. Sheluga, *The Miscomprehension of Televised Communication* (New York: American Association of Advertising Agencies, 1980); and Jacob Jacoby and Wayne D. Hoyer, "Viewer Miscomprehension of Televised Communication: Selected Findings," *Journal of Marketing,* 46, Fall 1982, pp. 12–26.

33. Gary T. Ford and Richard Yalch, "Viewer Miscomprehension of Televised Communication—A Comment," *Journal of Marketing,* 46, Fall 1982, pp. 27–31.

34. Richard W. Mizerski, "Viewer Miscomprehension Findings Are Measurement Bound," *Journal of Marketing,* 46, Fall 1982, p. 32.

35. This section draws upon Dorothy Cohen, "The FTC's Advertising Substantiation Program" *Journal of Marketing,* Winter 1980, pp. 26–35.

36. John S. Healey and Harold H. Kassarjian, "Advertising Substantiation and Advertiser Response: A Content Analysis of Magazine Advertisements," *Journal of Marketing,* 47, Winter 1983, pp. 107–117.

37. *Carter Products Inc.* v. *FTC,* 186 F. 2d 821 (7th Cir. 1951).

38. Cohen, "Substantiation," p. 31.

39. Robert F. Wilkes and James B. Wilcox, "Recent FTC Actions: Implications for the Advertising Strategist," *Journal of Marketing,* 38, January 1974.

40. Kenrec Sports, Inc. et al., 3 Trade Reg. Rep. 19.971 (1972).

41. For an excellent review of corrective advertising from which much of this section draws, see William L. Wilkie, Dennis L. McNeill, and Michael B. Mazis, "Marketing's 'Scarlet Letter' the Theory and Practice of Corrective Advertising," *Journal of Marketing,* 48, Spring 1984, pp. 11–31.

42. ITT Continental Baking Co. (1973), 8860, 83 FTC 865.

43. Ibid.

44. Warner-Lambert (1975), 8891, 86 FTC 1398.

45. Michael B. Mazis, Dennis L. McNeill, and Kenneth Bernhardt, "Day after Recall of Listerine Corrective Commercials," Working Paper (Washington, D.C.: American University, 1981).

46. Gary M. Armstrong, Metin N. Gurol, and Frederick A. Russ, "Detecting and Correcting Deceptive Advertising," *Journal of Consumer Research,* 6, December 1979, pp. 237–246.

47. Michael B. Mazis, "The Effects of FTC's Listerine Corrective Advertising Order," a Report to the FTC, Washington, D.C., 1981.

48. William L. Wilkie, *Consumer Research and Corrective Advertising* (Cambridge, Mass: Marketing Science Institute, 1973).

49. RJR Foods Inc. (1973), C2424 (July 13).

50. Thomas C. Kinnear, James Taylor, and Odee Gur-Arie, "Affirmative Disclosure: Long-term Monitoring of Residual Effects," *Journal of Business Policy and Marketing,* 2, forthcoming.

51. The 1972 Annual Report of the National Advertising Review Board.

52. "Pillsbury Loses Some Brownie Points at NAD," *Advertising Age,* March 17, 1980, p. 10.

53. Stanley E. Cohen, "Advertising Regulation: Changing, Growing Area," *Advertising Age,* April 30, 1980, p. 218.

54. Ibid.

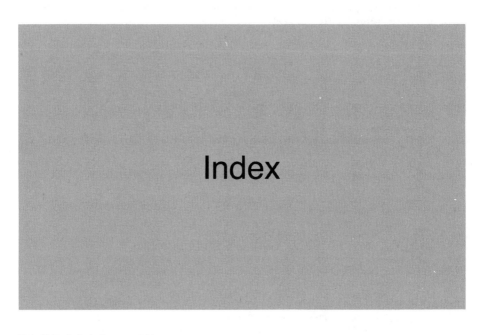

Index

Note: Italics indicate figures or tables.